an invitation to

THE CATHEDRAL CITIES
of Southern England

Edited by Joy David

"Let your light so shine before men,
that they may see your good works."

St. Matthew iv. 17

Acknowledgements

The writer and editor, Joy David, wishes to thank her fellow contributors to this book; John Theobald, Jane Drake, Bernard Fullerton, Dick Benson-Gyles, Sally Dunsmore. Their enthusiasm for the subject has been an inspiration. To Hassina Carder and Adrian Carey for their loyalty and hard work in the compilation and production. The researchers, Rose Dennis, Scott Anthony, Nancy Pavey, Tracie Keene, Guy Horton, Sue Looms, Cath Mitchell, Ruth Bowden. Christine Scobling, Barbara Bowden, Alison Troth and Hilary Kent whose unceasing efforts have provided the material.

Thanks are also given to Emma Macleod-Johnstone and David Williams for the superb work on the link illustrations. Rose Dennis, David Williams, Carlos Escobar, David Moore and Andrew Forsythe for the remaining illustrations without which the book would be a "poorer place!"

To Emma, a special thank you for the pleasure and fun she and I had whilst we were unearthing suitable quotations for each cathedral.

Finally a sincere thank you for the generous assistance in time and material that the Cathedrals themselves have given me.

ISBN 1 873491 60 3
First published in 1993
Copyright Griffin Publishing Ltd
All rights reserved

All information is included in good faith and is believed to be correct at the time of going to press. No responsibility can be accepted for error.

Typeset by Griffin Publishing Ltd, Devon. Tel: (0752) 256177 / 256188
and Typestyle (The P.C. Bureau), Devon. Tel: (0752) 698668 - Fax (0752) 698669
Printed and bound in Great Britain by Witherby & Co, London. Tel: (071) 253 4513

Contents

Introduction

The Cathedrals of the British Isles spell out our history almost more than any other part of our glorious heritage. The opportunity to visit and write about them throughout the length and breadth of the land is one of the most satisfying tasks I have ever dealt with in my long life. It has been an unforgettable privilege both for me and for the five other writers who have contributed to this book.

For each of us there has been an especial love of the cathedrals about which we have chosen to write, although I must confess to drawing the short straw occasionally, and finding myself on unfamiliar ground, but if I arrived as a stranger I felt richly rewarded by the experience. Every cathedral, whether old or of this century, has a great deal to offer and for many different reasons.

The other purpose of this book is to help you enjoy the cities in which the cathedrals are situated and in many cases some of the interesting and beautiful countryside within striking distance. We have added a number of hotels, restaurants and inns as well as museums and other attractions that we hope you will also enjoy.

Millions of people from this country and overseas visit our cathedrals every year, of all creeds and cultures. For those who already enjoy visiting the cathedral cities, we hope this book will enhance their pleasure. For those who newly discover this rich heritage of ours, we hope it will make easier their understanding of the history and the beauty and introduce to them, those who live their lives in the close knit cathedral communities.

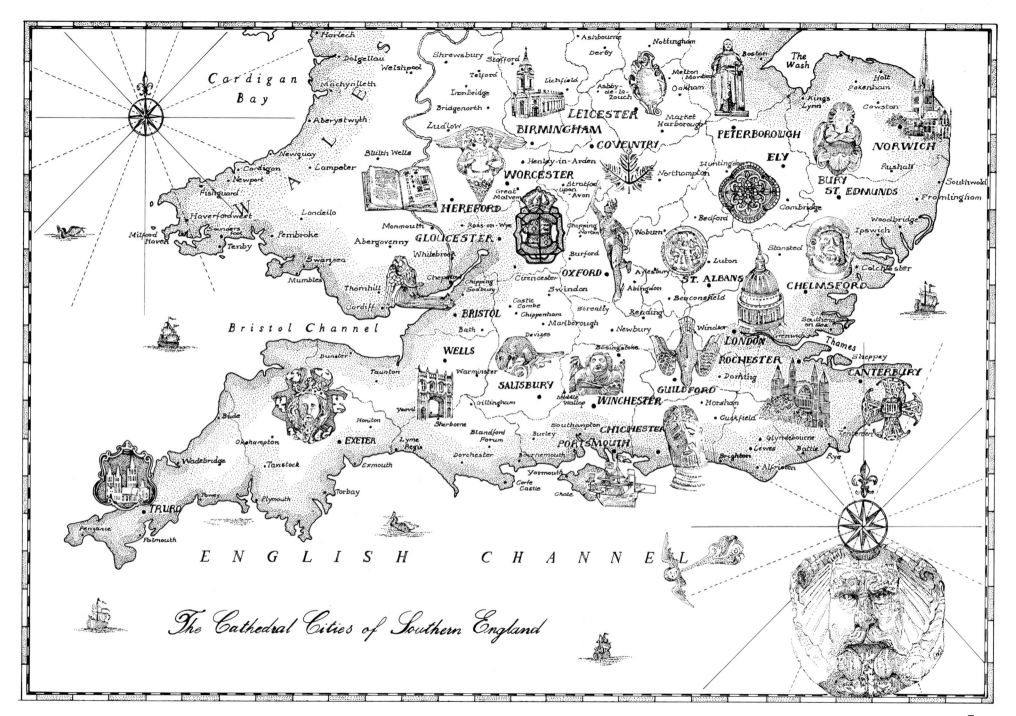

The Cathedral Cities of Southern England

Birmingham Cathedral

Birmingham

"Men's eyes were made to look,
and let them gaze;"

William Shakespeare

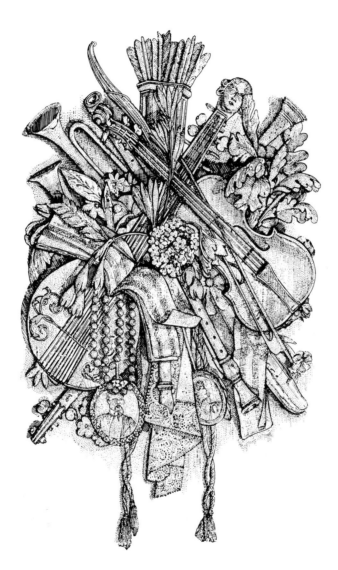

The City of Birmingham

by Joy David

Birmingham is one of Britain's premier meeting places. Its excellent communications by air, rail and road make it a natural choice for business men and women seeking a central location in which to gather. It is also becoming increasingly popular as an excellent place to visit in order to unearth its remarkable heritage. One tends not to think about Birmingham with a past but it is there for all those who wish to seek it out. I was amazed and delighted in the time I spent in the city. It has so much to offer.

This is a city that is home to nearly one million people and as one of the city's illustrated brochures says to 'more than one million histories'. Since its origins in the 7th century, as a small river-crossing until its present development as an international city, Birmingham's people have created lasting landmarks in both buildings and thinking.

The heritage survives in the historic buildings, splendid museum collections and monuments of industry and art, both in the heart of Birmingham and out towards the city boundaries.

Exploring the past and the present in today's city centre reveals a proud heritage and an exciting future. As I found, there are many ways to seek out Birmingham's heritage. Museums show off the city's history, the worlds of other cultures, important milestones in technology, treasures from the world of nature and masterpieces of the arts and crafts. Art galleries abound showing works of local artists and the great masters as well as sometimes provoking experimental works, by international figures. There are the churches, the impressive mass of the INTERNATIONAL CONVENTION CENTRE. Canals, themselves major feats of engineering, thread their way through a hidden Birmingham, giving another view of the city at work and fostering canalside wildlife. Birmingham has more miles of canals than Venice!

BRUMMAGEM BOATS at Sherborne Street Wharf, Sherborne Street have two longboats the 'Euphrates Packet' and 'Jericho - the Brummagem Fly' which will transport you from the quayside at the International Convention Centre through the 200 year old network of waterways. From this unique moving viewpoint you can explore the ins and outs of Birmingham's industrial past in a new found tranquillity, where unexpected glimpses of nature are more than rewarding and it also gives you time to think about the days before motorways and rail when these canals provided Britain's inland trade links. There are public trips from Easter to October at 11.30am, 2pm and 4pm from the ICC quayside.

Bold modern statues bring art into the everyday life of this vibrant city, while memorials to war and peace remind one that a world exists outside the city. In Centenary Square THE HALL OF MEMORY rises as a lasting tribute to the Birmingham men and women who gave their lives during the two World Wars. The bronze statues outside represent Army, Navy, Air Force and Nursing. Beyond the weighty bronze doors, the cool interior creates a fitting atmosphere in which to contemplate their courage. The Hall is open all year from Monday to Saturday 10am-4pm. 'Lest we forget'.

If you want to take a fresh look at art and begin to appreciate that modern art is not 'child's play' then THE IKON GALLERY in John Bright Street is the place for you. You must have an open mind and revel in surprises because you certainly will get some. From temporary exhibitions to more outlandish events (sometimes involving music and drama), The Ikon's three white walled caverns provide the ideal setting in which to experience the work of living artists. It is open all year from Tuesday to Saturday from 11am-6pm and 8pm on Thursdays.

If you want somewhere to lunch or dine after a vist to The Ikon then I suggest LA GALLERIA RESTAURANT AND WINE BAR in Paradise Place. It is within easy walking distance of all the main hotels and it has been a centre of excellence for many years. It has the true ambience of an Italian restaurant.

As I drove towards Birmingham my thoughts were on how much coverage THE NATIONAL EXHIBITION CENTRE, THE INTERNATIONAL CONVENTION CENTRE and THE NATIONAL INDOOR ARENA were given. Sometimes to the detriment of the city. These impressive and still expanding facilities are equipped to the highest standards and play host to a multitude of events as diverse as opera, international athletics and CRUFT'S DOG SHOW as well as numerous conferences and trade shows which attract several million people a year, representing some 95 countries! Nevertheless these massive centres are not alone and it is typical of Birmingham's ability to react to market demand that numerous other conference venues are available, from five star hotels to stately homes, together with an impressive infrastructure that covers everything necessary, such as accommodation, travel, leisure facilities and marketing. Perhaps more than any other skill, it is this ability in the market place that has brought Birmingham from being a 'vill of ten adults' and valued at £1 in 1086 to today's priceless 65,000 acre metropolis of one million inhabitants. The basis of Birmingham's wealth was established with the granting of a market charter in 1166 and initial trading would have been in cattle and sheep which then led to the establishment of the first manufacturing industries of leather and cloth. Exploitation of the Black Country's mineral wealth combined with a plentiful supply of water-power, attracted skilled metal-workers and men of vision who founded the first factories, mass-producing goods for the nation and overseas. The adaptability of the city (declared so by Queen Victoria) was reflected in its innovatory attitude to industry - steam and coal gas were utilised in manufacturing processes before anywhere else, and it's enlightened attitude towards city planning and provision for houses and services were far in advance of their time. Cutlery and fastenings were joined by more sophisticated trades of gunmaking and jewellery until by 1873 there

were more than 745 listed trades and professions; the 20th century adding yet more with the invention of the internal combustion engine and the establishment of the motor industry. To this day, the city provides a home to both mass-production and the individual craftsman together with those of the space-age and the facilities and services already mentioned.

The city is constantly changing and intensely alive and it is difficult to know where to start but my main purpose was to discover and explore its Anglican Cathedral in Colmore Row which is open every day of the year from 6.30am until 7pm for those who want to worship, sit and contemplate or just enjoy this English Baroque Church of St Philip's, built in 1709-1715, which became BIRMINGHAM CATHEDRAL in 1905.

If you look at the inscription above the inner door of the South West porch you will see it proclaims;

'His most Excellent Majesty, King George upon the kind application of Sir Richard Gough to the Rt Honourable Sir Robert Walpole gave £600 towards finishing this Church A.D. 1725'

This fine new church was consecrated in 1715, and the tower completed ten years later, thanks to the munificence of the King. It beggars belief that such a little sum of money could have made so much difference to its welfare, but it was so. Money had a very different value in those days.

The decision to build the church came about because of the growth of the little town of Birmingham in the 17th century. At that time the life of the town was centred around the Bull Ring and the old parish church of St Martin within it. As industry developed and the town began to expand further afield a new church was needed

in what was known as High Town, and so an Act of Parliament in 1708 created the new parish. One, Thomas Archer from Warwickshire, a great exponent of English Baroque was commissioned as the architect. This was a man who had travelled widely on the continent and was heavily influenced by the work of the great masters, Bernini and Boromini. You can see their style in Archer's design for the north front at Chatsworth in Derbyshire, Heythrop House in Oxfordshire and in London at St John's Church, Smith Square and St Paul's Deptford. It was this talent he brought to his design for St Philip's, and the magnificent result is now Birmingham Cathedral, the centre of the diocese created in 1905. Today the Cathedral is surrounded by Victorian buildings but there is much to admire. Thomas Archer designed a rectangular building with a shallow apsidal sanctuary and a vast galleried nave to allow seating for the ever growing number of church going people of the developing town. When one considers all that was happening in growth throughout England, it must have been a rare compliment to the town, and a respect for its value to the country, that prompted King George to present the church with such a generous gift.

Doric pilasters, round-headed windows, a balustraded parapet capped with urns all catch the eye. At the west end there is a projection under the tower with a curved pediment; on either side are pedimented doorways, with beautiful oval windows, with generously and enchantingly carved surrounds. The tower soars trying to reach the heavens, with twin Corinthian pilasters adorning the corner buttresses. An impertinent and arrogant gilded weather vane sporting a boar's head dominates the leaded dome - the boar's head is the crest of Sir Richard Gough who was Lord of the Manor of Edgbaston and had much to do with the Prime Minister recommending that King George presented his £600 to the church.

In 1883 the church was enlarged with the architect J.A. Chatwin displaying a sympathetic understanding, and his chancel is built in strict harmony with Archer's design. The thing that struck me more than anything else about the interior of this Cathedral was the four spectacular and stunning stained glass windows, designed by Burne Jones and made by Morris & Co. They are almost a hundred years old and must have sent shafts of coloured light throughout the church then as they do today, imbuing it with a warmth which otherwise would be lacking. Three of these gorgeous windows are in the sanctuary, and another at the west end. The designs are dramatic and tell the story of the Ascension at the east end, the judgement at the west with the Nativity and the Crucifixion on either side of the sanctuary. When I first looked at them it was the brilliance of the colour, red, green and blue, which stunned me rather more than the design. The whole is nothing short of magnificent. The more you look at them, the more detail you pick out; the beautifully detailed angels' wings, the brilliantly coloured banners of the soldiers. I wondered how Burne Jones felt about it when he saw his designs completed.

Do not go to the Cathedral expecting to find beautiful furnishings. You will be sadly disillusioned if you do. There is a superb organ case by Thomas Schwarbrick in 1715 in the chancel and another which came from another church in the north gallery. In keeping with modern liturgical thinking the High Altar has been removed from the Sanctuary. The beautiful railings which once guarded the altar are now there merely as a decoration to enclose a chair and an uninteresting table. There are some fine pictures and a splendid and vast tapestry finished and hung in 1975.

One thing that does not disappoint is the music of the cathedral. Nothing ever fills me with such a sense of the presence of God than fine church music sung by able choristers letting their voices soar aloft.

Whilst this book is essentially about Anglican Cathedrals it would be unworthy not to tell you about ST CHAD'S CATHEDRAL at Queensway. Bishop Walsh made a brave decision in 1838 to appoint the celebrated A.W. Pugin to design the first Roman Catholic Cathedral in Britain to be built since the Reformation. What he produced was a Victorian masterpiece in red brick, which is a testimony of faith, with its spires rising above the city centre. Much of its contents are far and away older and have been given or worked for. In particular one should notice the 15th century carved Flemish pulpit. St Chad's is open every day throuhout the year from 9am-6.30pm and people of all denominations, colour and creed are welcome.

Birmingham is blessed with several fine churches and not the least of them is the most ancient ST MARTIN'S-IN-THE-BULL RING which has been the focal point of the markets area since the 12th century. Inside, the oldest monument in the city, a 1325 effigy of Lord of the Manor Sir William de Bermingham, lies opposite a beautiful Burne-Jones designed window. The present building dates from 1875. It is the Parish Church of Birmingham and is also home to the world's only change ringing peal of 16 bells.

ST THOMAS in Bath Row is no longer a church in use. It is a facade made so by the bombers of the German Luftwaffe in World War II. Today doves fly, an elephant dances and a horse prances in ornate steel at the PEACE GARDEN which surrounds it. It is a place of hope and peace. The Birmingham-made railings depict issues of war and peace connecting the memorial colonnade to the facade of the church. Here in St Thomas' Peace Garden you will see messages from around the world holding out the hand of friendship and peace to the people of Birmingham. The Peace Garden is open daily from dawn to dusk.

'The Jewellers Church' is how ST PAULS CHURCH is described. It stands at the heart of St Paul's Square, the only remaining Georgian Square in Birmingham. At first a fashionable centre for culture, later the church was a focus for the fight against 19th century poverty. Manners, metal and music sum up the essence of this fine building which is at the gateway to the Jewellery Quarter. Inside the church the wooden pews used by many of Birmingham's famous citizens are still there. The church is open all year Mondays, Wednesdays and Fridays from 12-2.30pm and on Sundays according to the times stated on the notice board outside the church.

For nearly two hundred years the streets of THE JEWELLERY QUARTER have been the home of Britain's jewellery industry. THE JEWELLERY QUARTER DISCOVERY CENTRE,is Birmingham's newest heritage attraction. Tiny workshops and factories house a concentration of highly skilled craftspeople producing beautiful jewellery and silverware. There are over 100 shops selling a wide range of gold and silver jewellery, clocks and watches. You can even commission your own design or have your favourite piece repaired.

At the Jewellery Quarter Discovery Centre, two floors of displays outline the history of the Quarter and introduce you to the jeweller's craft which can be traced back over thousands of years. Your visit includes a tour of the former Smith & Pepper jewellery works, little changed from 1914. When it closed in 1980, the departing jewellers left behind on the benches, their tools, equipment and personal belonging. This small factory has been preserved to allow visitors a rare glimpse of life in a jewellery workshop. With the help of demonstrators, you can see the processes involved in producing a finished piece of jewellery. The Jewellery Quarter Discovery Centre information will also provide you with visitor information about the many things to see and do in the Quarter. It is the ideal place from which to start your exploration of this historic part of Birmingham.

You will find The Jewellery Discovery Centre is situated near the Great Hampton Street end of Vyse Street between the junctions of Branston Street and Spencer Street. On foot it is only a short walk from the City Centre. It took me about fifteen minutes at a gentle pace. You will see pedestrian fingerposts for the Jewellery Quarter from St Philip's Cathedral and Newhall Street. If you drive there parking is available in the Vyse Street multi-storey car park close to the Jewllery Quarter Discovery Centre. There are also frequent buses from the city centre. Services 74, 78 and 79 stop on Great Hampton Street close to the end of Vyse Street.

The opening hours from Monday to Saturday are from 10am-5pm. There is full access and toilets for the disabled.

The past can be seen in places like ASTON HALL, a fine Jacobean house furnished with tapestries and pictures. Imagine going for a walk in your own home when it's raining outside. In his Long Gallery, Sir Thomas Holte, who built this mansion in between 1618 and 1635, could do just that. Aston Hall, with over 20 furnished rooms, bears witness to Civil War intrigues and the visits of monarchs. Sharp-eyed visitors can spot the marks of Roundhead cannon shot upon the staircase balustrade.

The address is Trinity Road, **Aston** and it is open from 27th March-31st October daily from 2-5pm.

In Aston there is also THE ASTON MANOR ROAD

TRANSPORT MUSEUM at 208-216 Witton Lane, Aston. It pays tribute to public transport. In the old tram depot, restored lorries, buses, vans, coaches and trams rest on cobbles and tram tracks. Dedicated volunteers work hard on preserving these gems of the past and an electric model tramway operates most weekends. If you are lucky you may be invited to sit in the driving seat of your favourite vehicle. It is open to the public all year from 11am-5pm on Saturdays and Sundays and Bank Holiday Mondays with the exception of the 18th and 19th September and December 25th-27th inclusive.

While I am writing about transport it is a good moment to mention one fascinating place. THE BIRMINGHAM RAILWAY MUSEUM at 670 Warwick road, **Tyseley** which opens all year, daily from 10am until 5pm and dusk in winter. Here yesterday comes steaming back, when you hear whistles blow at the former great Western Railway Steam and Locomotive works. Outside you can explore the gleaming engines around an operational turntable. Inside watch as the workshop echoes to the sound of repairs. If you have ever wanted to be an engine driver now is your chance. Adults can enrol for a one day locomotive driving course.

WEST MIDLANDS POLICE MUSEUM is another place which attracts people. It is sited in Sparkhill Police

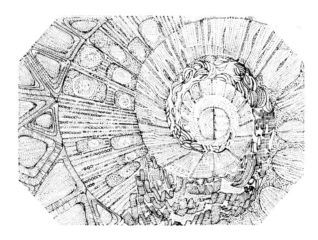

The embroidered panel on the east wall of the south nave, by Carole Raymond. Has the theme 'creative energy of God'.

Station at 641 Stratford Road and is open all year by prior appointment. Ring 021-626-7181. All the methods of policing in the past are on show with an unpleasant looking birching stool, a spiked helmet and some very unpleasant prisoners' leg irons. An old magistrate's court now houses a collection of police memorabilia from 1839 to the present day. Don't miss the 1900's book of persistent drunks complete with photos or the case of 'conviction by chocolate' as explained by a resident policeman.

In Chamberlain Square BIRMINGHAM MUSEUM AND ART GALLERY opens its doors to the general public all the year round, Monday to Saturday from 11am-5pm and on Sundays from 11am-5.30pm. It is a remarkable place which covers a myriad of subjects and cultures from the ancient to the 20th century with arts and crafts from the Natural World to the story of Birmingham, through Africa, America and Oceania to India and the Far East: in the Museum and Art Gallery, you can discover much more than artefacts and art. Gallery 33 takes a new look at people's beliefs, customs and values and you are invited to leave your own mark. I understand from October 1993 the Gas Hall will be open for spectacular exhibitions on novel themes. I made a beeline for the Edwardian Tea Room which is stylish, welcoming and gave me the best cup of tea I had tasted in ages.

THE BIRMINGHAM SHAKESPEARE MEMORIAL ROOM is also in Chamberlain Square. It very nearly came to a sad end in the 1970s but was rescued and restored in 1973-74. Designed in 1879 it was meant as a tribute to the great playwright. The carved oak panels, restored plasterwork and elegant Elizabethan style marquetry make it worth a visit. It is open all year Monday to Saturday from 9am-5pm by prior appointment. Ring 021-235-3392

At 69A New Street, THE ROYAL BIRMINGHAM SOCIETY OF ARTISTS is home to many Midland Art Societies and in the light gallery it is a pleasure to look at the constantly changing exhibitions. Open all year; during exhibition periods from Monday to Saturday 10.30am-5pm.

A total change of atmosphere and purpose is THE MUSEUM OF SCIENCE AND INDUSTRY at Newhall Street. Here the halls ring to the myriad sounds of machines with a constant banging, clicking and hissing. Nothing peaceful about it but it is exciting to get to grips with power, energy and forces at work in this wealth of interactive technology, past and present. If you are more intelligent than I am you will be able to work out the wonders of the hands-on 'Light on Science', marvel at the Smethwick Engine, the oldest working steam engine in the world, and see the 'City of Birmingham' locomotive in motion. Open all year, Monday to Saturday from 11am-5pm and Sundays from 11-5.30pm.

From the wonders of science to PERROTTS FOLLY in Waterworks Road, **Edgbaston** which is called Birmingham's most eccentric building. This 29m high tower was built in 1758 by wealthy landowner, John Perrott, purely to provide a bird's eye view of the city and beyond. From 1884 it was one of the world's first weather stations. Don't be daunted by the 139 steps - the climb is eased at each of the folly's seven levels. I wonder what John Perrott, now looking down from above, thinks of today's panorama?

In Pershore Road, THE BIRMINGHAM NATURE CENTRE invites you to take a look at the geese, picnic with the pygmy goats and chatter to the chickens in the Nature Centre's new open paddocks. With over 150 species of animals and plants to choose from, everybody will find a favourite. Special underwater viewing points mean you can be a David Attenborough and watch the otters watching you at close quarters. The centre is open daily from March 31st to the end of October, from 10am-4.30pm and in winter on Saturdays and Sundays from 10am-4.30pm.

If you have ever wondered what wandered around Birmingham before mankind ever existed then look no further than LAPWORTH MUSEUM at the School of Earth Sciences at the University of Birmingham, Edgbaston. Its venerable wooden cabinets contain fossils, minerals and rocks from the West Midlands and all over the world. You can see a dinosaur's footprint, a shoal of stony fish, some skulls of our distant ancestors, and admire the spectacular colours of the crystals. Lapworth Museum is open all year except Christmas and Easter weeks from Monday to Friday 9am-5pm.

THE BARBER INSTITUTE also at the University suggests you muse over a Monet, puzzle over a Poussin, be bemused by a Bellini, or simply delighted by a Degas. The Barber Institute is a treasure trove of artistic gems and ranks among the finest small picture galleries in Britain. The paintings, sculptures, drawings and prints are regularly rearranged to provoke a different reaction so one visit will never be enough. The Barber Institute is open all year except for Christmas and Easter weeks, Monday to Friday from 10am-5pm and Saturday from 10am-1pm.

Still in Edgbaston you should see THE BIRMINGHAM BOTANICAL GARDENS AND GLASSHOUSES in Westbourne Road. It is a 15 acre oasis of delight. The Botanical Gardens boast plants and birds from around the world. You can take a trip to the steamy Amazonian jungle in the Tropical House and Palm House, visit the fruit orchards of southern Europe in the Orangery and then dry off in the desert heat of the Cactus House. Outside it is just sheer pleasure to meander along through all manner of gardens, frequently accompanied by or glared at by the peacocks. It is open all year daily from 9am-8pm or dusk if earlier. Sunday it opens at 10am.

At **Bournville** there is SELLY MANOR AND MINWORTH GREAVES in Maple Road. Times have changed since Thomas Jouettes - a local tax collector - lived in Selly Manor 600 years ago. The 'post and truss' house, Selly Manor and the 'cruck' house Minworth Greaves, were saved and reconstructed in Bournville by George Cadbury. The two houses preserve a slice of English medieval life. You can find out what a witch's mark is and discover the hiding place. Imagine banqueting at one of the largest tables ever cut from a single tree. It is a wonderful sight. The houses are open all the year except mid-December to mid-January from Tuesday-Friday and Bank Holiday Mondays from 10am-5pm. Still thinking about Cadbury, CADBURY WORLD in Linden Road is in the heart of Bournville's 'factory in the garden'. Here you immerse yourself in the Chocolate Experience - the story of chocolate from the first 'chocolate' drinkers in Aztec America to the modern advertising campaigns of the now famous brands. You can learn what part the Cadbury family played in cocoa's history, see a mini packaging plant in action and chocolates being made by hand – sampling is actively encouraged! It is advisable to telephone for opening times and days. The number is 021-459-9116.

It was after I had been to see THE BIRMINGHAM ORATORY in Hagley Road which is 'Little Rome in Birmingham' and a memorial to Cardinal Newman, that I discovered THE STUDIO RESTAURANT AND LODGE which was built as a hostelry welcoming travellers in 1890. Since then three generations of the Creed family have developed this fine establishment into an outstanding restaurant with accommodation. No one who comes here to dine or stay feels anything but cossetted and welcomed.

I discovered another oasis at **Bearwood** THE BEARWOOD COURT HOTEL with its own restaurant, is a well converted hotel that was originally 4 Victorian terrace houses. It is only three miles from the city centre and ideal as a base from which to explore all the places I am writing about.

There are all sorts of oddities, if the owners will excuse the expression, that are good to visit. SAREHOLE MILL is one of them. You will find it a Cole Bank Road, **Hall Green**, and it is open from the end of March until the end of October daily from 2-5pm. It is Birmingham's only surviving watermill. I was entranced by the rushing water and the creaking cog as the old wheel turns. You can discover what part the pit, willow, spur and crown played in turning corn into flour. During the Industrial Revolution I was told that the mill also made rough metal smooth and rolled metal flat - it seems a far cry from grinding corn. The views across the pond are a delight and it is a place that J.R.R. Tolkien, the author of The Hobbit, visited regularly in his childhood and treasured the memory.

MOSELEY HALL DOVECOTE must rank as one of the oddities. It stands discreetly at the entrance of Moseley Hall Hospital. It is octagonal and built of red brick and seems to serve no purpose other than a monument to the doves and pigeons once used as a source of fresh meat in winter long before the invention of the deep freeze. Beside it stands the cowhouse which now houses temporary exhibitions of local artist's work.

Still in **Moseley** at Number 4 Yew Tree road is HIGHBURY, the home of the revered politician Joseph Chamberlain and his family from completion in 1880 until his death in 1914. It has extensive and beautifully kept gardens and one can well imagine what a restful place it must have been to the great man after the hurly burly of politics. I understand he used it frequently to entertain important guests. It is open seldom and perhaps it might be as well to ring to confirm dates before going. The number is 021-449-6549. The Park in which it stands is open all the year round from dawn to dusk.

CASTLE BROMWICH HALL GARDENS in Chester Road, Castle Bromwich, I found enchanting. It is a vision of genteel leisure of 300 years ago. The Gardens are hidden behind the Hall walls and only plants available before 1730 are grown. They recreate one of the few formal English

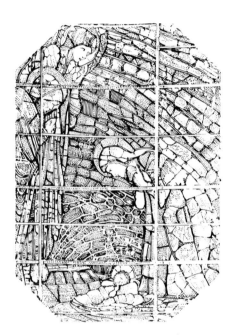

A detail from the Nativity Window, one of the three pre-Raphaelite windows, designed by Burne-Jones and created by William Morris

garden layouts to survive the 'naturalist' hand of later landscaping. Only 2 minutes from the M6 you can wander in perfect peace where melons and marrows slowly ripen. It is open from Easter until the end of September; Monday to Thursday 1.30pm-4.30pm, Saturday, Sunday and Public Holidays from 2pm-6pm.

BLAKESLEY HALL in Blakesley Road, **Yardley** is somewhere else that takes one back into the past. Hair and dung bind together the woven hazel and wooden joints of this timber-framed farmhouse in old Yardley village. You step over the threshold and meet the staff in period costume. It is charming and welcoming. The Hall itself was built in 1590 by Richard Smallbroke; today's furnishings date from an inventory of 1684. All twelve rooms - from the painted Chamber to the Boulting House- tell their own story. Blakesley Hall is open from the end of March until the end of October daily from 2-5pm.

My last visit in this mammoth exploration was to DUDLEY ZOO and CASTLE a fascinating place in its own right and made even more delightful by the wealth of history associated with it. Industrial, political and social history all combine at **Dudley** in the heart of the Black Country, together with varied architecture and attractions. The ruined castle standing on a wooden rise above the busy industrial town, dates back to the 11th centuy although the basic structure that we can see today is principally 14th century. DUDLEY CASTLE has had a long and chequered history and was first destroyed in 1175 when the then owner made the tactical error of backng Prince Henry in the revolt against his father, Henry II. A century later, rebuilding began but proceeded slowly; one of the reasons being the unpopularity of the bullying and dishonest John de Somery, whose forcible taxations and reluctance to settle debts led to a natural dis-inclination on the part of the locals to help with construction. The Dudley family took over during the reign of Henry VIII, but John Dudley followed in the footsteps of his predecessors by backing Lady Jane Grey for the throne and paid the supreme penalty.

The family fortunes like those of the castle, must have declined somewhat, for in 1585 a report was submitted that the castle was unfit for Mary Queen of Scots to visit - and she was a prisoner at the time! However, the increasing value of the surrounding mineral and manufacturing wealth soon put things right and the castle survived (apart from a slight Civil War battering) as a residence until a severe fire brought about its downfall in July 1750. Rumour has it that this was caused by counterfeit coiners working in the dungeons; but whatever the cause, the massive ruins still stand and are well worth a visit - particularly as they are now part of the well known DUDLEY ZOO; the two being connected by a chair lift.

Birmingham's GRAND HOTEL is one of the most distinguished in the city. Redolent of the past, with al the comfort of the present it is an ideal place in which to stay while you unearth the treasures Birmingham has to offer and perhaps go a little outside to see some lovely countryside. Near Alcester at **Temple Grafton,** THE BLUE BOAR is a delightful hostelry, at **Bewdley,** a small town rich in good things, has a lively and different pub, THE LITTLE PACK HORSE which is one of

thirteen belonging to Mad O'Rourke. Each is fun and if you visit them all you become a member of a select club! I wonder if you would still be sober enough to appreciate the award. Between Birmingham and Coventry is **Wootton Wawen** at the heart of the reclaimed Birmingham and Stratford Canal where THE NAVIGATION INN plays host to many visitors all year round within its welcoming walls.

Birmingham has rewarded me beyond my wildest dreams with its rich heritage, even if I was a little disappointed in its cathedral. Even that disappointment was assuaged by the superb Burne-Jones windows and the wonderful music. Somewhere I will never forget.

360-366 Bearwood Road, Bearwood,
Birmingham, West Midlands, B66 4ET.

Tel: (021) 429 9731
Fax: (021) 429 6175

THE BEARWOOD COURT HOTEL
Hotel & Restaurant

Four elegant Victorian town houses with a distinctive green frontage have been married together to produce The Bearwood Hotel. Situated on the A4030 in Bearwood, Warley, and just three miles from the centre of the city of Birmingham, this family run hotel has the sort of atmosphere that anyone staying away from home will appreciate. The 24 rooms, mainly en-suite, are all individually furnished in a comfortable fashion and complete with TV, telephone, clock radio and that most welcome of sights, tea and coffee making facilities.

The owners, Dan and Margo Doyle have been here 13 years and they improve the standard all the time. They are helped in the operation by their two charming and competent daughters. This is a hotel which will be as good for business people as it is for visitors. Children are very welcome and cots and highchairs are available on request.

The Bearwood is full licensed and it is very pleasant to come back here in the evening after visiting the city or undertaking business matters to take a drink either into the conservatory lounge or into the pretty garden where there are tables and chairs. Snacks and sandwiches are available at any time but certainly after the excellent breakfast, it is unlikely that you will want to eat until the evening! At dinner which is served from 7-9pm you will be offered traditional home-cooked food with what the owners describe as 'a little bit extra'. The wine list is well chosen and special menus are available for vegetarian and diabetic needs.

USEFUL INFORMATION

OPEN: All year. Breakfast 7-9am
Dinner 7-9pm
CHILDREN: Welcome. Cots & highchairs available
CREDIT CARDS: Visa/Access/Master
LICENSED: Full On Licence
ACCOMMODATION: 24 rooms, mainly en-suite

RESTAURANT: Home-cooked, traditional style, with a little bit extra
BAR FOOD: Snacks & sandwiches anytime
VEGETARIAN: Daily selection
DISABLED ACCESS: Level entrance to all public areas
GARDEN: Yes, with tables & chairs

---

31 High Street, Bewdley,
Worcestershire, DY12 2D4.

Tel: (0299) 403762
Fax: (0299) 401728

THE LITTLE PACK HORSE
Public House

Thirteen years ago 'Mad' Colum O'Rourke purchased this early 17th century coaching inn in the heart of Bewdley and went on to purchase 13 more, known collectively as The Little Pub Co. Each pub is an experience and if you are brave enough to embark on the Little Pub Tour, calling in at every one of the thirteen and have the Landlord witness your signature and stamp a passport provided, you will not only have great fun but be presented with a 'Lucky Member's Plaque' limited strictly to those who complete the tour, and once having done so you become a member of the most exclusive society in Europe.

The Little Pack Horse is full of atmosphere with original oak beams, low ceilings, lots of paraphernalia, old pews and a bar made from old beer barrels and railway sleepers! There is an open log fire and always many regular customers who are happy to share the warmth and bon homie of the pub with you. Visitors from all over the world come to pubs within The Little Pub Co and most of them have been introduced by friends who have been before them. The Real Ales are well kept and the food is genuinely home-made. The Little Pack Horse is especially famous for its Desperate Dan Game Pies. One item you will never find on the menu here is chips!

Bewdley has something for everyone from the Severn Valley Railway and memorable river trips, to idyllic countryside walks; from white-knuckle rides and exotic animals at West Midlands Safari and Leisure Park to fascinating craft museums in the town itself. A thriving inland port bypassed by the Industrial Revolution, Bewdley retains to this day its Georgian elegance.

USEFUL INFORMATION

OPEN: Mon-Sat: 11-3pm & 6-11pm, May to Sept 11-11pm
CHILDREN: At the landlord's discretion
CREDIT CARDS: All major cards except Amex
LICENSED: Full On Licence
ACCOMMODATION: Not applicable

RESTAURANT: Not applicable
BAR FOOD: Fresh, home-made. No chips!
VEGETARIAN: 4-5 dishes daily
DISABLED ACCESS: All ground floor. Happy to assist
GARDEN: No

LA GALLERIA

Restaurant & Wine Bar

Paradise Place,
Birmingham, West Midlands, B3 3HJ.

Tel: (021) 236 1006
Fax: (021) 212 1275

USEFUL INFORMATION

OPEN: 12-2.30pm & 6.30-11pm.
Wine Bar & Bistro: 5.30pm-11pm
CHILDREN: Welcome, One of 2 in
Birmingham where children are permitted
CREDIT CARDS: All Major cards
LICENSED: Full On Licence
ACCOMMODATION: Not applicable

RESTAURANT: Italian & International
BAR FOOD: Bistro meals, Dishes of
the Day
VEGETARIAN: Always available
DISABLED ACCESS: Yes & toilets
GARDEN: Outside seating front & rear

A few minutes from the ICC Symphony Hall and the NIA, La Galleria in Paradise Place has been a centre of excellence for many years. It has the true ambience of an Italian restaurant, owned and run by Marcello and Kay Manca, whose love of good food and expert knowledge of wine has given endless pleasure to their regular customers and a desire to enjoy more for those who come here for the first time.

It always seems to those who delight in eating in Italian restaurants, that the Patron manages to retain the same staff year after year, something that is quite unusual in the catering business. The effect this has is very noticeable; a sense of permanency and well being ensues which is reassuring to the clientele. Recently refurbished La Galleria is elegant, stylish and relaxing. All the food is fresh and prepared on the premises. Fish and meat is delivered daily and as well as traditional Italian dishes, Marcello and Kay Manca offer an extensive international menu.

Situated as it is in the heart of the city within easy walking distance of all the main hotels, La Galleria is a very popular rendezvous for business people seeking a lunchtime 'Menu Rapide' and ideally placed for theatre and concert goers in the evenings. It is very pleasant to enjoy a glass of wine whilst sitting in the sun, either in the front or to the rear of the building. For those who relish the relaxed atmosphere of the Wine Bar and Bistro, they are open from 5.30pm whilst the restaurant opens from 12-2.30pm and 6.30pm-11pm

THE GRAND HOTEL

Hotel

Colmore Row, Birmingham,
West Midlands, B3 2DA.

Tel: (021) 236 7951
Fax: (021) 233 1465

USEFUL INFORMATION

OPEN: All year 24 hours
CHILDREN: Welcome
CREDIT CARDS: All major cards
LICENSED: Full On Licence
ACCOMMODATION: 173 en-suite
bathrooms including 2 suites

RESTAURANT: Superb food in elegant
surroundings
BAR FOOD: Colmores lounge bar for tea
coffee and sandwiches at all times & hot
and cold menus at lunchtime
VEGETARIAN: Choices every day
DISABLED ACCESS: Yes
GARDEN: Not applicable

This stately hotel was built in 1876 and to this day is considered one of Birmingham's principal hotels. Situated in the city centre across the road from St Philip's Cathedral it was built over an artesian well which still supplies all the water for The Grand - over 15,000,000 gallons a year. The Grand Hotel became part of the Queens Moat House group in April 1982 and under the able management of Stephen Rees and his team it has blossomed. During the last few years a great deal of money has gone into the careful refurbishment of some of the bedrooms and all of the ground floor. What is so good is the retention of some of the Victorian splendour of years gone by and at the same time providing the modern facilities expected by customers today.

The hotel has three main venues from which to choose to eat. Colmores lounge bar is ideal for those wishing to eat in informal surroundings offering tea, coffee and sandwiches at all times and a hot and cold menu at lunchtime. The Carvery Restaurant offers traditional roasted joints as well as meat and fish entrées, vegetarian choices and salads. It offers quality food at excellent value for money. Chamberlains restaurant is a high class restaurant offering a la carte and table d'hote menus as well as winter and summer specials. The Grand is extremely proud of its conference and banqueting facilities. There are 22 rooms in all, catering for 5-500 people. Over the years many eminent statesman have spoken in the Listed Grosvenor suite with its magnificent ceiling. Over the years the Grand has had a number of important visitors including members of the Royal family as well as celebrities from the world of show business.

Linden Road, Bournville,
Birmingham, B30 2LD.

Tel: (021) 433 4334

CADBURY WORLD

Exhibition & Visitor Attraction

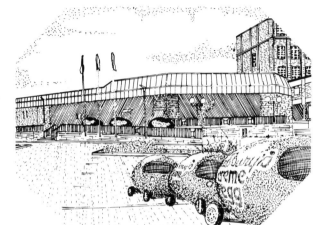

Cadbury World is a permanent exhibition devoted to chocolate. It tells how the Spanish found chocolate in central America and introduced it to Europe; how George and Richard Cadbury built 'The Factory in a Garden', and how the business grew to become 'The first name in chocolate'. What is written here is just a taster to the feast that is in store for you when you explore and examine with the help of people in the know, how Cadbury grew, how it sets about its advertising campaigns and cares for its employees. A truly great visitor attraction that should not be missed.

The chocolate trail begins at the Court of the Aztec Emperor Montezuma, where you can try for yourself the ancient spicy drink of chocolatl. You will discover how chocolate became all the rage in Europe before arriving at the beginning of the Cadbury story in Victorian England. Then discover how Cadbury transformed the chocolate drink into the world famous taste of Cadbury's Dairy Milk. Nowadays at Bournville many highly mechanized methods of chocolate making are inaccessible and not so interesting to look at. However, as well as the exhibition, there is a guided tour where visitors can see two production areas in which Cadbury's exclusive range of hand-made chocolates is produced, including the best selling Cadbury World Assortment.

Cadbury's advertising has been famous for over 100 years. Here you will have an inside view of how they make one of the best loved TV advertisements - Milk Tray's 'Man in Black' - as well as showing you some of those famous campaigns of the past and present. There is a restaurant, a chocolate shop and a collection of wonderful memorabilia.

USEFUL INFORMATION

OPEN: 10am -5.30pm, last ticket 4pm, opening days vary ring (021) 4514159 for admission details & reservations service. Entry not guaranteed without reservations. Closed throughout January 1994

CHILDREN: Welcome. Baby changing facilities. Children's Birthday parties by appointment

CREDIT CARDS: Access/Visa/Switch

LICENSED: Restaurant

ACCOMMODATION: Not applicable

RESTAURANT: Large selection self-service light meals and refreshments

BAR FOOD: Not applicable

VEGETARIAN: Available

DISABLED ACCESS: Everywhere except packaging plant. Toilets.

GARDEN: Large play area, picnic area

---

2 The Broadway, Dudley,
West Midlands, DY1 4QB.

Tel: (0384) 252401
Fax: (0384) 456048

DUDLEY ZOO & CASTLE

Zoo and Castle

Castle Hill provides a superb setting for Dudley Zoo - home to one of the most varied collection of animals in the country. The survival of many of these species is threatened in the wild and their hope of survival may depend on the breeding programmes in which the Zoo participates. Alongside the threatened species such as the Arabian Gazelle, Snow Leopard and Maned Wolf are many of the worlds well loved animals. Only by appreciating the height of a Giraffe and the aquatic agility of a Sea-lion or Penguin can we fully appreciate what will be lost if we do not conserve natural habitats.

In the Geochrom visitors can walk through a recreation of tropical rainforest where exotic birds fly amongst the foliage and the pools and streams are home to shoals of tropical fish. The Zoo is an ideal setting for a family day out and gives everyone the chance to see and learn about animals from every continent. There are tree-lined pathways and a free land train or chair-lift to take visitors to the top of the hill. Refreshments are available at the Queen Mary Restaurant and the Safari Cafeteria or there are many picnic areas with tables and benches.

Some people ask why have a Zoo? Here Dudley Zoo answers that it plays a vital role in ensuring the survival of many of the world's threatened species. Zoos allow us to study animals closely so that we understand their needs and behaviour thus helping us to help them in their natural habitat. Many zoos, like Dudley Zoo, provide sanctuary for animals that have nowhere left to live in the wild.

USEFUL INFORMATION

OPEN: Every day from 10am. Last admission in winter 3.30pm & summer 4.30. Closed Christmas Day

CHILDREN: Very welcome. Education service

CREDIT CARDS: All Major cards

LICENSED: Restaurant

SHOP: Souvenir shop

RESTAURANT: Yes, plus Safari Cafe serving a wide range of food. Queen Mary suite available for private functions daytime and evenings

VEGETARIAN: Selection available

DISABLED ACCESS: Yes, plus facilities

GARDEN: Acres of ground. Picnic areas. Land train ride

STUDIO RESTAURANT & LODGE

Restaurant & Lodge

616 Hagley Road West, Quinton, Oldbury,
Warley, West Midlands, B68 0BS.

Tel: (021) 422 2926
Fax: (021) 423 1902

USEFUL INFORMATION

OPEN: Restaurant: Tue-Sat from 7.30pm
Studio Rest: Daily breakfast from 7.30am
CHILDREN: Welcome
CREDIT CARDS: Access/Visa/Amex
LICENSED: Full On Licence
ACCOMMODATION: 5 self-contained
suites in the Lodge

RESTAURANT: Traditional & unusual
BAR FOOD: Not applicable
VEGETARIAN: Dishes available
DISABLED ACCESS: Yes, + 1 suite
GARDEN: Yes. Seating only

The Studio was built in 1890 as a hostelry welcoming travellers. Since then three generations of the Creed family have developed this fine establishment into an outstanding restaurant. No one who comes here feels anything but cossetted and welcomed. It is not only people from this country who have enjoyed The Studio Restaurant and Lodge but many from nations all round the globe.

The Creeds are justifiably proud that they are now able to compliment the Restaurant with a splendid Lodge within the grounds comprising of superior studio-style suites. Retaining the charm and elegance of yesteryear, the Lodge is handsomely built in fine old English brick with little dorma Georgian Windows shedding light onto a gallery in each room for you to work, relax or just 'think'. The latter is of enormous importance to those of us who work away from home. It is also wonderful for visitors who have spent a day exploring Birmingham and its cathedral and want to mull over and digest all that they have seen. Adding another nice touch, the suites are all named after an artist, four famous and others not so famous yet.

The Restaurant is delightful and has that wonderful sense of being away from the city of Birmingham and yet still a part of it. You will find it on the A456, half a mile from Junction 3 of the M5. It is a restful, intimate place and serves dishes which have been created with loving care and attention. The choice is wide, some traditional and some new found favourites. Naturally there is a list of fine wines.

THE BLUE BOAR

Inn & Restaurant

Temple Grafton, Alcester,
Warwickshire, B49 6NR.

Tel: (0789) 750010

USEFUL INFORMATION

OPEN: Mon-Sat: 11.30-2.30pm & 6-11pm
Sun: 12-3pm & 7-10.30pm
CHILDREN: Welcome
CREDIT CARDS: Access/Visa/Amex
LICENSED: Full on Licence
ACCOMMODATION: None available

RESTAURANT: Traditional with
International variations
BAR FOOD: Separate menu available
VEGETARIAN: Selection available
DISABLED ACCESS: Level access to bar
areas only
GARDEN: Patio Garden with
tables and chairs

Shakespeare was married in Temple Grafton church to Anna Whateley in 1582. The name Whateley incidentally is a corruption of the name Hathaway. The oldest part of the village inn, The Blue Boar dates from the early 1600's and records show that it has been an ale house since that time. It is possible to trace the names of the individual landlords and their families since 1776. This long association with the life of Temple Grafton has produced a unique and wonderful atmosphere within the Blue Boar; something that is remarked upon by every newcomer and relished by those who have been fortunate to have been there before.

The Blue Boar Inn represents what every one dreams of in an old English Country tavern. Traditional values survive and the service is as friendly and welcoming as it would have been hundreds of years ago. One doubts though that the food could possibly have reached the standard of today. The Inn is renowned for its fine food and has a wide ranging a la carte and international menu catering for all tastes including vegetarian, together with a good selection of pub meals served in the bar areas.

It is a fascinating experience to peer into the glass covered well in the restaurant which is some 35 feet deep and its pure water has been used in the brewing process for many years. The onset of the cooler Autumn days brings to life some of the four open fires in the bar and the restaurant areas, whereas the sunshine of Spring offers opportunity to relax outside in our patio garden and enjoy the extensive views towards the Cotswold Hills.

670 Warwick Road, Tyseley,
Birmingham, West Midlands, B11 2HL.

Tel: (021) 707 4696
Fax: (021) 764 4645

THE BIRMINGHAM RAILWAY MUSEUM
Visitor Attraction

This is an irresistible museum for anyone who enjoys the age of steam engines and even for those who are not afflicted with this fascination, it is still a tremendous place to visit. The museum is located on the site of a former Great Western Railway steam shed and is home to several steam locomotives, a reconstructed turntable and signal boxes as well as a well equipped information centre and locomotive sheds which are all open to the public.

The exhibits are many and varied including a Royal Coach Saloon used by Edward VII and at the other end of the scale a mail coach used in The Great Train Robbery - at its time the most daring robbery ever and later the subject of a film. The Museum runs many 'Steam Days' during the year which are always well attended and for the youngsters there are much loved Thomas Tank Engine days when the engines don the appropriate faces to delight the children - and not a few adults!

Another different facet of this exciting museum is the Steam Locomotive Driving Courses. You can choose to spend a whole day learning the art of driving and firing the GWR Castle class' 'Defiant', drive a small tank engine and discover how to operate a signal box and the technical explanation of steam engine principles. This is just one of the courses available, some are just one or two hours. All periods of driving are arranged for groups of up to three trainees, plus the instructor. Whatever the time you can afford to spend will be memorable. Corporate enquiries are welcome and all bookings are handled by the Birmingham Railway Museum.

USEFUL INFORMATION

OPEN: 10-5pm, closed Christmas day, Boxing day and New Years day
CHILDREN: Positively encouraged
CREDIT CARDS: Visa/Access
LICENSED: Not applicable
ACCOMMODATION: Not applicable

RESTAURANT: Snack type food, hot and cold
BAR FOOD: Not applicable
VEGETARIAN: Daily selection
DISABLED ACCESS: Level with some facilities
GARDEN: Picnic area at the trackside

Stratford Road, Wootton Wawen,
West Midlands, B95 6B2.

Tel: (0564) 792676

THE NAVIGATION INN
Public House & Restaurant

Wootton Wawen is a pretty country village on the main Stratford-Birmingham Road just one mile south of Henley in Arden. It is 19 miles from Birmingham and 17 miles from Coventry so it is ideally situated for anyone wanting to explore either or both city's remarkable Cathedrals.

The Navigation Inn was built in the 1830's especially for the men working on the Birmingham and Stratford Canal and was once owned by the Great Western Railway Company. One can imagine how busy it was then pulling pints for work weary and thirsty men who would stream into the bar at the end of their shifts. All that died away with the changing times. For thirty years the canal remained closed and unloved until the late 1960's when the National Trust bought the southern section of the Canal, although they left it to the Birmingham Water Board to operate. This gave a new lease of life to The Navigation Inn which is now owned by Whitbreads but has had Mark Smith as a tenant for the last ten years. He has made the pub lively and very popular with a Jazz night on the 2nd Monday of each month. It is right by the Canal and Narrowboats moor alongside during the summer months. It is actually a terminus for the Anglo-Welsh Narrowboat Company but you will find the canal is closed between November 1st and mid-March.

The food at The Navigation is memorable. They specialise in Sea food and high quality Grills. Everything is cooked to order and almost everything is home-made. The restaurant seats 50 comfortably.

USEFUL INFORMATION

OPEN: Apr-Oct, Mon-Sat: 11-11pm. Nov to March 11-3pm & 6-11pm. Sun: 12-3pm & 7-10.30pm
CHILDREN: Children's menu. Play area. High chairs in restaurant
CREDIT CARDS: All major cards
LICENSED: Full On Licence
ACCOMMODATION: None

RESTAURANT: Large, varied menu
BAR FOOD: Wide choice, mainly home-made
VEGETARIAN: Several dishes
DISABLED ACCESS: Few steps so limited access
GARDEN: Big garden by canal

Bristol Cathedral

Bristol

"Consider the lilies of the field...
even Solomon in all his glory was not
arrayed like one of these."

St. Matthew Vi v.28

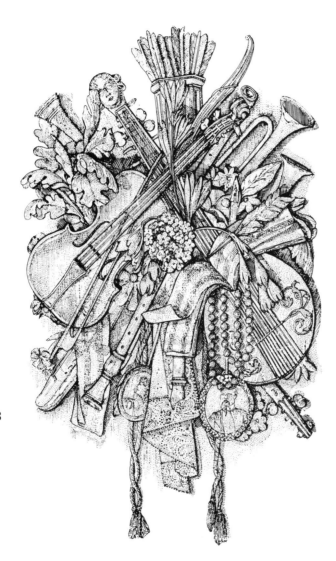

The City of Bristol

by Joy David

Bristol's geographical position has made it a place of importance over the centuries, each of which has added charm to this major city of the west. Nor has it tried to emulate its larger cousins. In fact Bristolians would be insulted to be thought of as in the same league as London, Birmingham or Manchester. The 15th century saw it as a time of seafaring drama, the 17th and 18th were blighted by the slave trade, civil wars and the arrogance of the merchants. Now it is alive with a thrust towards the 21st century. New industry and redevelopment of old warehouses along the docks has produced a new environment which marks the City as an important place to visit as well as to carry out its business.

More than 250,000 years ago primitive man settled in the valley of Bristol Avon; one can see the attraction, rich alluvial soil ripe for cultivation good clean spring water and a wealth of vegetation. The original settlement was built by Brennus a British Prince, in 380 BC. It was first mentioned as a fortified city in 430AD. variously called Caer Oder and Caer Brito, British City, by far the most delightful name was the Saxon, Brigstowe or 'pleasant place'. The name Avon appears elsewhere in the country, sometimes with a different spelling but the origin is the same, from the Celtic word for river. This Avon is born in the South Eastern Cotswolds, near **Malmesbury**. From here it describes a wide arc through **Chippenham**, **Melksham**, **Bradford on Avon** and **Bath**. Over the millenia the river has carved a deep, narrow channel through the limestone ridge, and it makes its stately progress through Bristol until it spills past Avonmouth and relinquishes its identity at the confluence with the vast expanse of the Severn.

From these auspicious beginnings the vibrant port of Bristol developed and continued to grow for the next 800 years. Its story along the way is fascinating, sometimes harsh but almost always thrilling. At one time the Tolsey would have been the centre of trade for the town and the crush of merchants would have been oppressive. Here they conducted the business of the day with speed, bargaining and bartering until the deal was struck with cut throat precision. At this moment the cash was 'paid on the nail', and the merchants counted their money on ancient tables forged from bronze. Outside this throng other gentlemen would meet in the popular coffee houses where they would discuss the latest news, a pastime much enriched when William Bonny introduced the Bristol Post Boy, the first newspaper to be published outside London. In the streets the ever increasing populace made negotiating the narrow alleyways a hazardous procedure; a situation not helped by small traders who resorted to dragging their wares through the town on 'geehoes', or sleds. Wheeled vehicles were not allowed in the streets because of the comb of cellars beneath them.

At that time the cellars and wharves would have been overflowing with more and more ships arriving to discharge their cargo on a daily basis. It was reported that at certain times of the year over a thousand ships could be found tied up at Kingroad and Hungroad, their masts like a forest along the river. Had you been able to see inside the storehouses your eyes would have gazed on hogsheads of wine from Spain and France, bales of wool, fine silks, Flanders' linen and skeins of thread. The exotic fragrance of almonds, saffron and liquorice would have filled the air. While the more prosaic, pots, pans, oil and tar would have been discussed in the same breath as the miserable pathetic human cargo of slaves, arriving in their hundreds to swell the coffers of the already fabulously wealthy.

In medieval days Bristol was enclosed by walls, pierced at intervals by gates. Above these gates were built churches and of these THE CHURCH OF ST JOHN still stands. The four main streets met at an intersection to which the townspeople would flock to listen to the bellman read proclamations, here too stood the High Cross, and any event of social interest took pleace beneath it. Visiting Monarchs were received with great ceremony or an unfortunate vagrant dealt a flogging, attracting the crowds equally, although the latter no doubt produced a somewhat less respectful response. Overseeing these events stood three of England's oldest churches, ALL SAINTS, CHRISTCHURCH and ST EWENS. The effigy of Edmund Blanket in ST

STEPHENS CHURCH offers a good example of the characteristic dress of the wealthy merchants of the 14th century. Over his tight sleeved tunic he wore a 'cote lardie; across his shoulders a small falling cape fastened in front'. Below the waist he sported a handsome jewelled belt, this denoted him as a man of importance and substantial wealth. Under the sumptuary laws of Edward III the wearing of such belts was forbidden to anyone below the rank of knight or possessed of less than £200. If you think the laws were a little severe, I can assure you they were considerably worse in the days of 844BC when it was ordained that no woman should walk in the street attended by more than one maid unless she was drunk!

It must have come as quite a shock to the gentry of Bristol when Henry VII imposed fines for the excessive finery worn by the merchants and their wives. Until then they had delighted in their conspicuous riches, far from hiding their light under a bushel, or woolsack or wine barrel, anything for that matter by which they had earned their money, frequently commemorating these items on shields and merchant marks.

Of all the churches in the area ST MARY REDCLIFFE is renowned for its beauty and reputed to be one of the largest in the land. Its massive tower is richly embellished and crowned with a spectacular spire which soars 285 feet toward heaven. When Elizabeth I saw St Mary Redcliffe in 1574 she described it as 'the fairest, goodliest and most famous parish church in England.'

Among its many memorable features is a tomb to the church cat, who was resident from 1912-27. The church was built between the early 13th century and 15th century on the Avon's red cliffs, when Redcliffe was inhabited by wealthy mechants. If you think the exterior is magnificent you will find the interior equally inspiring. Arches and pillars soar in exquisite slenderness and grace to the ribbed vaults, which are studded with more than 1200 bosses, each different. These were covered in pure gold when in 1740 Bristol women gave their jewellery for melting down.

The American Chapel contains a ship's figurehead of Elizabeth I and many fragments of medieval glass make up a window. The tomb of William Penn senior is in the South transept. It was his son, William, who founded Pennsylvania. The whale rib brought back by the Cabots, who sailed from Redcliffe Harbour in 1497 and discovered Newfoundland, is under the tower. The Royal Arms of Charles II are gorgeously coloured and framed. There are two effigies of William Canynges, a vastly wealthy merchant, who restored the church after the spire was struck by lightning in 1446 and for some reason there is the tombstone of his cook, with knife and colander on it. This is not a church just to behold in awe. It is a place in which to worship and enjoy the many concerts and recitals particularly in July when it is the setting for the annual music festival.

It was in the muniment room above the north porch that the precocious teenager Thomas Chatterton was inspired to write the verses that would lead to his downfall. Discovering some suitably distressed materials, Chatterton put quill to parchment and began to compose poetry in the style of Thomas Rowley, monk. These 'newly discovered' masterpieces were received with great excitement by the literati of the time. Sadly for the entrepreneurial youth, Rowley was proved to be a fiction and Chatterton having travelled to London to make his fortune was so disillusioned he committed suicide in a Holborn garret. A moral there for those who wish to see it! The fame he sought in life has been afforded to him posthumously and his birthplace at Chatterton Place is now a museum.

If Chatterton created a minor stir in the literary world it was undoubtedly John Wesley who made one in the relgious. John, his brother Charles and George Whitfield were friends at Oxford. While they were there they had been part of a group known as 'Methodists'. John spent two years in America and on his return, fired with a great revivalist zeal, attracted a crowd of 3,000 to hear him preach. The eloquence and fervent commitment that emanated from him not surprisingly produced a hostile reaction from the established church. His presence was not accepted in the parish churches, possibly because of this his followers grew rapidly in number. It became imperative for Wesley to find his own premises and when he eventually bought land at Horsefair, the first Methodist church was built. He travelled far and wide spreading the word and his famous Journal records the

One of the many hidden jewels amidst the magnificence of Bristol Cathedral

often depressing forays he made into the dismal underworld at **Knowle** where French prisoners were held in appalling conditions. He did much to improve education in the county. Despite this contribution to society he constantly met with hatred and suspicion, and it was not until after his death that the congregations became permanently established. 36, Horsefair, the sight of his 'New Room', now has two fine bronze statues to John and Charles.

18th century Bristol society displayed the dichotomy one would expect to find in a feudal society turned capitalist, and the atmosphere produced a fertile breeding ground for dissent among the poorer classes. In Octber 1831 the catalyst appeared when Sir Charles Wetherall, the Recorder, entered the city. By opposing the Reform Bill he had alienated himself from the people. The ensuing riots were catastrophic. The Mansion House was fired and looted as was the Customs House and other buildings in Queens Square, even the Bishops Palace went up in flames. The troops were called in and the Riot Act read, but Colonel Brereton refused to fire on the mob. For this act of compassion he was later rewarded by a court martial, the shame of which resulted in his suicide, a sad time. The mob which had indulged freely of the wine liberated from the Mansion House rampaged on to the

Strange Folk! A wood carving jousting scene:
Man on sow with pitchfork against a woman with
distaff mounted on a goose

prisons and many convicts were released. After three days of looting and destruction they were finally brought to order, over one hundred homes had been raised to the ground and 500 people lost their lives. So great was the fire in the city that it could be seen in Cardiff. Charles Kingsley who was a schoolboy in Bristol at the time described the scene as being like Dante's Inferno.

This was a dark period for the city but it rallied as usual. The world was expanding at a breathtaking pace, and in every quarter the conversation turned to exploration and adventure. This expeditionary zeal seems to be inherent in the hearts of Bristolians, how else could the Venetian John Cabot have arrived in the city, as a newly adopted son of Bristol who convinced the merchants of the 15th century to sponsor his expedition across the unchartered Atlantic. On May 2nd 1497 his little ship, The Matthew, set sail. He and his crew of eighteen had embarked on a perilous voyage into the unknown, and I expect their families secretly despaired of ever seeing them alive again. Imagine their excitement when, after a terrible period of waiting, the ship was first sighted returning to her home port. Fear and trepidation would have turned to pride when reports of the voyage became known. John Cabot had sighted land after fifty two days at sea, and on going ashore had ordered his men to hoist the flag of England and St Mark

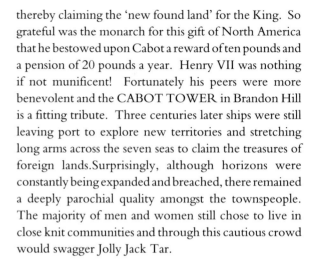

thereby claiming the 'new found land' for the King. So grateful was the monarch for this gift of North America that he bestowed upon Cabot a reward of ten pounds and a pension of 20 pounds a year. Henry VII was nothing if not munificent! Fortunately his peers were more benevolent and the CABOT TOWER in Brandon Hill is a fitting tribute. Three centuries later ships were still leaving port to explore new territories and stretching long arms across the seven seas to claim the treasures of foreign lands. Surprisingly, although horizons were constantly being expanded and breached, there remained a deeply parochial quality amongst the townspeople. The majority of men and women still chose to live in close knit communities and through this cautious crowd would swagger Jolly Jack Tar.

There can be little about his chosen career to earn the average merchant seaman the epithet 'Jolly'. It probably had more to do with his essence of bravado and occasionally altered emotional state after a brief exposure to alchohol. He carried about him the air of a true man of the world for he had seen jungles and white beaches, the raging oceans and the deep blue seas of the West Indies. He stood apart from other men, and developed characteristics and a uniform peculiar to himself. The wide bottomed trousers were tarred against insinuating damp, he wore a heavy 'fearnought' jacket and a Monmouth cap. On his forearms he displayed tatoos, made by scratching a design on his tough skin and rubbing in pigments or gunpowder. His face proclaimed him a seafarer battered by the salt winds, and burnt the colour of ochre by the sun; he was indeed a marked man. An occupational hazard which often, resulted in him waking up on slave ships embarked on yet another voyage, courtesy of the press gangs who roamed the alleys searching out unwilling recipients of the King's shilling. There would have been almost 2,000 seamen living in the town at that time and as night fell they

24

would have been looking for cheap lodgings, hot food and a jug or two of ale. They might well have staggered along between the close thronged houses in King Street, one of Bristol's oldest streets, passing the doors of the historic LLANDOGER TROW one of Bristol's oldest and most famous inns, believed to have been the model for the 'Admiral Benbow' in R.L. Stevenson's 'Treasure Island'. Perhaps they would have been tempted to open the door and go in for their ale. When they eventually fell out into the street they would have wandered on past the THEATRE ROYAL, Britain's oldest working theatre, through the passages and into CHRISTMAS STEPS. Their voices raised as the result of their carousing causing some upstairs windows to be flung open and the helpful occupants suggesting to them some alternative routes! They might even have tested the patience of the hospitable gentlewoman who runs MCCREADIES WHOLEFOOD RESTAURANT at number 3, but I doubt it! Here you can sample vegetarian and wholefood cooking at its very best and be welcomed by one of the nicest women in the business. Christmas Steps, completed in 1669, is enchanting and a fascinating place to linger and browse among the antique shops. At the top is the tiny 15th century CHAPEL OF THE THREE KINGS OF COLOGNE which is only 18ft by 22ft.

Outside the town in those days **Redcliff** would still have had a fine hostelry THE BELL, a place of merriment and bonhomie. It is in an area known locally as Cathay and was famous for the Bristol Blue Glass. The health giving properties of Bristol's spring waters was renowned by this time and demand for bottles provided more employment in the glass factory. The workers would have enjoyed the Bell. One wonders if they realised that while they were supping their ale, far beneath their feet in the deep cellars all manner of nefarious goings on were afoot, for this was the golden age of smuggling and not only brandy and wine. Indeed it was suggested that in

England and America there is not a man or woman who has not drunk smuggled tea, smoked smuggled tobacco, or ever owned a silk hankerchief which had not passed through customs.

This trading by stealth acknowledged no social or economic barriers, and as such is simlar to another form of free enterprise, poaching. Pickpockets were everywhere undoubtedly doing a brisk trade close to the fine Theatre Royal or even a carriage ride out at **Hotwells**. Since Catherine of Braganza first visited the springs which gush out of the cliff near the mouth of Avon Gorge, Hotwells became a fashionable place to be seen. Many of our great literary names frequented the spa. Perhaps they would have taken wine in THE ROSE OF DENMARK.

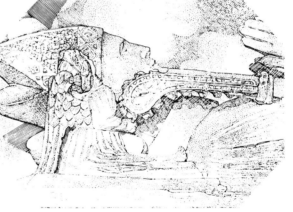

Gradually the architecture of Bristol changed. As the merchants poured money into improvement schemes a form of official planning developed and the random structure made way for a more formal design of elegant squares, without sweeping away the ancient city. The great COLSTON HALL and ST NICHOLAS ALMSHOUSES built by Edward Colston survived. It has always puzzled me how you can equate philanthropy with the slave-trade. Edward Colston, Bristol's greatest benefactor, found no difficulty with his conscience in the money he made from this evil business nor did Bristol

A Bishop at peace with his heavenly guardian

mind accepting his generosity. He was a bigoted high Churchman who ruled with a firm hand and gave his money without ceasing to found charities which still survive today. In Bristol you cannot escape his name, there are schools, almshouses, Colston Hall of course, renowned for its concerts, Colston Avenue where he is remembered in a great bronze showing him leaning on a cane, and Colston Parade. He laid down stringent conditions as to where his money went. Only Anglicans, for example, could attend his schools. Bristol certainly gained but I wonder if you can buy your way into the next world using money garnered from the misery of others?

Whatever changes in Bristol THE CATHEDRAL is a firm foundation. Once the Abbey Church of St Augustine, founded in 1140, it was given cathedral status by Henry VIII in 1542 at the same time as Gloucester, Chester, Oxford and Peterborough. It was Robert FitzHardinge who was responsible for building the grand Norman church of which important parts still remain. We can still see the great gatehouse, the entrance to the Abbot's lodging, the walls of the south transept and the east walk of the cloister, and the Chapter House.

In the early 13th century the Elder Lady Chapel came into being, opening out of the north transept in the Early English style. At the end of the same century the rebuilding of the entire chancel began and it is from this moment that Bristol Cathedral became unique and superlative among the cathedrals of our land.

When you get your first glimpse of this wonderful building, in the heart of the old city, you will see it stands full length in its splendour, on College Green. You would be forgiven if you thought after a glance that its three towers, long traceried windows, the full height of the building, pinnacled, embattled parapets, pinnacled, embattled transept with an earlier chapel extending on its east side, were all one piece. It is a deeper look that will tell you that the two west towers for instance are Victorian, indeed the whole nave is Victorian too. Do not be disappointed the whole is wonderful and the history of how it came about, thrilling.

In most medieval churches the central aisle rises above those at the side, but this is a hall-church in which the aisles are as high as the central space and the external buttresses are replaced by stone bridges carrying transverse tunnel vaults across the aisles. The central space itself has the earliest lierne vault in England. We can only stand and stare and relish the heritage that is ours because of the master craftsmen of these far gone times. Men who created a sense of space, elegance, and in spite of the grandeur, a light hearted expression of their belief in themselves and their undoubted faith in the Almighty.

Rebuilding work was abandoned at the time of the Dissolution, the west arch of the crossing was walled up, two bays of the Norman nave were entrusted as buttresses and the church had to do without a nave. It was not until 1868 that G.E. Street was appointed architect to build what had been begun over three hundred years earlier and even he did not live to see his towers completed in 1888.

26

The West front with its rose window and vast central porch reminds me of a French church but it is when you enter by the North west porch and step into the nave that you are stunned by what you see. There before you is the great wide nave, long aisle windows which bring the daylight dancing into the church and above, the sweeping vault spreading itself like a tree clad in its summer coat. Slowly, in a euphoric state, you will walk ahead to the chancel with the Lady Chapel beyond, knowing that you are reaching something that is unique.

Everywhere you turn you will find beauty, some will touch you more than another. Throughout the cathedral there are notable monuments covering every century, and in memory of those past citizens of Bristol to whom today's city owes so much. One visit here is insufficient. You could spend weeks and still find something new to wonder at and then each return visit would renew a love affair that would continue until you left these mortal coils.

Before you leave on your first visit, find a narrow door in the south transept, which leads down to the cloisters where only the east and part of the north walks survive. These are Perpendicular, but the east wall is Norman, and a fine Norman vestibule leads you into the Norman Chapter House, one of the most magnificent Norman interiors in England, with its walls arcaded and intricately carved and ornamented dating from about 1150. From the cloisters you will go to a tiny precinct, to the south of which stands the Cathedral School, and to the west the Abbey gatehouse with a sturdy Norman arch, and above, the house itself built about 1500 with its mullioned windows and panelled, pinnacled parapet. From here you are back in the Bristol of today in College Green. Refreshed? Maybe that is not the word. I never fail to emerge humbled by the Cathedral's present beauty and astounded at the physical effort, let alone the talent of the people who designed it and carried out the work.

Bristol has many fine churches including St Mary Redcliffe about which I have already written. In Broad Street in the heart of the city is CHRIST CHURCH with ST EWEN which was rebuilt in 1791 by Bristol architect, William Paty. The dragon vane on the spire was brought from the earlier church as well as the Quarter Jacks of 1728, the Renatus Harris organ and fine case, and the Lord Mayor's sword rest. It is quite lovely with a sublime white and gold domed interior influenced by Wren.

ALL SAINTS CHURCH in Corn Street is partially Norman and part Perpendicular. The north tower topped by a cupola, is of the early 18th century, and the chancel was built in the mid-19th century. The most outstanding monument is by the Belgian sculptor Ryusbrack to Edward Colston who died in 1721, designed by the architect James Gibbs. The church is now a Diocesan Study Centre.

THE CHURCH OF ST MARK, The Lord Mayor's Chapel, originally belonged to Gaunt's Hospital, but at the Dissolution became the property of the City Corporation - it is the only church in England owned by a corporation - and from 1721 their official place of worship. There have been many alterations to the original 13th century building. A tower in the Perpendicular style was built in 1487 and in the 16th century the Poyntz Chapel, floored with Spanish tiles came into being. There is a wealth of stained glass, some of which came from the collection of the eccentric millionaire William Beckford's Fonthill Abbey. There are monuments everywhere, making this one of the most important churches for monumental sculpture.

You need time to explore Bristol. I have spoken already of its beautiful and gracious squares but not of Frogmore Street which has the 17th century HATCHET INN, once part of a row. Then there is ORCHARD STREET which has to be the loveliest Georgian Street in Bristol. In some ways it might be advisable to take advantage of the many very good museums before you start seeking out the treasures of the city. THE CITY MUSEUM AND ART GALLERY is the major museum of the area with displays representing applied art, fine art, oriental art, archaeology, geology and natural history. It has an outstanding collection of European ceramics and glass, and particularly noteworthy are the galleries of archeology and natural history. Open 10am-5pm except Sundays.

THE GEORGIAN HOUSE, just off Park Street, built 1789-91, is fully furnished in the elegant style of the period and is maintained as a museum. Open 10am-1pm & 2pm-5pm. Closed Sundays.

Backing onto The Lord Mayor's Chapel in Park Street is HARVEY'S WINE MUSEUM housed in the 13th-century cellars of the Gaunt's Hospital. This unique place contains displays of antique corkscrews, bottles, decanters, drinking glasses etc. It is normally open to the public by appointment only. However, visitors over 18 are welcome on Friday mornings without prior appointment.

Also in Park Street is the famous bookshop of WILLIAM GEORGE & SON, a wonderful place in which to browse, to seek out a special book or buy a present for oneself or others. I have a particular liking for it, perhaps because my grandfather was a William George - no relation I hasten to add.

Do you enjoy riddles? If so I will quote you this one from a brochure recently given to me. Question: Which Bristol building can boast a 400 year history during which it has been a home, a lecture theatre, a finishing school for young ladies, a mecca for scientists and the first reform school for girl's in the country? Which Bristol

building can boast one of the finest rooms in the South West? Answer: THE RED LODGE. It is one of Bristol's few remaining 16th century buildings, once forming part of a great estate and the 'finest room' is an astonishing example of interior decoration. From the icing sugar plasterwork of the ceiling to the carved oak wall panels there is seemingly no end to the intricate embellishments. When you have become quite dizzy with the splendour it is as well to remember the walled Tudor garden which has been lovingly created outside. In June and July the garden is open to visitors and where better to sit and unwind than among the wafting perfume of old roses and honeysuckle.

THE MARITIME CENTRE is essential visiting. Here Isambard Kingdom Brunel's restored GREAT BRITAIN lies in Bristol Docks near a reconstructed dredger, also designed by Brunel, and a display of ship models and paintings accumulated by the shipbuilder, Charles Hill.

*The majesty of the West Front's
rose window*

The centre of Bristol is excellent for shopping and nowhere better than BROADMEAD which has been massively reconstructed over the last few years giving Bristolians and visitors the opportunity to shop in a pedestrianised area amongst stores and individual businesses offering everything one could wish for. In the midst of the newness is JOHN WESLEY'S CHAPEL, the famous New Room, which was the first Methodist

church in the world. Of particular interest is the double-decked pulpit from which Wesley preached. Outside in the courtyard is a fine bronze equestrian statue of the man himself. It is no distance from there to QUAKER'S FRIAR which is part of the Dominican Friary founded in 1227.

Bristol harbour is two and a half miles of calm, deep, waterway right in the heart of the city, the legacy of Bristol's maritime past. No longer is it one of the world's busiest harbours. Those days have gone but what has emerged is an imaginatively transformed major leisure and recreation centre. Where once John Cabot departed to discover North America there are now shops, museums, cinemas and arts centre, an exhibition centre, pubs and restaurants. It is lively and a fun place to be.

One of my favourite ways of seeing it is to take one of the Bristol ferry boats from ST AUGUSTINES REACH. It stops at fourteen landing stages and allows you a chance to sit back and take in much that you might otherwise miss. At the head of the Reach is one of Bristol's best loved landmarks, NEPTUNE'S STATUE. There are some picturesque dock cottages dating from 1831. You will see some of the places about which I have written including the SS Great Britian and occasionally at weekends you will see the restored locomotive Henbury, steaming along from the INDUSTRIAL MUSEUM to the Great Britain. Permanently moored in the floating harbour going towards

Castle Park is a lightship which once gave warning to seafarers in the North sea. It plays a very different role today as a pub and restaurant moored in the Welshback.

Away from the centre is **Clifton** with its Downs, a 400 acre green expanse, and wonderful houses, particularly the terrace of Regency houses known as The Paragon where the fronts are concave and the porches curve the other way, with convex double doors. Clifton is elegant and gracious and almost like a village, yet it is a place of many contrasts. Architects must have had a sense of theatre when they built Royal York Crescent and Windsor Terrace on the cliff over the Gorge. In Canynge Square there are dainty, balconied houses and rows of very squat, rather boring Victorian villas. It has some excellent restaurants and delightful pubs and wine bars. None better than the very different COLONEL JASPERS. If you still have the energy you can carry on and visit BRISTOL ZOO on the downs. One of the foremost in the country it is a super place. Go far enough and you will come to Brunel's graceful and miraculous SUSPENSION BRIDGE which hangs right across the Avon Gorge at a height of 245 feet and incorporates chains from the old Hungerford suspension bridge in London.

There are many places close to Bristol which should be included in your itinerary. The pretty village of **Almondsbury,** for example, and whilst there a little refreshment at the welcoming BOWL INN would not go amiss.

Instead of staying in Bristol - although I hasten to say that the city has many first class hotels - I always try to stay outside and if I am on good terms with my bank manager then I would not hesitate to go to THORNBURY CASTLE in the small, thriving market town of the same name, just north of Bristol. It has managed to achieve a certain isolation which has allowed it to keep its old streets and buildings. The main street layout has not changed since medieval times.

In 1511 Edward Stafford, 3rd Duke of Buckingham, started to build his castle and ten years later he was beheaded for treason. Henry VIII appropriated the castle and brought Anne Boleyn to stay here in 1535. Mary Tudor lived here for some years and when she became Queen she returned the castle to the descendants of the late Duke. Today, with its own vineyard and the oldest Tudor garden in England, Thornbury is the only Tudor Castle to be run as an hotel. As you would suspect it is superb, and is rated as one of the best 300 hotels in the world.

No one should visit Bristol without also visiting **Bath**. It is always with a certain amount of impatience and eager anticipation that I seek out this incomparable city. Georgian Bath is wonderful, not because of the individual buildings but the whole architectural assembly. Take a walk down through Laura Place, looking at the houses in which society used to dwell in its heyday when Bath was a fashionable watering place, cross Argyle Street and so to Pultney Bridge which spans the Avon. You could be forgiven for thinking you were in Florence as you cross this enchanting bridge which has small shops on either side not unlike the Ponte Vecchio. The Abbey must come on your list of places to see. It is probably the most beautiful place in the city. There is more glass than stone in the walls which fill it with light. I have no hesitation in recommending four superb hotels, each with its individual charm. DUKES HOTEL in Gt Pultney Street, NEWBRIDGE HOUSE in Kelston Road, THE QUEENSBERRY HOTEL in Russel Street and THE REDCAR HOTEL which includes BENTLEYS RESTAURANT at 27, Henrietta Street. Something totally different for you and so very English is the enchanting ENGLISH TEDDY BEAR COMPANY at 8, Abbey Churchyard. I doubt you will leave the shop without purchasing a bear to join your family or delight another.

Wherever you stay and whatever you do it is always the magnificence, the history and the charm of Bristol, its Cathedral, Bath and its Abbey and the many pretty villages and small towns making up this part of Avon which will draw you back relentlessly.

Church Road, Almondsbury,
Bristol, Avon, BS12 4DT.

Tel: (0454) 612757/613717
Fax: (0454) 619910

THE BOWL INN

Inn & Restaurant

Almondsbury is a delightful place, as pretty as its name and deserves to have a good hostelry. The Bowl Inn answers this need admirably. Built by Monks centuries ago it has aged well and has both a great atmosphere and a warmth that has built up over the years.

The eight en-suite bedrooms are recommended by the English Tourist Board; three crowns - commended. Comfortably furnished they provide an excellent place in which to stay either for business or pleasure. For most people though this is the place to eat and drink in attractive and historic surroundings. People of all age groups seem to make up the clientele. The inn is always busy with people in the bars enjoying the well kept Real Ales and in the Restaurant the wide ranging menu tempts even the most pernickety of diners.

Fourteen starters make the choice difficult but exciting. Stilton and garlic mushrooms - button mushrooms sauted in Stilton and garlic butter and succulent slices of smoked chicken breasts served with a quince and orange jelly, are two very popular choices. Fish, fresh from the market, prime Scotch beer, English lamb and veal, and a range of Bowl Specialities together with vegetarian main courses, make up the menu in the restaurant. An equally good selection of dishes is on offer in the bar. With the comprehensive and fine selection of wines, you will leave The Bowl totally contented.

USEFUL INFORMATION

OPEN: 11-3pm & 5-11pm,
  Sat: 11-3pm & 6-11pm,
  Sun: 12-3 & 7-10.30pm
CHILDREN: Welcome
CREDIT CARDS: All major cards
LICENSED: Full On Licence
ACCOMMODATION: 6 twin, 2 double,
  en-suite

RESTAURANT: A la carte. Home-cooked
  International cuisine
BAR FOOD: Full Bar menu
VEGETARIAN: 7 dishes
DISABLED ACCESS: Level & loos
GARDEN: Patio. Barbecues

27-29 Henrietta Street,
Bath, Avon, BA2 6LR.

Tel: (0225) 469151
Fax: (0225) 461424

BENTLEY'S RESTAURANT & THE REDCAR HOTEL

Hotel & Restaurant

Apart from the undoubted comfort and service of staying in a hotel of this calibre, there is the added pleasure in learning about its history. Its architect and designer, the redoubtable Sir William Pultney, who also designed Great Pultney Street, would no doubt be very surprised that the three houses numbers 27-29 had changed from individual buildings into this elegant establishment which gives pleasure to visitors from all over the world, all the year round.

Centrally situated at the end of Laura Place, a street beloved by Regency society, The Redcar is versatile. It has 31 bedrooms each furnished beautifully and with every modern facility. It is an ideal venue for small conferences, where meetings can be held in quiet surroundings. It accommodates 70 people theatre style and 50 boardroom. The rooms are also excellent for a dinner dance or a wedding reception.

Bentley's Restaurant is somewhere that is popular with residents of Bath. They know it is tranquil, delightfully appointed and it is somewhere that they can be sure of the freshest of ingredients in all the interesting dishes that are produced by the Head Chef and his Brigade. Every dish on the a la carte menu is a masterpiece and an excellent table d'hote menu is also available. The bar is a meeting place for friends who want to enjoy comfort, a drink and probably indulge in one of the tasty lunchtime specials.

USEFUL INFORMATION

OPEN: All day
CHILDREN: Welcome
CREDIT CARDS: All major cards
LICENSED: Full On Licence
ACCOMMODATION: 31 rooms,
  22 en-suite

RESTAURANT: A la Carte & Table d'Hote
BAR FOOD: Lunchtime specials
VEGETARIAN: Always available
DISABLED ACCESS: No
GARDEN: Henrietta Park next door

DUKES' HOTEL
Hotel

Great Pulteney Street,
Bath, Avon, BA2 4DN.

Tel: (0225) 463512
Fax: (0225) 483733

USEFUL INFORMATION

OPEN: All year
CHILDREN: Welcome
CREDIT CARDS: All major cards
LICENSED: Full On Licence
ACCOMMODATION: 22 en-suite,
3 star rating

RESTAURANT: Fixed price, delicious
BAR FOOD: Not applicable
VEGETARIAN: Always available
DISABLED ACCESS: No
GARDEN: Two parks very close

There is nowhere in Bath that exemplifies its architecture more than Great Pulteney Street, a classical Georgian parade without a single building dating from later than the 18th century. It is here that you will find Dukes' Hotel. Until you experience it for yourself you will find it difficult to envisage how zealously it has been preserved inside and out. It is truly beautiful in every way. You can enter through an elegant doorway with an impressive staircase almost immediately ahead of you. The bar is warm and friendly, the drawing room impressive but restful. It is a hotel that has won acclaim throughout the world and it is not unusual to find celebrities staying here.

It is never easy to adapt old buildings to cope with the demands of modern day life. Somehow Tim and Rosalind Forester, the resident proprietors, have managed to incorporate private bathrooms and showers, central heating and superb modern kitchens without in anyway detracting from the beauty of the house.

You will dine here on beautifully presented food, sleep peacefully in comfortable beds and awake in the morning looking forward to a day in this lovely Georgian city, after breakfasting exceedingly well. As part of their tariff, Duke's offers 'Daysaway' breaks, which include accommodation, breakfast and dinner for two nights at generous rates; an offer that is well worth taking. There is no doubt that you will be well cared for here.

THE ENGLISH TEDDY BEAR COMPANY
Shop

8 Abbey Churchyard, Bath,
Avon, BA1 1LY.

Tel: (0225) 338655

USEFUL INFORMATION

OPEN: 10-7pm daily
CHILDREN: Welcome
CREDIT CARDS: All major cards
DISABLED ACCESS: Good

SPECIAL SERVICES: Gift boxing
available, Made to order service,
Mail Order Catalogue available –
Contact branch for further information
on availability.

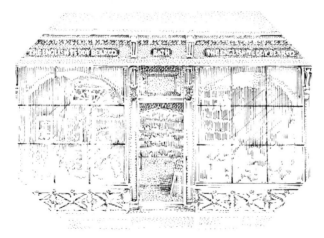

The beautiful Abbey Churchyard exactly opposite the Roman Baths and Pump Room is the appropriate setting for The English Teddy Bear Company's shop in the glorious city of Bath. The shop is in a beautiful Georgian building with a shopfront dating from 1830. Inside, the shop is like a ballroom for Teddy Bears. Classically proportioned furniture houses these most proud of Teddy Bears. One's eyes light up with pleasure, not only at the Teddy Bears but at the wonderful blue panelling and Austrian crystal chandeliers which lend countenance to this most elegant of shops.

The English Teddy Bear Company creates traditional Teddy Bears in a variety of cloths, all English and the Bears are made with traditional features like long snouts, embroidered noses and jointed limbs and head. Since the bears are hand made, no two are alike and each bear comes with its own birth certificate! The company also makes an eccentric range of stylish Teddy Bear clothes. Silk waistcoats, bow ties, smoking jackets, cricket jumpers, boaters and much more make up the essential English Teddy Bears' wardrobe! The Teddy Bear's appetites are also considered – there are the most delicious traditional English biscuits, jams and marmalades on sale. And if you do not wish to be free of Teddy Bears in any situation, they produce a fun and stylish range of all cotton T shirts for children and adults. Each shop has designs exclusive to that town and these make affordable and easily transported gifts.

To visit one of The English Teddy Bear Company's shops is to return, all too briefly, to an ideal childhood world. Seek out the four others in Oxford, Canterbury, Cambridge and London. It is a rare treat.

35 Kelston Road, Newbridge,
Bath, Avon, BA1 3QH.

Tel: (0225) 446676
Fax: (0225) 447541

NEWBRIDGE HOUSE HOTEL

Hotel & Restaurant

Newbridge House was one the home of Lord and Lady Kirkwood and is noted within the City for its true Georgian Architecture. It is a period Georgian 1770 Graded Listed Building, set in a peaceful location and those who stay within its hallowed portals feel privileged. Of course, much of the pleasure is in staying in such an elegant building but that pleasure would be severely diminished if one did not have all the other ingredients that brothers, Colin and Nigel Day have brought to the hotel.

Some people describe the hotel as a reminder of old Colonial Singapore - Raffles perhaps. In the Reception room is a splendid grand piano, vast and very comfortable settees invite people to sit down and everywhere there are fresh flowers, and added to their scent is the gentle fragrance from bowls of pot-pourri. There are eleven en-suite bedrooms, some with open fires and four-poster beds. The charming restaurant, which is open to non-residents, overlooks the gardens and the breakfast room opens out onto a terrace where pergolas, water fountains, Chinese Buddhas and figurines bedeck the lawns. The beef trolley on Sunday is something that the people of Bath will tell you is not to be missed.

This truly beautiful hotel has three rooms available for small meetings and conferences. There are two formal dining rooms with open fires and one of these has a full length balcony commanding stunning views of the countryside.

USEFUL INFORMATION

OPEN: All year
CHILDREN: Any age welcome
CREDIT CARDS: All major cards
LICENSED: Full On Licence
ACCOMMODATION: 11 en-suite rooms

RESTAURANT: Superb cuisine
BAR FOOD: Not applicable
VEGETARIAN: On request
DISABLED ACCESS: 2 ground floor
rooms
GARDEN: Beautiful garden & terrace.
No playing!

Russel Street, Bath,
Avon, BA21 2QF.

Tel: (0225) 447928
Fax: (0225) 446065

QUEENSBERRY HOTEL

Hotel & Restaurant

The very name of Bath conjures up a vision of elegance both materially and architecturally. The Queensberry Hotel is the epitome of this style and charm. Your bedroom will be huge, beautifully furnished with a vast draped bed and well appointed bathroom. The whole house is quietly luxurious.

The house was built in 1722 for the Marquis of Queensberry who employed the renowned architect, John Wood to create a unique town house. Little did the Marquess know that he would be giving so much pleasure to so many people in this era; people who come to stay find themselves supremely cared for in a quiet, un-pompous but efficient manner. The position is marvellous too for you are just a few minutes walk from the Royal Crescent, Circus, and the Assembly Rooms, yet it is sublimely quiet.

In 1992 the hotel won the 'Best Newcomer Award for the South West. Sitting in the courtyard garden on a warm summer evening, you may forget that you are in the middle of Bath. You may not know that the Queensberry is rather less traditional than its surroundings; whether it is first class bathrooms, laundry and room service or up-to-date office support for executives, the hotel-keeping is certainly contemporary. The Olive Tree is what Stephen and Penny Ross, the owners, conceive as a contemporary restaurant - informal, modestly priced with English cooking that combines their own excellent produce with the robustness of the Mediterranean.

USEFUL INFORMATION

OPEN: All year
CHILDREN: All ages welcome
CREDIT CARDS: All major cards except
Diners
LICENSED: Full On Licence
ACCOMMODATION: 22 en-suite rooms

RESTAURANT: Contemporary - informal
BAR FOOD: Not applicable
VEGETARIAN: Always available
DISABLED ACCESS: Limited
GARDEN: Yes with seating. Not playing.

WILLIAM GEORGES & SON

Bookshop

89 Park Street,
Bristol, BS1 5PW.

Tel: (0272) 276602
Fax: (0272) 251854

USEFUL INFORMATION

OPEN: Mon-Sat: 9-5.30pm
CHILDREN: Very welcome.
Special department
CREDIT CARDS: Access/Barclay/Amex
Visa/Switch
DISABLED ACCESS: Yes.
SPECIAL SERVICES: International Mail
Order service

George's Bookshop in Park Street is a legend in its own time. The long story of George's begins in 1830, when William George was born in Somerset learning his business from his uncle William Strong who had a bookselling and publishing business. By the time he was seventeen he 'took the shop at 16 Bath Street, on Nov 1st 1847 - rent 3/6d per week'. The shop was opened for business on 15th November 1847, and his first day's takings were nine shillings and two pence! When William George died in 1900 it was his son Charles George who bore the repsonsibility for the business until 1929, when, his daughter Peggy invited Basil Blackwell of Oxford to assume responsibility for the future of the company.

The site has expanded and been improved and now has five specialist shops in Park Street. The General and New Books department stocks as wide a range of new and important hardback books. The paperback department stocks all the major new titles and has without doubt the largest stock of paperbacks in the United Kingdom outside London. Cookery and wine books are also housed here. Literature on wine is a speciality of George's. The Children's Department carries one of the largest fiction, non fiction and educational stocks in the country. There is a Languages and Education Department, and The Park Street Computer Bookshop. The Academic Shop has everything for the student including revision aids and The Scientific & Technical Department is highly rated. Medicine, the arts and literature all have their own department. It is fascinating, efficient and William George would have been proud of it.

COLONEL JASPERS

Restaurant & Wine Bar

3 Beacon House, (Below Habitat),Queens Avenue,
Clifton, Bristol, BS8 1QU.

Tel: (0272) 731289

USEFUL INFORMATION

OPEN: Mon-Fri: 11.30-3pm & 5-11pm
Sat: 11.30-3pm & 7-11pm
CHILDREN: Yes in Dining Room &
Wine Vaults. High Chairs. Menu
CREDIT CARDS: All major cards
LICENSED: Full on Licence
ACCOMMODATION: Not applicable

RESTAURANT: Traditional English
Fare. Good Quality & Home-made
BAR FOOD: Traditional, fresh,
value for money
VEGETARIAN: Daily Special
DISABLED ACCESS: No
GARDEN: No

Within easy walking distance, just north of the Cathedral, Colonel Jaspers is ideal for those seeking respite from the ardours of ecclesiastical exploration! You will find it located directly beneath the Habitat Store and pleasantly situated in the Queens Road shopping area with Clifton and Isambard Kingdom Brunel's stunning Suspension Bridge not far off.

Colonel Jaspers is based on a Victorian Ale and Port House with rich and highly polished mahogany furniture, sawdust covered floors and candlelight, all of which serves to produce a very special and memorable atmosphere. It is part of the Davys of London Group and as such is able to offer all the benefits of Davy Club discounts and promotions on wines and meals. It is somewhere much loved by Bristolians and equally by the many visitors who have discovered its presence. For confidential business lunches, private offices are available in the dining room.

Behind the counter Old Jollop Bitter Ale, N.A.T.S Lager and a selection of Davy's fine foreign wines is on offer. At present Colonel Jaspers provides two menus. A fixed price one, two or three course, and an a la carte with traditional pies, charcoal grill steaks and other delicious dishes. The bar snacks are traditional in the main, always freshly cooked and very good value for money. For vegetarians there is always a Daily Special. You will find the staff efficient, friendly and providing excellent service.

Thornbury, Nr Bristol,
Avon, BS12 1HH.

Tel: (0454) 281182
Fax: (0454) 416188

THORNBURY CASTLE
Hotel & Restaurant

Castles are immediately romantic in one's mind. The reality of that romantic image is Thornbury Castle. The focal point of a small, market town, 12 miles north of Bristol, Thornbury Castle stands in 15 acres of regal splendour with its own vineyard and the oldest Tudor garden in England. It was built in 1511 by Edward Stafford, third Duke of Buckingham and later owned by Henry VIII who stayed here with Anne Boleyn in 1535.

It is like entering a magical world, but with every realistic modern comfort, when you make the decision to stay or dine in the only Tudor castle in England operating as an hotel. It is renowned, quite rightly, for its high standards, luxurious accommodation, efficient, friendly but unobtrusive service and for its award winning cuisine.

The staff at Thornbury are as proud and devoted to its well being as the owners, the Baron and Baroness of Portlethen. John, the maintenance man who also tends the vineyard and the sheep, has been at Thornbury Castle for 25 years and knows as much about the castle and the surrounding area as anyone. Pepe, the Spanish waiter, has a mere 19 years of service - with no days off sick - an undoubted tribute to the caring spirit of Thornbury Castle which in turn pleases everyone who chooses to stay. For those who come just to dine, it is a gastronomic experience and it is superb for private dinner parties or for small conferences.

USEFUL INFORMATION

OPEN: All year round, except two days in January - ring first to check dates
CHILDREN: Not under 12 unless they are known
CREDIT CARDS: All major cards
LICENSED: Full On Licence
ACCOMMODATION: 18 en-suite bed-chambers

RESTAURANT: Classic English/French cuisine
BAR FOOD: Not applicable
VEGETARIAN: Full menu on request + One dish on usual menu
DISABLED ACCESS: None
GARDEN: The oldest Tudor garden in England. Pre-dinner drinks in summer

Bury St Edmunds Cathedral

Bury St Edmunds

"When Time, who steals our years away,
shall steal our pleasures too,
The memory of the past will stay
And half our joys renew"

Thomas Moore

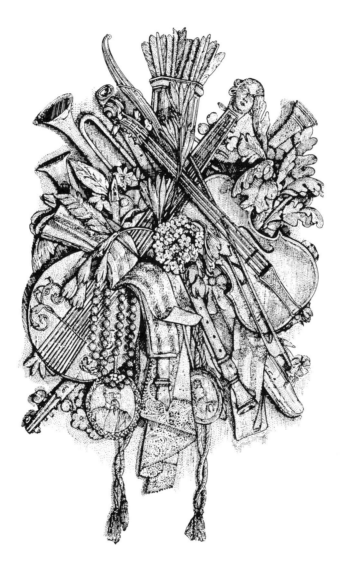

The City of Bury St Edmunds

by John Theobald

Bring a sense of history with you to this delightful and beautiful town for here is the very spirit of East Anglia. It is where the region's last king reigned and both the Borough and Cathedral of St Edmundsbury are named after him.

King Edmund died at the hands of invading Danes near Diss in AD896 and the visitor quickly realises that town and cathedral still pay homage to a man who for centuries was the patron saint of England. After Edmunds' body was brought to the monastery his shrine became a place of pilgrimage long before Canterbury and the Saxon settlement of Beodricksworth which was chosen as a monastic centre in AD636 steadily grew in religious importance when the mummified corpse of St Edmund - for he was canonised - became a symbol of resistance.

Miracles were ascribed to the dead king and so revered was his memory that when the monastery became an abbey King Canute was present when the remains were placed in the abbey church. Edward the Confessor, too, had honoured the dead king's memory and a third king was to pay him even greater homage. By now St Edmund was the country's patron saint and was to remain so until replaced by St George several centuries later.

When the Norman invasion took place, by great good fortune Abbot Baldwin was French, and his good influence saved St Edmundsbury from destruction. Instead the Normans recognised its religious importance and decided to build a great abbey here. They constructed the Benedictine foundation on the site of the seventh century monastery that had been founded by an earlier monarch, King Sigebert of East Anglia. As the huge walled abbey took shape the Abbot planned the town outside on Roman lines and his eleventh century street gridplan and the five abbey gates give the modern borough its charm and charcter.

Long vistas of varied architecture are presented to the modern visitor, and today almost 1,000 buildings have preservation orders on them. It is full of treasures, not least the CATHEDRAL OF ST. EDMUNDSBURY itself.

The Cathedral was founded in 1913 when the new diocese was created and the parish church of St James raised to become the new diocesan centre. It is at the heart of the now ruined abbey whose most important relic is the magnificent Norman tower which today serves the Cathedral as its bell tower. Built in the reign of a Norman king on the site of a monastery founded by a Saxon king, the abbey was dissolved by yet another king, Henry the Eighth. Thus ended its importance as a shrine to a saint, a centre of great religious influence, and its role as a cultural centre. Manuscripts written and illuminated by twelfth century monks under Bishop Anselm are now in

museums in London, New York, the Vatican, and Oxford and Cambridge Universities.

Church and constitution are married in Bury St Edmunds in a unique way, for it was here that a group of powerful barons met with the Archbishop of C a n t e r b u r y , ostensibly to celebrate St. Edmund's Day and resolved to curb the powers of King John.

The historic meeting at **Runnymede** followed with the signing of the Magna Carta. That meeting in the abbey led to James the First granting the town's Latin motto, Sacrarium Regis, Cunabula Legis (Shrine of a King, Cradle of the Law).

As you will see the abbey covered a considerable area; in medieval times there were three churches within its walls. Two remain and they are the present Cathedral, and ST MARY'S CHURCH, a 15th century b uilding where Henry the Eight's sister, Mary Tudor, was buried. St Mary's is a wonderful church lit by myriad tall windows with a hammerbeam roof embellished in blue and gold with angels, saints, dragons and unicorns.

One hundred years later the church of St James was built. Both had replaced earlier churches and were supported by burghers prospering from the local cloth-making industry. The left nave was created by the 15th century architect responsible for the glorious fan-vaulting in King's College Chapel at Caimbridge. In this century the chancel has been rebuilt and all the roofs painted in glowing colours.

In the Cathedral, which has a coffee shop open from Wednesday to Saturday where you can relax during your exploration, do not miss that memorial to the meeting of the barons. It is near the alter. Not far from the Norman Tower, once the main gateway to the abbey, is the Abbey Gateway leading from Angel Hill. This was built, too, in the 15th century and leads to the ruins now surrounded by beautiful gardens.

These are the ABBEY GARDENS. The Botanical Gardens have rare trees, many of them labelled, and they include a 'Chinese Tree of Heaven' planted 160 years ago. In the Applebury Rose Gardens are a profusion of these lovely blooms in season. This garden was funded by the sales of a best-seller written by a US serviceman, John Applebury, who was stationed nearby in World War II. Its title was 'Suffolk Summer'. Children can feed the ducks on the River Lark and it is all very peaceful, but the abbey knew stormy days and has witnessed tempestuous scenes, one of which had a virtual battle.

In 1327 the monks and the townspeople fell out. The monks were a militant lot and stormed the parish church and set about the worshipper. The angry parishioners in turn attacked the abbey in revenge and caused tremendous destruction. It fell victim again when one of those horrific fires which so often swept medieval towns, with flames leaping from one timbered building to another in the narrow crowded streets, consumed abbey buildings.

The abbey was rebuilt in 1538 and was fifty feet longer than NORWICH CATHEDRAL when it was completed. Only its west front, stripped of its facing stone, is left, as well as a few columns and a Norman Crypt.

North of the abbey ruins are an aviary and a tea shop not far from a medieval dovecote. The abbey wall leads to the ABBOT'S BRIDGE across the River Lark. This fortified bridge is one of the better preserved remains of the Abbey and should not be missed. Outside the Abbey walls is a town that was built on the medieval scheme of two squares with a grid of interlocking streets. One square was for God and one for man.

That for God is right outside the Abbey and today is called Angel Hill while that for man is today's nearby market place. Many delights wait you as you explore a town full of treasures. In Angel Hill, a row of charming houses, you are invited to stay at TWELVE ANGEL HILL which has six ensuite bedrooms and the additional pleasure of a very pretty, secluded walled garden with ivy clinging lovingly to the walls. Dinner is not served here but there are many good restaurants in Bury. What you will have, after a wonderful night's sleep, is a sumptuous breakfast. Here also in Angel Hill is the Tourist Information Centre from which guided walks begin on Tuesday and Thursday afternoons from June to September and on Sunday mornings from July to September. They take about 90 minutes and it is best to book in advance although you can join at the last moment if the tour is not full. These, of course, take place in the Abbey gardens.

The splendid nave roof, recently and gloriously painted, was erected 1862-84, designed by Sir George Gilbert Scott

There are walks for groups which are more specialised and take a closer look at literary, artistic or religious life in Bury St Edmunds. One of the giants of the Victorian literary world immortalised the ANGEL HOTEL, which is as good a place as any for us to begin our own tour of the town.

The Angel is a splendid and traditional hostelry where Charles Dickens twice stayed and you can see the very four-poster in which he slept. He came here twice to give one of his famous readings from his own works at the local assembly rooms, the Athenaeum, one of the graceful Georgian houses around Chequer Square.

In the later Pickwick Papers he had Sam Weller meet Job Trotter at the Angel where he had stayed in Room 15. Angel Hill leads you on a journey through the history of Bury and past some outstanding architecture. THE ONE BULL INN is an old coaching house built in the 17th century. Turn left past the many Georgian buildings and you arrive back at the Angel Hotel and the Norman Tower.

Some of these Georgian houses, incidentally, are in fact much older. In the Angel, for instance, you can see 13th century vaulting in the restaurant. Continue along Crown Street past Chequer Square and the Athenaeum I have already mentioned, and it will bring you to St Marys Church which I described earlier. In Honey Hill is the newly opened MANOR HOUSE MUSEUM OF ART AND HOROLOGY. The house was built in 1738 by John Hervey, first Earl of Bristol, and it and neighbouring buildings have been turned into a marvellous museum. The fabulous collection of watches and clocks is remarkable with timepieces of every description ranging from a portable sundial to a pocket watch more than 300 years old. The Time Machine is a hands on gallery that explains the technology of time-keeping that will intrigue and fascinate you. Computer screens tell you all about the exhibits which also include paintings, furniture, costume, ceramics and art objects from many periods.

The ballroom puts on exhibitions of art and there are all kinds of events taking place all the time. The courtyard cafe will feed you and the museum shop offers you a good selection of gifts and publications. The museum is open every day except Christmas Day, Boxing Day and Good Friday from 10 am to 5 pm on weekdays and from 2 pm to 5 pm on Sundays. There is an admission fee.

Another interesting place is THE BURY ST EDMUNDS ART GALLERY in The Market Cross. The building itself is of great historical significance and considerable architectural interest. Standing guard over the market place, it has witnessed centuries of social change as well as commercial and cultural activity. From 1734 to 1818 it was used for the Duke of Grafton's 'Company of Comedians', which originated in Cambridge. It was subsequently used as a public room for concerts and recitals and has been the home to the Bury St Edmunds Art Gallery Trust since 1971. Today the gallery features a wide range of work by artists and crafts-people both British and foreign; from oil, watercolour and etching to ceramic, glass and wood.

Sparhawk Street beyond Honey Hill has a number of ancient houses including the delightful CHANTRY HOTEL. This Georgian house has been given back its dignity after being sadly neglected for some time. Much love and hard work has transformed this elegant Grade II Listed property into a residential hotel of much character. Sparhawk Street leads into an old Saxon market place, St Mary's Square. In THE DOG AND PARTRIDGE INN you can try the excellent beer brewed by the famous East Anglian brewers, Greene King and Sons across the road and sample the good local sausages as you admire the brasses and other mementoes of brewery dray horses.

Turn right into Wesgate Street and you come to what I believe is the only theatre owned by the National Trust, the THEATRE ROYAL, which is in a Regency building. The theatre was designed and built in 1819 by the architect who designed London's National Gallery. He is William Wilkins and his building was restored and re-opened in 1965 when the Greene King brewery opposite gave it to the National Trust. It is the country's third oldest theatre and with many original features intact is one of the loveliest and most historic theatres in the world.

Today it has the essential addition of plentiful street parking after 6 pm and municipal car parks close by. Its programmes are impressive and embrace everything from opera to pantomime, and from films to country and western music. Marion Montgomery, the jazz singer, opened this year's autumn season and the pantomime Aladdin, closes it. Beyond the theatre on the right is College Street which was laid out in Norman times and has houses of many periods. Guildhall Street is also Norman.

The Guildhall was built in the 15th century and its two wings were added in 1807. Its porch is Tudor and is ornamented, with the town's shield portrayed over the entrance. College Street brings you to one of the loveliest shopping streets in the country, Abbeygate. Here you will find THE BUTLER'S CELLAR in the basement of number 22. It was an established practice years ago that when a child was born to parents of means, a pipe of port was laid down for them. The port would be non-aged and would come to maturity on the child's twenty first birthday. Such pipes were laid down in the vaults of what is now The Butler's Cellar, beneath the wine merchants, Threshers. These cellars were the vaults of old Bury and they are supposed to be haunted; many people have felt the presence, but no one knows who it is who finds the need to remain present. Possibly a child whose father drank the port before he reached maturity? Whatever it is it makes no difference to the very pleasing atmopshere that prevails here. In the Traverse off Abbeygate Street is THE NUTSHELL, a hostelry which vies with a pub in Dorset for the title of the country's smallest licensed premises.

No one could be anything less than contented after visiting THE OLDE WHITE HART HOTEL in Southgate Street. Some 800 years ago the Medieval chapel of St Botolph (the patron saint of travellers) was built, welcoming travellers to this beautiful town. Today the Olde White Hart continues this tradition. It is a hotel steeped in history and each room is a delight. Wonderful old beamed ceilings, hidden doors, thick walls and winding staircases makes this a building you will have to explore. Three of the rooms are built over the original chapel and the 18th century landlords' stables have been cleverly converted into sumptuous accommodation.

The VICTORIAN CORN EXCHANGE is still in use and is evidence of the importance of the surrounding agricultural area to the town. It was built in classical style and stands in the Norman market place. Opposite is the 17th century CUPOLA HOUSE with its overhanging balcony and, of course, cupola. The third important public building here is the Robert Adam-designed ART GALLERY which holds art exhibitions and presents concerts, about which I have already written.

Turn right into Cornhill and you will find the 17th century MOYSES HALL. It was built about 1190 and has been occupied since as a merchant's house, an inn and a police station. It is probably the oldest domestic house in East Anglia and is now a museum with exhibits that span many thousands of years. There are Bronze Age artefacts, monastic writings from the 13th century, natural history collections and a display devoted to a celebrated Victorian murder.

A squire's son in the area had his wicked way with a maiden and he went to the gallows for killing her. The murder was followed by a sensational trial and this East Anglian crime of the century was celebrated in a famous Victorian melodrama, Maria Marten or The Murder in the Red Barn. It kept audiences entranced well into this century. The museum is opened every day except Christmas Day, Boxing Day and Good Friday from 10 am to 5 pm on weekdays and from 2 pm to 5 pm on Sundays. Admission is free.

The BUTTER MARKET has stalls twice a week. Across Abbeygate Street you find Whiting Street, named after the once-familiar whitening chalk powder that was made here and used on so many front doorsteps and family cutlery. In Churchgate Street you are on one of the oldest approaches to the abbey.

Do note the UNITARIAN MEETING HOUSE, one of the finest of the non-conformist chapels in the borough, and the county for that matter. It was built in

1711 and has a double-decker pulpit. The SUFFOLK REGIMENT MUSEUM is in Gibraltar Barracks at Out Risby Gate and has all kinds of regimental mementoes. Check with Tel 0284 752394 for opening times.

Bury is the centre of a beautiful rural area with many villages of great character and appeal, and some outstanding country houses. One building which would be extraordinary anywhere is **Ickworth** three miles south west on the A143. It was built by the 4th Earl of Bristol, the eccentric Frederick Augustus Hervey who became Bishop of Derry in Ireland and died in a peasant's hut in Italy. He decided in 1792 to build this 700 ft long building to house his superb collection of paintings and sculpture. Its centrepiece was a 100 ft high rotunda with a central hall from which the main rooms are reached.

Work began in 1794 on land his family had owned for three centuries and the earl, who had a great taste for travel, was abroad as construction went ahead. He was in Rome when Napoleon captured it, imprisoned the earl - and confiscated his collection. When he returned to England he ordered its construction to continue but it was only half completed when he died in 1803. Some years later the 1st Marquess of Bristol had work re-started and it was completed in 1830.

He furnished the main rooms, and an important art collection was established in the opulent rooms which

Carved on the Bishop's throne: a ferocious wolk guards King Edmund's head - as told in the earliest life of St Edmund

now also have on display, in addition to works by painters such as Titian and Hogarth, Regency furniture, beautiful Georgian silver and many objets d'art.

The park in which this huge private art gallery stands was landscaped by Capability Brown and there are miles of walks. There is an Orangery, Italian gardens, a deer enclosure and marvellous views of the Rotunda from many spots. Ickworth is now a National Trust property and there is a shop and restaurant. For admission times to the house and the park, which vary according to the time of the year, and details of admission charges it is best to get the details from the Information Centre or to write or telephone the Administrator at Ickworth, Horringer, Bury St Edmunds, IP29 5QE. (Tel 0284 735270)

HENGRAVE HALL three miles north west of Bury St Edmunds is a lovely Tudor house used as a conference centre but can be visited by appointment Tel (0284) 701561.

A country park and Anglo-Saxon village awaits you at **West Stow** a few miles away. It covers 125 acres on the site of an Anglo-Saxon settlement which has been excavated and since then reconstructed by the West Stow Anglo-Saxon Village Trust, shedding light on a little known period of our history.

You can see how these early people lived and farmed, and you will sometimes find costumed Anglo-Saxons in the houses. The visitor centre and village are open daily from 10 am to 5 pm and there is an admission fee. There are many facilities for visitors and other attractions such as a nature trail and a wildfowl reserve. The ancient borough of Bury St Edmunds is a marvellous centre for visiting so many lovely and fascinating attractions.

Within a short distance to the east is **Thurston** where THE GRANGE HOTEL stands surrounded by peaceful and beautiful Suffolk countryside offering anyone who wishes to stay here the opportunity to relax and enjoy one of the nicest hotels in the county. The Grange is an attractive Tudor style country house set in its own grounds and has a resident Chef-Proprietor Gordon Wagstaff who with his wife Wanda, has been welcoming guests for 19 years. It is this personal touch that makes The Grange so special. The food is wonderful and the hotel specialises in local produce using local meat, fish and fresh vegetables. Even the bread is home-made from flour that comes from a local mill. Gordon Wagstaff is an inspired chef and every meal is memorable.

Imaginative country cuisine at it's best is to be found at THE FOX PUBLIC HOUSE & RESTAURANT at **Pakenham**. It is just seven miles outside Bury and

At the south side of the nave is a stained glass representation of St Edmund

situated charmingly between a water mill and a windmill. PAKENHAM MILL is still working and open to the public and it is from here that the Fox purchases its flour from which it makes bread - the smell is wonderful! The pub is very popular with locals and visitors, all of whom are happy to join in the fun with family games in the garden i.e: football, cricket and badminton etc. or barbecue evenings with themes - 'Country & Western' or 'Jazz' and not to be forgotten the wonderful and colourful Morris Dancers.

Pakenham Water Mill is worthy of a visit in its own right and offers visitors an insight into times gone by.

Just slightly north is **Wattisfield** where HENRY WATSON'S POTTERY AND COFFEE SHOP is full of interest. In fact this may well be one of the highlights of your visit to Suffolk and to the Cathedral City of Bury St Edmunds. To visit here is to step back into the past that has produced the excellence of the present. Watson's Pottery is an old established company dating back over 180 years. It is rumoured that the fascinating story of the ancient Wattisfield potters is lost in the mists of antiquity, but thanks to the techniques of modern archaeology, some light can now be shed on their activities. In their search for clay, the pits have yielded pottery fragments dating back to the Neolithic period (4000-2500 BC) and the flints with which the clay was presumably dug. The 'Beaker People' named after the

pottery beakers found among their remains, lived and worked here in the 2nd millennium, and the Iron Age fragments found demonstrate the long history of ancient pottery manufacture in the area. Whatever the past, the Watson family have been firmly entrenched for almost two centuries. A tour of the premises, by prior appointment, is wonderful. You can browse round the factory and enjoy a cup of tea or coffee in the coffee shop.

You really are spoilt for choice. Should it be the picture postcard village of **Cavendish** to the south where the SUE RYDER FOUNDATION MUSEUM tells of the achievements of this outstanding woman and her partnership with an extraordinary man, Group Capt Leonard Cheshire VC who died as Lord Cheshire? Or should it be nearby **Clare** with its country park, ANCIENT HOUSE MUSEUM, CAVENDISH MANOR VINEYARDS and the beautiful scenery of the River Stour valley?

I can promise you that when you finally leave the attractive Cathedral town of Bury St Edmunds and the lovely county of Suffolk you will wish to return.

THE BURY ST EDMUNDS ART GALLERY
Gallery

The Market Cross, Bury St Edmunds,
Suffolk, IP33 1BT.

Tel: (0284) 762081

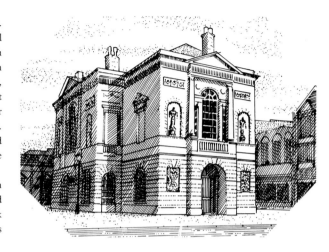

The Market Cross is a building of great historical significance and considerable architectural interest. Standing guard over the market place, it has witnessed centuries of social change as well as commercial and cultural activity. From 1734 to 1818 it was used for the Duke of Grafton's Company of Comedians, which originated in Cambridge. It was subsequently used as a public room for concerts and recitals and has been the home to the Bury St Edmunds Art Gallery Trust since 1971. Inspired by the 10th and 11th Duke of Grafton, a sum of £15,000 was raised by public subscription to restore the top floor of the Market Cross to its Robert Adam splendour and to establish it as a centre for the Arts. The rooms were officially opened in 1972 by Sir John Wolfenden with a loan exhibition entitled 200 years of Suffolk Art - from Gainsborough to Munnings. Prime examples of the work of Gainsborough, George Frost, John Constable, Thomas Churchyard, Edward and Thomas Smythe, John Moore, Alfred Munnings and many others were on view, thus setting the scene for the ensuing years.

Today the gallery continues to feature a wide range of work by artists and crafts-people both British and foreign; from oil, watercolour and etching to ceramic, glass and wood. Industrial and commercial art and photography are also represented from time to time. An important part of the gallery's work is the strong link it has with the local schools and colleges, offering a venue for exhibitions by budding artists as well as a means of understanding art. It is an exciting gallery and the setting in the Market Cross is perfect.

USEFUL INFORMATION

OPEN: Tues-Sat: 10.30-4.30pm
CHILDREN: Welcome. Workshops and
school visits
CREDIT CARDS: None taken
RESTAURANT: No
DISABLED ACCESS: 1st floor gallery.
Chair lift access
SHOP: Craft and gift shop

THE BUTLERS CELLAR
Wine Bar & Restaurant

The Wine Vaults, 22 Abbeygate Street,
Bury St Edmunds, Suffolk, IP33 1UN.

Tel: (0284) 702331

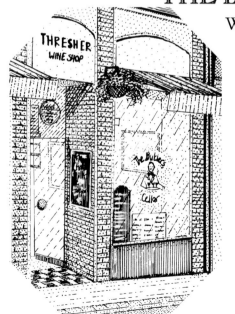

It was an established practice years ago that when a child was born to parents of means, a pipe of port was laid down for them. The port would be non-aged and would come to maturity on the child's twenty first birthday. Such pipes were laid down in the vaults of what is now The Butlers Cellar, beneath the wine merchants, Threshers in Abbeygate Street. These cellars were the wine vaults of old Bury and they are supposed to be haunted; many people have felt the presence but no one knows who it is who finds the need to remain present. Possibly a child whose father drank the port before he reached maturity? Whatever it is, it makes no difference to the very pleasing atmosphere that prevails in The Butlers Cellar.

Felicity and Colin Jordan, the proprietors have built up a great following. They have a widerange of wines and beers and if their list does not contain what you require they are always prepared to whip up to Threshers and see if they have it. It is that sort of business, run with great efficiency but with a friendly informality that makes it a pleasure to be there. The food served is in the style of modern English and includes old favourites such as steak and kidney pie along with more unusual dishes such as roulade of smoked haddock and watercress, rack of lamb with a herb crust or warm camembert with sweet and sour sauce. Fresh, local and seasonal produce is used wherever possible. Their home-made soups and salads are very popular.

With good sense Felicity and Colin have made sure that there is a non-smoking area - particularly important in a cellar. One can visit The Butler's Cellars for morning coffee from 10.30am, stay for lunch and perhaps return for tea if it is a Wednesday, Friday or Saturday. Dinners are available for parties by arrangement.

USEFUL INFORMATION

OPEN: Coffee: 10.30-12 noon, Lunch: 12
noon-2.45pm, Teas: 3-6pm Wed, Fri &
Sat.Closed on Thursdays.
CHILDREN: Children are welcome
CREDIT CARDS: All Major cards
LICENSED: Full On Licence
ACCOMMODATION: Not applicable

RESTAURANT: Home-cooked, nothing
fried. Fresh & seasonal foods
BAR FOOD: Good selection. Morning
coffee, afternoon tea
VEGETARIAN: Always a selection
DISABLED ACCESS: Very difficult.
Spiral staircase
GARDEN: Not applicable

CHANTRY HOTEL
Hotel

8 Sparhawk Street, Bury St Edmunds,
Suffolk, IP33 1RY.

Tel: (0284) 767427
Fax: (0284) 760946

USEFUL INFORMATION

OPEN: All year
CHILDREN: Yes
CREDIT CARDS: Diner, Visa
& Access
LICENSED: Residents
ACCOMMODATION: 17 rooms
en-suite

RESTAURANT: Open to residents only
BAR FOOD: Yes
VEGETARIAN: Yes - selection
DISABLED ACCESS: No
GARDEN: Parking only

This Georgian house has been given back it's dignity after being sadly neglected for some time. Much love and hard work has transformed this elegant property into a residential hotel of much character. The main building is listed grade 11 Georgian and is adjoined by houses over 400 years old. The owners Nigel & Valerie Jackson have recently purchased one of these houses, tastefully converting it for further accommodation. Now known as the Tudor Annex it includes the De Carle Suite named after a local coach builder who lived on the site in the 1800's. All rooms in the Chantry Hotel are comfortable and sympathetically decorated in colours and furnishings of the period. The seventeen bedrooms are all en-suite and have colour T.V., tea and coffee making facilities and direct dial telephone.

Situated in the heart of Bury St Edmunds, guests will find it easy to discover the town centre and Cathedral. Because everything is within a few minutes walking distance it means you can leave your car in the car park, thus avoiding the hassle of parking.

After an enjoyable day discovering this lovely town, why not relax in the residents lounge and enjoy a pre-dinner drink before partaking of your freshly prepared evening meal. All cuisine is traditional English with a light French flavour. Choose from starters, delicious main meals, salads, bar meals, light snacks and of course special of the day. It means you will be happily satisfied with the service the hotel has to offer. The owners and staff are dedicated to the well being of their customers and ensure that your stay will be remembered with pleasure.

THE MANOR HOUSE MUSEUM
Museum

Honey Hill, Bury St Edmunds,
Suffolk, IP33 1HF.

Tel: (0284) 757072
Fax: (0284) 757079

USEFUL INFORMATION

OPEN: Mon-Sat: 10-5pm, Sun: 2-5pm
CHILDREN: Yes
CREDIT CARDS: Access/Visa
LICENSED: Restaurant Licence
ACCOMMODATION: Not applicable

RESTAURANT: Light snacks
BAR FOOD: Not applicable
VEGETARIAN: Always 2-3 dishes
DISABLED ACCESS: Yes. Fully with
a lift
GARDEN: Georgian garden

Four minutes walk from the Cathedral is The Manor House Museum, with fabulous Collections of art and horology. After two years of careful restoration and refurbishment this fine Georgian mansion, together with neighbouring historic buildings has been transformed into a magnificent centre where you can discover clocks, watches and paintings, furniture, costume, ceramics and objects d'art from the seventeenth to the twentieth century.

Computer screens put a wealth of knowledge about the exhibits at your fingertips. Some displays are beautiful and challenging, others are quite different. A 'hands on' gallery, The Time Machine, introduces the technology of time keeping in ways that are intriguing and fun. Special exhibitions in the magnificent Ballroom or 'Saloon' bring the works of great artists to a local audience for the first time. Here too will be a new venue for musical recitals and other events, opening up a fabulous museum to a wider audience than ever before.

Displays, study areas, workshops, talks, activities, events, whatever your level of interest the Museum hopes to offer something new throughout the year. Finally the Courtyard Cafe will always give you a warm welcome, and so too will the Museum Shop with its wide range of gifts and publications, even if you are just passing. The Manor House Museum is fascinating and very different. It is a place to inform and entertain all ages.

35 Southgate Street, Bury St Edmunds,
Suffolk, IP33 2AZ.

Tel: (0284) 755547
Fax: (0284) 724770

THE OLDE WHITE HART HOTEL
Hotel

Step into the atmosphere of a bygone age. Some 800 years ago the Medieval chapel of St Botolph (the patron saint of travellers) was built, welcoming travellers to this beautiful town. Today the Olde White Hart continues the tradition. The present day building is part medieval (c.1250) and the main Tudor house dates back to 1530.

Today the Olde White Hart is a hotel which is steeped in history; each room is a delight. Wonderful old beamed ceilings, hidden doors, thick walls and winding staircases makes this a building you will just have to explore. Relax in one of the many deep upholstered sofas and soak up the atmosphere in the guest lounge; allow your eyes to wander over the historic timbers. Three of the rooms are built over the original chapel and the 18th century landlords stables have been cleverly converted into sumptuous accommodation.

This delightful hotel can easily be found. Leave the A45 at the east exit; at the first roundabout take the last exit into Southgate Street. You can park your car behind the hotel. You will find The Olde White Hart is within easy reach of the Cathedral and the town centre - just a five minute stroll.

Arthur and Carole Cannell and their housekeeper Wendy extend a warm welcome to this ancient and fascinating hotel. All 10 rooms are en-suite and have tea and coffee making facilities, colour TV and a direct dial telephone.

Breakfast is a real feast. You make your own choice, in your own time. Each breakfast is individually cooked and the menu includes traditional English, kippers and fruit. Bury St Edmunds is the eating centre of East Anglia. The Olde White Hart publishes a free restaurant guide and town map of 30 town centre restaurants - available to you with your reservation.

USEFUL INFORMATION

OPEN: All year
CHILDREN: Yes, welcome
CREDIT CARDS: Visa/Amex/Access/ Diners
LICENSED: Residential
ACCOMMODATION: 10 en-suite rooms. Some rooms are no smoking

RESTAURANT: Residents only
BAR FOOD: Not applicable
VEGETARIAN: Yes
DISABLED ACCESS: Yes. Ground floor accommodation
GARDEN: Yes, attractive town garden. Car park at rear. Only guide dogs are allowed

---

12 Angel Hill, Bury St Edmunds,
Suffolk, IP33 1UZ.

Tel: (0284) 704088
Fax: (0284) 725549

TWELVE ANGEL HILL
Hotel

Twelve Angel Hill occupies an attractive house in a mellow brick terrace close to the Cathedral and the centre of Bury St Edmunds. Georgian in the front and Tudor at the rear, it opened as a hotel in 1988 after a complete renovation. It is the most attractive place in which to stay with the additional pleasure of a very pretty, secluded walled garden with ivy clinging lovingly to the walls.

The six en-suite bedrooms are spacious and welcoming, one being a suite whilst a second is complete with a fine four poster bed. The furniture is antique or sympathetic reproduction and the wall coverings and fabrics are bold floral, rich in design and colour and absolutely right for bedrooms in a house of this age. Unlike the 15th century when the house was first built and would not have been warm in winter, central heating now keeps the whole house at a comfortable temperature.

Bernie and John Clarke are the resident proprietors and it is their cheerful and welcoming presence that makes Twelve Angel Hill so pleasant to return to after a days exploration of the Cathedral or the many delights of historic Bury St Edmunds or after a days business. Dinner is not served here but there are many good restaurants in Bury. What you will have at number Twelve is a wonderful, sumptuous breakfast that will set you up for the day.

USEFUL INFORMATION

OPEN: All year
CHILDREN: No
CREDIT CARDS: All major cards
LICENSED: Residential
ACCOMMODATION: 6 en-suite rooms

RESTAURANT: Breakfast only. First class English breakfast
BAR FOOD: Not applicable
VEGETARIAN: Yes
DISABLED ACCESS: No
GARDEN: Very pretty walled garden

THE FOX

Public House & Restaurant

The Street, Pakenham, Bury St Edmunds,
Suffolk, IP31 2JU.

Tel: (0359) 30347

USEFUL INFORMATION

OPEN: 11am-3pm & 6pm-11pm
CHILDREN: Play area - children's menu
CREDIT CARDS: None
LICENSED: Full on Licence
ACCOMMODATION: Not applicable

RESTAURANT: Imaginative
Country Cuisine at it's best
BAR FOOD: Large selection
VEGETARIAN: Good variety
DISABLED ACCESS: Ramp - not toilets
GARDEN: Yes, scented at night,
plus patio

Imaginative country cuisine at it's best will be found at The Fox Public House and Restaurant situated in the heart of the village of Pakenham. This delightful village is just seven miles from Bury St Edmunds with it's Cathedral and town centre. The Fox is in a chosen position nestling comfortably between a water mill and a windmill adding to the charm and interest of this delightful public house. Pakenham Mills is still working and open to the public, flour from the Mill is purchased by The Fox and each day the wonderful smell of fresh bread drifts through the village. The Fox is not only renowned for it's bread, it also bakes the famous Pakenham Pie.

Lynden and Howard extend a warm welcome to all their customers and provide a vast amount of entertainment. This is very popular with both the locals and visitors alike, join in the fun with family games in the garden ie: football, cricket, badminton etc. or BBQ evenings with themes - Country & Western or Jazz and not to be forgotten the wonderful and very colourful Morris Dancers.

Great care is given to the preparation and presentation of outstanding cuisine, Lynden is well travelled, collecting experience and recipes worldwide. Home made cakes and pastries are served with morning coffee. The bar menu is large and varied offering traditional and more imaginative fare. As for the Restaurant Menu, this will delight you, a treat not to be missed.

THE GRANGE HOTEL

Country House Hotel

Barton Road, Thurston, Bury St Edmunds,
Suffolk, IP31 3PQ.

Tel: (0359) 31260
Fax: (0359) 31260

USEFUL INFORMATION

OPEN: All year
CHILDREN: Yes. Special meals
CREDIT CARDS: Visa/Access
LICENSED: Full On Licence
ACCOMMODATION: 15 rooms,
12 en-suite

RESTAURANT: English with French
overtones
BAR FOOD: Home-made bar meals
VEGETARIAN: Yes. Several
DISABLED ACCESS: Eating areas &
toilets, not to bedrooms
GARDEN: Patio for eating & drinks.
BBQ's in summer

Four miles from the heart of the historic market town of Bury St Edmunds is The Grange Hotel. It stands surrounded by peaceful and beautiful Suffolk countryside offering anyone who wishes to stay here the opportunity to relax and enjoy one of the nicest hotels in the county. The Grange is an attractive Tudor style country house set in its own grounds and has a resident Chef-Proprietor Gordon Wagstaff who with his wife Wanda, has been welcoming and caring for guests here for 19 years. It is this personal touch that makes The Grange so special.

There are two lounge bars which open on to the terrace and garden, and where a varied bar menu is available; and the restaurant, whose main feature, apart from the food is an Adam fireplace, and where a la carte lunches and dinners are served, as well as a traditional lunch on Sundays. The banquet room is a popular venue for wedding receptions, dinner dances and Christmas parties, and serves also as a conference room; the coffee room is an attractive lounge facing the garden, which can accommodate up to 20 people for a private dinner party, conference or meeting. All 15 bedrooms are individually decorated and furnished, each one with a charm of its own. All the bedrooms have every modern convenience and all but two have private bathrooms.

The food is wonderful and the hotel specialises in local produce using local meat and fish and fresh vegetables. Even the bread is home-made from flour that comes from a local mill.

HENRY WATSON'S POTTERY & COFFEE SHOP

Pottery & Coffee Shop

Wattisfield,
Suffolk, IP22 1MH.

Tel: (0359) 51239
Fax: (0359) 50984

This will be one of the highlights of your visit to Suffolk and to the cathedral city of Bury St Edmunds. Wattisfield lies on the A143 on the Diss road from Bury. To visit here is to step back into the past and then be reminded that it is the past that has produced the excellence of the present. Watson's Pottery is an old established company dating back over 180 years. It is rumoured that the fascinating story of the ancient Wattisfield potters is lost in the mists of antiquity, but thanks to the techniques of modern archaeology, some light can now be shed on their activities. In their search for clay, the pits have yielded pottery fragments dating back to the Neolithic period (4000-2500 BC) and the flints with which the clay was presumably dug. The 'Beaker People' named after the pottery beakers found among their remains, lived and worked here in the 2nd millennium, and the Iron Age fragments found demonstrate the long history of ancient pottery manufacture in the area.

The discovery of Romano-British pottery in Wattisfield, nearby Rickinghall, and Hinderclay is evidence of Roman settlement and industry. The Roman invaders may well have arrived to find the local clay being worked, and built on the old foundations of the earlier potters. The Saxon and medieval pottery shards leave only the riddle of the dark ages before continuous pottery in Wattisfield can be finally established. Whatever the past, the Watson family have been firmly entrenched for almost two centuries. A tour of the premises, by prior appointment is wonderful. You can browse round the factory shop and enjoy a cup of tea or coffee in the coffee shop.

USEFUL INFORMATION

OPEN: Mon-Sat: 9.30-4.30pm. Closed on Sun, Good Friday, Xmas & New Year
CHILDREN: Welcome
CREDIT CARDS: Visa/Access
LICENSED: Not applicable
ACCOMMODATION: Not applicable

RESTAURANT: Not applicable
BAR FOOD: Coffee shop, light snacks, teas & coffees
VEGETARIAN: No
DISABLED ACCESS: Level entrance & WC's
GARDEN: No

Canterbury Cathedral

Canterbury

"And these were the dishes wherein to me,
...they served up the sun and the moon."

St Augustine

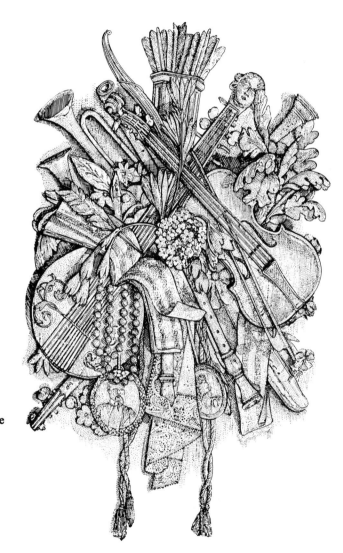

The City of Canterbury

by John Theobald

The English have an appalling habit of not recognising how wonderful their heritage is. I have seen this indifference to beauty, style and magnificence throughout my travels and perhaps it was brought home to me personally when I accompanied a Canadian friend to **Canterbury**. His stunned silence when he first caught glimpse of the Cathedral reawakened my awareness of how truly wonderful it is. It underlined how lacking the New World is in historical background and how privileged we are. I have visited Canterbury many times in my long life, frissons of pleasure have coursed through me as I have gazed at the sheer beauty of the building, but I have tended to take it for granted and accepted that it is there and easily accessible.

Canterbury was welcoming pilgrims 900 years ago and even then it was an ancient city. Chaucer with his Canterbury Tales, immortalised it 600 years ago. Today they come from all parts of the globe to visit this Mother Church of England, the mother church of the Anglican Communion. The Cathedral dominates the city and is the spiritual centre for Christians who belong to the Church of England in many countries. It is Canterbury Cathedral that enshrines one of the Churches' greatest martyrs, Thomas a Becket, murdered within its walls by four knights who heeded Henry II's plea to rid him of 'this low born priest.' For today's pilgrims the problem is that the city presents them with a feast of riches.

There is the Cathedral itself which was rebuilt in 1067, with a crypt that is the largest in the world. There is the city's spectacular West Gate built in the time of Edward III. There are the medieval remains of the oldest parts of the city, the Roman remains of a town house, the ruined St Augustine's Abbey, museums, fascinating lanes and a pedestrianised shopping centre that is hugely attractive.

Great writers have always been associated with Canterbury. Its theatre is named after Christopher Marlowe, the 16th century playwright who was born here. Much of the story of Charles Dickens great novel, 'David Copperfield' is set in Canterbury. The House of Agnes in St Dunstan's street belonged to his heroine. One of our greatest novelists, Joseph Conrad, lived near the city and lies in its cemetery. The famous King's School was where Somerset Maugham, novelist and playwright was educated. Kings and Queens, noblemen, scholars, statesmen and men and women of all ranks have been among the city's guests, and they will continue to be until the end of time.

Canterbury's beginnings go back to the Iron Age and oddly enough the damage caused by German bombs in World War II which destroyed almost a third of its buildings, assisted archaeologists. The craters disclosed foundations more than a thousand years old and enabled them to trace its history from the time man first settled there long before the birth of Christ.

There was a church in Canterbury when St Augustine arrived from Rome in 561AD and this ultimately became a cathedral which was burnt to the ground in 1011 by invading Danes, and its archbishop murdered. Ironically it was the Danish King Canute who gave and helped raise money to build the new Cathedral. By then the city had been the metropolitan centre of the English Church for more than 400 years.

Soon after, the Normans built a castle to protect its citizens from other marauders for it stood four-square on the great route to and from the Continent. But the Normans themselves were to be the last marauders and only ruins remain of their castle.

So bring with you to Canterbury a sense of time, for you are looking at the work of many ages. There can not be any problem in deciding where first to look. It must be the Cathedral with its great towers which dominate the city. Then must come the huge West Gate. Between them and beyond West Gate are streets and buildings by the dozen that on no account must you miss. I stayed in THE THANINGTON HOTEL at 140 Wincheap, just ten minutes walk from the Cathedral, and made sure that every morning I donned comfortable walking shoes before I set out.

One cannot pretend that visiting the Cathedral is tiring; the wealth of beauty tends to give you mental indigestion. I tend to spend several days in Canterbury and alternate with a day spent in the Cathedral and the next day either browsing round the city or going outside into the superb Kent countryside. Returning to The Thanington is always a pleasure especially on a fine day when the garden, which is always ablaze with flowers in summer, is a wonderful place in which to sit to rest one's weary feet. Lunch at THE QUEENS HEAD INN at **Boughton**, going west from Canterbury towards **Faversham**, is one of my treats. Another is a short drive out to the pretty village of **Bridge** where there are many Listed Buildings and the whole village has a sense of permanence. None more so than SKIPPERS OF BRIDGE which is wonderful, either for lunch or dinner.

Had I not wanted to stay in Canterbury itself this time, I would have made for **Petham** and THE OLD POOR HOUSE - a misnomer if ever there was one! Petham lies just south of Canterbury. The Old Poor House is a superb place in which to eat, has four ensuite bedrooms and a magnificent Dutch Garden. The whole is quite unique and an experience.

A little further south is another of my favourite haunts, THE FLYING HORSE at **Boughton Aluph**. Here Howard and Christine Smith welcome everyone to their 15th century inn complete with its oak beams and log fires during the winter. There is an excellent range of gourmet cooking available seven days a week both in the bar and dining room. Go there on Boxing Day and you will find cricket being played on the green opposite the inn - this also happens in summer, of course. The Flying Horse has 4 bedrooms which overlook the green; very comfortable but not ensuite. 15th century inns do not lend themselves too easily to the modern attributes that our sybaritic souls require. It does not matter a jot here,

the welcome and the atmosphere make up for the lack of ensuite rooms.

While I am talking about places where one can eat or drink, in Canterbury itself is STOWAWAYS and THE CANTERBURY TALES two splendid establishments and definitely worth visiting.

Returning to the Cathedral, Thomas a Becket and his story is of never failing interest. He died because of the great conflict of his time between state and religion. The priests were men of education and power who refused to acknowledge that they were answerable to the civil power. They acknowledged only the Pope. For King Henry II this was an intolerable situation and he exiled Becket to France in 1164.

Born in London, Becket was clever and able. His ability and self assurance enabled him to rise swiftly in the Church after becoming secretary to Archbishop Theobald at Canterbury. Before he was 40 he was Archdeacon of Canterbury and a great magnifico, enjoying considerable power and great luxury. He succeeded Theobald in 1161 and three years later was so hostile to King Henry's determination to clip the wings of the clergy resulting in his exile. His power did not diminish even in exile and he threatened to excommunicate Henry himself. He was not successful

Canterbury's most famous royal monument: The effigy of the Black Prince

and his unpopularity was such that it was six years before he returned to Dover and his medieval court in Canterbury.

Exile had been a salutary experience, he returned a changed man. Instead of the gorgeous trappings of office that he had previously enjoyed, he now scourged himself with a hair shirt and clothing so neglected to show his humility, it was verminous. His humility did not go so far as to deter him in his campaign to prevent civil law being applied to the priesthood and his aggressive sermons led Henry to ask in rage, 'Are there none to free me of this low born priest?'

It did not take long before the plea was answered. Four knights made their plans and in what is now known as the Martyrdom, put him to a violent death after unsuccessfully trying to drag him into the cloister to avoid sacrilege. One can imagine the scene. The man had to die but the knights, much as they revered their King, had no wish to commit murder before God and find themselves condemned to purgatory.

Within days Becket's death turned Canterbury into a place of pilgrimage. He was canonised in 1173 and a year later a remorseful King Henry himself made the pilgrimage in an act of penance. The pilgrims were to help make Canterbury one of the richest and most magnificent churches of medieval times.

King Henry's repentance had led to his recognition of the final authority of the Church which remained the dominant power until another Henry, Henry VIII clashed with the pope. By then Canterbury was the centre of English Christianity and had grown in influence and wealth, reflected in all its added architectural glories. It was the income from the pilgrim's offerings which allowed, in the 14th century, the nave and transepts, the south west tower and central tower to be rebuilt in glorious Perpendicular. There was a certain hesitation about rebuilding the north transept because it had been hallowed as the scene of the Martyrdom, but this was carried out in 1468.

Becket's tomb behind the High Altar became a shrine with the ability to work miracles! In 1220 his remains were removed to Trinity Chapel where one of the 12 Miracle Windows portrays his life and death. The shrine, encrusted with gold and jewels which must have been an incredible sight, was destroyed by Henry VIII. To give you some idea of its splendour it had taken 26 carts to carry away the gold, jewels, silver and rich ornamentation that had so awed the pilgrims who had gazed on it over the centuries. Where did the matchless haul go? Simple - straight into the coffers at the Royal Treasury.

A modern sculpture in the Martyrdom, designed by Giles Blomfield and dedicated in 1986, of swords hanging from a cross, marks the spot where Becket was murdered. So holy was the spot it was decided that the body of a national hero, the Black Prince, the warrior son of Henry II should be buried near it, in 1376.

The stole screens in the chapel of Our Lady were a gift from the Black Prince who had an early Norman chapel altered and take his name as the Black Prince's Chantry. When one considers the bitterness and the destruction caused by the dis-establishment of the Roman Catholic church in the time of Henry VIII and the still continuing bitterness between the Catholics and Protestants in Northern Ireland, the Muslims and the Serbs in Bosnia, it is encouraging to know that in May 1982, The Pope and Archbishop Runcie, then Archbishop of Canterbury, prayed together on the site of Becket's murder and you can see a plaque which records this historic meeting.

The famous 'Bell Harry' Tower was built at the very end of the 15th century and completed in 1503 and whereas Henry Yevele was master mason of the nave, John Wastell worked on 'Bell Harry'. You will see how this slender, soaring central tower pulls the whole building together; the lofty nave the long straggling choir and retrochoir, the corona, the double transepts. There are those who have been heard to say that the lack of architectural unity makes for a 'higgledy piggledy' appearance but for me this is one of the great charms of this complex building.

From the Martyrdom you should explore the Great Cloister which was rebuilt long after Becket's death but is still of great antiquity. The Water Tower was built by the monks in the 12th century and still supplies water to the Cathedral.

You may think that Canterbury Cathedral holds the record for the number of steps one climbs up and down during your tour of the building. There are steps up the chancel, steps down to the transepts and a flight of steps ascending to the pulpitum. It is a journey of never ending thrills, stunning architecture, glorious glass and always this awareness that the Almighty is gazing upon us.

From the south transept you enter St Michael's Chapel, known as the Warrior Chapel in which I always feel engulfed in the splendour of the tombs and the monuments. From the north the wonderful, fan vaulted Lady Chapel makes one feel that it would be useful to have a neck like a giraffe seeking the heights to imbibe the beauty. Once in the chancel you may think you are in another church; the building is so different, and I do not believe it has its equal anywhere in England. This is the choir built by the Frenchman, William of Sens who was given the task of overseeing the rebuilding after the fire. It resemble nothing English, some of it is Romanesque and half is Gothic. The rich ornamentation, the Corinthian capitals, the lancet windows all speak of France. The only English adjunct is the use of grey and brown Purbeck marble. Steps lead to the sanctuary where the dominant arcades curve inwards. The retrochoir is narrower and runs into the eastern apse. Apparently it was built this way to preserve the small extruding chapels. I have no great understanding of architecture but it gives one nothing but pleasure, the remembrance of which lasts long after your visit is over.

In the Trinity Chapel, the ambulatories, the Corona, and the eastern transepts is the finest 13th century glass in England. The richness of the medallion glass throws unexpected shafts of colour everywhere and adds to both the enjoyment and the extraordinary atmosphere of the unique Cathedral.

Underneath all this wonderment is another church: the crypt at Canterbury is the largest and most remarkable in England. The major crypt lies under the chancel and is part of Anselm's early 12th century building. Steps lead down from the crossing on the north and south sides into a gigantic undercroft held up by massive pillars adorned with carved capitals. Look closely and you will see that some of the carvings are foliage and others intricate human figures or animals - some playing musical instruments.

In the centre of all this glory is the Chapel of Our Lady Undercroft separated from the rest by 14th century carved stone screens. Smaller chapels stand at the sides.

It is time to leave, your feet are aching, your brain buzzing and your nostrils still filled with the very special smell of the cathedral. CHRIST CHURCH GATEWAY built in the 16th century will serve as your exit point; built as a memorial to Henry VII's son, Prince Arthur. Look up and you will see the sculpted head of the Prince and that of Catherine of Aragon, his fiancee. His younger brother, Henry VIII, married her and her failure to provide him with a male heir and his divorce led to his breach with the Catholic Church, and the martyrdom of another great English figure, Sir Thomas More, who was also canonised.

Time to have a break perhaps at Stowaways in Cogan House, St Peter's Street - more of that later - or The Canterbury Tales before spending the afternoon browsing in the city. Immediately leaving the cathedral you are in Mercery Lane, which is typical of the city's old narrow streets with overhanging roofs and was the home of medieval mercers who dealt in textiles.

Here the pilgrims could buy flasks of holy water and trinkets marking their pilgrimage. The shops in this street became prosperous through trade with them, as indeed, did the whole of Canterbury. An inn once standing on the corner of the lane where there is now a tobacconist's shop, was mentioned in the Canterbury Tales, and on the opposite corner the premises occupied by Boots contain a medieval well and cellar.

The High Street is an unending source of delight. At No 37 High Street is a 12th century crypt and across the road is the BEANEY INSTITUTE where archaeological items such as Roman glass, silver and Saxon finds from local excavations are exhibited. The museum and the library were funded by a Canterbury man called Beaney who made his fortune as a Victorian emigrant to Australia. Another intriguing place is a shoe shop on the corner of Guildhall; nothing remarkable about the shop although I am sure it sells first class wares, but it stands on the site where once stood the Guildhall from which the city was administered for hundreds of years.

Cross over High Street into St Margaret Street and you will find a former church which houses 'THE PILGRIM'S WAY', a fascinating exhibition portraying both the Canterbury Tales and medieval life generally. Back in the High Street, where you turn left, is a little precinct on the right where stands the Royal East Yeomanry War Memorial on the site of an old church. Just past the Yeomanry War memorial is Queen Elizabeth's Guest Chamber which began as a fifteenth century inn and was modernised in Restoration times. According to legend Queen Elizabeth I was entertained here and there is certainly a Royal monogram in the plaster of a first storey ceiling. The architecture is typical of an old merchant's house.

Grim characters for The Wife of Bath's tale: Canterbury Tales Exhibition

To the right, back in the High Street, is St George's Street. At its end is the tower of a church, blitzed in World War II, where the playwright Marlowe was baptised.

Butchery Lane is the site of a Roman mosaic pavement which was revealed by the German bombs that helped destroy that church.

Before you cross over the River Stour where the High Street becomes St Peter's Street, is THE ENGLISH TEDDY BEAR COMPANY at number 4, situated beside the charming Weaver's building and the River Stour. EASTBRIDGE HOSPITAL on the left was built in the 12th century, it was not a hospital in the modern sense but a place where poor pilgrims lodged. Its crypt, chapel and infirmary hall are open to the public free of charge. It became an almshouse after being used as a school during the 16th century. Today's pensioners receive a small pension from the 12th century endowment. From Eastbridge Hospital a walk along Stour Street will bring you to the Poor Priest's Hospital which today houses one of the city's most popular museums, THE CANTERBURY HERITAGE, which tells of the city's history and architecture.

Across the River Stour by the King's Bridge is a group of half-timbered cottages, the WEAVERS' HOUSES. They were built in the 16th century for the Huguenots who fled here from France to escape religious persecution. Earlier refugees from Spanish persecution in what is now Belgium, had already introduced weaving skills which brought added prosperity to the city, and the Huguenots developed silk weaving. There is an old ducking stool here and you can buy from the shop, a ticket for a boat trip.

Turn into All Saint's Lane where you will find a beautifully restored half-timbered building in All Saint's Court. It was originally built in the 15th century.

Across the road is the COGAN HOUSE which houses stowaways. Except for the Precincts, Cogan House is the only existing early stone house of Canterbury in part remaining - it is the hall house type built around 1200. The story of the house is fascinating and I will try to describe it to you with its history. I am helped in doing this by a super little book, researched and written by Peta McFarlane in 1991.

One needs to roll back the eight centuries and picture Hereditary Alderman William Cokyn of the Worthgate Ward surveying a site close by the King's Highway where on to build his new stone house - in 1200 rather a rarity. There were few such houses about in the 13th century, usually lived in by the City's high ranking officials; historians have recorded and written about these personages and Cogan House boasts of many Mayors and Aldermen who have been in residence.

A detail of the Becket window in the north aisle the only surviving 12th century 'portrait' of a saint

For about 175 years afterwards between 1230 and 1404 members of William Samuel's family used Cokyn's house as a private residence and it continued thus for a further 250 years until 1657 with 14 different tenants or owners. Loving care was taken of the house over the years and an Elizabethan housewife's will around this time makes it quite clear that she did not want there to be any waste, 'nether removing or taking awaye eyther wynscott or glasse wyndowes, to the deorderings of my house, but to lett all such still to remayne in as good Ordre as they nowe be.' This is no doubt why the parchemin panelling and John Thomas' frieze have come down in such good condition. The legacy John Thomas (the point maker) left whilst in Cokyn's House from 1536-1568 was the carved oak frieze which crowns the parchemin panelling. You will notice that the frieze is now in two sections. In the centre the Royal arms which is split in half and on either side a shield representing tools of his trade. He was also a hosier, hence the sheep and the woolsacks, one of which has the initials JT. There are two shields representing bear-baiting and hunting, no doubt his hobbies. Busts of himself and his wife are featured. John Thomas is accredited with the Tudor wing.

In medieval times the house was set back from St Peter's Street. There was a courtyard and there were gables and dormer widows. A lane called Cokyn's Lane ran alongside down to Greyfriars and the river; at one time it was reputed to be 40ft wide but it was built upon and reduced to 5ft. A side entrance in the grounds led onto it. Cogan House in medieval times would have had a very pleasing appearance with its black and white gabled frontage as compared to what we look at nowadays.

In 1626 a great change took place when John Cogan, a Londoner, became the owner and named it 'Cogan House'. Upon his death in 1657 it was decreed the house should again become a Hospital – this time to provide for six widows of the clergy 'men of honest godly conversation and painful diligent preachers of God's word' and that they be 'honest women of quiet peaceful life'. A room in the house was to be reserved for each widow with strict rules about habitation. A separate coal shed was provided for each and some of these can still be seen in the garden. It was not the easiest of establishments to run and it became dilapidated and so bad was it that at one time there was only one widow living in the house. Eventually in 1870 the widows were rehoused and Cogan house returned to private usage. Considerable alterations were made, the old black and white front was removed and red brick facing substituted. The tips of the two original gables can still be seen. It has always been a house with a wonderful atmosphere and it must have suffered a slight cultural shock when in the 1980's it underwent so much surgery it outgrew its role as a family home and became altogether a commercial proposition.

The shops at street level which have been there since 1882 have followed an interesting variety of trades, outfitters, jewellers, a ladies hairdresser, a curtain shop, shoe shop, fireplaces and beneath the old beams one can browse amongst remaindered books. It had a slightly chequered career until 1988 when the property was leased to Dianne Leamon and her late partner Dave Foreman. Cogan House has blossomed since then helped by their imagination and energy as they designed and fashioned the STOWAWAYS SEAFOOD RESTAURANT and OYSTER BAR.

Now with the Tudor Tea Room and Garden as well, people can sit amidst the roses and apple trees on the lawn to enjoy a meal or walk across the aisled hall into the old Tudor dining room. A suitable occupation for this fascinating old building.

From here you go past the lovely classical exterior of the Methodist Church and on to the early Norman church of St Peter's, with its modest tower.

Then there is the Sidney Cooper building opposite Black Griffin Lane named after a local artist and which, at one time, used to house the Canterbury College of Art.

St Peter's Street ends with the city's only surviving gate and one of the finest city gates left in England. There were once eight gates and this was built - or rebuilt - in about 1380. It has been used as a jail and is now a museum containing collections of arms and armour. The view from the roof is nothing short of panoramic.

St Dunstan's Street has the FALSTAFF HOTEL where pilgrims who arrived after the gate was shut, could stay. In the 17th century it was a suburban street for prosperous merchants and some good examples of the houses remain. WESTGATE HOUSE is Georgian and the House of Agnes, where David Copperfield's rather pallid heroine lived is now an hotel and restaurant. It is a most attractive street with so many types of architecture.

In Burgate THE CATHEDRAL GATE HOTEL is dignified and welcoming the sort of place where comfort and hospitality are paramount.

By Canterbury West Station is the site of the Whitstable-Canterbury railway, one of the world's first passenger railways. Beyond the level crossing is the ROPER GATEWAY, all that is left of the Tudor home of Margaret Roper, daughter of the martyred Thomas More. It was she who brought his head to nearby St Dunstan's Church after he was beheaded on the orders of the King, Henry VIII. His head still lies there in the chapel founded by the Ropers. A modern window celebrates Canterbury's second saint.

You will need many days and many walks if you are to uncover all Canterbury's treasures. On each of them you will discover many fresh delights and reminders of past ages. Nothing is further than twenty minutes from the heart of the city when you take a walk round the city walls which enclosed the original Roman town.

St Augustine's Chair,
where every Archbishop of Canterbury
is enthroned

One walk took me from the Westgate and I went anticlockwise past the largely restored Holy Cross Church and into WESTGATE GARDENS where you see the Tower House. This is of 19th century construction and is used as the Mayor's Parlour. Part of the city wall adjoins it. With the river on your left you pass over a stone set in the grass that indicates where the wall ran and as you continue along the course of the river you are also following the line of

the wall. Another stone is passed and a few paces on is a little Roman gate with a stone that states it is the site of the London Gate.

The old wall continued under what is now Rheims Way. Go through the bridge here and follow the path until you cross the Stour by the next bridge. Across the river is a Victorian tannery as you turn into Church lane that leads to one of the city's oldest churches. St Mildred was a well loved Kentish saint and the church that takes her name is at least twelve centuries old. Much of it has been rebuilt. Izaak Walton, who wrote the Compleat Angler, was wed here. Next to it is an old school. Walking back along Church Lane and turning into Gas Street you reach the ruined castle, built by William the Conqueror. It guarded the old Wincheap Gate in the city walls and remains an impressive structure. It covered a huge area but little is left of the other fortifications that surrounded the keep which was one of the largest in the country. The keep's three storeys became a prison in the Middle Ages. Its Norman name was 'Donjon' which became corrupted into Dane John. It has had little military significance beyond being attacked by Wat Tyler in the 14th century and occupied by the Royalists during the Civil War. It latterly suffered the indignity of being used by the gas company as a coal store.

Enter Castle Street by turning right out of Gas Street and at its end is CASTLE HOUSE where a plaque indicates the site of Worthgate. A footpath takes you to the Wincheap Gate from where you enter Dane John Gardens surmounted by Dane John Mound. You are now on the city ramparts which bring you to the memorial to the murdered playwright, Marlowe, who was educated at the King's School. The houses that face the gardens belong to a late Regency terrace.

The road from Dover entered through the Ridingate. This is Watling Street, now crossed by a footbridge from where you can see the University of Kent founded just over thirty years ago. The ramparts bring you to St George's Gate site where cisterns supplied the city with its water. The bastion near Zoar Baptist Chapel housed a water tower long after the gate was demolished.

The next gate along Burgate Lane is the Borough Gate - or Burgate - and Broad Street follows the city wall past another bastion which is now a Memorial Chapel to the dead of the first World War. Broad Street, which has earlier brought you past the remains of yet another gate, Queningate, continues to Northgate. To the north was an ancient crowded residential area just outside the city walls and this was one of the city's busiest gates. It was at this gate Royalty arriving from Thanet would receive the keys of the city. The original Roman gate was incorporated into the church of St Mary Northgate. Past the church a path brings you to a restaurant which occupies a timber-framed building that was once the 15th century St Radigund's Hall.

Continue along the street, cross the river and soon you will come to Westgate from which this walk started.

During these walks you will pass so much that is inviting. You will find lovely houses from every architectural period, all part of a lively and prosperous community. It is a community that has always had strong links with the surrounding countryside and many of the villages are well worth visiting. **Forwich on the Stour** for example was the city's port, **Hackington** near the University, was once a village in its own right. **Harbledown** appears in the Canterbury Tales as the last village before the destination of the pilgrims and it was here they would get their first glimpse of the Cathedral.

To the east of Canterbury the village of **Wingham** is home to THE FOUR SEASONS RESTAURANT which opens at night only and has superb food in a wonderful setting.

To the west at **Hernhill** near Faversham MOUNT EPHRAIM GARDENS at the heart of an 800 acre estate comprising the house and gardens, a progressive fruit farm, woodland and grazing, acts like a magnet to those who enjoy the glory of a garden which lies on a superb site. The house, rebuilt in 1870, but the home of the Dawes family for 300 years, commands a magnificent view over woodland parks, orchards and the Swale and Thames Estuary. Rose terraces enclosed by yew hedges, slope down to a lake with a woodland area as a backdrop. A Japanese rock garden, ornamented with stone lanterns and based on a series of pools, follow an alternative, gently winding route. The topiary garden contains a wide herbaceous border and a small vineyard produces a good quality white wine. The water garden planned only in 1989 is a new and exciting area. Many mature trees have mercifully survived the 1987 hurricane and replanting has been carried on for the last 36 years. Planting throughout is extensive giving colour and interest during the whole year. The gardens have a wonderful atmosphere of peace and charm.

Open Daily from mid-April until the end of September from 2-6pm. Teas are served every afternoon and lunches on Bank Holiday Sundays and Mondays only. Mount Ephraim wine is available and there is a craft centre, orchard walks and a vineyard which all adds to the attraction of this delightful place. Mount Ephraim Gardens are not specially set up for disabled visitors as there is a limited access for wheelchairs.

The joy of Canterbury is unending.

73 High Street, Bridge,
Canterbury, Kent, CT4 5LB.

Tel: (0227) 830788

SKIPPERS OF BRIDGE

Restaurant

Bridge is undoubtedly a beautiful village and adding to its charm is Skippers of Bridge, right in the main street. Many of the buildings here are Listed and Skippers is no exception. Built about 200 years ago it has a sense of permanence about it; a place that will continue to delight long after we have gone. It has been described by local people as somewhere one goes as if to a dinner party rather than going out for a meal.

At lunchtime every day an attractive menu is available. One can choose from a whole range of delicious dishes at a set price for two courses or three. Each dish comes to the table beautifully presented and one has to admit that if you have a sweet tooth, Skipper's famous Bread and Butter Pudding must be included in your choice - in which case it would be better to opt for the two course option!

On Sundays at lunchtime the traditional roast is a popular meal and it is advisable to book. People come from quite a distance to enjoy the food and the very genuine welcome one receives. At night the atmosphere changes and becomes perhaps a little more relaxed. There is more time to linger over dinner and truly relish both the food and the well selected wine list which has considered people's pockets as well as their palates!

Gary and Tina Skipper have certainly brought their own brand of magic to the restaurant aided and abetted by their staff who make everyone feel special.

USEFUL INFORMATION

OPEN: Every day 8pm until late.
    Lunch: Mon-Sat: 12-2pm, Sun: Lunch 1pm
CHILDREN: Yes, but it is a long evening
CREDIT CARDS: All Major cards
LICENSED: Restaurant
ACCOMMODATION: Not applicable

RESTAURANT: Delicious, innovative
BAR FOOD: Not applicable
VEGETARIAN: Always available
DISABLED ACCESS: Yes
GARDEN: None

---

111 The Street, Boughton-under-Blean,
Faversham, Kent, ME13 9BH.

Tel: (0227) 751369

QUEEN'S HEAD

Inn

This historic village on the old A2 London to Dover road, is ideally situated for an assortment of local facilities such as golf, fishing, Mount Ephraim Gardens and the ferry ports of Dover and Ramsgate. It has an ancient 16th century hostelry, the Queen's Head; a most welcoming place. It is easily reached being just one mile from the end of the M2 and six miles from Canterbury and two miles from Faversham. The inn has recently been refurbished by Elizabeth Sabey, the landlord. She has taken the most enormous trouble to bring it back to its original state and it certainly gives the impression of being a 16th century Inn. The atmosphere is great and the welcome genuine.

Elizabeth has been here for eight years during which she has built up a vast clientele who appreciate what the Queen's Head offers. It is such an easy run out from either Faversham or Canterbury that many business people just lift the phone, ring through their lunch order, and leave their offices knowing that lunch will be ready on their arrival. It is a very popular service. Elizabeth's staff have been with her for years and none longer than Jackie, the chef whose meals are renowned. She believes in good, straightforward home-cooking using the best ingredients available and local produce if possible.

Visitors have discovered that the Queen's Head is close enough to Canterbury for them to use the availability of the letting rooms as a base for exploring Canterbury and its magnificent Cathedral. Whilst the bedrooms are not en-suite they all have hand basins, TV, and that blessing; tea and coffee making facilities. The rooms are all centrally heated so they are ideal for a winter break.

USEFUL INFORMATION

OPEN: Mon-Thurs, 11-3pm & 6-11pm,
    Fri-Sat, 11-5pm & 6-11pm. Normal
    Sunday hours
CHILDREN: Welcome in gdn & restaurant
CREDIT CARDS: Access/Visa
LICENSED: Full On Licence
ACCOMMODATION: 4 letting rooms
    - not en-suite

RESTAURANT: 26 covers, open Mon-
    Sat 12-2pm & 7-9pm. Sunday lunches
    12-2.30pm. Booking advisable Fri-Sun
BAR FOOD: Traditional English. Daily
    Specials
VEGETARIAN: Always available
DISABLED ACCESS: Yes, not to rooms
GARDEN: Beautiful. Landscaped, seating

THE FLYING HORSE

Inn & Restaurant

Boughton Aluph, Ashford,
Kent, TN25 4ET.

Tel: (0233) 620914
Fax: (0233) 661010

USEFUL INFORMATION

OPEN: Mon-Fri: 11-3pm & 6-11pm.
All day Saturday in summer.
Sun: 12-3pm & 7-10.30pm
CHILDREN: Well behaved and
gagged welcome!
CREDIT CARDS: Access/Visa
LICENSED: Full On Licence
ACCOMMODATION: 4 rooms, 3 dbl,
1 twn. 2 with showers

RESTAURANT: Separate dining room
Excellent food. Fish a speciality
BAR FOOD: Wide range
VEGETARIAN: 4 dishes daily
DISABLED ACCESS: Good
GARDEN: Big & Beautiful for eating and
drinking. BBQ's

Cricket has been played on the village green at Boughton Aluph for over 250 years and enthusiasts have been able to enjoy a pint in The Flying Horse at the same time as watching the cricket. It is a delightful setting and the building has been there since the 15th century when it was on the Pilgrims Way from Winchester to Canterbury. The inn would have been a stopping place for weary travellers who would then gather together to continue their journey because the route through the woods was dangerous, and those travelling alone were frequently set upon by villains. Between the 15th and 17th century they used to brew beer on the premises and recently two wells in the rear of The Flying Horse have been uncovered, one of them 15th century, which would have supplied water for the brewing. The Flying Horse is converting this area into a garden bar which will feature these ancient finds.

Six Real Ales are on offer as well as a limited but interesting selection of wines. Many people come here just for the pleasure of the company, the atmosphere and the welcome but many more have discovered how good the food is. Fresh Fish of all kind is the speciality of the house, but the home-made pies come high on the list of favourites. Those who like international food will find them frequently on the menu - their Indonesian food is delicious. Every day the Blackboard advertises the home-cooked specials which are tasty and value for money.

Ashford is sufficiently near to Canterbury to make The Flying Horse a base while you explore the magnificent Cathedral and all that the city has to offer. There are four comfortable bedrooms two of which have en-suite showers.

THE CANTERBURY TALES

Visitor Attraction & Gift Shop

St Margaret's Street, Canterbury,
Kent, CT1 2TG.

Tel: (0227) 454888
Fax: (0227) 765584

USEFUL INFORMATION

OPEN: 7 days a week, throughout the year
CHILDREN: Very welcome. Special
childrens' commentary
CREDIT CARDS: Visa/Access
LICENSED: The Medieval Wine
Merchant within the Gift Shop

RESTAURANT: Yes
DISABLED ACCESS: Yes
GIFT SHOP: Incorporating The Medieval
Wine Merchant and The Medieval Market
LANGUAGES: Foreign language
commentries in Dutch, French,
German, Italian, Japanese and Spanish

In 1989, Canterbury Cathedral, St Augustines Abbey and St Martin's Church in Canterbury were designated world heritage sites - an accolade shared only with Stonehenge, The Giant's Causeway and, at the time, just nine other sites in the United Kingdom. The jewel in the City's crown is, of course, the Cathedral but no visit to Canterbury is complete without a visit to the award winning, The Canterbury Tales.

The Canterbury Tales is one of Kent's most popular visitor attractions - currently attracting more than 160,000 visitors a year, from all over the world. Housed in an ancient listed building in the heart of old Canterbury, less than 200 metres from the Cathedral, it is an extraordinary re-creation of life in medieval England conjured up - using the latest electronic wizardry - in light, sound and smells!! You embark on a 14th century pilgrimage to the shrine of St. Thomas Becket and along the way are able to listen to Chaucer's colourful stories brought dramatically to life by characters from The Tales.

There are five classic stories to hear of chivalry, romance, jealousy, pride and avarice, vividly described in turn by the courtly Knight, the bawdy Miller, the Wife of Bath, the Nun's Priest and the Pardoner. The pilgrimage lasts approximately 40 minutes with commentaries provided by such celebrated actors as Roy Kinnear, Prunella Scales and Robert Powell. This new style visitor attraction combines academic and historic accuracy with skilful interpretation and presentation. It is entertaining and educational, but most of all it represents an unusual fun day out for all the family.

THE CATHEDRAL GATE HOTEL

Hotel

36 Burgate, Canterbury,
Kent, CT1 2HA.

Tel: (0227) 464381
Fax: (0227) 462800

Tucked beside the great medieval gateway of Canterbury Cathedral is a row of shops and restaurants, above part of which is the small and delightful Cathedral Gate Hotel. Built in 1438 this hotel has for centuries stood between the tranquil haven of the Cathedral and its precincts and the busy commercial life of the city. The site is recorded from Saxon times and linkage with the Cathedral is recorded over a millennium. In medieval times the inn was called 'Sonne Hospice', the name later moving to an inn in neighbouring Sun Street, one of the English tea houses, written about by Dickens.

On the Cathedral side several rooms directly overlook the South Porch and the main West Entrance across the Precincts lawns. On the city side, the hotel adjoins the Christchurch Gateway, entrance to the Precincts, and overlooks the Butter-market and Burgate. Most of Canterbury's premium shops are to be found here; famous names from London's West End.

Every room reminds one of its medieval construction with sloping floors, massive oak beams and winding corridors. There is nothing about the comfort of the beds, the attractive furnishings and other facilities that is remotely reminiscent of medieval times; some 12 of the 24 bedrooms are en-suite, 2 have showers only and the rest hot and cold water. Every room has TV and tea and coffee making facilities, direct dial telephones and central heating. Evening meals are served although the area abounds with good restaurants. The hotel has its own car park about seven minutes walk away. Staying here is an enjoyable experience.

USEFUL INFORMATION

OPEN: All year round 7.30-11pm
(guests have own keys)
CHILDREN: Welcome. Highchairs, cots
CREDIT CARDS: Access/Visa/Diners/
Amex
LICENSED: Residents Licence
ACCOMMODATION: 24 rooms.
12 en-suite, 2 with showers, 10 H&C

RESTAURANT: Residents only. Evening
meal by request
BAR FOOD: Not applicable
VEGETARIAN: Any diet if notice is given
DISABLED ACCESS: Not suitable
GARDEN: No. Rear gate to Cathedral
precinct

THE ENGLISH TEDDY BEAR COMPANY

Shop

4 St Peter's Street, Canterbury,
Kent, CT1 2AT.

Tel: (0227) 784640

The English Teddy Bear Company is situated beside the charming Weaver's building and the River Stour. The delightful building houses two levels. The Teddy Bears on the ground floor delight and enthral visitors. The ground floor is intimate and oak beamed, and has a very cosy and friendly atmosphere. Upstairs there is rather more room and a splendid Tea Room called The Teddy Bear's Picnic. Here you can take Tea with Teddies and look down on the bustling High Street below. Since there are only six tables you are always assured of a friendly and personal welcome as well as delicious foods that Teddy Bears do love so much! Some of these you can take home with you like delicious shortbread biscuits, Honey Tea and Strawberry Jam!

If you have never discovered this wonderful world of Teddy Bears before you should know that The English Teddy Bear Company creates traditional style English Teddy Bears in a variety of cloths, all English, from acrylic to top quality mohair. The Teddy Bears are made with traditional features like long snouts, embroidered noses and jointed limbs and head. This company specialises in recreating special companions. Since all bears are hand made, no two are alike and each bear comes with its own birth certificate!

The English Teddy Bear Company also makes an eccentric range of stylish Teddy Bear clothes. Silk waistcoats, bow ties, smoking jackets, cricket jumpers, boaters and much more make up the essential English Teddy Bear's wardrobe! There are Teddy Bear emporiums currently in Oxford, Bath, London and Cambridge as well as in Canterbury.

USEFUL INFORMATION

OPEN: 10-7pm daily
CHILDREN: Welcome
CREDIT CARDS: All major cards
DISABLED ACCESS: Good

SPECIAL SERVICES: Gift boxing
available, Made to order service,
Mail Order catalogue avaliable- Contact
branch for further information on availability.

STOWAWAYS

Oyster Bar, Restaurant, &Tea Rooms

Cogan House, St Peters Street, Canterbury, Kent, CT1 2BE.

Tel: (0227) 764459

USEFUL INFORMATION

OPEN: Mon-Sat from 10am. Last orders 9pm
Sun: 11-6pm
CHILDREN: Yes
CREDIT CARDS: All Major cards
LICENSED: Throughout
ACCOMMODATION: Not applicable

RESTAURANT: Seafood a speciality.
Home-cooked. Fresh produce
BAR FOOD: Whitstable Oysters,
shellfish & snacks
VEGETARIAN: Always available
DISABLED ACCESS: Yes but no
special WCs
GARDEN: Yes, beautiful

Except for the Precincts, Cogan House is the only existing early stone house of Canterbury in part remaining - it is the hall house type built around 1200. A large proportion of the solid walls of the hall, made of flint and chalk and two feet three inches thick, still exists. The small Gothic doorway is the original entrance.

In the summer of 1990 Stowaways opened the Tudor Tea Room and Garden which was a joy to visit with tables set on the lawn amidst the roses and apple trees. Today people come into Cogan House directly from the street, pass under the small Gothic archway, walk across the aisled hall, into the old Tudor Dining Room and out through the old greenhouse into the peaceful garden to sit and take refreshment and perhaps to ponder at the vast expanse of the Kent peg tiled roof faithfully enveloping and guarding all the secrets of the old house.

Downstairs is an original Tudor Tea Room and up the stairs past the original oak panelling there is a super Oyster Bar with two restaurant rooms overlooking the garden. It is quite wonderful and somewhere that is a joy to visit even if you did not want to partake of the excellent food and wine, not to mention the Whitstable Oysters. Everything is home-made and attractively served. The sense of history is always about you - an excellent aid to the digestion. An unforgettable experience.

THANINGTON HOTEL

Bed & Breakfast Hotel

140 Wincheap, Canterbury, Kent, CT1 3RY.

Tel: (0227) 453227
Fax: (0227) 453225

USEFUL INFORMATION

OPEN: All year
CHILDREN: Welcome
CREDIT CARDS: Access/Visa/Amex/
Diners/JCB
LICENSED: Residents Licence
ACCOMMODATION: 3 twins, 2 family,
5 doubles. All en-suite

RESTAURANT: Not applicable
BAR FOOD: Not applicable
VEGETARIAN: Not aplicable
DISABLED ACCESS: No
GARDEN: Beautiful flower garden.
Swimming pool

Situated just outside the city walls of Canterbury on the A28 going towards Ashford and only a pleasant ten minutes walk from the Cathedral and the city centre, Thanington Hotel is ideal as a base for visitors. It is a Georgian grade II Listed building built in 1810 and was originally a farmhouse.

The hotel has ten en-suite bedrooms all attractively and comfortably furnished and deserves its AA Selected and 2 Crown Highly Commended Awards. It also has its own swimming pool which is a great attraction for people of all ages. David and Jill Jenkins run the hotel themselves and are always there to give their guests a warm welcome. Perhaps it is because they are so deeply involved personally with the well-being of the house that gives it a very special ambience. It is run efficiently and professionally, but also in the manner of a well loved home. The garden which is ablaze with flowers in the summer is tended by people who obviously have green fingers and is a very special place in which to sit, perhaps after a delightful but tiring day exploring the Cathedral.

It is almost an insult to suggest that breakfast in an establishment like this could be anything other than a first class meal. The choice is wide, everything is freshly cooked and there is as much as anybody could possibly want to eat. It is worth mentioning that dogs are permitted but in the bedrooms only.

Kane Street, Petham,
Canterbury, Kent, CT4 5RY.

Tel: (0227) 700413

THE OLD POOR HOUSE
Hotel & Restaurant

The Old Poor House is a complete misnomer for this super establishment. It's only justification for the name is that once is was a workhouse! Almost impossible to believe that this was so when you enter the now attractive building and see how beautifully it has been converted. It is quite unique within the county of Kent. One of its loveliest features is the Dutch Garden, a place of tranquillity and somewhere that is obviously tended with loving care. The hotel is surrounded by trees, flowering shrubs and grassland.

Whenever one stays away a genuine welcome and a comfortable bed is all important. These two ingredients are certainly there. Apart from that the restaurant offers an excellent meal. The dishes are all freshly prepared, using as much local produce as possible. The choice is wide with a tempting list of starters which includes 'Succulent Pink Prawns' served on crisp lettuce with a fan of avocado pear or perhaps 'Fresh Mussels' gently cooked with shallots, white wine and cream. If you follow that with 'Roast Rack of English Lamb' with fresh Rosemary served with a plum sauce and a selection of fresh Kentish vegetables you have a meal fit for a king. The menu always has a choice for vegetarians such as 'Mushroom and Celery Stroganoff' served with Basmati rice, or 'Wholemeal Spaghetti' with a sauce of tomato, fresh basil and zuccini.

In addition to the four elegant en-suite bedrooms there are well equipped facilities for small conferences.

USEFUL INFORMATION

OPEN: All year round
CHILDREN: Welcome
CREDIT CARDS: Visa/Access
LICENSED: Restaurant
ACCOMMODATION: 4 en-suite rooms,
 Conference facilities

RESTAURANT: A la Carte, Table d'Hote,
 fresh produce
BAR FOOD: Not applicable
VEGETARIAN: Always available
DISABLED ACCESS: No
GARDEN: Beautiful Garden

Chelmsford Cathedral

Chelmsford

"He builded better than he knows;-
The conscious stone to beauty grew."

Ralph Emerson

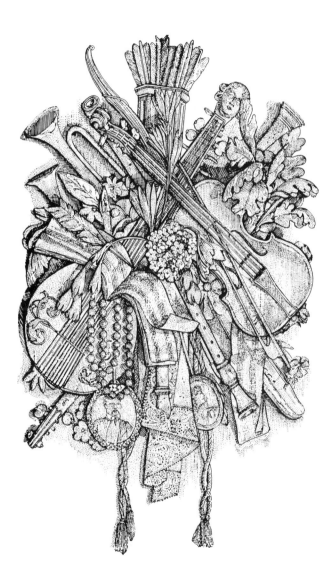

The City of Chelmsford

by John Theobald

When is a Cathedral City not a City? When it is a reluctant town, is the answer. When we started this book it was with the intention of including every English Anglican Cathedral in what we believed were cities. It was not until we came to take a look at **Chelmsford** that we found that not so many years ago it had lost the battle to become a city, to **Sunderland** in the north. That it hurt civic pride has been quite apparent to us as we have chatted to people, but Chelmsford is very much a place in its own right and should never do anything but hold its head up high, be proud of its achievments and its community spirit. It should also not dismiss its Cathedral.

CHELMSFORD CATHEDRAL is one of eleven old parish churches that were selected to serve new dioceses needed to meet the demands of a growing population. It was upgraded in 1913 and plays an important role in this busy and lively town, and a prosperous rural area with many important population centres.

Much of the ancient parish church collapsed in 1800. The nave collapsed without warning, on the opening of a vault under the south arcade. It was rebuilt by John Johnson, then the county surveyor. He did a fine job using Coade stone for the south arcade. I particularly liked the charming plaster ceiling. So much of what we see today is a result of the rebuilding that went on then, and some can be attributed to the major internal reorganisation and restoration which took place about twelve years ago. There are those who will tell you that the latest restoration was nothing short of a massacre, but beauty is in the eye of the beholder and we all have different sight!

The west tower, built in the 15th century, is magnificent and can truly be said to be the glory of the cathedral. Its little spire was added in the 18th century. In the south porch is a 17th century library, and monuments in the church date back to the 16th century. The church is full of interest for architecture of many periods is represented and it is a place of peaceful beauty.

The east end of the church was designed by Sir Charles Nicholson who also extended the parish church of St Peter and Paul at Sheffield when that too was raised to cathedral status. He added two extra bays and also designed the Chapter Room and Vestries which form, as it were, a large north transept.

Six decades after the Cathedral was founded the diocese was the second most popular diocese in England. The first bishop was the Rt St John Watts-Ditchfield and his statue faces the impressive Bishop's throne.

St Cedd, Bishop of the East Saxons, who brought Christianity to Essex, came from Northumbria in the seventh century, and a dedication to him was made as recently as 1954. You will find it in the chapel on the north side of the chancel. At the gates to the cathedral, beside the Shire Hall, you will find a monument of Thomas Hooker, who founded the American state of Connecticut. Hooker was a fellow of Emmanuel College at Cambridge and for three years was a non-conformist lecturer at Chelmsford. In 1630 he went to Holland and in 1633 sailed for New England where he became a Puritan preacher at St Cambridge, Massachusetts. He and his congregation moved south to what is now Hartford, Connecticut, and he became founder of the town and state in 1636.

If you come to Chelmsford especially for its Cathedral you will be further rewarded by taking a look at the various church buildings within the Diocese which stretches quite a distance. There are seven that should be considered. The first is BLACKMORE PRIORY which is unique among English monastic churches for its superb 15th century timber bell tower. It stands plump and beautiful above the meadows and the priory church. This was founded in the 12th century for Augustinian Canons by the de Samford family. You will find it at the end of the village street, a street of timbered or later houses and be quite surprised at its appearance. It looks almost like a three tier square wedding cake with the timber providing the decoration.

It certainly does not look grim and monastic as one might have supposed. The nave has a 14th century north aisle and the south has an unusual brick arcade of the 16th century, and was built after the Dissolution, when the Canon's choir was pulled down. What will probably interest you most will be the two Norman west bays of the nave and the west wall with its Norman doorway and twin windows above. The most exciting thing is to gaze up at the extraordinary interior of the bell tower which is a marvel of timber construction. It has massive posts, arched braces and cross-beams. It never fails to amaze me how the work was ever carried out in those times.

LITTLE COGGLESHALL ABBEY comes next. Not that anything remains of this church of the Cistercians founded by King Stephen about 1140. The only survivor is the monastic chapel of St Nicholas, now the parish church. Wear your wellies to reach it down the end of a muddy lane and through a field. You will see it signposted in the village, **Coggleshall Hamlet**. There is nothing grand about it, but a quiet rustic beauty assails your eyes and then when you go inside the brilliance of the east window depicting the Crucifixion dominates the whole interior.

In alphabetcial order LITTLE DUNMOW PRIORY comes next. Here a minor road between **Braintree** and **Great Dunmow** leads off to **Little Dunmow**. At the end of the village a little ancient church stands and this is all that remains of what was once a large cruciform church founded for Augustinian Canons by Geoffrey Baynard in 1106. It is the Lady Chapel which remains and it is a thing of beauty with an arcade of bays dating to round about 1200. The rest, in the Decorated style, dates from 1360. The great east

window and four others fill this lovely place with a light that can rightly be described as heavenly. In the sanctuary is the famous Dunmow Flitch chair. According to tradition dating back to Norman times, a flitch of bacon was presented to a married couple who, a year and a day after their marriage, could vow that not for one moment had they regretted their marriage nor had a cross word in the preceding year. There have not always been many takers!

HATFIELD BROAD OAK PRIORY was the home of the Benedictine order and the Priory was founded in 1135 by Aubrey de Vere. Today you will see an impressive Perpendicular church with a vast tower which in fact was the nave of the Priory. The monastic chancel is no more and only the 12th century crossing piers, built into the outside of the east wall, remind us of what was there once upon a time. The most outstanding feature is the superb 18th century brass candelabra together with a fine George III Royal Arms and a profusion of distinguished 18th century monuments.

HATFIELD PEVEREL PRIORY is partly still in being. It stands to the south of the village on the edge of the parkland which surrounds the 18th century Priory house. The nave remains and was founded by one of the Peverel family in the 12th century as a cell of St Albans. There

St Peter guarding the south east corner of the south trancept carved by Thomas Huxlry-Jones

is a mixture of architecture and it is the old glass which is memorable. In the south aisle two windows are filled with fragments of mainly foreign glass of the 16th and 17th century. It appears to be a complicated composition but none the less beautiful.

TILTY ABBEY belonged to the Cistercians and was founded in 1153 surrounded by the beauty of this green valley. Nothing much remains other than the monastic chapel of the Abbey which is now the parish church. The simple, tiny nave which has Early English lancets was joined by the much more important chancel added in the 14th century, with a wonderful traceried east window and carved niches in the adjoining buttresses. With this mixture of grandeur and simplicity the odd little 18th century cupola seems to sit uneasily. Inside it is white everywhere and the effect of sunlight streaming in through the plain glass windows lights up the furnishings. It is a place of peace and serenity.

Finally WALTHAM ABBEY has almost been eaten up by North East London but it firmly resists the challenge and the town of the same name remains firmly in Essex. You need to go to the Market Place to see what remains of the great abbey of the Augustinian Canons. It was at one time one of the most important monastic foundations in England established with the arrival of a college of secular canons in 1030. In 1177 it was refounded as an act of penance by Henry II for his role in the murder of Thomas a Becket. Today only the early Norman nave survives, walled off at the end of the West crossing. Even this is magnificent. Do not be disappointed by the exterior, the majesty of the interior will reward you with its enormous round pillars, lofty triforium and clerestory. There is much, much more to see and a splendid mix of anything from Norman times to the Victorians. One seems to be a foil to the other.

Away from the abbeys, the priorys and the churches there is much else of interest within reach of Chelmsford. A day out to THE BASILDON ZOO AND GARDENS will give enjoyment to all ages. You will find it on the London Road at **Vange**, two miles south west of **Basildon**.

Chelmsford has always been home to pioneers, the town was dominated by the industries that were set up by some of them. First and foremost was the Marconi works, the world's first wireless factory. Guigiliemo Marchese Marconi, the Italian physicist and inventor was responsible for a number of firsts.

He made his first successful experiments with wireless telegraphy in Bologna in 1895 after developing the discovery by Heinrich Hertz of electromagnetic waves. In 1899, after transmitting signals across the English Channel, he formed the Marconi Telegraph Company in London. Two years later he bridged the Atlantic with signals sent in morse code from Cornwall. He had bought an old factory in Hall Street in Chelmsford and it was here that the commercial development of his apparatus began. Thirteen years later the company had outgrown these premises and larger ones were opened in New Street. In its laboratories and workshops were developed the world's first short-wave radio equipment and the work done there established a world-wide radio telegraph system for the British Government.

The BBC was set up to control the public broadcasting that Marconi pioneered - the first broadcast programme was made here in Chelmsford.

In the 1920's every schoolboy had a crystal set with a delicate cat's whisker and on mine I listened to the conversations between engineers in New Street and their colleagues at Writtle, where transmitters had been built. The conversations were mundane, often with messages asking some-one to let his wife know he would be late home from tea, but even then you knew you were in at the birth of something pretty exciting.

By 1930 there were few homes without a wireless set in a bulky cabinet - sometimes bakelite, sometimes fretted wood - with hefty acid batteries that had to be re-charged professionally.

Marconi's is now part of an international conglomerate but the electronics headquarters remain here and the original works have expanded into separate sections for various branches, built both in Chelmsford and surrounding spots such as Great Baddow, Writtle, Billericay, Basildon, Maldon and Benfleet.

Radar, missiles, television and computers - they are just some of the 20th century inventions in which Marconi research and components have played a vital part. The worlds first wireless factory still stands in New Street and on the left of the White building is a plaque commemorating the "Father of Wireless", Marconi. His life was a colourful one and in his latter years he lived aboard his yacht, suitably named the Ellectra.

One of the two other major pioneers who set up factories in Chelmsford were Ernest Hoffman who manufactured roller bearings. These ball bearings became vital in engineering and by the end of the first World War the factory had doubled in size. It also is now part of a huge concern - RHP Ltd. The other, Colonel Rookes Crompton served in the army in India and was a natural inventor. On his return to England he became one of the most important figures in refrigeration and distribution of electricity and his works were opened in Anchor Street.

All three works opened in the town at much the same time in the last years of Queen Victoria's reign. Hoffman's factory opened in Globe House in New Street where a plaque commemorates the Swiss-American inventor who was to play such a major role in engineering in the transport industry. All three companies made major contributions to the work of the fighting services in two world wars.

Yet another industry, far older than them all, has been a major influence on the development of Chelmsford - agriculture. For Chelmsford was an important market town with its Corn Exchange and a big market. Farmland came to the edge of the town and the rich soil produces a big cereal crop. The first show organised by the Essex Agricultural Society was held in Chelmsford in 1858.

This sturdy, prosperous town has much to offer the visitor and residents alike. Where to stay and where to eat in this part of England is important to any visitor so I have chosen one or two I like particularly.

There is a pleasant Country House Hotel at **Great Baddow** almost immediately south of Chelmsford which is to be recommended for anyone wanting to stay in the area. PONTLANDS PARK COUNTRY HOTEL is a welcoming, informally run house where guests of all ages are catered for with thought and professionalism. It stands in extensive grounds which are delightful; somewhere in which to wander and throw off the stress of the day. As good for those in the area on business as for those lucky enough to be taking a break.

It did not take Egon Ronay long to discover the virtues of dining at FRANCINES in the High Street of **Maldon**. It is housed in one of the oldest buildings in this small town dating back to 1350. It cannot have changed much over the centuries. The ceilings are low, the beams are not friendly towards those who are tall but the whole atmosphere is redolent of history at its best and an ideal setting for a meal that will leave you wondering why it has taken you so long to discover the venue. There are only 24 covers which make it both intimate and somewhere where John Brotherton, Le Patron, will certainly remember you and you him. John's wife Sara comes from Thailand and a Thai dinner is featured on the 3rd and 4th Wednesday of the month.

Colchester should always be visited when you are in Essex for several reasons. It is England's oldest recorded town and very proud of its Roman and Norman history. It has been the centre of military activity for centuries. Many of its buildings are of great interest and none more so than THE WAREHOUSE BRASSERIE in Chapel Street North just off St Johns Street. It literally was a chapel built in 1903 and has been a restaurant for 5 years. Relaxed, welcoming and full of atmosphere it is a splendid place in which to eat. You will find it has two levels, the second would have looked down on the main body of the church and still has much of the wood that was there originally enriching the decor which is mainly a soft pink and green in hue. Lovely at night when the soft lights are on.

Just north of Colchester you are virtually in John Constable country, a beautiful area with lovely villages, pretty streams and flowing rivers. Having discovered GLADWINS FARM at Harpers Hill, **Nayland** with its charming accommodation both self-catering and in the farmhouse itself, I doubt if I would look for anywhere else to stay. It is centrally situated for visiting more than one of our great Cathedrals. **Bury St Edmunds** is just up the A134, **Chelmsford** is within easy striking distance and not much farther afield is **Norwich**.

The old Suffolk village of Nayland is at the western end of Dedham Vale. The village is known for the beautiful altarpiece painted by Constable which is on display in St James' Church.

Gladwins itself, no longer a working farm, nevertheless possesses much of interest for the visitor. The house which faces south over the valley, and the 500 year old Suffolk barn and stable block are centred in the 22 acres of wooded grounds which the owners are restoring, and through which guests are welcome to wander. Bed and breakfast accommodation is offered in the farmhouse and self-catering accommodation is available in the six cottages in the barn and stable block which have been converted to modern standards of comfort whilst retaining the old character of the buildings.

The human soul rising from the river of death and lifted into paradise. The theme for a wondrous window by Henry Holliday

In Mill Lane, **Dedham** is THE MARLBOROUGH HEAD HOTEL where part of the present structure incorporates the Royal Square room and entrance hall which is known to have been built around 1465. This has been investigated and corroborated by the form of end joints of the common joists which are the same form first used for the ceiling of the library above the South East Cloister range at Wells Cathedral in Somerset which was constructed about the same time. The area now occupied by the Royal Square room was originally the Wool Hall and 'Ordinary' which was an open walled market where all the local trade was transacted.

The diagonal or dragon beam remains in position, intact, and was used for weighing bales of wool amongst other things. From there, the skeins of wool were taken into the storage chamber, now the main bar area, where they were hung from the roof by tenterhooks, (hence the expression 'On tenterhooks') The large cellars housed wooden vats used for dyeing the finished material.

The building was originally the house of a leading clothier and wool merchant when Dedham was a centre of the east Aglian Wool trade during the 15th to 17th centuries, after which the industry fell into decline due to the fierce competition from the woollen mills of

Lancashire and Yorkshire. In 1704 it was turned into an inn and since this was the year of the Duke of Marlborough's famous victory over the French at the Battle of Blenheim, it seemed fitting to name the establishment after the hero of the hour, John Churchill, 1st Duke of Marlborough. History has it that at some time a dispute arose as to whether the inn sign should depict a bust of the Duke or his Coat of Arms and it is interesting to observe that the present sign at the front of the building shows the head of the Duke while the sign at the rear illustrates his Armorial bearings.

This is a fine hotel whether or not you are interested in history. Here you will be well fed, enjoy superb wines and find that the owners aim has always been, and will continue to be, to provide the public with traditional English Fare, served at reasonable prices and consumed in a pleasant, convivial olde world environment.

Alighting in this corner of England is a bonus for anyone who enjoys both history and the glorious countryside.

London Road, Vange,
Basildon, Essex, SS16 4QA.

Tel: (0268) 553985

BASILDON ZOO & GARDENS
Visitor Attraction

On the old A13 road to Southend from Basildon you will find Basildon Zoo and Gardens which once used to be the gardens of the old Vange Rectory. Twenty five years ago one of the vicars was very interested in the botanical aspect and he set about planting and building one of the finest gardens in the county. Some of the trees and shrubs have been identified by Kew Gardens and are very rare. For example there is a magnificent Red Oak. Because of this interest and rarity a preservation scheme is maintained.

This is essentially a family run business and when John and Yolande Surcouf took over in 1986 they made sure that children visiting here would have the benefit of a 'Hands on Exercise' and get to know as many animals as possible. Children love it when the animals are brought out and the adults too get a thrill of seeing these contented, well fed and loved creatures. The Surcouf's daughter is the Head Keeper and quite clearly loves her job and has a good rapport with the animals and the visitors. Some of the animals in her care have appeared on TV and in films.

The Zoo has much to offer, and not the least is the facility for children to have birthday parties in the cafe when, having eaten a super meal, they can go and see the animals. The food on offer to visitors is simple and wholesome and the prices are sensible. One can also eat outside the cafe where there are tables and chairs and close by is an enclosed sandpit where small ones can play in safety. The whole place has been well thought out and because it is not too big it has a friendly atmosphere about it.

USEFUL INFORMATION

OPEN: Summer 10-6pm, winter 10am until
    1 hour before dusk, seven days a week
CHILDREN: Yes. Play area, adventure
    playground, picnic area, baby changing
    facilities in mens & womens toilets .
CREDIT CARDS: None taken
LICENSED: Not licensed
ACCOMMODATION: Not applicable

RESTAURANT: Cafe offering light snacks
BAR FOOD: Not applicable
VEGETARIAN: Yes, snacks
DISABLED ACCESS: Yes & WC
GARDEN: Yes. Play area.

Chapel St North, Colchester,
Essex, C02 7AT.

Tel: (0206) 765656

THE WAREHOUSE BRASSERIE
Brasserie

This exciting Brasserie in the centre of Colchester just off St John's Street, was originally a chapel, built in 1903. It was not until 1988 that it became The Warehouse Brasserie and one of the most popular venues in the town. It is lively, relaxed, informal and buzzing with the chatter of contented customers.

The conversion from chapel to brasserie has provided two levels; the second is a gallery, attractively furnished. The colours throughout are soft pinks and greens and in the evening there is the added attraction of soft lighting which just serves to enhance an already pleasing atmosphere. The only thing that reminds one now that this was once a place of worship is the vast windows. Anthony and Mel the proprietors trained together, and always had the desire to own their own restaurant. This has been achieved and the two men have made an outstanding success of the venture. Anthony is the chef while Mel tends the Front of the House. It is a good balance and the result is an ever growing number of regular customers who come to enjoy both the food and the company.

The menu matches the establishment with eight tempting Starters followed by some interesting light main courses or perhaps a chargrill or one of 5 exciting dishes which includes a grillade of gish with a fennel dressing, a mushroom and hazelnut strudel, roast wild mallard or marinated chicken breast.

Every dish is freshly cooked and the presentation is superb. Naturally the well chosen wine list complements the food perfectly. The Warehouse Brasserie certainly deserves its entry in the Good Food Guide, Egon Ronay and Michelin 1994.

USEFUL INFORMATION

OPEN: Mon-Sat: 12-2pm & 7-10pm,
    Sun: 12-2pm only
CHILDREN: Welcome. Special meals on
    request
CREDIT CARDS: Access/Visa. Switch to
    the value of £35
LICENSED: Restaurant
ACCOMMODATION: Not applicable

RESTAURANT: European cuisine
BAR FOOD: Light lunches
VEGETARIAN: 3 starters & 3 main courses
DISABLED ACCESS: 1 small step
GARDEN: None

THE MARLBOROUGH HEAD HOTEL

Public House & Hotel

Mill Lane, Dedham,
Colchester, Essex, CO7 6DH.

Tel: (0206) 323124

USEFUL INFORMATION

OPEN: All year. 11-2.30pm & 6-11pm
CHILDREN: Yes. Family room
CREDIT CARDS: All major cards
LICENSED: Full On Licence
ACCOMMODATION: 3 en-suite rooms

RESTAURANT: Country English
BAR FOOD: Yes. Wide range
VEGETARIAN: 2-3 dishes daily
DISABLED ACCESS: One step
GARDEN: Yes with tables & chairs. Patio area

Right in the centre of the pretty village of Dedham and just 5 miles north of Colchester is the Marlborough Head Hotel, a wonderful half-timbered building with a long history. Part of the present structure incorporating the Royal Square room and entrance hall is known to have been built around 1465. This has been investigated and corroborated by the form of end joints of the common joists which are of the same form first used for the ceiling of the library above the South East Cloister range at Wells Cathedral in Somerset. The area now occupied by the Royal Square room was originally the Wool Hall and 'Ordinary', which was an open walled market where all the local trade was transacted. The building was originally the house of a leading Clothier and Wool merchant when Dedham was a centre of the East Anglian Wool trade during the 15th-17th centuries, after which the Industry fell into decline. It was turned into an inn in 1704 and since this was the year of the Duke of Marlborough's famous victory over the French at the Battle of Blenheim, it seems fitting to name the establishment after John Churchill, the 1st Duke.

The hotel has been run by Brian and Jackie Wills for the past 15 years and they have now been joined by Mrs Linda Mower. Their aim has always been and will continue to be to provide the public with traditional English fare, served at reasonable prices and consumed in a pleasant, convivial and olde world environment. There is informal eating in all areas, a large car park and the hotel layout is suitable for the disabled with wheelchairs. The large Patio is a delight in summer and children play happily in the fenced area.

PONTLANDS PARK COUNTRY HOTEL

Country Hotel & Restaurant

West Hanningfield Road,
Great Baddow, Nr Chelmsford, CM2 8HR.

Tel: (0245) 476444
Fax: (0245) 478393

USEFUL INFORMATION

OPEN: All year except Dec 27th-Jan 4th. Open New Year's Eve
CHILDREN: No facilities but welcome
CREDIT CARDS: Access/Visa/Amex/ Switch/ Connect
LICENSED: Full Licence
ACCOMMODATION: 17 rooms, all en-suite

RESTAURANT: A la carte
BAR FOOD: Not applicable
VEGETARIAN: Yes
DISABLED ACCESS: Yes. Assistance available
GARDEN: Yes. Extensive grounds

This fine Victorian mansion was built in 1879 for the Thomasin-Foster family and judging by the very pleasant and friendly atmosphere it must have been a friendly and welcoming house then, as it is now. It became a hotel in 1981. Wherever one looks one can see that the Victorian theme has been adhered to, tempered with the best of contemporary styling. Every room has been designed with the comfort of guests in mind. The public rooms are immaculate and yet have a pleasing informality. Beautifully furnished bedrooms have co-ordinated fabrics and well-defined colour schemes. Diners are offered a selection of imaginative and frequently innovative menus, always with fine wines and attentive but unobtrusive service. If you dine here on Fridays or Saturdays you will find it is Italian night and the dishes come from every region of that country with wines to match. It is always a popular evening.

Within the grounds, Trimmers Leisure Centre has indoor and outdoor swimming pools, Jacuzzis, saunas and a solarium. The beauty salon offers figure-toning, hair-styling and beauty treatments. Portlands Park has a very efficient and well organised facility for meetings, private dinners from two to 36 guests and if you have a large function in mind, 200 people can be accommodated in a marquee.

Pontlands Park is open all the year round with the exception of the week commencing December 27th until January 4th although by public demand they are always open for New Year's Eve.

1a High Street, Maldon,
Essex, CM9 7PB.

Tel: (0621) 856605

FRANCINES
Restaurant

Francines is set in one of the oldest buildings in Maldon dating back to 1350. It cannot have changed all that much through the centuries. The ceilings are low, the beams are not friendly towards those who are tall but the whole atmosphere is redolent of history at its best and an ideal setting for a meal that will leave you wondering why it has taken you so long to discover the venue. There are only 24 covers which make it both intimate and somewhere where the patron will certainly remember you and you him. Maldon is within easy reach of Chelmsford which we always thought was a Cathedral City but we have learnt it is not. Yes, it does have a fine cathedral but the status of city was lost in competition to Sunderland. However if this disappoints you, dining at Francines will not.

The menu is tantalisingly small but when you study it closely you will realise that only a master in his craft could possibly have gathered together such a delicious selection. The menu is changed on the first Tuesday in every month and each succeeding month produces some established favourites but always adds or something new that one has not tried before. One of the most sensible things is the fixed price for a two course and a three course meal. This makes it easy for people who need to think about what they are spending - and most of us do have to do so today.

It did not take Egon Ronay long to spot this excellent restaurant. John Brotherton and his wife Sara who comes from Thailand, have been here for six years. A Thai dinner is featured on the 3rd and 4th Wednesday of the month, and is delicious. The wine list has 28 carefully selected choices.

USEFUL INFORMATION

OPEN: Tues-Sat evenings: 7.30-last orders 9.30pm. Lunch by appointment
CHILDREN: If well behaved
CREDIT CARDS: Access/Visa/Master
LICENSED: Restaurant
ACCOMMODATION: Not applicable

RESTAURANT: Modern French. Excellent presentation
BAR FOOD: Not applicable
VEGETARIAN: By prior arrangement
DISABLED ACCESS: No
GARDEN: No. Small car park at rear, access via Gate Street, by police station

---

Nayland,
Suffolk, CO6 4NU.

Tel: (0206) 262261
Fax: (0206) 263001

GLADWINS FARM
Country House & Self Catering Accommodation

Set in the heart of some of Suffolk's loveliest countryside at the western end of the Dedham Vale and on the outskirts of the old village of Nayland, Gladwins Farm is an oasis in which anyone would find comfort and relaxation. Although well into East Anglia with its variety of attractions, Gladwins is well placed for visiting all parts of the region and giving you an opportunity to take a look at the Cathedrals of Chelmsford in Essex, Bury St Edmunds in Suffolk and Norwich Cathedral in the heart of Norfolk.

Gladwins is no longer a working farm, nevertheless it possesses much of interest for the visitor. The house which faces south over the valley, and the 500 year old Suffolk barn and stable block, are centred in the 22 acres of wooded grounds which the owners are restoring and through which guests are welcome to wander. The Trout Lake is available for anglers, picnic areas on the edge of the woodland enjoy beautiful views over the valley, the tennis court and boules area offer that little bit of activity, and to keep the children happy there is the adventure playground, and pets' corner, where they can help with the care of the animals.

Bed and breakfast accommodation is offered in the farmhouse and self-catering is available in the six cottages in the barn and stable block which have been converted to modern standards of comfort whilst retaining the old character of the buildings. The bedrooms in the house are comfortably furnished, two are en-suite, and the cottages are completely self-contained, opening onto terrace or private patio with garden furniture and barbecue.

USEFUL INFORMATION

OPEN: All year
CHILDREN: Yes, play area, pets corner, horses (riding instruction available)
CREDIT CARDS: All major cards
LICENSED: Restricted licence being applied for at time of press
ACCOMMODATION: 6 self-catering. 2 en-suite rooms. 1 Family, 2 single

RESTAURANT: Not applicable
BAR FOOD: Snacks etc by arrangement
VEGETARIAN: Catered for
DISABLED ACCESS: Yes. 1 suitable cottage
GARDEN: Extensive grounds. BBQs

Chichester Cathedral

Chichester

"All the beautiful time is yours for always, for it is life that takes away, changes and spoils so often- not death, which is really the warden and not the thief of our treasures."

Jeremy Taylor

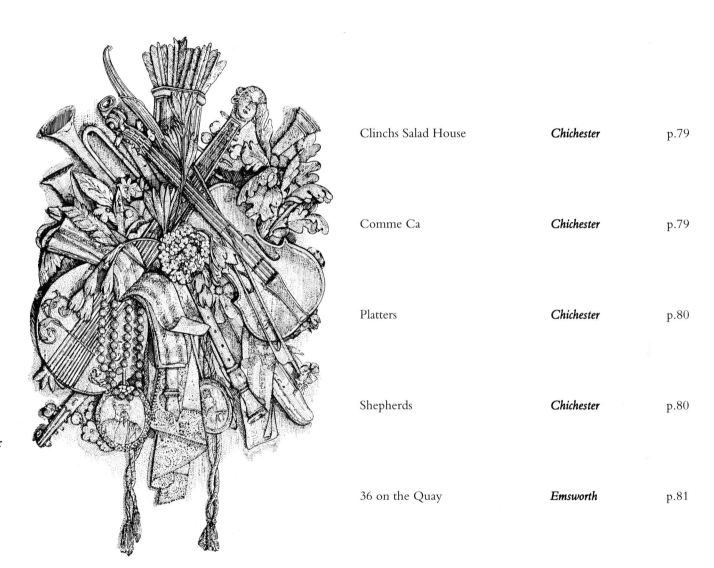

The City of Chichester

by John Theobald

This is a stylish and handsome city, dominated by its beautiful Cathedral, and influenced by Roman planners and medieval and Georgian builders. It is the centre of a prosperous agricultural area, set in lovely countryside and has one of the most distinguished theatres to be found outside **London**. This too is a place of many delights, many attractions and many outstanding buildings. First and foremost is its CATHEDRAL which follows the Continental pattern of being part of the city, rather than being set aside in its own precincts.

The Cathedral was founded in the eleventh century and is much the same as it was under its first Bishop, Ralph de Luffa. Changes there have been, of course, but the nave and choir are as they ever were. It is substantially a Norman construction but its front is 18th century. The Puritans badly damaged many of its monuments. The church was probably patterned on St. Stephens at Caen in Normandy but the stone came not from there, as at Canterbury, but from the **Isle of Wight**.

Purbeck stone is widely used in its columns. There are many works of art in the Cathedral, ranging from ancient carvings to modern paintings, sculptures, tapestries and stained glass windows. The Bishop's palace has beautiful gardens which, like the gateway, is now shared by the Bishop of Chichester and a theological college.

The Cathedral is the third widest in England and its choir is over one hundred feet long and rich in woodwork. The lovely St Clement's Chapel adjoins the impressive tomb of Bishop Durnford, a Victorian Bishop who ruled the diocese for twenty five years. St Clement's effigy is at the altar between Bishops Anselm and Alphege.

St George's Chapel is a memorial to 6,000 Sussex men who died in two world wars and to the men of the Sussex Regiment. St George himself is carved in wood. There is much woodwork in the choir beneath the central tower, which was rebuilt after both the tower and spire collapsed in 1861. The North West Tower which had fallen down in the 17th century was also rebuilt and the carved spire was then added.

The choir's stalls are well worth studying with their beautiful 14th century carvings ranging from harpists, a fiddler, and animals at play, to clowns and demons. The reredos was designed by John Piper and its tapestry was specially woven for it. The French-made tapestry was given to the Cathedral in 1966 and consists of seven strips, all heavy in symbols.

Bishop Bell, one of the best-known and most controversial clerics of his time, who was Bishop for nearly thirty years until 1958, was a great patron of the arts. There is a painting of Christ by Graham Sutherland in the St Mary Magdalene Chapel, a window by Chagall by the choir, and a tapestry behind the alter which was the work of both German and Sussex weavers as a sign of Anglo-German unity to which Bishop Bell was dedicated.

A modern font in black stone commemorates the centenary of BishopBell's birth. In the two transepts are huge paintings commissioned by a Tudor bishop. In the choir aisle are magnificent stone panels carved in the 12th century showing the Raising of Lazarus, and Christ at the home of Martha and Mary with his disciples. In the north aisle are tombs to a 13th century Countess of Arundel and a 14th century Earl of Arundel and his Countess.In the north transept are buried the ashes of the musician Gustav Holst and there is a memorial to the first man to be killed by a train. He was William Huskisson, MP for Liverpool who died from the injuries he received when the train knocked him over at the opening of the Liverpool and Manchester Railway in 1830. He had earlier been the Member of Parliament for Chichester.

No other Cathedral has a bell tower standing on its own. The 15th century tower is 120 feet high with one bell pre-dating the Spanish Armada and a huge bell, Big Walter, on which the hours are struck. The covered cloisters honour the patron saint of Sussex, St. Richard, whose shrine in the Cathedral was for two centuries a place of pilgrimage.

The Cathedral is open daily and there are guided tours on week-days. The visitor's shop is off the Cloisters and there is a shop in the bell tower.

Chichester is a county town, for it is the administrative centre of West Sussex. It was founded by the Romans who built the first city walls which were rebuilt in medieval times. Today you can walk along parts of these walls and it is a walk that will give you an illuminating introduction to the city. The old city is a compact area bisected to the south and north and the east and west by two streets that follow the Roman plan and intersect at the elaborate Market Cross built in Tudor times by a Bishop to give shelter to the country people who brought their goods to sell to the townspeople.

Over fifty feet high, the cross is the city's best-known landmark after the Cathedral. Bishop Storey, its donor, was Bishop of Chichester in the late 15th century. The bust of Charles I was erected after his death and the four clocks in stone frames were added in the mid-eighteenth century.

North Street will take you to the 13th century Guildhall which was built as a monastic chapel and stands in PRIORY PARK. It became the town hall and court and is now a museum with a collection of Roman artefacts.

From Priory Park a short walk takes you into **Little London** where an 18th century corn house is now the city and district museum which tells the story of the area from its earliest times. There are constant exhibitions here and a permanent display of Roman-British pottery and coins. A set of wheeled stocks is on display. Malefactors were locked into them and townspeople hurled rubbish and insults at them as they went by.

Some good furniture is also on display and two galleries are devoted to the history of the Royal Sussex Regiment.

Based in the Cathedral, the Chichester Festivities are one of the great art festivals of the year. The 1993 Festival began with a Festival Eucharist with the Cathedral Choir in the morning, and a brass band concert in the Cathedral in the evening. On the second day the London Mozart Players presented a concert with the BBC's Young Musician finalists. The third day included a champagne reception at GOODWOOD HOUSE at which the Britten Quartet played.

A choral, candlelit concert was featured the next day with a lecture by Germaine Greer as an alternative event. The Syd Lawrence Orchestra introduced big band music in the Cathedral on the fifth day and for those who were not devotees of the late and great Glenn Miller's type of music, there was a talk on nonsense verse by the distinguished critic Peter Levi.

On the Friday night there was the annual fireworks spectacular at GOODWOOD RACECOURSE with entertainment throughout the evening, including the band of the Royal Artillery.

Haydn's "Creation" was performed in the Cathedral on the Saturday, and on the Sunday night the Chelsea Opera Group staged the opera, "Benvenute Cellini".

The attractions the following day included the ACADEMY OF ST. MARTIN IN THE FIELDS and on the Tuesday there was another champagne reception in the Goodwood House ballroom, this time largely featuring jazz from Gershwin to Kern.

The city of London Sinfonia on Wednesday was followed the next evening by an operatic recital by the diva Rita Hunter - across the road at the Bishop's Palace George Melly was giving a lecture.

So, it went on, opera followed jazz, an open day arranged by the auctioneers - Christies, Gilbert and Sullivan, the brilliant Dillie Keane, numbers from the great British musicals presented by Richard Baker, and a Festival Finale that featured Rita Hunter with the Central Band of The Royal British Legion, and a poetry reading by Alan Bennett.

Throughout the Festival there were many other events, displays and exhibitions and it is difficult to think of a more exciting and broadly spread programme.
That was just for this year but each suceeding year seems to produce an even bigger and better festival. Certainly a good reason to visit Chichester.

After you have explored the Cathedral, its Cloisters, its precincts and the Bishop's Palace gardens cross over South Street and enter the Pallants, an area of lovely Georgian buildings. It gets its name because it once belonged to the Archbishop of Canterbury, whose palatine it thus was. It is a city in miniature with four narrow streets crowded with houses mostly built two hundred years or so ago.

In North Pallant is the most splendid of them all, PALLANT HOUSE built in 1712 by a wine merchant, Henry Peckham. He had stone birds added to the gateway to represent the ostriches on the family crest. But locals thought them decidely odd and nicknamed the residence Dodo House, a name that still sticks today. The interior has been beautifully restored and houses many fine pieces of furniture, porcelain, glassware and other antiques, and has an art gallery with an important modern collection.

You will find many other merchant houses close by. In Little London is the CHICHESTER DISTRICT MUSEUM, showing how townspeople lived and worked in the past. It is one of several Chichester museums and is probably the most important. It was once a corn store and outside is a carving by John Skelton of a tall piece of Westmorland slate in the form of a pair of hands thrusting up from the cobbled pavement.

Among the exibits inside is a huge lantern that preceded the Mayor when he went about his municipal duties after dark. It earnt it the name of "The municipal moon".

There is a statue of a pupil at Horsham's famous CHRIST'S CHURCH SCHOOL where the pupils still wear the medieval gowns that led to their being called Bluecoat Boys. This pupil supposedly told a lie and was turned into the statue you see as a result.

The museum stages many exhibitions and is open all the year round from 10 am to 5.30 pm, from Tuesday to Saturday.

The head of Christ from Chichester's distinguished Romanesque carvings

Little London is also the home of SHEPHERDS TEA ROOMS housed in a fine old Georgian Listed Building. This is a tea room run in the very best tradition with wonderful home-made cakes, scones and a whole variety of tasty dishes. It is tranquil and elegant and there can be no nicer place to rest awhile after the exertions of exploring Chichester Cathedral or the towns many antique shops.

Two other very different eateries are CLINCH'S SALAD HOUSE at 14, Southgate where ninety nine per cent of the dishes on offer are vegetarian and everything is home produced. The only meat dish is the delicious and succulent home-cooked ham which is served on a platter with salad. It would be hard in this establishment to choose anything that would not please the palate.

Number 15 Southgate is a 200 year old cottage which has been treated with imagination and courage by the owner Nik Westcott and has become the intimate restaurant PLATTERS. It could not be a more pleasant place in which to eat. Friendly, welcoming and with an ever changing menu at sensible prices, it has a following who would be devastated if they found the doors closed.

In St Martin's Street you will find ST MARTIN'S TEA ROOMS, a non smoking establishment which might appear as a traditional tea room from the outside but

inside the food is much more than cakes and scones. Savouries are mainly vegetarian, except for wild smoked salmon. Organic produce is used as much as possible. Every day there are delicious specials such as prawn salad. St Martin's bakes everything produced including their own bread, scones, carrot cake, vegan cake amd chocolate sponge cake.

The lovely 13th century building in Priory Park was built and used by monks and then became the city's Guildhall where aldermen and councillors met and courts sat. One man who was tried here was the poet, artist and visionary William Blake who lived at **Felpham** near **Bognor** for three years. He was little regarded by his contemporaries and his views were thought of as heretical. He had arrived in Sussex to make engravings for a wealthy patron but eventually fell out with him and his neighbours of whom he wrote:

*"The Sussex men are noted fools,
and weak in their brain-pan."*

The Guildhall, is open from June 1st to September 30th in the afternoons from Tuesday to Saturday. It is well worth exploring and has interesting historical displays.

The monks who built the church which is now the Guildhall were Greyfriars and the park is named after their priory. It is now a branch of the district museum. The park, an area of about ten acres, was given to the city at the end of the First World War as a memorial to that conflict, by the Duke of Richmond and Gordon, whose family still own GOODWOOD PARK. Part of the old city wall forms a section of its boundary.

In St Martin's Square is ST. MARY'S HOSPITAL, built in the 13th century. Four centuries later its infirmary was converted into homes for the old and they remain little changed.

There are two other museums. That of the CORPS OF ROYAL MILITARY POLICE MUSEUM celebrates the history of Provost Marshals since the first was appointed in the 14th century, and of the Royal Corps of Military Police. Uniforms, equipment, medals and much material of considerable interest of a body of men whose responsibilities took them into the battle area of two world wars are on display.

The 'Mechanical Music and Doll' collection features fairground and ballroom organs, musical boxes and street barrel-pianos all in full working order. There is a magnificent colection of dolls which contains many Victorian and Edwardian specimens beautifully costumed, and much else that entertained our great grandparents.

One nice thing I have discovered already about Chichester is its tea-shops; attractive and restful places. The shopping too is excellent and there are some particularly pleasant arcades such as ST PETER'S MARKET, once a church, in West Street, and SADLERS WALK off East Street. There is a splendid selection of restaurants and wine bars and some delightful pubs.

One restaurant at 67 Broyle Road is a most unusual business. COMME CA is a delightful French restaurant where the chef patron, Michel is assisted by his wife Jane, and a small but friendly French staff. It also has a bar in which you are invited to taste the 140 bins of superb wines including those from the New World. Of course it is for the food and wine that one goes here but it is much more. There is a 'Je ne sais quoi' that encompasses the whole and delights everyone who comes here. In the summer it is charming with the additional attraction of a beautiful private garden. However it is probably the warmth of the welcome on a cold winter's night that makes it extra special. An enormous open wood fire crackles away and the smell alone entices. Pre and post theatre bookings are welcomed. Comme Ca is just behind Chichester's famous theatre.

CHICHESTER FESTIVAL THEATRE stands on parkland which was once the site of the annual Sloe Fair and was opened in July, 1962 with a revolutionary design. Its first season was directed by Laurence Olivier and immediately put Chichester on the theatrical map. In its second season it became the summer home of the newly founded National Theatre and its story since is one long triumph with the greatest of the world's actors, actresses and entertainers appearing there year after year during the next three decades. The current season has featured plays by Shaw, Noel Coward, and Thornton Wilder, with a galaxy of West End stars, and a musical, "Pickwick", staring Sir Harry Seccombe.

The 1400 seater theatre has a stage surrounded on three sides by its audience, and it is complemented by the recently built Minerva Theatre which is experimental and intimate and puts on its own productions. The architecture of the Festival Theatre is innovative and striking and is surrounded by the beautiful lawns of Oakland Park. There is a stylish restaurant, bars and a gift shop and excellent facilities for the disabled, hard of hearing and partially sighted. Car parking is generous. You can book accommodation in the city and seats at the theatre with one phone call to 0243 778830 where you will get expert advice on both hotels and theatre seating.

"When the restorer has joined together",
Fitzlan monument C14 & C19

The Festival Theatre's stage is in sections of Canadian maple which can be re-arranged and added to for different productions and was the gift of the Shakespeare Memorial Theatre in Stratford, Ontario.

Chichester's near neighbour **Emsworth** hides much of its light under a bushel. It is quaint and attractive and has a good harbour but perhaps does not have the cachet of its wealthier sisters **Lymington**, **Cowes** and **The Hamble**. Nonetheless it is somewhere you should visit and if for no better reason than to sample 36 ON THE QUAY.

This is probably the best restaurant between Brighton and Southampton. The dining room of this yachting village cottage is full of surprises. Perhaps the Regency setting is unexpected for a cottage. Here the colours are predominantly duck-egg blue and yellow and the walls are hung with some good prints. What appears to be a bookcase opens to reveal a door to the wine cellar - with over 200 excellent wines at prices from £11-£155. It is appealing and provides the right ambience for the dishes which come out of the kitchen.

What surprises one most is that Emsworth can sustain a restaurant of such high standing, as it is not exactly The Hamble, but Emsworth offers berths to yachts that are definitely not as posh.

There are local people who delight in 36 On the Quay but the majority of its discerning and very satisfied customers come from far and wide.

One of the most interesting museums near Chichester is the MILITARY AVIATION MUSEUM at **Tangmere**. Tangmere and Goodwood House, just to the north would make an excellent day's excursion. Take the A285 from the city and you arrive shortly at Tangmere which was a front line Battle of Britain fighter station. Many Special Operations Executive agents were flown into occupied Europe from here.

It has not been an operational airfield for more than 20 years but its history and that of military flying is told in detail. There are many exibits to see and some beautiful high speed aircraft on show. There is a model of the Mohne Dam and a replica of the bouncing bomb designed by Barnes Wallis which destroyed it. It was one of the most famous bomber raids of World War II and was led by Wing Commander Guy Gibson who won the VC for his bravery and leadership at this dam and a second German dam. The museum is open daily from 10 am to 5.30 pm from February 1st to November 30th.

Goodwood House, its lovely park and the rest of the huge estate of the Duke of Richmond dominates this area. The famous racecourse - Glorious Goodwood - is on the edge of the park and there are race meetings throughout the summer, May until autumn when the last meeting is held in October.

Goodwood House is less than four miles from the city but its grandeur contains quite as many treasures as there are in Chichester itself. It began as a 12th century hunting lodge and was bought by the first Duke in 1697 but was not until the end of the 18th century that the present house was built by the third Duke who used James Wyatt as the architect, and Sussex flintstone as material.

The Duke bought twenty four square miles of land around the house for which his plans were so ambitious that they were never completed. Wyatt had designed an enormous octagon but less than half was completed and this has resulted in an odd and sprawling but fascinating building far smaller than was intended. One of the portraits in the house is that of the first Duke's mother, Louise de Querouialle who became the favourite mistress of Charles II who created her Duchess of Portsmouth. In a letter from him on display Charles calls her his "dearest, dearest fubs".

It is one of many paintings which include a marvellous collection of Vandycks. Canaletto panoramas and Stubb's paintings of racehorses among others.

There is a wealth of lovely furniture, Gobelin tapestries and Sevres porcelain.

It was the wife of the fourth Duke who gave the famous ball the night before the battle of Waterloo, and a standard presented to his troops by Napoleon is on display in the front hall, while the silver breakfast service used by Napoleon on the eve of the battle is in the drawing room. They were given to the Duke by Wellington.

The Peninsular War is celebrated by a table centre in the Long Hall, a gift from old soldiers for whom the fifth Duke obtained them medals to mark their part in the campaign. The house has played host many times to royalty, both for race-meetings and balls. The magnificent ballroom is now fully restored and plays its part during the Chichester Festivities.

There was once a zoo near the house which is now an amphitheatre with a stone figure of a lion to mark its past. An enclosure beside the race-course on a hilltop called the Trundle was once an Iron Age fortified camp.

The park itself is six miles in circumference. Between the race-course and Goodwood House is the SHELL HOUSE built by an earlier duchess for her daughters. The floor is paved with horse teeth and the walls of shell give their name to the house from which, like The Trundle , there is a marvellous view of countryside, city and coast stretching from **Portsmouth** to **Littlehampton**.

As well as the race-course there is a motor racing circuit and an airfield. The vast acres also takes in HALNAKER PARK in which stands the ruins of a Tudor mansion. A beautiful avenue leads to the ruined mansion and is nearly two miles long. On **Halnaker** (pronounced Hannaker: it means, oddly, half-naked) **Hill** overlooking the park is a windmill that was commemorated by the poet Hilaire Belloc. The mill was built in the 18th century and its tower and sails are a landmark for many a mile.

To the south of the A285 and mid-way between Goodwood House and Tangmere is Boxgrove church which forms the remains of the magnificent Boxgrove Priory, built soon after the Norman Conquest.

The CHURCH OF ST. MARY AND BLAISE has an Early English choir and a clerestory that uses Purbeck marble. The De La Warr chantry is a Tudor chapel with paintings of all kinds of figures and flowers. Of all the parish churches of Sussex this is the finest and one of the most beautiful in the country. Legend has it that a two mile tunnel runs from the old Priory to Goodwood House itself.

Five or six miles north of Chichester on the A286 are two outstanding attractions within a mile of each other, the WEALD AND DOWNLAND OPEN AIR MUSEUM and WEST DEAN GARDENS and WEST DEAN COLLEGE. The open air museum is just outside the village of **Singleton** and consists of a collection of historic buildings on a 60 acre parkland site. They range from a sixteenth century market to a watermill and you will find many traditional crafts being carried out that include charcoal kilns supply for industrial and medical uses. There is a nature trail and exhibitions of all kinds. Check with 0243 63348 for the opening times which in winter time vary from the daily 11 am to 5 pm openings from March 1 to October 31.

West Dean Gardens and West Dean College are a mile back to Chichester. The college is a huge mansion built in 1804 by the ducal architect, James Wyatt, and was established for residential courses in the arts and crafts, particularly country crafts. The gardens are extensive and impressive and will interest all flower lovers and gardens. You can buy both plants and refreshments. They are open daily from March 1 to October 31 from 11 am to 6 pm but the college itself is not open to visitors.

On the western edge of Chichester is FISHBOURNE ROMAN PALACE AND MUSEUM and the A27, one of the most important archaeological discoveries of the 20th century.

The first century palace was vast with mosaic floors and heating systems under them and was built around AD 75. Its story is told in a fascinating audio visual display and by museum exhibits. It first came to light in 1960 when a workman digging a trench found Roman tiles. Some of the once superb garden has been re-planted. It is open through much of the year but the times vary from month to month and it is best to check them by ringing 0243 785858.

Nearby is beautiful **Bosham** with a Saxon church, village green and a marine scene that has always attracted artists. It is here that Canute, asked to hold back the tide, rebuked the courtiers at his palace. Bosham, whose church features in the Bayeux Tapestry - Harold prayed at the church before sailing to meet the Norman king who was to become William the Conqueror - stands on one of three peninsulas jutting into Chichester Harbour.

The whole scene swarms with boats of all kinds and there is a 50 mile coastline on which stand many attractive villages. A canal from the harbour to Chichester carried cargo when there was much commercial traffic. Now the harbour is a huge leisure centre and there is a marina that is one of the biggest in Europe and a major bird sanctuary. Fisherman both professional and amateur, are based here. There is a waterbus and daily water tours from **Itchenor**.

North of **Thorney Island**, the westernmost point of Chichester Harbour, is **Westbourne** on the boundary of Sussex and Hampshire, an attractive village. A little further on is STANSTED PARK, the home of the Earl and Countess of Bessborough. The original house was built in the late 17th century, was destroyed by fire in 1900 and rebuilt in 1903. It is filled with fine furniture, paintings, porcelain and tapestries. The house is open at Easter and then on Sunday, Monday and Tuesday afternoons from 2 pm to 5.30pm from May to the end of September. All kinds of events are held here.

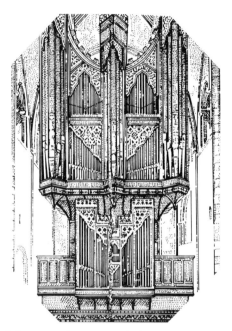

The restored organ with the Hill case & painted Renatus Harris pipes (1638)

Perhaps its most interesting feature is the chapel which is part Tudor, part Regency and part modern. Keats, the poet, was present at its dedications and celebrated it in two poems. The beach avenue west of the house is the longest in England but there are many gaps in its two mile length because of the disastrous storm of 1987.

Another stately home in the Chichester area is the grandest of them all, home for more than half a millenium to the Dukes of Norfolk.

ARUNDEL CASTLE is eleven miles to the east of Chichester and is incredibly romantic, towering over the town. It is a scene that seems little changed from medieval times and you expect to see men in armour and ladies in gowns and whimples strolling along the town's steep main street. The building of this huge fortress began in the reign of Edward the Confessor and it was besieged by Cromwell's men and burnt. So much reconstruction has been carried out since, that the castle is much changed but its magnificence has been unimpaired.

The early Dukes led a stormy life because of their opposition to the Crown but they have held the office of Earl Marshal, arranging all coronations, for several hundred years. The castle is full of works of arts and the huge apartments are open to the public. The picture gallery runs the width of the castle and here generations of Fitzalan-Howards are portrayed.

Van Dyck, Gainsborough and Reynolds were among the many great artists commissioned to paint them. In the billiard room is a portrait of Mary Queen of Scots and among the possessions of this tragic Catholic queen – the fourth Duke of Norfolk was among her suitors – are the rosary she gave him and the crucifix she was holding when the axe fell.

The family tombs are in the Fitzalen Chapel which occupies part of the parish church from which a screen separates it. One of the oldest parts of the castle is the keep, a crenellated building that goes back to Norman times.

The castle's park covers about a thousand acres and includes a cricket ground, a beautiful lake and grazing deer. In the castle grounds some of the events of the Arundel Festival are held each summer when the arts are celebrated by artists of international repute.

The castle is open from Easter until late October but for precise dates and times it is best to ring the Tourist Information Office in Arundel on 0903 882268.

The town itself is an attractive shopping centre and there are two museums and a 75 acre nature reserve created by the Wildfowl and Wetlands Trust. It has good bookshops and splendid antique centres.

You can row on SWANBOURNE LAKE or cruise on the River Arun. All in all, **Arundel** for a town of its size has as much to offer as many far larger towns.

Chichester has proved to be a very enjoyable experience and a welcome opportunity to visit the places within easy striking distance. I wish that I might have spent more time in Arundel for example but that will come when I start writing 'Invitation to the Castle Towns of Great Britain' hopefully in 1994.

14 Southgate Chichester,
West Sussex, PO19 1ES.

Tel: (0243) 788822

CLINCHS SALAD HOUSE

Salad Bar

Southgate is full of Listed buildings which delight the eye. Number 14 - Clinchs Salad House is an unusual venue which has found favour with both local people and visitors over the 15 years that it has been owned by the Ellis family. From here you are two minutes walk away from the cathedral and so Clinchs is ideal as somewhere in which to rest and enjoy good food after touring the magnificent cathedral. Such magnificence can give one mental indigestion but at Clinchs food will never do anything but assist the digestion.

Ninety nine percent of the dishes on offer are vegetarian and all are home produced. There is a changing menu both in the hot and cold dishes, but you will always find fish on the menu on Fridays. The only meat dish is the delicious and succulent home-cooked ham which is served on a platter with salad. There are always mouthwatering flans and pizzas with variable fillings. Sometimes you will find a beautifully cooked nut roast served with a delicious sauce which varies depending on the chef's mood - perhaps a delicate orange sauce. Stuffed tomatoes with a mushroom sauce is popular and so too is the vegetable lasagne and the courgette and pasta bake. In fact it would be hard to choose anything that would not please the palate. Macaroni cheese is one of the daily specials that is a favourite with local people.

Apart from the main meals there are some delectable sweets and trifles as well as light, freshly baked scones and delicious home-made cakes. The bread is cooked on the premises so is always fresh and delicious. It is a very friendly establishment with excellent service. Children are welcome and high chairs are available.

USEFUL INFORMATION

OPEN: 8am-5.30pm, Mon-Sat
CHILDREN: Welcome, highchairs
CREDIT CARDS: None taken
LICENSED: Restaurant. Wine, cider, beer & lager
ACCOMMODATION: Not applicable

RESTAURANT: Excellent hot & cold platters, fish & deserts. All home-made. The only meat is home cooked ham
BAR FOOD: Not applicable
VEGETARIAN: 99% vegetarian
DISABLED ACCESS: Yes, but not for wheelchairs
GARDEN: No

---

67 Broyle Road, Chichester,
West Sussex, PO19 4BD.

Tel: (0243) 788724
Fax: (0243) 530052

COMME CA

Restaurant & Bar

Here we have a most unusual business. It is a delightful French restaurant where the chef patron, Michel, is assisted by his wife Jane, and a small but friendly French staff and also a bar in which you are invited to taste the 140 bins of superb wines including those from the New World. The wine list is stated to be the best in Chichester. Of course it is for the food and wine that one goes here but it is much more. There is a 'je ne sais quoi' that encompasses the whole and delights everyone who comes here. In the summer it is charming with the additional attraction of a beautiful private garden. However it is probably the warmth of the welcome on a cold winter's night that makes it extra special. An enormous open wood fire crackles away and the smell alone entices. On a more mundane note there is a very large car park.

Pre and post theatre bookings are welcomed. Comme Ca is just behind Chichester's famous theatre. On Sunday there is a traditional French family lunch for you and les enfants which is leisurely, relaxed and delicious. It is a set price with a special price for children. Bar lunches are available from Tuesday to Saturday from a menu that can be as simple as a cold poached salmon salad or more richly, Filet Dijon, a fillet of Beef topped with Dijon mustard, caramelized and flambed. Set menus are available at lunchtimes should one wish.

To dine here, knowing that you have all the time in the world to enjoy the food and the wine, is one of life's treats. It will take you a considerable time to decide what to have but that difficulty can be eased by having an aperitif or sampling a bottle of wine. Everything is freshly delivered daily and prepared the same day so there is time between each course to take stock and relish the moment. Comme Ca is a find.

USEFUL INFORMATION

OPEN: Tue-Sat: 11-2pm & 5.30 until after the theatre. Sunday Lunch: 12 noon. Closed all day Monday
CHILDREN: Welcome
CREDIT CARDS: All Major cards
LICENSED: Full & Supper Licence
ACCOMMODATION: Not applicable

RESTAURANT: Beautifully prepared French cuisine
BAR FOOD: At least 12 specials daily
VEGETARIAN: Always available
DISABLED ACCESS: Yes, but toilets difficult
GARDEN: Beautiful private garden

79

PLATTERS
Restaurant

15 Southgate, Chichester,
West Sussex, PO19 1ES.

Tel: (0243) 530430

USEFUL INFORMATION

OPEN: 12-2pm & 7pm until theatre closes.
Closed Sunday and Tuesday
CHILDREN: Well behaved welcome
CREDIT CARDS: Amex/Visa/Access
LICENSED: Restaurant
ACCOMMODATION: Not applicable

RESTAURANT: Exciting, imaginative
Dinner menu changed every 6 weeks
Set price lunch menu changed daily
BAR FOOD: Light bites and snacks available
VEGETARIAN: Always available
DISABLED ACCESS: No
GARDEN: Yes. Seating for drinks & eating

A 200 year old cottage has been treated with imagination and courage by the owner Nik Westacott and become an intimate restaurant with the original wooden staircase going through the middle. It could not be a more pleasant place to eat. Friendly, welcoming, and with an ever changing menu it has a following who would be devastated if they found the doors closed.

Nik has considered all options when selecting his dishes. One consideration is the pocket of his regular clientele and no one can ever complain about his prices. Visitors coming here will be delighted not only at this but at the quality of the food they are offered. A regular visitor to the Downs and the Forests, Nik finds wonderful wild mushrooms, chanterelles, horn of plenty, parasols and hedgehogs which feature prominently on the menu at times. Every platter that comes to your table will be beautifully presented. This sumptuous feast is served for two or more people and is served on huge platters. This dish changes daily according to Nik's imagination and to what is good on the market.

Nik's menu changes every six weeks to keep up with the seasons. They always feature a range of nine starters and 10 main dishes. Usually featured are two fresh fish dishes, English Lamb, Scottish steaks and local poultry and game. All the dishes are cooked with care and imagination which is why Platters is a must.

The wine list is also worth noting. New wines are constantly appearing from all over the world.

SHEPHERDS
Tea Rooms & Gift Shop

35 Little London, Chichester,
West Sussex, PO19 1PL.

Tel: (0243) 774761

USEFUL INFORMATION

OPEN: Mon-Fri: 9.15-5pm, Sat: 8-5pm
CHILDREN: Welcome
CREDIT CARDS: None taken
LICENSED: Restaurant
ACCOMMODATION: Not applicable

RESTAURANT: This award winning
tea room is exceptional
BAR FOOD: Not applicable
VEGETARIAN: Always available
DISABLED ACCESS: Yes
GARDEN: Not applicable

Queen Elizabeth I named Chichester 'Little London' because she found it such a busy metropolis. It is still a very busy place but at No 35, Little London, Shepherds tea rooms is an oasis of everything that is tranquil and elegant. This Listed Building houses the award winning 'Top Tea Place of the Year'. There can be no nicer place to rest awhile after the exertions of exploring Chichester Cathedral or its many antique shops.

Shepherds opens at 9.15am and is frequently the place where business people are to be found enjoying their morning coffee break. It is also the place where residents meet for a natter and a first class cup of tea from the wide range of teas. The owners, Richard and Yvonne Spence, pride themselves on the quality of teas that they serve, only the best ingredients are used. Your choice may be the traditional English Breakfast Tea, Earl Grey or finest Darjeeling but you will also find China Black, Camomile, Green Teas and many more including some exotic teas. Coffee is of equal importance and you may have anything from Viennese to iced coffee.

Depending on what time of day you are there you have a wide selection of dishes to choose from. At lunchtime there are always blackboard specials but in addition jacket potatoes, rarebits, salads and sandwiches are beautifully made and served. There is an all day breakfast, hot toasted muffins, hot filled croissants and a mouthwatering tuna melt. For those with a sweet tooth the traditional cream tea is almost irresistible and the cakes certainly are. Shepherds is a find, and had it been there in Elizabeth I's time it would have a received a Royal Warrant undoubtedly.

South Street, Emsworth,
Hampshire, PO10 7EG.

Tel: (0243) 375592

36 ON THE QUAY
Restaurant

This is probably the best restaurant between Brighton and Southampton. The dining room of this yachting village cottage is full of surprises. Perhaps the Regency setting is unexpected for a cottage. Here the colours are predominantly duck-egg blue and yellow and the walls are hung with some good prints. What appears to be a bookcase opens to reveal a door to the wine cellar - with over 200 excellent wines at prices from £11 to £155! It is all appealing and provides the right ambience for the dishes which come out of the kitchen.

What surprises one most is that Emsworth can sustain a restaurant of such high standing, as it is not exactly the Hamble, but Emsworth offers berths to yachts that are definitely not as posh. There are local people who delight in 36 On The Quay but the majority of its discerning and very satisfied customers come from far and wide

The very grand cooking is executed with an ease that speaks of the true and dedicated professional. There are courses of amuse-bouches and friandises and between them lightly fried scallops and bacon with herb noodles, salmon with olive oil dressing and potato souffle with superb smoked salmon. If you enjoy sauces there are no better in the county especially with meat dishes. You really should try the Grand Marnier souffle afterwards.

The service is perfection, though a trifle pretentious - but who can fault this standard of excellence. 36 On The Quay is a memorable experience.

USEFUL INFORMATION

OPEN: Lunch: Mon-Sun. Dinner: Mon, Wed, Thurs, Fri, Sat. Closed Tue & Sun
CHILDREN: Over 11 & must eat from menu
CREDIT CARDS: All major cards
LICENSED: Full Restaurant
ACCOMMODATION: Not applicable

RESTAURANT: Superb menu, highest quality
BAR FOOD: Not applicable
VEGETARIAN: Yes
DISABLED ACCESS: Yes, welcome
GARDEN: Small

Coventry Cathedral

Coventry

"Though nothing can bring back the hour
of splendour in the grass, or glory in the flower;
we will grieve not, rather find
Strength in what remains behind;
In the primal sympathy
which having been must ever be;"

William Wordsworth

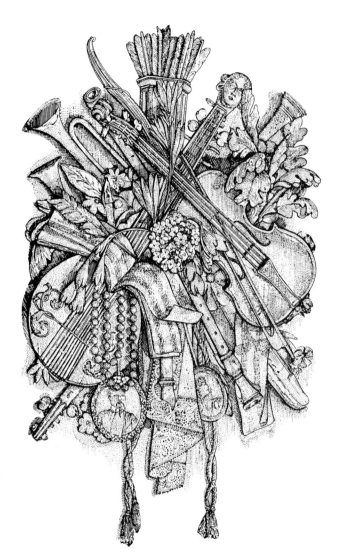

The City of Coventry

by Joy David

Essentially **Coventry** is a bright, modern, industrial city and has become known as the 'City in Shakespeare Country', a name which allows it to reach out its enterprising arms and make it possible for those who live in Coventry, those who come here on business and would be visitors, to experience and enjoy to the full, both what is in the city and what surrounds it.

As a Plymothian, living in that city during World War II, I experienced the horror and devastation brought about by the German Luftwaffe, night after night. We stood firm and so did Coventry who saw their ancient city disappear. Plymouth was lucky in that it retained some of its oldest treasures. Coventry did not, but like a Phoenix rising from the ashes a new, vibrant, colourful, cosmopolitan and cultural Coventry arose. It is an exciting place in which to live and for those who come to see it. Just occasionally amongst its tall, clean office blocks, fresh roads, smart shops and spacious parks one will catch a glimpse of medieval houses and old churches that are the only remains of the past.

A symbol of the town's regeneration is the new CATHEDRAL OF COVENTRY. Designed by Sir Basil Spence, it is a striking piece of modern architecture which stands in proud contrast to the ruins of the old Cathedral destroyed in the Blitz of 1940. It proves that contemporary craftsmen are as capable of creating a physical and spiritual experience, as their medieval counterparts. I find the Cathedral both inspiring and irritating. Brilliant in its concept it somehow misses a simple chapel or siding in which one can have a 'working pray'. Basil Spence, who won the competition for rebuilding the Cathedral in 1951 was inspired in his idea to preserve the ruins of the bombed old church and to use the shell as a paved, open forecourt leading into the new cathedral. At one end of the forecourt you will see the apse and at the other the slender 300ft spire which refused to bend to the might of the German bombers. It is a perfect example of late Gothic architecture with a lofty, slim tower, a little octagon and then the mystical spire, supported by flying buttresses.

This was a church that was begun in 1371 and was completed about 1430. More rebuilding was carried out and completed in the early 16th century. Steps descend from the old North aisle to the West front of the new church and are joined by a flight of steps up from the street and so the old and the new marry in harmony.

The Cathedral was consecrated in 1962 and has continued to give the more orthodox a shock when they see it for the first time. It looks like a vast pink rock with rugged and sometimes jagged sides. This is because the side windows, rising to the full height of the building, are angled in 'saw-tooth' fashion. This is not the only shock; the new cathedral has no truck with medieval buildings. Near the West end is the enormous bow-fronted window of the Baptistry by John Piper which represents the light of God, Jesus Christ, breaking into his world. Between that and the porch stands Epstein's bronze figure of St Michael trampling Lucifer. A porch covered by the oddest canopy and supported by slender columns leads to the great glass screen designed by John Hutton in which the images of patriachs, saints and angels affirm the continuity of Christianity down the ages. It is a link between the old and the new cathedrals almost as if it is reminding us of the Christian message of the resurrection. This mighty work forms the West Wall and the principal entrance through which one can see the interior of the Cathedral and sometimes the reflection of the gaping perpendicular windows in the glass.

My immediate reaction on entering the cathedral was its size and yet it is misleading. It is not large, only 270 feet in length but Sir Basil has somehow contrived to make it seem vast and spacious. It reminded me of the medieval hall-church an example of which is to be seen in Bristol Cathedral. The glass of the eastward facing windows is richly coloured and spreads its warmth throughout, long thin columns uphold a wide shallow vault, and at the end of the aisle is Graham Sutherland's vast tapestry 'Christ in Glory' which is best viewed from the nave. Christ, who was the carpenter of Nazareth is shown seated, wearing a workman's apron, surrounded by the symbols of the four Evangelists - John, Mark, Luke and Matthew. St Michael casting out the Devil can be seen below the eagle. Through his death and resurrection Christ won for all people the way of restoration to a living relationship with God. He is therefore shown seated in majesty. His hands are raised in a gesture of commissioning and blessing. The colours are all greens and golds and reds and browns and make the interior fabulous. The tapestry seems to reach out and speak to everyone who comes to the cathedral. Christ's commanding presence fills the church. Everything leads to this figure, the font at the West end in front of the Baptistry window is a boulder from the hillside above Bethlehem, the Tablets of the Word carved in bold lettering by Ralph Beyer on the splays of the angular windows. They contain eight of the great sayings of Jesus. The old lettering reminds us that from simple beginnings these truths have endured through the centuries and still speak to us today. The Altar with its large gilded cross contains the original Cross of Nails. This was made from three medieval nails collected from the ruins of the old Cathedral, and has become the symbol of reconciliation in Coventry and worldwide. It is only as one is returning from the altar having taken communion that one sees the gorgeously rich stained glass in the saw-tooth windows.

The immensity of this building takes one over but not always for the right reason. I hated the choir stall canopies for example which are supposed to resemble stars but look, from a distance, like one of those protective walls built with struts coming out of them which prevent intruders from getting in. I also find the outside stark and unwelcoming but all that is as nothing when it comes to the thrilling beauty that is before you as you gaze into the interior through the

glass screen at night, when the candles are lit and the music fills every tiny corner.

The new Cathedral is famed as a centre for 'International Peace and Reconciliation' and the old Cathedral ruins are often the setting for major special events such as the internationally-acclaimed triannual Mystery Plays.

Coventry Cathedral's new visitor's centre aims to increase the appreciation and understanding of the past, along with the present and future of this great Benedictine Monastery with its unique international reputation. Leading designers and experts in high technology have come together to create the new visitor's centre. Holograms have become the norm but here is a world first sculpture/holography project. It is almost beyond me and all I could do was to wonder at the walkaway of the mystery of art and technology in combination - three dimensional images made with laser light. I read about how a hologram is made and saw the 'Stations of the Cross' in three dimensional images. Beautiful holograms tell the story of what happened between the sentencing to death and burial of Jesus Christ.

The Spirit of Coventry is told in an audio-visual spectacular which runs for eighteen minutes in the new audio visual theatre. Through this award winning show you

Helen Jennings' sculpture: Christ crucified, with the baptistry window far distant

learn the importance and meaning of the historical events which took place in Coventry.

A feature of the post-war reconstruction, the extensive traffic free shopping precincts, are wonderful. Over a mile in length, this pleasantly terraced and arcaded shopping area, which is constantly being developed, caters for every possible demand, while fountains, murals, and open-air chess create a diversion from the shops. One of the most successful developments is WEST ORCHARDS the home of Debenhams where just about everything seems to be under one roof. Close by is MARKS AND SPENCERS and BRITISH HOME STORES with WOOLWORTHS across the street. Part of West Orchards is OSCARS FOOD COURT operated by a smart and friendly team who have been trained to provide the best customer care and service to the highest standards. The range of food, consisting of 8 kiosks have all manner of foods. Traditional English fare in FOOD GLORIOUS FOOD, Italian food in the ITALIAN JOB, GOLDEN BOY has jacket potatoes, MANHATTAN deals with American burgers, PRETTY PINK sells ince-cream sundaes- sandwiches and baguettes are to be found in the cafe metropole, you go to CHINATOWN for Chinese cuisine and HIGH SOCIETY has fresh cream cakes and patisserie. In fact something for everyone. The CATHEDRAL LANES SHOP-

PING CENTRE is another favoured spot for shopping, meeting and eating in the heart of Coventry.

The City Gallery has an exhibition 'A History of the City beyond the Millenium' which is opening in the Spring of 1994. It is the best and most prestigious exhibition ever to be seen in the HERBERT ART GALLERY AND MUSEUM. It will tell the story of the city from the days of Lady Godiva to the 21st century and will be a permanent attraction in the historic heart of Coventry. Of particular interest will be the evocation of Coventry's craft based skills as they were passed seamlessly from generation to generation; from the great medieval textile city of 'Coventre' through the clock, watch and ribbon trades to the twentieth century 'Car City'. The story will be brought alive using audio tours and the latest video interactives, supporting the unique collection of real objects specially assembled for the permanent exhibition. One of the many high points will be the popular Lady Godiva paintings and artefacts displayed together for the first time.

A badge of the cathedral seal depicting St Michael the Archangel

Audio cassette tours will provide a short, interesting insight into Coventry and its people. Those with more time can enjoy the richer depth of knowledge provided in the text, graphic and video form. Careful thought has also been given to the needs of disabled and older people. It should be a memorable visit.

Most of the ancient city has gone, but there are still significant remains and these have under-gone, and benefited from, considerable conservation work. The medieval GUILDHALL is more than worth visiting. It contains a splendour of old glass, a wealth of carving and a minstrel's gallery. A unique Arras tapestry dating from the 15th century can also be found there. Its tower once imprisoned Mary Queen of Scots and it has a restored 600-year old crypt. The Great North Window and the oak ceiling were rebuilt after wartime bombing with the original wooden carvings still intact. Suits of armour are on display in the Minstrel's Gallery. Open daily from April to October and Easter holiday. Guides are available.

Close to the Guildhall is THE GOLDEN CROSS INN which possibly dates from the 17th century. According to tradition it was built on the site of an ancient Coventry mint. It is a popular and welcoming hostelry open to the public during normal licensing hours.

BOND'S HOSPITAL in Hill Street is a beautiful 16th century Tudor almshouse, still in use as a home for the elderly. The exterior and the courtyard are there to be seen but the inside is private. At FORD'S HOSPITAL in Greyfriars Lane it is also the exterior that can be seen. It is a half-timbered Tudor almshouse founded in 1509 by Coventry merchant William Ford. It was repaired after wartime damage and is still used as an almshouse for old ladies. It is considered to be one of the finest examples of domestic architecture.

The medieval SPON STREET is a living museum of the city's heritage and contains 15th and 16th century buildings which are now gaining a new lease of life as shops, art galleries and restaurants. It is a sheer delight to wander along and enjoy its beauty and activity.

WHITEFRIARS in London Road is a renovated 14th century Carmelite friary with one remaining cloister. It is in use throughout the year for temporary exhibitions, sculpture displays and special events. It is open all year from Thursday to Saturday.

SWANSWELL GATE STUDIOS is a unique 14th century studio which houses the work of local artists and crafts people. There are working artists on site and arts and crafts are for sale. It opens in the summer from 8-6pm 7 days and in winter from Monday to Friday 9-5pm and Saturdays 9-12 noon.

There is another attractive half-timbered building in New Union Street. CHEYLESMORE MANOR HOUSE once belonged to the Black Prince when he was Lord of the Manor. It is now in use as the register office and it is the oldest one in Britain dating back to 1250.

If you have a liking for the theatre THE BELGRADE THEATRE was the first civic theatre opened in Britain after the war and has an annual calendar of plays and concerts. Sports enthusiasts will enjoy THE FAIRFAX STREET SPORTS CENTRE with bowls, badminton, squash, two swimming complexes, a sauna suite and a solarium.

A busy city needs good places to stay. Many hotels can offer you a choice of bedrooms but few can offer you a choice of history! BROOKLANDS GRANGE in Holyhead Road, can do just that. The bedrooms in the original part of the house were built around the 16th century, each room is completely different, full of character and charm and with that special atmosphere only old oak beams and low ceilings can evoke. The Victorians added on more rooms and the owner, Lesley Jackson has had a lot of pleasure in enhancing and highlighting the bigger and grander style they favoured. However if you are one of those people who think history should be in the past then the new bedrooms are just the place for you. No matter what your choice every room has an ensuite bathroom and all the modern facilities and certainly plumbing and heating circa 1990!

The city of Coventry is renowned for its many fine restaurants and not the least of these is THE FERNLEAF, a Peking and Cantonese restaurant which is run by Richard and Susan Ngun. You will find it some two miles from the centre of Coventry, on the main Walsgrave road, in the **Ball Hill** area. The food is excellent and value for money. It also has a first class take away.

With everything that happens in Coventry one should never forget that the city is the acknowledged 'home' of British road transport and perhaps it is appropriate to reflect on the reasons why this now universal industry centred itself in Coventry.

Coventry has been a manufacturing city since the middle ages and at one time, was the sixth largest town in England. During the early and middle part of the 19th century, the city was committed to the watch making and textile industries, which fell into decline during the 1860's and the city looked set for a severe depression with most of its skilled labour force losing their jobs.

However, in 1865 the Velocipede had been invented in France and the cycle trade abroad had started to grow apace. A young Englishman, Rowley Turner worked for one of these French manufacturers during a period when the company was having difficulty meeting its production demands. Visting his uncle, Josiah who managed a Coventry company known as the Coventry Sewing Machine Company, he sought his help in manufacturing 400 of these new fangled machines. Josiah seeing his falling order book, readily agreed and changed the Articles of Association of the company to permit the inclusion of manufacturing bicycles. The Franco-Prussian war brought the collapse of the French and European market for these Velocipedes and so the new machines had to be sold on the home market. The British bicycle industry was born in Coventry.

Turner's partner in the Sewing Machine Company which had become Coventry Machinists had an inventive genius and he was to earn himself the name of 'Father of the Cycle Industry'. In the years that followed over 300 individual cycle manufacturers opened up businesses and earned Coventry the title of 'Cycle Capital of the World'. Until 1896 the cycle industry was the most significant employer in Coventry but around 1896, a slump set in. However conditions were changing and aided by the repeal of the notorious 'Red Flag Act' which had inhibited the development of Coventry's motor vehicle industry. A

The Apse of St Michaels' with the alter of reconciliation and charred cross

young Warwickshire engineer, F.R. Simms had acquired the patent rights for the manufacture of Daimler engines in the United Kingdom and in 1893 he set up the Daimler Motor Syndicate. The obvious location for his manufacturing plant was a city where both inventive skills and suitable premises were available in abundance. Coventry offered both and in January 1896, it was the registration of the Daimler Company which effectively gave birth to Britain's motor vehicle industry in the City of Coventry.

Since that time well over 120 individual motor vehicle manufacturers have made their homes in Coventry and the city's reputation also brought a host of motorcycle and commercial vehicle manufacturers. In addition, the needs of these burgeoning industries required a whole range of engineering manufacturers of tyres, wheels, bodies and engines etc. and service industries to support the development. From a town of some 30,000 inhabitants just before the turn of the century, the city's population grew to in excess of 300,000 thus confirming the road transport industries as being both the economic and social backbone of Coventry throughout the twentieth century.

This unique story is told vividly and accurately in THE MUSEUM OF BRITISH ROAD TRANSPORT of which Coventry is justly proud. Here you can see the largest display of British made road transport vehicles in the world, all under one roof. There are more than 150 cars, 75 motorcycles and 200 cycles. You can live the history through the famous marques of Alvis, Daimler, Hillman, Humber, Jaguar, Riley, Rover, Standard, Triumph and many more. It goes from little to large with an impressive display of old and new road transport items. I was amazed how big the collection is. You will need to allow several hours to really explore all it has to offer.

Another fascinating museum is at Coventry Airport where THE MIDLAND AIR MUSEUM which incorporates the SIR FRANK WHITTLE JET HERITAGE CENTRE, houses a unique collection of aircraft, engines and supporting exhibits illustrating the exhilirating story of the jet age. On display is something to interest everyone from the wartime Meteo to the supersonic Lightning, including such classics as the Vulcan, Canberra, Hunter and Starfighter.

Local aviation history is strongly represented, too. There is a wealth of Coventry-produced aircraft and other exhibits, dominated by the giant Armstrong-Whitworth built Argosy freighter of 1959. During World War II, Baginton Aerodrome was an RAF fighter station. Today as Coventry Airport, it is a busy general aviation centre and the museum provides an excellent vantage point for watching the wide variety of aircraft using the airfield.

When you come here you will experience the fascinating appeal of historic aircraft. You can get further details about the museum, its admission prices and events calendar from the Midland Air Museum, Coventry Airport, Baginton, Warwickshire. Tel: (0203) 301033

On the lighter side of things you can enjoy a splendid medieval banquet at COOMBE ABBEY, Brinklow

Road, **Binley**. Nr. Coventry. It is a night you will never forget. Coombe Abbey has won international awards for their banquets and one can understand why. Here you dine by candlelight in this Cistercian Abbey, enjoy professional singing and good humour presented by the Court Chamberlain, musicians and ladies of the court, all in traditional costume. The food is a feast and you will find not only wine but medieval mead. Evening performances commence at 8pm and the Abbey and bar open from 7pm. There is a special fully inclusive price. For reservations ring 0203 452406.

Coombe Abbey is also part of a fine country park and is a jewel in Warwickshire's beautiful countryside. It has taken ten centuries and the vision of many individuals for the park to reach its present splendour. After thoroughly exploring Coventry Cathedral it is the most refreshing place to be with its beautiful garden, woodland and lakeside walks. There are plants, animals and birds in abundance and everyone has a chance to get close to nature. Most of the parkland is classified as a 'Site of Special Scientific Interest' in recognition of its importance to wildlife.

Coombe Abbey Country Park is easily accessible and opens every day from 7.30am to dusk. Pay and display charges are in operation. The visitor centre is open 7 days a week from 9am-7pm April to September and from 9am-5pm October to March except Christmas Day.

Having spent a day in the country park you might well be rewarded by a visit to LINO'S RESTAURANT at number 5 Brinklow Road, Binley, where in what was an old thatched cottage Lino Gomez has produced a charming, intimate restaurant where the food is of gourmet standing and the wines superb. Lino frequently buys wines at auction and your choice comes from some of the finest in the world and mostly at affordable prices

although No 107 on the list is a Chateau Talbot 1949 Grand Cru Classe Saint Julien at £895 a bottle! The restaurant is open in the evenings only.

Lino Gomez also owns a comfortable small hotel THE GRAPEVINE HOTEL AND RESTAURANT in **Lower Highhead** where you will be well cared for and well fed.

RYTON ORGANIC GARDENS at **Ryton-on-Dunsmore**, the home of Channel 4 TV series 'All Muck and Magic' is a wonderful place for a day out within easy reach of Coventry. Whether you are an experienced gardener or not you will enjoy it. It is more than just a garden. Its eight acres are carefully laid out to show you the mysteries of compost making and how to protect your plants from pests and diseases, by methods which are cheap and easy and will not harm the environment. It is run by The Henry Doubleday Research Association, Europe's largest organic gardening organisation, whose patron is Prince Charles.

It is the scents of the roses and lavender in the rose garden which was almost as appealing to me as the flowers themselves. They seem to intermingle in the most delicious manner. All the plants grown here have been selected so that they avoid diseases, so saving money on fungicides. At its best from July onwards, it's a delight to visit for most of the year.

One tends to forget that seeds, like animals, can become extinct but here at Ryton you can see varieties of threatened vegetables, that might have been grown by your grandfather and are unobtainable today except through Ryton's Heritage Seed programme. Vegetables have strange names from time to time and I was reminded about 'Prolific Penelope' and the 'Lazy Housewife'! Ryton has its own livestock to provide organic manure or more correctly I should say that in the spring and summer months rare breeds are on loan to Ryton from the COTSWOLD FARM PARK. They are all animals on the list of the Rare Breeds Survival Trust.

Modern farming methods have led to the virtual extinction of many wild flowers that were readily seen when I was a child but here at Ryton Organic Gardens they have recaptured the beauty of a wildflower meadow and a cornfield, before the age of sprays. Ryton will even teach you to create your own garden haven for wildlife, which is not a mass of weeds!

After you have spent an idyllic time in the gardens it is time to visit the cafe where you will discover that their commitment to organic growing does not stop in the gardens. Almost all of the home-made food in the cafe is organically grown.

Ryton Organic Gardens are open every day except during Christmas week from 10am-5.30pm

Both Coombe Abbey Country Park and Ryton Organic Gardens are delightful places to spend a day within easy reach of Coventry but there are many more in what is known as Shakespeare Country. BADDESLEY CLINTON HALL at **Lapworth** is a medieval moated manor house little changed sine 1634. It is open from Wednesday to Sunday in the afternoons from April until the end of October.

19th century converted farm buildings have been turned into a successful and exciting number of craft workshops at HATTON CRAFT CENTRE at**Hatton**. The centre has a rare breeds park and there are shops and cafes. It is open daily throughout the year.

Hockley Heath is proud of PACKWOOD HOUSE which belongs to the National Trust. This is a charming Tudor timber-framed house with a remarkable Yew garden dating from 1650 which represents the Sermon on the Mount. It is open Wednesday to Sunday and Bank Holiday Monday afternoons from April to the end of October and Easter.

Visiting the stately RAGLEY HALL at **Alcester** is one of those rare treats. It was built in 1680 and is a joy to walk through with its fine paintings, china furniture and library. The gardens, beautifully kept, lead to a lake, the park and an advetnure wood which children love. There is a 3-D maze and a country trail. All the ingredients for a magical day out. It is open daily except Monday and Friday from Easter until the end of September, but open Bank Holiday Monday.

One of my treats having visited Ragley Hall, is a short drive to the pretty village of **Temple Grafton** and one of my favourite establishments, THE BLUE BOAR which has a superb atmosphere and the food is wonderful.

STANFORD HALL at **Lutterworth** is a house built in the 1690's and has an 1898 'Flying Machine' on display in the motor cycle and car museum. It also has a beautiful walled rose garden leading to the old forge and crafts

Part of the Swedish windows by Einar Forseth, here is St Sigfrid, a 11th century English Missionary in Sweden

centre. Open Bank Holiday weekend and Thursday afternoons from Easter until the end of September.

There is no lack of castles within easy reach of Coventry. The glorious 12th century KENILWORTH CASTLE is open daily. WARWICK CASTLE which has changed little since the 14th century has towers and dungeons to excite visitors and State apartments which contain some of Reubens' finest work as well as Van Dyke and the 'Royal Weekend Party 1898' tableau by Tussauds. Capability Brown was responsible for the landscaping of the gardens. There are picnic areas, riverside walks. It is open daily.

TAMWORTH CASTLE is Norman with later additions including a Tudor banqueting hall and Jacobean state apartments housing a local history museum. It is also open every day.

Lying at the heart of England, it is in the area around Coventry that the agricultural south meets the industrial north. As a result, the countryside comprises a variety of scenery as well as the historial interest I have just written about. Warwickshire's gentle landscapes and fertile pastures lie within easy reach of the city, and to the south, you will find secluded villages such as **Wootton Wawen**, Alcester and **Hampton Lucy** where THE BOARS HEAD is somewhere not to be missed. It has belonged to St Peter ad Vincula, Hampton Lucy, since it was erected over 450 years ago. The pub stands within 50 yards of the church which is widely known as the 'cathedral in the country'. It is a delightful spot, less than four miles from Stratford and a half a mile from CARLECOTE HOUSE AND PARK. The Boar is much as it was a century ago, the oak beams and open fireplace give it a timeless beauty. There is nothing fussy or elaborate about its character, it is unashamedly a pub enjoyed and amply supported by the locals, although many travellers throughout the world have, at one time or another, partaken and thoroughly enjoyed its hospitality.

At **Kenilworth** the modern town centre seems to have been absorbed by the ruined red sandstone castle and the town of **Warwick** is dominated by that mighty castle. Although it does have one of my favourite places FANSHAWES RESTAURANT in Market Place. The approach to Fanshawes in the summer is enhanced by the colourful hanging baskets but at anytime of the year it would be welcoming. The owners, David and Susan Fanshawe who share the cooking between them, have created a very special restaurant. It is small and intimate and a place in which to relax in the certain knowledge that the food will be memorable.

One of my other favourite places is elegant **Leamington Spa** with its fine terraces of Regency and Victorian buildings which grace this once fashionable health resort. Even today the town's mineral waters are revered for their medicinal properties. If you are looking for a truly splendid meal while you are in Leamington Spa then I can wholeheartedly recommend LES PLANTAGENETS, a superb French restaurant, specialising in authentic French cooking with regard to method and the capture of the true appetising flavour. Everyone

from Remy Loth, the chef/proprietor to the waiters is French. The atmosphere is marvellous and everyone who comes to this truly Gallic establishment is imbued with the excitement that only the French can produce about food.

It is not too far to **Stratford-upon-Avon** where everything is linked somehow to the greatest of all English playwrights, William Shakespeare. A wonderful experience for any visitor especially if it is for the first time. It is here that apart from the theatre and Shakespeare THE TEDDY BEAR MUSEUM should not be missed. In an original Elizabethan setting hundreds of teddy bears are to be seen many of whom have come from across the world. It is open daily and attracts children of all ages!

The Cotswolds are within reach and here amongst the glorious scenery are peaceful market towns like **Chipping Campden** and **Fenny Compton** with their hone-coloured stone cottages so typical of this beautiful area.

I always prefer the country south of Coventry but there are many who will sing the praises of the mainly man-made landscape to the north of the city. I have to admit that even here there is an odd sort of beauty which is distinctively English and can still be seen around **Wolvey** and **Market Bosworth**. It is here that you can take a look at BOSWORTH BATTLEFIELD AND VISITOR CENTRE where there is a splendid interpretation of the famous battle of 1485. Check the opening times with the Information Centre at Market Bosworth. Tel: (0455) 292239

If you enjoy visits to battlefields you may care to take a look at EDGEHILL BATTLE MUSEUM at **Farnborough**, Banbury where there are dramatic displays of arms and armour, costumes and other memorabilia all associated with this famous battle of 1642. Open April to

September, Wednesday and Saturday afternoons only.

Nuneaton was the home of George Eliot and ARBURY HALL, an 18th century Gothic mansion was George Eliot's 'Cheverel Manor'. It is open Sunday and Bank Holiday afternoons Easter to October.

Dr Johnson was born at **Lichfield** with its wonderful Cathedral which will be featured in the Northern England book in this series. Just east of Coventry is **Rugby**, whose name is synonymous with its famous school and as the home of Tom Brown's Schooldays. For most people however it is known as the birthplace of the game of Rugby.

Holyhead Road, Coventry,
Warwickshire, CV5 8HX.

Tel: (0203) 601601
Fax: (0203) 601277

BROOKLANDS GRANGE
Hotel & Restaurant

Many hotels can offer you a choice of bedrooms but few can offer you a choice of history! Brooklands Grange can do just that. The bedrooms in the original part of the house were built around the 16th century, each room is completely different, full of character and charm and with that special atmosphere that only old oak beams and low ceilings can evoke. The Victorians added on more rooms and the owner, Lesley Jackson has had a lot of pleasure in enhancing and highlighting the bigger and grander style they favoured. However if you are one of those people who think history is a thing of the past then the new bedrooms are just the place for you. No matter what your choice every room has an en-suite bathroom and all the modern facilities and certainly the plumbing and heating is circa 1990!

Everything about this elegant and comfortable hotel is meticulously handled. It is ideally located for easy and direct access to Birmingham International Airport, The National Exhibition Centre, The National Agricultural Centre and the City of Coventry. It is equally well placed for a visit to either Birmingham or Coventry Cathedral and the very many local historic attractions such as Warwick Castle and Stratford upon Avon, both of which are only a short drive away.

Brooklands Grange restaurant is outstanding and highly thought out, offering the best in Continental and English cooking. With a selective and creative menu they take pride in everything they serve. It is a perfect place for weddings and for seminars, product launches and many other business occasions.

USEFUL INFORMATION

OPEN: All Year round except Boxing Day
CHILDREN: Welcome. Special meals, cots
CREDIT CARDS: All major cards
LICENSED: Full On Licence
ACCOMMODATION: All en-suite, direct dial telephone, TV, trouser press

RESTAURANT: Brasserie serving Continental and English cooking
BAR FOOD: Light meals
VEGETARIAN: Yes 2 - 3 dishes daily
DISABLED ACCESS: Yes, ramp. Disabled toilet. One bedroom
GARDEN: Yes, chairs & tables

---

74 Walsgrave Road, Ball Hill,
Coventry, CV2 4ED.

Tel: (0203) 650199

THE FERNLEAF
Peking & Cantonese Restaurant

The City of Coventry is renowned for its many fine restaurants and not the least of these is The Fernleaf, a Peking and Cantonese restaurant which is run by Richard and Susan Ngun. You will find the restaurant some two miles from the centre of Coventry, on the main Walsgrave Road in the Ball Hill area. It is just over a year ago that the Ngun's became the proud owners of The Fernleaf and in that time they have brought their ten years catering experience to bear on providing an atmosphere which their ever growing number of regular customers have learned to appreciate and rely upon.

The interior is decorated tastefully with soft shades of pink being evident throughout. The restaurant is light and airy and at the same time extremely relaxing. It is Susan's role to oversee the front of house and welcome everyone, a task she obviously enjoys. In the kitchen, Richard is in charge, and with his team they produce a whole range of tempting dishes. The menu is extensive and everything is cooked to order.

The Fernleaf is well known for its business lunches with a House Special on each days menu. You may choose from the house specialities, the seafood, duck, chicken, pork sweet and sour. Sizzling platters are very popular and so too is the Birds Nest . In case you get lost in their a la carte menu, there are a number of set dinners to suit everyone. Mixed appertisers, Yuk Sung and fillet steak Cantonese style is a must if you are into Peking and Cantonese food. Whatever you choose you will find it delicious and excellent value for money including the Take Away.

USEFUL INFORMATION

OPEN: Lunch: Wed-Sat: 12-2pm & 6-11.30pm Mon-Sat: 6-11.30pm. Closed Sundays
CHILDREN: Well behaved welcome
CREDIT CARDS: Visa/Mastercard/Amex
LICENSED: Full Restaurant Licence
ACCOMMODATION: Not applicable

RESTAURANT: Top Class Peking & Cantonese
BAR FOOD: Not applicable
VEGETARIAN: Five main dishes
DISABLED ACCESS: Willing to assist
GARDEN: No

THE GRAPEVINE HOTEL

Hotel

28 Lower Holyhead Road,
Coventry, Warwickshire, CV1 3AW.

Tel: (0203) 555654

USEFUL INFORMATION

OPEN: All year
CHILDREN: Welcome
CREDIT CARDS: Access/Visa
LICENSED: Full On Licence
ACCOMMODATION: 11 rooms,
    2 en-suite doubles

RESTAURANT: International cuisine.
    A la carte
BAR FOOD: Not applicable
VEGETARIAN: 15 dishes
DISABLED ACCESS: No
GARDEN: Patio for BBQ's

The Grapevine Hotel is just a quarter of a mile from the cathedral and runs off Spon Street which is the medieval part of the city. It stands in a quiet cul de sac, Lower Holyhead Road, which offers a quiet retreat yet no distance from the centre of all the tourist attractions. The hotel was built in Victorian times and managed to survive the bombing of World War II. It has all the natural elegance with which the Victorians embellished their buildings. The rooms are all spacious with high ceilings. Sensibly the furnishing of The Grapevine has been carried out in a manner which has an understanding of Victorian times, without making one suffer the discomfort of the Horsehair chairs which were so prevalent at that time. Nor are there any aspidistras! Instead there are flowers and plants, comfortable chairs, warm rooms and beds which ensure that one has a restful night's sleep.

There are 11 rooms, two of which are en-suite. The Restaurant which has a following of local people as well as residents, seats 35 with ease and you will enjoy beautifully cooked meals from an a la carte menu which is definitely international. Everything is freshly cooked and prepared with the finest fresh ingredients available. The Chef/Manager has that essential ability to combine his talent and artistry in the kitchen with a friendly approach to his clientele. The staff are all welcoming and more than willing to help visitors find there way about and get the best out of any visit. There is so much to see and do in Coventry and visiting the striking cathedral is a must on anyone's itinerary.

LINO'S RESTAURANT

Restaurant

5 Brinklow Road, Binley,
Coventry, CV3 2HZ.

Tel: (0203) 635760

USEFUL INFORMATION

OPEN: Seven days of the week
    except Sunday evenings
CHILDREN: Yes. Special menus
CREDIT CARDS: All major cards
LICENSED: Full on licence
ACCOMMODATION: Not applicable

RESTAURANT: English, French &
    Continental cuisine
BAR FOOD: Not applicable
VEGETARIAN: Yes. 4 - 5 dishes
DISABLED ACCESS: Yes. Level entrance
GARDEN: Yes. For eating & drinking

Once upon a time Lino's was an old thatched cottage and today in its role as a restaurant it still has a cosy charm. Having spent the day exploring the thrilling interior of Coventry Cathedral there can be no better place to dine than at Lino's. Easily found on the edge of Coventry on the A4027 Brinklow Road, less than one mile from the M6/M69 motorway intersection and within easy reach of Birmingham, the National Exhibition Centre and the National Agricultural Centre at Stoneleigh. The totally relaxed air of wellbeing is wonderful. The low ceiling restaurant is attractively furnished and the tables are comfortably large. The decor is soft with pretty drapes, pink chairs, immaculate table linen set off with shining cutlery and sparkling glass.

Before you go in for dinner it is very pleasant to sit in the intimate bar, enjoying a pre-dinner drink and enjoying the chance of some quiet conversation and an opportunity to mull over the events of the day. The first class traditional and continental cuisine is in the control of Lino Gomez who is Les Gastronomes de la Mer 1993; an award well deserved. Everything is freshly prepared and you are waited on by a discreet, efficient and friendly staff. The Wine List is especially interesting. Lino frequently buys wines at auction and your choice comes from some of the finest in the world and mostly at affordable prices although No 107 on the list is a Chateau Talbot 1949 Grand Cru Classe Saint Julien at £895 a bottle! Many regular guests have discovered the advantage of celebrating special occasions or entertaining clients at Lino's. Reservations are advised both for lunch and dinner.

MUSEUM OF BRITISH ROAD TRANSPORT

Museum

St Agnes Lane, Hale Street,
Coventry, West Midlands, CV1 1PN.

Tel: (0203) 832425
Fax: (0203) 832465

Coventry is the home of the British Road Transport Industry and it is fitting therefore that it should also be home to this outstanding museum. Here you will delight in the largest display of British made road transport in the world, all under one roof. With more than 150 motor cars, 75 motorcycles and 200 cycles, the Museum tells the fascinating story of Coventry's contribution to Britain's road transport heritage.

Step back in time to the pioneering years of the first motor cars, trace the fascinating story of Edwardian motoring and the glamour of the 30's. Here you can see how Royalty rode in style in Queen Mary's Daimler Limousine and King George VI's State Landaulette, and reflect on the family cars of the 50's and 60's, then marvel at today's high-tech advantages.

You are invited to follow the enthralling story of Thrust 2 on its dramatic 633m.p.h. Run. The magic of the latest audio-visual techniques brings the record-breaking run, in which Richard Noble reclaimed the World Land Speed Record for Britain, back to life.

One of the latest exhibitions recreates the devastating air raid on Coventry during World War II. You will experience the smoke and hear the sirens, bombs and crackle of flames. It also has the effect of bringing home forcibly why Coventry's manufacturing industries were such an important wartime objective.

The vehicles in the Museum are not just full sized. It is the home of the World famous Tiatsa model collection. Built up over the past 50 years this collection of Dinky, Corgi, Matchbox and many other makes of models portray the complete history of road transport in miniature.

USEFUL INFORMATION

OPEN: Seven days a week, 10am-5pm
CHILDREN: Welcome. Education facilities available
CREDIT CARDS: None taken
LICENSED: Not applicable
ACCOMMODATION: Conference /Exhbition facilities

RESTAURANT: No. Refreshment area
BAR FOOD: No. Drinks vending machine, tea, coffee etc.
VEGETARIAN: Not applicable
DISABLED ACCESS: All areas via ramps or lifts. Toilet facilites
GARDEN: Not applicable

OSCARS FOOD COURT

Food Court

West Orchards Shopping Centre, Smithford Way,
Coventry, Warwickshire, CV1 1QX.

Tel: (0203) 231133
Fax: (0203) 231463

This exciting venue is in the heart of the city centre of Coventry, close to all the shopping areas and only a few minutes away from either the bus or train station. If you are approaching by car, take Junction 2 or 9 off the Coventry ring road and you will see West Orchards clearly sign-posted.

The Centre opened in 1991 and with its 100 foot high atrium, it is the home of the largest glass retail dome in Europe. In 1992 it won the BCSC award for the 'Best New Shopping Centre'. Live from Oscars Food Court is BBC CWR, a local radio station which has a studio on the food court and broadcasts daily to listeners around The Centre and the local area. This shopping centre is an exciting venture and extremely efficiently thought out. There is parking for 660 cars, a creche for children next to the Food Court, and a wide variety of shops within the Centre.

The Food Court is operated by a smart, friendly and competent team who have been trained to provide the best customer care and service to the highest standards. The range of food, consisting of 8 kiosks have all manner of foods. Traditional English fare in Food Glorious Food, Italian food in the Italian Job, Golden Boy has jacket potatoes, Manhattan deals with American burgers, Pretty Pink sells ice-cream sundaes - sandwiches and baguettes, are to be found in the Cafe Metropole, you go to Chinatown for Chinese Cuisine and High Society has fresh cream cakes and patisserie. In fact something for everyone. It is not licensed.

USEFUL INFORMATION

OPEN: Mon-Sat: 9am-5.30pm except Wed 9am-6.30pm
CHILDREN: Welcome and catered for
CREDIT CARDS: Luncheon vouchers at most kiosks
LICENSED: Not applicable
ACCOMMODATION: Not applicable

RESTAURANT: 8 different kiosks
BAR FOOD: Not applicable
VEGETARIAN: 10 dishes
DISABLED ACCESS: Full access, toilets
GARDEN: Not applicable

THE BOARS HEAD

Public House

Church Street, Hampton Lucy, Warwick,
Warwickshire, CV35 8BE.

Tel: (0789) 840533

USEFUL INFORMATION

OPEN: Mon-Sat: 11-3pm & 5.30-11pm
Sun:12-3pm & 7.30-10.30pm
CHILDREN: Well behaved
CREDIT CARDS: None taken
LICENSED: Full On Licence
ACCOMMODATION: Not applicable

RESTAURANT: Not applicable
BAR FOOD: Home-made specalities
VEGETARIAN: Various
DISABLED ACCESS: Flat, and willing to assist
GARDEN: Yes. No dogs. BBQ's

The Boars Head has belonged to St Peter ad Vincula, Hampton Lucy, since it was erected over 450 years ago. The pub stands within 50 yards of the church which is known widely, as the 'Cathedral in the country'. It is a delightful spot, less than four miles from Stratford and half a mile from Charlecote House and Park. It is also within a mile or so for the well known Wellesbourne air base used in World War II.

The Boar is much as it was a century ago, the oak beams and open fire places give it a timeless beauty. There is nothing fussy or elaborate about its character; it is unashamedly a pub enjoyed and amply supported by the locals, although many travellers throughout the world have, at one time or another, partaken and thoroughly enjoyed, its hospitality. Sally Gilliam became the landlady after her mother, Thelma retired. It was Thelma who first produced the recipe for steak and kidney pies which Sally makes today but are still known as 'Thelma's Pies'. The name Hampton Lucy, conjures up something of beauty and this is so true of this pretty and unspoilt village. The Boar has its own pool team and , they hold regular fun quiz nights, open to the casual visitor, with impromptu barbecues through the summer. The wide and varied menu, caters for all tastes including vegetarians.

Everything is freshly cooked and local produce is used wherever possible. It is very busy from Easter through the summer months but a visit during other periods will undoubtedly reward any hungry visitor with excellent personal service and a quiet tranquillity, so rare in these days of hustle and bustle.

LES PLANTAGENETS

Restaurant

15 Dormer Place, Leamington Spa,
Warwickshire, CV32 5AA.

Tel: (0926) 451792

USEFUL INFORMATION

OPEN: Lunch: Monday-Friday.
Dinner: Monday-Saturday.
CHILDREN: Welcome
CREDIT CARDS: All major cards
LICENSED: Restaurant Licence
ACCOMMODATION: Not applicable

RESTAURANT: French cuisine
BAR FOOD: Not applicable
VEGETARIAN: Yes. Available on request
DISABLED ACCESS: No stairs
GARDEN: No

Leamington Spa is a delightful town just 12 miles from Coventry. It is full of attractive buildings and among them in Dormer Place is Les Plantagenets, a superb French restaurant, specialising in authentic French cooking with regard to method and the capture of the true appetising flavour. Everyone from Remy Loth, the chef/proprietor to the waiters are French. The atmosphere is superb and everyone who comes to this truly Gallic establishment is imbued with the excitement that only the French can produce about food. Remy Loth was trained in France to the highest standards of Cuisine and it is his pride and joy to place before you a masterpiece of culinary art. You have only to talk to him to realise that his flair and imagination knows no bounds. You are encouraged to take time over your meal, to savour the various flavours and to relish the excellent wines.

Special menus are created for special occasions just as common-sense is applied to business lunches, which are increasingly a popular feature of Les Plantagenets. It is an ideal venue for those wanting a small conference and equally good for an intimate wedding reception. The decor is charming and at the same time unpretentious and naturally the wine list is as illustrious as the food. Remy has taken great care to make sure that the wines fit every occasion and also do not cause too much of a financial drain!

Everything about Les Plantagenets is to be recommended and it is quite obvious that the growing number of regular clients appreciate everything that Remy Loth and his staff do to make dining at the restaurant memorable.

22 Market Place, Warwick,
Warwickshire, CV34 4SL.

Tel: (0926) 410590

FANSHAWES RESTAURANT

Restaurant

The approach to Fanshawes in the summer is enhanced by the colourful hanging baskets but at anytime of the year it would be welcoming. The owners, David and Susan Fanshawe who share the cooking between them, have created a very special restaurant. It is small and intimate and a place in which to relax in the certain knowledge that the food will be memorable. It is right in the heart of Warwick and only five minutes walking distance from the red-stone Warwick Castle which has dominated the town for centuries. There are some 25-30 covers and Fanshawes has gained a tremendous reputation locally for the quality and the imagination of the dishes on offer.

Sensibly there is a set price menu as well as an a la carte choice. Whatever you choose it will be freshly prepared. You will certainly find some unusual dishes including a herb pancake, wrapping up a filling of salmon, beansprouts, spring onion and tomato, laced with a creamy dill sauce or thin slices of veal with parma ham masked with a fresh sage sauce. Familiar favourites also adorn this interesting menu in which is a selection of tempting sweets and cheeses. Vegetarians have a menu of their own but for the true Vegan a little notice would be appreciated. Fanshawes also have 'Nipper Nosh' a menu for children which has all the time honoured favourites.

Early evening meals are served especially to allow children to join their parents up to 7.30pm and there are few better places to book for a special occasion than Fanshawes.

USEFUL INFORMATION

OPEN: Tues–Sat: Lunch & evenings.
  Closed Sunday & Monday
CHILDREN: Yes. Special separate menu
CREDIT CARDS: Amex/Visa/Access
LICENSED: Restaurant Licence
ACCOMMODATION: Not applicable

RESTAURANT: English &
  French cuisine
BAR FOOD: Not applicable
VEGETARIAN: Yes. Separate menu
DISABLED ACCESS: Small step.
  Willing to assist
GARDEN: No

Ely Cathedral

E

Ely

"O thou art fairer than the evening air,
Clad in the beauty of a thousand stars."

Christopher Marlowe

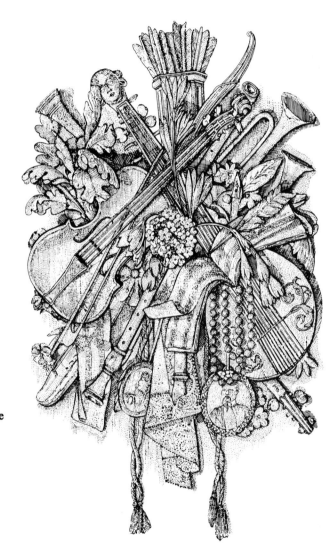

The City of Ely

by Dick Benson Gyles

Ely, the sentinel city of East Anglia's fenlands, is overshadowed by the worldwide celebrity of its neighbour, **Cambridge**, but once, long ago, it was a defiant standard-bearer of that stubborn, insular independence of spirit for which the British are renowned.

Cambridge boasts the second oldest university in England and its proud history of academic achievement down the centuries and the singular beauty of its colleges and its setting on the river Cam are justly praised, but Ely has an altogether more subtle seductivness. Imagine, just for a moment, that with the mysterious technological magic of a 'Back to the Future' film you have time-travelled more than 900 years to find yourself in the Ely of the Norman Conquest.

All around you is stillness, silence and mist-blanketed water stretching away as far as the eye can see to a dimly discernible horizon where water, mist and sky become indistinguishably one. You know instinctively that you are somewhere far away from the centre of things, that to leave this place you risk getting hopelessly lost in strange, forbidding wetlands where distance and direction are dangerously deceptive.

It is 1066 and far off to the South a losing battle is being waged against the invading armies of the Norman, William the Conqueror. Alarming rumours, multiplied and blown up in their tortuous passage through Saxon England, speak of a ruthless, irresistible army and daunting, mail-clad knights on horseback. But here, in the quiet but treacherous fenlands of the East, William can make no inroads. For a heady moment in history the last hurrah of a dying Saxon world is defiantly shouted across the wide open skies and remote fastnesses of Ely.

Ely is a centre of Anglo-Saxon resistance under Hereward the Wake, who is mounting a fierce, rearguard action against the Norman invaders from the security of his island bastion above the fens. Woe betide any stranger, Norman or otherwise, who, ignorant of their secret ways, tries to brave these impassable, watery wastes. So successful is Hereward's campaign that William himself is forced to come to Ely to put down what he views as an upstart rebellion. However, Hereward's brave, willow-the-wisp resistance is, in the perspective of history, only a moment of defiance, but it lives on in our National folklore and in the subtle independence of spirit of fenmen, even today. The Norman advance was not to be stayed and William installed his own abbot in the ancient abbey and swept irresistibly on to conquer England and ultimately to leave the glorious architectual heritage which is our Norman cathedrals.

Ely's history has been dominated by the fens, and by its great cathedral. The all-pervasive influence of the fenlands is even present in the city's name. Ely was once called Elge or Elig, because of the many eels caught in the surrounding waters. Elig in fact means eel island. Sixteen miles north of Cambridge, this island rises to about 80ft above the flatlands around it and it is the sentinel of the cathedral which dominates the view, the city, everything. Ely's ecclesiastical beginnings go back at least to 673 and the pious St Etheldreda, Queen of East Anglia, who started a religious community on the hill-top site. Like many early church luminaries, she seems to have been quite a character. She married twice, each time unsuccessfully, and, on the breakdown of the second relationship, she ran off and became a nun. She then built an abbey on her own estates at Ely and installed herself as the first abbess.

Etheldreda was reputed to have been also known as St Audrey. The word 'tawdry' derives from the apparently cheapjack clothes that were on sale at an annual fair on St Audrey's day. There is very little left to remind us of Etheldreda's time but there is extant, part of an inscribed cross from her reign, which is now to be seen in the Cathedral's south aisle. Etheldreda's abbey, the real beginning of Ely's ecclesiastical importance, was sacked during the many Danish raids on the East coast of England in the ninth century. However, 100 years later the Benedictine monks re-established the abbey, and the building of the splended edifice we know today as ELY CATHEDRAL was started in 1081 under the guiding hand of Abbott Simeon after Hereward's brave last stand had been consigned to history.

The Middle Ages were a time of prosperity for the burgeoning fen capital, which was rapidly becoming one of the main monastic houses in England and whose wealth was lavished on building and decorating the new cathedral and the surrounding monastery property. A visit to Ely today by the historically-minded, reveals that St Mary's Street to the West of the cathedral, together with Palace Green, was once a large triangular open space which has been reduced and almost destroyed by later development. The present ST MARY'S CHURCH, which is located on the South side of this 'green', probably stands on the site of the original church of the very first settlement.

The next stage in the city's development was probably eastwards to Market Street, High Street and the Market Place. A searching look reveals that this area has all the giveaway signs of medieval urban development. Proof positive in the High Street of medieval times is the timber-framed building which houses STEEPLEGATE, a delightful craft gallery and tea room. It is made beautifully simple with white-washed walls hung with watercolours of local landscapes; its sloping floors just adding to the ambience. Steeplegate is full of interest everywhere but none so fascinating as the Vault downstairs which is used for art exhibitions and houses the work of local artists. It is a place in which to browse and then to relax over a piping hot pot of tea and a delicious home-made cake or delectable gateaux. The area is generally

rectangular and consists of lanes and alleys as well as buildings. Look at the names: Chequers Lane and Butchers Row are surely indications that the rectangle as a whole was once a large and open marketplace. However, temporary stalls and edifices in time became permanent and so the impressive size of the original medieval market was whittled away, even as far back as the 13th century. A survey of 1251 tells that there were 20 freeholders with stalls and booths, 16 of them registered as 'butchers' stalls. Between 1086 and 1251 the population of Ely trebled and the market must have been a flourishing place. The market was owned not by the Abbey but by the Bishops of Ely. It may even have been established by the church to contribute to the episcopal treasury. One thing is certain, by the middle of the 13th century Ely was achieving considerable importance. The 1251 survey talks of merchants galore in the city - tanners, glaziers, craftsmen of all sorts; there is also mentioned what at first sight appears to be an anomoly - a spice dealer - but which, on reflection, is proof that trade was now covering great distances - via the myriad waterways of the fens.

The best view of all into this medieval world of Ely is contained in the wonderful survey of 1416, which describes the city in minute detail, street by street and

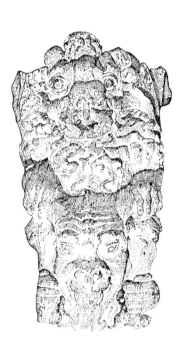

The 'Ely Imps', a carving from the south side of the choir

building by building. The old 'green' and the subsequent marketplace are both scrutinised, revealing many more houses and stalls. The key factor, however, is the shift of trading activity from the old ecclesiastical centres to an area to the east, down Fore Hill to the very edge of the notorious fens and the River Ouse. The little lanes all running down to the river are named - Castle, Stock Hythes, Monk's Broad and many others - and it is clear that they were all the sites of wharves.

Water-borne trade now became the order of the day and endured for centuries. An interesting factor, and what seems initially to be a quirk of local geography, encouraged this new trade: the realignment of a river. The River Ouse today arcs West along the edges of the fens and thus dovetails with all these wharves, but in very early days its course was more to the South East. You can still see the outline of the old course in the form of a drainage ditch. It is quite probable that it was the Bishops of Ely who were responsible for this realignment, carried out to encourage trade. This part of the city is fascinating to those with eyes to see, in many ways, and certainly archaeologically, more interesting than the cathedral and its Close. It speaks so nostalgically and vividly of the old inland port of Ely with its thriving trade. For example, to the North Fore Hill becomes

Waterside, a long, open expanse with an eastern quay. What is left of 17th and 18th century warehouses and barns still line it.

Think of those slightly self-important Victorian narrative paintings of British seaports and this part of Ely will come to life for you. Here is an inland port colourfully displaying all the trappings of the seaport, with men and goods coming and going, barges being loaded and unloaded, orders being shouted along the quaysides in the peculiar fenland acent, which even today seems unique, and everywhere there's a thriving hustle and bustle. Today all this is gone, all gone, to be replaced - as is the order of our day - by museums and memories of the past. But in those far-off days Ely was not for tourists, it was too busy to accommodate sightseeers. The tourist is a 20th century phenomenon. To medieval man such a thing would have appeared most bizarre. Ely then was a very busy place. Cloth came from **Bury St Edmunds** and **Newmarket**, glass from **Yarmouth**, lead from **Boston** in Lincolnshire, canvas from **Huntingdonshire**, tin from **King's Lynn**, limestone from **Peterborough**, and bricks from **Wisbech**, and a huge number of goods came from the great Stourbridge Fair at **Cambridge**, including metals and spices.

During the dissolution of the monasteries in the reign of Henry VIII the cathedral was lucky in suffering less damage than most, but the monastery was to be no more. Of course, Henry was not the only famous - or notorious - historical figure seriously to affect the progress of the city. Oliver Cromwell not only did his usual puritanical bit to diminish the artistic glories of the place, he also lived there! This was before he rose to become the most powerful man in the land as Lord Protector in 1653

- not bad for a man who started life as a farmer. If you cross PALACE GREEN with the 15th century Bishop's Palace to your left, you will come across a sizable half-timbered house. This was Cromwell's home from 1636 to 1647. His New Model Army went on exercises in the surrounding countryside and he even had relatives on his mother's side who collected dues for Ely Cathedral. In keeping with that stiff, martinet, kill-joy reputation which has come intact to us down the centuries, Cromwell, who hated anything which spoke of High Church or colourful decor in the House of God, closed down the cathedral for 17 years from 1644.

The old house is worth a visit. Some rooms have been refurbished in Cromwellian style to show features of the house which Cromwell would have been familiar with. An audio-visual presentation gives you a peep into the domestic, military and political side of the great man's life. Displays also recount the rest of the house's history. It has medieval origins and Cromwell was not its only occupant. Built in the 14th century for the collection of tithes, it was also used as a brewery and an inn in the 19th century. You can still see the Cromwell Arms inn sign. And it was even used as a vicarage until quite recently - for the adjoining church of St Mary's.

While I am talking about St Mary's I am reminded of the excellent Brasserie and restaurant at Number 8 St Mary's Street, DOMINIQUE'S is a non-smoking establishment which is attractively modern and refreshing in this ancient city. Years ago we are told it used to be a clothes shop but no one would ever believe it today. Now it has furnishings that are conducive to the atmosphere of a first class brasserie and restaurant. During the daytime you will find it light and airy and at night the whole

atmosphere changes with the advent of candlelight which produces a delightfully intimate feeling. Afternoon tea, cream teas and traditional patisserie are all available as well as brunch, tasty snacks and a whole range of daily specials. At night the menu is a constantly changing table d'hote. The dishes are all interesting and presented quite beautifully. The wine list includes some very good French wines as well as Australian and New Zealand, plus an unusual Lebanese red wine. A patio terrace allows for outside eating on sunny days.

St Mary's Street is also the home of THE OLD FIRE ENGINE HOUSE an excellent restaurant which has just recently celebrated its 25th year. Most regulars will tell you that it has always been a part of their lives and that many of the 20 or so local ladies who do the cooking in shifts have been there since the inception of this classic eating house. It is renowned for its homeliness and informality. You wander into the dining room through the kitchen so that you can see the cheerful culinary team rolling the pastry, chopping the vegetables and roasting the meat and dealing with the hundred and one tasks that produce food that is delicious, and probably best described as English Farmhouse style. The wines are a personal enthusiasm of the owner with more than 100 bins primarily from France but with examples from many other of the worlds wine producing regions. The Restaurant is a must for visitors to add to their list. It stands at the west end of the Palace Green, about two minutes walk from the West door of Ely Cathedral.

On the down side of any assessment of life in the Ely of the past must be the damp and waterlogged conditions created by those same fens which had often so often been a protective barrier. In the 16th century the fens were still largely undrained and there were some scarifying travellers tales to come out of visits to the city. That indomitable horse-riding lady-about-England, Celia Fiennes, didn't think much of old Ely at all ! She had to negotiate waterlogged streets and ended up at night in a slug-infested bedroom - hardly calculated to endear a place to you ! The fen drainage began in earnest in the 18th century and markedly enhanced its standing. From then Ely grew in leaps and bounds. The arrival of the railway last century effectively finished off the city's heyday and prosperity as a port, and today it is really a local market town with an ace up its sleeve - its cathedral and its history.

In some ways Ely's limited development as a town - relative to other larger ones - has been a blessing in disguise and has helped preserve the cathedral precincts, much of which today are occupied by the King's School, as are many of the remaining monastic buildings. The original priory gatehouse, which dates from 1397 and is known as THE PORTA, is still the entrance from the South. Prior Crauden's ornate Chapel, which is open to visitors, also belongs to the school and has a tall undercroft of 11-century origin. The great cathedral, often called 'the ship of the fens', is quite stunning. Completed in 1189, just over 100 years after the first foundation stones were laid, the cathedral now stands as a superb example of Romanesque architecture.

The most remarkable feature of this remarkable building is clearly the Octagon, which was built to replace the Norman tower which collapsed in 1322. The sheer scale, engineering genius, and sublime beauty of it will take your breath away. The Octagon seems to hang in the air, shot through from every angle by outside light. What

vision its creator, Alan of Walsingham, had. He was also responsible for the early construction of the much admired 14th century Lady Chapel, the largest of its kind in England. Look for the series of intricate stone carvings, which have been beheaded, it would appear. They once showed scenes from the life of the Virgin Mary but vandalism during the Reformation, when the monastery fell under the axe, was responsible for their mutilation. Poor Oliver Cromwell, blamed for so much church desecration, is often accused of defacing these carvings but, for once, was not guilty. As for Alan of Walsingham, you can see his burial place in the East end of the nave.

The cathedral is full of joys and wonders. Beyond the Octagon and the Lady Chapel is ST EDMUND'S CHAPEL, which retains several wall paintings from the 12th century; then there is the Prior's Door - the main entrance from the cloister - which has delightful Norman decorative figures. Part of the cathedral has now been turned into a museum of stained glass with a separate entrance fee.

There is a wide range of glass from a 14th century Annunciation to the Gothic Revival and the Pre-Raphaelites. There is even some modern stained glass and some early 20th century examples of the art. This museum is in the NORTH TRIFORIUM which has

The 'Prior's Door' c.1150, one of Ely Cathedral's greatest treasures

some fascinating views of the cathedral often missed by the visitor in too much of a hurry. Like much of our ecclesiastical architecture, Ely Cathedral, because of its age, is urgently in need of repair and millions of pounds of restoration work will eventually have to be carried out. As a result, money has become an overriding priority and some of the touristisation of the cathedral does detract from the otherwise wonderful atmosphere of the building. However, the book shop is excellent and the staff are helpful. But we haven't finished yet. Gaze upward at the painted Nave ceiling and gaze into BISHOP WEST'S CHANTRY CHAPEL. And not forgetting St Ovin's Cross - the only piece of Saxon stonework in the cathedral.

In the 1990s the cathedral is the heart of a great Diocese and Christian worship and musical appreciation continue here as they have done for centuries. The building is set within the walls of the Benedictine Monastery and a walk round the College will reveal that Ely has the largest collection of medieval domestic architecture in England. The Porta was the Monastery's original main entrance and PRIOR CRAUDEN'S CHAPEL is nearby. POWCHERS HALL, the OLD BARN, THE ALMONRY and all the other medieval buildings are wonderful and living monuments to the Middle Ages and to a community who lived, worked and worshipped together over 600 years ago.

At the end of your visit to this stunning Cathedral a visit to THE ALMONTRY RESTAURANT and THE CATHEDRAL REFECTORY will reward you with excellent food in The Chapter House. Something not to be missed.

To come back to earth and to the materialist 20th century, there are plenty of places where shopping is a pleasure in this delight of a little city with its tiny, 11,000 population. The main shopping areas are High Street, Market Street, Market Place and Fore Hill. And there is a bustling market every Thursday in Market Place, selling fruit, vegetables, fish and much more, while the Saturday market offers an unusual range of crafts and antiques.

And there are plenty of historical buildings to see in addition to Cromwell's House: THE MALTINGS on the riverside walk is an intriguing example of what to do with a defunct former brewery - convert it into a public hall and conference centre. It is open to the public for meals, snacks and drinks, regular cinema evenings and occasional exhibitions; THE MONKS' GRANARY, used by the King's School and 14th century; THE MONKS' INFIRMARY, which is 12th century and to be found near the cathedral South door; then there's the 13th century GREAT HALL, now the Bishop's residence, and the 14th century QUEEN'S HALL, said to have been built to entertain Queen Phillippa, wife of Edward III. It is now the Kings's School headmaster's house. WALSINGHAM HOUSE and the painted chamber built in the 14th century is also now a part of the school.

And if you wish to visit the Dean of the Cathedral, you should go to the Chapel of the Infirmary - 12th century.

And so it goes, on and on. A veritable parade of medieval architecture beautifully preserved for posterity - The Almonry, the GOLDSMITH'S TOWER and SACRIST'S GATE, the STEEPLE GATE, the PALACE.

There is, too, and also within the cathedral precincts and part of the historic range of buildings we have just toured, the ELY MUSEUM in the High Street, close to Barclays Bank. Currently on show here are a huge range of assorted historical artefacts and displays - such as vintage racing bicycles, a complete Roman burial, a history of the Cambridgeshire Regiment, old films on Ely and the Fens; examples of 18th century prison punishment; a 100 year old Market Place clock; local 17th century trade tokens; unique muniments chests, a Hereward the Wake display; local crafts tools, and aspects of local archaeology.

Be sure to see the cathedral from outside and at a distance. Walk round the outside of the great building and see all the monastic buildings at the heart of this ancient city. Look back across the meadows - only recently saved for the nation by vigorous campaigning. Climb the lower slope of CHERRY HILL - the site of one of Ely's Norman Castles - for a view towards Stuntney. Visit Palace Green, ouside the old Bishop's Palace, with its cannon brought back from the Crimean War. You might even stroll along the river bank and maybe you'll see the Cambridge University and King's School rowing eights out for a practice!

And so we return full circle to those watery wastes which make the island cathedral city of Ely unique and, even

today, still somehow lend it a vestigial air of remoteness and mystery. The nature of the Fens is very special. No other part of rural England has changed quite so fundamentally as theses great waterlands over the centuries. Once they were misty, waterlogged marshes, the haunt of wild birds and wild men. Now they are transformed into huge swathes of rich farmland, a lot of it below sea level and depending for its continued existence on a drainage network of drains, dykes and pumping engines.

The Romans first attempted drainage here but the real reclamation took place in the 17th and 18th centuries. A group of entrepreneurs, led by the 4th Earl of Bedford and Dutchman Cornelius Vermuyden, built huge channels to drain off the water. They were known as the Bedford Levels. It all started in 1636 and has continued unabated ever since. To this day the fight against inundation by the sea still goes on. The Fens today are man-made but yet retain a haunting beauty all their own. On still Summer nights, and sometimes through the dripping rains of a black Winter's evening, if you listen very carefully, you may hear the distant sound of horses hooves and the cry of Saxon horsemen, as Hereward the Wake gathers his men against the Norman invaders.

Having made the decision to come to Ely you should also explore the many delightful places within striking distance. **Cambridge** is a short drive and I do not need to tell you how full of history it is. If you decide to go there you will need refreshment and where better than LA MARGHERITA in Magdalene Street. This attractive brasserie style restaurant has been styled out of an old building. It is in the heart of the town centre and just a short walk from Cambridge's Market Square, classed as the old part of this historic town, it is a mixture of purposes. On the one side you have an Italian ice cream counter and patisserie offering irresistible commodities. On the other is the restaurant and a large bar, whilst upstairs two rooms have become intimate eating areas. Everything about LA MARGHARITA is stylish but it also has the ebullience of an Italian eaterie and the staff employed are friendly smiling people who have the Latin approach to customers.

I know of few people who have not at sometime in their lives enjoyed Teddy Bears. Many of us later in life still have the battered and beloved bear that became part of our lives in the nursery. THE ENGLISH TEDDY BEAR COMPANY in Kings Parade is a must for any Teddy Bear afficionado, and an experience for those who have never met with them before. Here in Cambridge the Teddy Bears clearly feel the setting is right for them. Here they await your visit. Don't fail them; it is truly an experience.

Almost on the outskirts of Ely, there is one of my favourite places NEEDHAMS FARM RESTAURANT. It is part of the quiet village of **Witchford**. Set in its own grounds it was once a farmhouse and has been lovingly and carefully restored, losing none of its bewitching charm en-route. One of this restaurant's great attributes is the window in the lounge bar through which one can see the chef at work. It is quite tantalising and certainly whets the appetite for the meal that is to come. The window also has a more practical purpose, you can open it and enquire within about anything to do with your forthcoming meal, or indeed anything else.

FIVE MILES FROM ANYWHERE NO HURRY INN must attract you if only for the name. You will find it at **Upware**, just off the A10 from Cambridge and one mile into the country. You will see it on your map just south of Ely. The fabulous lawn and gardens at the rear of the pub back onto the River Cam and so you have the choice of approach by road or bringing your boat here with the option of mooring overnight. During the day the pub is a peaceful plan with time to stand and stare and watch the water flow gently by whilst you enjoy food and drink. At night it buzzes with people and entertainment. It is an extraordinary establishment with a long history. An inn has stood on the site since the 28th century but it has been totally rebuilt and now has two modern bars, an upstairs snooker club, a delightful riverside restaurant, a patio, children's playground and good entertainment at the weekends. If you read up its history you will discover that Richard Ramsey-Fielder declared Upware a republic in the 1700's and at the same time declared himself 'King of Upware' - a slight contradiction of terms!

Waterbeach, an attractive village, 4 miles from Cambridge and ten miles from Ely, is a little way south down the River Cam from Upware. One of the focal points is THE WHITE HORSE, a friendly pub with a nice restaurant. It was built about 1911 and over the years has had various extensions, including the new restaurant. Good food, good wine and good company are the hallmarks of The White Horse.

An experience never to be forgotten is STOCKS in the small village of **Bottisham**. Everyone here knows Dickie Jeeps and his wife who are the proprietors of this friendly and most popular eating house, but the world knows Ruchard Eric Gaultry Jeeps CBE as a name to be conjured with in the world of Rugby. As a great player in his time, and latterly as a revered President of the Rugby Union, he had class and style on and off the field and he has brought the same class and style to the running of Stocks. The menu is based on modern English and Fremch cuisine and the wine list is international. Traditional Sunday lunches, which include the traditional puddings, are sought after occasions, as is membership of The Connoisseurs Club whose members are invited once a month to theme evenings which may be anything from a barbecue to music and dancing. Stocks is first among equals.

The Prior Crauden's Chapel built in 1324

One other charming place in which to eat or drink is THE CHESTNUTS at **Needingworth**, close to St Ives. This was originally a farmhouse built in 1710 during the reign of Queen Anne. A grade 2 listed building and one of the few to survive the great fire which destroyed much of the village about a century ago. There was once a forest of sweet chestnuts surrounding the farm. Now the tree of interest is an acacia of considerable age which dominates the attractive patio and beer garden. Facilities are available for small conferences, private parties and weddings in a pleasant environment. There are no juke boxes, fruit machines or pool tables. Background music merely complements a conversation; it does not destroy it.

Enjoy Ely, it is mystical, magical and quite unique.

STOCKS

Restaurant

76 High Street, Bottisham,
Cambridgeshire, CB5 9BA.

Tel: (0223) 811202
Fax: (0223) 811202

USEFUL INFORMATION

OPEN: Weekdays & Sundays 12-2pm,
Evenings: Tues-Sat 7pm – late
CHILDREN: Welcome. Highchairs
CREDIT CARDS: Access/Visa/Amex
LICENSED: Restaurant
ACCOMMODATION: 2 en-suite rooms,
one with four-poster

RESTAURANT: Modern English &
French
BAR FOOD: Not aplicable
VEGETARIAN: Own a la carte menu
DISABLED ACCESS: Limited but welcome
GARDEN: Swimming pool & winter
gardens

People in and around the small village of Bottisham know Dickie Jeeps and his wife Jenny as the proprietors of Stocks, one of the friendliest and most popular eating houses, but the world knows Richard Eric Gaultry Jeeps CBE as a name to be conjured with in the world of Rugby. As a great player in his time and latterly as a revered President of the Rugby Union. He had class and style on and off the field and he has brought the same class and style to the running of Stocks.

The restaurant is housed in a building which first came into being in 1478. The exterior is deceiving as it is no longer the original but inside it is all natural oak beams. The decor is elegant and restrained. The flowers which are everywhere bring a grace and charm of their own and are arranged with skill by Jenny. It is a very special restaurant in which to dine, lunch or stay; there are two pretty en-suite bedrooms one of which has a splendid four-poster. The food is fabulous but if you talk to the regular customers – and there are many of them - you will find they come as much for the atmosphere created by Dickie and Jenny as they do for the food. It is such an easy going informal atmosphere and the Jeeps are simply natural hosts who treat the business as though they were entertaining guests in their own home. The menu is based on Modern English and French cuisine and the wine list is international. Traditional Sunday lunches, which include the traditional puddings, are sought after occasions, as is membership of The Connoisseurs Club whose members are invited once a month to theme evenings which may be anything from a barbecue to music and dancing. Stocks is first among equals.

THE ENGLISH TEDDY BEAR COMPANY

Shop

1 King's Parade,
Cambridge.
CM2 1SJ
Tel: (0223) 300908

USEFUL INFORMATION

OPEN: 10-7pm daily
CHILDREN: Welcome
CREDIT CARDS: All major cards
DISABLED ACCESS: Good

SPECIAL SERVICES: Gift boxing
available, Made to order service,
Mail Order catalogue available - Contact
branch for further information on availability.

The Cambridge shop of The English Teddy Bear Company is as gracious and elegant as all the other four in Oxford, Canterbury, Bath and London. Each has its own special characteristic and it is difficult, if you have had the good fortune to visit them all, to decide which is one's favourite. Here in Cambridge it is in the heart of the town surrounded by the beauty of the famed and historic University Colleges. The Teddy Bears clearly feel that it is the right setting for them. Here they await your visit. The company specialises in recreating special companions in all manner of cloths, all English, from acrylic to top quality mohair. The Teddy Bears are made with traditional features like long snouts, embroidered noses and jointed limbs and head. The Teddy Bear is a popular gift that has lasted almost a century and which is given equally to adults as well as children. Since all the bears are hand made, no two are alike and each bear comes with its own birth certificate!

The English Teddy Bear Company also makes an eccentric range of stylish Teddy Bear clothes. Silk waistcoats, bow ties, smoking jackets, cricket jumpers, boaters and much more make up the essential English Teddy Bear's wardrobe! The Teddy Bears' appetites are also considered. Here you will find the most delicious traditional English biscuits, jams, marmalades and teas so that each bear can be sure of a good tea! And if you do not wish to be free of Teddy Bears in any situation, they produce a fun and stylish range of all cotton T shirts for children and adults. Each shop has designs exclusive to that town and these make affordable and easily transported gifts. To visit one of these shops is to recapture childhood.

LA MARGHERITA
Restaurant

15 Magdalene Street, Cambridge,
Cambridgeshire, CB3 0AF.

Tel: (0223) 315232

An attractive brasserie style restaurant has been styled out of an old building in Magdalene Street and become the popular and welcoming, La Margherita. It is in the heart of the town centre and just a short walk from Cambridge's Market Square, classed as the old part of this historic town. The walls may be white and modern but no attempt has been made to disguise the charm of the original beams and stone tiled floors.

It is a mixture of purposes. On the one side you have an Italian ice cream counter and patisserie offering irresistible commodities. On the other is the restaurant and a large bar whilst upstairs, two rooms have become intimate eating areas. Everything about La Margherita is stylish but it also has the ebullience of an Italian eaterie and the staff employed are friendly smiling people who have the Latin approach to customers.

La Margherita has become a meeting place for local people of all ages and somewhere to purchase delicious patisserie if one is entertaining or merely wishing to indulge. Amongst the many enticing dishes on the changing menu is the house speciality, 'Tiramisu' a home-made dessert for which the restaurant is renowned. For those wanting just a light lunch there are toasted sandwiches richly and generously filled or Pizzette - pizza slices, and freshly made sandwiches or rolls. One of the favourite lunchtime purchases is 'La Margherita' special - Italian bread filled with parma ham, salami, provolone cheese and mixed salad. La Margherita is ideal for private parties held in the upstairs rooms and for business lunches which can be eaten in a private room.

USEFUL INFORMATION

OPEN: 11-3pm & 6-late, 7 days a week
CHILDREN: Welcome
CREDIT CARDS: All major cards
LICENSED: Restaurant
ACCOMMODATION: Not applicable

RESTAURANT: Italian cuisine
BAR FOOD: Snack menu, daytime only
VEGETARIAN: Wide selection & special requests
DISABLED ACCESS: Limited, welcome
GARDEN: No

THE ALMONRY RESTAURANT
Cathedral Restaurant & Tea Rooms

High Street, Ely,
Cambridgeshire, CB7 4JU.

Tel: (0353) 666360
Fax: (0353) 665658

Although the Almonry is centrally located next to Ely's Market Place it also forms part of the cathedral's extensive range of buildings - known as the 'College' - with beautifully landscaped and planted gardens to the south, below the eastern prospect of the magnificent cathedral, its unique octagon and lantern tower rising above. In monastic days, the Almoner and his servants would have used the building as a centre from which to care for poor townsfolk. In later years, the much-altered Almonry became a splendid residence for Cathedral clergy. Since 1989, visitors have been able to enjoy lunches in the beautiful 12th century vaulted undercroft, whilst morning coffee and afternoon tea are served in the south-facing garden room, with its french windows leading to the gardens (tables are placed outside in summer) and the Cathedral.

The setting is superb with tables and chairs set beneath the fine vaulting, the menu varied with a choice of interesting starters. The Main Courses, where meat is concerned, can be served hot or cold. Fenland steak and kidney pie is one of the favourite dishes. There are fresh seasonal vegetables and a choice of fresh home-made salads. The home-made sweets tempt everyone and a meal is rounded off beautifully with fresh brewed coffee and cream or tea. Ely cathedral also offers light lunches, teas and coffees in the cosy and friendly Cathedral refectory within the cathedral.

USEFUL INFORMATION

OPEN: Mon-Sat: 10-5pm, Sun: 11-5pm, Lunch 12-2pm
CHILDREN: Welcome
CREDIT CARDS: None taken
LICENSED: Full Table Licence
ACCOMMODATION: None
'Blue Room' available for small meetings. Whole restaurant may be hired for wedding receptions

RESTAURANT: Honest, wholesome fare. Excellent value
BAR FOOD: Not applicable
VEGETARIAN: Several dishes
DISABLED ACCESS: Via College entrance; some steps inside
GARDEN: Large garden with tables in summer

105

DOMINIQUE'S

Brasserie &Restaurant

8 St Mary's Street,
Ely, Cambridgeshire, CB7 4ES.

Tel: (0353) 665011

USEFUL INFORMATION

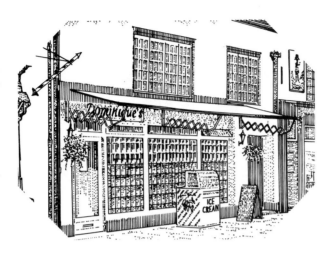

OPEN: Wed-Fri: 11-3pm & 7-9pm.
Sat: 10.30-5pm & 7-9pm, Sun: 10.30-
5.30pm. Closed Mon & Tue. Latest times
given are for last orders of food
CHILDREN: Welcome
CREDIT CARDS: None taken
LICENSED: Full On Licence
ACCOMMODATION: Not applicable

RESTAURANT: English/French with flair
BAR FOOD: No, but delicious snacks
available all day. Baguettes a speciality
VEGETARIAN: 1-2 daily
DISABLED ACCESS: Ramped entrance.
No special WC
GARDEN: Patio terrace for utside eating

One minute's walk from Ely's magical Cathedral is Dominique's, a non-smoking restaurant and brasserie which is attractively modern and refreshing in this ancient city. Years ago we are told it used to be a clothes shop but no one would ever believe it today. Now it has furnishings that are conducive to the atmosphere of a first class Brasserie and Restaurant.

Jo and Dominique Bregeon run this friendly place together. During the daytime you will find it light and airy - always strictly non-smoking - and at night the whole atmosphere changes with the advent of candlelight which produces a delightfully intimate feeling. The daytime menu includes brunch and tasty snacks which may well be hot grilled Baquettes with various toppings, Welsh Rarebit or simple scrambled eggs. There are well filled sandwiches, omelettes, salads, baked tatties with a host of fillings, and everyday the blackboard tells you what are the freshly prepared specialities.

Afternoon tea, cream teas and traditional patisserie are all available. It really is a pleasant place to visit. The evening menu which is table d'hote changes every two weeks. The dishes are all interesting and presented quite beautifully. The wine list includes some very good French wines as well as Australian and New Zealand, plus an unusual Lebanese red wine. A patio terrace allows for outside eating on sunny days.

THE OLD FIRE ENGINE HOUSE

Restaurant

St Marys Street, Ely,
Cambridgeshire, CB7 4ER.

Tel: (0353) 662582

USEFUL INFORMATION

OPEN: Mon-Sat: 10.30-5.30pm & 7.30-9pm
Sun: 12.30-5.30pm. Closed bank holi-
days and 2 weeks after Christmas
CHILDREN: Allowed. Welcome,
half portions, half price
CREDIT CARDS: Visa/Access/Eurocard
LICENSED: Restaurant
ACCOMMODATION: Not applicable

RESTAURANT: English farmhouse style
BAR FOOD: Not applicable
VEGETARIAN: 1 dish at lunch and dinner
DISABLED ACCESS: Wheelchair access,
but not on one level
GARDEN: Large mature walled garden.
Meals outside weather permitting. Swing

The Old Fire Engine House recently celebrated its 25th year as a restaurant. Most regulars will tell you that it has always been a part of their lives and that many of the 20 or so local ladies who do the cooking in shifts have been there since the inception of this classic eating house. It is renowned for its homeliness, and informality is a feature of the day-to-day operation. You wander into the dining room through the kitchen so you can see the cheerful culinary team rolling the pastry, chopping the vegetables, roasting the meat and dealing with the hundred and one tasks that produce food that is delicious, and probably best described as 'English Farmhouse' in style.

Menus change with every meal, but they are all built around a core of thirty or so from dishes which recur frequently. Casseroles, pies and plain roasts form the backbone of most menus; fresh fish, poultry, and a vegetarian dish are always available. Menus are always as seasonable as possible making good use of local game, local fruit and vegetables throughout the year; asparagus, marsh samphire, pike, eels, and North Sea mussels in their various seasons. The ingredients are always of the highest quality which is quite evident in the dishes which are fairly simply prepared.

The wines are a personal enthusiasm of the owner, with more than 100 bins; primarily from France, but with examples from many other of the world's wine producing regions. The Restaurant is a must for visitors to add to their list. It stands at the west end of the Palace Green, about two minutes walk from the West Door of Ely Cathedral.

16-18 High Street, Ely,
Cambridgeshire, CB7 4JU.

Tel: (0353) 664731

STEEPLEGATE
Craft Gallery & Tea Room

This delightful Craft Gallery and Tea Room is housed in a medieval timber-framed building, made beautifully simple with white-washed walls hung with watercolours of local landscapes; its sloping floors just adding to the ambience. Steeplegate is full of charm with something of interest everywhere but none so fascinating as the Vault downstairs which is used for art exhibitions, and houses the work of local artists. There are modern sculptures, craft and woodwork displays, pottery, ceramics, and a splendid display of tasteful and high quality gifts. It is a place in which to browse and then to relax over a piping hot pot of tea and a delicious home-made cake or a delectable gateau.

At lunch time there are light, home-cooked meals, soups, salads, jacket potatoes, toasted sandwiches with a range of fillings. The food is well cooked and beautifully presented. The Tea Rooms make an ideal place to visit after a morning or an afternoon looking round and taking in the magical beauty of Ely Cathedral which is situated to the rear of the building.

On Saturday afternoons the Vault has demonstrations of wood turning and indeed, Steeplegate is renowned for its wide range of beautiful wooden items. The work of these men and women is quite breathtaking and makes one realise the level of skill involved. Steeplegate is a must on every visitor's list in Ely.

USEFUL INFORMATION

OPEN: Shop: Mon-Sat: 9-5.30pm, Tea
   Rooms: 10-5pm. Open Bank Holidays
CHILDREN: Welcome
CREDIT CARDS: Access/Visa/Euro/
   Master
LICENSED: No
ACCOMMODATION: Not applicable

RESTAURANT: Tea Room serving light
   lunches, teas etc. All home-made
BAR FOOD: Not applicable
VEGETARIAN: Yes, dishes available daily
DISABLED ACCESS: Gift shop only
GARDEN: No

---

85 High Street, Needingworth,
Cambridgeshire, PE17 3SB.

Tel: (0480) 463456

THE CHESTNUTS
Bar & Restaurant

A place of enchantment, beautiful food, excellent wines and proprietor, Joyce Edwards with her Chef and staff, make The Chestnuts an establishment not to be missed. The Chestnuts was originally a farmhouse in 1710 during the reign of Queen Anne. It is a Grade Two Listed Building and one of the few to survive the great fire which destroyed much of the village of Needingworth about a century ago. There was once a forest of sweet chestnuts surrounding the farm. Now, the tree of interest is an Acacia of considerable age which dominates the attractive patio and beer garden. The tree is a considerable talking point for those who are fortunate enough to enjoy a drink on the sunkissed patio in the summer months,

One of the nicest things about The Chestnuts is the absence of jukeboxes, fruit machines and pool tables. The only sound apart from the contented hum of conversation is the gentle background music. Everything about The Chestnuts is done well. The furnishings, Queen Anne in style, are very elegant, attractive and fitting for the building. The subtle shades of pinks, rose for the carpet and a softer pink for the table linen, the china and sparkling glass are immaculate, and the superb atmosphere comes from a job well done. Damon MacGowan, the Chef is a perfectionist and he cooks with imagination and flair producing mouthwatering dishes in an ever changing menu. For those who do not wish to eat a major meal or who would like to but do not have the time, the Bar Meals are an extension of the a la carte menu. At the moment there is no accommodation but it is hoped to rectify this shortly - an added bonus for anyone wanting to dine here and sample the fine wines.

USEFUL INFORMATION

OPEN: Bar: Mon-Sat: 11am-11pm
   Sun: 12-3pm & 7-10.30pm
   Food: 12.30-2.30pm & 7.30-10pm
CHILDREN: Well behaved welcome
CREDIT CARDS: Visa/Access
LICENSED: Full On Licence
ACCOMMODATION: Not at present

RESTAURANT: English &
   Continental cuisine
BAR FOOD: English & Continental
VEGETARIAN: Imaginative
   selection available
DISABLED ACCESS: Very limited
GARDEN: Attractive Patio &
   Beer Garden

FIVE MILES FROM ANYWHERE NO HURRY INN

Public House & Restaurant

Upware, Wicken,
Cambridgeshire, CB7 5YQ.

Tel: (0353) 721654

USEFUL INFORMATION

OPEN: Normal hours + restaurant extension & late licence Fri & Sat until 2am
CHILDREN: Very welcome. Play area
CREDIT CARDS: None taken
LICENSED: Full On Licence. Restaurant, Club 2am licence
ACCOMMODATION: Not applicable, overnight mooring for 14 boats

RESTAURANT: Extensive menu. Home-Cooked, catering to all tastes
BAR FOOD: Stop-gaps Bar menu
VEGETARIAN: Separate menu
DISABLED ACCESS: Ramp & WC
GARDEN: Huge patio & riverside garden

The very name of this different and delightful place tells you that it is going to be an experience. You will find it just off the A10 from Cambridge and one mile into the country. The fabulous lawn and gardens at the rear of the Five Miles from Anywhere No Hurry Inn, back onto the River Cam and so you have the choice of approach by road or bringing your boat here with the option of mooring overnight. During the day the pub is a peaceful place with time to stand and stare and watch the water flow gently by whilst you enjoy food and drink. At night it buzzes with people and entertainment.

There is a long history to the Five Miles. An inn has stood on the site since the 14th century. The Old Five Miles burnt to the ground in 1956 and a new building was erected in 1979 which has two modern bars, an upstairs function room, a delightful riverside restaurant, a patio, children's playground and good entertainment at the weekends. If you read up its history you will discover that Richard Ramsey-Fielder declared Upware a republic in the 1700's and at the same time declared himself 'King of Upware' - a slight contradiction of terms !

Eric and Marion are known to everyone in the area. In spite of the size of the pub they have created a friendly family atmosphere and they like it to be known as a family style pub. The restaurant serves good, home-cooked, substantial meals at realistic prices. You need not drink alcohol to enjoy The Five Miles; Coffee is available from the bar always. The licence runs until 2 am which makes it a popular place for weddings and other special occasions.

THE WHITE HORSE

Public House & Restaurant

12 Greenside, Waterbeach,
Cambridgeshire, CB5 9HP.

Tel: (0223) 860603

USEFUL INFORMATION

OPEN: 11-2.30pm & 6-11pm.
Sat: 11-3pm, & 7-11pm.
Sun: 12-3pm & 7-10.30pm
CHILDREN: To eat at lunchtime
CREDIT CARDS: None taken
LICENSED: Full Licence
ACCOMMODATION: Not applicable

RESTAURANT: Mainly home-prepared
BAR FOOD: Traditional pub food
VEGETARIAN: Six dishes
DISABLED ACCESS: Via back gate
GARDEN: Yes, for meals

Waterbeach is an attractive village just off the A10, four miles from Cambridge and 10 miles from Ely. One of the focal points of the place is the White Horse, a friendly pub with a nice restaurant. It was built about 1911 and over the years has had various extensions, including the latest, a new restaurant.

There is a warmth of welcome as soon as you walk through the doors into the bars which are full of character with many interesting brasses and other nic-naks. One of the bars is the regular haunt of locals, with a wooden floor that adds much to its atmosphere. With an army barracks nearby, many of the customers are from there and you get the feeling that they treat it like a second home. This is not surprising because Alan and Chris Ibberson, the proprietors, are just the right sort of people to be running an establishment of this kind. Even if you are a first time visitor to the White Horse you will be made to feel welcome very quickly. If you are sports minded you will get on well with Alan who is an ex-pro-golfer and the chef, a keen football fan. It's all good fun with a lot of friendly banter. At lunch time the food is good, home cooked fare with various fish dishes, steak and mushroom pies, ploughman's, etc as well as daily specials. In the evening, steaks from the local butcher are tremendously popular. Additionally you can have all kinds of well cooked dishes including medallions of lamb served on a cream of mint sauce with fresh vegetables and new potatoes. There are always vegetarian dishes and children are welcome to eat at lunch times.

186 Main Street,
Witchford, Cambridgeshire, CB6 2HT.

Tel: (0353) 661405

NEEDHAMS FARM RESTAURANT

Restaurant

The quiet village of Witchford is two miles out of the tiny city of Ely with its magnificent cathedral that dominates the skyline for miles. Needhams Farm Restaurant is part of this village. Set in its own grounds, it was once a farmhouse and has been lovingly and carefully restored, losing none of its bewitching charm en route. It can boast original beams throughout and has that air of homeliness that can only be achieved if the owners are contented people. Barny and Carol Smith answer that proviso.

One of Needhams Farm's great attributes is the window in the lounge bar through which one can see the chef at work. It is quite tantalising and certainly whets the appetite for the meal that is to come. The window also has a more practical purpose; you can open it and enquire within about anything to do with your forthcoming meal, or indeed anything else.

The menu is a pleasure to read and the joyful anticipation of the arrival on the table of your choice, never disappoints. Scallops and prawns in filo pastry followed by chicken breast with cheese and asparagus filling perhaps, or garlic mushrooms and roast rack of lamb with a herb crust. The selection is varied and whatever you may decide upon will be delicious. A number of home-made desserts are offered or a choice from the cheese board. Accompanied by a first class bottle of wine from the remarkable wine list, your meal will be memorable. There are conference facilities and a function room for 100 people. Wonderful for wedding receptions and parties.

USEFUL INFORMATION

OPEN: 12-2pm & 7-9.30pm
CHILDREN: Welcome
CREDIT CARDS: Not at present
LICENSED: Restaurant & Supper Licence
ACCOMMODATION: 1 twin room

RESTAURANT: English with a strong
   hint of French at its best
BAR FOOD: Not applicable
VEGETARIAN: On request
DISABLED ACCESS: Disabled ramp
   & WC
GARDEN: Yes. Large car park at rear

Exeter Cathedral

Exeter

"A thing of beauty is a joy forever:
It's lovliness increases, it will never
Pass into nothingness;"

John Keats

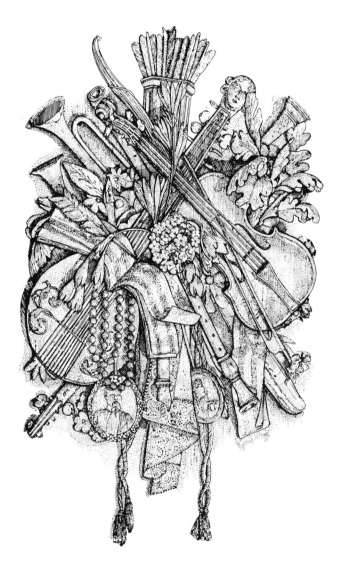

The City of Exeter

by Joy David

There are many counties envious of Devon's good fortune in having **Exeter** as its capital. It has everything. The River Exe wends its gracious way through the heart of the city, stopping every now and again to prepare itself for the opening of the swing bridge which permits small coasters to sail upstream for unloading, much in the way it has for centuries. The jewel in the crown of this beloved city is the magnificent cathedral which dominates the city centre and dictates much of the life-style immediately around it.

Exeter is Roman, Saxon and Norman; it has walls and a tower built by Athelstan, the first King of England, but most of all it is Medieval. There are still miles of quaint streets and passageways, rambling walls and a plethora of churches and of course, the cathedral, bequeathed to us by seven generations of the first English builders, apart from its Norman walls and tower. Of course the 20th century has crept in and much has had to be changed, but on the whole it has been done with the greatest of care and dedication to the preservation of all that is good. One of the reasons that it can sustain its beautiful buildings is because of the ever increasing business that comes to the city.

Industry and commerce have flourished in Exeter for centuries but probably never so forcefully as today. Companies throughout the U.K. seek to relocate here. There is little opposition from their staff either, once they have seen the amenities that Exeter has to offer and the glorious areas within easy reach of the city in which they can live.

Shopping is a pleasure, with the big stores living comfortably alongside medieval buildings. As in most county towns there are innumerable small shops which entice - most of them hidden away in enchanting alleyways like Gandy Street. Sadly, much of the medieval city was destroyed by German bombs but much of beauty survives. In and around the High Street, the modern commonplace, has in no way swamped the 16th century GUILDHALL which still stands on its granite columns astride the pavement, leaving you in no doubt of the importance and the prosperity of the medieval guilds and merchants. Its walls go back 600 years although it was much rebuilt about 550 years ago. Its great door is magnificent and older than the Spanish Armada.

Next door to it is THE TURK'S HEAD, now owned by a modern company but still a beautiful old inn, in which the floors are uneven, the ceilings slope, the old doors are still in existence and the nooks and crannies make it a splendid place to drink or to enjoy a meal. The resident ghost has never given up and even today can be relied upon to cause mayhem in the staff quarters. No one quite knows who or what he is, but I wondered if it was the spirit of the Turk who was the last man to be decapitated in Exeter, hence the name of the pub.

Modernity can from time to time be a blessing, the newest hotel in Exeter is the impressive Forte Hotel, which sits at the bottom of Southernhay and is very popular with me because parking is easy! In all fairness that does play a part but the hotel is welcoming, informal and a great place to meet one's friends for a drink or lunch and certainly lives up to the standards of the Forte chain when it comes to the bedrooms. I have not dined there but I am told the service is excellent and the food good.

The oldest hotel without question is THE ROYAL CLARENCE in Cathedral Yard. To stay here in one of its bedrooms overlooking the floodlit cathedral, is a privilege. Two hundred years ago the Royal Clarence was the first inn in Britain to receive the title 'hotel'. Lord Nelson stayed here and so have many other Royals including Czar Nicholas I. If you are an architectural buff you will be intrigued and delighted by the differing styles which have been introduced ever since the original building in the 14th century. You will see that every one of the 56 bedrooms and suites is richly furnished in Tudor, Georgian or Victorian style, which in their own way tell the story of the colourful history of the Royal Clarence.

Dining in the Raleigh Restaurant is to be gastronomically spoilt, waited on by quietly efficient staff, who unobtrusively see to your every need. It says on their brochure 'Peaceful elegance and undisturbed comfort makes the Royal Clarence more than worthy of its distinguished reputation'. It could not have been better phrased.

An indestructible part of the tradition of Exeter is the dignified ROUGEMONT HOTEL, just a few yards from the High Street. David Reynolds has been the Manager here for well over twelve years; backed by the Mount Charlotte Group, he has steadily enhanced the hotel's image, bringing it in line with the very best of modern day hotels and yet never once allowing the dramatic quality of its splendid rooms to be decimated. His impeccable standards are reflected throughout the hotel and he demands nothing from his staff that he is not personally prepared to give.

It is not so much the hotel I want to talk about but its intriguing history. Originally the site was occupied by a debtors prison and was said by one occupant, that it was the worst he knew in all England. To this day some of the basement areas of the hotel remain as they were in the days of the prison. There is a tunnel which runs from the basement to the present site of the museum situated across the road. No one knows quite what its purpose was, but it could have been an escape route for prisoners or even a safe place for wealthy guests. One person who might know, if only she could talk, is The Grey Lady, who is sometimes seen walking the staircase in the early hours of the morning. She was a guest when the hotel was first opened, but for some reason she gassed herself in her room and has never found peace since. The flagpole stands at the front of the hotel on the grisly spot where prisoners were hanged, and in the cellar of the Drake's Bar, until quite recently, old shackling irons were still attached to the walls.

In 1876 the building of the hotel commenced and for the sum of £21,000 plus another £11,000 for furnishings and fitting the Rougemont was able to open its doors on the 29th May 1877. It was a splendid occasion and the local paper stated that, 'If the venture was not attended with success this would be due to an ungrateful public, and not any fault of the directors.' It has flourished ever since, although there have been times when its prestige slipped a little. Today however, I am happy to report that this hotel is very much alive and kicking and offering an excellent service to anyone who stays within its hallowed portals.

In one of the little pamphlets which the hotel gives its guests, there is a suggested walk which really takes you into the heart of the city. It is quite a way so you will need comfortable shoes, but it is more than worthwhile. From the front of the hotel you turn right into Queen Street, leaving the museum on your left and coming to the High Street. This allows you to see some of the most exquisite timber-framed Merchants Houses of the 16th and 17th century; on your right there is quite a mishmash of shop fronts which vary from the 16th to 20th century. Turn right and you come to the Guildhall with the Turk's Head next door. Further down on the same side is Parliament Street, the narrowest street in the world - so be careful you don't miss it.

Detail from the minstrel's gallery showing some of the angels playing their 14th century instruments

At the bottom where the four ancient main streets meet, you turn right into ST NICHOLAS PRIORY built about 1070, the surviving west range of which is now a museum. Bartholomew Street next and then into Fore Street again and down West Street to the bottom of the cobbled Stepcote Hill, once the main thoroughfare leading to the West Gate and the river crossing. At the bottom of the hill is the 'HOUSE THAT MOVED'. A wonderful house that got in the way of progress but was far too historically valuable to demolish, so literally it was rolled to its present position in the 1960's.

On december 9th 1961, the problem was solved. Very gently the house was jacked up from its foundations, lifted onto a vehicle that had iron wheels, and moved inch by inch the 100 yards along the road to its present site in West Street. It took four days to move the 100 yards but it stands safe now and is one of the finest jewels of this already treasure rich city.

Next on the Quay. This area, with its massive warehouses and beautiful Customs Houses built in 1675, reminds you sharply of the one time importance of the maritime trade to the city. It may also remind some readers that this area was used extensively in filming 'The Onedin Line' for television some years ago. If you have time you can take the little ferry across the river and visit THE MARITIME MUSEUM which is fascinating.

Leave the Quay by the steps alongside the 'Prospect' and continue up Southernhay. From here you pass into Cathedral Close dominated by the superb Gothic Cathedral

113

with its 11th-century towers. I am leaving talking about this wonderful building until a little later in this chapter.

In Princesshay there are underground passages and the line of the old Town Wall is marked by crazy paving. A left turn takes you into Castle Street and there is the Norman castle, or what remains of it. Left again brings you to the Rougemont Gardens, laid in the 18th century. On the right is the only remaining piece of the Norman Castle defences, the Gatehouse. Rougemont House to the left contains pictures of archaeology and history of the City and County. If you go through the small gate cut into the Town Wall and into Northernhay Gardens, a turn left will bring you back to the Rougemont Hotel more than ready for a meal, a large drink, or even a cup of tea.

THE WHITE HART HOTEL in South Street is one of Exeter's most ancient inns. It is a few yards from the site of the South Gate through which Henry VI entered the city in 1452. Everything about this fine establishment appeals. Stay here and enjoy comfort in an atmosphere steeped in history, and with such service, you may think belonged to bygone days. Two of the more notable features are the 15th century wine room and an adjoining wall with an early stone fireplace, now incorporated in the bar. In a city that is not the easiest for parking, one modern benefit of the White Hart is its large car park.

South-east crossing corbel, 1309-13
Exeter Cathedral

Exeter has reason to be exceptionally proud of its University which has spread its arms out far and wide with different faculties in different places as well in the busy Campus of the University itself. It is recognised throughout the world for its excellence and students count themselves fortunate to be living and studying in this beautiful city.

On land given to it by the University and from money donated by the Northcott family, the interesting NORTHCOTT THEATRE was built in the 1960s much to the delight of people living in the South West. Here was a shining chance for good theatre to return to the west. It was the first theatre built for many a year and we all hoped that it would encourage first rate productions to come west of **Bristol**. For years Touring Companies of any stature had avoided the tortuous journey. **Plymouth** still had the old Palace theatre and a little Civic Theatre on Plymouth Hoe, but it was all shabby and second rate. the Northcott was to be the shining star.

Over the years the star has grown less bright and The Northcott has struggled to find its true place in the community. Many a time those who controlled it and produced the shows must have wondered whether their allegiance was to the city or to the University.

The advent of Plymouth's Theatre Royal, newly built and one of the finest provincial theatres in the country diminished the brilliance of The Northcott. It had the good fortune to acquire the services of the especially talented Roger Redfarn who has consistently brought new and often award winning, productions to the stage of the Theatre Royal, frequently as a forerunner to successful runs in the West End.

The question has always remained in my mind, why Plymouth and not Exeter? Exeter is a wealthier city and one has always been led to believe, culturally more aware than its bigger neighbour. I have talked to one or two people about this and it seems to me that because it is on the Campus and parking is horrific, the Northcott has found itself isolated from the people of Exeter. The student population make little use of it and the lack of parking does not encourage any but the most ardent of theatregoers from the city to make the trek to the campus.

I have always felt that the theatre does not keep a sufficiently high profile in the city or its surrounding areas. If you were to run a market research exercise you would find that the vast majority of the people of Exeter know of the theatre's existence but they have not a clue where it is nor what it offers. It is a great pity because The Northcott has everything it could wish for except a good site. It would be splendid if the image of the theatre could receive several shots of adrenalin and make the people of Exeter wake up to the fact that they have a splendid theatre in their midst which should be used for seeing productions and as a meeting place for friends.

All my walks and discoveries in the city have led me nearer and nearer to my goal - the cathedral. Such is its dimension that I find it hard to do it justice on paper. THE CATHEDRAL stands behind the High Street and in many ways quietly concealed behind the houses in

Cathedral Yard. Its dominance is not because it stands tall but because the aura and authority of the cathedral is so much part of the life of Exeter. I love walking along the little Cathedral Close and Southernhay with its beautiful buildings, almost entirely occupied by professional people rather than residents. Perhaps I will walk in the garden of the 14th century BISHOP'S PALACE, with its fine trees taking shade from the great walls of the cathedral. Certainly I will look at THE DEANERY where Catherine of Aragon stayed a night on her way to meet her fate. Her mind must have been on her fiance Prince Arthur. Little would she have expected to find herself married to Henry VIII.

Gazing at the outside one should remember that here is a See that was founded in 1050 when the ancient Bishopric of Crediton and Cornwall was transferred to Exeter. Bishop William Warelwast, the nephew of William the Conqueror built a Norman Cathedral on the site of an ancient Saxon church which goes back to at least the 7th century. St Boniface was educated here and it was in the small Saxon Minster, west of the present Cathedral, that Leofric was enthroned as the first Bishop, by Edward the Confessor. It must have been an impressive sight as Edward and his Queen Editha led the Saxon Bishop to his throne.

There are Norman arches that lead into cobbled courtyards with graceful wisterias creeping up the walls.If you are allowed a glimpse of the room in which the librarian works above the cloister, surrounded by 8000 books, you will see one that is treasured above all others. It is the wonderful Exeter book that Leofric gave to the cathedral. It is beautifully written in ink and contains about a third of our Saxon literature. You may also see among these books the chalice and signet ring of a prelate of the 13th century, taken from the coffin of Bishop Bitton was was buried here in 1307.

The two great Norman towers, one of which has 100 arches, have stood for eight centuries; the piers and arches and the roof for six. There are angels, prophets, soldiers and kings, fighting for their places amidst the priests and apostles. St Peter sits above them, almost as if he is looking down on an unruly mob.

In the time of Bishop Bronescombe between 1257 and 1280 the Dean and Canons were dissatisfied with what they demmed to be an old fashioned building. They started to rebuild it, beginning with the new Lady Chapel at the east end. Bishop Bronescombe's fine tomb is on the south side of this chapel. In less than 100 years the whole building was remodelled in the 'Decorated' style, with large windows and pillars of sixteen shafts of Purbeck marble. The new building contained a great deal of scupture, much of it coloured, in bosses, corbels and finally the image screen of the West front. the Norman towers were kept, but they were incorporated in the new building as transepts. No other English cathedral has 'lateral' towers of this kind. the absence of a heavy central tower or spire has prevented certain arhitectural problems, and gives us 300 feet of unbroken stone vaulting – the longest stretch of its kind in the world.

The creative period of cathedral building had ended by 1400. The religious troubles of the 16th century brought it some trouble and caused some damage and in

Coronation of the Virgin: roof boss from presbytery, Exeter Cathedral

Cromwell's time it lost its cloisters. But its basic purpose and constitution continued and in recent years, like other great churches, it has been the object of much tender loving care by its many devotees. Worldwide interest has been generated in its needs and has helped funds to be raised over the last fifteen years to assist in the cleaning and washing with water of the building and also extensive conservation work. The image screen, which was much eroded by smoke and the weather, has been put into good order and netted against the pigeons. The Norman South Tower, which houses the cathedral's ring of fourteen bells, also suffered much stone erosion and is being repaired by stone quarried from the original site near the Devon coast.

Music has always been one of the strong points of Exeter Cathedral and the soaring sound of the 17th century organ entwined by the pure and lyrical voices of the choirboys and choristers fills me with intense pleasure and a sense of being closer to the Almighty, everytime I go there. In the Quire is the 60 foot Bishop's Throne, given by Bishop Walter Stapledon in 1320. The east window has the best stained glass in the South West of England. It sends shafts of wondrous light seeking out the hidden places of this awe inspiring building.

This is a Cathedral that despite its magnificence remains welcoming and a joy to be in. I never fail to be mesmerised by the beauty around me. It is almost like being in a heaven in which modern man is allowed to go about an ordered, peaceful existence which in no way lacks purpose. There is no strife, no threat of war, no anger, just a great sense of the presence of God in the most wonderful surroundings. If there is any cry for help it comes from the need to keep this treasure safe. The years are telling on it and constant war is waged against decay. This takes an enormous amount of money which is mainly raised by the public. It is not only money that is needed, craftsmen are continually at work and some of them are getting too old for their task. Finding replacements becomes quite a battle in itself.

Exeter Cathedral has all the beauty of Devon in it. Its original builders, masons, carpenters and glaziers, painter and sculptors, were all Devon men. Today they come from all over the place. Times have changed but the love of these great buildings remains and I am sure that men and women will always be drawn to this work of repair and maintenance which is almost a vocation.

You must not ignore the Chapter House of the cathedral, built in 1224 and reconstructed in 1412. It was also extensively renovated in 1969 and should be seen if only to view the sculptures of the stages of the Creation, as told in both Old and New testaments. They were installed during 1974 and are the work of a local sculptor, Kenneth Carter.

Another modern edition to the cathedral is a series of cushions known as the Exeter Rondels which in 1989 were placed on the stone plinth of the Nave. The tapestry work on these cushions was designed by Marjorie Dyer, and tells the whole history of the cathedral in its National and local setting.

During the summer there are free guided tours at 11am and 2.30pm from Monday to Friday and at 11am only on Saturdays. The insight you get into the working of this mighty building and its history makes such a tour invaluable. I have only touched on what the cathedral has to offer; there is so much more and all beautiful.

Exeter is blessed with many fine churches, some of which are never used but most have stories attached to them. One entrance to the Close is by the tiny church of St Martin with its porch looking across to the cathedral. It is quite easy to disregard this little gem because of the stunning beauty of the Elizabethan structure alongside, which was known once as Moll's Coffee House. The tiers of windows lean out and are crowned by a little gallery. Its front reminds one of an old ship - not surprising because it was here that Drake used to meet his captains. Nothing much has changed since his time. The oak panelling is almost black with age, and there is an intriguing gallery painted with 46 different coats of arms. The most fascinating sight though is the whole front of the low room, which is glass. I am told there are no less than 230 panes and no two the same size.

ST PETROCK'S CHURCH has a bell that is more than 500 years old, yet its parish is no bigger than the ground the church stands upon. Then there is the Norman priory of ST NICHOLAS IN THE MINT which is 900 years old and an excellent example of a medieval Monastic Guesthouse. A priory was first founded on this spot during the reign of William the Conqueror, but after the Reformation the domestic buildings became a town house. The vaulted Norman Undercroft dates from 1100 while the kitchen was rebuilt in the 15th century. The splendid Guest Hall has, for the time being, 17th century furnishings and so I could continue with ST MARY ARCHES, the curious church of ST MARY-AT-STEPPES and the quaint 16th century CHURCH OF ST THOMAS - a church with a difference. It is the only one in the county in which a vicar was hanged from his own tower in the rebellion of 1549. There is another little piece of history attached to this church. General Gordon of Khartoum fame arrived at the door of this church with the intention of seeing his grandfather's grave. Before he could cross the threshold he was handed a telegram summoning him to the War Office in London. Once there he was ordered to Khartoum from where he never returned.

Exeter's four Valley Parks are close to people's homes and provide areas for informal countryside recreation with a variety of leisurely walks in attractive surroundings. MINCINGLAKE VALLEY PARK extends down from Stoke Hill between Mincinglake Road and Mile Lane. The lower valley is wooded, whilst the upper part comprises meadowland rich in wild flowers and insects. At LUDWELL VALLEY PARK you will find it is an 'island' of agriculture within the City located between Wonford and Rydon Lane and affords fine views of the City and the Estuary. Some land in the Park is privately owned and access is only allowed into a field when a stile or kissgate is provided. RIVERSIDE VALLEY PARK is the largest, it stretches from the Canal Basin to Topsham ferry. The character changes down its length becoming more informal and richer in wildlife. There are some fine circular walks with longer routes for the more ambitious walker. At DURYARD VALLEY PARK the rich meadows and woodland are host to a wide range of wildlife which thrives in the quiet valleys. Most of the land is in private ownership and access is restricted to the roads which skirt the valleys except where stiles and signs show otherwise.

No one should come to Exeter without taking time to drive a little distance to **Doddiscombsleigh** where the NOBODY INN is superb both as a hostelry offering wonderful food and wine and as somewhere in which to stay. The village is peaceful and the buildings lovely.

For me KILLERTON HOUSE on the west side of the B3181 Exeter-Cullompton road is one of the most glorious houses in Devon. It is a National Trust property and one from which they carry out the administration for all their properties in Devon. How I envy those who work here. The house was rebuilt in 1778 to the design of John Johnson and is the home of the Acland family. Its wonderful, gracious rooms, house superb paintings and furniture and, in add ition, the Paulise de Bush collection of costumes, shown is a series of room tableaux of different periods from the 18th century to the present day. The materials of the earlier costumes put to shame the man-made fibres we use today and the workmanship that went into the design and creation of each outfit is incredible.

The park is open all year during daylight hours and the house opens on Good Friday and closes at the end of October. It is as well to remember that the house is only open to visitors from Wednesday to Monday 11-6pm.

No one must come into the Exeter area either without visiting POWDERHAM CASTLE, one of the quiet glories of Devon. Built between 1390 and 1420. It has been the home of the Courtenay family ever since. Sir Philip Courtenay was the first occupant, the sixth son of the second Earl of Devon, from whom the present Earl of Devon is directly descended. Actually, what I am saying is not strictly accurate, because about five years ago, the present earl who is 75, decided to move out and make way for his heir. He has not moved far - merely

to a house on the estate, but it has meant changes within the castle and some modernisation in the wing of the castle in which the younger family live. I am told that guests staying there now do not have to go on safari to find a loo!

If you take a look at the castle you will see that every generation has made some form of alteration in order to keep up with the changes of their time. None of this has detracted from its beauty. The story of the Courtenays is so extraordinary that it has inspired writers for centuries to tell the tale. Gibbon traces the rise of the house from a root established near Paris, Crusading Governors in Mesopotamia and giving a king to Jerusalem, as well as rulers to Constantinople. One branch came to England and for 600 years they have played their part in the history of this country.

Thomas was killed fighting for the Red Rose in the Wars of the Roses. Richard, beloved of Henry V, died in his presence at the Battle of Harfleur. Henry fell foul of Henry VIII and was executed in the Tower. His son, Edward fell in love with Mary Tudor and might well have married her had it not been in England's interest for her to wed Philip of Spain. Some say he might have become the Consort of Elizabeth I. The family has produced many bishops, one of whom became Archbishop of Canterbury in the 14th century. Other Courtenays too have played their part in the

Detail from the 14th century North Porch Exeter, showing one of the statues (a patron saint of the Allies: World War I) given by Archdeacon Saunders in 1918 in thanksgiving for the survival of his two sons

Affairs of State. A visit to Powderham will always remain in your mind as a red letter day.

I love genuine tea rooms and at **Topsham** on the outskirts of Exeter I found THE GEORGIAN TEA ROOMS in the High Street, housed in Broadway House. This elegant pre-Georgian High Street should not be missed. It is full of beautiful buildings and none more so than Broadway House. It was built in 1777 by a Dutch merchant at a cost of £3, 000, who then could not afford to live in it! Heather and Gerald Knee bought the house in 1982 to use as a home for young people who needed a bed-sit in a Christian environment. Today five rooms are are still occupied by youngsters some of whom are long term residents. It was Heather's dream to have a tea room and when a friend suggested using the house itself with its prime main street position, the dream became a reality.

On the road that leads to Sidmouth one could take a slight detour and make instead for OTTERTON MILL CRAFT CENTRE at **Otterton** quite close to **Budleigh Salterton**, a charming, small seaside resort in its own right. Otterton Mill is the last working mill on the River Otter. Restored in 1977, this large village cornmill has been grinding grain in the lower Otter Valley since before the Norman Conquest. Its machinery has been turned by the River Otter ever since. It is a fascinating place to visit with much of interest including the opportunity of a guided tour of the mill and occasionally seeing the milling being carried out. There are studio workshops, 'Millhands' craft shop, and the delightful 'Duckery Restaurant and Bakery', which uses the products of the mill and the results of the baking are on sale. I never leave here without taking home at least some of the wonderful scones. Otterton Mill also has a bookshop and a gallery, offering a varied programme of fine art and craft exhibitions. Thanks to the east Devon District Council's Otter Project there is going to be a wildlife pond in Otterton Mill's lower meadow. The banks will be planted with willow and waterside plants and offers of plants are eagerly sought. The idea is to encourage local schools to use the pond for field studies. There is already a large population of moorhens who spend their time in the lower meadow every winter.

Sidmouth is one of those places that seems never to change. It still has the look and the atmosphere of a Victorian holiday resort. I enjoy it because it is so peaceful except for one time of the year when it springs into frenetic activity for the annual Folk Festival which has become the Mecca for entrants worldwide. The first time that I saw it I could not believe that there were so many different variations of Morris Dancing and folk singing, let alone the clacking of Clog Dancers.

Once over Sidmouth returns to its demure, elegant self. You can stroll along the Regency Esplanade where, as a child, Queen Victoria was pushed as a little child, by her father, the Duke of Kent. Their house is now The ROYAL GLEN HOTEL. However it is not about the hotel I wish to tell you, but rather THE HUNTERS MOON HOTEL on Sid Road. This is a family run, early Georgian residence set in two acres of wooded lawns. It is positioned approximately ten minutes level walk from the sea front and shops. The hotel lies along a beautiful National Trust walk following the River Sid and the grounds offer seclusion in

which to sit and relax with refreshments available throughout the day. Hunters Moon is friendly and informal, somewhere to unwind and enjoy a holiday in this superb area.

On the Plymouth side of Exeter, I am a devotee of THE SEVEN STARS at **Kennford**. This has been a village inn for approximately 100 years and there are rumours of a nightly ghostly visitor, but Norma Whitfield the proprietor, has not yet been introduced! It is near Exeter Cathedral, adjacent to the Exe estuary, and within reach of Haldon Woods, famous for forest walks.

THE LORD HALDON HOTEL AT **Dunchideock** is a splendid country house, formerly the home of the Lords Of haldon, and was built in 1737 for Sir George Chudleigh by Sir Robert Adam, and enlarged in 1772 by Sir Robert Palk. It was modelled on Buckingham Palace and was thus one of the largest and finest houses in Devonshire. Sadly the majority of perished in a fire leaving only the west wing and arch by Adam. It is only ten minutes drive from the heart of Exeter. The setting is so tranquil and a wonderful place to seek out, both for those who want to stay away from a busy city and for those who just want to drive out for a meal and a drink.

Finally on the old A30 Exeter to Okehampton Road you will find THE OLD THATCH INN at **Cheriton Bishop** just ten miles from Exeter and inside the Eastern Border of Dartmoor National Park. From here you can set forth to explore the scenic beauty of this wild and rugged area - Fingle Bridge for example, which R.D. Blackmore describes as 'the finest scene in all England'. Then there is Castle Drogo, the last castle to be built in England. One of Sir Edward Lutyens triumphs built for Julius Drewe famous for his chain of shops, The Home and Colonial Stores. The Old Thatch Inn is run under the personal supervision of Hazel and Brian, now in their second decade at the inn. Their aim is to maintain the high standards that they have always set and no one can doubt their success.

My visit to Exeter has come to an end but living as I do in Devon, I know, thankfully, that other visits will not be long delayed.

Otterton Mill, Otterton,
Nr. Budleigh Salterton, Devon, EX9 7HG.

Tel: (0395) 68521/67041

OTTERTON MILL
Craft Centre

The last working mill on the River Otter, restored in 1977, this large village cornmill has been grinding grain in the lower Otter Valley since before the Norman Conquest. Its machinery has been turned by the River Otter in East Devon ever since and it is now one of the few surviving, working watermills in the English countryside. The two water wheels, three metres in diameter were made by Bodley Bros. of Exeter in the early 19th century. A part of the mill machinery is wooden and part cast iron. The wheels vary in age from the 18th-19th centuries. The great spur and crown wheel have applewood cogs. Milling is done, on average three days a week, but the machinery and restored wheel turns every day. There are three pairs of stones, four feet in diameter. Two are French burr stones, with rhymed dedications on them, and the third, which they use, are composition stones. In the mill museum one can discover much more, both visually and with the aid of a tape/slide sequence. The miller takes guided tours for groups, which have to be booked.

There are studio workshops, 'Millhands Craft Shop' and a delightful 'Duckery Restaurant and Bakery'. Otterton Mill also has a bookshop and a gallery offering a varied programme of fine art and craft exhibitions. Thanks to the East Devon District Council's Otter Project there is going to be a wildlife pond in Otterton Mill's lower meadow. The banks will be planted with willow and waterside plants and both help and offers of suitable plants are eagerly sought. The idea is to encourage local schools to use the pond for field studies. There is already a large population of moorhens who spend a great deal of time in the lower meadow every winter.

USEFUL INFORMATION

OPEN: Easter–October 31st: 10.30-5.30pm.
Nov 1-Easter: 11.30-4.30pm
CHILDREN: Actively encouraged
CREDIT CARDS: Yes
LICENSED: None

RESTAURANT: Home-made fare using flour from the mill
BAR FOOD: Not applicable
VEGETARIAN: Always several choices
DISABLED ACCESS: Yes, sometimes difficult
GARDEN: Acres of delightful land
SHOPS: Craftshops, bookshop, gallery, exhibitions

Cheriton Bishop, Nr Exeter,
Devon, EX6 6HJ.

Tel: (0647) 24204

THE OLD THATCH INN
Inn

This truly rural and very pretty 16th Century thatched Free House is believed to have been built as a coaching house and is now a Grade II Listed building. You will find it on the old A30 Exeter to Okehampton road just 10 miles from Exeter and inside the eastern border of Dartmoor National Park. From The Old Thatch Inn you can set forth to explore the scenic beauty of this wild and rugged area - Fingle Bridge which R.D. Blackmore describes as 'The finest scene in all England' is only three and a half miles away. A visit to Drogo Castle, the last castle to be built in England, is wonderful. You can fish in the nearby upper reaches of the River Teign for sea or brown trout or salmon; or stroll through the ancient cathedral city of Exeter with its many tourist attractions, just 15 minutes away by car.

The bar and lounge with their beamed ceilings and decor in keeping with the inn's history, are separated by a large open stone fireplace, with a log fire in the cooler months. The emphasis on home-cooking ensures that the food is exceptional. Quality, choice, and value for money are the keynotes of the menus, served in the bar, lounge or Travellers' Nook. If you decided to stay a night or two in one of the three, en-suite bedrooms, breakfast is served in the Travellers' Nook, or in your room if you prefer it. Wherever you have it, you will find breakfast is a delicious and sustaining meal which will set you up well for a day's exploration anywhere.

The Old Thatch is run under the personal supervision of resident proprietors Hazel and Brian, now in their second decade at the inn. Their aim is to maintain the high standards of hygiene, quality food and drink, plus a friendly, unobtrusive hospitality and service. They succeed admirably.

USEFUL INFORMATION

OPEN: Summer: Mon-Sun: 12-3pm
& 6.30pm– 11pm
CHILDREN: No children under 14
CREDIT CARDS: Visa/Access
LICENSED: Full On Licence
ACCOMMODATION: 3 en-suite double rooms

RESTAURANT: Home-cooked traditional recipies. Booking advisable
BAR FOOD: From a snack to a full meal
VEGETARIAN: 2 choices daily
DISABLED ACCESS: Yes. Level entrance if required
GARDEN: Small area at front

THE NOBODY INN

Inn

Doddiscombsleigh,
Nr Exeter, Devon, EX6 7PS.

Tel: (0647) 52394

USEFUL INFORMATION

OPEN: 12-2pm & 6-11pm, 7pm in winter
CHILDREN: No
CREDIT CARDS: Visa/Access/Master
LICENSED: Full. 220 whiskies, 700 wines
ACCOMMODATION: 7 en-suite rooms

RESTAURANT: Finest, fresh, local
   ingredients
BAR FOOD: Delicious & varied
VEGETARIAN: Numerous dishes
DISABLED ACCESS: Level entrance
GARDEN: Patio terrace

According to legend an unknown purchaser was reputed to have closed and locked the doors and refused hospitality to weary travellers seeking bed or refreshment. They, upon receiving no answer to their knocking continued on their journeys in the belief that there was nobody in, and 'Nobody Inn' it has remained since then.

This renowned 16th Century Inn is six miles from Exeter and within a short drive from Dartmoor and the coast. It has long since outlived its reputation for its inhospitable past, and today's traveller is assured of a warm and genuine welcome. Food can be enjoyed in the bar, a favourite spot in the winter months being near the huge and imposing inglenook fireplace, under the beams that were old when Drake was busy 'Singeing the King of Spain's beard'. The old world ambience of the dining room provides a relaxed atmosphere in which to enjoy good food. The restaurant offers an a la carte menu with dishes cooked from the finest, fresh local ingredients, complemented by informal but quietly efficient service. Open from Tuesday to Saturday 7.30-9.30pm, it is advisable to make a reservation in advance. For special occasions or business meetings there is a private dining room. The bar and cellar rank with the finest in the country. There are a limited number of charming bedrooms, mostly en-suite, in the inn and more in the nearby manor house owned by the Nobody. Breakfast is served in the room.

In addition The Nobody offers about 40 varieties of delicious Devon cheeses which are a must to try, both these and a vast selection of wines can be purchased to take away.

THE GEORGIAN TEA ROOMS

Tea Rooms & Restaurant

Broadway House, 35 High Street,
Topsham, Nr Exeter, EX3 0ED.

Tel: (0392) 873465

USEFUL INFORMATION

OPEN: Mon-Sat: 9.30-5pm. Closed Sunday
CHILDREN: Yes. High chairs, bibs,
   box of toys
CREDIT CARDS: None taken
LICENSED: None
ACCOMMODATION: Not applicable

RESTAURANT: Coffee, lunches, cream
   teas. Fresh meals served daily from 12pm
   including roast dinners served on
   Tuesday & Thursday
BAR FOOD: Not applicable
VEGETARIAN: Approx 6 daily
DISABLED ACCESS: Side entrance
   available. Help if required
GARDEN: Large walled garden with patio
   tables for the summer months

The elegant pre-Georgian High Street in Topsham is a part of Exeter that must not be missed. It is full of beautiful buildings and none more so than Broadway House a fine Georgian detached house built in 1777 by a Dutch merchant man at a cost of £3,000 who then could not afford to live in it! The horses were kept at the rear of the building which had its own coach house, laundry and two wells making the early occupants self-sufficient. Today it houses The Georgian Tea Rooms.

Heather and Gerald Knee bought the house in 1982 to use as a home for young people to have a comfortable bed-sit in a Christian environment. Today five rooms are still occupied by youngsters some of whom are long-term residents enjoying the surroundings. It was Heather's dream to open tea-rooms and when a friend suggested using the house itself with its prime main street position, the dream became a reality. Heather's aim is to produce a home-cooked menu as varied and healthy as possible, she produces a wide selection of home-made cakes and jam. The cooked meals are all produced with the emphasis on variety and freshness. All fresh vegetables are used and vegetarians are well-catered for with a choice of meals daily.

The quiet ambience of the tearooms combined with elegant tableware and delightful friendly staff make a simple cup of coffee or pot of tea an occasion. The 'Heartbeat Award' an achievement awarded by the local Environmental Health Authority has been given to the Tea-Rooms three years running.

Dunchideock, Exeter,
Devon, EX6 7YF.

Tel: (0392) 832483
Fax: (0392) 833765

THE LORD HALDON HOTEL
Hotel

This lovely country house hotel, formerly the home of the Lords of Haldon, was built in 1737 for Sir George Chudleigh by Sir Robert Adam and enlarged in 1772 by Sir Robert Palk. It was modelled on Buckingham Palace and was thus one of the largest and finest houses in Devonshire. Sadly the majority perished in a fire leaving only the west wing and an arch by Adam. These remaining parts have been beautifully converted into an hotel by the current owners Michael and Simon Preece. It is only ten minutes drive from the heart of Exeter with its magnificent Cathedral. The setting is so tranquil and a wonderful place to seek out, both for those who want to stay away from a busy city and for those who just want to drive out for a meal or a drink.

The 22 bedrooms are all en suite and have every modern comfort. The Cocktail and Lounge Bars are welcoming places for a quiet drink or somewhere in which to relax whilst waiting for a meal. The food is renowned and fresh produce is used wherever possible. The restaurant is a delightful place in which to dine but the food in the bars is equally good with very substantial platefuls on offer. On a fine day there is nothing more enjoyable than having a meal or a drink on the large patio overlooking the beautifully kept gardens. There is a purpose built conference suite which is separate from the accommodation.

Speciality evenings are very popular with different themes occurring throughout the year. For those who like outdoor activities there is golf and horse riding close by and the wild and rugged beauty of Dartmoor is just a twenty minute drive.

USEFUL INFORMATION

OPEN: Restaurant: 12.30-2.30pm & 7-9.30pm, snacks: 12-2.30pm & 7-10pm
CHILDREN: Yes. No special facilities
CREDIT CARDS: Access/Visa/Amex
LICENSED: Full On Licence
ACCOMMODATION: 22 en-suite rooms

RESTAURANT: Home-cooking. Fresh produce wherever possible. High quality
BAR FOOD: Wide choice. Generous portions
VEGETARIAN: 3-4 dishes daily
DISABLED ACCESS: Level entrance. Toilets possible for wheelchairs
GARDEN: Large with patio for alfresco eating and drinking. No play area

---

Powderham Castle,
Exeter, EX6 8JQ.

Tel: (0626) 890243

POWDERHAM CASTLE
Castle

Powderham Castle is one of Devon's most cherished treasures. In a tranquil and beautiful setting beside the picturesque estuary of the River Exe, this medieval castle stands serene for all to see as they travel by train along the coast line from Plymouth to Exeter. It is easily approached by road from Exeter. An ancient deer park surrounds the Castle providing a home for a long established herd of fallow deer and other wildlife. Many heron and waterfowl can be seen on the river Kenn which lazily runs it's way through this delightful parkland. In front of the Castle is a terraced English Rose Garden filled with older, stronger scented varieties of roses. Here you may come across Timothy the Tortoise. At the age of at least 140 years he is the Castle's oldest resident!

Inside the Castle you are invited to visit a succession of magnificent Halls and State Rooms filled with lavish furnishings, tapestries and historic portraits of the fascinating Courtenay family. The Castle has been their home for over six hundred years and the present Earl of Devon is a direct descendant of Sir Philip Courtenay, who built the Castle between 1390 and 1420. It was extensively damaged during the Civil War and considerable restoration and alterations followed during the 18th and 19th centuries.

During the season various exciting events are held in the park. Horse Trials, Class Vehicle Rallies, Concerts and Craft & Design Fairs occur at intervals. Send for a programme. The castle is available for a variety of functions - a memorable setting for any occasion.

USEFUL INFORMATION

OPEN: Easter to early October: Every day except Saturday from 10am-5.30pm
CHILDREN: Welcome
CREDIT CARDS: Visa/Mastercard
LICENSED: Not applicable
ACCOMMODATION: Five individual holiday cottages throughout the year

RESTAURANT: Light lunches & teas
BAR FOOD: Not applicable
VEGETARIAN: On request
DISABLED ACCESS: Ring for details
GARDEN: Rose Garden, picnics & lake

THE WHITE HART HOTEL

Hotel & Inn

South Street,
Exeter, Devon, EX1 1EE.

Tel: (0392) 79897

USEFUL INFORMATION

OPEN: All year round
CHILDREN: Welcome, highchair, baby listening service
CREDIT CARDS: All major cards
LICENSED: Full On Licence
ACCOMMODATION: Modern bedrooms all en-suite

RESTAURANT: Home-cooked, traditional fare
BAR FOOD: Extensive bar snacks & meal menus
VEGETARIAN: Vegetarian menu
DISABLED ACCESS: Limited but always willing to assist
GARDEN: 14th century cobbled courtyard

The 15th century White Hart Hotel is one of Exeter's most ancient Inns. It is situated in a central position within the old city wall and a few yards from the site of the South Gate, through which Henry VI entered the city in 1452. Everything about this fine establishment appeals. Two of the more notable features are the 15th century wine room and an adjoining wall with an early stone fireplace, now incorporated in the bar.

In a city that is not the easiest for parking, one modern benefit of the White Hart is its large car park. A new wing offers excellent bedroom accommodation, tastefully furnished with private bathrooms en-suite, radios, colour TV and telephone etc. The White Hart has many facets. The dining room, the grill room or the bars offer traditional meals, excellently prepared, cooked and served in the proper manner, together with the finest wines, port, madeira, sherry etc. The atmosphere is wonderful and with such service, you may think belongs to bygone days.

For a delightful venue Bottlescrue Bills Wine Bar and Garden, off the car park is very special. 'Davy's Old Wallop' - English bitter ale - is served by the pewter tankard or half gallon copper jug. There is a varied list of Davy's house wines by the glass or bottle. Port, sherry and madeira are served from the wood. For more serious moments, an elegantly proportioned boardroom is available for conferences and for celebrations. It is superb for a wedding reception, or a dinner party for example, with superb food and service.

THE SEVEN STARS

Inn

Kennford, Exeter,
Devon, EX6 7TR.

Tel: (0392) 833246

USEFUL INFORMATION

OPEN: Mon-Thur: 11-3pm. Fri-Sat: 11-11pm. Sun: 12-3pm & 7-10.30pm.
CHILDREN: Welcome
CREDIT CARDS: None taken
LICENSED: Fully Licensed
ACCOMMODATION: Not applicable

RESTAURANT: Not applicable
BAR FOOD: Home-made specialities
VEGETARIAN: Yes, upon request
DISABLED ACCESS: Yes
GARDEN: Yes

The country village inn, The Seven Stars at Kennford, not only offers you good food but it could not be better situated. It is near the Cathedral city of Exeter, adjacent to the Exe Estuary, and within reach of Haldon Woods, famous for forest walks. It is also only 20 miles from Dartmoor where ponies wander freely, and just twelve miles from the nearest beach.

The Seven Stars has been a village inn for approximately 100 years and there are rumours of a nightly, ghostly visitor, but Norma Whitfield, the proprietor, has not yet been introduced!

With 16 years in the licensed trade and a caterer since her college days, Norma knows exactly what pleases her customers, gastronomically. She has always been conscious of the need to produce good home cooking using fresh meats and vegetables, and most of all to make sure that prices are comfortable for all.

There is a varied menu every day which includes chicken and fresh fish from Brixham. On Sundays there is a choice of three roasted meats served with fresh vegetables and followed by delectable home-made sweets; all for approximately £5 per person with reduced prices for children. Bar snacks are also available.

Sid Road, Sidmouth,
Devon, EX10 9AA.

Tel: (0395) 513380
Fax: (0395) 514270

HUNTERS MOON HOTEL
Hotel

Sidmouth lies at the heart of the Heritage Coast, nestling between sandstone cliffs on a softly curving bay. Walkers will discover the many coastal and inland paths. The town itself offers a pleasant place to browse amongst fine Regency architecture amd many interesting shops.

Hunters Moon is a family run, early Georgian residence set in two acres of wooded lawns. It is positioned approximately ten minutes level walk from the sea- front and shops. The hotel lies alongside a beautiful National Trust walk following the River Sid, the grounds offer seclusion in which to sit and relax with refreshments available throughout the day. Hunters Moon is a friendly informal hotel where you can unwind and enjoy your holiday.

For the more competetive, the hotel offers a private floodlit bowling green where beginners and experienced bowlers can enjoy this popular game - or alternatively a nine hole putting green is available for the whole family. The hotel dining room, with its typical Georgian ceiling, offers a varied menu, utilising fine Devon produce and freshly caught fish. All of the comfortable bedrooms enjoy private facilities and good views of the garden or surrounding hills.

The Hunters Moon makes an ideal base for exploring the picturesque Devon countryside and numerous historic towns and villages. One can travel from the wild beauty of Dartmoor and Exmoor to the landscaped splendour of Bicton Gardens and the magnificence of Exeter Cathedral.

USEFUL INFORMATION

OPEN: March until the end of October
CHILDREN: Always welcome
CREDIT CARDS: None taken
LICENSED: Table Licence
ACCOMMODATION: Comfortable
ensuite rooms

RESTAURANT: Open to non-residents
BAR FOOD: No but snacks available
VEGETARIAN: Always a choice of dishes
daily
DISABLED ACCESS: Easy access. Ground
floor bedrooms
GARDEN: Large gardens

Gloucester Cathedral

Gloucester

" - From worlds not quickened by the sun
A portion of the gift is won;
An intermingling of Heaven's pomp is spread
On ground which British shepherds tread."

William Wordsworth

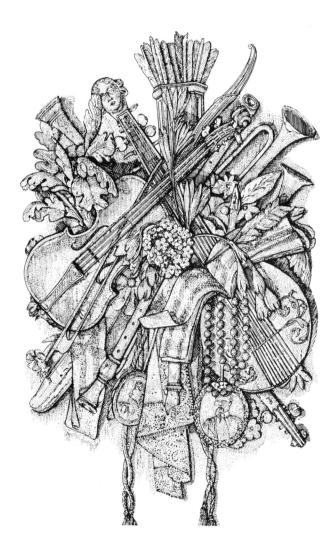

The City of Gloucester

by Joy David

They say that 42 Kings have visited **Gloucester**, to say nothing of Queens, Princes, Princesses and other Royal personages. The Saxon Kings had their own royal palace here, giving their name to the district of Kingsholm. Gloucester owes much to one Saxon 'royal', Aethelflaeda, daughter of Alfred the Great, who undertook the restoration of the City after its period of decline. The City had no particular connections with the Vikings although Guthrum visited here at one time. Towards the end of the Saxon-Danish period, Edward the Confessor held 'Witans' (Parliaments) here regularly.

We have to thank a Christmas Witan for the commissioning of the Domesday Book by William the Conqueror in or around the Abbey Church of St Peter in 1085. Gloucester's own entry described the City as a prosperous town of some 3,000 souls. William built a castle at the south-west corner of the old Roman town. Henry I built another, while Henry II gave Gloucester the first of their very long line of Royal Charters. Henry III was crowned in GLOUCESTER CATHEDRAL and no other coronation has taken place outside Westminster since. Richard III's most famous entry into the City was a triumph. Gloucester had supported him during the Wars of the Roses and in 1483 he rewarded Gloucester by granting them Letters Patent. Henry VIII

brought Anne Boleyn here and Eliabeth I gave the City the status as a Port. It was the arrival of the Stuarts that upset Gloucester's long and happy association with Royals.

Charles I was denied entry although he tried hard to gain access. It rained that August of 1643 and the two young princes, later Charles II and James II were kept within the walls of Matson House by the weather and also as a protection against possible kidnappers. Given the humiliation of their ignominious retreat, and the sheer boredom of their confinement it was not very surprising that Gloucester was not their favourite place after the Restoration, or that Charles took his revenge by reducing the boundaries and ordering the destruction of the City Walls. Good relationships have been continued with the House of Windsor and in 1988 the Prince of Wales opened the magnificent BRITISH WATERWAYS MUSEUM.

Gloucester sits in an envious position and is able to claim it is part of the West Country as well as being in the Heart of England. Whichever it chooses to be it is bustling and prosperous. A wonderful base from which to explore so many places. Close to the Cotswolds, no distance from the Severn Vale, and a short drive to the Royal Forest of Dean. Wherever you are in the city you cannot miss the Cathedral.

Whatever one's opinion of the less than sympathetically developed city of Gloucester nothing can detract from the magnificent grandeur of the body nor the glorious

symmetry of the cathedral tower. Inside it has so much beauty that one is left almost bereft of speech and it takes a while to re-adjust to the hurly burly of the twentieth century when you leave its hallowed portals.

Gloucester is one of the Cathedrals like Oxford, Peterborough, Chester and Bristol which were granted Cathedral status by Henry VIII. A great Benedictine abbey church originally Henry nominated this as the cathedral church for a new diocese carved out of the ancient see of Worcester. The charter issued proclaimed that 'considering the site of the said late monastery in which many famous monuments of our renowned ancestors, Kings of England, are erected, is a very fit and proper place...we have decreed that the site of the said monastery be an episcopal see... and we also will and ordain that the said Dean and Prebendaries, and their successors shall forever hereafter be called the Dean and Chapter of the Holy and Undivided Trinity of Gloucester.'

The history goes way back to a monastery founded here by Osric, Prince of Mercia, as early as 681, and though the foundation had a far from tranquil history, with the church and monastic buildings destroyed twice, the strategic importance of Gloucester as one of the main cities of Saxon England was undoubted. It was rapidly refounded, first in 823 and then. as a Benedictine house in 1048. King Alfred's daughter Ethelfleda was buried in the church of St Peter. William the Conqueror recognised the importance of Gloucester's strategic position and although by the time of the Battle of Hastings in 1066, the monastery was almost extinct with only two monks remaining, he ensured its future by placing his own chaplain Serlo, from Mont Saint Michel, as abbot and steadily the numbers increased. By the time of his death there were over a hundred monks in residence and a magnificent new church was dedicated in 1100.

Of this church only the crypt remains and that was strengthened to take the weight of the building above. It was the Benedictines in the 12th century to whom we have to give thanks for the nave with its inspiring and massive pillars round the arches.

William the Conqueror was not best pleased with his eldest son Curthose who inherited none of the Conqueror's strength and was over blessed by a treacherous and weak nature. However it is a pointer to the importance of Gloucester that when he died he was laid to rest in the abbey church.

Gloucester did not escape the ravages of fire which caused such destruction to so many wooden-roofed churches of Saxon and Norman England. Fire swept through during evensong one evening in 1122 when the monks were singing and it destroyed the whole monastery. Nearly 70 years later in 1190 another fire destroyed most of the city and many of the buildings of the new monastery. It was the desire to circumvent this happening again that between 1242 and 1245 the nave was given a new stone vault erected by the monks themselves. No one can do anything but admire their labouring skills but they were not good at getting their proportions right, and today it is a scar on the wondrous beauty of the nave.

Royal events have regularly taken place at Gloucester. In 1216 following the sudden death of King John at

Newark on the 28th October, his son, a mere nine years old, was crowned in the abbey church and became Henry III. If you look you will see there is a Victorian window in the south aisle of the nave which commemorates the event. It seems to indicate that he was crowned not with a crown but with his mother's bracelet.

It is strange that in death those who have been reviled and despised seem to take on a new persona. When Edward II, a man of straw and addicted to sodomy, was murdered at the instigation of his wife, Isabella and her lover, Roger, Earl Mortimer, he was buried amid great scenes of panoply and solemnity in this great church in the presence of his 'grieving' widow and his young son, Edward III. A suitably splendid monument was ordered by Edward in memory of his father and within a few years this tomb had become a shrine to the martyr King. Gloucester benefited and became a centre for pilgrims. Always a profitable business the money gained from the hordes of pilgrims went to the glorious building of the cathedral that we see today.

The great round columns of the nave lead us to the choir where the beauty is so wondrous it is almost miraculous. There are soaring columns, a great lierne vault and the largest stained glass window in England which somehow has survived six centuries, and is still full of superb 14th

Found at the base of the Great East window, this stained glass roundel depicts a 14th century youth playing with bat and ball

century glass. It is known as the Crecy window because it was probably a gift of Lord Bradstone who fought with his friend, Sir Maurice Berkely, at Crecy in 1346, and he too is commemorated. The window shows the coronation of the Virgin, the twelve apostles surrounded by saints and under them abbots of Gloucester and bishops of Worcester. There are flying arches and angelic musicians form the bosses in the vault above the high altar. There are no adequate words to describe such beauty. It is for you to see and make up your own mind.

For me, the cloisters which were finished in 1420 are especially wonderful, and memorable. As you pass along see the fantastic fan vaulting above and envy the monks who would have worked in the little recesses at their wooden desks on one side. There is also the lavatorium where they washed. I wonder sometimes if they registered so much beauty every day, or were they sated by it and then would they have treated their working environment with the the contempt that familiarity brings. Whenever I vist Gloucester I make for the cloisters and never fail to be enriched but I just wonder.......

Work continued on extending and enriching this great abbey church with the West Front in place between 1450 and 1460 and then the central tower; one of the most beautiful in Europe. The final icing on this glorious cake was the Lady Chapel finished at the very end of the 15th century. Its Perpendicular at its very best with its superb vaulted roof and an elegant bridge which links the north and south triforia across the chapel, and has the effect of producing a whispering gallery.

1540 must have been a terrible year for Gloucester when the abbey church was surrendered to the king. Perhaps because of its royal associations it suffered less than it might have done. Along with all the other buildings of this great Benedictine house it lost the name of St Peters and became the Cathedral of the Holy and Undivided Trinity. It has led a charmed life. The Civil War saw it lose much glass and almost the Lady Chapel. Even the 18th and 19th century could not harm it. I read in a guide book of 1897 something which amused me. It said 'Gloucester has suffered somewhat at the hands of Sir Gilbert Scott, but probably not a tithe what would have been inflicted upon it had Wyatt been turned loose with an absolutely free hand.'

Gloucester Cathedral is one of my favourites and in amongst its beauty and magnificence there are some very simple and moving things to see as well. For example only a few steps away from the tomb of Edward II, perhaps the finest of all medieval royal effigies, is a very different piece of stonemasonry - a tiny cross, obviously fashioned by a loving but amateur hand. This is the cross of Colonel Carne, carved with a nail in the Chinese prison camps by the brave and valourous Commanding Officer of the Glorious Gloucesters, who preferred to go into captivity with his men rather than escape to freedom after the heroic battle at Solm-ri on the Imjin River during the Korean War in April 1951. He was later awarded the Victoria Cross.

There are two fine exhibitions which should not be missed. The Treasury Exhibition is open every day except Sundays from April to September and The Cathedral Exhibition is the other, which encapsulates the whole history of the Abbey and Cathedral.

Your neck will be aching from gazing towards the heavens and your feet will be sore but the time spent in the cathedral will never be forgotten. If you need refreshment after your wanderings, The Undercroft Restaurant will take care of that. It serves wonderful home-made cakes and a first class cup of tea as well as light meals.

With a love of things eccesiastical it would be a pity not to take a look at Gloucester's fine churches. There is an old saying which is supposed to relate to the amazing number of churches in Gloucestershire. 'As Sure as God's in Gloucestershire'; something that certainly applies to the number and variety in this County capital. At the north-west corner of the Cathedral precincts, is the green of ST MARY'S SQUARE with a massive memorial to the martyred Bishop Hooper and it also has a small and pleasant church, ST MARY DE LODE which just might be the site of one of the earliest places of Christian worship in Britain.

In 1982 the church was found to have a rising damp problem and workmen excavating the nave to get to the root of the trouble unearthed a lovely Roman pavement. It is this find that has led to the speculation of the origin of the site.

Just a short stroll from the Cathedral you will come to the ruined priory church of ST OSWALD'S which is Gloucester's oldest building. THE PRIORY, founded in AD 909 is dedicated to the martyred King of Northumbria. It stood close to the royal palace of the Saxon kings after which the area of Kingsholm is named.

English Heritage have the care of BLACKFRIARS, the most perfectly preserved example of a Dominican Friary in Britain, and careful development work constantly unearths more important remains.

GREYFRIARS is a fine example of an early 16th century Franciscan Friary, ruined after the Dissolution. It forms a most dramatic backdrop to the delicate beauty of ST MARY DE CRYPT church and the modern architecture of EASTERGATE MARKET. You will find St Mary de Crypt in Southgate Street. It is one of Glolucester's oldest churches and the site of several fine murals. George Whitfield, the Great Evangelist and friend of John and Charles Wesley, preached his first sermon here and the Founder of Sunday Schools, Robert Raikes, is buried here along with Charles Hoare, whose family sailed on the Mayflower.

LLANTHONY PRIORY has undergone a massive programme of restoration after years of neglect. The funds have come both from the City Council and English Heritage. It is known as Llanthony Secunda to distinguish it from its Welsh parent foundation. You approach it by way of a walk along Hempstead Lane. It is a distinctive medieval building, with later additions and the intention is to turn it into an archaeology centre. The ruined barn, restored pond - now a nature reserve - and the fine ruined arch fronting Hempstead Lane are well worth a visit.

Probably the most intriguing of all Tourist Information Centres in the country is in ST MICHAEL'S TOWER, all that remains of a medieval church. The tradition has it that ST JOHN'S in Northgate Street was founded by the Saxon King Athelstan, in about AD 931 and later rebuilt by the Normans. No less than seven mayors of Gloucester are buried here, but the pulpit is all that remains of the original 'three decker' from which both George Whitfield and John Wesley are known to have preached.

The redundant ST NICHOLAS' CHURCH opposite the FOLK MUSEUM in Westgate Street has an extraordinary leaning tower and a fine sanctuary knocker was found in the church, which is now in the protective custody of the City Museum.

Gloucester is a multi-racial city and many new churches have been welcomed into it. It is a fascinating pilgrimage to see these different places of worship embodying and glorifying the different faiths. The buildings have certainly added a new, handsome and spectacular dimension to the architecture of Gloucester. None of these is more remarkable than the MOSQUE JAMA, which adds its own distinctive spire and dome to the eastward skyline of the Barton area.

One of my favourites is the delightful, tiny MARINERS' CHURCH which is incorporated into the redevelopment of Gloucester Docks. It is a Victorian foundation, provided for the spiritual well-being of the sailors and dock workers, who perhaps felt uncomfortable in the town churches. Gloucestershire poet and composer, Ivor Gurney, was choirmaster here for a while.

You could travel all over Britain and Europe today and see nothing quite like GLOUCESTER DOCKS. They represent a resource of national importance and one of England's most exciting new tourist attractions. However that is not how Charles Dickens would have seen this last Victorian port. His description says it infinitely better than I can and from his words you will be able to understand the changes that have been wrought:

" You will see, suddenly appearing, as if in a dream. long ranges of warehouses, with cranes attached, endless intricacies of dock, miles of tramroad, wildernesses of timber in stacks, and huge, three masted ships, wedged into little canals, floating with no apparent means of propulsion, and without a sail to bless themselves with."

That was Gloucester Docks at the height of their wealth and prestige. Now where dockers and mariners once toiled and strived tourists can sit and stroll at leisure. Where grain, salt and timber were stored, there are bars, restaurants, an antiques centre and three museums. Dickens ' long range warehouses' have been restored to their former glory and this is only one part of the miracle that has occurred. A decade or so ago public opinion was so strong that the acres of dereliction which existed were nearly demolished with the objective of starting something new from scratch. Fortunately there was an acceptable alternative made possible by British Waterways Board and the Gloucester City Council, and so now we are able to see the most complete example of a Victorian Dockland in existence anywhere in the world.

The Docks are a Mecca for film and TV companies who have used the Docks as a period setting on many occasions including the memorable 'Onedin Line'.

The above is a detail of the effigy of King Edward II, one of the most beautiful 14th century alabaster figures

Walking down Eastgate Street you will be amazed to find that the ground floor of Gloucester's century old Guildhall now houses the main branch of the Cheltenham and Gloucester Building Society. THE GUILDHALL ARTS CENTRE is there too and it will seem odd at first sight. Why would the City move its traditional headquarters to make room for these newcomers? The reason was the challenge of Gloucester Docks. The city had to do something about the acres of decay so close to the city centre. The development potential of the Docks site was enormous but the cost of tackling it astronomical.

Bravely the City Council decided to move to the Docks, financing the project with the resources obtained from leasing the Guildhall's ground floor to the building society. British Waterways co-operated, selling the derelict, but strategic, North Warehouse to the City for just £1. This has given Gloucester one of the most imaginative civic headquarters in Britain.

This success encouraged the city to acquire three more warehouses, the adjoining Herbery, Kimberley and Phillpotts warehouses and centralise almost all the Council administration within the Docks Complex. This project was completed in 1988. The City Council's courage had the effect of opening the flood doors. Leisure and Retail interest was immediately shown and the resulting developments have brought prosperity to where decay once reigned. As an example of co-operation between local, national and private interests, the Gloucester Dock project has few equals. Visitors come here in their thousands, marvelling at the museums, having a quiet meal or drink, pouring over bygones, or simply admiring the architecture of the warehouses themselves. It is stunning.

THE NATIONAL WATERWAYS MUSEUM is housed in one of these wonderful old warehouses. The Museum building is a part of the display and where you can follow in the path of the people who once worked the canals. The Nation's Waterway collection is housed on three floors of the warehouse. There are vast timber beams, wooden floors and cast iron pillars which form the backdrop to displays, simulators and models. You are encouraged to see if you could steer a narrow boat - not as easy as you think and opening paddles and gates on a lock could spell disaster if you get the things in the wrong order - fortunately your effort will be on a simulator! The Museum provides hours of fun for all ages, and a few suprises as well.

Around the warehouse, at the quayside are moored a variety of narrowboats, barges and the massive Number 4 Steam Dredger. To one side of the main building is LLANTHONY YARD where you will find a forge, Engine house and workshops, with regular demonstrations of the skills needed on and around the waterways. Peter the shire horse who spends his days in a stable at Llanthony is happy to pull a cart in which you may ride. You are invited to take a 40 minute cruise on the Gloucester and Sharpness Canal on board the Queen Boadicea II, one of the Dunkirk little ships. You join the boat at Merchants Quay and travel down the canal through Hempstead Bridge and back.

You can take one of these trips any day from Easter to October leaving at 1.30pm, 2.30pm and 3.30pm. Morning and more frequent trips are available in the peak season and at weekends. In winter the boats operate at weekends only. All trips leave Merchants Quay and these can includ some delightful Evening River Cruises which are invariably musical, varying from jazz to 80's disco and 'Country and Western'. There are longer cruises too and details of these may be obtained from The National Waterways Museum by telephoning 0452 307009.

The museum shop sells a wide range of souvenirs, books, and clothes, and an amazing variety of traditional items and ornaments from the canal era. The waterside cafe serves everything from a pot of tea to a full range of appetising snacks and meals. There are activities and displays on most days.

The National Waterways Museum is open daily from 10am-6pm throughout the year but in the winter it closes at 5pm.

MERCHANTS QUAY is a new green steel and glass pavilion on the edge of the main dock basin and forms the heart of Docks shopping. Here you can hire a ball gown, buy a postcard, enjoy a cup of freshly ground coffee with a doughnut, have a pizza or relax with a pint looking out across the water from DR FOSTER'S PUBLIC HOUSE AND RESTAURANT.

THE ROBERT OPIE COLLECTION - MUSEUM OF ADVERTISING AND PACKAGING is a nostalgic journey through childhood memories as one looks at a century of shopping basket history. It is entirely devoted to the preservation of products anbd packaging from the Victorian era onwards. It is the only museum of its kind in the world. Old advertisments and packages greet you

at every turn. I wonder how many you will remember? They certainly brought memories crowding back to me. Housed in a Dockside warehouse the opening hours are 10am-5pm (6pm in summer). Closed Mondays, Christmas Day and Boxing Day. Contact: (0452) 302309.

THE REGIMENTS OF GLOUCESTERSHIRE MUSEUM overlooks the Docks and here you will experience a unique British tradition - the County Regiments. I read in the Daily Telegraph yesterday that Robert Keegan, the eminent military historian believes that the Regiments of the Army and the men and women who serve them are a breed apart. I agree and this wonderful Museum underlines this.

Here in a colourful, award winning exhibition, you can follow in the footsteps of the Gloucester men who have become soldiers of the Gloucestershire Regiment and the Royal Gloucestershire Hussars over the past 300 years. Life-size displays show how they lived and fought in all corners of the globe. You will see the clothes they wore, the weapons they used, the medals they won and the souvenirs they sent back home. You will find out how a soldier's family lived 200 years ago. You can walk through a World War I trench and peer into a dugout. Archive film of the Korean War allows you to hear Colonel Carne talk about his experiences as a prisoner-of-war. A visit to this museum is a must once you have seen the cross he carved in captivity, now on display in the Cathedral. The museum is open from 10am-5pm. Closed Mondays, Christmas Day and Boxing Day. Contact: (0452) 522682

Not a museum but certainly a place for the lover of Antiques is THE GLOUCESTER ANTIQUES CENTRE where 67 dealers sell antiques and collectables under one roof. Opening hours: 9.30am-5pm Monday-

Saturday. 1pm-5pm Sunday. Closed: Christmas Day, Boxing Day and New Year's Day. Contact (0452) 529716.

There is no doubt that Gloucester Docks offers a very lively day out and the fact that there is ample car and visitor coach parking makes life much easier! Parking is free after 6pm and on Sundays.

There are many more treasures in Gloucester, NATURE IN ART for example which is to be found on the outskirts of the City at Wallsworth Hall, an imposing Georgian mansion now gracefully converted to a National Heritage Centre for widlife art. In Longsmith Street is GLOUCESTER'S TRANSPORT MUSEUM housed in a disused fire station.

THE CITY MUSEUM AND ART GALLERY is centrally sited in Brunswick Road and actually built over excavated sections of the original city wall. The Archaeology Gallery displays a remarkable array of artefacts dating from prehistoric times. Other departments present a colourful panorama of Gloucester's history, including some exceptionally fine Roman mosaics and sculptures.

THE FOLK MUSEUM in Westgate Street is housed in a Tudor half-timbered building, this is said to be where the martyred 16th-century Protestant Bishop John Hooper, spent his last night before being burnt at the stake. In the 18th and 19th centuries, these buildings were converted into a pin factory.

A fascinating range of material illustrates the social, agricultural and industrial life of the city and county over 500 years. Special exhibitions and demonstrations are run throughout the year. On the top floor is a period reconstruction of a Victorian schoolroom complete with a stern Victorian schoolmaster. Outside there is a little courtyard planted with its own herb garden; a wonderful place to sit and contemplate after a visit here.

Anyone who was brought up on the books of Beatrix Potter, or indeed is only now making the acquaintance of her magical world, must visit THE HOUSE OF THE TAILOR OF GLOUCESTER at 9 College Court. It is one of Gloucester's best known landmarks. This tiny shop is situated at the end of College Court, next to the Cathedral Gate, and is the home that Beatrix Potter chose for the tailor in her famous story, The Tailor of Gloucester. Since 1979 it has been a Beatrix Potter Gift Shop featuring many exhibits of the author's life and work, with hundreds of gifts based on all the favourite Beatrix Potter characters.

All around the building are display panels giving biographical information and pictures of this lady's life and work. First editions of her books are on show as well as a beautifully sewn waistcoat, a replica of the one in her tale. There is a working model of the mice busy sewing and the kitchen is laid out exactly as in the illustrations from the book, complete with Simpkin the cat. There are an amazing number of items that make great gifts all featuring favourite characters, Peter Rabbit, Tom Kitten, Jemima Puddle-duck. All the stories are stocked as wall as many books about the life of Beatrix Potter and her extraordinary

Above Gloucestor's High Alter: (Christ in Glory)

artistic ability. And there is also a selection of paperback Puffin Books - ideal for young visitors to the shop.

Opening hours are from 9.30am-5.30pm Monday to Saturday.

Exploration inevitably produces a thirst and Gloucester is full of historic Inns. In Northgate Street is THE NEW INN built around 1450 to accommodate pilgrims visiting the tomb of Edward II. You can stay here as people have done for the last 500 years. It has a fine galleried courtyard which is a wonderful spot for a quiet drink on a sunny morning.

In a fine old timber-framed building in Cross Keys Lane, off Southgate Street, is THE CROSS KEYS INN, a good traditional pub and in Southgate Street itself is THE GOLDEN CROSS occupying a 16th century house which was once owned by the founder of Sunday Schools, Robert Raikes and in Longsmith Street is THE MALT AND HOPS famous for the quality of its Real Ales.

THE FLEECE HOTEL on Westgate Street can claim to be one of Gloucester's oldest inns, dating from the 16th century. Here you can stay in comfort, dine on delicious food and take a drink in an old cellar bar that was known as 'The Monks Retreat'. Supposedly there was a tunnel that ran from here directly to the Crypt of the Cathedral for the benefit of the monks!

Also in Westgate Street is THE FOUNTAIN in a 17th century building with a much later frontage. It has an entrance in Berkeley Street and is the site of Mistress Savage's Alehouse, and the oldest hostelry of which the City has records. If you look carefully you will see a plaque of a gentleman riding a white horse. This is said to represent William III riding up a set of stairs which existed nearby.

In a 13th century house which was once the home of the Whittington family - the famous 'Dick' was born at **Pauntley** a few miles to the west - the DICK WHITTINGTON is a popular haunt. In the 19th century during renovations a small piece of statuary was found depicting a small boy and a cat. Tradition has it that this represents Dick Whittington and his cat. The piece is now in the safe hands of The Folk Museum.

A simple, comfortable home from home is how I would describe THE DENMARK HOTEL at 36 Denmark Road. Dawn and David Mallett have no need for glossy brochures, they rely on word of mouth and a friendly letter to people who enquire about staying here. It is beautifully run and has been awarded three crowns and approved by the English Tourist Board. The Malletts do not employ any staff so you are sure of their undivided personal attention and they certainly have a vested interest in making sure their guests want to return.

Looking for somewhere to eat in the centre of Gloucester I suggest you try BERRYS RESTAURANT in Southgate Street. Do not be put off by the fact that it does not have a car park; you can usually find a place in Spa Road or Llanthony Road, or you can walk the short distance from the city centre. Berrys stands on the corner of Southgate Street and Spa Road, a busy locality, but the moment you enter the door you are encompassed by a warm, relaxed atmosphere which makes you forget the bustle of the world outside. An ideal place to eat having spent some time in the Cathedral or exploring the historic docks.

Finally no one should come to Gloucester without visiting the amusing and entertaining DR FOSTERS - named after the nursery rhyme. This lively pub and restaurant has something for everyone.

Gloucester is an exciting city and one to which I could easily become addicted especially as it is surrounded by so much wonderful countryside. I took time out to visit some favourite places that I have visited for years and others that were new but will certainly be on my visiting list!

Cheltenham three hundred years ago was just an ordinary village and not the elegant place we know today. The story of how it became a Spa is undoubtedly far fetched but nonetheless an enjoyable thought. A resident watched a flock of pigeons who appeared particularly healthy. Daily they came to drink from the same spring. Samples of the water were taken and it was found that it had health giving minerals. This brought people flocking to the town to gain the same benefits as the pigeons and so the Spa town was born. You may not believe it but Cheltonians do - they have seen fit to include a pigeon on the town's crest. By the end of 1783 the first PUMP ROOM was established and it attracted such distinguished visitors as George III and the Duke Of Wellington. There is no question that the waters were beneficial and still are.

Today you can take the waters at the TOWN HALL as well as the Pittville Pump Room which has to be the most notable of all the Regency buildings. It also houses the PITTVILLE PUMP ROOM MUSEUM OF FASHION on its upper floors where the history of this Regency town is told through two and three dimensional displays of costumes, fashion accessories and jewellery. It is open from April 1st until the end of September, Tuesday-Sunday from 10.30am-5pm and from October 1st-31st March on Tuesday-Saturday from 10.30am-5pm.

The whole town has an air of elegance with its fine crescents and distinguished mansions. The finest Regency building without doubt is The Promenade, laid out in 1818, it must be one of the most gracious and superior thoroughfares in Britain. It was built as a carriage drive leading from the High Street up to the Spa, now the sight of the Queens Hotel.

Cheltenham is a town of flowers and has many times won awards in Britain in Bloom competitions. You need go no further than THE IMPERIAL GARDENS in the heart of the town to enjoy wonderful floral displays. Two museums are worthy of your attention. THE GUSTAV HOLST BIRTHPLACE MUSEUM is to be found in the house in which the composer was born and is open all year round Tuesdays to Fridays from Noon to 5.30pm and 11am-5.30pm on Saturdays. THE CHELTENHAM ART GALLERY AND MUSEUM contains a vast range of displays of arts and crafts as well as an eclectic mix of furniture. Open all the year round Monday to Saturday 10am-5.30pm.

A charming house known as HALEWELL CLOSE in **Withington**, Cheltenham is a private guest house which I can sincerely recommend. It belonged to the church until the late 1920s and was closely aligned to the monastery across the road for many moons before that. It has a tranquil quality about it that has perhaps been inbred over the years but much of it is because of the serenity of the present owner Elizabeth Carey-Wilson who runs the house as a home, with an unerring sense of what her guests will like.

CLEEVEWAY HOUSE RESTAURANT at **Bishop's Cleeve**, is a charming manor house. Nowhere could you feel more a part of the English landscape than here. Originally belonging to the Bishops of Worcester it has seen many changes which have culminated in its development into a restaurant with hotel accommodation and an atmosphere of peace and tranquillity. It is the aim of the owner that you will enjoy the pleasure of this fine old house to the full. They succeed admirably.

Guiting Power is a small place not far from Cheltenham on the A40 Oxford to Andoversford road, from there turn left onto the A436 for Stow on the Wold. After 4 miles turn left again onto the B4068, and 8 miles later turn left and follow the signs. Your destination is THE COTSWOLD FARM PARK a rare breeds survival centre owned and run by Miss Henson, a daughter of Joe Henson, founder and chairman of the Rare Breed Survival Trust. It is a fascinating and informative experience for anyone who comes here. The ignoramus might think that having seen one sheep you have seen them all but that misconception is soon corrected when you discover that Cotswold farm Park has nearly fifty breeding flocks, a herd of our rarest and most interesting British breeds of sheep, cattle, pigs, goats, horses, poultry and waterfowl.

Who could not love **Tewkesbury**. Situated where the Avon meets the Severn, it is the northern gate to the Cotswolds. It grew up around the Abbey, first founded in the 8th century, one of England's most magnificent Norman churches which was saved from sacking at the time of the Dissolution when the townspeople decided to buy it. It cost them the vast sum of £453! Everything about it is beautiful. Each time I visit I find something new but perhaps the beautiful Quire windows - seven of them, all of which have 14th century stained glass, and the dazzling splendour of the Beauchamp Chapel, are my favourites.

Two good museums here. Tewkesbury prospered particularly in the 15th and 16th centuries as you can see from the fine buildings. To see what such a home would look like inside, visit THE LITTLE MUSEUM in Church Street which was built in 1450 and restored this century. Open from Easter-October, Tuesday-Saturday from 10am-5pm. The other is THE JOHN MOORE MUSEUM with displays based on the extracts form this fine writer's books which are all about this part of the country. Portrait of Elmbury was always one that I enjoyed - and still do. The museum is open Easter-October, Tuesday to Saturday from 10am-1pm and 2pm-5pm.

Tewkesbury is surrounded by wonderful villages. Equidistant from Gloucester and Tewkesbury is **Corse Lawn** a small village where the CORSE LAWN HOTEL is situated, and in which it is a privilege to stay. Owned and run by an ebullient Frenchman, Denis Hine, and his English wife, Baba, the essence of success here is the relaxed family atmosphere. It is efficiently run but it is that quality that perhaps allows it to be so informal and jolly.

THE HAW BRIDGE INN at **Tirley** is wonderful. Idyllic is not a word to be used lightly but in the case of the setting of the inn, it is the adjective to describe it. Nestling in the banks of the River Severn it lies some 8 miles from Gloucester Cathedral and 8 miles from Cheltenham and not so many miles from the splendour of Tewkesbury Abbey.

The south walk of the Great Cloistor, showing the beautiful fan vaulting for which it is renowned

Whatever your needs, a family outing, a drink with friends, or a private function, THE FARMERS ARMS at **Apperley**, near Tewkesbury, will make your visit one to remember. You can read that in their brochure - but it is a fact. 'Mayhem's Real Ale' is brewed on the sight and is a recent addition to the Farmers Arms. The Brew House is situated in the grounds of the pub and is open for customers to enter the viewing gallery and see the brewing process.

South of Cheltenham and to the east of Gloucester are three more places I would like you to enjoy. KINGSHEAD HOUSE at **Birdlip** is just off the A417 on the B4070. The setting is delightful and this 17th century former coaching inn is the home and restaurant of Warren and Judy Knock. It is not in the least pretentious; blessed with the original oak beams, it has a reassuring air of stability. Here you can enjoy excellent English cooking prepared by the chef-patron Judy. Her imaginative menu changes twice-weekly and everything is home-made from the rolls to the julienne of carrots. There is one ensuite, spacious bedroom for anyone who wants not only to enjoy the food but also imbibe some super wine from Warren Knock's expertly compiled list.

Eric and Mary Bird run the exceptionally pleasing COLESBOURNE INN at **Colesbourne** in true, traditional innkeeping manner. The earliest record of Colesbourne shows that it was given to the Abbot Balham of Kempsey in 799AD and was then held by various churches until 1537 when it was given by Henry VIII to Thomas Guise for 'services rendered'. In 1565 Queen Elizabeth I granted the manor to Thomas Reeve from whom it passed to a number of families until being acquired by the present owning Elwes family in 1789. It is a super place in which to eat, drink or stay.

To find NOTLEY HOUSE & COACH HOUSE, an admirable guest house, one needs to locate the A417 to the east of Gloucester. Follow the signs to Gloucester Trading Estate, at the roundabout by the estate is Hucclecote Road, five miles from the M5. Notley House was established four years ago by Alyn and Jackie George who had the talent and the discernment to retain the character of the house. It has not taken long for Notley House to become well known and is now synonymous with warmth and comfort, innovative food and a friendly atmosphere. Two of the charming bedrooms have four-poster beds.

As always I am reluctant to leave Gloucestershire. It has so much to offer and is such a warm-hearted county. However I am heartened by the fact that I am off to Hereford and Worcester both of which are old friends.

Apperley, Nr Tewkesbury,
Gloucestershire, GL19 4DR.

Tel: (0452) 780307
Fax: (0452) 780307

THE FARMERS ARMS
Country Inn

Whatever your needs, a family outing, a drink with friends, or a private function, The Farmers Arms will make your visit one to remember. You can read that on their brochure - but it is fact. It is situated on the edge of the village of Apperley in the heart of Gloucestershire's most picturesque countryside, between the Cotswolds and the Malvern Hills. It is within easy reach of Tewkesbury and its superb Abbey, the elegant town of Cheltenham and Gloucester itself with its glorious Cathedral.

Recently The Farmers Arms has been given a loving refurbishment, and it is both comfortable and appealing; one of the nicest country inns in the area in which a wide range of good food, real ale and fine local wine is served. The fully landscaped grounds with ample parking have a play area for younger guests complete with a wendy house. The garden is well furnished with tables and seating to provide the ideal spot for warm evenings. The traditional ales brewed on site go down well with the extensive range of traditional and continental food served lunchtime and evening, seven days a week. You should try the fresh fish and real chips - a speciality of the house. Not served in newspaper but they taste just as good! The Farmers Arms can cater for private functions for up to 120 guests in comfort; ideal for wedding receptions, business lunches or just a good Christmas party.

Mayhem's real ale brewed on site, is a recent addition to the Farmers Arms. The Brew House is situated in the grounds of the pub and is open for customers to enter the viewing gallery and see the brewing process.

USEFUL INFORMATION

OPEN: All year round. Food served all day
CHILDREN: Yes, special menu
CREDIT CARDS: All major cards
LICENSED: Full On Licence
ACCOMMODATION: Not applicable

RESTAURANT: Sunday Roast, Country fare. Home-cooked dishes with a Continental influence
BAR FOOD: Specials of the day
VEGETARIAN: Vegetarian menu
DISABLED ACCESS: Yes. Level entrance
GARDEN: Yes. Patio for eating & drinking. Play area, wendy house

---

Birdlip,
Gloucestershire, GL4 8JH.

Tel: (0452) 862299

KINGSHEAD HOUSE RESTAURANT
Restaurant with Accommodation

Kingshead House is to be found just off the A417 on the B4070, 8 miles from Gloucester and Cheltenham. Made of Cotswold stone, this 17th-century former coaching inn is the home and restaurant of Warren and Judy Knock. The setting is delightful; close to the Cotswold Path along the edge of the hill, from where there are fine views over the Severn Valley. The restaurant is not in the least pretentious; blessed with the original oak beams, it has a reassuring air of stability. Here you can enjoy excellent English cooking prepared by the chef-patron Judy. Her imaginative menu changes twice-weekly, offering up to four courses with perhaps five delicious choices for each course. Judy insists on fresh produce, with fish delivered from Abergavenny, meat from the local butcher and vegetables from a local farm. Everything from home-made rolls to the julienne of carrots is rich in flavour. Main courses range from hot cheese tourte to guinea fowl with braised red cabbage, while for a starter there may be a delicious hot liver chicken and spinach pate.

Puddings are equally appealing, with such tempting delights as hot strawberries sauteed in kirsch served on a hazelnut meringue, filled with raspberry sorbet, or caramelised bread pudding with cream. There is one ensuite bedroom, spacious and comfortably furnished, ideal for those who wish to enjoy to the full this excellent fare and at the same time sample Warren Knock's expertly compiled wine list. It offers an especially good selection of half-bottles. From reasonably priced house wines to more specialised vintages, there is something to suit every palate.

USEFUL INFORMATION

OPEN: Tues-Fri: 12-15-2pm. Tues-Sat: 7.30-10pm last orders. Sunday Lunch 12-1.45pm
CHILDREN: Welcome
CREDIT CARDS: Amex/Diners/Visa/ Master
LICENSED: Restaurant
ACCOMMODATION: 1 ensuite room

RESTAURANT: Superb English cooking using fresh produce
BAR FOOD: From snacks to full lunch
VEGETARIAN: 2-3 courses daily
DISABLED ACCESS: Slight step. Willing to assist
GARDEN: Yes with seating. Car park

COTSWOLD FARM PARK

Farm Park

Guiting Power, Cheltenham,
Gloucestershire, GL54 5UG.

Tel: (0451) 850307

USEFUL INFORMATION

OPEN: April- Sept
CHILDREN: Welcome. Adventure
    playground, pets corner
CREDIT CARDS: All major cards
LICENSED: Not applicable
ACCOMMODATION: Not applicable

RESTAURANT: Self service cafe. Healthy
    range of food
BAR FOOD: Not applicable
VEGETARIAN: Several dishes
DISABLED ACCESS: Yes. Free access
GARDEN: Picnic area with facilties for
    eatingand drinking, play area

This is a rare breeds survival centre owned and run by Joe Henson, Founder Chairman of the Rare Breed Survival Trust. A fascinating and informative experience for anyone who comes here. The ignoramus might think that having seen one sheep you have seen them all but that misconception is soon corrected when you discover that Cotswold Farm Park has nearly fifty breeding flocks, and herds of our rarest and most interesting British breeds of sheep, cattle, pigs, goats, horses, poultry and waterfowl.

Set on the very top of the Cotswold Hills with magnificent views this is the perfect opportunity to get to know a Bagot goat, cuddle a Cotswold lamb, stroke a mighty Longhorn ox, or simply admire generations of our agricultural heritage. Cotswold Farm Park is part of Bemborough Farm who have attempted to leave the farm park area unaltered with its sheltered hollows and scattered thorn bushes, ideal for picnicking, and have only planted small groups of forest trees to enhance the wild beauty of the park.

There is so much to see and do here. Children of all ages find it absorbing. You are invited to come and see the babies galore; fluffy chicks and baby bunnies, new born lambs and goat kids in April, spring calves in May, foals in June and cheeky piglets throughout the year. There is a pets corner, a children's shop, a tots corner, an adventure playground and a nature trail.

Before you leave Cotswold Farm Park you will probably wish to visit the self service cafe where they specialize in home made food.

CLEEVEWAY HOUSE RESTAURANT

Country House Restaurant Hotel

Bishops Cleeve, Cheltenham,
Gloucestershire, GL52 4SA.

Tel: (0242) 672585

USEFUL INFORMATION

OPEN: All year round
CHILDREN: Yes
CREDIT CARDS: All major cards
LICENSED: Full On Licence
ACCOMMODATION: 3 en-suite. Space
    for conferences, wedding etc.
    Pets permitted

RESTAURANT: English with French
    influence
BAR FOOD: Yes
VEGETARIAN: Several dishes
DISABLED ACCESS: Level entrance.
    Will willingly assist
GARDEN: Four acres

Nowhere could you feel more a part of the English landscape than at Cleeveway House Restaurant, a most charming manor house. Built in the early 18th century from golden Cotswold stone and originally belonging to the Bishops of Worcester it has seen many changes over the years, which have culminated in its development into a restaurant with hotel accommodation and an atmosphere of peace and tranquillity. It is their aim that you should enjoy the pleasures of this fine old house to the full.

You will not find a reception desk on arrival, just comfortable sitting rooms to feel at home in. You are invited to relax in the drawing room over a drink before and after a meal in the excellent restaurant. Gazing through the large windows at the specimen trees you should allow your eyes to wander across the five acres of quiet green lawns, rose gardens and herbaceous borders. During the winter months crackling log fires complete your relaxation.

Lovers of freshly cooked food will find inspiration in the delicious and imaginative menus. Each course is prepared from the finest ingredients and everything from crisp rolls to mouthwatering ice creams are made in the hotel's kitchens. Season game, fresh fish, shellfish, tender cuts of prime meats marry with the produce of the garden and locally grown vegetables. There are delicious, light desserts, summer puddings, sorbets, ice cream and fresh fruits. A fine cheese board tempt one to indulge in some excellent port. There is an interesting list of fine wines. This is somewhere to come and enjoy yourselves, it won't break the bank.

Colesbourne, Nr Cheltenham,
Gloucestershire, GL53 9NP.

Tel: (0242) 870376
Fax: (0242) 870397

COLESBOURNE INN

Hotel & Restaurant

Eric and Mary Bird run this exceptionally pleasing hotel which is a true, traditional Cotswold Inn. The inn stands proudly by the side of the main A435 Cheltenham to Cirencester road amidst beautiful Cotswold countryside steeped in history stretching back to Mesolithic times (8000 BC).

The earliest record of Colesbourne shows that it was given to the Abbot Balham of Kempsey in 799 AD and was then held by various Churches until 1537 when it was given by Henry VIII to Thomas Guise for 'services rendered'. In 1565 Queen Elizabeth I granted the manor to Thomas Reeve, from whom it passed to a number of families until being acquired by the present owning Elwes family, in 1789.

The inn was built approximately 200 years ago to serve the then new main road from Cheltenham to Cirencester, brought about by George III's visit to the spa town of Cheltenham and its subsequent rapid development. Today the inn retains all the charm of a traditional Cotswold inn and the recent conversion of the old stable block, with its rare 'Lunnet' windows, to form 10 extremely comfortable en-suite bedrooms now enables the Colesbourne to fulfil its potential as a real inn in the true sense of the word. All the bedrooms are beautifully appointed to ETB 4 Crown standard. The bar is full of atmosphere with ale from the wood, real log fires and super food. Brambles restaurant with its large patio overlooking lovely countryside copes superbly with those wanting to dine in style. Home grown produce is the order of the day. Wonderful place for wedding receptions, parties, business meetings or seminars.

USEFUL INFORMATION

OPEN: All year round
CHILDREN: Yes
CREDIT CARDS: All major cards
LICENSED: Full On Licence
ACCOMMODATION: 10 en-suite rooms

RESTAURANT: A la carte & Table d'hote, Cold table in Summer
BAR FOOD: Yes
VEGETARIAN: 2-3 daily selections
DISABLED ACCESS: Onestep. Willng to help
GARDEN: Patio & Garden overlooking Churn Valley

Corse Lawn,
Gloucestershire, GL19 4LZ.

Tel: (0452) 780771
Fax: (0452) 780840

CORSE LAWN HOUSE

Country House Hotel & Restaurant with Bistro

Gloucester has its magnificent Cathedral and Tewkesbury has an abbey which is as fine as any cathedral in the country. Both these are equidistant from Corse Lawn House Hotel, a delightful establishment owned and run by an ebullient Frenchman Denis Hine, and his English wife Baba. The essence of success here is the relaxed family atmosphere. It is efficiently run but it is that quality that perhaps allows it to be so informal and jolly. You would be very difficult to please if you were unable to appreciate what Corse Lawn House has to offer.

Corse Lawn was rebuilt in 1745 in the Queen Anne style, after a fire destroyed the earlier building which was a Tudor Inn. In 1745 it was an attractive coaching inn and that charm has been added to with the most recent additions to the house, being very carefully constructed in the old Queen Anne style with the old 'Coach Wash' in the front being retained as an unusual and ornamental pond, around which drinks and light meals are served.

To stay in this beautiful house is a privilege. It has 19 luxury bedrooms, three drawing rooms, two private dining rooms cum conference rooms, a stunningly attractive bar, and, of course, the renowned restaurant. The hotel and restaurant are open seven days a week and they are happy to arrange menus for private parties, small business functions and wedding receptions. Conference facilities for up to 40 delegates are available. With Baba being English and Denis French, they have always provided a fairly mid-Channel selection of food for obvious reasons.

USEFUL INFORMATION

OPEN: All year round
CHILDREN: Yes. Special meals
CREDIT CARDS: All major cards
LICENSED: Full On Licence
ACCOMMODATION: 19 rooms en-suite, two private dining rooms

RESTAURANT: English, modern with French overtones
BAR FOOD: Many dishes available
VEGETARIAN: Vegetarian menu
DISABLED ACCESS: Level entrance, 5 downstairs rooms
GARDEN: Lovely patios & gardens with tables & chairs

BERRYS RESTAURANT

Restaurant

117-119 Southgate Street,
Gloucester, Gloucestershire, GL1 1UT.

Tel: (0452) 520894

USEFUL INFORMATION

OPEN: Tues-Sat: 12-2pm & 7-last orders at 9.30pm. Sunday lunch 12-2pm
CHILDREN: Yes. Children's menu
CREDIT CARDS: Visa/Access/Diners/Amex
LICENSED: Restaurant
ACCOMMODATION: Not applicable

RESTAURANT: Traditional English & Continental cuisine
BAR FOOD: Special bar menu
VEGETARIAN: 3-4 dishes
DISABLED ACCESS: Level entrance, steps to toilet
GARDEN: No

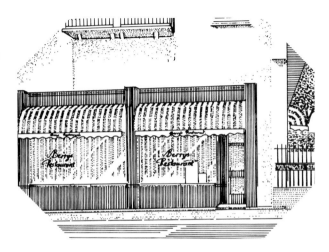

Do not be put off by the fact that this delightful restaurant does not have a car park; you can usually find a space in Spa Road or Llanthony Road close by, or you can walk down from the city centre which is really no distance. Berrys stands on the corner of Southgate Street and Spa Road, a busy locality but the moment you enter the door you are encompassed by a warm, relaxed atmosphere which makes you forget the bustle of the world outside. It is an ideal place to go having spent sometime in the cathedral or exploring the historic docks.

It is a restaurant that is obviously popular with local people; you will see several diners who are immediately on friendly terms with the staff. It does not take the stranger long to become a familiar face in this small and cosy establishment.

At Berry's they specialise in their own home-cooked food using fresh produce whenever possible. The dishes are interesting, especially the House Specials like Chicken Creole or Butterfly Lamb Chop - a double Lamb Chop served with tomatoes stuffed with bacon, onions and parsley. All the main courses are served with a selection of fresh vegetables and potatoes. There are children's meals and simple dishes like Fishermen's Pie and feather light omelettes. For those who are weight conscious crisp salads are available. Vegetarians too will be pleased to know that Berry's has plenty to offer them. Beside the comprehensive menu they offer an excellent two-course lunch. There is no doubt that Berry's will not ask you to dig too deep in your wallet and whatever you have is value for money.

DENMARK HOTEL

Residential Family Hotel

36 Denmark Road,
Gloucester, Gloucestershire, GL1 3JQ.

Tel: (0452) 303808

USEFUL INFORMATION

OPEN: All year round
CHILDREN: Yes, welcome
CREDIT CARDS: Visa/Master/Euro
LICENSED: Not applicable
ACCOMMODATION: 10 rooms, 5 en-suite

RESTAURANT: Residents only. Traditional English
BAR FOOD: Not applicable
VEGETARIAN: On request
DISABLED ACCESS: Level entrance. Ground floor room. Will assist willingly
GARDEN: Private, but large car park

Dawn and David Mallett do not have glossy brochures for this comfortable, family hotel. They rely on word of mouth and a friendly letter to people who enquire about staying here. It is beautifully run and has been awarded three Crowns and approved by the English Tourist Board. It is a small family hotel with 10 bedrooms and it is also the Mallett's home. They do not employ any staff so you are sure of having their undivided personal attention and they certainly have a vested interest in making sure their guests want to return for another visit.

The Mallett Motto is 'Home from Home'. This is something they have worked hard to achieve and it is certainly the impression you get immediately you arrive. There are more up-market hotels but there will be few that can rival the standards here or the prices. The Denmark is situated in a quiet residential area just a few hundred yards from the city centre and extremely convenient for visiting the cathedral. There is a large car park at the hotel which means that you can leave you car here rather than cope with the hassle of parking in the centre - something for which Gloucester is notorious.

Breakfast is a generous meal and one that will certainly set you up for the day. In the evenings there is a table d'hote menu served at 6pm. It is traditional English fare using fresh food and fresh vegetables which are purchased daily. Five of the bedrooms are en-suite.

Kimberley Warehouse, Gloucester Docks,
Gloucester, Gloucestershire, GL1 2ES.

Tel: (0452) 300990

DR FOSTERS
Public House & Restaurant

We take the liberty of quoting 'Gloucester's Very Public Poet' Carol Ann Blackshaw who in 1991 described this extraordinary establishment in verse.

"Doctor Foster came to Gloucester in the pouring rain.
He stepped in a puddle right up to his middle and
swore he would never return again.
Travelling far and wide with home-made medicinal brews in his bags full of herbs,
When his horse shired - he was thrown down a sewer.. he just
climbed back stepping up the kerbs.
But Doctor Foster was really Edward the First known as the
'Forts maker'... he really did care.
He built a castle here and a castle there...
In fact he built them just about everywhere!
In this splendid building - once a warehouse but now
exclusively 'The Doctor Foster'
With a background of glorious serenity in the
tranquillity of the docks here in the city of Gloucester."

It is a fascinating hostelry with a restaurant that seats 100 comfortably. Here you will find good spirits - liquid and human! good food and a cheerful, friendly service from the lively staff. It still has beams that were in the old warehouse, many artefacts including a flour press and a spinning wheel. It is hugely popular with local people and definitely somewhere the visitor should discover.

USEFUL INFORMATION

OPEN: All year
CHILDREN: Yes. Conservatory area of Restaurant
CREDIT CARDS: All major cards
LICENSED: Full On and Off Licence
ACCOMMODATION: Not applicable

RESTAURANT: Home-made - own recipes.
Modern English & International
BAR FOOD: Home-made speicals
VEGETARIAN: Always four dishes in restaurant & bar
DISABLED ACCESS: Yes. WC & ramp
GARDEN: Conservatory & courtyard - spacious

---

93 Hucclecote Road,
Hucclecote, Gloucestershire, GL3 3TR.

Tel: (0452) 611584

NOTLEY HOUSE & COACH HOUSE
Guest House

To find this admirable guest house locate the A417 to the east of the city. Follow signs to Gloucester Trading Estate, at the roundabout by the estate is Hucclecote Road, five minutes from the M5. Notley House was established four years ago by Alyn and Jaki George. It had once been one of the seven private schools which existed in the Hucclecote area.

The Georges had the talent and the discernment to retain the character of the house with its cottage and beam appearance. Fully aware that today's visitors are demanding in their desire for modern facilities, these have been introduced wherever possible and the seven bedrooms are each equipped with a private shower and most have a toilet en-suite. It did not take very long before they received their first guests, and for the name of Notley House to become synonymous with warmth and comfort, delicious, innovative food and a friendly atmosphere.

Children are very welcome at Notley Guest House. Cots and highchairs are available free of charge. You are welcome to use the ironing board, a hair dryer and shoe cleaning equipment. The most recent addition to this successful business is the development of the two level coach house which is situated in the grounds. This new high standard accommodation makes an ideal relocation base for business people moving into the area. It would be equally good for a romantic weekend or perhaps for a honeymoon - with champagne provided by the Georges! You might wish to take advantage of one of the four-poster bedroom suites for such a special occasion. The award of the 'Three Crowns' highly commended for quality by the English Tourist Board is well deserved. The price is reasonable and the food delicious.

USEFUL INFORMATION

OPEN: All year round
CHILDREN: Yes. Special meals if required
CREDIT CARDS: All major cards except Amex
LICENSED: None. Bring your own wine
ACCOMMODATION: 6 rooms plus coach house including 2 four-posters. No pets. Non smoking rooms

RESTAURANT: Not applicable - residents only
BAR FOOD: Not applicable
VEGETARIAN: Yes. Breakfast & meals
DISABLED ACCESS: No
GARDEN: Lovely garden. Grass lawns

139

HAW BRIDGE INN
Country Pub

Haw Bridge, Tirley,
Gloucestershire, GL19 4HJ.

Tel: (0452) 780316

USEFUL INFORMATION

OPEN: Mon-Sat: 11-3pm & 6-11pm,
Sun: 12-2.30pm & 7-10.30pm
CHILDREN: Well behaved
CREDIT CARDS: None taken
LICENSED: Full On Licence
ACCOMMODATION: Small, beautifully
laid out, touring caravan area

RESTAURANT: Wide, imaginative.
A la crte
BAR FOOD: Vast choice. Daily specials
VEGETARIAN: 3-4 dishes daily
DISABLED ACCESS: Slight step. Willing
to assist
GARDEN: Yes. Extenisve seating

Idyllic is not a word to be used lightly but in the case of the setting of the Haw Bridge Inn at Tirley, it is exactly the adjective to describe it. Nestling on the banks of the River Severn, it lies some 8 miles from Gloucester Cathedral, approximately 8 miles from Regency Cheltenham and not so many miles from the splendour of Tewkesbury Abbey.

Built in 1622 and with deeds that go back to 1749 The Haw Bridge Inn has been lovingly and painstakingly redesigned and refurbished in the caring hands of Richard and Mavis Pope over the last five years. They have achieved their goal without losing one iota of the old world charm that has always been so much a part of the inn. Richard's association with horses is evident in the cosy bar area which has a massive open fire in the lounge end and a super wood burner at the other. Just off the lounge up a few steps is 'The Pink Room', an intimate little restaurant with 17 covers and somewhere in which one can enjoy a relaxed meal from the first class a la carte menu. There is a function room which sometimes becomes a restaurant.

The food is imaginative and the choice of dishes wide ranging from Daily Specials which include Kidneys in Madeira Sauce, Game Casserole and many other favourites. Roast Lamb with mint and rosemary is one of the most popular joints on the menu served with a selection of no less than eight vegetables. Finally, do ask how the marmalade cat is. He is absolutely massive and is not allowed in during opening hours. His size is due to the quality of the scraps according to Mavis Pope. This pub really does have something to please everyone.

NATURE IN ART
Museum

Wallsworth Hall, Twigworth,
Gloucester, Gloucestershire, GL2 9PA.

Tel: (0452) 731422
Fax: (0452) 730937

USEFUL INFORMATION

OPEN: Tues-Sun: 10-5pm and Bank
Holidays. Closed December 24-26th
CHILDREN: Welcome
CREDIT CARDS: None
LICENSED: Restaurant
ACCOMMODATION: Not applicable

RESTAURANT: Delightful home-made
meals and snacks served all day
BAR FOOD: Not applicable
VEGETARIAN: A selection
DISABLED ACCESS: Yes
GARDEN: Nature garden and pond.
Play area. Life size sculptures

Wallsworth Hall is the home of Nature in Art, The centre for international wildlife art, the world's first museum dedicated exclusively to art inspired by nature. Its unrivalled collection is constantly growing. At the start of 1993 it embraced work in all media from over 40 countries by around 400 artists spanning 1,500 years. The ever changing exhibits are unique in scope, appeal and stature. A regular programme of temporary exhibitions, also of truly international standards, and loan exhibits from other collections around the world, ensure that a visit to Wallsworth Hall is a stimulating experience for all those interested in art and wildlife. Complementing the fine exhibits is a unique programme of artists in residence from home and abroad who, between February and November, work in the studios demonstrating a huge variety of media.

Nature in Art is a winner of Special Commendation in the National Heritage Museum of the Year awards. It is fully accessible to wheelchair users, has ample free parking, a licensed coffee shop, a well stocked museum shop and a membership scheme. Groups are welcome by arrangement both during the day and evening. A successful and comprehensive range of educational services is also offered to schools and groups of young people. From the grandeur of the wildlife landscape to the detail of oriental treasures; from the best in contemporary sculpture to the complexity of the ancient mosaic; from the variety of the early illustrations to present day abstract interpretations; from the intricacy of glass engraving to giant nature canvases, you will be enthralled by this collection.

Withington, Cheltenham,
Gloucestershire, GL54 4BN.

Tel: (0242) 890238
Fax: (0242) 890332

HALEWELL CLOSE
Private Guest House

This is a fascinating establishment. It belonged to the church until the late 1920's and was closely aligned to the convent and monastery across the road for many moons before that. The word 'Close' in its true form would be Cloister. It has a tranquil quality about it that has perhaps been inbred over the years but much of it is because of the serenity of the present owner Mrs Elizabeth Carey-Wilson who runs it with an unerring sense of what her guests will like.

Halewell is essentially a home and everything about it tells you that it is to be regarded as such. It is relaxed, friendly and without any tiresome rules. It is small but because of the way in which the house is designed it is possible to provide a private suite for three adults with a double room, a single room and bathroom. There is another for double and single occupancy with a dressing rooms en-suite for family groups. If you would like to bring your dog with you, please let them know in advance.

Fishing can be arranged at £20 per day and a Thames River Board Licence is required. With Gloucester Cathedral, Worcester Cathedral and Tewkesbury Abbey so close, it is an ideal place to stay for those who enjoy ecclesiastical perfection. Race-goers will certainly appreciate its convenience for the Cheltenham meetings and it would be a wonderful place to spend Christmas. Elizabeth Carey-Wilson does all the cooking and her food is traditional. It is for residents only but you are welcome to invite guests by prior arrangement. They will envy you your choice of Guest House.

USEFUL INFORMATION

OPEN: All year round
CHILDREN: Welcome. Dogs by prior arrangement
CREDIT CARDS: Access/Visa/Amex
LICENSED: Residential Licence
ACCOMMODATION: Rooms & suites

RESTAURANT: Dining en famille for residents
BAR FOOD: Not applicable
VEGETARIAN: Not applicable
DISABLED ACCESS: Level entrance. Special bedroom, complies with Social Services
GARDEN: 50 acres

Guildford Cathedral

Guildford

"Let me enjoy ... no less
Because that all-enacting Might
That fashioned forth its loveliness
Had other aims than my delight"

Thomas Hardy

The City of Guildford

by John Theobald

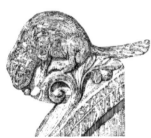

Guildford is the largest and most important town in Surrey and is a happy marriage of the ancient and modern, old buildings in its busy streets harmonising with 20th century commerce. It was a borough a thousand years ago. Its lovely Cathedral on Stag Hill was consecrated long after the end of World War II.

The Saxons built a settlement here, the Normans constructed a castle, and its 20th century citizens built both the Cathedral and a spanking theatre. It has long been a prosperous place ready to pay homage to the church, commerce and the arts and they are all reflected in its steep High Street which has been described as one of the finest in Southern England.

Here are the gabled merchant's houses, a magnificent 17th century town hall and almshouses and a grammar school with a medieval chained library. All are in the heart of a superb shopping area and important business and administrative centre.

In Jeffries Passage just off the High Street is CHAPPLE'S a splendid wine bar. It is a comfortable place and has a degree of intimacy that makes it especially pleasant for those who want a quiet drink and a simple meal.

Particularly welcome after exploring Guildford. It is not always easy to put one's finger on the one ingredient that makes a wine bar, or indeed any other establishment, remain in one's mind. In the case of Chapples it is several different things but none so important as the friendliness with which one is greeted. You will never feel a stranger here for long. There is always a contented buzz from the chatter going on, sometimes from the regulars who know Chapples well but more often a combination of those who have just discovered the bar, talking to habitues.

Guildford Cathedral stands on Stag Hill and with its clean and simple lines, this red brick edifice looms over the River Wey and the campus of the University of Surrey. It is only the second Anglican Cathedral to be built on a new site since Henry the Eighth's reformation and one of four Cathedrals built in the 20th century. The land was presented by the Earl of Onslow, of nearby Clandon Park, after the formation of the new diocese in the 1920's and Sir Edward Maufe was appointed as the architect in 1933.

I remember going on a guided tour of the shell of the Cathedral of the Holy Spirit way before it was finally consecrated in 1961 and it has played a prominent role in the life of the borough and the county since.

The simple Gothic style of the exterior conceals many glories. Among the work decorating it is Eric Gill's St John the Bapist outside the south transept, and the sculpture around the circular east window. There are other stone carvings by a number of artists. The bronze Great West Doors have glass engraved by John Hutton, who engraved the glass screen at Coventry Cathedral.

The font was carved by Alan Collins and there is stained glass by Moira Forsyth and Rosemary Rutherford.

The great Guildford sanctuary carpet was designed by the architect who used honey coloured stone for the interior and floors of marble.

You have an immediate impression of lightness and cool grandeur and of vast high acres. There are free tours each day by knowledgeable guides and a video programme about the Cathedral. A gift shop and a refectory restaurant are open daily, as is a brass rubbing centre. You are welcome at the services. The Cathedral is open each day from 8.30 am to 5.30 pm.

Now back to the town. Let us walk along that cobbled High Street with its 18th century air and some magnificent buildings.

At its top is Guildford Grammar School which has one of the country's three surviving medieval chained libraries - the books were chained to prevent theft. It was founded in 1507 by a wealthy merchant and endowed by Edward the Sixth and its distinguished scholars include a number of bishops and one Speaker of the

House of Commons. The Royal Grammar School, to give it is proper title, is open by appointment.

THE HOSPITAL OF THE BLESSED TRINITY has a massive Tudor facade and super Jacobean architecture. Known as the Abbot's Hospital, it was founded in 1619 by George Abbot, Archbishop of Canterbury, as almshouses. The Archbishop had been born in Guildford and he is commemorated by a Latin inscription in the dining room which, translated, reads, we call Abbot our father. The whole nation owes the Archbishop a debt for he was one of the translators of the magnificent King James Bible. The dress of the male residents is a Tudor hat and a coat bearing the Abbot's emblems.

There are guided tours by arrangement and you will see some beautiful stained glass in the Chapel. GUILDFORD HOUSE was built in 1660 as a private residence but for more than a hundred years has been used for commercial purposes.

Across the road is TUNSATE ARCH which was once the facade of the corn market. The outstanding building in the High Street is, of course, THE GUILDHALL with that huge gilded clock reaching over the street. The Guildhall's exterior is 17th century but it hides a lovely 16th century structure. The court room has its original panelling and stained glass windows. From this building the borough was governed, justice administered and fires fought, for its entrance was used as a fire station.

There are free guided tours of the Guildhall every Tuesday and Thursday afternoon when you will learn more of its history and be able to see its civic treasures. There are guided tours from Tunsgate Arch which take in all of the borough's most interesting features. They are arranged during the summer months and you should enquire at the Tourist Information Centre for precise details.

But, we will continue on our own tour which now takes in the MEDIEVAL UNDERCROFT in which the Information Centre is housed. It dates from the 13th century and English Heritage has called it the finest medieval building of its kind. This was once a shop under a wealthy merchant's house and across the road is another fine undercroft. This is now part of the lovely ANGEL HOTEL, the only remaining coaching house for which Guildford, lying on the important route from London to Portsmouth, was famous.

It was in the equivalent of a 17th century Good Pub Guide. John Taylor, the poet who wrote it, was once a publican in Oxford and London so was a good judge.

Across the road is the Angel Gate, a good example of the narrow passage ways called gates in Guildford. This one leads to a courtyard in which there are some delightful shops. Back in the High Street you can turn into Chapel Street just below the Medieval Undercroft and it will take you to the CASTLE KEEP and CASTLE GROUNDS. Only the Keep, 70 feet high and walls up to 14 feet thick, built by Henry II, remains of the royal castle where Edward I and his Queen Eleanor, often stayed. At its entrance three wall plaques show how the castle looked, and there is a sundial featuring the royal couple. Plaques and sundial were sculptured by a local artist. The castle grounds are beautiful and are a lovely leisure area.

One feature is a giant open air chess board. In them, too, stands a statue of Alice in Wonderland, whose creator, the Reverend Charles Dodgson, better known as Lewis Carroll, frequently stayed at The Chestnuts on Castle Hill, the home of his sisters. He preached at St Mary's Church which is on the way back to the High Street.

The baptistry and the font

Characters from his classic story are featured on a memorial plaque outside the house, which is privately owned and is not open to the public. The author spent the last years of his life here where he died in 1898. He is buried nearby. There is a fascinating collection of letters by him and other relics in the GUILDFORD MUSEUM in Quarry Street.

The museum is in one of a number of old houses in this interesting street. It stands beside the Castle Gateway which is believed to be 13th century and is a scheduled ancient monument. This house was built in 1630 and as well as being the borough museum is the headquarters of the Surrey Archaelogical Society.

In the Muniment Room there are over 100,000 documents relating to the area. In CASTLE CLIFFE GARDENS, which you enter from Castle Hill, excavations have uncovered a royal apartment and part of a ditch that may have protected the castle. There is evidence here of other royal buildings.

Racks Close off these gardens takes its name from the wool trade which brought such prosperity to Guildford and it was here that the cloth was dried on racks after it had been dyed.

Walk back past The Chestnuts and into Quarry Street and past the museum and the Castle Arc and admire the gabled buildings as you walk down to ST MARY'S CHURCH. In Rosemary Alley clay pipes on display in the museum used to be baked in a kiln here.

St Mary's Church tower is Saxon but most of it is Norman. The church and the keep are the borough's two oldest buildings.

Back along Millbrook are the TOWN MILL and the YVONNE ARNAUD THEATRE. There were four mills from Saxon times until the end of the last century and a fuller's mill harnessed the water here. Later after the death of the cloth trade it became a corn mill.

The foundation stone laid in 1936 to the holy spirit: a dedication unique amongst English cathedrals

Across the channel is the Yvonne Arnaud Theatre, one of the best known provincial theatres in which West End stars regularly appear. The productions for 1993, for instance, end with the pantomime Peter Pan starring Brian Blessed as Captain Hook and Toyah Wilcox as Peter in Barrie's classic entertainment. The theatre overlooks the River Wey and has a first class, elegant ground floor restaurant serving lunch and dinner. It is open to non-theatre goers and Figaro's the Italian-style restaurant on the top floor with a piano bar has a varied menu for those lunching or dining.

Near the junction of Millbrook and Quarry Street is the GUILDFORD BOAT HOUSE where you can get waterborne and explore the peaceful waters of the Wey Navigation. You can hire craft ranging from rowing boat to a narrow canal boat or dine on a cruiser. Some 20 miles of the river are owned and administered by the National Trust and there are 12 locks, river and canal which make a lovely leisure area. The waterways were once important trade routes between the town and London and are now a sanctuary for wild flowers and bird-life.

Back in the town let us have a look at the North Street area. The CLOTH HALL behind Abbot's Hospital was also built by Archbishop Abbot to provide jobs for medieval cloth workers. Guildford market is held in North Street on Fridays and Saturdays. At the bottom of North Street is the FRIARY CENTRE, where a Dominican religious house once stood. It is now an excellent shopping centre. It is one of several good shopping centres.

In addition to the Yvonne Arnaud Theatre, where plays are tried out before going to the West End, Guildford is host to an arts festival in July, a music festival and a book festival.

The CIVIC HALL is the home of the Guildford Philharmonic Orchestra and concerts and other entertainments are staged throughout the year. You should visit GALLERY 90 in Ward Street where exhibitions of every type of art are held. Admission is free.

There are recitals at the University and the Cathedral and concerts and other events at National Trust properties in the area. Before leaving the town THE MUSEUM OF THE WOMEN'S ROYAL ARMY CORPS in Queen Elizabeth Park should be visited. Among the items devoted to the Corps is the uniform the Queen wore when she was a member in World War II.

Guildford is set in glorious countryside with the North Downs providing magnificent walks, and there are many beautiful villages close at hand and some outstanding houses and gardens. The countryside here was discovered in the 19th century by ramblers and hikers in the London area for it could easily be reached from the metropolis.

Men of letters in Victorian times led the way with Carlyle, Robert Louis Stevenson, Hilaire Belloc and George Meredith among them: it is a tradition that continues. First among the great houses in the area and as close at hand as any is CLANDON PARK, an outstanding National Trust property in West Clandon just outside Guildford on its east.

It began as an Elizabethan manor and was then transformed by the Venetian architect Giacomo Leoni for the second Lord Onslow into the classical Palladian mansion you see today.

Its real riches are its interior, in particular the two-storey marble hall, one of the most impressive rooms created in the 18th century. There is a fine collection of furniture, paintings and other valuables and in its basement is THE MUSEUM OF THE QUEEN'S ROYAL SURREY REGIMENT with a fine display of weapons and medals. There is a restaurant and shop and you should check with 0483 222482 for opening times. The park was landscaped by Capability Brown.

Adjacent to Clandon Park is a splendid hostelry which is instantly recognisable in summer by its beautiful and colourful hanging baskets. THE BULLS HEAD was built in 1530 and as soon as one enters, the atmosphere of years is endorsed by the presence of beamed low ceilings and cosy bars. It must have always been a contented place to enjoy a drink and the present landlords, Brian and Sylvia Wheeler have made sure the tradition of centuries continues.

Just off the A2246 at **East Clandon** is HATCHLANDS, another National Trust property. Its handsome exterior has superb interiors by Robert Adam, a remarkable collection of keyboard instruments and a splendid garden. For opening times telephone 0483 222482.

Eight further miles along the A246 is POLESDEN LACEY at **Great Bookham**. This beautiful Regency house standing on land owned by the playwright Richard Brinsley Sheridan was from 1906 to 1942 the home of the Hon Mrs Ronnie Greville, a leading society hostess of her time. She was extremely wealthy, an appalling snob and often abominably rude but her guests included many members of the Royal Family.

The Queen Mother and her husband, George VI, spent their honeymoon here. It is also a National Trust property, with a magnificent collection of exquisite valuables and antiques. An open air theatre season is held in its extensive grounds in the summer.

LOSELEY HOUSE just off the A3100 road to **Godalming** is still privately owned. Sir William More, a kinsman of the martyred Sir Thomas More had this house built in the 1560's and set it in a beautiful park. His descendants, the More-Molyneeux family, still live here and welcome visitors and the income they bring, that enables the glorious house with its lovely ceilings, Elizabethan panelling from a royal palace, fine furniture and tapestries, to survive.

The owners describe it as a family home and country house with a friendly atmosphere. There are tours of the house, and tours of the farms, where 700 Jersey cattle graze in 1400 acres of pasture and woodland, on foot and by tractor and trailer. There is a farm shop selling dairy, cereal and meat products. The restaurant is in a magnificent tithe barn which adjoins the house.

For information on opening times and all tours telephone 0483 505501.

The nearby village of **Compton** is considered to be one of the most beautiful of villages and it is here you will find THE WATTS GALLERY, which commemorates the paintings and sculpture of the Victorian artist G.F. Watts who lies in a remarkable art nouveau chapel nearby. Part of the old potteries where the gallery is housed also has a charming TEA SHOP where you can enjoy delicious food in pleasant surroundings which are enhanced in summer by the opportunity of sitting at a table outside marveling at the fabulous

Part of the children's window in the "Children's Chapel"

countryside with The Pilgrim's Way next door. This runs, as it has for centuries from Winchester to Canterbury. The Potteries were famed for many years for their terracotta pottery and tombstones. To this day there are terracotta candelabras from the potteries in Adelaide Cathedral in Australia.

THE MARY WOND-RAUSCH POTTERY is also in this lovely village and a shop sells the 17th century style earthern-ware pottery.

ST NICHOLAS CHURCH is Norman with fascinating and unique features that make it one of the most important churches in the county. Its west tower is Saxon and there is a Norman screen below a tow-storey chancel, and a carving scratched on a chancel pillar of a Norman soldier.

Looking for somewhere to stay which would suit parents with young children I was recommended to THE SQUIRRELS RESTAURANT AND COUNTRY HOTEL at **Hurtmore** near Godalming. It was a dislike for the manner in which David and Jane Barnes were treated as guests in hotels and particularly as parents of young children that made them determined to oprate this refreshing establishment with a standard of service that they themselves require. Squirrels is everything that anyone could wish for and far more than somewhere in which to stay and have a good meal. The welcome counts for a lot and there are the well equipped bedrooms, each of which has a unique character. Eight of them are in a row of restored 17th century cottages and the rest in the main building. In winter an open fire throws out a welcoming warmth in the cosy lounge where a profusion of books and board games is available. All sorts of activities can be organised from hot air ballooning to wine tasting. HURTMORE GOLF CLUB surrounds Squirrels on three sides.

There are a number of other excellent establishments in this area. For example LE BERGER in the High Street at **Bramley**, owned and run by Peter and Mary Hirth. An inspired chef with a lot of experience, Peter had always dreamt of having his own restaurant. That dream is now reality and he has delighted many people with his imaginative and innovative dishes. The restaurant is charming and on a summer's day it is very pleasant to have a drink in the pretty garden complete with a babbling brook.

A little way south is the delightful village of **Dunsfold** surrounded by some beautiful country, ideal for walking. There, overlooking the cricket green is THE SUN INN, a happy mix of 15th, 17th and 18th century architecture. This is an inn which has dispensed hospitality for centuries and continues that tradition today in the capable hands of Judith Dunne. It is a pub beloved by the locals and a regular haunt for people who come from quite a distance to enjoy its food, drink and hospitality.

At **Haslemere** THE LYTHE HILL HOTEL on the Petworth Road stands in 20 acres of glorious grounds with lovely views over the Blackdown Hills. It is a fascinating ancient house listed as an historic monument which has remained unspoilt for 600 years. The early

history of the house is conjectural, but the half-timbered work of the early part of the building is of the late 14th century. It was in 1580 that the east wing was added, presenting a striking contrast, with its square and circle patterned timbering, to the earlier part. The fact that it has been brought so beautifully into the 20th century with all its demands for modern conveniences, is a tribute to the caring owners. The house is warm, comfortable and the food in the hands of a talented continental chef is outstanding. The wines are equally superb.

Within a few miles of Lythe Hill there is polo at Cowdray Park, racing at **Goodwood** and **Sandown**. Portsmouth has its famous ships lying alongside, the Farnborough Air Show is not far off and Guildford with its splendid Cathedral is just twelve miles. There are several golf courses, riding stables, hunting and fishing available in the immediate neighbourhood.

I have always had a great liking for **Petersfield** which is south of Guildford. It is a nice old town and has its fair ratio of attractive buildings. It was therefore not surprising to find THE DONKEY CART RESTAURANT housed in a 16th century Tudor building in the square. Not only does it offer good food at reasonable prices all day long, it also has a banqueting hall where you are invited to attend a Medieval feast. Such an occasion is memorable and if you wish to attend in costume then they can arrange for you to hire

To the north of Guildford is **Cobham** and THE CRICKETERS. Traditional pubs are at a premium and one is lucky to find such a good example as this one. Cobham is only ten miles from Guildford and it is well worthwhile making the effort to drive here. The

Cricketers answers everyone's dream of a country pub with its low beams, many horse brasses and in winter, a large open fire with crackling logs that waft into the air their unmistakable smell. Wonderful.

One of the great joys about visiting Guildford, apart from the glories of the cathedral and the attractive town, is the ease with which one can reach many places. The countryside is stunning and yet it is no distance to **London**, **Portsmouth**, **Winchester**, **Chichester** or **Salisbury**. A plethora of cathedral magnificence to enjoy or maybe too much when seen one after the other. For me it is always the aftermath that I especially relish, when I can mull over all that I have seen, stimulate my memory with the aid of the various books and postcards I have purchased in each House of God. How lucky we are with this wonderful heritage.

LE BERGER
Restaurant

4a The High Street, Bramley,
Nr Guildford, Surrey, GU5 0HB.

Tel: (0483) 894037

The bustling village of Bramley is sited some three miles south of Guildford and in the heart of the village lies Le Berger, a particularly special restaurant run by Peter and Mary Hirth. Peter began his career as an apprentice with the Roux brothers at the Waterside Inn restaurant at Bray. When he was 25 and working as chef-de-partie at the Gavroche in London he was recommended to the Rothschild family who were seeking a 'young chef with inspiration', within a short time he set up and is still running a successful city outside-catering business renowned for high quality and beautifully presented food.

In 1988 Peter's dream came true when he and Mary opened Le Berger. Intimate and beautifully appointed, this delightful restaurant has 24 covers, you can therefore confidently expect individual attention. To the rear of the restaurant, french doors take you onto a terrace area and charming garden complete with a babbling brook, it is a delightful spot for a quiet evening drink.

The menu and wine list are both extensive and imaginative. All food is prepared using only fresh, raw ingredients, predominantly from France, fish is delivered daily from the French fish markets. Peter even bakes bread and makes home-made ice-cream. Menus are changed monthly and Peter holds gastronomic evenings every few weeks. This is a place where you can really wine and dine at leisure, every carefully prepared dish is presented with a flair worthy of a picture in a glossy magazine. This special restaurant deserved more than one visit as every dish chosen promises to delight. Le Berger was chosen as County Restaurant of the Year in the Good Food Guide in 1991, a worthy winner

USEFUL INFORMATION

OPEN: Tue-Sat: 7-9.30pm. Lunches by prior
    booking
CHILDREN: Well behaved welcome
CREDIT CARDS: All Major cards
LICENSED: Full On Licence
ACCOMMODATION: Not applicable

RESTAURANT: Haute cuisine. Menu
    changes monthly
BAR FOOD: None available
VEGETARIAN: As requested
DISABLED ACCESS: Yes. Willing to
    assist
GARDEN: Attractive secluded garden
    with patio

THE CRICKETERS
Public House

Downside, Cobham,
Surrey, KT11 3NX.

Tel: (0932) 862105
Fax: (0932) 868186

Traditional pubs are at a premium and one is lucky to find such a good example as The Cricketers at Cobham just ten miles from Guildford with its magnificent Cathedral. It is an attractive area and the pub is well known not only to locals but also many people who drive out especially to enjoy its friendly, welcoming hospitality. The Cricketers answers everyone's dream of a country pub with its low beams, many horse brasses and in winter a large open fire with crackling logs that send into the air that unmistakable smell.

Brian and Wendy Luxford are mine hosts and it is their talent for innkeeping that undoubtedly makes it such a sought after venue. The buffet offers a very extensive range of hot and cold snacks with changing daily dishes and seasonal specials. The experienced chef makes every possible use of what is available in the market and his dishes have the touch of a man who loves his profession. Dining in the elegant restaurant with its exposed brickwork is sheer pleasure. The tables are immaculately laid, shining silver and sparkling cut glass add the finishing touches. The menu mixes English and Continental styles, with starters such as creamy courgette and stilton soup, avocado and crab thermidor, or cornets of smoked salmon filled with cream cheese and chives. Typical of the main courses on offer is Veal Amaretto, escallop of veal in amaretta liquer with tomatoes and sultanas and glazed with mozzarella cheese. Several fresh fish choices include a delicious Sole Waleska. If, after such delicious starters and main courses you can bear to look at the Dessert Trolley you will find it laden with almost irresistible delicacies.

USEFUL INFORMATION

OPEN: Mon-Sat: 11-2.30pm & 6-11pm
    Sun: 12-2.30pm & 7-10.30pm
CHILDREN: Well behaved welcome
CREDIT CARDS: All major cards taken
LICENSED: Full On Licence
ACCOMMODATION: Not applicable

RESTAURANT: Wide ranging.
    Innovative. Specials according to
    market availability
BAR FOOD: Extensive Bar Menu
VEGETARIAN: 3-4 daily. Others
    on request
DISABLED ACCESS: Yes. Always
    willing to assist
GARDEN: Patio Area

THE TEA SHOP

Tea Shop

The Old Potteries, Watts Gallery, Down Lane,
Compton, Nr Guildford, Surrey, GU3 1DQ.

Tel: (0483) 811030

USEFUL INFORMATION

OPEN: Mon-Sun: 10.30-5.30pm
CHILDREN: Well behaved
CREDIT CARDS: None taken
LICENSED: Not licenced
ACCOMMODATION: Not applicable

RESTAURANT: Tea Room. All home-made food
BAR FOOD: Not applicable
VEGETARIAN: Always catered for
DISABLED ACCESS: Willing to assist
GARDEN: Next door to Pilgrim's Way, Winchester to Canterbury

The sleepy village of Compton is situated but a 15 minute drive from the centre of Guildford and nestling in the leafy woods at one end of the village is The Tea Shop. Here Sally Porter and her daughter Catherine and son, Timothy, run the tearoom which is at the heart of The Old Potteries. These Potteries for many years were famed for their terracotta pottery and tombstones and is known worldwide. To this day there are terracotta candelabras from the Potteries in Adelaide Cathedral in Australia.

The Tea Shop has room for 170 visitors during good weather when one is able to marvel at the beautiful countryside from your table in the open air and right next door is The Pilgrim's Way which runs from Winchester to Canterbury. The whole area is steeped in history and just begging to be explored. On an inclement day the inside is cosy and comfortable. Sally Porter is a mine of information and never too busy to spare time for her customers.

An exceptionally varied menu is something that the Tea Shop is renowned for. Absolutely everything is home-made even down to the jam! There are items on offer to suit all tastes and very realistically priced. It is a splendid place in which to spend a morning or afternoon in the tranquillity of this delightful setting, yet still so close to the heart of Guildford. Many visitors find their way here after revelling in the majesty and architectural beauty of Guildford Cathedral.

THE SUN INN

Inn

The Common, Dunsfold,
Surrey, GU8 4LE.

Tel: (0483) 200242

USEFUL INFORMATION

OPEN: 11-3pm & 6-11pm. Normal Sunday hours
CHILDREN: Yes
CREDIT CARDS: Master/Barclay/Amex
LICENSED: Full
ACCOMMODATION: Not applicable

RESTAURANT: Not applicable
BAR FOOD: Good blackboard menu. Charcoal Grill, home-cooked
VEGETARIAN: Always avaiable
DISABLED ACCESS: Level access
GARDEN: Beer garden. BBQ's & spit roasts

Dunsfold is a pretty village surrounded by some beautiful country walks and overlooking the Cricket Green, is The Sun Inn, a happy mixture of 15th, 17th and 18th century architecture. This is an inn which has been dispensing hospitality for centuries. At one time it was a stopping point for the Portsmouth to London coaches. One can still imagine the busy atmosphere which would have prevailed as a coach pulled in with its horses champing at the bit, and its weary passengers only too happy to dismount and take sustenance inside its welcoming doors.

In the friendly hands of Judith Dunne, The Sun still offers that warmth of hospitality. It is a pub much loved by the locals and finding a great deal of favour with the many people who come from quite a distance to enjoy its atmosphere. There are always 4 Real Ales and the wine list is one of the most interesting in the neighbourhood. In addition to the familiar European wines there is a plethora of New World wines as well.

Food is always important and Judith Dunne recognises the fact that people like home-cooking. This you will certainly find at The Sun with a whole range of favourite dishes available daily, as well as Charcoal Grills. Fresh Fish is added to the list at weekends. The Garden in summer attracts many people especially for the informal Barbecues and Spit Roasts. You will see the road opposite the pub is cobblestoned - another reminder of the old days, for it was here the carriages were cleaned.

SQUIRRELS RESTAURANT & COUNTRY HOTEL
Restaurant & Country Hotel

Hurtmore, Nr Godalming,
Surrey, GU7 2RN.

Tel: (0483) 860223
Fax: (0483) 860592

A dislike for the manner in which David and Jane Barnes were treated as guests in hotels, and particularly as parents of young children made them quite determined to operate this refreshing establishment with a standard of service that they themselves require. Squirrels is everything that anyone could wish for and far more than just somewhere in which to have a good meal. The welcome counts for a lot and then there are the well-equipped bedrooms, each of which has a unique character. Eight of them are in a row of restored 17th century cottages and the rest in the main building. In winter an open fire throws out a welcoming warmth in the cosy lounge where a profusion of books and board games is available. Hot-air ballooning, laser shooting, croquet parties, wine tastings and theme days and nights are some of the regularly arranged events for the enjoyment of guests. Hurtmore Golf Club surrounds Squirrels on three sides. Temporary membership can be arranged at a nearby health club. There is a good, safe children's play area, baby listening service, a stock of baby essentials and a 'Rumpus' room provided at weekends.

The restaurant is open seven days a week for breakfast, lunch and dinner and has an ever changing menu with dishes that will suit all tastes and ages. The house speciality is 'stone cooking' - a delicious style of table-top cooking which always entertains the partaker. The wine list is well chosen. You can elect to dine in the Cellar with its wine memorabilia or the Bunker with its golfing paraphernalia.

USEFUL INFORMATION

OPEN: 7am for breakfast + 8am on Sat
Mon-Fri: 11-3pm & 6-11pm. Sun: 12-3pm & 7-10.30pm
CHILDREN: Very welcome. Children's room.Changing facilities
CREDIT CARDS: All major cards
LICENSED: Full On Licence
ACCOMMODATION: Yes. Delightful en-suite bedrooms

RESTAURANT: A la carte & table d'hote
BAR FOOD: Extensive range
VEGETARIAN: Choice on all courses
DISABLED ACCESS: Yes, willing to assist
GARDEN: Play area for children

CHAPPLES
Wine Bar

8/9 Jeffries Passage, Guildford,
Surrey, GL1 4AP.

Tel: (0483) 35025

Chapples has an immediate ambience as you walk through the doors. It is very comfortable and has a degree of intimacy that makes it especially pleasant for those who want a quiet drink and a simple meal. Chapples is easily found in a walkway from the main High Street to North Square.

It is not always easy to put one's finger on the one ingredient that makes a wine bar, or indeed any other establishment, remain in one's mind. In the case of Chapples it is several different things but none so important as the friendliness with which one is greeted. You will never feel a stranger here for long. There is always a contented buzz of chatter going on, sometimes from local people who know Chapples well but more often a combination of those who have just discovered the bar, talking to regulars.

The food is a happy mixture of Continental and English dishes. Huevos Ensalada Caliente - curried eggs in mayonnaise with a crisp salad or Deep Fried Camembert perhaps, Chapples Pommes du Terre - potato jackets with a difference, served with soured cream and chives dip with all sorts of different and delectable fillings. Maybe you are an Ensalada worshipper in which case the selection of fillings is delicious and served with salads, French bread or cornbread. There are pastas galore, steaks and chicken. In fact a very good menu at sensible prices.

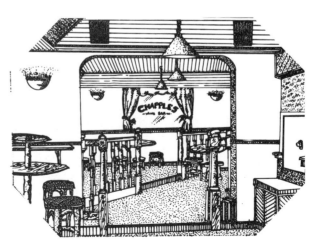

USEFUL INFORMATION

OPEN: Mon-Thurs: 11-3pm & 5.30-11pm, Fri-Sat: 11-11pm, closed Sundays
CHILDREN: Saturday lunchtime only
CREDIT CARDS: Access/Visa/Master/Amex
LICENSED: Restaurant Licence
ACCOMMODATION: Not applicable

RESTAURANT: Interesting English/Continental/Mexican
BAR FOOD: Daily Specials plus a wide range
VEGETARIAN: At least 6 daily
DISABLED ACCESS: No
GARDEN: Not applicable

LYTHE HILL HOTEL

Hotel

Petworth Road, Haslemere,
Nr Guildford, Surrey, GU27 3BQ.

Tel: (0428) 651251
Fax: (0428) 644131

USEFUL INFORMATION

OPEN: All year
CHILDREN: Yes. Cots & extra beds if required
CREDIT CARDS: All major cards except Diners
LICENSED: Full On Licence
ACCOMMODATION: 40 en-suite rooms including 14 suites. Pets permitted. Purpose built Conference Suites

RESTAURANT: Classic French in 'Auberge de France' Imaginative English fayre in dining room
BAR FOOD: Not applicable
VEGETARIAN: Made to order as required
DISABLED ACCESS: No
GARDEN: 20 acres. Several eating areas etc

With lovely views over the Blackdown Hills and far across Sussex and the South Downs, lying in 20 acres of glorious grounds, Lythe Hill Hotel and Restaurant is an experience enjoyed by people from all over the world, and one that should not be missed. It is a fascinating ancient house listed as a historic monument which has remained unspoilt for 600 years. The early history of the house is conjectural, but the half-timbered work of the early part of the building is of the late 14th century. It was about 1580 that the East Wing was added, presenting a striking contrast, with its square and circle patterned timbering, to the earlier part. It is presumed locally that in the 18th century the premises were used as a court-house, and in the dining room is the bench set into the wall, where the miscreants sat awaiting trial. Antiques furnish the house throughout, and a large collection of Copper and Pewter, match the old oak beams, and the genuine oak panelling of the house.

The fact that it has been brought so beautifully into the 20th century with all its demands for modern conveniences, is a tribute to the caring owners. The house is warm and comfortable and has outstanding views over Blackdown Hills, a National Trust beauty spot. The food, in the talented hands of the Chef, is outstanding. and is complemented by the equally superb wines.

Within a few miles of Lythe Hill there is polo at Cowdrey Park and racing at Goodwood and Sandown. Portsmouth, with its flotilla of ships is a drive away whilst Guildford Cathedral is approximately 12 miles. There are several golf courses, riding stables, and many stately homes to visit in the immediate neighbourhood.

DONKEY CART RESTAURANT

Restaurant & Medieval Banquet Hall

The Square, Petersfield,
Hampshire, GU32 2HJ.

Tel: (0730) 260930

USEFUL INFORMATION

OPEN: Mon-Fri: 8-5pm & 7-midnight.
Sat: 8.30-5pm & 7-12pm.
Sun: 12-3pmClosed Monday eve.
CHILDREN: Welcome
CREDIT CARDS: None
LICENSED: Full
ACCOMMODATION: Not applicable

RESTAURANT: Traditional English & Medieval Banquets
BAR FOOD: Wide range, snacks, etc
VEGETARIAN: Usually 3. Includes Vegan
DISABLED ACCESS: Unfortunately, no
GARDEN: None

There are many stories told about the fabulous 16th century building which houses The Donkey Cart Restaurant. It is thought to have been a farmhouse attached to Castle House which was demolished at the beginning of the century to make way for the new Post Office. Some of the timbers used to build the house were originally meant for one of Henry VIII's naval vessels. This would date the building in the first half of the 16th century and makes it one of the oldest surviving buildings in the town and one of the finest preserved. This may be due in part to the fact that the building spent a large portion of its time plastered over. It was not until the previous owner uncovered it that the full extent of its beauty was revealed.

Earlier still on this site, a religious dwelling with a connecting tunnel to the church on the other side of the Square, is supposed to have stood. Parts of a possible tunnel were unearthed when it was knocked down. Samuel Pepys makes a mention in one of his diaries that Charles II and his Lady, whilst on their way to Portsmouth, played bowls in the garden of Castle House.

Coming here is an experience, both gastronomic and aesthetic. The Elizabethan style Banquet is a feast of extravagance and merriment. As we go to print in October 1993, the price per head is £21 and you will be entertained by live musicians in a style that will surprise you. The restaurant itself has traditional English fare of a very high standard including some of the best casserole dishes you will ever taste and opens in the mornings very early for breakfasts and food throughout the day. Who could not enjoy eating here.

The Street, West Clandon,
Surrey, GU4 7ST.

Tel: (0483) 222444

THE BULLS HEAD
Public House

Instantly recognisable in the summer by its beautiful and colourful hanging baskets. The Bulls Head is situated just eight miles from Guildford and adjacent to the historic Clandon Park. The village, to which it belongs, West Clandon is attractive and it is fitting that it should have such a nice village pub as its focal point.

The Bulls Head was built in 1530 and as soon as one enters, the atmosphere of years is endorsed by the presence of beamed low ceilings and cosy bars. It must have always been a contented place to enjoy a drink and the present landlords, Brian and Sylvia Wheeler have made sure the tradition of centuries continues. Four hundred years ago the food would not have been as plentiful or varied as today. There are two exciting dishes and one can guarantee that there will be something to suit every taste. Much of the fare is genuinely home-made and served on plates rather than dishes. The portions are more than generous and it is exceptional value for money.

To the rear of the Bulls Head is a garden, neatly laid out with tables and chairs, swings and a Wendy House for the youngsters. Wonderful for a warm day. There is ample car parking so please do ask Brian or Sylvia if you may leave your car there while you take off for one of the many pretty walks that abound round West Clandon and don't forget to visit the National Trust at Hatchlands and the famous Clandon Park.

USEFUL INFORMATION

OPEN: Mon-Fri: 11-2.30pm & 5.30-11pm
  Sat: 11-3m & 6-11pm,
  Sun: 12-3pm & 7-10.30pm
CHILDREN: Well behaved
CREDIT CARDS: None taken
LICENSED: Full On Licence
ACCOMMODATION: Not applicable

RESTAURANT: Not applicable
BAR FOOD: Vast selection. None on
  Sunday night
VEGETARIAN: Six choices of Omlettes,
  ploughmans, salads
DISABLED ACCESS: Rear entrance level
GARDEN: Play area, swings, wendy house,
  tables and chairs

Hereford Cathedral

Hereford

"I'be lived it through; and nevermore
can harsher fate destroy
The glory that has gone before
or afterglow of joy."

**Frank Ashton - Swakin's translation
of Petronius**

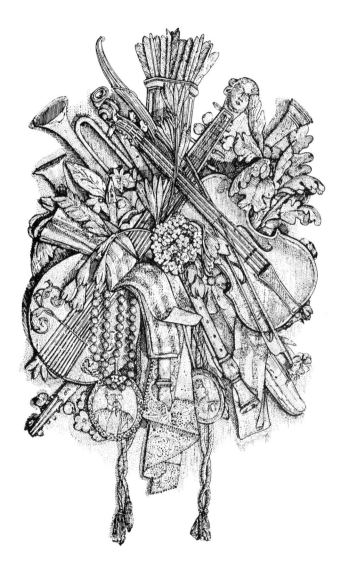

The City of Hereford

by Joy David

Herefordshire is an enchanting county full of beautiful places and things. It has a host of remarkable churches some of them to me even more magnificent than the great CATHEDRAL OF HEREFORD which is the purpose of my visit this time. If you approach Hereford from the north, the road has cider orchards alongside and hints at one of the city's major industries. BULMER'S have been making cider in **Hereford** for well over a century, and their premises in Plough Lane are open for tours and sampling. The contrast with modern automated production techniques with those of yesteryear are enormous, and a visit to THE CIDER MUSEUM AND KING OFFA DISTILLERY, in Ryelands Street, is a real eye-opener. There are numerous displays and reconstructions, including a farm Cider House, and an apple orchard, massive presses and mills and cellars where Champagne Cider was stored. The Distillery is where Cider Brandy is made in a 40 gallon copper pot, brought over from the Calvados region of France. The spirit was popular in the 16th and 17th centuries but now has been revived under licence from HM Customs and Excise - who were responsible for enforcing the whopping taxes that led to the original demise of the liquor!

Open: April-October daily 10am-5.30pm November - March, Monday - Saturday 1pm-5pm. Pre-booked parties at any time.

Any town or city engaged in the convivial pursuits of brewing or distilling has a rather jolly atmosphere, and Hereford is no exception, although its early history would suggest otherwise. Never free of strife until the end of the Civil War in 1651, the city suffered numerous attacks and sieges over the preceding centuries, yet during that time managed to become one of the most thriving medieval cities in England; a centre for both trade and scholarship.

Its tactical importance can be judged by its name, which means an 'army river crossing'. The Saxons built the earliest defence against the Welsh, who managed to destroy them in 1055, and in 1067. The power of these Lords of the Marches grew rapidly and they were rightly perceived as a threat to the Crown, for their rule was absolute and they commanded large and well-disciplined armies whilst their allegiance was often doubtful. Their weakness was in the fact that they quarelled as often with each other as they did with Celt or Crown; feudal law existed in the Marches long after the rest of England had peaceably settled down. One result of this was that the unfortunate citizens of Hereford, and indeed of the entire region, were subject to attack, not only by the Welsh, but by forces of the rival barons, seizing an opportunity to take a neighbour's property. Hereford and its castle were

attacked many times, and changed hands with (almost) monotonous regularity. The last time the castle was rebuilt was in 1402, during Owen Glendower's Welsh revolt. It suffered its final seige during the Civil War and was demolished in 1660, with a large part of the city walls being removed for redevelopment in the 18th century. CASTLE GREEN, east of the Cathedral, bears no trace of the long-suffering fortress which stood guard by the Wye - but does have a monument to a famous freeman of the city, Admiral Lord Nelson. Unfortunately, money ran out so the sixty-foot column has an urn rather than a bust at the top.

For many years 'Roaring Meg', an immense siege mortar that fired 200 pound cannon balls, was to be found on the Green. Responsible for inflicting much damage to Royalist strongholds during the Civil War, including Goodrich Castle, the huge weapon has been moved to the peaceful, if slightly incongruous surrounds of CHURCHILL GARDENS. Here the museum is full of fine furniture, costumes and paintings of the late 18th and 19th centuries. There are late 18th and 19th century rooms, the Sandford Collection of Straw Work, a special Barometer Exhibition and a new Costume Exhibition gallery which has been opened recently. The Victorian nursery, parlour, butler's pantry and kitchen gives you an insight to the domestic life of Victorian times. THE HATTON GALLERY is devoted to work of local artist Brian Hatton who was killed in the First World War. Whilst at CHURCHILL

GARDENS visit the Fragrant Garden with its wonderful smells, somewhere that is suitable for visits by the blind and disabled.

Open: Tuesday to Saturday 2pm-5pm. Summer Sundays from 2pm-5pm. Open Bank Holiday Mondays. The Fragrant Garden is open daily until dusk throughout the year.

Other items relating to the turbulent past, as well as to more peaceful interests, such as bee-keeping, can be seen in THE HEREFORD CITY MUSEUM AND ART GALLERY in Broad Street. Natural history, archaeology and local history are featured in the Museum, whilst the art gallery includes collections of 19th-century watercolours and works by local artists. Exhibitions in the art gallery change monthly.

Open: Tuesday, Wednesday and Friday 10am-6pm. Thursday 10am-5pm. Saturday 10am-5pm in Summer and 4pm in Winter. Open Bank Holiday Mondays.

The modern military presence in the city is restricted to THE HEREFORDSHIRE REGIMENTAL MUSEUM at the TA Centre in Harold Street, and to the discreet gentlemen of the SAS, at Bradbury Lines. The Regimental Museum has a collection of uniforms, colours, medals, equipment, documents and photographs, together with the flag and pennant of Admiral Doenitz, the last Fuhrer of the Third Reich.

Open: Tuesdays, Wednesdays and Thursday 2pm-5pm by arrangement.

Hereford is rich in museums; apart from those already mentioned there is BULMER RAILWAY CENTRE, for steam enthusiasts where The Centre houses a collection of mainly industrial locomotive and rolling stock. The exhibits include the well known locomotive ex-LMS 6201 'Princess Elizabeth' and ex-GWR Pannier Tank 5786, both restored and normally kept in full working order, 6201 can at times, be absent working elsewhere.

Open: Easter/April to September inclusive, weekends and Bank Holidays only, normally for static displays, between 2pm and 5pm. However Brake Van steamings and Steam Open Days, are available on specified dates between 11am and 5pm. For details ask The Publicity Officer, 24 Rosemary Gardens, Hampton Dene, Hereford and please do include a stamped addressed envelope.

THE ST JOHN MEDIEVAL MUSEUM at **Coningsby** is in a 13th century building skilfully restored to show its extended use in the 17th century, with costumed models of Nell Gwynne (a famous native of Hereford) and the Coningsby pensioners who used the Hospital on the site, Armour, Emblazons, and information about the fascinating history of the Ancient Order of St John and its wars during the 300 years of the Crusades.

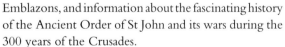

One of the roundels on the West Front of the Cathedral which records Dean Croft preaching to the soldiers during the Civil War

Open: Easter to September, daily 2pm-5pm except Mondays and Fridays.

THE OLD HOUSE built in 1621 is a fine specimen of Jacobean domestic architecture. Furnished in the style of the 17th century on three floors, the house includes a kitchen, hall and bedrooms with four-poster beds. It was originally part of Butcher's Row.

Open: Monday 10am-1pm, Tuesday to Saturday 10am-1pm and 2pm-5.30pm. Saturdays in winter until 1pm only. Open Bank Holiday Mondays.

The area around the Old House is a pedestrian precinct and in nearby St Peter's Close weary feet can be rested, thirsts quenched and hunger satisfied at GILBIES BISTRO AND BAR. A splendidly secluded spot with a distinctly Continental flavour, it has a continually changing menu which the proprietor modestly describes as 'good not great' and some real bargains in the wine-list.

HEREFORDSHIRE WATERWORKS MUSEUM has the restored Victorian Pumping Station, housing the giant Broomy Hill steam pumping engines and Lancashire boiler. There is a fascinating collection of pumps, some of which can be operated by visitors, gathered from all over the country to illustrate the development of the waterworks. Virtually all the Museum is acessible to those in wheelchairs.

Open: 2pm-5pm Saturdays, Sundays and Mondays between approxiamtely mid April and mid August. For details telephone (0432) 361147.

Water plays quite a part in the life of Hereford. THE LEISURE POOL COMPLEX in St Martins Avenue, has excellent facilities with a main swimming pool, leisure pool, diving pool, learner pool, squash sauna,solarium, sun bed, cafeteria and club room, table tennis and jogging.

A fishing platform for disabled anglers is provided by the HEREFORD & DISTRICT ANGLING ASSOC-IATION on the bank of the River Wye at King George V Playing Fields. For permission to use it and information ring (0432) 274152. Prior booking is necessary. KING GEORGE'S PLAYING FIELDS AND BISHOP'S MEADOWS are blissful for children with a paddling pool and playgrounds. There are also tennis courts both hard and grass Putting, Soccer and Cricket Pitches.

Every day throughout the summer Guides are on duty to show visitors around this historic City, and tell them about the houses and streets where people of interest once lived. Parties leave at 10.30am (2.30pm on Sundays) from the Shirehall forecourt for walks of about one and a half hours. You can book your place at the Tourist Information Centre. You will find it stimulating and probably have made new friends by the end of the tour.

The medieval visitors to the city – scholars, men-at-arms, and traders – would have had their numbers swelled by large numbers of pilgrims, visiting THE CATHEDRAL OF ST MARY THE VIRGIN AND ST ETHELBERT THE KING. The Cathedral was begun in the 11th century on Saxon foundations dating back to the 7th century - in fact, the appointment of the first Bishop of Hereford dates back to that time. Of the first Cathedral there is no trace, however there is some fine Norman work, dating from the middle of the 12th century. That was an important time for Hereford. Unwillingly the city got drawn politically into the struggle between King

Stephen and Matilda. In the sanctuary you will see an ancient wooden chair on which King Stephen is supposed to have sat when he was enthroned and crowned in the Cathedral on the Feast of Pentecost in 1138. It was also in this century that the Cathedral became renowned as a seat of learning. The gloriously rich library still has some ninety 12th century manuscripts.

The 13th century brought two very different Bishops to Hereford - there were more of course but these two were notable. In 1239 Peter Aquablanca was enthroned and so began a period of dissension but achievement. He was not popular but nonetheless managed to attain the rebuilding of the north transept, introduce a new and distinctive form of liturgy - which no one approved of - and reorganised the adminstration of the Cathedral in the teeth of stubborn resistance. Since his time two candles are lit before the bishop's throne whenever it is occupied - a tradition that is fiercely guarded today but I am not aware of why it happened in the first place.

A totally different kind of man became Bishop in 1175. Thomas Cantilupe was already a bishop when he came to Hereford. He had been Chancellor of the University of Oxford and briefly Chancellor of England. His time was short but he was revered as a good and pious man and after he died in Italy in 1282 his bones were returned to Hereford. Pilgrims flocked to his shrine and reported miracles. It became one of the most famous places of pilgrimage in the whole of England. As in Gloucester the money that accrued from these pilgrimages enabled the building of the great central tower. A little later in the 14th century a superb Lady Chapel was added but it was destroyed in the Civil War. Cloisters were added in the 15th century and the two fine Chantry Chapels of Bishop Stanbury and Bishop Audley were also built. The vaulting in both is fabulous and Bishop Audley's is further enhanced by a wonderful painted screen.

It was Bishop Booth who completed the medieval cathedral at the beginning of the sixteenth century adding the fine outer north porch and the bishop's cloister.

The Reformation was not a happy time for Hereford. Its deans and canons were not in favour of the doctrines and eventually the majority of them lost their livings. However the Cathedral's heyday came in the reign of Elizabth I. John Bull, one of the country's principal musicians was the organist and the academic ability of the canons attracted many scholars to Hereford, rapidly re-establishing it as a seat of learning. Hereford never wavered in its allegiance to the King in the 17th century although the town changed hands three times. One splendid battle saw the Scots repulsed by the Royalists who used melted down lead from the chapter house to make bullets. Even when the Parliamentarians did garrison the town they found themselves constantly rebuked by Dean Croft from a pulpit which is still in the nave.

In the same way that we are horrified by what people did to door panelling and fireplaces in the 1960's so was Hereford Cathedral the unfortunate recipient of improvements in the early 18th century. Bishop Bisse ordered the covering of the Norman pillars in the choir with panelling, he added more odd looking pillars and an altar piece, all of which was too heavy for the structure and weakened it considerably. The good news from the early 18th century onwards was the beginning of the now world famous Three Choirs Festival which now alternates between Hereford, **Worcester** and **Gloucester**.

Easter Monday 1786 is a day that will never be forgotten in the history of this cathedral. The west tower collapsed and brought with it the west front and much of the nave. The great architects Wyatt and Gilbert Scott both had a go at rebuilding and both should be ashamed of what they did. Wyatt's was the biggest sin when he removed the spire which had graced the central tower, probably the cathedral's finest feature. The present Victorian west front is entirely the work of Scott the younger. In 1967 George Gilbert Scott's screen was removed - today that would have been considered a masterpiece. How our tastes change!

I would not put Hereford Cathedral at the top of the league table but it is without question one of the most comfortable ones to visit and it has a great warmth and strength about it. Whatever alterations have taken place they have always managed to hang on to its original furniture. The misericords beneath the choir stalls are masterpieces in their own right and the magnificent 14th century bishop's throne stands proudly for all to see. There are inumerable interesting tombs but the greatest of Hereford's glory is its library of 1,500 chained books now kept in the upper transept and upper cloister rooms, still with the chains as they were when the library was housed in the exquisite 13th century Lady Chapel. The most precious book in this unequalled collection is a copy of the Four Gospels dating from the 8th century. The extraordinary Mappa Mundi is the finest treasure of the cathedral. It is a picture of the medieval world, a map drawn by Prebendary Richard of Haldingham at the end of the 13th century. It shows the earth as being flat with Jerusalem at the focal point with graphic representations of the Garden of Eden and the Tower of Babel.

More history is within easy reach of Hereford at DINEDOR CAMP, seven miles south of Hereford. This is an old scheduled Iron Age Fort, well worth exploring and an excellent place for picnicking.

Returning briefly to the Cathedral, I found that the fairly exhausting climb up to the top of the 13th century Tower was more than worthwhile. The views across the City and the surroundings are stupendous and beyond the boundary you can see the long ridge of the Black Mountains which divide England and Wales. Much as I loved being in Hereford the lure of Wales made me set forth next day towards the Brecon Beacons on a trip that was to take me almost in a circle to **Hay-on-Wye**, south to **Tretower** on to **Abergavenny**, on to **Monmouth,** then to **Ross-on-Wye** and finally back to Hereford.

I started by stopping! On the A438 I saw a signpost for **Credenhill** and here is THE NATIONAL SNAIL FARMING CENTRE formed by the two largest indoor snail farmers in the country and a biologist of long standing in the British snail farming industry. Combining the expertise of large scale production and trechnical knowledge, the Centre is acknowledged as a leading authority on snail farming. I never thought about anyone snail farming before I came here. I found it both entertaining - sometimes amusing - and always informative.

Fierce marcher lords, Anglo Norman feudal rulers of the Welsh border areas, rode out fro the old castle of Hay whenever the borders were disputed. The 12th century castle is now mostly in ruins. Modern Hay-

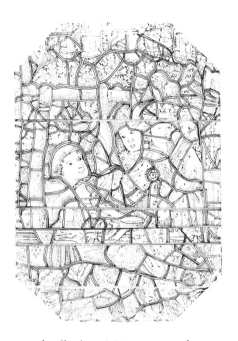

A collection of 15th century glass fragments, recently restored as a window. From the jumble can just be made out the scene where Joseph's brothers imprison him in a pit

on-Wye stands high above the southern bank of the river Wye.It is a pretty town of old buildings and narrow streets and has the world's largest second-hand bookshop, which has spread to more than six buildings.

If I were asked to name my favourite spot in the old market town of Abergavenny then I would certainly plump for Castle Meadows alongside the River Usk. On a summer's day there can be no more idyllic place and a picnic beneath tall trees on the gently sloping banks is certainly my idea of heaven. There is plenty to see and do here, for this is a very busy market town and despite its 900 years of history it does not believe in resting on its laurels. Both produce and livestock markets attract thousands of visitors - the produce market on Tuesdays and Fridays has a particularly fine setting; the Market Hall, a landmark with its own copper-canopied clock tower.

Of ABERGAVENNY CASTLE little remains. It was first built around 1090 by the Norman Lord Hemellen de Ballon. The castle was abandoned by the Royalists during the Civil War.

Had I decided to take the A465 from Abergavenny back to Hereford I would have come across **Walterstone** where ALLT-YR-YNYS, pronounced 'Allt-er-Innis' is many things to many people: Conference centre, country retreat, holiday hotel or activity holiday venue. The common thread is the personal involvement of the owners, John and Janet Manifold, and their staff - a guarantee that the interests of their guests are paramount. The setting is as fascinating as the history. On the English side, the rolling wooded farmland of Herefordshire gives way to the Malvern hills beyond. On the Welsh side the great Fwddog Ridge dominates the landscape. Part of the Black Mountains, it runs north to Hay-on-Wye, all within the Brecon Beacons National Park, with its interesting mountain centre. To match the superb setting and their historic house, the food and the wine is of the very highest standard.

Monmouth is a splendid town. It stands on the confluence of the Wye, Monnow and Trothy rivers, and this former county town of Monmouthshire boasts many well-preserved Tudor and Georgian buildings. Agincourt Square is elegant, bordered by a cluster of fine inns, the Shire Hall and Library, and a statue there is itself a tribute to a man who helped bring elegance to the motor industry: Charles Stewart Rolls, co-founder of Rolls-Royce, who was born at nearby Rockfield.

I took a look at THE NELSON MUSEUM AND LOCAL HISTORY CENTRE in Priory Street, and it was the last place I called at before leaving Monmouth. You may well ask, as I did, why there should be a Nelson Museum in Monmouth when the Admiral was born in Norfolk and buried in St Paul's Cathedral. The nearest I can get to an answer is that Horatio Nelson did pass through Monmouth in 1802 when he visited the Naval Temple on the 800foot Hill of Kymin which is about a mile to the east of the town. The bulk of the collection was formed by Lady Llangattock, who lived near Monmouth, and among many exhibits is Nelson's fighting sword. The Local History Centre is in the same

building, and as well as a comprehensive unfolding of the history of Monmouth there is also a considerable section devoted to Charles Stewart Rolls and his work.

This is wonderful countryside and driving alongside the Wye is an unforgettable experience. You will probably be tempted to leave the main road to take a look at **Symonds Yat.** The Wye loops its way round to enter this precipitous limestone gorge, one of the most beautiful and spectacular views in England. The 400-foot high Yat Rock (yat being Old English for a gate or gorge) is a favourite spot to admire the scenic splendour of the Wye curling its way sinuously through the wooded countryside. Peregrine falcons nest in the limestone cliffs and at the bottom of the path from the rock down to the river there is an unusual man-powered rope ferry.

Ross-on-Wye is another delightful market town, overlooking the River Wye. Agriculture, light industry and tourism form the basis of the local economy and Ross (from the Welsh ros, meaning a spit of land) is ideally situated for exploring the glorious country of the Wye Valley.

Its friendly and welcoming atmosphere owes much to the example set by the town's best loved inhabitant, John Kyrle (1637-1724). Trained as a lawyer, he inherited a small fortune and never practiced, preferring to spend his time and money on good works and acts of great public generosity. He died, a bachelor, at the age of 89, having given all his money away but never incurred a debt. He is remembered as the 'Man of Ross', and among his many philanthropies were the provision of a town water-supply, a causeway enabling the bridge to be used when flooding occurred, and a walled public garden, still known as Kyrle's Prospect. He built a summer-house in the grounds of his home, now known as KYRLE HOUSE, and paid the poor and unemployed to find

horse's teeth from animals killed in a nearby cavalry skirmish during the Civil War; these were then set into mortar to create a mosaic in the shape of a swan. Kyrle is buried in the CHURCH OF ST MARY'S, and his monument is modest and restrained.

Another benefactor was Frances, Duchess of Somerset, who provided the handsome sandstone 17th-century MARKET HALL, raised on sixteen pillars and where market-stalls gather to this day. In the north-eastern corner of the churchyard is a stone cross in memory of the 315 victims of an outbreak of the plaque in the year of John Kyrle's birth.

The little town in its steep rocky outcrop has been a favourite with visitors since the early Victorian era when, as now, the attractions of the surrounding countryside and the excellent salmon-fishing brought people back year after year, prompting a testy local parson, Thomas Fosbrooke, to comment in the 1830's that the tourists 'during summer and autumn poke about the Wye like snipes and woodcocks, and after rummaging through everything, re-emigrate to London.' Around that time, a conscious effort was made to romanticise the town by 'medievalising' constructing walls and a round tower. Thankfully, the soft red local sandstone has eroded fast and what could have looked uncomfortably twee now looks uncommonly like the real thing. Hotels, pubs and restaurants are plentiful, and I was impressed by the enthusiasm and high standards to be found. In Edde Cross street stands PHEASANTS RESTAURANT, a former 16th century Cider house converted firstly into a private house and then into a turn-of-the-century Dining Room. It is small, intimate and charming with exposed yew beams and an original stone fireplace. The atmosphere is super and the restaurant deservedly won the 'Country Restaurant of the year' in 1992. Upstairs the large toilet/bathroom is graced by over 100 hippos of various manifestations which gave the restaurant, the '1992 Restaurant Loo of the year' award!

Somewhere you should visit is THE LOST STREET MUSEUM, a charming and very well-thought out museum in the form of an arcade of Edwardian shops containing all manner of period items including amusement machines, musical boxes, toys, costumes and gramophones. For gardeners, HILL COURT GARDENS AND GARDEN CENTRE to the east of the town and HOW CAPLE COURT GARDENS are both a sheer delight.

The village of **Peterstow** is on the doorstep of Ross-on-Wye and if I wanted somewhere to stay I can think of nowhere nicer than PETERSTOW COUNTRY HOUSE, where Jeanne and Mike Denne have turned a dilapidated rectory into a masterpiece. The house sits next to the church of St Peter and the house on the adjoining land belongs to the farm where the Dunne's live, which is thought to be the original site of Peterstow village. A reward for all the hard work and the risks they took in achieving this beautiful restoration and making it a lovely home, has been the delight of the guests who come here from all over the world. Their pleasure and enthusiasm has put the seal on the success of this fine hotel.

Only four miles from Ross-on-Wye just north of Peterstow is the unspoilt village of **Hoarwithy** and in its midst THE OLD MILL dating from the 18th century which has been renovated to form a small country guest house offering every comfort and amenity whilst retaining its character and charm.

Either of these two delightful establishments would be ideal as a base for visiting Hereford and its Cathedral as well as enabling you to savour the glories of the Herefordshire countryside.

Two traditional inns are in this vicinity also. Either will please you. THE NEW INN at **St Owens Cross** is an establishment that answers every one's dream of an English country hostelry but has so much more, and attracts people from all walks of life. The charm comes from the genuine welcome of Nigel and Jane Donovan, the owners and the locals, who are all prepared to chat. It is the sort of place in which you might be a stranger when you arrive but you will leave having made new friends. You can stay here in two enchanting rooms, both ensuite and complete with fourposters. One room also has its own lounge and dining room.

THE HAREWOOD INN is just nine miles from Hereford, in the pretty village of **Harewood End**. Built about 400 years ago, it is a cheerful, welcoming pub where not only the beer is good but the food as well.

The road north of Hereford leads to **Leominster**, the county's second largest town. Pronounced 'Lemster' it is set amongst a gentle landscape of fields, hills and meadows where river, stream and brook wander. The town's fortunes were based on the fine quality of the wool from the local breed of sheep, the Ryeland, an animal that thrives on the poorer grazing to be found on the neighbouring hills and the less fertile outcrops of sandy soil from which the name is derived. The demand for this wool was so great that at one time the fleece was known as 'Lempster Ore'.

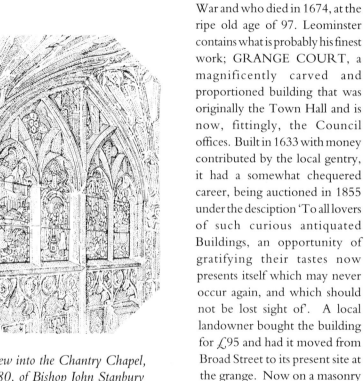

A view into the Chantry Chapel, c.1480, of Bishop John Stanbury

The area is also known locally as Jon Abel country after the master-craftsman who was responsible for many of the fine timber-framed buildings; a rural architectural genius who was awarded the title of 'King's Carpenter' for his works during the Civil War and who died in 1674, at the ripe old age of 97. Leominster contains what is probably his finest work; GRANGE COURT, a magnificently carved and proportioned building that was originally the Town Hall and is now, fittingly, the Council offices. Built in 1633 with money contributed by the local gentry, it had a somewhat chequered career, being auctioned in 1855 under the desciption 'To all lovers of such curious antiquated Buildings, an opportunity of gratifying their tastes now presents itself which may never occur again, and which should not be lost sight of'. A local landowner bought the building for £95 and had it moved from Broad Street to its present site at the grange. Now on a masonry base, it originally stood on massive wooden timbers, similar to the Market House at **Ledbury**. Leominster Council bought it in 1939, when there was a chance of it being sold and dismantled for export to the USA.

There are a good mix of architectural styles in the town, principally Jacobean and Georgian, and the High Street, CHURCH STREET and ETNAM STREET all contain good examples, and in the last-named sightseeing thirst and hunger can be appeased in the cheerful 14th century surrounds of THE WHITE LION INN. Very much a family pub, there is a large garden, children's play area, and a large patio for summer barbecues. THE LEOMINSTER FOLK MUSEUM is also in Etnam Street.

Leofric, Earl of Mercia, and husband of that well known naked equestrienne, Godiva, is supposed to have given his name to the town with the establishment of a religious order in the 9th century (Leofric's Minster). This is thought unlikely since the order was a nunnery (although he may have hoped that his wife would enter and stop embarrassing him) and anyway, the family cannot have been over popular in the area since Leofric's son promptly ran off with the Abbess! A second legend concerns a lion who cornered a Christian missionary but spared the man's life in return for a share of his bread, whereupon the missionary took this to be a remarkably good omen and founded a church on the spot (Leo's minster). The most likely story is rather more prosaic and has no connection with either embarrassed Saxon aristocrats or vegetarian lions; Leominster simply means 'the Church on the Lene' - Lene being the old name for the Arrow valley. Nevertheless, carved into the head of one of the huge pillars of the west entrance to LEOMINSTER PRIORY CHURCH are the figures of a monk and a lion.

The Priory succeeded earlier religious foundations, including Leofric's nunnery, that dated back to a Celtic settlement of about 660AD. Rebuilt as a monastery in the 11th century, it suffered much damage during the Dissolution and also as a result of a severe fire in 1699, but for all these disasters it remains a most handsome and dignified building. The unique tower reflects it's history incorporating work of the Early Norman, Transitional, Early English, Decorated and Perpendicular periods.

The south aisle contains extensive examples of a form of early 14th century decoration to be found all over Herefordshire - the ball-flower, a three petalled carving enclosing a ball. There is also a fine Chalice of the same period, and in the north aisle, the town's Ducking Stool. This was the last such stool to be used in England and the victim was one Jenny Pipes, immersed in the Arrow in 1809 (there would have been a later ducking in 1817, but the river was too low!).

On my way back to Hereford down the A4110, I stopped in the village of **Canon Pyon** and found THE NAGS HEAD, an old style country pub, a fine black and white building dating back to 1450. Here Fred the Ghost has no intention of retiring - he enjoys the friendliness of the pub far too much! Situated as it is so close to Hereford it is a good place to stay as well as have a drink or a meal. I certainly found the food good and the company relaxing.

The longer I stayed in Hereford, the more attached I became to it and its Cathedral. I leave it wanting to return and quite sure that I will do so to see not only the Cathedral's wonderful chained library but also the chance to listen to the music which fills every corner when the great organ plays and the choir raise their voices in triumphant sound.

Canon Pyon,
Herefordshire, HR4 8NY.

Tel: (0432) 830252

THE NAGS HEAD

Public House & Restaurant

The Nag's Head in the centre of the village of Canon Pyon, on the A4110 Hereford to Knighton road, five miles north of Hereford, is an old style country pub. It is one of those striking black and white buildings which has stood forever. In this case it was built about 1450 and although it has been altered over the centuries it has lost none of its nooks and crannies which makes it so appealing. It is enjoyed by the locals and the many visitors who have discovered it over the years, and by Fred the Ghost, who obviously has no intention of retiring from such a likeable hostelry! The Nag's Head has several interesting artefacts, amongst them a brass hand water pump in the corner of the bar.

If you are good at answering trivia questions you may well win yourself a free pint! The blackboard by the bar asks the question every day and the winner is suitably rewarded. It is all good fun and that is the general atmosphere of the pub. A thoroughly friendly establishment run by Mark and Hayley Bamber plus their in-laws. Apart from the good selection of ciders and real ales there is a wide selection of traditional food which is all home-cooked. For families it is ideal. Children are welcome and in the summer the large garden is open to everyone, and the children have their own play area.

Situated as it is so close to Hereford with its superb cathedral, and also to the wonderful surrounding countryside, The Nag's Head would make a good base for anyone who wants to stay. There are four letting rooms with one of the double rooms being en-suite. Breakfast is a feast to be remembered.

USEFUL INFORMATION

OPEN: 12-3pm & 7-11pm. 7 days a week
CHILDREN: Yes. Play area in garden
CREDIT CARDS: Access/Visa/Master/
Euro
LICENSED: Full On Licence
ACCOMMODATION: 1 double en-suite,
2 twin, 1 double. Reasonably priced

RESTAURANT: Wide selection of
traditional foods
BAR FOOD: All home-cooked meals
VEGETARIAN: Daily selection
DISABLED ACCESS: Level entrance
from car park. Access to rooms
GARDEN: Large with Children's play area

Credenhill,
Hereford, Herefordshire, HR4 7DN.

Tel: (0432) 760218
Fax: (0432) 760218

THE NATIONAL SNAIL FARMING CENTRE
Farm

Set on a farm in the glorious countryside of Herefordshire, with an unspoilt view to the Black Mountains of Wales, the unassuming exterior hides a hive of activity on a working farm.
If you have never given much thought to snails, this remarkable establishment will put that to rights. For example a snail likes to be warm and wet. Most snails are 'hermaphrodite' - both snails will lay eggs after mating. These eggs are usually buried in the earth. Snails mostly eat green plants but they will also eat paper and cardboard! All this and much more you will learn here.

The National Snail Farming Centre is formed by the two largest indoor snail farmers in the country and a biologist of long standing in the British Snail Farming Industry. Here at Credenhill guided tours, which take one and a half hours, are fascinating. You are taken along the Snail Trail and there you see snails in the wild. You learn about their habits, their uses and begin to understand why someone like Mr Vaughan, the owner of the centre has such a passion for his subject. You will also learn some delicious recipes using the English snail.

This is something truly different and while it conforms to the norm in welcoming visitors, having a picnic area and offering light refreshments, it is an experience you will never forget.

USEFUL INFORMATION

OPEN: All year round 11-6pm.
No weekends October to April
CHILDREN: Actively encouraged
CREDIT CARDS: None
LICENSED: Not applicable
ACCOMMODATION: Not applicable

RESTAURANT: Not applicable
BAR FOOD: Not applicable
VEGETARIAN: Not applicable
DISABLED ACCESS: No facilities
GARDEN: Picnic area. Free parking for
coaches and cars

THE HAREWOOD END INN

Inn

Harewood End,
Herefordshire, HR2 8JT.

Tel: (098 987) 637

USEFUL INFORMATION

OPEN: Weekday: 11-2.30pm & 6-11pm
Sundays: 12-3pm & 7-10.30pm
CHILDREN: Yes if well behaved
CREDIT CARDS: None taken
LICENSED: Full Licence
ACCOMMODATION: 5 dbls, 1twn, 1 sgl
all with en-suite facilities

RESTAURANT: Fresh food inc.
fish & game
BAR FOOD: Extensive & daily specials
VEGETARIAN: 6 dishes. Very
good choice
DISABLED ACCESS: Yes
GARDEN: Beer garden & mature
garden

There is a little inn that nestles into the countryside some four miles from Ross on Wye, and nine miles from Hereford, in the pretty and tranquil village of Harewood End. The pub bears the name of the village and is quite enchanting. Built about 400 years ago it exudes warmth and happiness in its combined lounge and bar. Old oak beams and a roaring open fire simply add to the atmosphere and the general well being of The Harewood Inn.

Surrounded by some of England's most beautiful countryside and with the River Wye and a major fruit growing area within 3/4 mile, this inn is just the place to visit, either for lunch or for an evening meal. If you know the place already, you will be aware that on four acres of land belonging to the pub, there is a registered Camp Site with space for 40 caravans. It must be wonderful to wake up here on a lovely summer's morning knowing that you have a blissful day ahead of you exploring the surrounding area. If you enjoy market towns then Hereford will suit you very well. This lovely, historic city has a Cathedral which is breathtaking.

David and Jill Headon are the cheerful and welcoming hosts. It falls to Jill's lot to produce the excellent food. Her insistence on fresh produce, including fish and game, has given her a reputation for miles around which is second to none. She obviously enjoys the task. As well as the restaurant menu there are 'Daily Specials' and a whole range of first class bar snacks. A traditional 'Sunday Lunch' is a firm favourite.

GILBIES BISTRO

Bistro

4 St Peter's Close, Commercial Street,
Hereford, HR1 4AT.

Tel: (0432) 277863

USEFUL INFORMATION

OPEN: 10am-11pm every day
CHILDREN: Good children welcome
CREDIT CARDS: Visa/Access
LICENSED: Full Licence
ACCOMMODATION: Not applicable

RESTAURANT: One menu
available all day
BAR FOOD: Competitive prices
VEGETARIAN: At least 3 daily
DISABLED ACCESS: Limited
GARDEN: Pleasant, secluded patio area

In the middle of the busy city of Hereford there is an oasis. Gilbies Bar and Bistro is something different and special. Somewhere you can go early in the morning for breakfast - as early as 7am if it is prearranged - have coffee, maybe a snack or a full meal throughout the whole day.

Modelled in many ways on the kind of Bistro you might find in any of the larger French or Spanish cities, Gilbies will make you feel a little more European, so flexible are the opening hours. Music also plays an important part in the everyday life of Gilbies. The music played is very much influenced by the customers. Regular jazz evenings are held on the first Wednesday of every month. The food, Kevan Gilbert, the proprietor describes as 'good but not great, at reasonable prices, eaten in a completely relaxed atmosphere'. Their menu changes hour by hour and always covers all style of cuisine: from steaks to kebabs - from fish to seafood or simple snacks like bacon sandwiches through to New Zealand Mussels. The drinks list includes 30 varieties of wine from all around the world and also a large selection of both traditional and unusual beers and lagers. The mixture of cuisine and culture under one roof is a piece of magic and a real asset to Hereford. Kevan Gilbert is to be congratulated.

Hoarwithy, Hereford,
Herefordshire, HR2 6QH.

Tel: (0432) 840602

THE OLD MILL
Guest House

The Old Mill, dating from the 18th century, has been renovated to form a small country guest house offering every comfort and amenity whilst still retaining its character and charm. Hoarwithy is a pleasant, unspoilt village on the banks of the tranquil River Wye. It lies in the heart of rural South Herefordshire, being only four miles from the town of Ross-on-Wye and 10 miles from the nearest city, Hereford.

Hoarwithy is an ideal base for those wishing to visit the market towns of the area, such as Hay on Wye and Ledbury, the beautiful countryside of the Welsh Marches and Symonds Yat, the black and white villages of Herefordshire and the many castles along the Welsh borders. The area is renowned for its beautiful scenery. It is an ideal area to discover by foot or car. Local facilities for leisure include fishing, canoeing, cycling, golf and horse riding.

With all this it makes very good sense to stay in the attractive confines of The Old Mill House right next to the River Wye. The bedrooms are comfortable with en-suite or showers in most rooms. All rooms have hot and cold water. The dining room is spacious and beamed with a french window opening onto the paved gardens. A large lawn and flower garden are for the use of residents. The beamed lounge is cosy with a large stone fireplace in which there is a log fire on colder days. Home cooking is a speciality with local produce being used whenever possible. Special diets are catered for if notice is given. It is a happy, friendly house offering excellent value.

USEFUL INFORMATION

OPEN: All year except Christmas
CHILDREN: Welcome
CREDIT CARDS: None taken
LICENSED: Bring your own wine for dinner
ACCOMMODATION: 1 db en-suite, 2dbl
with shower, 1 dbl with vanity unit,
1 twn en-suite

RESTAURANT: Home cooked, local
produce
BAR FOOD: Not applicable
VEGETARIAN: Yes, on request
DISABLED ACCESS: No
GARDEN: Yes, with cider mill & stream

Peterstow, Ross-on-Wye,
Herefordshire, HR9 6LB.

Tel: (0989) 62826
Fax: (0989) 67264

PETERSTOW COUNTRY HOUSE
Country House Hotel & Restaurant

How only a few years ago this wonderful house was a dilapidated rectory, is almost beyond comprehension. Jeanne and Mike Denne have thrown themselves hook, line and sinker, into creating this masterpiece. The house sits next to the church of St Peter and the house on the adjoining land belongs to the farm where the Denne's live, which is thought to be the original site of Peterstow village.

A reward for all the hard work and the risks they took in achieving this beautiful restoration and making it a lovely home, has been the delight of the guests who come here from all over the world. Their pleasure and enthusiasm has put the seal on the success of Peterstow Country House Hotel.

Undoubtedly the centrepiece of Peterstow is the restaurant. Here one dines on modern English and French cuisine from a kitchen where the chefs are continually searching for new ideas and tastes incorporating the seasonally available fresh vegetables and fruit from the kitchen garden and farm. Lunch or an evening meal is a memorable experience. Naturally there is an excellent wine list.

The spacious entrance hall with its flagstone floor and grand winding staircase leads you to the nine en-suite rooms, each individually styled, ranging from half tester suites, with their beautiful canopied beds to the charming double and twin-bedded rooms.

USEFUL INFORMATION

OPEN: All year round
CHILDREN: Welcome, over 7 yrs old
CREDIT CARDS: All major cards
LICENSED: Full On Licence
ACCOMMODATION: 9 en-suite rooms

RESTAURANT: Superb cuisine. Open to
non-residents
BAR FOOD: Not applicable
VEGETARIAN: Always a dish of the day
DISABLED ACCESS: Level entrance
Ground floor accommodation
GARDEN: 28 acres pasture, woodlands &
formal gardens

THE LOST STREET MUSEUM

Museum

Palma Court, 27 Brookend Street,
Ross-on-Wye, Herefordshire, HR9 7EE.

Tel: (0989) 62752

USEFUL INFORMATION

OPEN: Mon-Sat: 10-5pm, Sun: 11-5pm, Closed Dec. Jan/ Feb: Phone for times. Special rates for coach parties by prior arrangement

CHILDREN: Actively encouraged

CREDIT CARDS: None taken

LICENSED: None

ACCOMMODATION: Not applicable

RESTAURANT: Humble Pie Cafe. Delicious food. Hereford cream teas

BAR FOOD: Not applicable

VEGETARIAN: Limited

DISABLED ACCESS: Easy access ground floor

GARDEN: Courtyard cafe

Ross-on-Wye is beautiful and picturesque, and it is fitting that it should have The Lost Street Museum in a courtyard behind the main street. It is a veritable time capsule of shops dating from 1885 to 1935. To visit this cobbled street is a journey into the past of shopping. There is a tobacconist with all the old cigarettes, Woodbines, Senior Service, Goldflake, chocolate vending machines, sweet jars, chocolate boxes and pictorial tins. It also houses a collection of match boxes and unusual vesta cases. A grocery, where you are encouraged to sit down whilst ordering the week's groceries - a pound of sugar in a blue bag, all weighed up for you on scales, biscuits sold loose from a tin, sultanas scooped out from big boxes and butter cut from a big slab.

The Lillie Langtry pub, which originally stood in London's East End, is a fine example of a late Victorian public house, with a mahogany bar and magnificent etched mirrors. Then there is the glass shop, the toy shop - paradise for all children -. The chemist has always played an important part in the life of the community, and the shop in Lost Street is largely stocked with items put away by a local chemist some 60 years ago. The ladies outfitters, housed appropriately in a Bon Marche front from Cardiff, evokes an era of elegance, of long dresses, elbow length gloves and fine lace, and shows both dresses and accessories of the late Victorian period. It is all wonderful. The Museum has been designed to appeal to both Men and Women of all ages and to all children from 5 to 80! In July 1990 The Lost Street was awarded a Certificate of Merit in the 'Come to Britain Trophy' - the Oscars of the Tourist Industry - by the British Tourist Authority.

PHEASANTS

Restaurant with Accommodation

52 Edde Cross Street,
Ross-on-Wye, Herefordshire HR9 7BZ.

Tel: (0989) 65751

USEFUL INFORMATION

OPEN: Mar-Oct: Lunch 12.30-2pm. Winter bookings only. Evening: 7-10pm, Closed Dec 24-Jan 2nd

CHILDREN: Only with well behaved parents

CREDIT CARDS: Access/Visa/Diners/ Amex

LICENSED: Restaurant

ACCOMMODATION: 2 bedrooms

RESTAURANT: Simple, elegant, delicious

BAR FOOD: Brasserie style. Lunch: Tues-Fri, Dinner: Tues-Sat Nov-May (inclusive), bookings only at lunchtime

VEGETARIAN: At least 6 dishes

DISABLED ACCESS: Level entrance

GARDEN: Walled garden for use in summer

Pheasants is not just another restaurant but a new experience! It is almost impossible to believe that until quite recently Pheasants was just a tiny pub building. Its present owner, a woman of many surprises and talents, Eileen Brunnarius has created a Victorian style dining room with 8 neatly spaced tables, fronted by a dispense bar and a fireside lounge. She has deliberately made it a 'home from home' atmosphere into which you are not only welcomed by her but also BBC, the 'Big Black Cat' and the witty, whimsical waiter and wine-buff, Adrian Wells.

Pheasants is all about intimate dining whether at lunchtime or in the evening. Eileen's interest in old English recipes and the resulting delicious dishes brought Pheasants the 'Country Restaurant of the Year 1992' award. It was an accolade richly deserved. At lunchtime there are simple dishes ranging from a Brunch Pancake to Hazelnut and Mushroom Wellington or Old English Duck Pie, followed by Eileen's famous Bread and Butter Pudding'. Dinners are more varied, offering three different menus, brasserie style, the fixed price supper menu or the a la carte, each offering you the chance to sample some of the International wines - by the glass. In summer, the secluded walled courtyard is the most delightful and tranquil place in which to enjoy a meal. Pheasants is three minutes from the centre of Ross, and for those who wish to stay there are two attractive bedrooms. A 10% discount on evening meals is offered to those staying. An opportunity not to be missed even if you only have time for a quick lunch. You will want to return.

St Owens Cross,
Herefordshire, HR2 8LQ.

Tel: (0989) 87274

THE NEW INN
Inn & Restaurant

Nigel and Jane Donovan, the owners of this super inn, will tell you it is just a true traditional pub, but their modesty belies reality! Here we have an establishment that answers every one's dream of an English country hostelry but has so much more, yet attracts all walks of life. The charm of The New Inn which delights so many people, comes from the genuine welcome from the Dononvans and the locals, who are all prepared to chat. It is the sort of place that you may be a stranger when you arrive but you will leave having made new friends. The desire to return will be strong.

You have a choice of eating in the bar or in the more intimate and quieter atmosphere of the pretty restaurant. The food is delicious. The choice is not remarkable but it is the quality, the cooking and the presentation which is what makes it outstanding. You will never see a frozen vegetable, the bread is newly baked, the salads are crisp and even a simple sandwich is well filled and beautifully garnished. The portions are more than generous - you will be told it is because the locals have huge farmer's appetites! In addition the price is right!

There are two enchanting rooms here in which you can stay. Both are en-suite and complete with four posters. One also has its own lounge and dining area. There are oak beams on the ceilings and the walls - even in the bathroom. It would be wonderful to return to such a room in such a genuine inn at the end of a day of exploration.

USEFUL INFORMATION

OPEN: Mon-Sat: 12-2.30pm & 6-11pm,
Sun: 12-2.30pm & 7-10.30pm
CHILDREN: Welcome
CREDIT CARDS: Access/Visa
LICENSED: Full On Licence
ACCOMMODATION: The Oak Suite &
The Hentland Room

RESTAURANT: All home-cooked, fresh
produce
BAR FOOD: Wide selection
VEGETARIAN: Several dishes on menu
DISABLED ACCESS: Small step, willing
to assist
GARDEN: One acre with seating

Walterstone,
Herefordshire, HR2 0DU.

Tel: (0873) 890307

ALLT-YR-YNYS
Country House Hotel & Restaurant

Allt-yr-Ynys, pronounced 'Allt-er-Innis' is many things to many people: Conference centre, country retreat, holiday hotel or activity holiday venue. The common thread is the personal involvement of the owners, John and Janet Manifold, and their staff - a guarantee that the interests of their guests are paramount.

The Hotel as it is today was built about 1550 and was once the home of the Cecil family who became the Earls of Exeter in 1605 and found favour with Elizabeth I who was a house guest. The house retains much fine craftsmanship of the period. Individuality and tradition are much in evidence in the bedrooms. In the interests of comfort, a modern touch in each bedroom is the provision of an en-suite bathroom, telephone, colour television and radio. Each bedroom is furnished differently, for instance the master suite boasts a particularly fine Jacobean four-poster.

The setting is as fascinating as the history. On the English side, the rolling wooded farmland of Herefordshire gives way to the Malvern Hills beyond. On the Welsh side the great Fwddog Ridge dominates the landscape. Part of the Black Mountains, it runs north to Hay-on-Wye, all within the Brecon Beacons National Park, with its interesting mountain centre.

To match the superb setting and the historic house, the food and the wine is of the very highest standard. It is renowned for its clay pigeon range and known for the efficiency with which it runs its conference facilities. A wonderful place. You are welcome for drinks, to dine or stay.

USEFUL INFORMATION

OPEN: All year round. Non-resident
evening meal by reservation
CHILDREN: Welcome
CREDIT CARDS: Diners/Amex/Master/
Visa
LICENSED: Full On
ACCOMMODATION: All en-suite.
Four-posters

RESTAURANT: Fresh, local produce,
highest qualtiy
BAR FOOD: Bar snacks available
VEGETARIAN: Catered for
DISABLED ACCESS: No
GARDEN: 16 acres.Beautiful river setting

Leicester Cathedral

Leicester

"Nothing is worth more than this day"

Goethe

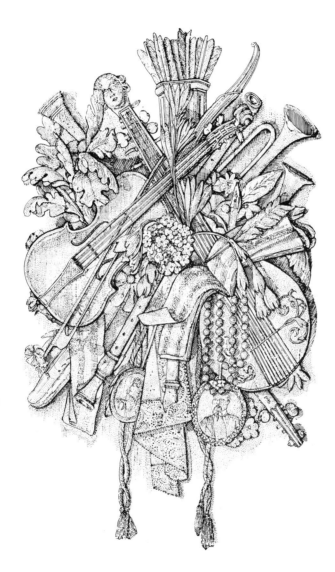

The City of Leicester

by Joy David

It is difficult to enthuse about LEICESTER CATHEDRAL having been so fortunate in my explorations elsewhere. Although St Martin's has a medieval plan, what one sees is almost entirely Victorian. Its finest attribute is the soaring spire between the nave and chancel, designed by Raphael Brandon in 1867, rising to 220feet; it manages to dig itself out and away from the ever encroaching buildings of the 20th century which cramp its style. Whilst St Martins in the main dates from 1867 it did not become a cathedral until 1927. The spire of the cathedral was once the most prominent of Leicester's landmarks but it is now hemmed in by so many modern blocks that the church has become quite difficult to find. You will find it close to the Clock Tower, in the very centre of the city.

It is a dignified church, furnished inside with handsome oak fittings, organ gallery, chancel screen, the Chapel of the Leicestershire Regiment and a medieval Lady Chapel which now serves as the Consistory Court, with endless rows of chairs and well polished parquet floors everywhere. I understand the the nave arcades are medieval but most of the rest of the church has been rebuilt or at best thoroughly restored. The chancel is filled with choir and canons' stalls and the Bishop's throne designed in 1927 by Sir Charles Nicholson. I heard it described once as 'it has the air of a well-furnished college chapel - small but dignified.'

Visitors are encouraged to tour the building and what impressed me most was the fine roof, the decent Victorian glass throughout the church and the stone and wood carvings. The North chapel contains many memorials to the old Leicester family of Herrick with the earliest dating to 1589, with many tomb slabs erected round the walls. The father of Robert Herrick, the poet was born in Leicester and the mother of Dean Swift, who was a Herrick, is buried here. The South chapel will reward you with its many 18th century monuments. Two windows by Christopher Whall should be looked for; the first is the east window and the other, the smaller one at the west end of the South aisle.

In the floor of the chancel is a slab inscribed:

RICHARD III
King of England
killed at Bosworth Field
in this county
22 August 1485
Buried in the church of the Grey Friars
in this parish.

What it does not tell you is that Richard's body was brought back to Leicester via Bow Bridge - where there is a plaque - after the battle of Bosworth. He was buried in Greyfriars Friary but his bones were later thrown into the River Soar from the bridge. The plaque recalls the spot near where 'lie the remains of Richard III, last of the Plantagenets, 1485.'

There are many more interesting monuments. For example in the North Aisle there is one to John Whatton dated 1656, signed by Joshua Marshall. In the chancel there is one of Rococo design to the son and wives of Gabriel Newton, Alderman of Leicester who died in 1746. He was the great benefactor to education in the city of Leicester. In the South Chapel is the tablet by Bacon erected in 1814 by the architect John Johnson to his parents. It also tells of the man himself 'late of the parish of St Mary-le-Bow, London'. He was the architect of Leicester's County Rooms and also of the Shire Hall in Chelmsford and rebuilder of the nave of Chelmsford Cathedral which you will have read about earlier. I always enjoy reading odd inscriptions on memorials and there are many of them here.

It is not just for the cathedral that you should visit **Leicester**. People have lived and worked here since before the Roman Conquest. The Romans established Ratae Corieltauvorum as a flourishing regional capital and remains of its public baths are still visible today at Jewry Wall. The Romans recognised its position as worthy because of its many trade routes. Today it still has an enviable central location within two and a half hours drive of many of Britain's largest centres of population. Leicester is Britain's first Environment City and it shows in its surroundings and green spaces - those used to more built up cities will be impressed by the parks and gardens, green wedges, foot and cycle paths and wildlife sanctuaries in the city centre itself.

Anglo Saxon times saw Leicester as the probable centre of a Saxon Bishopric and the arrival of the Danish Invaders established the town as one of the five principal Boroughs of the Danelaw.

Granted land by William the Conqueror, Hugh de Grantmesnil took steps to defend his possessions by building a simple 'motte and bailey' castle next to the River Soar at Leicester, the remains of which are visible today. Successive Earls of Leicester built the GREAT HALL and THE CHURCH OF ST MARY DE CASTRO nearby. Simon de Montfort; 'the founder of Parliament' became Earl of Leicester in 1231.

During the 14th and 15th centuries many more buildings sprang up around the castle and further afield outside the city walls, hence the 'New Work' or 'Newarke' the TRINITY HOSPITAL, THE MAGAZINE GATEWAY, PRINCE RUPERT'S GATEWAY, GATEWAY HOUSE and THE GUILDHALL belong to this period. During the Civil War, Leicester supported the Parliamentary cause and witnessed fierce fighting as the walls of the Newarke were breached by Prince Rupert. Scenes of violence and plunder followed and many citizens were ruthlessly murdered in the streets - all to no avail, for after the Battle of Naseby the King returned to Leicester in 1646 as a prisoner.

The growth of industry during the 18th and 19th centuries brought important changes to Castle Park and the development of the knitwear industry led to major expansion of the city. Canals, railways and factories were constructed to service these new industries, evidence of which can still be seen around the Park.

Leicester has some fourteen museums and a host of other places to see so I am going to take you along CASTLE PARK HERITAGE TRAIL in an attempt to cover as many as possible. This trail is some three miles long in the heart of the city. It endeavours to let you discover the role each place has played in the development of the city from Roman times to the present day. To make it simpler the trail has been divided into sections which allows you the opportunity to stop wherever you feel so inclined. I suggest you obtain a map from the Tourist Information Centre which will guide you although it is well signposted along the route of the trail. The trail makes use of pedestrian crossings throughout but care should be taken in crossing busy roads. Much of the trail is accessible by wheelchair although there are a number of difficult spots. Contact the T.I.C for further information; (0533) 511300.

In the Blue Section which takes you from St Martins to Newarke Houses starting at the T.I.C you turn right into Cank Street and follow the road to St Martins. The National Westminster Bank on your left stands on the site of G R E Y F R I A R S MONASTERY where the body of King Richard III was publicly displayed after his death on Bosworth Field in 1485. Legend tells that Richard III was leaving Leicester for the Battle of Bosworth, his spur hit a stone on the parapet of Bow Bridge. An old woman prophetised that his head would hit the same stone on the way back, and this apparently came true when his broken, stripped body was brought back from battle.

From St Martins you turn left into New Street. One of the last remaining remnants of the wall of GREYFRIARS MONASTERY can be seen at the back of a car park on your righthand side. Where New Street meets Friars Lane, turn right until the junction with Millstone Lane, where you will find the entrance to the subway to your left. The subway has recently been renovated, partly inspired by the many Roman mosaics which have been found around the city. At the mid-point of the subway climb the steps to THE MAGAZINE GATEWAY. The gateway was built in the 14th century. During the Civil War it was used for the storage of arms; hence its present name. It now houses THE MUSEUM OF THE ROYAL LEICESTERSHIRE REGIMENT. For many people with a military background this museum will appeal. The Regiment was once the 17th Foot and its history unfolds as you wander amongst the many exhibits and documents of this distinguished regiment.

When you leave The Magazine turn right and descend the steps, turn left at the bottom and take the first left into the tunnel. At the end of the tunnel, climb the steps to your right. At the top turn right where 50 metres on the left is THE JAIN CENTRE. What an extraordinary place this is. Originally it was built as a Congregational Chapel but has now been transformed by the Jain Community of Leicester into the first Jain Centre of Europe. Jainism is an ancient religion that teaches love to all living creatures and a way of life which rejects violence, self seeking and dishonesty. Fifty two beautiful hand-carved marble pillars, hand carved ceilings and domes, as well as stained glass windows andd other exhibits, now dominate this brick built 19th century building. Without doubt this Centre contains the finest examples of Indian traditional architecture in the western world. Open every day to devotees; visitors are welcome

Castle Gardens, originally part of the Castle area in Leicester

171

into the entrance lobby and can view the interior by appointment. Tel: (0533) 543091.

Once outside the Jain Centre and rejoining our hectic world, retrace your steps back to the subway. Descend the steps crossing over the central courtyard to the steps signposted 'Newarke Houses'. Climb the steps and continue along The Newarke. On your right are the Newarke Houses. Two fine Tudor Houses - The CHANTRY HOUSE of 1513 and SKEFFINGTON HOUSE of about 1600, have been carefully preserved and now house displays on the social history of Leicestershire from 1500, including 17th century panelled rooms, period furniture and a re-creation of a 19th-century Leicester Street.

Having left the museum continue along The Newarke, cross over the junction with Castle View, 50 metres on the right is TRINITY HOSPITAL. The hospital was founded in 1331 by Henry, Earl of Lancaster and Leicester. Much of the original hospital and its chapel survive. The hospital continues to provide residential accommodation. It can be viewed by appointment only.

Now turn right into CASTLE GARDENS. With the Castle Motte this was originally part of the castle area. If you follow the path to the right you can see Castle Motte, the remains of the artificial mound probably raised by William the Conqueror. The Motte is open to the public and interpretation boards explain its history. After visiting the Motte, return to the path. To your left you can see the statue of Richard III which commemorates his links with Leicester. The path will then take you to more steps at the top of which is a small section of the foundations of the medieval castle wall.

Leaving the Gardens by the gate at the top of the steps and following the road to the right you will arrive at CASTLE HOUSE which stands in front of the church. It is a fine early Georgian building with an attractive Tuscan-style porch.

Next ST MARY DE CASTRO CHURCH with its dramatic spire with crockets leaping up to a great height, which is in a wonderful setting beside the Norman Castle, above the River Soar. Founded in the early years of the 12th century by the first Earl of Leicester, as a Collegiate church attached to the castle. Many Norman features are still visible, and a walk around will reveal much of interest including some fascinating tombstones. Geoffrey Chaucer who wrote the Canterbury Tales was probably married in this church and in 1426 the four year old King Henry VI was knighted there.

GATEWAY HOUSE is an attractive timber framed house dating from 1447. It was originally separate from Castle House, to which it is now joined. If you walk through the archway you will come to THE GREAT HALL of the castle, which faces you on CASTLE GREEN - Castle Green incidentally was the site of many grisly executions in medieval times. It was built in the 12th century but substantially altered during the Middle Ages. In 1695 the East aisle was demolished and a new brick frontage built which can be seen today. Despite these changes the GREAT HALL is still recognised as one of the most important medieval secular buildings remaining in England.

THE TURRET GATEWAY was the southern gate to the castle dating from about 1423. Portcullis grooves can still be seen. Fierce encounters took place here during the Civil War and it was almost destroyed by a mob during the election riots in 1832. If you continue through the Gateway and walk through Castle view on your left you will be able to see the remains of a medieval wall, with holes cut in it during the Civil War for musket fire. You can enter the gardens of Newarke Houses on your left hand side.

Turn right when you reach the junction to the Newarke and walk past Trinity Hospital again. Continue past the entrance to Castle Gardens, cross the bridge and turn first left into Western Boulevard. Descend the steps on your left to the towpath. Here you come to the Riverside Walk to Jewry Wall Museum. Turn left at the bottom of the steps and follow the 'Mile Straight'. Rowing regattas are annually held here.

RIVERSIDE PARK is a fascinating stretch of eight miles along the footpaths of the River Soar and Grand Union Canal which passes through Castle Park and allows an insight into Leicester's early industrial history. The dominant Pex Factory was originally a worsted spinning factory providing yarn for the knitting trade. Goods were brought to and from the city by the major waterway network. The River Soar was 'canalised' in the late 19th century forming the 'Mile Straight'. This nearly destroyed a great reed bed although it is still possible to see a small part of it. The old line of the Great Central Railway has now been developed as a pedestrian walk and cycleway.

Continue along the towpath passing under both spans of the bridge and then climb the steps on your left which will bring you to THE DOULTON MERMAIDS, the original terracotta decoration from Leicester's old wholesale market was re-assembled on this site in 1982. On the main road, turn right and walk along Bow Bridge about which I have already written. Retrace your steps past the 'mermaids' and up the hill to ST NICHOLAS CIRCLE. Follow the footpath to bring you to the JEWRY WALL MUSEUM on your left. This is the county's Archaeological Museum which includes the Bronze Age Welby Hoard and Romano-British mosaics, in a modern building which overlooks the Roman baths site and the massive 2nd century Roman Jewry Wall. It is the largest civil Roman Structure surviving in Britain today. It is an interesting fact that over thirty Roman mosaics have been found in Leicester.

Leaving the museum continue along the road, turning left after the footbridge into St Nicholas Walk to gain a close up view of the Jewry Wall. On your right is ST NICHOLAS CHURCH. Enter the churchyard by the gate. This is the oldest church in Leicester dating from Anglo-Saxon times. Although much changed by the Normans and again altered in the 19th century, it retains examples of the Saxon world incorporating Roman tiles and bricks from the adjacent Roman bath site. Walk through the churchyard and leave by the gate to the main road. Use the three pedestrian crossings to cross the busy roads and walk around the car park to enter Applegate. WYGSTON'S HOUSE is in front of you.

This house is thought to have been the home of Roger Wygston, a fabulously rich medieval wool merchant and city benefactor. The rear wing is 15th century and the frontage 18th century. It now houses THE MUSEUM OF COSTUME which displays varied collections of costumes and textiles dating from the 18th century to the 20th century. There is a reconstructed 1920's draper's and shoe shop.

Crossing over into Guildhall Lane, after 20 metres on the right you will come to THE GUILDHALL where the original hall dates from about 1390. It was built by the Corpus Christi Guild as a meeting place. By 1500 it had begun to be used as the town hall and continued to be used as such until the new Town Hall was built in 1876. The Guildhall was greatly extended in about 1586 and a library and Mayor's parlour were added in the 1630's. From 1836 the newly established police force had its headquarters here and 19th century cells and police equipment can be seen. When the new Town Hall was built in 1876 the Guildhall continued to be used as a Domestic Science School for poor girls of the town.

Turn right when you leave the Guildhall and right again into St Martins West where, on the left, you will come to the entrance of the Cathedral grounds. You are now back virtually where you started from the Tourist Information Centre in St Martins.

There are many more places that have not come into this trail and which are worth seeking out. THE MUSEUM

OF TECHNOLOGY in the 1891 Abbey Pumping Station in Corporation Road, for example, where the Giant Beam Engines hold a fascination for many. There are four of them housed here.

Just 2 miles from the city centre off the A6 Loughborough road in Church Road is BELGRAVE HALL, a small Queen Anne country house built between 1709-13. It is delightful with its period furniture. Outside, coaches and agricultural implements are displayed in the stable block. The gardens are exquisite, whether it is the rock and water garden or the period and botanical gardens. It is open to the public every day with the exception of Christmas Day, Boxing Day and Good Friday, Monday-Saturday from 10-5.30pm and on Sundays from 2-5.30pm.

Something a bit more mundane is THE BRITISH GAS EAST MIDLANDS GAS MUSEUM in Aylestone Road. It is an extraordinary place showing the history of the gas industry in a wide range of exhibits. I was somewhat reluctant to go there because it sounded dull but how wrong I was and how much I learnt of this vital industry. It is open Tuesday-Friday 12.30-4.30pm.

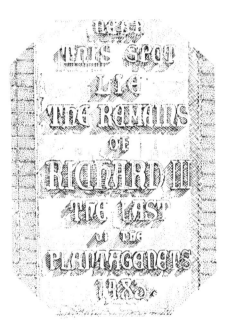

The plaque on Bow Bridge commemorating the site where Richad III's bones were thrown into the Soar.

The unassuming doors of THE COUNTRY RECORDS OFFICE at 57 New Walk open to display an extensive collection of private and public records together with urban and rural archives relating to the county. The opening hours are Monday-Thursday 9.15-5pm, Friday 9.15-4.45pm. It is open most Saturdays

from 9-15-12-15pm, but always closed on Bank Holiday weekends.

For lovers of fine paintings THE LEICESTERSHIRE MUSEUM AND ART GALLERY is the home of a wonderful collection of English art from the 16th century onwards, plus some Old masters and 19th and 20th century French paintings. There are important ethnic collections particularly Gujerati and also natural history and geology galleries.

Leicester is a city full of suprises. I had no idea until I came here to take a serious look that the city is one of the country's ten largest, or that it has the biggest and probably the finest covered market in Europe. I found that the variety found on the Market is reflected in the shopping experience throughout the city and Leicester's retailers are very much aware of how important value for money is to today's consumer.

Leicester has become the Renaissance city of England. A decade ago it looked tired, more than a little uninteresting and saddened by its contracting textile industry. Today it has risen to the challenge and found a new role as champion of urban regeneration and environmental concern. You can see evidence of it everywhere. There are restored buildings, pedestrianised streets and squares, a dazzling new shopping mall, and an abundance of trees and flowers show that this is a city with confidence and vision.

The renovated city centre has something for every taste and pocket. New shops offer innovative ideas at affordable prices especially for the young, style conscious customers. This is more and more a University town which brings the young to its midst but its older citizens have also benefited from fresh enterprises - from the department stores in THE SHIRES CENTRE which include The Body Shop, W H Smith, Miss Selfridge, Principles, Boots, Dolcis, and Olympus Sport, all complemented by a fascinating mix of smaller retail outlets, all offering quality merchandise.

The Shires is palatial, practical and convenient. Parking is easy in the centre's 1,900 space car park with immediate access to the shops. The centre's cafes and ice cream parlours are there to tempt you.

Nearby in the High Street and East Bond Street you can find additional interesting shops and restaurants. Dominoe's Toys will keep children happy for hours. I browsed around BLACKTHORN BOOKS which surprisingly, has a first class vegetarian restaurant in the basement known as BREAD AND ROSES!

ST MARTIN'S SQUARE is definitely the place to be when the sun shines. It is relaxed and there is nothing more pleasant than to sit at one of the pavement cafes and watch the passers by. Fine restored buildings and sympathetic additions help in creating this feeling of quality, well being, charm and style. All around the Square are the winding lanes of the medieval town. Loseby Lane has speciality shops and there is a pleasant cafe and a couple of traditional tea rooms.

Walk across the High Street from The Shires and you will discover possibly the best kept secret among Leicester treasure hunters. THE ARCADES are rich with unique and original gems if you appreciate the appeal of a good second hand book or fashion with an alternative edge. In Silver Street you wil find THE GLOBE one of Leicester's oldest pubs.

THE MARKET is a piece of living history. For over 700 years the tradespeople of Leicester have been selling their wares on this spot, and it remains as vibrant and lively as ever. Value and variety is the hallmark of The Market's Traders. You can buy apples and pears from the stall run by Gary Lineker's family. The rare and the exotic are commonplace here - Kenyan matoke, karelia, okra, saragwo and mooli are as everyday as cauliflower and potatoes. **Melton Mowbray,** not too far away from Leicester, is famous for its pork pies and you will find them sold on the stalls as well as the famous Red Leicester cheese and the local Stilton.

It is the chatter and buzz of the market that I find intoxicating. As the day progresses so the noise becomes greater. Prices change hourly and the stallholder's cheerful patter outweighs the conversation of the purchaser.

MARKET STREET has been pedestrianised and it is delightful with its seating, hanging baskets and period street lamps. Many of the buildings date from Victorian times and give the street considerable charm. Fenwicks department store is here and so too is one of my favourite bookshshops, Dillons. Camera buffs have three shops to choose from here and in neighbouring Belvoir Street so there is no excuse not to take pictures. Just around the corner is the magnificent Town Hall Square - worthy of the attention of any photographer.

GALLOWTREE GATE despite its macabre name is charming with its floral baskets and maturing trees; pedestrianised of course. You will often find crowds around the street entertainers and pavement artists, and there are plenty of benches where you can sit and take the weight off your feet. At night CHURCHGATE is alive with the sound of revelry from those who frequent its clubs and bars but by day it provides a peaceful pedestrian environment for shoppers.

THE HAYMARKET is the home of Leicester's theatre which is one of the leading provincial theatres in the country with an enviable record of quality productions that go direct to the West End. Tucked away from the grand Victorian houses of Stoneygate, a couple of miles from the city centre and just off London Road, is Allandale Road and Francis Street which contain a compact collection of small, up-market shops selling quality antiques, exclusive designs and interesting gifts.

Known as THE GOLDEN MILE, Belgrave Road, leading into Melton Road, is well worth taking a short bus ride from the Haymarket to visit. It is the busy centre of the city's Gujarati community. Displays of Indian culture abound in almost every shop window. Golden jewellery, fabulous silks, delicious sweetmeats and savouries are everywhere, but this is not a tourist attraction so much as a vibrant commercial centre which attracts visitors from all over the country and beyond.

One place you must certainly visit in the centre of Leicester is WELFORD PLACE at 9 Welford Park. It is a delightful Victorian building which is open to the public from early morning with food in perpetual motion, until late in the evening. Samuel Stephen Butler was the inspiration behind the construction of this house which was erected by Henry Herbert and opened on the 6th November 1877 as a private member's club. It is superb in its own right and there is an associated premises up the road in Lincoln, out of which was born the ideas being put into effect at Welford Place. Called the Wig and Mitre it is known and recognised by all publications of serious intent. What makes Welford Place particularly special is the thought, care and attention which is put into it.

GORSE HILL CITY FARM in Anstey Lane is a Voluntary Community Project with small scale humane farming and organic horticulture. On the attractive 3 acre site are rare breed animals, a cob walled hen house, an old carter's pond and picnic area as well as the Buttercup Hill Cafe. Admission is free but they badly need donations to cover their running costs. As a guide it is hoped that visitors can give at least £1 for adults and 50p for children. The farm is open 6 days a week and closed every Wednesday. Summer 10am-6pm Winter 10am-4pm

How can I ever have imagined that Leicester was dull? When you come to Leicester where are you going to stay? An important question. I have my favourites, and it is to those I am going to introduce you now but it does not mean to say that there are not many more excellent places.

In Leicester itself is one of the two Moat Houses I can recommend. THE LEICESTER FOREST MOAT HOUSE in Hinckley Road is comparatively small with just 34 tastefully furnished bedrooms. It is splendidly situated 3 miles from the Junction 21 interchange of the M1 and M69 motorways. The cosy bar is well stocked and next to it is the candlelit Restaurant Giverny renowned for its excellent and extensive choice of dishes. The lively Sportsmans Arms produces a totally different atmosphere and is very popular at lunchtimes when it serves a good selection of hot and cold meals at very reasonable prices.

I wanted to tell you about one or two places outside the city which you might otherwise not get to hear about. LEICESTER MOAT HOUSE at **Oadby** is reputed to have been built on the site of a dwelling for the monks who were engaged in the building of St Peters Church in 1400AD. It is just three and a half miles from the centre of Leicester and only four and a half miles from the M1 and M69 with both Birmingham and East Midlands airports easily accesible. It is a landmark in Oadby with its extensive grounds, pool and delightful walled gardens. It offers a high standard of accommodation, excellent food and service, and extensive conference and banqueting facilities.

THE EAST MIDLANDS HOTEL at **Loughborough** delights everyone who stays there. Family owned it has 53 super bedrooms. The olde worlde charm of the restaurant heightens your enjoyment of the excellent food. There is a first class leisure centre, banqueting and conference facilities. For most people the reception foyer is the heart of the hotel and it is wonderful to sit there and absorb the atmosphere. You will be lulled by the sound of gently cascading water from the fountains, the strains of soft music in the background and the sight of trellisingfoliage creeping from the lanternlight glass roof two storeys above.

The triangle that is bordered by the M69, M6 and M1 south of Leicester has a coterie of pleasing places to visit. There is HIGHCROSS HOUSE at **Lutterworth,** renowned for its comfort, food and atmosphere. THE COUNTRYMAN at **Sharnford** does not boast accommodation but has everything that a good country pub should have in a quiet village setting, surrounded by beautiful unspoilt countryside. It has the added bonus of the gentle babbling of Soar Brook running through its centre. Kingfishers nest on the stream and herbs and wildflowers grow in abundance in this rural backwater.

Seek out THE COVE PUBLIC HOUSE at Stoney Cove, **Stoney Stanton** not because it is a beautiful building for it is definitely not that, but what it does have is a friendly, welcoming interior which encourages you to stay and enjoy the hospitality it has to offer. It sits below a huge quarry face and on a nice day you can sit on one of the terrace's overlooking the lake which is now the setting for theNATIONAL DIVING CENTRE and water sports.

If one is allowed to have favourite places then I have to confess to a partiality for**Rutland Water** where alongside Europe's largest man made lake is THE NORMANTON PARK HOTEL on its South Shore. It is a converted Georgian coach house and stable block which commands superb views across the water. Once the hotel was part of Normanton Hall, the ancestral seat of the Earls of Ancaster. In 1927 the main Hall was demolished and rebuilt elsewhere. The stable block and coach house, both Grade II listed buildings, were converted in 1980 into what is assuredly one of the most gracious hotels in this area.

Also overlooking Rutland Water, BARNSDALE LODGE is delightfully different. It is a 17th-century farmhouse with barns, which have been completely renovated, totally in an Edwardian theme. There are exposed stone walls, flagstone floors, chunky old tables, highback, highly polished chairs, a cosy parlour with chaise longues and well upholstered Edwardian seats. There are three interconnecting dining rooms serving English dishes from the 'Edwardian Country Farmhouse Fare'. It is busy all day long with people popping in for coffee, bar lunches and afternoon teas which are served in the buttery. The 17 bedrooms, each furnished in Edwardian style, have private facilities and are exceptionally comfortable. Robert Reid, the owner, is also a director of the Normanton Park Hotel. The whole ambience of the Barnsdale is one of warmth, comfort and hospitality.

Wherever you go in Leicestershire you will find warmhearted people. Leicester proved to me that it is a great city. Yes, I was disappointed in the cathedral compared to the might of **Canterbury** and the beauty of **Wells** but it is still a joy to see and the regeneration of the city makes it a place that should come high on any visitor's itinerary.

HIGH CROSS HOUSE

Hotel

High Cross, Lutterworth,
Leicestershire, LE17 5AT.

Tel: (0455) 220840

USEFUL INFORMATION

OPEN: All year. Early morning until late at night
CHILDREN: Welcome. Catered for, high chairs, cots
CREDIT CARDS: None taken
LICENSED: Table Licence
ACCOMMODATION: 6 rooms, 3 en-suite

RESTAURANT: Traditional English. Generous portions
BAR FOOD: Snacks, sandwiches, Ploughmans
VEGETARIAN: Always a choice & Vegan
DISABLED ACCESS: Downstairs bedroom plus bathroom
GARDEN: Very large & walled garden

High Cross hamlet consists of four houses and the beautiful timber-framed High Cross House. Lutterworth is 6 miles away and the fascinating city of Leicester just 12 miles. For those wanting to take a look at Leicester's Cathedral and the many interesting facets to this, one of England's ten biggest cities, High Cross House would be a wonderful base. Apart from its attraction as an old listed building it has so much to offer. All the rooms are enormous in this house that used to be The Sun Inn. In the garden is a monument which reinforces the fact that this area was once the Roman centre of England.

Jain Galliford and her family are welcoming people and it is very much a home from home. The six beautifully furnished bedrooms are warm and one has an amazing antique four-poster bed. It has not been possible because of the restrictions of a listed building to make every room en-suite; three of them are and for the others the bathroom is close by. The house is run informally and yet with a professionalism that ensures that meals are beautifully cooked and everything in the house shines. There are three chocolate Labradors who will also make you feel at home. Quite frequently the whole house is taken over for weddings or special occasions – there is sufficient room to put up a marquee if needs be.

People who have stayed here will tell you that nothing is too much trouble when it comes to their comfort. Children are more than welcome and dogs by prior arrangement. There is always a choice of dishes for Vegetarians and Vegans as well. A thoroughly happy house in which to stay.

BRITISH GAS EAST MIDLANDS GAS MUSEUM

Museum

John Doran Museum, Leicester Service Centre,
Aylestone Road, Leicester, LE2 7QH.

Tel: (0533) 535506

USEFUL INFORMATION

OPEN: Tues-Fri: 12.30-4.30pm excluding Tuesdays after Bank Holidays and Good Friday.
CHILDREN: Welcome
CAR PARKING: Free
BUS ROUTES: Leicester Citybus No 37 passes the museum
PARTIES: Welcomed providing advance bookings are made

The John Doran Museum is Britain's first specialist gas museum which is regularly open to the public. It is housed in the gatehouse of the original Aylestone Road gasworks of Leicster Corporation, begun in 1878. The museum, which opened in April 1977, is devoted to the preservation of the heritage of the gas industry, both in the East Midlands and further afield.

On the ground floor you will find the hardware of the industry in its many forms. The display follows a logical sequence in the progress of gas from its production to the customer. One display illustrates the ways in which gas was made before the advent of natural gas, both from coal and oil, with examples of typical tools and equipment. Another shows Instrumentation in which the means of quality testing gas are illustrated, both for lighting quality and heating quality. This has aided the implementation of legal standards since 1860. There are also working examples of communication equipment used for passing information on gas pressures etc.

Distribution required a wide variety of tools and equipment and these are well displayed. The history of pipe jointing methods is of particular interest. A whole range of meters are to be seen and through the doorway in the end room a National Gas Engine is housed. At one time gas was used almost exclusively for lighting. Here there are working examples and finally all sorts of appliances are on show from fires to the unusual items such as hairdryers and magic lanterns. On the first floor is the archive and special display area providing endless surprises including a gas radio of 1939.

Leicester Promotions,
7-9 Every Street, Leicester, LE1 6AG.

Tel: (0533) 856734
Fax: (0533) 555726

CASTLE PARK
Heritage Trail

Leicester becomes more fascinating and worthy of visiting the more deeply you look into its past, its heritage and what it has to offer today. Castle Park, for example, has quiet corners in which you will find buildings and structures which are reminders of Leicester's continuous existence for 2,000 years. Museums reflect the social history of the area and informative displays provide background to the many historic buildings. The County and City Councils are developing Castle Park as a heritage centre to bring together the many surviving elements of the City's history.

The Heritage Trail takes you to some of Leicester's best known historic sites and buildings and explains the role each has played in the development of the City from Roman times to the present day, The trail is three miles long and it is possible to complete it in two hours, however you may wish to spend more time looking around certain buildings which you will find described in detail at the beginning of this chapter. The trail has been divided up into smaller section, (blue, orange, green, red, purple and brown) so that it is possible to begin and end it at any of the Information Points in Castle Park. The length of walk which you take can be varied according to how energetic you feel. There are signs along the route of the trail to keep you on the right path. The trail makes use of pedestrian crossings throughout but care should be taken in crossing busy roads.

You can start from the T.I.C. From the Cathedral or Jain Centre Information Points join the blue section where marked. From Newarke Houses Information Point begin at the orange section. From Jewry

Wall Information Point begin at the purple section. W.C's are situated in the Newarke subway and at the museums at Jewry Wall and Wygston's House.

All the museums on the trail are open from 10-5.30pm weekdays and 2-5.30pm on Sundays and are closed on Good Friday, Christmas and Boxing Day. The Cathedral is open every day, St Mary de Castro on Saturdays and Bank Holidays from Easter to the end of October and the Jain Centre entrance lobby from 9-5pm Monday-Friday. Much of the trail is accessible by wheelchair although there are a number of difficult spots. Contact the T.I.C for further information (0533) 511300. From January 1994 (0533) 650555

Leicester Promotions,
7-9 Every Street, Leicester, LE1 6AG.

Tel: (0533) 856734
Fax: (0533) 555726

THE GOLDEN MILE
Shopping Facilities

The Golden Mile is the name attributed to Belgrave Road which leads onto Melton Road. This busy commercial highway is in the heart of Leicester's Gujarati community. All manner of services may be purchased here including some of the best vegetarian restaurants in Britain. Bobbys recently won a mention in 'The Good Food Guide'. There are many Pann shops selling delicious sweetmeats and savouries. There are innumerable clothing, jewellery and food centres revealing some of the brilliance of Indian fashion and cuisine. There is a major centre of Asian music. It is possible to see displays of Indian culture in almost every shop window. This area contains major Indian banks as well as other commercial centres.

The area abounds in places of worship Brahma Samaj, Shree Swaminarayan Centre and other centres. There are two major mosques on the Loughborough Road nearby. This district is often packed with people seeing friends, chatting and shopping. There are also fast food centres and cafes such as the Chaat House that offers good food to those in a hurry. New exciting dance magazines are on sale as well as Gujarati games and sports magazines. Posters advertise Gurba, Raas and top singers from India who visit nearby centres to packed audiences. The newly refurbished Coliseum Centre was a major venue for Navrati and when the Diwali lights are switched on the effect is magical. Melton Road is going places but there is still time to stand still and absorb the age old culture of India in a modern setting.

USEFUL INFORMATION

OPEN: Normal Shop opening times

CHILDREN: Shoppers Playcentre in the Market, St Martins Sq. For details Telephone (0533) 533966

DISABLED ACCESS: Shop Mobility Scheme of free loan of Powered chairs etc. Telephone (0533) 526694 for details

LEICESTER FOREST MOAT HOUSE
Hotel

Hinckley Road, Leicester Forest East,
Leicester, LE3 3GH.

Tel: (0533) 394661
Fax: (0533) 394952

USEFUL INFORMATION

OPEN: 24 hours
CHILDREN: Welcome
CREDIT CARDS: All major cards
LICENSED: Full On Licence
ACCOMMODATION: 34 rooms with private bathrooms

RESTAURANT: Traditional, French, a la carte & Table d'Hote
BAR FOOD: Excellent home-cooked dishes. Lunchtime & evenings

VEGETARIAN: Always 20 choices
DISABLED ACCESS: Yes but not in rooms
GARDEN: Yes

Leicester Forest Moat House is what you choose to make it. You will find it as conducive to a weekend retreat as it is to most important business occasions. Staying here is a sheer pleasure whatever the reason and it is equally good as a meeting place in which to enjoy a drink or dinner with friends. You will find it situated on the Leicester-Hinckley Road four miles from the city centre. Three miles from junction 21 interchange of the M1 and M69 motorways. The National Exhibition Centre and Birmingham International Airport are both 30 miles away. Ample car parking awaits you at the Moat House.

There are 34 tastefully furnished bedrooms furnished with your comfort in mind, having direct dial telephones, remote control radio and television, and tea/coffee hospitality trays. Every room has a private bathroom complete with a shower and hair dryer.

At the end of a day's holiday or business, or even at lunchtime, the cosy, well stocked bar just next to the candlelit restaurant is an ideal place in which to relax. The Restaurant Giverny is renowned for its excellent and extensive choice of menus and has covers for 80. Everything is cooked using the freshest produce from local suppliers. The lively Sportsmans Arms provides a totally different atmosphere and is very popular at lunchtime when it serves a good selection of hot and cold meals at very reasonable prices. The Leicester Forest Moat House also excels at catering for banquets and wedding receptions.

WELFORD PLACE
Restaurant Pub of Rare Quality

9 Welford Place,
Leicester, LE1 6ZH.

Tel: (0533) 470758
Fax: (0533) 471843

USEFUL INFORMATION

OPEN: 8am-midnight. Sundays, Good Friday and Xmas Day
CHILDREN: Welcome if well behaved
CREDIT CARDS: All major cards
LICENSED: Full On Licence
ACCOMMODATION: Not applicable Private party rooms available

RESTAURANT: English with Italian, French and international influence
BAR FOOD: Breakfast, sandwiches, teas, and a wide range of daily specials
VEGETARIAN: Several dishes daily
DISABLED ACCESS: Yes
GARDEN: No

Welford Place, a delightful Victorian building situated in the heart of Leicester, is open to the public from early in the morning, with food in perpetual motion, until late in the evening. Samuel Stephen Bankart was the inspiration behind the constrution of this building which was erected by Henry Herbert and opened on the 6th November 1877 as a private member's club. It is superb in its own right and there is an associated premises up the road in Lincoln, out of which were born the ideas being put into effect at Welford Place. Called the Wig and Mitre it is known everywhere and is recognised by all publications of serious intent. It really is worth a visit.

Flexibility is important to people coming to Welford Place knowing it is open, civilised and reliable, in a variety of contexts. There is a wide range of food available from early in the morning continuously till the end of the evening. The staff are trained to care as well for those who need quick, slick service as for those who prefer to take things at a more leisurely pace. Cooking is English with Italian, French and international influence. There is an extensive wine list and function and private rooms which can cater for as few as six guests to as many as a hundred. What makes Welford Place particularly special is the thought, care and attention which is put into it.

Nottingham Road, Loughborough,
Leicestershire, LE11 1ET.

Tel: (0509) 233056
Fax: (0509) 268665

EAST MIDLANDS HOTEL
Hotel

The East Midlands Hotel delights every visitor who enters its portals by its tranquil atmosphere and the genuine warm welcome which greets you. It is a family owned hotel with a friendliness of service that is only surpassed by the assurance that a full team effort is provided to maintain the efficiency and attention to detail on which they pride themselves.

Loughborough is an historic market town, surrounded by rural English landscape and rolling countryside, meandering waterways, villages and quiet copses. The cathedral cities of Leicester, Derby and Lincoln are within easy distance and so is the old castle of Nottingham with its legend of Robin Hood. The East Midlands Hotel is ideal as a base also while you head for rugged Charnwood with its craggy outcrops, the celebrated scenery of Rutland Water, and the beautiful Vale of Belvoir. For the energetic, Alton Towers or the American Adventure Theme Park offer full days out.

Each of the 53 tastefully decorated guest bedrooms have bathrooms ensuite and every modern facility. There are two bars for your enjoyment with food and an entertainment programme. The olde worlde charm of the retaurants heightens your enjoyment of the excellent food. There is a first class leisure centre, banqueting and conference facilities. For most people the reception foyer is the heart of the hotel and it is wonderful to sit there and absorb the atmosphere. You will be lulled by the sound of gently cascading water from the fountains, the strains of soft music in the background and the sight of trellising foliage creeping from the lanternlight glass roof two storeys above.

USEFUL INFORMATION

OPEN: All Year
CHILDREN: Welcome. Highchairs
CREDIT CARDS: All cajor cards except Switch
LICENSED: Full On Licence
ACCOMMODATION: 53 ensuite rooms

RESTAURANT: Good wholesome fare. Rest:7-10pm: Mon-Sat & Sun lunch
BAR FOOD: Carvery: Mon-Fri: 12-2pm. Salads. Chef's specials
VEGETARIAN: 3 dishes daily
DISABLED ACCESS: No
GARDEN: No but central roofed open area with garden seating & fountain

---

Wigston Road, Oadby,
Leicester, LE2 5QE.

Tel: (0533) 719441
Fax: (0533) 720559

LEICESTERSHIRE MOAT HOUSE
Hotel

This comfortable hotel is reputed to have been built on the site of a dwelling for the monks who were engaged in the building of St Peters Church in 1400AD. During the early 19th century, the site housed a low, rambling house and in 1898, the present house was built and named 'Hermitage' from the site's original use It became a landmark in Oadby with its extensive grounds, pool and delightful walled gardens. It is still a landmark today, refurbished by Queens Moat Houses and offering a high standard of accommodation and public areas, with extensive conference and banqueting facilities.

Oadby is just three and a half miles from Leicester town centre and only four and a half miles from the M1 and M69 with both Birmingham and East Midlands airports easily accessible. There are many places of interest in and around Leicester including the famous Jewry Wall Museum, Rutland Water and Bosworth Battlefield. Visits to these and many more including Leicester's magnificent cathedral can be organised by the hotel.

'Czars Restaurant' within the Moat House is noted for the excellence of its cuisine and the adjoining cocktail bar offers a relaxing atmosphere for pre-dinner drinks. On the lower ground floor, the main bar offers a wide variety of drinks and local ales. All the well appointed bedrooms have a private bathroom and every modern facility. The Leicestershire Moat House is very conscious of standards and service especially when it comes to the business of meetings and banquets. There are several suites to choose from, catering for up to 500 persons in total. There is free open air parking for 160 cars.

USEFUL INFORMATION

OPEN: All Year. 24 hours
CHILDREN: Special Menu. Baby listening service
CREDIT CARDS: All major cards except Carte Blanche
LICENSED: Full On Licence
ACCOMMODATION: 57 rooms with private bathrooms
RESTAURANT: Superb international cuisine
BAR FOOD: Lunchtime only in bar
VEGETARIAN: Wide selection
DISABLED ACCESS: Yes. 1 purpose built bedroom. Access throughout
GARDEN: Patio adjacent to bar/restaurant plus general garden

BARNSDALE LODGE
Hotel

The Avenue, Rutland Water, Nr. Oakham,
Rutland, Leicestershire, LE15 8AH.

Tel: (0572) 724678
Fax: (0572) 724961

USEFUL INFORMATION

OPEN: 8am-midnight
CHILDREN: Yes. Highchairs, cots.
CREDIT CARDS: Visa/Access/Amex
LICENSED: Full On Licence
ACCOMMODATION: 17 ensuite rooms

RESTAURANT: Exciting. Special Table d'Hote Sundays
BAR FOOD: Farmhouse fare
VEGETARIAN: At least 2 dishes. Also vegan dishes.
DISABLED ACCESS: Yes + toilets
GARDEN: Delightful garden, patio, courtyard

Overlooking Rutland Water, Barnsdale Lodge is delightfully different. It is a 17th century farmhouse with barns which have been completely renovated, totally in an Edwardian theme. There are exposed stone walls, flagstone floors, chunky old tables, highback, highly polished chairs, a cosy parlour with chaise longues and well upholstered Edwardian seats. It is a wonderful place to stay and excellently situated for anyone wanting to explore the cathedral cities of Leicester, Lincoln, Ely and Peterborough.

There are three interconnecting dining rooms serving English dishes of 'Edwardian Country Farmhouse Fare'. It is busy all day long with people popping in for coffee, bar lunches, and afternoon teas which are served in the buttery. The 17 bedrooms, each furnished in Edwardian style, have private facilities and are exceptionally comfortable. Robert Reid, the owner, who is also a partner of the Normanton Park Hotel, is a tremendous character and is frequently to be seen in a splendid blazer and boater which he wears whilst overseeing lunches. The whole ambience of the Barnsdale is one of warmth, comfort and hospitality. The staff in black dresses and white aprons in keeping with the Edwardian era, are helpful and smiling. You are encouraged to choose whichever dining room you prefer. They are all different, all Edwardian and all have super food. Robert and Mandy Knowles, the head chef and restaurant manageress have been with Robert Reid for twelve years, as indeed have many of the team. It is their expertise and professionalism which makes it such a pleasure to be at the Barnsdale Lodge. Good food, good wines and a wonderful atmosphere; it is all here.

NORMANTON PARK HOTEL
Hotel

Rutland Water, South Shore,
Rutland, Leicestershire, LE15 8RP.

Tel: (0780) 720315
Fax: (0780) 721086

USEFUL INFORMATION

OPEN: 8am-midnight
CHILDREN: Welcome
CREDIT CARDS: Visa/Access/Amex
LICENSED: Full On Licence
ACCOMMODATION: Ensuite bedooms

RESTAURANT: English cuisine
BAR FOOD: Healthy, wholesome, varied fare
VEGETARIAN: 6 dishes daily
DISABLED ACCESS: Yes
GARDEN: Ensuite bedooms

This delightful hotel is a converted Georgian coach house and stable block on the south shore of Rutland Water. It commands superb views across the water, Europe's largest man-made lake. Once the hotel was part of Normanton Hall, the ancestral seat of the Earls of Ancaster. In 1927 the main hall was demolished and rebuilt elsewhere. The stable block and coach house, both Grade II Listed Buildings, were converted in 1980 into what is assuredly one of the most gracious hotels in this area. Normanton Park is well situated for anyone wanting to visit Leicester, Lincoln, Ely or Peterborough cathedrals.

Your hosts are Daniel and Jane Hales and their partner, Robert Reid, whose smooth efficiency make a visit here such a pleasure. Whether you stay or just decide to have a super meal, you will relish the warmth of the welcome. In the main restaurant you can savour the A La carte lunches and dinners, plus a three course Table d'Hote Sunday lunch. In the 'Sailing Bar' you can enjoy morning coffee, lunches, afternoon tea and suppers. Paul Huxtable, the head chef is a craftsman. His imaginative menus are meticulously chosen, offering a range of food that is both delicious and health conscious; low cholesterol ice cream yoghurts for example! The Fillet of Beef with a crown of puff pastry and a mixed peppercorn sauce, fish kebabs of salmon, scallops and bream on a bed of yoghurt dressing are just three of the variety of main dishes. Vegetarians can enjoy Gourmet Artichoke and Tomato Pie or a Spicy Black-Eyed Bean Casserole. Desserts are dangerously tempting. Freshly ground coffee and home-made chocolates complete a meal. The bar food menu has an equally wide range and is excellent.

Leicester Road, Sharnford,
Leicester, Leicestershire, LE10 3PP.

Tel: (0455) 272268

THE COUNTRYMAN
Public House

The name Sharnford was originally derived from Saxon origins (Scerneford). You will find this quiet village at the centre of the Shires, resting on the border of the olde Fosse slightly north of the 'Roman Centre of England' (part of the parish of Sharnford). It is a long winding village with the babbling Soar Brook running through its centre. Kingfishers nest on the stream and herbs and wild flowers grow in abundance in this rural backwater. Like all good villages it has a fine hostelry, The Countryman, which is the focal point of the village. Here in this one time coaching inn, Alan and Sally Anne Lawson are mine hosts. This likeable and welcoming couple have long time connections with the village; Alan was born in Sharnford and came to the pub some years ago, since when they have built not only a large local following but a recognition from those who live further away.

The Countryman is on the route of the 'Around Leicester' walk which is a 100 mile rural walk, just off the Fosse Way. Few people attempt this distance but many walk part of it and have found the pub to be an ideal stopping point. Here they know they will find not only a cheerful welcome but well kept ales and a wholesome menu, at sensible prices and generous portions. Speak to anyone who has sampled the Steak and Stilton with a Port Wine Sauce and they will tell you it was delicious. There is an ever changing choice from the blackboard which, and the set menu offers a choice of some 42 meals. There are always a choice of dishes for vegetarians, a choice of sweets and a wide range of freshly cut, well filled sandwiches and salads. For children there is an adventure play area in the garden which also has Long Alley Skittles.

USEFUL INFORMATION

OPEN: Mon-Thu: 11-3pm & 6-11pm. Fri & Sat: 11-11pm, Sun: 12-3pm & 7-10.30pm
CHILDREN: Well behaved welcome
CREDIT CARDS: None taken
LICENSED: Full On Licence
ACCOMMODATION: Not applicable

RESTAURANT: Not applicable
BAR FOOD: Wide range, home-made food at sensible prices
VEGETARIAN: Always available
DISABLED ACCESS: Yes. Willing to assist
GARDEN: Large. Seats 60, play area, Long Alley Skittles

Stoney Cove, Stoney Stanton,
Leicestershire, LE9 6DW

Tel: (0455) 274198
Fax: (0455) 274646

THE COVE PUBLIC HOUSE
Public House

The Cove has one of the prettiest locations in this part of the country. You go down a leafy lane and there it is. Certainly it is not the best looking building to be seen, but what it does have is a friendly, welcoming interior which encourages you to stay and enjoy the hospitality it has to offer. It sits below a huge quarry face and on a nice day you can sit on one of the terrace's overlooking the lake which is now the setting for the National Diving Centre and water sports.

The inviting, cosy corners in the comfortable lounge are warm and homely in wintertime and sufficiently intimate to allow private conversations. All sorts of things nautical festoon the walls and ceilings. There are ships' lanterns, charts, emblems plus many other ships artefacts, not forgetting the ship's wheel on the ceiling!

Sue Woodward, the landlady, with the assistance of her helpful staff, have made this out of the ordinary pub very special. They have won awards for the excellent food. The well kept cellar has not escaped the notice of people in the know and for the last three years The Cove has been one of the top 40 pubs in the country.

No one would ever call the menu sophisticated but it is traditional pub fare, all freshly cooked and plentiful. There is a particularly good steak and kidney pie, tender meat topped with a feather light lid, a spicy chicken curry, all sorts of sandwiches, and every day a tasty list of 'Blackboard Specials'.

USEFUL INFORMATION

OPEN: Winter: 11-2.30pm & 7-11pm. Summer: 11-2.30pm & 6.30-11pm. Normal Sunday hours
CHILDREN: Yes. Welcome away from the bar area
CREDIT CARDS: No
LICENSED: Full & Function Room
ACCOMMODATION: Not applicable

RESTAURANT: Not applicable
BAR FOOD: Wide range. 20 'Blackboard Specials' daily
VEGETARIAN: Always available
DISABLED ACCESS: Yes. Assistance given
GARDEN: No. 2 patios, back and front

St Pauls Cathedral

London

"Sir Christopher Wren
Said 'I am going to dine with some men.
If anybody calls
Say I am designing St Paul's"

Edmund Bentley

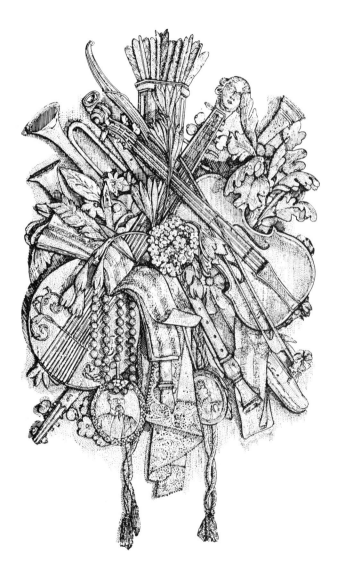

The City of London

by Bernard Fullerton

The Choristors Of St Paul's Cathedral:

So you are in ST PAUL'S CATHEDRAL, maybe for the first time, and you are overwhelmed with the magnificence, the dignity and the serenity of the whole place, and you also enjoy the opportunity for quiet reflection. I know how you feel. St Paul's has been part of my life since I was eight years old. It is an immense privilege and one which I truly enjoy. The sense of awe and wonder never goes, in fact it grows as the Cathedral becomes more and more like a home, a haven of peace. If this is your first visit you may be staying to attend a service. The choir and clergy will process into the stalls in the chancel. Thirty boys and eighteen men, and if you look further into the chancel eight probationers probably eight or nine years old. As you listen to the choir a number of thoughts may come into your mind such as 'how beautiful', 'how professional' and as you look at the probationers 'how sweet'! You may wonder where they come from, what they do outside the cathedral, where they go to school and many other aspects of the life of a St Paul's Cathedral Chorister. I can tell you because I was one from 1937 to 1942. Before the war, during the war, evacuation from London, bombs in the Cathedral... a unique period in the history of the Cathedral and the choir. Of course my experiences are not those of the chorister today, things change, generally for the better, but if you stay with me I will draw the comparisons so that you have a picture of THEN and NOW.

In April 1936 I was eight and already a chorister for two years at my local church. At the instigation of the vicar (himself a former St Paul's chorister), I was taken by my mother to a voice trial for the Cathedral. A written exam, singing in groups, a solo piece of your choice, note recognition, pitch etc.. and all the time they are looking for the quality and the potential. There were forty applicants and two vacancies. At that age you either have natural musical ability or you do not. It is those who select who have the problem, not you. I came third - with an invitation to try again next year. I did, and after the same extensive trial secured one of the two vacancies that year, again out of forty applicants.

September 1937 saw me arriving in Eton suit and wide stiff collar at CHOIR HOUSE in Carter Lane, (now the Central London Youth Hostel). St Paul's Cathedral Choir School was (and is) the establishment that provided accommodation and all the needs musical, educational and recreational for thirty-eight boys. It comprised two dormitories, five classrooms, library, basement playground and a rooftop playground completely surrounded by wire netting where we could play football, cricket and other sports. Until the war we were utterly spoiled. Our beds were made by chamber maids, our shoes cleaned, we were waited on at table and mothered by matron. What is more it cost parents almost nothing! The only expense was for instrumental tuition, (an instrument was compulsory), pocket money, clothing (pretty extensive) and any other extras. If the whole bill (apart from clothing) was more than £10 a term I was in trouble at home!

New boys were required to 'fag' for older boys. This involved simple tasks like fetching shoes or slippers, mortarboard and gown, collecting music or books and running internal errands as required. You also reported with clean hands and hair done at appropriate times, particularly before going to the Cathedral. Choristers all wore mortarboards and gowns for the walk to the Cathedral. A strategically placed policeman held up the traffic and we cascaded across the road and up the steps two at a time. Coming out was even more dramatic, the most rapid of descents being imperative. I never saw anybody fall, but it frightens me to think of it now. Time away from the school or Cathedral was important to us. A daily walk before breakfast down to The President on the embankment, unsupervised walks on a Sunday between evensongs when we managed to find the muddiest wharf or back street, occasionally getting lost. Best of all were the visits to **Bellingham** sports grounds on Monday mornings and Thursday afternoons for football or cricket, **Battersea** athletics track for sports, (Battersea power station only had three chimneys then), or to St Brides baths for swimming. It was a full programme by any standards, frighteningly so compared with today, but there are significant differences which I will come to later. In 1937 or '38 a typical weekday was:

7.00	Get up
7.30	Walk to Embankment
8.00	Prayers followed by breakfast
9.00	Lessons
10.00	Mattins in Cathedral
11.00	Lessons
1.15	Lunch followed by rest on bed
2.15	Choir practice
4.00	Evensong in Cathedral (broadcast on Wednesdays)
5.00	Tea in school or out with parents
	Free time until
6.30	Prep
8.00	Supper followed by prayers
9.00	Bed

Sundays were naturally fully occupied in the Cathedral:

10.30	Mattins followed by Holy Communion
3.00	Evensong
6.30	Second Evensong
8.00	Empire Service (Monthly broadcast)

Another aspect of the timetable in those days was the amount of time the Cathedral allowed itself without its choir. At Christmas the choir had two weeks holiday which started on the First of January. At Easter we had about three weeks starting after Easter Day. The month of August was the summer holiday. Probationers may in all cases have received about a week more holiday. At nine years old this is a busy life, not devoid of the habitual problems of home-sickness, bullying and plenty of tears. At the same time an immense amount of musical

knowledge is being injected, practised and absorbed. The learning process is assisted by the chap next to you who knows the work and can give you a sharp reminder with his foot whenever you get it wrong. There were compensations. Father Christmas came on schedule with not more than one gift from parents (the rest to wait till after 1 January) and a stocking from the Dean and Chapter. We were taken to a pantomime every year, the Bishop of London invited us to his annual ball, trips down the Thames, tea with various members of Chapter, visits to museums on rainy sports days and above all, kind members of staff who understood everything and did a lot to help. The capacity for learning is immense at that age and it was used to the full. In addition to the regular round of services there were annual performances of The Messiah, The St Matthew Passion, Brahms Requiem, Mendelssohn's St Paul and a host of others. In addition there were many 'Special Services' for groups, Orders and Associations who had a regular annual service. We did not have the concert tours, recordings and other public appearances that the choir has nowadays, but their regular schedule now is less than it was then.

After one year as a probationer I was formally admitted by the Dean as a chorister. Mortarboard and gown,

St Paul's Cathedrals' oldest book written over 800 years ago

prayer book, psalter and bible were presented (which I still have), and I took my place in the choir stalls next to the head boy as I was the most junior chorister. That process of determining where you sat was always controlled in that way until you got to the point when younger boys were being placed next to you. It was now September 1938 and my future at St Paul's looked settled for the next four years at least. The routine was by then well-established in my mind and the arrival of boys younger than yourself works wonders for the ego.

About this time Mr Chamberlain went to Munich and came back with "Peace in our time". The school was included in an evacuation scheme and we had bags packed, but it did not happen. So 1938 saw Compton, Edrich and Hutton scoring runs against Australia but still failing to win back the Ashes, HM Forces were taking advantage of twelve months respite to prepare for probable war and I sang my heart out well aware of the former but oblivious of the latter, as far as I can recall. King George VI, Queen Mary and the Duke and Duchess of Kent attended the Service of the Order of St Michael and St George which gave me my first close-up of members of the Royal Family, a pleasure which was a rare privilege for anyone in those days, but was to be repeated in St Paul's many times.

The Cathedral routine carried on entirely normally in 1939. Special Services (the Duke of Kent again), Messiah etc. all happened on schedule. Sports day was held in July and holidays were taken in August. Whilst on holiday parents were warned that an evacuation plan existed which would take us to **Truro** where we would join Truro Cathedral School and sing with the Cathedral choir there. On return to school at the end of August everything was planned for evacuation. Rucksacks, gas masks, labels in lapels were all necessities for the trip. Parents were not allowed to see us leave on Friday 1st of September - national evacuation day! We left school at noon walking in a crocodile with a banner at the head saying who we were. We walked to a school in **Holborn** to join others in our serial of the evacuation plan. Thence to Holborn underground and a tube train to Ealing Broadway where we took an evacuation train to **Newbury**. Thereafter we were expected to get to Truro under our own steam(!) with the help of GWR trains that might be going in the right direction. All this time we had five members of staff with us who were trying to keep us together and happy. I remember it well, but I cannot remember a minute of anguish or unhappiness, I was too busy being sick! We caught a train to **Bristol** which took hours but I was sleeping against a friendly lady, and then a mad dash to catch one to Truro. Luckily I knew the West Country so the names were all familiar to me and I did not feel so out of touch. We reached Truro at 2 am very weary. The following day was for recuperation. We first attended the Cathedral at Mattins and Communion on Sunday as members of the congregation, having just arrived. The sermon was about to start, but instead of a text the preacher read out the announcement that had just been made from Downing Street. We were at war with Germany. I was just over eleven years old and at that stage could not possibly know that later I would spend forty-two years of my life in the Army.

Truro was different for so many reasons. First of all it was a day school with a small boarding house for younger members. The choir for the Cathedral was part of the school but not its raison d'etre and was exclusively taken from day boys. The schedule of Cathedral services was nothing like that which we had performed in London. The choir was about twenty boys and twelve men whose repertoire was limited by comparison with ours. Because the school was really a day school, we effectively became day boys too. After our privileged and sheltered life style, albeit hard-working, this was a shock. We were billeted with families throughout Truro who were prepared to accommodate us for whatever the government (no doubt subsidised by the Dean and Chapter) were prepared to pay. We were in pairs normally, sometimes more in the larger homes that existed there with landed gentry generously sharing their facilities. Only the probationers and youngest choristers stayed in Trewinnard Court, the boarding element of the school. Billeting was like boarding school in that you were still away from home, but your 'in loco' parent could make a big difference to your happiness, after all it wasn't proper home, was it?

But there were other reasons why Truro was strange. There was a complete loss of identity. Truro Cathedral, built 1910 is no substitute for St Paul's, 1710. The musical training and discipline would undoubtedly suffer as a result of fewer services. Being day boys affected the cohesion of the school, our sporting achievements were always as a part of Truro's and not our own. The Dean and Chapter realised all this and I know that serious consideration was given to closing the school for the duration of the war. There was little obvious benefit and considerable cost to the Cathedral in keeping it going. However, the difficulties of eventually starting again from nothing were too great. Furthermore the decision was made that whenever it was safe to do so the choir

should return to the Cathedral for special events. These visits were to take place in school holidays, which were longer now that they conformed to Truro's requirements.

We settled in to a new way of life, but somewhat reluctantly I have to confess. School magazines of the time are full of longing to return to London and resume life as it was. Of course this was impossible, particularly as after a slow start the war was intensifying, particularly in respect of its effect on London. The Battle of Britain was being fought in summer skies in 1940 and heavy bombing raids continued well into 1941. Thereafter raids still occurred, followed by the terror of V1 and eventually V2. Any suggestion that the choir might return for special services had to be shelved until it was considered safe for us to return, however briefly.

Meantime our beloved Cathedral was not to escape the blitz. First of all a time bomb buried itself in front of the Cathedral, near the foundations at the west end, but it did not explode. Royal Engineers spent careful hours making it safe and then transporting it outside London for safe detonation. The first real blow occurred on October 10th 1940 when a bomb struck the Cathedral, piercing the lead roof and exploding against the centre of the arch immediately over the high altar. Huge chunks of masonry hurtled down completely destroying the high altar. Damage to everything in that area was considerable. The marble reredos behind the altar was badly damaged as were the Grinling Gibbons wood carvings. Dust was blown everywhere finding its way into the organ pipes, with the result that the main organ was not played again until after the war. Nobody was hurt, though there were many people in the Cathedral, mostly in the crypt. All services were immediately transferred to the crypt chapel. Shortly thereafter an altar was established in front of the steps to the chancel with a screen behind it. All services were held in that area until well after the war when the new high altar was built. At that time it was decided to remove the former reredos, rather than repair it because it did not fit the new design of an altar under a baldachino.

St Paul's was well prepared to combat bomb damage. Throughout the war a team of volunteer watchers were on duty every night to deal with the ever present danger of incendiary bombs. Many ricocheted off the dome only to embed themselves in lead roofing elsewhere. There is so much wood in the internal construction of the Cathedral so all incendiaries had to be identified and dealt with quickly. Reserve water tanks were strategically placed and a control room operated from dome level. Many members of the Cathedral staff volunteered for these duties which required twenty men every night. No serious fire occurred which they could not deal with. However, the Chapter House on the north side of the Cathedral was burnt out in 1940. (It has been rebuilt within the former structure). Residences in Amen Court for the organist, Mr J Dykes Bower and the Head Verger Mr Tanner were also destroyed by fire. The Choir School in Carter Lane received no damage at all. However worse was yet to come. In April 1941 a much larger bomb fell and pierced the roof in the middle of the north transept. It exploded after entry so the blast demolished the saucer dome which itself crashed to the floor of the Cathedral and through into the crypt below. The hole in the floor was about twenty feet across. Beneath it was the former choir practice room containing a grand piano which did not look at all well. I recorded a description of this damage myself in the school magazine at the time. I was impressed then by the fact that windows were broken all over the Cathedral and that some massive cornices at the tops of columns had been shifted many inches. The whole north transept was in due course sealed off from floor to ceiling. It was a long time after the end of the war that it was reopened to the public.

It is still possible to see exactly where the bombs came in. The saucer dome over the north transept still looks unfinished and the centre of the arch over the high altar looks relatively new. You look, the next time you are there.

The danger associated with London resulted in any visits to London for Special Services being postponed. In fact the first occurred just before returning to Truro in September 1941 at the end of the summer holidays. The occasion was the coming of age of His Majesty King Peter of Yugoslavia. No less than fourteen members of Royal Families including our own King and Queen were present as well as the Prime Minister (Mr Winston Churchill) and his cabinet, senior officers of the allied forces and members of the Diplomatic Corps. Such splendid occasions were rare during the war, but we enjoyed them when they happened. The temptation to convince oneself that you had received a direct smile from the Queen was hard to resist! At Christmas 1941 we returned again for several services, also at Easter and Christmas 1942. It was important that everyone should know that the choir was still in existence, and for the Dean and Chapter to know that our standards of performance were not deteriorating. Mr John Dykes Bower the Cathedral organist had joined the RAF early in the war so the musical responsibilities for London, with a men only choir, and our training and performance in Truro fell on

St Paul's brass eagle lectern, dating from 1719, with a glimpse of the organ, Wren's 'box of whistles', in the background.

the assistant organist Dr Douglas Hopkins. He could not be in Truro all the time so Mr Sydney Lovett, a former organist of Salisbury Cathedral was full time choir trainer there. Dr Hopkins came down frequently to ensure that we were up to scratch. We had quickly introduced annual performances of the major works that were performed in London and he was particularly keen to be in Truro for those.

In December 1942 I left the Choir School to go on to my Public School. Life in Truro continued in much the same way until the decision was made to return the choir to London at very short notice in May 1945, in order that they may rehearse the Victory Services which were to be held later that month. Out of the thirty-eight boys that returned only two left London with the evacuation and returned there in May 1945. One had been in the school three months before September 1939, the other only two days.

There have been many changes in the way of life at the school since those days. The school has new premises at the east end of the Cathedral in New Change, which it moved into in 1967. The school now admits day pupils who are not choristers. The choir is still thirty, with eight probationers, all of whom live in the choir school. The commitment for routine services is much reduced. They do not sing mattins on weekdays at all. Mattins is said in the crypt chapel apart from Saturdays when there are men's voices only. The boys sing evensong at 5 pm every weekday except Thursday. On Sundays the choir sings at Mattins at 10.30 followed by Holy Communion. They also sing evensong at 3.15. There are still many special services for Royal or other occasions, and the annual performances of Oratorios. The biggest difference in the last twenty years has been the opportunity for extensive overseas tours, special concerts throughout the country, recordings of the choir on compact disc or record and the use of soloists in support of television or radio programme theme music. Overseas tours have not only been an exciting experience for all concerned but they have served to expand the repertoire as well. Most importantly they have demonstrated to everyone the standard of excellence that the choir achieves in quality, interpretation and pure musicianship. This is largely due to the training they receive from the organist and his assistants. It is not surprising that about 8% of former choristers become professional musicians of one sort or another, and 2% become ordained into the priesthood.

When a boy leaves the school he is admitted to The Guild of the Companions of St Paul. The Guild was founded in 1891 with the objects of keeping former choristers in touch with each other and the Cathedral and helping them to preserve and develop their Christian commitment. It is an Old Boys' Association, with a difference. There can be no other such organisation which has an alma mater of such national significance. The pride which is created by service to the Cathedral is everlasting and the Guild endeavours to help its members to enjoy this feeling. The membership includes boys who are recent leavers as well as those perhaps in their nineties. I am now the Chairman of this Guild. We

meet in London once a year for an Annual General Meeting followed by evensong in the Cathedral at which (after rehearsal) we are included in some of the choral works. The Dean and Chapter then mix with us over a drink and then we have dinner together. This event attracts about seventy members. Such is the allegiance to Cathedral Choirs that there is also a Federation of Cathedral Old Choristers Associations. This organises a weekend annually in one of the Cathedral cities at which former members of many different choirs can participate in worship and enjoy other musical and social activities throughout the weekend.

Pride in membership of a Cathedral choir is inevitably rooted in the history of the Cathedral and the development of its choral tradition. St Paul's is the most perfect example of this historical development. It seems likely that what was called the Song School of St Paul's in London was founded at the same time as the See of London by St Augustine in 604 AD. This is recorded in a book by Dora Robertson called "Sarum Close". This makes the school older than the Houses of Parliament and indeed than the English nation. Little more is known until the 12th century when Richard de Belmeis, Bishop of London re-founded the School for the Choristers. Richard I (1189), Henry III (1216) and Edward II (1307) endowed the school which was by then referred to as the Almonry. Thereafter it continued in pre-Reformation times until Dean Colet, when founding St Paul's School (the present Public School) in 1509 was concerned also about the education of the Cathedral choristers. Subsequently in 1584 Dean Nowell ordered that they should attend St Paul's school to learn grammar, but that the Master of the Choristers should teach them Catechism, writing and music. This is the only recorded direct connection between the Choir

School and St Paul's (Colet's) School which shows that singing and education then involved both establishments, which were situated very close to each other. (Nowadays people often think that there is a link between the two, but that is no longer so.)

From earliest days the boys were used in plays to amuse Royalty and the aristocracy, both as young actors and singers. The endowments of the Court ensured their availability. Queen Elizabeth, in 1586 required the Master of the Children of St Paul's to instruct them for the entertainment of the Court so that they might serve her when she needed them. By 1626 it was thought to be inconsistent with their religious duties to continue to act in stage plays.

At about this time the Almonry, which was a boarding school, was situated on the north-west side of the Churchyard. This house was demolished about 1710. During the remainder of the 18th century the boys were moved from one place to another and the boarding facility lapsed due to insufficient funds. From 1812 things got a great deal better, mainly due to the efforts of Miss Maria Hackett who campaigned for proper education, accommodation and care for Cathedral choristers. Charing Cross, Adelphi Terrace, the Chapter House and Amen Court all featured as residential addresses for the school until 1875 when the purpose-built Choir House in Carter Lane was occupied. It was at this time that the size of the choir increased from twelve to thirty because Sir John Stainer had been appointed organist in 1872 and thought the increase necessary. The school was modernised in 1937 and boys stayed there (apart from the war) until 1967 when they moved to the existing premises in New Change.

All the information about the choir and its school has to be seen in the context of the Cathedral which was there at the time. The first was in 604 AD, founded by St Augustine. That burnt in 675 and was replaced in 685. That was ransacked by the Vikings and burnt in 962 but was replaced almost immediately, only to be burnt down in 1087. The replacement Cathedral, started in 1087 and finished in 1240 was in Norman style and is what we now call Old St Paul's. This also was burnt in the Great Fire of London in 1666. Wren's masterpiece was started in 1675 and finished in 1710.

Your visit to St Paul's or to any other Cathedral may now hold more interest for you as you think more deeply about the lives of those who sing so beautifully and the long history of which they are now part. Rest assured that they enjoy what they are doing, they are experiencing something which is going to be part of their lives for ever and they sincerely hope that hearing them may be a wonderful experience for you as well.

London is full of first class hotels but for people wanting to stay in the Capital and are looking for something a little out of the ordinary, we have chosen six which we think are the epitome of gracious living and English hospitality; we hope you agree. Placed in alphabetical order there is no favouritism!

THE BEAUFORT HOTEL at 33 Beaufort Gardens, **Knightsbridge**, is a quietly elegant hotel standing in a peaceful tree-lined Victorian Knightsbridge Square and since it opened in 1986 it has found favour with an ever growing number of famous but very low profile guests. It is they who appreciate the impeccable, discreet and efficient service. It is owned by the television presenter, Diana Wallis and under her careful guidance it has received many awards including "London's Top 'Hotel for Service'".

At 33 Roland Gardens, BLAKES HOTEL, which opened in the early 1980's is a personal statement about what good design can achieve. Anouska Hempel, television personality and now famous fashion designer, has created one of the distinctive hotels in the world, tucked away in London's **South Kensington**. BLAKES RESTAURANT is renowned for the originality and variety of its international cuisine, its wine list and its friendly and professional service.

THE CRANLEY HOTEL can be found at 10-12 Bira Gardens, South Kensington, a quiet residential street. Lovingly restored under the watchful eyes of the proprietors Bonnie and Peter de Loof, this delightful hotel was re-opened in 1990. The impression from outside is that of three private Georgian town houses, elegantly decorated and adorned with flowers and pots of miniature trees.

11 CADOGAN GARDENS was the first of the exclusive private town house hotels in London. It is set in a tree-lined square in the heart of **Chelsea**. The hotel was established by an eccentric Swiss gentleman in the summer of 1949 for his friends and ' such ladies and gentlemen as can furnish me with acceptable introductions'. It has been the London home to discerning visitors throughout the intervening years. With its own health and beauty spa at No 1. Synergy just a few doors away it provides a haven of peace and tranquillity amid

Big Tom,
the cathedral clock

the hustle and bustle of the city. Guests have free use of the facilities.

NUMBER SIXTEEN Sumner Place in South Kensington is an elegant town house hotel comprising 4 Victorian houses side by side in a quiet thoroughfare. The premises just ooze warmth and a sense of being in your own private dwelling cared for by an efficient and friendly staff.

SYDNEY HOUSE at 9-11 Sydney Street, Chelsea between the Kings Road and the Fulham Road is five minutes walk from South Kensington tube station and ten minutes from Westminster by train or taxi. It has been superbly restored and furnished by the Swiss owner, the designer and hotelier, Jean-Luc Aeby. Each room is unique and has a different theme with a wealth of unusual details. The hotel has all the requirements of modern living and an international staff providing unobtrusive, efficient and friendly service.

For something very different, THE PALM COURT AT THE WALDORF in **Aldwych** offers you Tea Dances, a truly unique experience, popular with Londoners and visitors alike. Held every Saturday and Sunday, the tea dance has also become a favourite pre-theatre venue - the Waldorf's location on the Aldwych, in the heart of theatreland, makes most theatres within easy walking distance.

189

ST MARTINS IN THE FIELD is one of London's best known and beloved churches. Music has always played a large part in the church's activity and every weekday, except Thursday, concerts are held from 1.05-2pm for which no charge is made. These concerts have not only given pleasure to the many listeners but have also allowed them to snatch precious time to sit within the walls of this old church and come to terms with the trauma of life in the capital. On Thursday, Friday and Saturday evenings there are candlelit concerts. St Martins is also the birthplace of the internationally renowned orchestra, The Academy of St Martin-in-the-Fields. THE CAFE IN THE CRYPT is open daily and provides excellent food at sensible prices. It is also capable of catering for a formal dinner for 80 or a buffet for 200. A venue so unusual that you can virtually guarantee your guests won't have been before. St Martins-in-the-Field is different and should not be missed by any visitor to London.

MAGNO'S BRASSERIE at 65a **Long Acre**, **Covent Garden** is a simple no nonsense French Brasserie in which over the years, the menu has evolved to include more sophisticated dishes, yet the restaurant has retained its overall simplicity and bistro ambience. It has a set price Pre-Theatre Menu and an A La Carte menu which features robust dishes such as Baked Roquefort Cheese in puff pastry, Coq au Vin with Sage Mash Potato and Confit of Duck with Choriza Sausage and Roasted Shallots. The wine list is extensive but user friendly and always includes a good value for money wine of the month.

A little on the light-hearted side may we suggest a visit to meet up with THE ENGLISH TEDDY BEAR COMPANY in **Regent Street**. You may well have met these teddy bears or their brothers in Canterbury, Cambridge and Bath and you will also do so in Oxford. If your teddy bear needs to be properly dressed for the theatre or opera you need look no further! This charming shop offers the full range of English Teddy Bear Company goods in a nautical setting. The shop is decorated like a cabin in a cruise liner with calming sea references and a miniature cruise liner from which you can choose your teddy.

Detail from the monument to Joyce Austin (1633), Southwark Cathedral

Before leaving London we must tell you about THE CATHEDRAL CHURCH OF ST SAVIOUR & ST MARY OVERIE, SOUTHWARK or more simply Southwark Cathedral. There has probably been a church on this site for more than a thousand years. The area was a suburb of the Roman City of Londinium and recent archaeological excavations have shown that it was a flourishing centre of trade. The Romans built the first London Bridge and some of the same roads of the present day still follow the lines of their roads to the south. A Roman villa stood on the site of the cathedral, and some of its pavement has been incorporated in the floor of the south choir aisle. In a well beneath the choir broken fragments probably put there in the fourth century were discovered in 1977. The largest was a statue of a pagan god and a replica is on display in the cathedral.

Southwark Cathedral

by Joy David

If one had to decide which of England's cities had the worst surroundings, there would be no contest. Inevitably **Southwark** would win. It is tucked into a corner by London Bridge, below road level and hemmed in by mucky buildings. It is noisy, never tranquil but if you believe in the church being amongst the people Southwark certainly answers that description. Architecturally it is splendid and will please any visitor. The interior has been restored over the centuries and is magnificent. Near the central simple altar are an icon of Christ, a gift from the Patriarch Justinian of Romania, and a statue of the Virgin and Child, the work of Peter Ball, given in 1989. Prominent in the centre at the back of the church is the font which not so long ago stood by the entrance but was moved to allow a memorial to the fifty one victims of the sinking of The Marchioness in the

Thames in 1989. The great nave is modern but blends perfectly with the older parts of the building. 13th century arcading can be seen in the south aisle and in the north aisle are the remains of two Norman doorways. Further along the north aisle is the elaborate medieval canopied tomb of John Gower (1408), an early English poet and a friend of Chaucer. The north transept is full of monuments and effigies but it is the magnificent Jacobean communion table with twisted legs that catches the eye. In the north choir aisle is one of the most interesting memorials in the cathedral. It is the wooden effigy of a knight of the 13th century. This is one of the earliest wooden effigies in England, and it may depict a member of the de Warenne family, who were benefactors of the church. The choir itself is a splendid example of early English work. There are five bays and the piers, alternately circular and octagonal, re-attached to triple vaulting shafts. Everything you see is a thing of beauty but above all it is the colour that emanates from the interior which would draw me back again to visit Southwark Cathedral.

One of Southwark Cathedral's medival roof bosses; the Devil swallows Judas Iscariot

It seems that it is because Southwark Cathedral is surrounded by all its 'inner city' problems that it draws on the affection and loyalty of so many people. It is South London's largest historic building. Its music soars and anyone listening to the sheer beauty of the voices singing in praise of God can only be uplifted and totally forget the misery of the outside world. Inside it is clean, warm and a great symbol of joy and hope. It has a regular congregation much as any parish church. In fact it has the duty to maintain daily worship, now as in Anglo-Saxon times. A Eucharist is celebrated on each weekday in the lunch hour, a time chosen because it makes it possible for those who work in the neighbourhood to attend. This is preceded by Morning Prayer. At the end of the day Evening Prayer is sung or said, another opportunity for celebration and refreshment. All this daily routine may be a reminder of the imagery in the revelation of St John the Divine (22:1-2): 'the river of the water of life, bright as crystal, flowing from the throne of God and of the lamb through the middle of the street of the city.'

THE PALM COURT AT THE WALDORF
Elegant Edwardian Style Lounge

Aldwych,
London. WC2B 4DD.

Tel: (071) 836 2400
Fax: (071) 836 7244

'Tea Dances' are synonymous with the Palm Court Lounge at The Waldorf Hotel. Taking tea and dancing the afternoon away in the magical terraced Palm Court is a truly unique experience, popular with Londoners and visitors alike. Held every Saturday and Sunday, the tea dance has also become a favourite pre-theatre venue - The Waldorf's location on the Aldwych, in the heart of theatreland, makes most theatres within easy walking distance.

The Waldorf's tea dance will always give people a chance to escape from the rigours of everyday life. The setting is superb and the tea dance has a long standing tradition at The Waldorf, dating back to 1913, when 'Tango Teas' first became popular at the hotel. Today it is the only weekly tea dance in London. It is a sparkling occasion as you step back in time to the early 1900's and step in time to the scintillating rhythms of Greg Davies and the Waldorfians. The traditional tea of finger sandwiches and bridge rolls, toasted crumpets and homemade scones and sweet pastries can be complemented by a glass of champagne, chosen from the menu's wide selection.

The Waldorf, which is the flagship hotel in the Forte Grand Collection of 29 International luxury hotels, has recently undergone a £12.5 million refurbishment programme to restore and enhance the original character of the hotel. The Palm Court Lounge was totally decorated in the refurbishment with great care taken to maintain and enhance the room's cherished character and traditions.

USEFUL INFORMATION

OPEN: All Year. Tea Dances: 3.30pm-6.30pm. Saturday and Sunday. Afternoon Tea: 3.30pm-6.30pm
CHILDREN: Well behaved
LICENSED: Full On Licence

RESTAURANT: Palm Court
BAR FOOD: Not applicable
VEGETARIAN: Yes
DISABLED ACCESS: Flat entrance. Willing to assist
GARDEN: Not applicable

ELEVEN CADOGAN GARDENS
Hotel

11 Cadogan Gardens, Sloane Square,
Chelsea, London, SW3 2RJ.

Tel: (071) 730 3426
Fax: (071) 730 5217

Eleven Cadogan Gardens was the first of the exclusive private Town House hotels in London. It is set in a tree-lined square in the heart of Chelsea, just a few minutes walk from Sloane Square, close to Harrods and the shopping delights of Knightsbridge and Kings Road, a seven minute taxi ride to the Roman Catholic Westminster Cathedral at Victoria and 25 minutes to St Paul's Cathedral.

The hotel was established by an eccentric Swiss gentleman in the summer of 1949 for his friends and 'such ladies and gentlemen as can furnish me with acceptable introductions'. It has been the London home to discerning visitors throughout the intervening years. With its own health and beauty spa at No 1 Synergy, just a few doors away it provides a haven of peace and tranquillity amid the hustle and bustle of the city. Guests have free use of the facilities.

There are 60 beautifully appointed rooms including 5 suites. Each has its en-suite bathroom and every modern comfort. There is a boardroom large enough to take 12 people and a Chauffeur driven limousine service.

Not suprisingly the service is impeccable, discreet and efficient. From the moment of arrival when the butler meets you at the door it is the epitome of Victorian hospitality. Room service is around the clock and can provide light meals and refreshments in a moment. The chauffeur driven limousine service is fantastic for those wanting to take in some sightseeing or a little shopping.

USEFUL INFORMATION

OPEN: 24 hours
CHILDREN: Yes. No special facilities
CREDIT CARDS: Amex/Visa/Diners/ Mastercard
LICENSED: Liquor Licence
ACCOMMODATION: 60 en-suite rooms including 5 suites

RESTAURANT: Room service only
BAR FOOD: No Bar
VEGETARIAN: Always vegetarian dish of the day
DISABLED ACCESS: None
GARDEN: Deck-chairs can be arranged in the communal gardens opposite

SYDNEY HOUSE

Hotel

9-11 Sydney Street, Chelsea,
London. SW6 5PU.

Tel: (071) 376 7711
Fax: (071) 376 4233

USEFUL INFORMATION

OPEN: All year
CHILDREN: Yes
CREDIT CARDS: All Major cards
LICENSED: Full on Licence
ACCOMMODATION: Twenty one differently designed bedrooms with marble bathrooms en-suite.

RESTAURANT: Breakfasts, light snacks.
BAR FOOD: Not applicable
VEGETARIAN: By arrangement
DISABLED ACCESS: No
GARDEN: No

Sydney House is located in the middle of Chelsea between the Kings Road and the Fulham Road. It is five minutes walk from South Kensington Tube Station and ten minutes away by train or taxi from Westminster. Sydney House is a particularly distinctive luxury town house hotel, part of a parade of mid-19th century houses. It has been restored and superbly furnished by the Swiss owner, the designer and hotelier, Jean-Luc Aeby.

Each room is unique and has a different theme. Intimate dark corridors lead you to light bedrooms designed to evoke other times, places and continents. A wealth of unusual details, the rich play of colours, the rare balance of a luxurious and stylised decor with a relaxed atmosphere, all the requirements of modern living and an international staff providing unobtrusive, efficient and friendly service are some of the elements which contribute to make the Sydney House Hotel a real 'Hotel de charme' and an exciting and different place to stay.

It is invidious to choose one room above another but just to give you an idea the Royal Room has a gilded four poster bed tented in silk and brocade. The Paris Room is a symphony of reds and Toile de Jouy. The Wedgwood Blue Room is totally restful and has the bonus of a charming balcony. The Chinese Leopard Room is a stunning mixture of warm yellows and Biedermeier furniture. Finally The Penthouse is delightful and has a large terrace overlooking the spectacular roofs of London.

BLAKES HOTEL

Hotel & Restaurant

33 Roland Gardens,
London, SW7 3PF.

Tel: (071) 370 6701
Fax: (071) 373 0442

USEFUL INFORMATION

OPEN: 7 days a week all year round, from breakfast until late at night
CHILDREN: Welcome
CREDIT CARDS: All major cards
LICENSED: Full On Licence
ACCOMMODATION: 52 individually designed rooms

RESTAURANT: Skilful blend of east and west. Imaginative, beautifully presented
BAR FOOD: Not applicable. Drinks & coffee served in the lively bar
VEGETARIAN: Several dishes
DISABLED ACCESS: No
GARDEN: None

Blakes Hotel which opened in the early 80's is a personal statement about what good design can achieve. Anouska Hempel, television personality and now famous fashion designer, has created one of the distinctive hotels in the world, tucked away in London's South Kensington. Internationally renowned, Blakes has become a model for the 'fashionable small hotel' in cities all over the world. Respected for protecting the privacy of its guests against the paparazzi, it is the London base of film stars such as Robert de Niro and Jack Nicholson and fashion designers Gianni Versace, Christian Lacroix and Jean Paul Gautier, earning the reputation as the 'couture hotel'. Each of the 52 bedrooms has been personally designed by Ms Hempel; every detail reconstructed to provide the ideal blend of colour, texture and atmosphere.

As one of London's top restaurants, Blakes is renowned for the originality and variety of its international cuisine, its wine list, its friendly and professional service. Its decor is a dramatic combination of modern and traditional; with rare costumes and jewellery of the mountain people of Thailand in frames on the walls to elegant black and white furniture and table settings.   It is particularly popular with late night diners after an evening at the theatre or opera. The cuisine, devised by Anouska Hempel, is a skilful blend of east and west, together with imaginative dishes of her own, all elegantly presented to look as good as they taste. It is a favourite venue for breakfasts (offering English and Continental breakfasts, as well as a special Japanese East/West menu) and a light lunch for the busy business person or traveller.

THE BEAUFORT HOTEL
Hotel

33 Beaufort Gardens, Knightsbridge,
London, SW3 1PP.

Tel: (071) 584 5252
Fax: (071) 589 2834

This quietly, elegant hotel stands in a peaceful tree-lined Victorian Knightsbridge Square right in the heart of London, yet it is untroubled by noise and since it opened in 1986 has found favour with an ever growing number of famous, but very low profile guests. It is they who appreciate the impeccable, discreet and efficient service which is there from the moment you arrive. It is owned by the television presenter, Diana Wallis and under her careful guidance it has received many awards including 'Londons Top Hotel for Service' and 'The Best City Hotel in Britain in the Good Hotel Guide.'

With 28 rooms, all en-suite and furnished delightfully in individual styles and colours it is small enough to feel like a private house. Guests have the complimentary use of a membership of a health club nearby. There is no restaurant but complimentary light snacks are available. A 24 hour complimentary drinks bar which includes champagne, is there for the use of guests. Children over the age of ten are welcome as well as babes in arms but those in the intervening years are not permitted. The room rates are from £115-£250 which includes everything other than telephone calls which are charged at cost.

From Beaufort Gardens it is easy to reach every part of the west end of London with its shops and theatres. It is also somewhere which has easy access to the routes in and out of the capital. No 33 will provide a memorable stay for anyone who comes for the first time - once that initial visit has been made you will always look to stay here again on another visit.

USEFUL INFORMATION

OPEN: All year except a week at Christmas
CHILDREN: Babes in arms or over 10 only
CREDIT CARDS: All Major cards
LICENSED: Residential
ACCOMMODATION: 28 en-suite rooms

RESTAURANT: No, but complimentary snacks
BAR FOOD: No, but complimentary drinks bar including champagne
VEGETARIAN: Not applicable
DISABLED ACCESS: No
GARDEN: Not applicable

MAGNO'S BRASSERIE
French Restaurant

65A Long Acre,
London, WC2E 9JH.

Tel: (071) 836 6077
Fax: (071) 379 6184

The loyal following behind Magno's is proof of the demand for such a simple, no nonsense French brasserie in London. For strangers wanting to discover the pleasure of eating in this truly Gallic environment they will find it in the heart of London in Long Acre. Once found it will become a regular venue whenever you are in London.

Over the years, the menu has evolved to include more sophisticated dishes yet the restaurant has retained its overall simplicity and bistro ambience. Only the finest of ingredients are used and seasonal changes are reflected in the choice of daily specials, for example 'Sauteed Scallops with Wild Mushrooms and Saffron' also 'Grilled Seabass with Fennel and Aniseed'.

The Al La Carte menu features more robust dishes such as 'Baked Roquefort Cheese in Puff Pastry', 'Coq au Vin with Sage Mash Potato' and 'Confit of Duck with Chorizo Sausage and Roasted Shallots'. The pre-theatre menu attracts many people and for less than £10 one can eat handsomely. There are thirty three theatres within walking distance. The furthest away is 15 minutes. It really does make for a special evenng to eat here first and walk to the theatre of your choice as a means of rounding it off.

All Magno's prices are common sense; something that is quite a rarity in London. In addition you get this wonderful atmosphere and a true and genuine welcome. The wine list, which has been chosen by a master, is extensive, user friendly and always includes a good value wine of the month.

USEFUL INFORMATION

OPEN: Lunch: Mon-Fri: 12-3pm.
Dinner: Mon-Sat: 5.30-11.30pm
CHILDREN: Yes. No Children's menus
CREDIT CARDS: All major cards
LICENSED: Restaurant Licence with Supper Hour
ACCOMMODATION: Not applicable

RESTAURANT: No nonsense French brasserie
BAR FOOD: Not applicable
VEGETARIAN: 3-4 dishes daily
DISABLED ACCESS: Yes. Level entrance. Willing to assist
GARDEN: Not applicable

THE ENGLISH TEDDY BEAR COMPANY
Shop

153 Regent Street,
London, WIR 7FD.

Tel: (071) 287 3273

USEFUL INFORMATION

OPEN: 10-7pm daily
CHILDREN: Welcome
CREDIT CARDS: All major cards
DISABLED ACCESS: Good

SPECIAL SERVICES: Gift boxing
available, Made to order service,
Mail Order catalogue available -
Contact branch for further information
on availability.

Situated right in the heart of Regent Street beside Burberry's, The English Teddy Bear Company is a welcome haven in such a big busy city. If your Teddy needs to be properly dressed for the theatre or opera, you need look no further! This charming shop offers the full range of English Teddy Bear Company goods in a nautical setting. The shop is decorated like a cabin in a cruise liner with calming sea references and a miniature cruise liner from which you can choose your Teddy!

The English Teddy Bear Company creates traditional English Teddy Bears in a variety of cloths, all English, from acrylic to top quality mohair. The Teddy Bears are made with traditional features like long snouts, embroidered noses and jointed limbs and head. The Teddy Bear is a very popular gift that has lasted almost a century and which is given equally to adults as well as children. The recreating of special companions is a particular feature of this company and since all the bears are hand made, no two are alike and each bear comes with its own birth certificate! They make an eccentric range of stylish Teddy Bear clothes. Silk waistcoats, bow ties, smoking jackets, cricket jumpers, boaters and much more to make up the essential English Teddy Bear's wardrobe. Even the Teddy Bears' appetites are considered with the most delicious home-made traditional English biscuits, jams, marmalades and teas so that each bear can leave the country well equipped for the journey abroad!

The English Teddy Bear Company has shops in the most attractive English towns, at their historic centres and in beautiful old buildings. Currently these are Oxford, Canterbury, Bath, Cambridge as well as London.

CRANLEY HOTEL
Hotel & Apartments

10-12 Bina Gardens, South Kensington,
London, SW5 0LA.

Tel: (071) 373 0123
Fax: (071) 373 9497

USEFUL INFORMATION

OPEN: All year, 24 hours
CHILDREN: Welcome. Cots, high chairs,
roll away beds, baby sitting service
CREDIT CARDS: Visa/Master/Amex/
Diners/Switch
LICENSED: Restaurant/redidential
ACCOMMODATION: 36 suites, all
en-suite

RESTAURANT: Not applicable
BAR FOOD: Room service; light snacks
and afternoon teas etc
VEGETARIAN: About 30% of menu
DISABLED ACCESS: No, but welcome
GARDEN: Small with dining area

The Cranley Hotel can be found in a quite residential street in the heart of London. Lovingly restored under the watchful eyes of the proprietors Bonnie and Peter De Loof, this delightful hotel was re-opened in 1990. The impression from outside is that of three private Georgian town houses, elegantly decorated and adorned with flowers and pots of miniature trees.

A warm homely feeling welcomes you within, a fireplace is lit in the reception and a graceful staircase take you to your luxurious room. Many of the original features have been retained including the floor to ceiling bay windows and Victorian fireplaces. Every room, hallway and stairwell is graced with oil paintings. The Cranley Hotel has both double rooms and one or two bedroom suites making 36 units in all, each exquisitely decorated and furnished with antiques. The bathrooms are luxurious also with deep tubs, showers, soft white towels and robes. All rooms are en-suite, have colour TV and well equipped concealed kitchenettes. Families will love to stay in one of the beautiful apartments, very upmarket but still with a homely feeling, a more reasonable deal than separate rooms.

Breakfast, light lunches and afternoon teas are available throughout the day and evening, served in your room or in the Petit Salon. The reception is open 24 hours and offers you every assistance from flower vases to baby sitters, hairdressers to food and drink.

Situated in South Kensington this is an ideal place for sightseeing or shopping. Close to many famous restaurants offering a variety of quality cuisines, a short stroll from Harrods and Harvey Nichols to mention just two of many and not forgetting the Victoria and Albert and Natural History Museums.

16 Sumner Place,
London, SW7 3EG.

Tel: (071) 589 5232
Fax: (071) 584 8615

NUMBER SIXTEEN

Town House Hotel

To find a quiet, tranquil haven in the heart of London is a godsend. Number Sixteen, Sumner Place in South Kensington is that place. This elegant 'Town House Hotel' comprises of 4 Victorian houses side by side in a quiet thoroughfare. The premises just ooze warmth and a sense of being in your own private dwelling cared for by an efficient and friendly staff.

The whole of Number Sixteen is decorated and furnished with exquisite, good taste. Guests are invited to pour themselves a drink from their 'Honour Bar' in the relaxed surroundings of the lounge, a perfect setting in which to meet friends or business associates. The comfortable informality of the drawing room will encourage you to curl up in front of the blazing fire with a book or the magazines thoughtfully provided.

The conservatory opens onto a secluded garden which has been tended with green fingers and loving care. It is no wonder that Number Sixteen is an award winner. In 1991 it won the prestigious 'Spencer Trophy' amd the 'London in Bloom' award. Both are well deserved, and only serve to confirm that there are few better places to stay in the metropolis than in the embracing comfort of this excellent hotel. Our American friends will tell you that in addition to the pleasure they get from staying in such an elegant environment, they think the sumptuous English breakfast is memorable.

USEFUL INFORMATION

OPEN: All year
CHILDREN: Over twelve
CREDIT CARDS: All major credit cards
LICENSED: Residential Licence
ACCOMMODATION: Elegant, spacious ensuite rooms

RESTAURANT: Hotel and breakfast only
BAR FOOD: Not applicable
VEGETARIAN: Not applicable
DISABLED ACCESS: No. Willing to assist
GARDEN: Secluded, award winning

St Martin-in-the-Fields,
Trafalgar Square, London. WC2N 4JJ

Tel: (071) 930 0089
Fax: (071) 839 5163

THE CAFE IN THE CRYPT

Church, Cafe and Concert Hall

To briefly remind one in historical terms, King George 1st was a church warden at St Martins and Nell Gwynn was buried in the Crypt. St Martins is a church that is well known throughout the world both for its ecclesiastical attributes and for its realistic approach to the modern needs of the people of London, especially the homeless. It is a church that has gone out to the people rather than waiting for the congregation to walk through its doors. The price of heritage is high. It receives no money from the Church of England or the government and relies entirely on the support of those who value the ministry.

Music has always played a large part in the church's activity and every weekday except Thursday concerts are held from 1.05-2pm for which no charge is made. These concerts have not only given pleasure to the many listeners but have also allowed them to snatch precious time to sit within the walls of this old church and come to terms with the trauma of life in the capital. On Thursday, Friday and Saturday evenings at 7.30pm there are candlelit concerts. St Martins is also the birthplace of the internationally renowned orchestra, The Academy of St Martin-in-the Fields.

The Cafe in the Crypt is open daily and provides excellent food at sensible prices. It is also capable of catering for a formal dinner for 80 or a buffet for 200. A venue so unusual that you can virtually guarantee your guests won't have been before. St Martins in the Fields is different and should not be missed by any visitor to London.

USEFUL INFORMATION

OPEN: Cafe: All year: 10am-8pm. Sunday: 12-6pm. Monday -Thursday, Christmas Day & Boxing Day: all day
Church: every day 8am-7pm
CHILDREN: Very welcome.
CREDIT CARDS: Mastercard/Visa
LICENSED: Full On Licence
ACCOMMODATION: Not applicable

RESTAURANT: Snacks, sandwiches, meals, home-made cakes. Value for money
BAR FOOD: Not applicable
VEGETARIAN: 1 hot/ 1 cold, each meal time + sandwiches
DISABLED ACCESS: Willing to assist
GARDEN: Courtyard market

Norwich Cathedral

Norwich

"Nothing is repeated, and everything is unparalled."

Goncourt Brothers Journal 1867

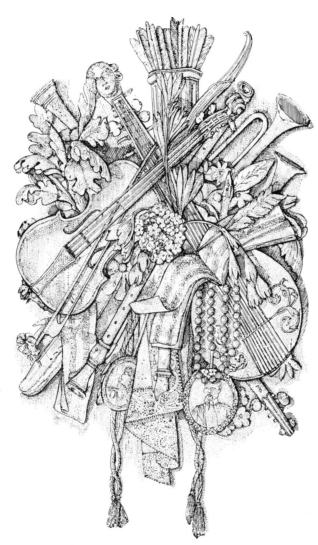

The City of Norwich

by Dick Benson–Gyles

Deep in the heart of the fastest-growing, most progressive region in Britain, East Anglia, lies a city which, paradoxically, offers all the unchanged and unchanging qualities sought after by more and more people desperate to escape life in today's fast lane. That city is **Norwich** and it is a city of marvellous contradictions. It pursues the modern and the technological with commendable ambition while cherishing at its heart a wonderful monument to the glories of the past and to those creations of mankind which defy both change and time.

Capital of the region, Norwich has a thousand jewels of interest to offer the visitor but the real gem is the cathedral. In a city which has a history stretching back more than 900 years, the great monument to both the power of religion in Norman and medieval times and the piety and skills of the craftsmen of East Anglia is the great hymn in stone which is Norwich Cathedral. From the vast dome of space capped by fountains of stone tracery which is the nave and its roof, to the immensity of the flying buttresses holding the vault in place and the soaring 315 ft spire, the cathedral is a perfect example of what the Victorian aesthete, John Ruskin, called the frozen music of Gothic architecture.

The spire, second only to Salisbury in England, dominates the city, which lies cradled in an arm of the River Wensum. Despite Norwich's hunger for the new and the hi-tech, the city fathers have shown an almost visionary foresight and wisdom about development. Where many 20th century towns and cities in Britain have been chopped and mutilated by over-zealous developers, bludgeoned by councils blinded by the glitter of progress, and ultimately fallen prey to the worst excesses of the Philistine, Norwich has managed a remarkable balance of past and present.

There is a wealth of medieval building still extant and there are many intriguing walks through the narrow, old streets and down by the river, from where boats busily ply to and from the Norfolk Broads via the River Yare. For the practised historical eye one of the great joys of Norwich is that you can still clearly make out the shape of the city of yesteryear in the busy criss-cross of today's thoroughfares. It was the level, fertile and very rich agricultural land of Norfolk which led to its capital's wealth and to its fine architectural heritage. This, in the main, is to be found in the North East section of the 'Wensum Loop', and, as in the City of London, parts of the old walls, once a mile square, are still standing.

Befitting a modern regional capital, the city has a large, and thriving shopping centre and a major development - Castle Mall - opened only this year (1993). It is a cultural centre with an appeal and reputation reaching well beyond East Anglia, with annual Arts, Jazz and Folk Festivals. Norwich also proudly boasts an Arts Centre, a major regional theatre and several small theatres and, of course, the famous Norwich Puppet Theatre, which is unique.

To eulogise Norwich is not to falsify the facts or embellish the truth in a bout of partisan fervour. As short a time ago as 1986 an EEC-commissioned study named the East Anglian capital as Britain's number one city for prosperity and attractiveness. It is full of good antique shops and very good restaurants and if you like eating game, Norwich is the place for you. With large estates like Sandringham in the surrounding countryside, the city's butchers are full of fresh game, from pheasant, snipe and woodcock to quail, hare and grouse. I would unhesitatingly recommend you to ADLARDS RESTAURANT in Upper St Giles Street where David Adlard produces meals you will never forget in a restaurant that is utterly charming.

A totally different sort of establishment but delighting its many admirers is THE ATTIC CARVERY AND BISTRO at 14-16 Lower Coat Lane. It is advisable to book for then the table is yours for the evening and you can indulge yourself in the relaxing atmosphere with the promise of a good meal. Each day the blackboard tells of affordable bar meals and specials and the restaurant is known for its carvery and Sunday lunches.

No 1 Old Post Office Yard, Bedford Street until seventeen years ago was a 17th century merchant's house and now it has been converted into BEDFORDS BRASSERIE AND BAR. Not being satisfied with being as old as the 17th century it goes one better and has below a 13th centuy crypt. It is an elegant and delightful place to be where the food is a happy blend of European cuisine with a definite local influence. In summer the pretty garden tucked away at the back makes eating outside a rare treat.

Tombland is an ancient word meaning open space and today The Tombland Experience is in the very heart of Norwich next to the cathedral. At its heart is BOSWELLS BRASSERIE, PIZZA ONE/PANCAKES TOO AND HY'S NIGHTCLUB. All this is to be found within a beautiful building datng back to 1541.

And if you have a rich palate and want to garnish your game, a visit to the famous Mustard Shop in Bridewell Alley in the old heart of the city is a must. Opened by Colman's of Norwich in 1973 to mark the 150th anniversary of the partnership between Jeremiah Colman and his nephew James, the shop is like something left over from Victorian times, full of mahogany shelving and marble tops, old chandeliers, timeless clock and ancient staircase. Doubling as a museum, the shop sells 20 different varieties of mustard, both powdered and prepared, and most are specially blended.

Norwich has already tasted the heady draught of celebrity and limelight. As far back as the 17th century it was England's second city, due in large part to the prosperity created by the textile industry, which had been given a big boost by the arrival of the so-called 'Strangers' from the Netherlands. The Strangers were religious refugees,

Protestants fleeing the persecution of the Duke of Alva in the Low Countries. At the start of 1579 there were 6000 of them - nearly 40 per cent of the city's total population of 16,000. They brought with them some strange new materials. A quaint description of these has survived in Queen's letters patent - granting some of the Strangers licence to practise their trade - and reads: "bays, arras, sayes, tapestry, mokadoes, stament, carsay and other such outlandish commodities as hath not bene used to be made within this realme of England."

If the newcomers, with their advanced weaving techniques, gave the city's prosperity a crucial fillip, they also aroused resentments and jealousies among the indigenous residents. They suffered what today we would call human rights abuses and it was not until 1598 that resident aliens could become freemen of the city on the same footing as the native pop-ulation. Their religious views also created disharmonies and it was some years before the residue of the Strangers had integrated into the community.

Norwich, like many cities of the Elizabethan era, had its share of poverty, unemployment and severe deprivation. Sometimes I think we don't know how lucky we are to be living in the 20th century, when you compare today's

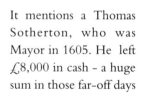

The knight and mythical Griffin in combat: one of the wood carvings at Norwich

living standards with those of earlier times. Contemporary accounts tell that in 1570 Norwich was swarming with tramps and a fifth of the population was living on charity. A municipal census in that year shows that there were 2,300 residents poor - as opposed to vagrants - from a total population of 12,360.

There was tragic irony in the fact that it was the plague of 1579 which came to the rescue of the hard-pressed city accountants. Many poor died and country people avoided Norwich. At this time the city was ruled by a small, rich oligarchy, most of whom had country estates as well as town houses. To give you an idea of the wealth of some of these powerful burghers, let me cite Norfolk Museums Service's publication 'Norwich, the growth of a city'.

It mentions a Thomas Sotherton, who was Mayor in 1605. He left £8,000 in cash - a huge sum in those far-off days - plate, jewels and land all over the place. Yet four fifths of the population were either poor or destitute.

For some while the population was kept down to about 11,000. Bubonic plage was the main culprit and it was so virulent that Norwich suffered more than any other provincial town in England. The 18th century saw

Norwich coming into its own. Its power and influence resulted directly from the prosperity brought by the spread of the worsted industry. Sales abroad took off and all over Europe Norwich stuffs cornered the market from Exeter serges. The key was cheap labour and handsome, well-made fabrics. By the end of the century Norwich was trading right across the known world. Other industries were now vyeing with wool for attention and leather-work and brewing were soon prominent. By the turn of the 18th century the good water off the chalk and Norfolk's top quality malting barley had combined to develop a boom business - beer.

As the 19th century dawned, there were at least half a dozen large breweries in Norwich and the city even supplied London. In 1801 one of the brewing houses actually topped some of the London firms, producing an astonishing 20,000 barrels.

Norfolk farmers were now in full swing and the city's markets for food, corn and livestock were becoming ever busier, especially after the turnpike movement of the 18th century saw the proliferation of roads into cities. Norwich was also becoming a place of butchers who put up stalls displaying their wares every weekday. On big market days the city must have come very close to our modern-day imaginings of 'Merrie England'. Beef, pork, veal, lamb, sausages, dressed poultry, sucking pigs, rabbits,

The Victorian pulpit, Norwich Cathedral

butter, cheese and eggs were all for sale. The farmers' wives would sit on the cobblestones with their goods in round baskets dubbed 'peds'. The market duly became the Ped Market and one of the sights of Norwich.

Insurance and banking - unusual in provincial cities at the time - now began to blossom. Gurneys bank was opened in 1775 by John and Henry Gurney and is still in existence today as part of Barclays Bank (Richard Gurney had married the only daughter of London banker, David Barclay), and in 1783 John Bignold, likewise a banker (and a wine merchant to boot), launched a series of businesses with yet another familiar ring to them: Norwich General Assurance Office, Norwich Union Fire Insurance Society, and Norwich Union Life Insurance Society.

Just over a century later, in 1887, the Norwich Union Life Office really took off. Agencies were set up in most European and many Commonwealth countries, and today the Union is the largest single employer in the city and one of the biggest insurance companies in England.

The well-to-do in 18th century Norwich could afford everything the burgeoning British Empire could provide from the increasing trade with far-flung outposts. The ships of the powerful East India Company brought exotic goods galore to the wealthy burghers. If you were invited in to the house of one of these city worthies, you could expect to see furniture of French walnut and other rare woods - especially mahogany - Oriental carpets, and the best in French wines, while a glimpse into Milady's wardrobe would reveal sumptuous velvet, lace and muslin from Europe and further afield.

As the 19th century got underway, the city's shape changed. The gates were removed, the walls were not maintained and parts of them collapsed, and building grew apace both inside and outside the old Norwich. However, cities like Norwich, until well into the 20th century, were very unhealthy places to live. There was precious little piped water and the poorer citizen had to rely on parish pumps or shallow wells. There was no sewerage as we know it, just cesspools and heaps of night soil. Disease was rife.

The arrival of the railways saw the city expand even further beyond its old confines. Norwich boasted three terminals by the mid-1880s. Thorpe Station was completed by 1844 on land east of the Wensum and Victoria Station was up and running just outside St Stephen's Gate in 1849. Then the Midland and Great Northern Railway built the City Station in 1882 on the west bank of the river, complete with new bridge and approach road. Yet today, despite the flight of population from London to the provinces, particularly East Anglia, there is only one passenger station left in the city.

Norwich's earlier pride and joy - the textile industry - had also shrunk by the end of Victoria's reign. In 1750 worsted weaving was the city's prime industry; at the start of the Edwardian decade there wasn't one worsted weaver worth the name left in Norwich. Machined cloth was cheaper and the North had taken on the East's mantle. Boots, shoes, beer, soap, paper, agricultural machinery and the famous Colman's mustard, were chief among the staples of the 19th century Norwich economy.

Towards the end of the century the population had risen to 90,000 or more and by 1921 had rocketed to 121,000. The Great War was a watershed for Norwich, as it was everywhere in Britain and the Western world in general. Living conditions had been bad for the lower classes before the war but now the Corporation was to launch a drive for slum clearance and rehousing. However, it is this century which has seen the most radical change to the face of the city. 'Spread' is the key word. Development has pushed out into the surrounding countryside in all directions.

The Second World War was a nasty interruption to the city's growth, with Norwich taking a hammering from German bombs. More than 2000 houses were damaged beyond repair and several churches were destroyed, with others, notably St Michael at Thorn and St Benedict, never being rebuilt. Today some of the redundant churches have been turned productively to other uses: St Peter Hungate, for one, is a museum of church art.

And, like many another city centre in our over-populated land, the heart of Norwich has come under heavy siege from the motor car and traffic of every sort. Despite a complex one-way system, congestion is increasing and those ugly, characterless deserts known as urban car parks have proliferated. However, an earlier ring road and the conversion of some of the old city centre streets into pedestrian preserves have helped maintain Norwich's medieval ambience and kept the worst depredations of modern development at bay.

Returning for a moment to the matter of travel in and out of the city, if the passenger rail service has declined, the conversion of part of the old RAF airfield at Horsham St Faiths has created a busy civil airport with connections to both domestic and Continental destinations.

So much for a whistle-stop tour of 500 years of Norwich history. Today anyone who visits the city with a keen eye and an open and enquiring mind will be well rewarded. Many, if not most, of our county towns and cities can boast heritages choc-a-bloc with architecture and artefact, but Norwich really can claim to be, if not in a league of its own, certainly a leader in the top echelon. And this boast is no idle one: The city has the finest group of medieval churches in Europe; Britain's second best collection of civic plate and portraits; England's largest six-day open air market; Europe's first pedestrianised streets; and one of the best provincial museums in the country.

It is associated with such historical and literary luminaries as Admiral Lord Nelson, Elizabeth Fry, Edith Cavell, George Borrow and Round Table founder, Louis Marchesi.

On the modern and media front Norwich is right there too: It is at the heart of the region's communications networks with both Anglia Television and Eastern Counties Newspapers based there, and industry is well represented. There is major investment in food processing, shoe manufacture, insurance, printing, window manufacture, chemicals and banking.

In all this I have, of course, left out the jewel in Norwich's crown - one of the finest Norman cathedrals in England. It is a tried, if not always tested, dictum about great art that its genius and greatness is immediately

The Flemish lectern, circa 1450: a Pelican feeding its young made of Lattern

obvious without need of knowledge or scholarship. This is especially true of NORWICH CATHEDRAL. The cathedral is a working community, a living entity, still as actively promoting the word of Jesus Christ now as it was 600 years ago. It is by no means just a monument for tourist consumption. All over Europe from 1050 to 1350 there was the most unprecedented boom in cathedral building. Eighty of them, not to mention countless churches, were built.

As you gaze at a cathedral like Norwich and realise what went into its building in the form of commitment, expertise, architectural genius, craftsmanship, not to mention the sheer volume of manpower and richness of invention and ingenuity needed to raise such a huge edifice in those far-off days, you can only marvel in awestruck silence. The cathedral lies off Tombland, the very picturesque street you come to from Princes Street at the top of the equally ancient and beautiful Elm Hill. In fact, you would be well advised to approach the great cathedral edifice by a sort of historico-architectural route, a walk down the centuries to Norman England and a glorious hymn in stone.

And so we find ourselves surrounded by memories of the city's past. They are on all sides. George Borrow, that extraordinary 19th century writer and promoter of the bible abroad - who could teach most modern salesmen a trick or two - was the author of the enduring 'Romany Rye', 'Lavengro' and 'The Bible in Spain'. In between his wanderings he found time to pen some touching words on the city of his boyhood in the early 19th century:

"...It shows best from the east, where the ground, bold and elevated, overlooks the fair and fertile valley in which it stands...Yes, there it spreads from north to south, with its venerable houses, its numerous gardens, its thrice twelve churches, its mighty mound...There is a grey old castle upon the top of that mighty mound; and yonder rising three hundred feet above the soil, from among these noble forest trees, behold that Norman masterwork, that cloud-encircled cathedral spire, around which a garrulous army of rooks and choughs continually wheel their flight. Now who can wonder that the children of that fine old city are proud of her and offer up prayers for her prosperity."

Approach the city centre from the West and make your way along St Benedict's Street - one of the earliest areas of settlement in Norwich (the city's name probably derives from the Saxon North-wic) - and you will pass through part of the old walls. Look carefully and here you will see, better than anywhere else, signs of the old Norwich in the narrow thoroughfares which wend towards Pottergate and St Giles Street. Here is the hallmark of the ancient city - its many churches, so many sadly redundant: Diminutive St Swithin's without a tower metamorphosed into the Norwich Arts Centre; St Margaret's, a gymnasium; and the large and grand St Laurence's, perhaps the finest of the unused churches and now tragically vacant.

All about are the architectueral indicators of historical Norwich. St Gregory's Church, now an arts centre, The Quakers Meeting House behind St Gregory's in Upper Goat Lane; and continuing eastwards, Charing, or more correctly, Shearing Cross. Then the Strangers Hall - a 15th and 16th century house and at present a very good Folk Museum - and behind it the Maddermarket Theatre, home of the Norwich Players. All the names crowded into this central area tell of the Norwich of old: Shearing Cross, where the shearers worked, Pottergate, the potters' street, and Maddermarket, which speaks of weaving and dyes. At St John Maddermarket Church are to be found the finest collection of monunmental brasses in the city.

Next and happily still a working church is spacious St Andrew's with its fine cambered roof tie-beam. If you walk round to the right you will see the church of St Michael-at-Plea; converted into yet another arts centre, it has a fine south porch and owes its quaint name to the fact that the Archdeacon used to hold his courts here. The medieval paintings this church once boasted are now in the cathedral.

So, turning yet again eastward we come full circle, as it were, to Elm Hill and the approaches to the great Norman cathedral. However, to delay you just once more, you may, if you so wish, arc round via Bank Plain to take in the great castle on its mound. The Norman keep of about 1160 was refaced in the 1830s and part of it, designed by Sir John Soane, served as the gaol. Today it is a fine museum. Worth seeing here is the marvellous collection of Norwich School paintings.

We cannot walk away and up Elm Hill without a mention of Norwich's superb market place with all its many stalls, surrounded by the 15th century Guildhall, the modern City Hall and a great medieval church. The vistas down the little sidestreets to distant churches are fascinating. Now go back to St Andrew's Church and the adjoining Bridewell Alley - still redolent of the Middle Ages and still, as in those distant times, basically a shopping street and containing, as already mentioned, The Mustard Shop..

I have kept you waiting far too long. Make your way now down St Andrew's Hill to St Andrew's Street and thence to St George's Street and the river, spanned by the graceful bridge in Portland Stone designed by Soane in 1784. From here are plainly visible the medieval backs of the houses on Elm Hill. Turn into Colegate and re-cross the Wensum by the Fye Bridge. Elm Hill will now be to your right. It is the most splendid example of a cobbled medieval street you could hope to see. There are, however, a lot of Victorian shop fronts to the picturesque houses, with the exception of the Elizabethan Strangers' Club.

Turn left into Princes Street and walk to Tombland. Now begin the glories. The Cathedral Close is entered through the tall arch of the Erpingham Gate, or via the vaulted roof of Ethelbert Gate. Despite the depredations of the motor car and the fact that some of the buildings have been converted for office use, the 18th century atmosphere of the Close is still all around you.

This unexampled jewel of church housing is in fact the biggest and most intimate collection of cathedral houses in Europe. With its eighty dwellings, some medieval, including the Deanery - which is the oldest inhabited house in Norwich - it's a bit like a small but bustling village.

And now to the star of the show, the cathedral! Herbert de Losinga, first Bishop of Norwich, obtained, free of local control, a grant of land, which he wanted in order to found a Benedictine monastery for fifty monks. Then, when his hugely ambitious building project - the cathedral - came to be launched in 1096, he used Norfolk flint for the core, while the pristine white stone which gives Norwich such a fine finish, was brought all the way from Caen in Normandy. Stone was also brought from Barnack in Northamptonshire and Yorkshire.

Let us start with the Close. Into this medieval village we step, as through magic portals into another world. The Bishop's Gate (from Palace Street), the famous Erpingham Gate, or St Ethelbert's Gate - any of these will usher us into this little, private remnant of an almost forgotten England with its simple, no-nonsense English names - Upper Close, Lower Close, Green Yard, Almery Green, Hook's Walk. Gardens and gables, mullions and mellow brick, nooks and alleys, all await exploration.

Norwich Cathedral, you will notice straight away from the outside, has a very long nave and by comparison a short chancel. Great flying buttresses reach up to steady the weight of the nave masonry and the east end is a delight of shape and artifice with its chevet, apse, chapels and traceried windows; Then the wide arms of the transept and the crowning Norman central tower and the soaring 15th century spire. The main body of the church was completed by the mid-12th century. 200 years went by and then a catastrophe - which ultimately turned out to be a blessing in disguise - struck. The spire tumbled down, damaging the chancel clerestory in the process. The incident provided a heaven(?)-sent opportunity to recreate the east end of the great cathedral in the imposing form we know it today.

The cloisters had been begun half a century earlier but, with the collapsed spire and subsequent rebuilding, were only finished in 1430. Thirty years on and disaster struck again, this time in the form of a fire which completely destroyed the original timber roof. Again it may have been a blessing in disguise because it initiated the building of what is arguably the cathedral's greatest glory - its 14th/15th century vault.

Not even the most virulent atheist and only the most intractable Philistine could fail to be moved by the nave at Norwich, particularly its roof, where finely-honed fountains of stone seem to burst forth from the great columns to create a dizzying tunnel of masonry above your head forever defying gravity - frozen music indeed!

Matching the nave roof for symmetry and rhythm are the Norman arcades with the great triforium above and the high clerestory above that again. And yet the columns, triforium and clerestory were all finished by 1250. It is amazing that this uncluttered Norman austerity should be so perfectly matched by the profuse riches of the 15th century vault with its wonderful bosses. The roof was built during the time of Bishop Lyhart, whose motif - a deer couched in water - can be spied by the eagle eye at the head of every third pillar.

Everywhere there are Perpendicular windows, in particular note the west window which has Victorian glass of 1854 in it, recalling pictorial windows of a previous century. The choir is a masterpiece in its own right, gorgeously filled with 15th century canopied stalls with notable misericords. All around the apse and altar and triforium is a marvellous synthesis between the Norman and the Perpendicular.

'The grim jaws of Hell' - A roof Boss, one of many wonderful examples found in Norwich Cathedral

The chapels in the chevet are apsidal Norman with basic stone arcading, some consider these among the most beautiful features of the Cathedral. The chapels are both intimate and imposing and boast superb, and rare, medieval painted panels.

No English Cathedral would be complete without its monuments and there are some suitably grand ones in Norwich: Bishop Goldwell slumbers below his alabaster effigy atop a painted tomb under a vaulted canopy, while a Bishop of nearly 350 years later, Bishop Bathurst, sits not far off and Bishop Pelham (1896) reclines nearby.

The walls are throughout graced by a fascinating gathering of largely 18th century monuments by Norwich sculptors. Note particularly the fine tablet by William Stanton to Dean Fairfax in the south arcade. Close at hand are the cloisters. These really are special and among the best in England. Although they were built up over many years, they show a wonderful harmony of style. The window tracery is remarkable, from the early Geometrical to Curvilinear and Perpendicular. Look up at the vaulting and the profusion of superb bosses. Perhaps one of the most perfect Gothic entrances anywhere is the north-east doorway of the cloisters leading into the nave. Let your eyes feast on the stunning radiation of carved figures under crocketed canopies adorning the arch.

A final memory of Norwich Cathedral should perhaps be a view of it from the south side. It is superb. The two-storeyed cloister, then the the lofted south aisle with the windows of the triforium and clerestory rising up to the pitched roof.

Arcaded, battlemented, buttressed,like a vast mountain-face it reaches ever upwards to its crowning, soaring spire. No, you will not forget Norwich Cathedral easily.

To more mundane matters after so much that is rich. THE OASIS SPORTS AND LEISURE CENTRE at **Thorpe** just outside Norwich will answer your need to get exercise and at the same time enjoy the social side of this complex which has everything. It is on the road to Great Yarmouth.

If you have time, wend your way towards the Norfolk Broads and the many wonderful sights there. Just 20 minutes from the centre of Norwich you will find WROXHAM BARNS where in splendid surroundings you will get the oportunity to see craftsmen at work. It is home to 13 or 14 resident craftsmen all offering different skills. There is an excellent Tea Room and a 'Junior Farm' where visitors can wander among young animals and help at feeding times. It will provide a very special day out.

If you enjoy a drink and food in a village pub then make for **Strumpshaw** where THE SHOULDER OF MUTTON where you will always be warmly welcomed and meet a cross-section of people.

There are three places some considerable way from Norwich which should be included in anybody's itinerary in Norfolk. They each are unique in their way and not to be missed.

NORFOLK LAVENDER at Caley Mill, **Heacham** is England's Lavender Farm. Here you will discover the history of the traditional uses of lavender in England through the ages. Learn about the early days of Norfolk lavender and get to understand about the growing of

English lavender and the producing of English lavender oil, which is prized above all other lavenders. You will also find useful hints and ideas for growing plants and using lavender at home. It is a fantastic place. To get to Heacham from Norwich take to A47 to **Kings Lynn** and then the A 17 a little further on towards **Terrington St Clement**.

If you take the same road out of Norwich and when you reach **Swaffham** turn right onto the A1065 you will come to **Fakenham** and from there the A148 will take you to **Thursford** where THE THURSFORD COLLECTION is an experience that should certainly not be missed. This interesting collection has been described as a 'sight and sound spectacular'. It is unlike any museum you have ever seen - or will find anywhere else in the world. It is full of mechanical pipe organs, gleaming with gilt and rich colours. Thurston has nine of these wonderful organs and offers you daily music starring Robert Wolfe in The Wurlitzer Show. Evening musical events throughout the year should be noted in your diary. This is not all - there is much more and it is something for you to seek out.

A little further north, almost up to one of my favourite places **Wells-next-the-Sea** is LANGHAM GLASS in The Long Barn, North Street, **Langham.** The beautiful old flint barns hold all the secrets of glass making and you can see how it has been done traditionally for hundreds of years.

Norwich and its Cathedral are unforgettable but the icing on the cake has to be that they are situated in Norfolk, a beautiful county.

Thursford Green, Thursford, Nr Fakenham,
Norfolk, NR21 0AS.

Tel: (0328) 878477

THE THURSFORD COLLECTION
Historic Complex & Coffee Shop

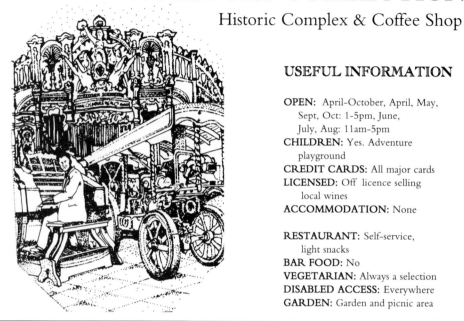

This interesting collection has been described as 'a sight and sound spectacular'. The Thursford Collection is like no museum you've ever seen - or will find anywhere else in the world. Enter a world of magic and nostalgia, fun and majesty of bygone years. Walk into a glittering Aladdins's Cave and enjoy all that is within.

The first thing to catch your eye must be one of the many mechanical pipe organs, gleaming with gilt and rich colours, coloured in exuberant carvings, a pleasure to behold. Thursford has nine of these wonderful organs and offers you daily music starring Robert Wolfe in The Wurlitzer Show. Evening musical entertainment throughout the year is not to be missed featuring a variety of artists, the opening night in June gets off with a champagne reception and towards the end of the year a spectacular fireworks display gets the concert off with a bang.

Many other exciting exhibits are awaiting your attention, how about the majestic old road engines, standing proud in all their glory, well loved and tenderly cared for, these fine machines deserve much attention. Take a nostalgic trip back to childhood on the switchback roundabout, with it's Venetian gondolas, exotic in gold and myriad colours. Visit the mini village with a touch of Charles Dicken, many delightful shops are within, offering a vast selection of quality goods ranging from local fruit wines, special preserves, sweets, records and gifts. Time for refreshments? Cream teas are served on the lawn, light snacks can be found in the barn and home-made ices in the parlour. A visit will surpass all your expectations.

USEFUL INFORMATION

OPEN: April-October, April, May, Sept, Oct: 1-5pm, June, July, Aug: 11am-5pm
CHILDREN: Yes. Adventure playground
CREDIT CARDS: All major cards
LICENSED: Off licence selling local wines
ACCOMMODATION: None

RESTAURANT: Self-service, light snacks
BAR FOOD: No
VEGETARIAN: Always a selection
DISABLED ACCESS: Everywhere
GARDEN: Garden and picnic area

Caley Mill, Heacham,
Norfolk, PE31 7JE.

Tel: (0485) 70384
Fax: (0485) 71176

NORFOLK LAVENDER
Visitor Attraction

Caley Mill, the headquarters of Norfolk Lavender, was originally a water mill for grinding corn. Built of the local carrstone in the early 19th century, it is now set in gardens of lavender, roses and herbs, and has become a distinctive Norfolk landmark. To come here is to discover a different world of sight, sound and smell and an experience you will never forget.

Until 1955 bushes were planted singly, to give the maximum space for each bush. From then on all replanting was done in rows to produce lavender hedges in anticipation of a suitable mechanical cutter. By 1989 Norfolk Lavender had almost 100 acres in full production, including 50 acres at Sandringham. Five varieties are grown for distilling, and two additional varieties for drying. The weather plays a vital part. Sun is essential to enable the plant to make its oil. Heavy rain at harvest time can be a disaster, reducing yields by more than half as the damp causes the florets to turn brown.

In the grounds are the National Collection of Lavenders. There are about 50 different lavenders to see and one of the most popular features of a visit is a wander around the plant sales area beside the Conservatory where they sell many types of lavender in different sizes of pots to suit all requirements. The Distillery is open in July and August when the harvest is in progress. The Herb Garden has almost 60 individual beds laid out like an old monastery garden. In the centre is a locally made sundial. Few visitors leave Norfolk Lavender without having first experienced one of the famous cream teas and also the delightful gift shop. Guided tours are available from the end of May to September.

USEFUL INFORMATION

OPEN: All year round. Closed during the first two weeks of January
CHILDREN: Welcome
CREDIT CARDS: Access/Visa/Switch
LICENSED: None
ACCOMMODATION: No. Super gift shop

RESTAURANT: Tea room with home-made cakes, scones etc
BAR FOOD: Not applicable
VEGETARIAN: Yes, several dishes
DISABLED ACCESS: Yes, everywhere
GARDEN: Patio for eating & garden by the river for picnics

WROXHAM BARNS

Craft & Gift Centre

Tunstead Road, Hoveton,
Norwich, NR12 8QU.

Tel: (0603) 783762
Fax: (0603) 783911

USEFUL INFORMATION

OPEN: All year except Christmas and
Boxing Day
CHILDREN: Yes. Playground, old
fashioned fair and farm
CREDIT CARDS: Visa/Access (not
Switch or Connect)
LICENSED: Restaurant
ACCOMMODATION: Not applicable

RESTAURANT: Traditional English
BAR FOOD: Not applicable
VEGETARIAN: Yes
DISABLED ACCESS: Most areas
GARDEN: Just over 10 acres. Picnic area

Situated within easy reach of the Norfolk Broads and only twenty minutes from the centre of Norfolk, you will find Wroxham Barns. Once a dairy farm, it was discovered in a very bad state in 1982, and after a lot of hard work was opened as a number of craft workshops, set in ten acres of parkland. Parking and entrance is free; entry to the Junior Farm is £1.50 (at October 1993). This is a perfect opportunity to see craftsmen at work. Today Wroxham Barns is home to 13 or 14 resident craftsmen, all offering different skills including; stitchcraft, sketch printing, perfumery, gemstone jewellery, bookbinding, painting in enamel, woodturning, pottery, glassmaking, classic wooden boatbuilding, wooden toys, flower remedies and oils. Visiting craftsmen often can be found in the bottom courtyard. All the work on display is for sale: if you can't find that special something, you will find the artists only too willing to help. Visitors are welcome to watch the craftsmen and chat about their work.

Time to sit down? Need a cup of tea? Visit the Old Barn Tea Room, for morning coffee, fresh home-made food (but of course), light lunches, including a vegetarian meal of the day and afternoon teas. Picnic facilities are by the duck pond . There is also a kiosk serving snacks. Next, take a stroll through The Gallery Collection and Craft Shop. The ground floor has a wonderful selection of exciting quality gifts and upstairs you will delight at the designer knitwear and clothing. Recently opened 'Junior Farm' is very popular with both young and old. Visitors can wander among the young animals and help at feeding time. What better way to end your day than a visit to the traditional fun fair and penny machines. A truly special day not to be forgotten.

LANGHAM GLASS

Fine Hand–Made Crystal

The Long Barn, North Street,
Langham, Norfolk, NR25 7DG.

Tel: (0328) 830511
Fax: (0328) 830787

USEFUL INFORMATION

OPEN: All year
CHILDREN: Welcome
CREDIT CARDS: Switch only
LICENSED: Restaurant Licence
ACCOMMODATION: Not applicable

RESTAURANT: Light lunches.
Traditional English
BAR FOOD: Not applicable
VEGETARIAN: 2/3 dishes
DISABLED ACCESS: Yes, level
GARDEN: Yes with barbeque

Set between Blakeney and Holt, Langham Glass is a working glass factory. The whole site was conceived as a tourist attraction; having all the amenities associated with a great family day out, plus the added attraction of actually seeing the glass works in action from a viewing gallery with a running explanatory commentary provided by the 'Master' working the molten glass.

An adventure playground, museum, video centre, tea room/restaurant and substantial gift shop make Langham Glass, in its early 18th century complex, an ideal visit whether it's a sunny or rainy day; with plenty of free parking!

Over Bank Holidays and from May 1 to November 1 the factory and all facilities are open 7 days a week together with the shop, adventure playground and restaurant.

Paul Miller – founding owner of Langham Glass in the late 1970's , is widely recognised as one of the finest glass blowers in the UK. His crystal creations have ben presented as gifts to foreign dignitaries from around the world. But don't worry, Langham craftsmen hand create gifts for every pocket including such delights as perfume bottles, drinking glasses, swans and pandas. They also provide an engraving service. A great day out whatever your age!

Langham Glass is only 27 miles from the Cathedral in Norwich and five miles from Holt. In spring 1994 Langham are opening a new glassworks in the centre of Cambridge.

79 Upper St Giles Street,
Norwich, Norfolk, NR2 1AB.

Tel: (0603) 633522

ADLARD'S RESTAURANT
Restaurant

Tucked away in a busy cul-de-sac under the tower of the quaint church of St Giles-on-the-Hill is Adlard's one of England's highest rated restaurants. The whole area is one of charm with the Roman Catholic Cathedral of St John the Baptist at the far end of the street. The restaurant is 200 yards south of the City Hall and just a gentle ten to fifteen minutes walk from Norwich's superb Anglican Cathedral. Attractively furnished Adlard's has an ambience which is to be envied and is certainly conducive to relaxing, enjoying a pre-dinner drink and studying the menu to decide on your meal. The decision is always going to pose a problem because, whilst the choice is not vast, it is made up of a number of very interesting dishes which change constantly.

David Adlard was trained in the French Classical tradition and offers a menu of Modern British Interpretations based on fresh, local ingredients if possible. Who could resist Escalope of Salmon with Mussels and Sorrel Sauce or Grilled Teal with 'Salsa Verde' and Pinenuts, Herb Salad for starters followed by Rack of English Lamb with a Tapenade Crust and Tart of Onion Confit and Glazed Baby Onions, Gratin Dauphinois or Seafood with Braised Organic Fennel, Lobster Fumet and Fresh Tagliatelli. The sweets are equally delicious and if you can possibly find room you may be able to taste one of the best Summer Puddings ever, accompanied with Lime Syllabub. The eclectic wine list covers the Classic Wine Regions as well as Australian, New Zealand, Californian and South American. The Lunch Menu is equally as good and both at lunch and dinner there is a fixed price.

USEFUL INFORMATION

OPEN: Lunch: Tues-Fri: 12.30-1.45pm,
Dinner: Tues-Sat: 7.30-10.30pm
CHILDREN: Welcome
CREDIT CARDS: Visa/Access/Amex
LICENSED: Restaurant
ACCOMMODATION: Not aplicable

RESTAURANT: Modern British. Fresh produce
BAR FOOD: Not applicable
VEGETARIAN: On application
DISABLED ACCESS: Level entrance. WC slightly more difficult
GARDEN: Not applicable

14-16 Lower Goat Lane,
Norwich, Norfolk. NR1 1EL.

Tel: (0603) 666802

THE ATTIC CARVERY AND BISTRO
Bistro & Carvery

As the name suggests The Attic Carvery and Bistro is upstairs. This delightful restaurant was once a DIY store, impossible to imagine now. Situated in a very central position and a couple of minutes from the market square, theatre or cathedral, makes this a perfect retreat for the weary sightseer. The 'romantic at heart' also enjoy The Attic Carvery and Bistro, for the gentle lighting and comfortable surroundings lend themselves to a warm, intimate evening for two. Enjoy a pre-dinner drink in the little bar if you wish before relaxing at your table. It is advisable to book, for then the table is yours for the evening, Shinuna and Tony don't rush their guests. Indulge yourself in the relaxing atmosphere with the promise of a good meal.

Tony is the chef and prides himself on freshly cooked, delicious food. The menu is exciting with a large range of tempting dishes. The Chicken and Walnut Pate served with toast catches my eye as an unusual starter and for the main meal it is an impossible choice from, salmon, steaks, duck etc. all prepared as part of mouth watering recipes. The children have a separate menu and Tony always makes sure that vegetarians are not forgotten. Each day the blackboard tells of affordable bar meals and specials including lasagne, pies etc. The Attic Carvery and Bistro is well known for its carvery and Sunday lunches, all reasonably priced. They also cater for birthdays, weddings, conferences and buffets in the sit-down function room.

Shinuna and Tony make sure you get value for money and give all their guests a warm welcome.

USEFUL INFORMATION

OPEN: All year. Tue-Sun: 12-2.30pm.
Wed-Sat: 7-10.30pm.
CHILDREN: Yes. Children's menu
CREDIT CARDS: All major cards except Amex
LICENSED: Full On Licence
ACCOMMODATION: Not applicable

RESTAURANT: Traditional English, with A La Carte
BAR FOOD: Yes. Separate bar menu
VEGETARIAN: Yes
DISABLED ACCESS: No (upstairs)
GARDEN: No

BEDFORDS BRASSERIE AND BAR

No 1 Old Post Office Yard, Bedford Street, Norwich, Norfolk, NR2 1FL.

Tel: (0603) 666869

Brasserie and Bar

USEFUL INFORMATION

OPEN: All year Mon-Sat: 12-3pm & 5-11pm. Closed on Sundays
CHILDREN: Garden only
CREDIT CARDS: All major cards
LICENSED: Full On Licence
ACCOMMODATION: Not applicable

RESTAURANT: European cuisine with local influence
BAR FOOD: Yes. Wide choice
VEGETARIAN: 3-4 daily
DISABLED ACCESS: Garden but not restaurant
GARDEN: Patio, tables and chairs outside for eating

Seventeen years ago this fascinating 17th century merchant's house was converted into Bedford's Brasserie and Bar. Not satisfied with being as old as the 17th century it goes one better and has below, a 13th century crypt. One has to admit that it has suffered several indignities over the centuries not the least being used for rope making as late as the 1940s. Today it is an elegant, intimate and delightful place to be.

It has many things about it that are not run of the mill. For a very old house it has amazingly high ceilings which manage to produce an air of spaciousness that does not really exist. The whole decor and furnishings have been brought together in harmony to produce a refined and relaxed atmosphere in which anyone would feel good.

The food is a happy blend of European cuisine with a definite local influence. Only the best of ingredients are used and everything is freshly prepared. The wine list is made up from wines procured from a local company, Adnams. They are constantly sourcing wine which means that what is on offer to the Brasserie and Bar is very special - almost unique.

In summer there is an additional attraction at Bedfords. The pretty garden tucked away at the back makes eating outside a rare treat. It is only in this garden that children are allowed. Sadly too it is really the only area suitable for disabled people; the age of the building makes elsewhere impossible. Bedford's Brasserie is a very happy find in Norwich - one that local people know and love already.

BOSWELLS & PIZZA ONE PANCAKES TOO! & HY'S

Tombland, Norwich, Norfolk, NR3 1RF.

Tel: (0603) 626099
Fax: (0603) 665683

Live Music Jazz Cafe, Bar, Restaurant & Nightclub

USEFUL INFORMATION

OPEN: All year round
CHILDREN: Yes
CREDIT CARDS: All major cards
LICENSED: Fully licenced until 2am
ACCOMMODATION: Not applicable

RESTAURANT: Yes. Pizza/Pancake Too and Boswells
BAR FOOD: A selection at night
VEGETARIAN: Yes
DISABLED ACCESS: Yes
GARDEN: Licensed forecourt for eating and drinking

The Tombland Experience is in the very heart of Norwich along the front of the Cathedral wall. Tombland is an ancient word meaning 'open space' and has become *the* meeting place. At the heart of Tombland is "Boswells", "Pizza One Pancakes Too!" and "hy's" nightclub. All are situated within this beautiful ancient building dating back to 1541. Hy Kurzner, travelling through Norwich in 1976, saw Boswells up for sale and fell in love with the building. He bought, re-opened and soon made a talking point of the new "Boswells". Then disaster struck one Saturday in 1978 when a raging fire consumed much of the heart and roof of the building. Nine months later the total reconstruction was completed and "Boswells" re-opened to greater acclaim than ever. In 1979 "Pizza One Pancakes Too!" was created and "hy's" in 1983. Today all three have become "the place to be" in Norwich.

"Boswells" is a pub with a difference. It offers music, a cafe, and an excellent restaurant with a mouth-watering selection of high quality yet reasonably priced meals. Open all day, even for breakfast on Sundays. Every night is music night at "Boswells" (and Sunday lunch time too!) with live bands playing the entire gamut of jazz and blues.

"Pizza One Pancakes Too!" is popular with everyone. It features delicious pizzas, pastas, as well as sweet and savoury crepes and is open 7 days a week all the year round. It is without doubt Norwich's premier eating place for value for money and ambience.

"Hy's" nightclub is an exciting night time venue with all the latest music, an armour plated glass sound graphic dance floor, which was the first of its kind in any UK club and a spectacular overhead light and laser show producing stunning visual effects. Combine this with luxurious, quiet seating areas, two plush bars and two restaurants, and you have a great night out waiting for you.

Norwich Road, Strumpshaw,
Norwich, NR13 4NT.

Tel: (0603) 712274

THE SHOULDER OF MUTTON
Village Pub

Strumpshaw is a typical Norfolk village just seven miles outside Norwich and off the A47 Great Yarmouth Road. It has a fine church with a spire that makes it the highest point in Norfolk. Equally important in the life of the village is the friendly village hostelry, The Shoulder of Mutton. Built in 1876 it is thought to have been the home of a member of the Whitbread family who is buried in the churchyard. He would have approved of the happy atmosphere in the Shoulder of Mutton today where you will always see and meet an interesting cross section of people, all enjoying a drink and quite probably one of the many well-cooked dishes on offer daily. Anne Miller does all the cooking and whenever possible she uses the vegetables out of the pub's garden. So prolific is the crop that customers are welcome to buy the home-grown vegetables in season. One of the favourite recipes Anne produces is 'Smokies' a delicious combination of Smoked Haddock creamed and covered with a cheese sauce. There is a roast most days and always a good steak menu. On Sundays there is always the traditional meal complete with crisp roast potatoes and Yorkshire Pudding. There is a separate dining area.

The Shoulder of Mutton is a sporting pub where Petangue is very popular and brings out the competitive spirit amongst the locals. They also belong to the local league teams for darts, pool and crib. Real Ale enthusiasts come to the pub knowing that Rod has 4 Real Ales which are local to the area.

USEFUL INFORMATION

OPEN: All year: 11am-11pm
CHILDREN: Welcome
CREDIT CARDS: None taken
LICENSED: Full On Licence
ACCOMMODATION: Not applicable

RESTAURANT: Separate dining area. Always fresh food
BAR FOOD: Wide range of traditional food
VEGETARIAN: Several dishes
DISABLED ACCESS: Level entrance
GARDEN: Extensive garden with tables and chairs

Pound Lane, Thorpe,
Norwich, NR7 0UB.

Tel: (0603) 37738
Fax: (0603) 700264

OASIS SPORTS AND LEISURE CENTRE
Sports and Leisure, with Bar & Restaurant

The comprehensive brochure for this well established, carefully planned and well executed sports and leisure centre which has super facilities states "Here's Health, Here's Oasis". It is conveniently situated in beautiful wooded grounds off the main Norwich ring road, at Pound Lane, which runs between the Yarmouth Road A47 at Thorpe to the B1140 Plumstead Road.

Here there are squash courts, badminton, tennis, table tennis, 2 indoor swimming pools, sauna baths, spa bath, steam room, solariums, ladies and men's fitness studio, aerobics, yoga, Tae Kwon Do, beauticians, men's and ladies hairdressing, sport shop, club lounge bar, restaurant, gardens and grounds. There is extensive free car parking. The Mirage Restaurant is open to non-members for Sunday lunch.

Steve Gedge runs the Mirage Restaurant and Bedouins Restaurant within his company 'The Art of Food'. Here is a man brought up in Norwich who has gained wide experience with hotels and restaurants in London and Norfolk. His work and training have made him a skilled chef in all aspects, bringing flair and imagination to the art of food. Through his company Oasis clients now benefit from a professional chef service which enables them to entertain at home, at the Mirage Restaurant or Bedouins to standards normally expected only in the most exclusive restaurants. Clients will have a unique menu fashioned exclusively for them to suit their tastes and the occasion. Oasis offers you the opportunity to join a most comprehensive health, sport and leisure complex.

USEFUL INFORMATION

OPEN: Lunch. Mon-Sun: 12-2.30pm. Eve: Mon-Sat:7-9.30pm last orders
CHILDREN: Restriction on sports facilities. Well behaved in bar & rest:
CREDIT CARDS: Rest: All major cards. Sports: Access/Visa only
LICENSED: Full On & Restaurant
ACCOMMODATION: Not applicable

RESTAURANT: Imaginative cuisine. High standard
BAR FOOD: Good food, sensible prices
VEGETARIAN: Always a choice
DISABLED ACCESS: Yes. No special facilities for sport
GARDEN: 5 acres. Trampoline, swings, BBQ

Oxford Cathedral

Oxford

"Beautiful City! so venerable, so lovely...
whispering from her towers the last
enchantments of the Middle Age."

Matthew Arnold

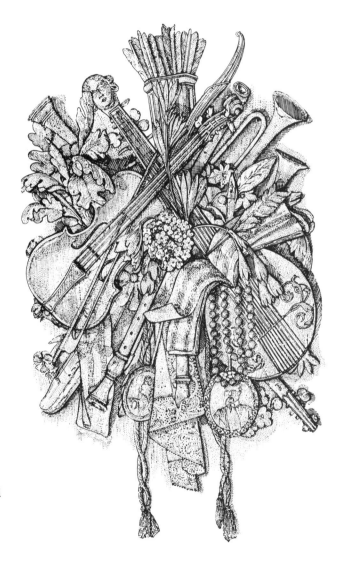

The City of Oxford

by Sally Dunsmore

OXFORD - City of Dreaming Spires

Oxford is one of the world's great cities. Famous for its University, its history and magnificent architecture. Within one square mile Oxford has more than 600 buildings of architectural interest and Oxford University consists of 35 different colleges sited throughout the city. The colleges' peaceful quadrangles and stunning gardens contribute to the atmosphere of England's foremost seat of learning.

Oxford has extraordinary variety. Against the backdrop of a city steeped in history and heritage, lies an immense range of culture that is very much contemporary. From world-famous international contemporary exhibitions, theatre, pre-West End musical premieres, film and music to student fringe events held in the college gardens. The old and new of Oxford complement each other and provide the visitor with a wealth of culture to be discovered. It is this unique variety that I invite you to explore.

Whether you arrive by car, bus or train, Oxford is best seen on foot. As you wander through the city, you will discover hidden cobbled passageways, ancient towers from which you can enjoy the most magnificent views of the city and of course the University's splendid colleges.

My first view of Oxford was 10 years ago when I came to live and work here. As I was driven down St Giles', I was struck by its beauty. It seemed the perfect approach to Oxford. An outstanding street lined with trees exploding into the red and gold colours of autumn and a "series" of impressive architectural wonders gave only a hint of what was still to come. It left an indelible impression on me and as you can tell I have not left since.

St Giles' is an unusually wide street as it was the place where cattle and sheep used to be herded before they were driven into the city for sale at the market. It is now one of the main routes into Oxford. However, St Giles' is closed to traffic for 2 days in September for the customary St Giles' Fair which evolved in the 18th century from St Giles' parish wake.

If you approach Oxford from the Banbury Road, just before entering St Giles you will find one of the most delightful and attractive hotels in Oxford, THE OLD PARSONAGE. It is small and intimate and is ideal for those who enjoy the personal and yet unobtrusive attention such a hotel offers. Under the watchful eye of its General Manager, Michael Thompson, the hotel continues to flourish and has become a welcome retreat for local Oxford residents looking for a relaxing environment in which to enjoy a drink or meal. The staff are efficient, friendly and dignified. The Parsonage Bar is both charming and sophisticated, a style that is reflected throughout the hotel. All the bedrooms are appointed to the highest standard and the marble bathrooms are exquisite.

During the summer months the front terrace is open where, as in the Parsonage Bar, food and drink are served throughout the day. The menu changes daily and offers a variety of interesting dishes to whet the appetite.

The hotel has become quite the favourite with a number of well-known actors. Sir Anthony Hopkins, Debra Winger and Lord Attenborough stayed there during the making of Shadowlands, Lord Attenborough's new film about the life of C S Lewis. Dudley Moore, Michael Palin and Diana Rigg are amongst others who have also resided at the hotel. It is rumoured that Oscar Wilde stayed there during his time at Oxford.

Not far from the Old Parsonage in Banbury Road is GEE'S BRASSERIE. Originally a Victorian conservatory, the restaurant has a unique style of its own and is a particularly elegant environment in which to eat. The atmosphere is sophisticated and relaxed, the food simple and delicious.

Running parallel alongside the Banbury Road and behind the Old Parsonage is the Woodstock Road where you will find BROWNS RESTAURANT - perhaps Oxford's liveliest and most popular restaurant. Browns is an Oxford institution remembered with affection by generations of graduates. Probably best known for its legendary queues on busy nights. It is good value for money and worth the wait, if you are seeking an exuberant atmosphere.

MAISON BLANC, the bread shop and patisserie, is next door and serves real French bread and a mouth-watering selection of traditional French patisserie.

Just round the corner is Little Clarendon Street known fondly by the locals as Little Trendy Street. Its range of shops include GEORGE AND DAVIS - a haven for those who adore ice cream - restaurants and exclusive designer clothes shops.

If you turn right into Walton Street at the end of Little Clarendon Street, you will come across one of Oxford's 4 cinemas, THE PHOENIX, an independent cinema that offers an inspired programme of European and English film.

Alternatively if you cross the road into Walton Crescent you will discover one of Oxford's hidden restaurants, AL-SHAMI. Serving Lebanese food, Al-Shami is very popular with the locals. Their range of starters are particularly good and whenever I eat there with friends we share an enormous selection of entrees - it makes an ample and delicious meal. However, I recommend you book before you go.

If you continue down St Giles; you will pass the 1650s inn THE EAGLE AND CHILD which C S Lewis and J R R Tolkein frequented. Opposite St John's College lies Beaumont Street where the magnificent ASHMOLEAN MUSEUM is situated. Founded in

1683 by Dr Johnson's great friend Elias Ashmole, the Ashmolean is the oldest museum still open to the public in Great Britain. No less than 73 rooms house the cream of Oxford University's archaeology and art treasures. Its collections of paintings which include old master drawings by Leonardo, Michaelangelo and Raphael, and works of the French Impressionists and Pre-Raphaelites are world-famous. The collections of Greek, Roman and Egyptian antiquities are fascinating as is the collection of Oriental art which includes Chinese and Japanese ceramics. Regular guided talks are available and are certainly worth joining for an illuminating tour of the exhibitions.

THE RANDOLPH HOTEL, Oxford's most famous hotel for over a century, looks out over the Ashmolean and onto St Giles. Its public rooms and bedrooms are impressive and the hotel is the ideal place to stay if you want to be right in the centre of Oxford. Tea is served daily in their glorious drawing room where you can enjoy the delights of cucumber sandwiches, cakes and scones.

A delightful 17th century conversation peice in the East Window

Theatre and art play a big part in the cultural life of Oxford and situated only yards from the Randolph Hotel in Beaumont Street is one of Britain's best known theatres THE OXFORD PLAYHOUSE. The theatre reopened in 1991 and is associated with some of the most famous names in the theatre world - Peggy Ashcroft,

Elizabeth Taylor, Dirk Bogarde, Janet Suzman and Sir John Gielgude. Under its dynamic young co-directors, Hedda Beeby and Trish Francis, it continues to remain true to its reputation as a theatre that presents a broad range of top quality performing arts. From one week to the next you can see anything from classic and contemporary drama to musicals and comedy to opera and dance to pre-West End hits. The range is phenomenal.

Oxford's very own highly acclaimed company of actors - The Oxford Stage Company- regularly perform at the Playhouse. The company frequently tour the world with their internationally renowned productions of Shakespeare's plays which have won great praise from audiences and critics alike. If they happen to be performing at the Playhouse when you visit Oxford - don't miss the opportunity of a trip to the theatre.

Just down the road from the Playhouse at the bottom of Beaumont Street lies WORCESTER COLLEGE, a particularly attractive college which, in spite of being in the city centre, is set in 26 acres of grounds and gardens. Worcester is home not only to undergraduates but also to a variety of wildlife including ducks and swans which are attracted to the picturesque lake - the only one of its type to be found in the grounds of an Oxford College.

Just round the corner from the Playhouse is Gloucester Street which leads into Gloucester Square, a European style square, conveniently situated next to the Bus Station, with cafes and restaurants, some unusual shops and a cinema. THE OLD FIRE STATION THEATRE looks over the square. It opened in 1991 and has emerged as one of the most important theatres in the country for the development of musical theatre.

The theatre was a development by Apollo Leisure UK Ltd. in association with the Mackintosh Foundation and the Oxford City Council. The Foundation was set up by Cameron Mackintosh, the famous impresario who produced such hits as Cats, Phantom of the Opera and Les Miserables and who endowed a Chair of Theatre Studies for Oxford University.

The Old Fire Station premieres major pre-West End musicals and celebrated its first birthday with the world premiere of Stephen Sondheim's Putting it Together directed by Julia Mackenzie, produced by Cameron Mackintosh with a West End cast including Diana Rigg.

The theatre is small and very comfortable. I particularly love the intimacy and closeness with the actors that such a theatre can offer - a special atmosphere a large London theatre can never produce.
Curioxity, also based at the Old Fire Station, is Oxford's

Tom Tower, Christchurch

hands-on science exhibition offering a unique opportunity to explore the fascinating world of science and technology. It is a great place for children who love to touch and investigate the exhibits.

If you walk through the square into George Street, you will come across yet another theatre THE APOLLO. With 1800 seats the Apollo is well equipped to cope with the demands for tickets for its programme of major operatic productions, ballet, pop concerts and musicals such as Evita and Showboat.

Cornmarket Street at the top of George Street is one of the main shopping areas in Oxford. During Medieval times the corn market was held here hence its name.

One of Oxford's more unusual places to eat is THE CRYPT, which is situated in a small passageway called Frewin Court off Cornmarket. A restaurant and brasserie The Crypt serves an interesting selection of wines and is housed in the cellars next to the Oxford Union - the headquarters of the famous University debating society founded in 1825. Past holders of the Presidency of the Union include William Gladstone, Sir Robin Day and Benazir Bhutto. Its magnificent debating hall has recently been privileged to witness the presence of Mother Teresa and in total contrast that of Warren Beatty and Jerry Hall.

The most famous debate at the Oxford Union was in 1933, on the motion: "This House will in no circumstances fight for King and Country." It was carried 275 - 152 and Winston Churchill denounced the result as "disquieting, disgusting, squalid, shameless and abject."

GOLDEN CROSS, a charming courtyard of small interesting shops including The Oxford Collection was originally the courtyard of the 12th century Golden Cross Inn. Its entrance sits in Cornmarket and leads into the Covered Market.

The Oxford Collection was appointed by the University to design and develop a range of merchandise bearing the University's Coat of Arms. Silverware, ceramics, scarves, pewter, sweatshirts, t-shirts and even stationary, with designs based on 19th century caricatures of Oxford dons, are just some of the items you will find in this fascinating collection. The collection is well-designed and the quality successfully reflects the University's standing as a world renowned centre of learning.

If you continue down Cornmarket, you will approach what can be considered the City Centre - Carfax. Derived from the Latin word quadrifurcus (four-forked), Carfax is Oxford's central crossroads where the ancient church of St Martin once stood. Carfax Tower is all that remains of this medieval church. However, I do recommend you climb the Tower for an extraordinary bird's eye view of Oxford and you will then certainly understand Matthew Arnold's now famous reference to Oxford's dreaming spires in his poem 'Thyrsis'.

The Tourist Information Centre is a useful stop for those wishing to find more information about the city and is to be found in St Aldate's, one of the streets forming the crossroads at Carfax.

Opposite is the MUSEUM OF OXFORD which tells the story of the city and the University. The past is brought to life on this unique journey through Oxford's history by the clever use of authentically re-created rooms, period music and sound effects.

Just around the corner from the Tourist Information Centre in Pembroke Street, is THE MUSEUM OF MODERN ART, also known as MOMA. Housed in a former 19th century brewery MOMA is one of the world's most prestigious and exciting contemporary art galleries. Despite its name the museum does not have a permanent collection of its own. Instead it shows an innovative range of exhibitions that includes 20th century painting, sculpture, photography, design, film, video and in particular art from different cultures.

MOMA shows art that is at the cutting edge of contemporary culture and expresses the spirit of its time. David Elliott, Director since 1976, is rare in his ability to look ahead and anticipate that spirit. MOMA shows important and relevant exhibitions, which have often never been seen in Britain before, just as major historical events occur in the world. As their show 'Art from South Africa' opened, which included the works of both white and black artists, Nelson Mandella walked free from years of imprisonment. During 'Engineers of the Human Soul: Soviet Socialist Realist Painting 1930-1970' - a vast exhibition of richly coloured paintings depicting Stalin's false interpretation of life under communism - the world witnessed the break-up of the Soviet Union.

It is Elliott's unique and daring approach to art that has contributed to MOMA's reputation as one of the most influential museums.

The museum's cafe, Café MOMA, serves a wide variety of freshly prepared food that is not only good for you but

also tastes delicious. Try their mushroom and courgette bake or their lentil curry and end your meal with one of their homemade cakes or extremely wicked pavlova. Illey, well-known suppliers of coffee to most bars, cafes and restaurants throughout Italy, also sell their delectable beans to MOMA. The coffee is excellent and Café MOMA is a mecca for those seeking a really good cup of coffee.

BOOKHOUSE can be found at the entrance to the galleries and specialises in books on contemporary culture including art and literature. Amongst the books you will also find unusual gifts such as art umbrellas, posters, calendars and a good selection of art postcards.

CHRIST CHURCH is the largest University College and is often referred to by dons and undergraduates as The House. With its imposing Tom Tower above the main entrance in St Aldate's, Christ Church is quite magnificent and has enormous presence. Tom Tower was designed by Sir Christopher Wren and houses the huge bell Great Tom which was cast in 1680. It chimes 101 times every night at 9.05pm commemorating the original number of scholars.

CHRIST CHURCH CATHEDRAL is the smallest in England and the only college chapel in the world designated as a Cathedral. Attached to it is the 13th

Mercury, looking towards Fell's Tower, in the Great Quachangle (Tom Quad)

century Chapter House which contains a permanent exhibition of the treasures of the cathedral and college and a souvenir shop.

Christ Church supports its own college choir of undergraduates, dons and gifted young boys from its school situated close to the college. The quality of their singing is outstanding and you can hear their spiritual offering at Evensong in the Cathedral. It is a worthwhile and magical experience.

When visiting the Cathedral, do see the great medieval hall where undergraduates and dons partake in the daily ritual of dining. Lined along the wooden panelled walls are portraits of famous members of the college including 2 prime ministers and that of Charles Dodgson who taught mathematics at Christ Church. It was under the pseudonym of Lewis Carroll that Dodgson created Alice's Adventures in Wonderland originally for the Dean's daughter Alice Liddell.

Set in the Dean's garden is CHRIST CHURCH PICTURE GALLERY which houses the college's collection of Old Masters and at the same time shows a frequently changing programme of exhibitions.

Christ Church Meadow is a delightful open space, where cattle are put out to graze, consisting of wide gravelled paths that lead to the Rivers Thames and Cherwell. The Broad Walk runs alongside Christ Church Meadow Buildings.

Along the River Thames lie the college boat houses. During the months of February and May when the rowing races known as Torpids and Eights Week are held between the colleges, the boat houses and river banks are crowded with undergraduates supporting and cheering their colleges. The Pimms flows and much passion is spent - the atmosphere is electric.

Punting is a favourite pastime in Oxford and is the perfect way to spend a gloriously sunny day. It can be hard work for the person actually punting, but if you take a picnic and plenty of wine - an essential part of this famous Oxford tradition - you will have the perfect excuse for tying your punt up alongside the riverbank for some sustenance and a well-earned rest. Punts are available for hire at Folly Bridge at the end of St Aldate's, Magdalen Bridge and the Cherwell Boathouse in Bardwell Road.

Alternatively, you could take a trip along the Thames to **Abingdon** on one of Slater Bros steamers which run daily from May to September. Salter Bros have been operating their passenger service since 1888 and are also based on Folly Bridge.

From the Broad Walk in Christ Church Meadows, a small passageway will lead you through wrought-iron gates into Merton Street where CORPUS CHRISTI, ORIEL and MERTON colleges reside. Merton Street is a charming cobbled lane and Merton College is thought to be the oldest college in Oxford.

Undergraduates sit their degree examinations in the Examination Schools the rear of which is situated on the corner of Merton Street. The main entrance is on the High Street. At the end of June, the High Street - known affectionately by undergraduates as The High and considered to be one of the most architecturally outstanding streets in the world - is crowded with undergraduates celebrating the completion of finals as they revel in the street to the sound of popping corks. The intoxicating and delicious scent of champagne lingers in The High long after the celebrations are over.

If you turn right in The High you will come across THE BOTANIC GARDEN. Founded in 1621, the Botanic Garden is the oldest in Britain and is set alongside the River Cherwell. Its rare collection of plants and glasshouses full of ferns, palms and orchids are quite remarkable.

MAGDALEN COLLEGE, pronounced "Maudlin" is opposite the Botanic Garden and is immersed in extensive grounds including its very own deer park. Its tower presides high over Magdalen Bridge and plays an important role in an old Oxford custom - May Morning.

On May Day, locals and undergraduates throng to Magdalen at six o'clock in the morning to hear the college choir sing carols and madrigals from the top of the tower. Spring is welcomed and the celebrations continue in the various cafes and restaurants that have opened specially to serve breakfast.

If you head back along the High Street towards the City Centre, you will pass Queen's Lane (in which you will discover St Edmund Hall, known as Teddy Hall), The ENGLISH TEDDY BEAR COMPANY - a shop brimming with teddy bears of all sizes - QUEEN'S COLLEGE and UNIVERSITY COLLEGE before reaching the UNIVERSITY CHURCH OF ST MARY THE VIRGIN. Climb the steep steps of St Mary's

Tower for another outstanding rooftop view of Oxford. Further along The High is the VICTORIAN COVERED MARKET which is entered by one of four avenues and offers a fascinating variety of stalls and shops selling anything from clothes and jewellery to second hand books and flowers.

The market enjoys an excellent reputation for its food. Its variety of fruit, vegetables, herbs, pastas, fish, game, French bread, coffee and wonderful warm chocolate cookies are proof that its reputation is well-founded. If you love food, you will not be disappointed.

Behind St Mary's Church lies Radcliffe Square, with 2 colleges ALL SOULS and BRASENOSE on either side and Radcliffe Camera siting majestically in the centre. The Radcliffe Camera is the earliest example of a round reading room and is the reading room for the BODLEIAN LIBRARY - one of the world's great libraries. Standing opposite the entrance to the camera, the Bodleian is the main library of the University. Home to millions of books, it receives a copy of every new book published in the United Kingdom and also has an outstanding collection of manuscripts.

HERTFORD COLLEGE is to be found in Catte Street at the top of Radcliffe Square away from The High. Its 2 buildings are linked by Oxford's own version of Venice's Bridge of Sighs. Often used as a backdrop in the television series Inspector Morse, regular viewers will recognise the bridge as they recall Morse driving under it along New College Lane in his red Jaguar. In actual fact, it is not possible to drive down New College Lane - I suppose television directors are allowed a little poetic licence. However, I strongly recommend that you do wander down this delightful backwater almost hidden in the centre of Oxford.

Past Hertford College on your right is Holywell Street where you will find BLACKWELL'S MUSIC SHOP and the 18th century HOLYWELL MUSIC ROOM – the first room built specifically for the performance of music. Music can still be heard here. The Coffee Morning Concerts held regularly on Sunday mornings are particularly popular.

Bath Place is opposite the Holywell Music Room and is a delightful cobbled yard surrounded by 16th and 17th century houses that lead to the excellent BATH PLACE HOTEL and THE TURF TAVERN. The Turf is a charming small timbered inn and a great favourite with the students and indeed Inspector Morse.

Opposite Catte Street, in Parks Road lies WADHAM COLLEGE, which was filmed for the well-known television series Brideshead Revisited, and the UNIVERSITY MUSEUM with its striking and distinctive glass roof. Fossils, gemstones and the remains of the extinct dodo are just some of the items you will find in this fascinating museum. The skeletons of dinosaurs are especially popular with children since the furore over Steven Spielberg's Jurassic Park.

Behind The University Museum lies THE PITT RIVERS MUSEUM. Its world famous anthropology collection includes masks, weapons, hunting trophies, carving and sculpture. Many of the objects were brought back by explorers in the 19th century from Africa, Asia and South America. A number of exhibits collected by Captain Cook are shown in this collection.

The great SHELDONIAN THEATRE stands in Broad Street and is one of Sir Christopher Wren's first works of architecture. It is here that the University degree

ceremonies take place. One of the most impressive is the Enacaenia Ceremony held in June where honorary degrees are awarded to distinguished people from all over the world.

Dons and dignitaries of the University wear the most elaborate robes for the ceremony. The crimson and scarlet of their dress look magnificent against the rich golden colour of the stone of the ancient buildings as they proceed through the city streets to the Sheldonian.

Music is one of the highlights of Oxford life and the Sheldonian Theatre provides a unique space for it to be heard.

Music at Oxford present an enormous range of classical concerts including an array of internationally acclaimed musicians and regularly hold concerts here and also in Christ Church Cathedral. To celebrate their 10th anniversary and Handel's visit to Oxford

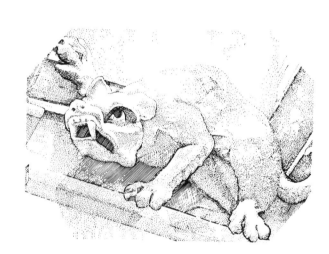

A demonic resident of Oxford

and the Sheldonian Theatre in July 1733, Music at Oxford presented the choirs of Christ Church Cathedral, Magdalen College and New College in a performance of Handel's Coronation Anthems at the Sheldonian. It was only the third time the 3 choirs had sung together. The Sheldonian was bursting with the rousing sound of the choristers voices - it was incredible.

Oxford's very own orchestra, The City of Oxford Orchestra, also perform frequently at the Sheldonian Theatre and has been a cornerstone in the musical life of Oxford for over a quarter of a century. The quality of its playing has been consistently acclaimed by both critics and audiences, and Nigel Kennedy, Simon Rattle, Jane Glover and Julian Lloyd Webber are just a few of the distinguished guest artists who have appeared with the orchestra.

Their programme has included for the past couple of years a summer season of 'Beautiful Music in Beautiful Places' featuring historical and famous settings such as the Holywell Music Room, Merton College Chapel, Christ Church Meadows and of course the Sheldonian Theatre.

Opposite the Sheldonian lies BLACKWELL'S BOOKSHOP which inspite of its success as one of the world's finest and largest booksellers, is still owned by the Blackwell family who live locally in Oxfordshire. The selection of books is enormous and do not be surprised if you find that you have spent an entire afternoon lost amongst this treasure trove of books.

In St Michael's Street, THE NOSEBAG RESTAURANT is probably one of the longest in continuous operation in Oxford. It is certainly one of the most popular with a clientele that is very much across the board. You will find the student population happily mixing with the professions and making tourists feel part and parcel of the Oxford experience.

The Turl links Broad Street to The High. Three colleges line the street EXETER, JESUS and LINCOLN, and WHITES RESTAURANT, which opened just over year ago, can also be found here. Whites serve an unusually good range of fish and their deserts are inspired. Both the owners Robert Patterson and Michael White are committed to producing good quality food and it shows. Their wine cellar is Oxford's oldest wineshop and contains part of the 13th century city walls. It also contains over 500 fine and rare wines and their own delicious selection of extra virgin oils.

THE OXFORD STORY in Broad Street offers a different and unusual introduction to the history and present-day life of Oxford University. It propels you back in time to the 13th century for a fascinating journey through 8 centuries of Oxford. Moving scholars desks take you through the sights, sounds and even the smells of Oxford as you relive its past. The whole experience is very successful and fun too.

There are many places worth visiting on the outskirts of Oxford and there are 3 that I feel compelled to mention - THE TROUT, ROSAMUND THE FAIR and THE HARCOURT ARMS at **Stanton Harcourt**. The Trout is a cosy inn set alongside the river on the edge of the small village of **Wolvercote**. Its garden, river and peacocks make it a particularly delightful place to enjoy a drink.

Rosamund The Fair is a unique cruising restaurant moored at The Trout from where it picks up diners. The name of the barge owes its origin to the romantic legend of a beautiful novice nun who became the mistress of King Henry II and died at the hands of his jealous queen, Eleanor of Aquitaine.

"Since then, 'tis said, her ghost doth roam
Along the river there,
And you mayhap may see her shade,
Or her sad weeping hear."

Its two young chefs Tim Matthews and Sophia Goodford produce wonderful and imaginative food – and all from a 6 by 9 foot galley – while you cruise through some of the prettiest stretches of waterway in and around Oxford.

A little more rural is THE HARCOURT ARMS at Stanton Harcourt. In this quiet village it is the manor house belonging to the Harcourt family that is famous for its gardens where many people come to spend happy hours enjoying the wonderful flowers and shrubs and the tranquil atmosphere. However, people come equally to enjoy the warm welcome and splendid atmosphere of The Harcourt Arms which stands just across the road from the Manor House.

In these few pages about Oxford I have attempted to give you an insight into this great city. I could have written so much more but alas limited space has prevented me from doing so. Sadly I didn't tell you about Port Meadow or Oxford's canal, the Antiques' Centre or the University Parks, the all-night June Balls or of the many plays performed in the college gardens – but perhaps there is something to be said for leaving you the pleasure and joy of discovering a part of Oxford that I have not mentioned here.

Oxford, seething with tradition and the wisdom of the past and at the same time thriving on the new and vibrant, is a city that remains extraordinary and beautiful throughout the changing seasons of the English climate. As Matthew Arnold wrote:

*"And that sweet City with her dreaming spires
She needs not June for beauty's heightening"*

(NB   Times of opening are dependent on the time of year.)

Beaumont Street,
Oxford, OX1 2PH.

Tel: (0865) 278000
Fax: (0865) 278018

THE ASHMOLEAN MUSEUM
Museum & Art Gallery

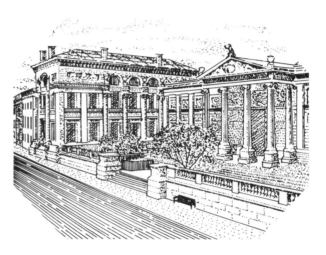

The Ashmolean is one of the most famous and respected museums in the world. The treasures have been accumulated over three centuries, since its foundation by Elias Ashmole in 1683. It is the oldest museum to be opened to the public in Britain, and may be the oldest in the world. It is a museum that will provide many hours of happy browsing for anyone interested in art, archaeology, or for visitors who are specialists in all kinds of fields from Old Master drawings to Oriental lacquer, Greek coins to Iranian bronzes, it offers collections of international importance.

The treasures range from the earliest implements of man, made about five hundred thousand years ago, to twentieth-century works of art. They include curiosities like Guy Fawke's lantern and unique relics like the Alfred Jewel. There are collections of antiquities from Egypt, Greece, Rome and the Near East; British and European paintings from the Middle Ages to the present day; Oriental art, including Chinese bronzes, Islamic and Japanese ceramics, and Indian sculpture; applied art (silver, glass, porcelain, etc) and European stringed instruments.

The Ashmolean's handsome building was designed by C.R. Cockerell and completed in 1845. It is one of the finest examples of neo-classical architecture in the country, and provides a very sympathetic interior for the display of works of art and antiquities.

The main entrance is opposite that of the Randolph Hotel. Having explored and browsed do remember to visit the museum shop before you leave. It sells postcards, books, replicas, prints, souvenirs and gifts.

USEFUL INFORMATION

OPEN: Tues-Sat: 10am-4pm. Sundays: 2pm-4pm. Bank Holiday Mondays in summer: 2pm-5pm
CHILDREN: Welcome
CREDIT CARDS: Access/Visa
LICENSED: Not applicable
RESTAURANT: No
DISABLED ACCESS: Ramp to ground floor & lift inside. Ground floor toilet

---

50 Broad Street,
Oxford, OX1 3BQ.

Tel: (0865) 792792
Fax: (0865) 790937

BLACKWELL'S
Bookshop

Blackwell's is one of the largest and best-known bookshops in the world. Still family owned and privately run, it is perfectly situated in the heart of the University, surrounded by Trinity, Balliol, Exeter, Hertford and Wadham Colleges, opposite the 17th century Ashmolean building and Sir Christopher Wren's Sheldonian Theatre. Blackwell's is half a mile through the city centre from the cathedral, and they are the second most visited tourist attractions after the University.

With Blackwell's background it is hardly surprising that famous literary figures have always been among Blackwell's customers and the shop itself has been the subject of many writings. John Masefield wrote:
'There in the broad, within whose booky house
Half England's scholars nibble books or browse;
Where'er they wander blessed fortune theirs....'
Bishop Stubbs accorded Blackwell's as 'the Literary man's public house.' Other well known customers in the past have included A.E. Houseman, Oscar Wilde, Bernard Shaw and Lewis Carroll. More recently visitors to Blackwell's have included Sir David Attenborough, Desmond Tutu, David Bellamy, Rolf Harris, Sir Michael Tippett and Kurt Vonnegut all of whom came to sign copies of their latest books. Blackwell's is Oxford's biggest bookshop, with more than 200,000 titles in stock covering every subject, discipline and interest. You are invited to browse at your leisure. Unless you ask for help, the staff will not disturb you - a tradition at Blackwell's for over a century.

USEFUL INFORMATION

OPEN: Mon-Sat: 9-6pm. Tues: 9.30-6pm
CHILDREN: Welcome
CREDIT CARDS: All major cards except Diners
DISABLED ACCESS: Yes

THE CRYPT
Wine & Steak Vaults

Frewin Court, Off Cornmarket Street,
Oxford, OX1 3JB.

Tel: (0865) 251000

USEFUL INFORMATION

OPEN: Mon-Fri: 11.30-3pm & 5.30-11pm
Sat: 11.30-3pm & 6-11pm
CHILDREN: Childrens portions
CREDIT CARDS: Amex/Diners/
Visa/Master/Switch
LICENSED: Full On Licence
ACCOMMODATION: Not applicable

RESTAURANT: Celebrated Pies,
Smoked & Fresh Salmon,
Steaks, Lamb & Duck
BAR FOOD: Wholemeal Sandwiches.
Filled Potatoes, Salads
VEGETARIAN: One dish
DISABLED ACCESS: No
GARDEN: No

In the 1950's Michael Heseltine ran a Jazz Club in part of the basement which is now a successful wine and steak bar. Oxford is full of interesting places in which to eat and drink but this has to be one of the most atmospheric, with its sawdust covered floors, candlelight and an enchanting mixture of Dickensian and Victoriana making one think that this is what Old England once was.

A love of good wine is perhaps a prerequisite of total enjoyment here, but even if you are a teetotaller you will relish the happy buzz of conversation around you emanating from a broad cross-section of people who have turned The Crypt into a meeting place for friends - and those who might be strangers on arrival will certainly not leave that way.

Whether you have a liking for Champagne, Hock, Claret, Burgundy or wines from around the world, the list has something for everyone. The prices are realistic. Vintage Ports are decanted daily, one can have a tankard of Bucks Fizz, a large glass of excellent sherry or the Naturally Aged Traditionally Strong, Davy's Lager known as NATS for short! The food is as good as the wines with succulent Steaks prominent on the menu, but perhaps one of the most popular and famous dishes of The Crypt is its Chicken and Chestnut Pie under a flaky pastry lid served with a Baked Jacket Potato. There is a delectable cold table, a fine salad selection, snacks, sandwiches and, for the sweet tooth, several choices including Treacle Tart. The Management team would be delighted to discuss any 'special occasions' and offer menus from informal cheese and wine gatherings to a grand buffet.

THE ENGLISH TEDDY BEAR COMPANY
Shop

84 High Street, Oxford,
Oxfordshire, OX1 4BG.

Tel: (0865) 201321

USEFUL INFORMATION

OPEN: 10-7pm daily
CHILDREN: Welcome
CREDIT CARDS: All major cards
DISABLED ACCESS: Good

SPECIAL SERVICES: Gift boxing
available, Made to order service,
Mail Order catalogue available -
Contact branch for further information
on availability.

The English Teddy Bear Company is situated in Oxford's most historic shop. Until very recently it was the Oxford Marmalade Shop of Frank Cooper who began trading in these premises in 1874. The shop has tremendously high ceilings, supported by four marbled ionic columns. Outside the listed shop-front is very prominent, reaching over 20 feet high and marked by four Corinthian columns. Inside the shop you can buy anything from an Oxford T Shirt to an academic dress for your Teddy Bear. Or you may wish to really get into the spirit of things and buy your Teddy a boater and silk waistcoat and bow tie! Marmalade is still sold, along with all other foods to which Teddy Bears are partial! If you do not wish to be free of Teddy Bears in any situation, The English Teddy Bear Company produces a fun and stylish range of all cotton T shirts for children and adults. Each of the current English Teddy Bear Company's branches has designs exclusive to that town and these make affordable and easily transportable gifts. You will find the shops in beautiful old buildings in Canterbury, Bath, London and Cambridge as well as in Oxford.

The creation of traditional English Teddy Bears is a very serious business and is carried out in all sorts of cloths, all English, from acrylic to top quality mohair. The Teddy Bears are made with traditional features like long snouts, embroidered noses and jointed limbs and head. Special companions are recreated and since all the bears are hand made, no two are alike and each bear comes with its own birth certificate!

61A Banbury Road,
Oxford, OX2 6PE.

Tel: (0865) 53540

GEE'S BRASSERIE
Restaurant

It is not usual to find a Victorian nursery and plant shop built in 1892 which appears again almost a century later as a most attractive restaurant making the very best use of the conservatory. Gee's has done just this and has the benefit too of not being quite in the centre of town, and is therefore not burdened by the lack of parking space that haunts the centre of Oxford. It will take you no longer than ten minutes to walk to the Cathedral or to take a look at the colleges - an excellent way of getting some exercise after a very good lunch!

Gee's has acquired a very interesting clientele with a mixture of academics, students, business and professional people. It could fairly be stated as one of the top and most fashionable restaurants in the city, yet it has a happy informality that is relaxing and conducive to contented eating. In addition to an interesting and well planned menu, Gee's has also introduced the excellent habit of 'Brunch' and 'Light Lunch' on Saturdays and Sundays. Ideal for those who enjoy meeting friends, reading the newspapers and being thoroughly entertained. The traditional English breakfast is beautifully cooked and presented but probably one of the most favourite dishes is the light, feathery scrambled eggs with smoked salmon.

Everything is good on the menu from the distinctive and interesting selection of breads, to the starters and salads, the delicious pastas, the varied main courses and the delectable puddings. A children's menu is available on request and there are always dishes for vegetarians.

USEFUL INFORMATION

OPEN: Mon-Fri: 12-2.30pm & 6-11.30pm
Sat: 10.30am-11.30pm. Sun: 10.30am-
11pm
CHILDREN: Welcome, high chairs
CREDIT CARDS: Access/Visa
LICENSED: Full Restaurant Licence
ACCOMMODATION: Not applicable

RESTAURANT: Robust & rustic
BAR FOOD: Not applicable
VEGETARIAN: 8 dishes
DISABLED ACCESS: Ground floor toilet
GARDEN: No

---

30 Pembroke Street,
Oxford, OX1 1BP.

Tel: (0865) 722733
Fax: (0865) 722573

MUSEUM OF MODERN ART
Museum

The Museum of Modern Art, situated in Pembroke Street, a few minutes walk from Christ Church Cathedral, has played and continues to play a pioneering role in the presentation and development of visual arts and culture in Britain. In the 1960's and early 1970's, MOMA became the leading 'Alternative Space' in Britain.

Since the mid 1970's, under the award-winning directorship of David Elliott, the museum has taken a leading role in exhibiting 'World Art'. Many important international artists were given their first British showing here; Richard Long (1989 Turner prize winer) made an early mud spiral and Sol Le Witt his earliest wall drawings in the museum's large upper galleries . The Museum of Modern Art's exhibition programme, covers 20th century painting, sculpture, photography, architecture, design, advertising, folk art and craft and in particular art from other cultures (Russia, Japan, Africa, India, South America and China) and is supported by a lively schedule of lectures, film, music and performance.

Cafe MOMA, which also shows contemporary young and local artists work, has become one of the most popular restaurants in the centre of Oxford. Serving a range of vegetarian and non-vegetaian foods, home-made cakes, beers, wines and Italian style coffee. Book House is situated at the entrance to MOMA and sells a wide variety of books on contemporary culture and literature.

USEFUL INFORMATION

OPEN: Tues-Sat: 10am-6pm. Thurs: 10am-
9pm. Sun: 2pm-6pm. Closed Mondays
CHILDREN: Yes. Free entrance under 16
CREDIT CARDS: Visa/Mastercard/
Access
LICENSED: Licence for wine and beer.
ACCOMMODATION: Not applicable

RESTAURANT: Cafe Moma offers whole-
some food, home-made cakes. 'Daily
Specials'
BOOK SHOP: 'Book House' sells a wide
range of books on contemporary culture
VEGETARIAN: 5 dishes daily
DISABLED ACCESS: Yes
GARDEN: None

THE NOSEBAG RESTAURANT

Restaurant

6-8 St. Michael's Street,
Oxford, OX1 2DU.

Tel: (0865) 721033

USEFUL INFORMATION

OPEN: Mon: 9.30-5.30pm Tues-Thurs:
9.30am-10pm Fri-Sat: 9.30am-10.30pm
Sun: 9.30am-9pm
CHILDREN: Welcome
CREDIT CARDS: No
LICENSED: Restaurant
ACCOMMODATION: Not applicable

RESTAURANT: Traditional,
International, Home-cooked
BAR FOOD: Not applicable
VEGETARIAN: One during the
day, four at night
DISABLED ACCESS: No
GARDEN: Not applicable

St Michael's Street is just ten minutes walk to the Cathedral and just off Cornmarket. More importantly it is the home of The Nosebag, a restaurant that is probably one of the longest in continuous operation in Oxford. It is certainly one of the most popular with a clientele that is very much across the board. You will find the student population happily mixing with the professions and making tourists feel part and parcel of the Oxford experience.

Mary Brunt is the cheerful, welcoming manageress who has been here for over 8 years and has many regular customers who have become friends. Some of them are real characters, for example a poet who always leaves a verse for the waitress! She and her team are young and dedicated. The Nosebag is always busy and at lunchtime there is almost always a queue but don't let that put you off; the service is fast and the turnover runs smoothly. It is one of the most relaxed places to be found anywhere.

Every dish is freshly cooked and made on the premises apart from the bread. It is wholesome, wide in choice and the menu changes constantly. You would be hard-pressed to find nothing on the menu that tempted you. The home-made cakes are especially popular with a moist, delicious carrot cake one of the favourites. Children are very welcome and there is always a dish for Vegetarians.

THE OLD PARSONAGE

Hotel

1 Banbury Road,
Oxford, OX2 6NN.

Tel: (0865) 310210
Fax: (0865) 311262

USEFUL INFORMATION

OPEN: All day every day
CHILDREN: Allowed. No special facilities
CREDIT CARDS: Amex/Diners/Visa/
Barclaycard/Access/Mastercard
LICENSED: Full On Licence
ACCOMMODATION: 30 en-suite rooms
equipped to international standards

RESTAURANT: The informal Parsonage
Bar is the heart of the hotel. 7am-11pm
BAR FOOD: Light snacks available
VEGETARIAN: Always vegetarian choice
DISABLED ACCESS: Not good
GARDEN: Front terrace for al fresco
eating. Roof garden, walled garden for
residents

The Old Parsonage has stood on the present site in the leafy St Giles part of Oxford since 1660 when Edward Selwood the prosperous chef of nearby St John's College, completed the original and principal part of the house which he had commenced twenty years earlier. The land on which Selwood built his house was owned by University College, one of Oxford's oldest seats of learning, which had bought the land as an endowment for their early scholars. The College has remained the ground landlord for over six centuries. Until the mid-14th century the priest of the medieval hospice which had reputedly stood on the site since the Norman Conquest, had his dwelling here next to the ancient church of St Giles, hence the name 'Old Parsonage'.

In one way or another it has provided lodgings for many people including undergraduates, one of whom is traditionally said to have been Oscar Wilde. In 1989 the old Parsonage was acquired by the successful restaurateur, Jeremy Mogford, whose family have been well known hoteliers for three generations. With his architect Roger Stretton he set about a refurbishing scheme to restore the character of the old building. The emphasis throughout the restoration has been to display the quality and interest of the original features while creating a comfortable, attractive ambience which respects the history of the building. The Old Parsonage, which has become a well-loved feature of Oxford remains closely connected to the University. From Edward Selwood's 17th century guest house to the present elegant hotel, the Old Parsonage continues to be a haven of good hospitality.

Stanton Harcourt,
Oxford, OX8 1RJ.

Tel: (0865) 881931

THE HARCOURT ARMS
Inn & Restaurant

The quiet village of Stanton Harcourt is famous for the gardens of the Manor House belonging to the Harcourt family. Naturally many people come here specially to spend happy hours enjoying the wonderful flowers and shrubs and the tranquil atmosphere. Equally people come to Stanton Harcourt, which is only seven and a half miles from Oxford, to enjoy the warm welcome and the splendid atmosphere of The Harcourt Arms, which stands just across the road from the Manor House.

This is an inn which is known for its grace and style and because of the food. It is somewhere that will always surprise you with something out of the ordinary. The knowledgable and friendly staff will do their best to give you what you want. It also has special evenings when for ten pounds you can enjoy a super banquet, complete with one of the restaurant's famous puddings. Wine is also of major importance here. The list of some 80 wines covers mainly the traditional French and German vineyards and also those from around the world, allowing you to try out something new.

Whilst the menu is comprehensive and almost entirely English, it is renowned for king prawns. Pink, succulent and delicious, they are virtually irresistible. The large garden is somewhere to escape in summer and somewhere in which to eat and drink whilst enjoying the sunshine. Occasional barbecues are very popular with regular visitors to the Harcourt and they are good fun, even for total strangers.

USEFUL INFORMATION

OPEN: 12-2.30pm & 6-11pm
CHILDREN: Welcome
CREDIT CARDS: All major cards
& Switch
LICENSED: Full On Licence
ACCOMMODATION: Not applicable

RESTAURANT: Comprehensive English
menu. Home-cooked
BAR FOOD: Delicious and varied. King
prawns a speciality
VEGETARIAN: At least 3 dishes
DISABLED ACCESS: Easy access. Help
available
GARDEN: Large with ten tables and
occasional barbecues

Peterborough Cathedral

Peterborough

"Tis a visionary blessing;
A dream that's past expressing;"

John Gay

The City of Peterborough

by John Theobald

PETERBOROUGH CATHEDRAL is at the heart of this ancient borough which was created a city by Henry the Eigth. It is one of the most impressive of all our great Cathedrals and was the burial place of two Queens. It left an overwhelming impression of beauty and dignity from the moment I first entered it from its beautiful close. Laughing choristers had been making their way across the close, leaving an unforgettable memory of graceful youth and magnificent age in harmony.

Much the same could be said of the city itself which is now very modern but with its roots in a 7th century monastic community established by the King of Mercia in an area where man first settled in the Bronze Age.

The Romans were here and their legionnaires marched to a terrible defeat by the forces of Queen Boudicca who reigned in Norfolk, Suffolk and part of Cambridgeshire. The city takes its name from the Cathedral Church of St. Peter, St. Paul and St. Andrew, one of the finest and most sophisticated Norman buildings in the country. Under its transept are the remains of a church built by King Edgar and destroyed by a fire in 1116 which began in the abbey bakery, destroyed one timbered building after

another and started a fire that burnt for nine days in the church.

The third church here which is the present Cathedral was begun two years later and became one of the great Benedictine abbey churches. The master masons erected the cathedral at roughly ten feet of height each year, working from east to west. Thus the nave was not completed until 50 years after work started.

Some parts of the earlier abbot's and prior's lodgings remain as well as various gateways. The abbey church was dissolved by Henry the Eighth in 1539 and re-founded by him as a Cathedral two years later. Perhaps he was moved to do so because Katherine of Aragon, his first queen, lay buried here. But, Henry the Eighth knew Peterborough well and had spent much of his boyhood with his grandmother in the area. The city's connections with its sovereigns were always strong. Cromwell's soldiers destroyed stained glass, statues, the High Altar, the Lady Chapel and the Cloisters during the Civil War and it is the loss of most of the stained glass from large windows that had replaced the smaller, earlier Norman ones that allows such an airy, light interior.

It is the West Front of the Cathedral which is its most magnificent architectural achievement with three huge 85 feet high arches dominating the Gothic front. The centre arch is narrower than its neighbours but the corner towers offset any cramped effect. On top of the gables are

the figures of the three saints from whom the Cathedral takes its name. The Gothic porch was added in the 14th century. Inside much of the original Norman fabric remains. The nave was completed in the 12th century and is a superb example of Romanesque design.

The stone used in its building came from the monks' own quarry and its warmth and light colour gives the interior its distinctively gracious character. Paintings decorating the high wooden roof go back to 1220 and have been beautifully restored. This ceiling is one of only three remaining in Europe.

Monsters, saints, musicians, animals and kings and queens are portrayed against a glowing sky. A gallery runs round the inside of the central tower offering views over the fens to **Ely**. This tower was rebuilt in the 1880's and the Bishop's Throne, choir stall and the High Altar were installed ten years later.

The choir sings every week-day evening at 5.30pm and at weekends at 3.30pm and you are welcome at the services. The crucifix that now hangs in the nave was placed there in 1975 but the medieval brass eagle lectern is one of only about 40 of its type that survive. There is by the sanctuary an effigy of the 12th century abbot, Benedict, who built most of the nave. A little way on at the eastern end of the church is the tomb of Queen Katherine and the banners include those of the King of Aragon. Her coffin had arrived from Kimbolton in a procession led by sixteen priests followed by a party that included numerous heralds. The black covered wagon with a huge silver cross was drawn by six horses and accompanied by fifty servants carrying torches. Three bishops awaited the cortege at the Cathedral and Masses were said for two days as the coffin lay under a canopy with the words Humble et Loyale' embroidered in gold letters. Four hundred candles surrounded her coffin.

At the farthest point with its marvellous fan vaulting is the Hedda Stone, a Saxon sculpture. Christ, the Virgin Mary and the Apostles are represented in the carvings. The building was begun with the apse and the tapestries hanging in it are Flemish from the 17th century. Sir Gilbert Scott's painting, replaces the painted medieval ceiling destroyed in 1643.

Mary Queen of Scots who had been imprisoned in Fotheringay Castle where she was beheaded, was buried beside the sanctuary in 1587. The coffin had left Fotheringay Castle at night and was accompanied by forty bare-headed riders carrying torches and led by Garter King of Arms. The Arms of Scotland were embroidered on the black velvet cloth that covered a specially built vehicle drawn by four horses. Into the vault in the South Aisle the coffin was lowered and here officers threw in their staves of office. The Countess of Bedford led the procession of one hundred mourners from the Bishop's Palace to the funeral service. The beautiful and accomplished Queen was a focal point for Catholics in England after Mary had escaped from Scotland and sought the protection of Queen Elizabeth. She was to become a prisoner for life until the English queen signed her death warrant.

In 1612 her son, James II, had her trunk and severed head moved to the chapel of Westminster Abbey where they still remain.

Mary is one of the most tragic figures in history, regarded by some as a Catholic traitor, by others as a Catholic martyr.

There are three chapels in the South Transept which is 12th century with its original wooden ceiling. There is a watch tower here from which monks guarded a sacred relic, now lost for several hundred years, and a Saxon sculpture 1200 years old. On the wall facing you as you leave is a striking painting of Robert Scarlett, the 16th century sexton who dug the graves of two queens. He too, lies buried in the Cathedral. He had died at the age of 98 and he had buried many people in his long life. He had tolled the bells for the sick and later dug their graves, in between keeping the Cathedral and churchyard tidy. When he was 89 he married his second wife. He must have been a remarkable man.

Above the entrance porch in a former chapel is the cathedral treasury in which a collection of its silver is housed. There is an extensive library with many rare tracts and some of its earliet books are on permanent loan to Cambridge University.
The Cathedral clock is not as ancient as many think and is in fact little over forty years old.

The Cathedral is open from 7 am to 8 pm on weekdays from May to September but closed after Evensong on

Sundays. From October to April it opens at 7 am but closes every day after Evensong. Guided tours are available for parties. There is a bookshop in the precincts and above it is a cafe. Visitors are warmly welcomed at all services. Because the upkeep of this great structure is costly, every visitor is asked to donate at least one pound towards its maintenance.

There is a visitor centre in the 14th century Almoner's Hall south of the Cloisters where a permanent exhibition tells the story of Peterborough Cathedral. Models show how it was built and how the creamy-white stone was brought by barge along the River Nene from Barnack limestone quarry nine miles away. The quarry and the places which grew the timber are now English Nature Reserves and English Nature, too, have a display here. A herb garden is used to display how the monks used them for various purposes and the daily life of the monks is depicted. There is an admission fee and entry times are from 11 am to 4 pm from Monday to Saturday from Easter to October 31st and from November 1st to Easter, Saturdays only by prior arrangement. Tel: (0733) 897337/3433420.

The Cathedral church was completed during the rule of Abbot Martin of Bec and it was he who moved the Burgh, or town to the west of the abbey and laid out a

Roof Boss of Holy Trinity (c.1380) in the inner bay of the porch

market place, around which a road system grew that became the basis of the town centre for centuries. The earlier town had grown up around the abbey from about the seventh century.

There had been Bronze Age and Iron Age settlements before the Romans built their own small town covering about 44 acres. It was finally deserted and little is known about it. The Saxons took over and **Peterborough** emerged as a town then named Medeshamstede in the seventh century. The history of the present city is unbroken from that time. Tom Lock's Spring became another central feature of the Abbot's new town and two bridges crossed this stream which supplied both drainage and a water supply. The abbot was almost the supreme power in both civil and ecclesiastical matters, answering to the king only, to whom he would regularly be host. Relations between burghers and monks were sometimes strained as a result and on at least one occasion the abbey was attacked.

Today in the words of a former Mayor, "Peterborough is a fine and beautiful city in which the historic and modern elements combine to provide an exciting place to live and work." Many national and international companies have made their home here and it is now an important tourist centre with many leisure facilities and attractions. For centuries Peterborough's importance rested on its repute as a market centre and it was heavily dependent on a rich agricultural area for its prosperity. By 1700 its industries were based on wool manufacturing, some of which was exported to the continent from **Kings Lynn**. It also traded with London in malt, and wild ducks caught in the Fens. The arrival of the railways brought more manufacturers, and the brickmaking that had used the local Lower Oxford seam of clay, was developed on a large scale in Victorian times and became a vital industry.

Fletton bricks from Peterborough have been used in millions of British homes for over a hundred years. Frank Perkins Ltd is now one of the world's biggest makers of diesel engines on which Frank Perkins had begun work in 1932 in the city, eventually to give employment to thousands. He was a local man of genius who, to prove the worth of his new engine, installed it in a car which he drove to the Russian capital. Today the company he founded is a part of the Varity Corporation which exports engines made here all over the world. The city retains its links with agriculture, particularly through the East of England Agricultural Society which has a 300 acre showground on the city's edge. When the Peterborough Development Corporation was set up, Peterborough saw a transformation that resulted in its population increasing from 86,000 in 1970 to 135,000 in 1988 when it was reported that £1,000 million had been spent on introducing a New Town and expanding the city's industrial and commercial base.

Thousands of new jobs have been created. A typical example was the re-location of the huge Pearl Assurance Company. Even the late Roy Kinnear had been used in TV commericals to promote the city. Thomas Cook the travel agents, have their headquarters here and Hotpoint has long been a familiar name in Peterborough. Today the job of attracting industry and commerce is carried on by the Peterborough Development Agency.

PETERBOROUGH'S MUSEUM AND ART GALLERY tells in detail of the city's history and you will find it at Priestgate housed in a large Regency house that was once a private dwelling.

There is a unique collection of carved bonework and straw marquetry made for sale by Napoleonic prisoners of war held in Norman Cross Barracks. There is an archaeological collection of items from the Romano-British and Anglo-Saxon periods and fossil reptiles from local clay which date back to the time of the dinosaur when Peterborough lay under a warm sea. One extraordinary exhibit is the skeleton of a plesiosaur excavated from a brickpit at **Dogsthorpe**. Memorabilia connected with Mary Queen of Scots and John Clare, the rural poet, are on display. The art gallery holds many exhibitions and shows the work of modern artists in addition to its own permanent collection of paintings and English ceramics.

A visit to a museum is always thirsty work and so I wholeheartedly recommend you to visit the oddly named WAYWARD FROG AND RIBBITS which is just opposite. Its name comes from the nickname 'Wayward' bestowed upon the owner Peter Hayward, and his partner and brother-in-law, a Frenchman, the combination quite easily became 'The Wayward Frog'. For the last twenty five years, this family run business has been giving pleasure to the people of Peterborough and the many visitors who have found the welcoming atmopshere of this splendid wine bar just what is required.

Another fairly unique experience, just two minutes from the Cathedral is CHARTERS CAFE BAR at Town Bridge. It is a large floating, continental barge moored against this historic old bridge on the Nene River. It is an enchanting place to be. The barge was converted by the owner, Peter Hook, in 1990 and it has taken no time to become one of the places to be in Peterborough. You approach it either on the pedestrianised south side of the Cathedral or, if you wish, from the floating pontoon where you may moor your boat before enjoying the pleasures of Charters. It was originally a commercial barge which sailed the rivers of Holland, Germany and Belgium, carrying 616 tonnes of cargo including sand, grain and other such bulk items. How did it get where it is? Ask a silly question and you get a silly answer. There are many stories but we are told to look for the obvious - by rolling tree trunks, pulled by a herd of African elephants!!!

At FLAG FEN two miles east of the city centre is a working excavation site where the visitor can watch archaeologists at work uncovering Bronze Age workings. Three thousand years ago prehistoric people drove massive posts into the waters of **Flag Fen** to construct a huge tidal barrier. Around the posts they made offerings and sacrifices to their Gods. Then at about 900BC the waters rose so fast that everything - seeds, leaves, twigs, even pollen grains became pickled in peaty mud. There is no site like it anywhere in Europe. Exciting finds continue to be made. In the visitor centre there is a unique display of the many finds that have been made here. There are guided tours of the excavation from Easter to the end of October. The visitor centre, for which there is an admission fee, is open with the landscape park every day except Christmas and Boxing Day from 11 am to 4 pm. There is a gift shop, and in the landscape park there are reconstructions of prehistoric buildings and ancient breeds of domestic animals such as sheep, pigs and horses.

Back in the city the 17th century GUILDHALL stands in Cathedral Square, the old market place, and is classed as an ancient monument, for it was rebuilt as the first Market Cross, with room above it, used as a council chamber. THE LONG CAUSEWAY SHOPPING CENTRE is a mix of the old and the new but the QUEENSGATE CENTRE is totally modern. In 1982 it won the title of the best new covered market in Europe and in marble air conditioned malls are all the major stores, well over 100 other shops selling every type of goods. There is parking for thousands of cars and it is close to the railway station and a bus station.

On the banks of the River Nene stands the KEY THEATRE which puts on everything from drama and operas to musicals and pantomime. There is a restaurant which serves snacks and full meals, and you can drink in the RIVERSIDE BAR. West of the city is the great leisure centre of NENE PARK running for six miles beside the River Nene with golf courses, fishing, a big Caravan Club site, a watersports centre, and facilities for the walker, cyclist, dinghy sailor or windsurfer. There are cafes in which to relax after taking part in any of the many activities on offer. The Nene Valley Railway has seven and a half miles of track along which steam engines operate services on weekends from March to the end of October. Children can meet Thomas the Tank Engine and there is a Santa Special at Christmas. It is run by volunteers determined to preserve a slice of England's railway history, including a museum which has recreated street scenes from long ago. There are British and continental locomotives, and the controls of one of them was taken over by Prince Edward on a visit.

The railway has been used as the location for a number of films and televison programmes. Telephone 0780 782854 for the talking timetable. No-one should visit Peterborough without making time to visit one of the grandest of Elizabethan homes, BURGHLEY HOUSE famous for its art collection and the annual three-day horse trials.

Standing just outside **Stamford** in a beautiful park landscaped by Capability Brown it is a superb example of Elizabethan domestic architecture. It has been the home of the Cecil and Exeter families for over 400 years since it was built in the 16th century by a Cecil who was Lord High Treasurer to Queen Elizabeth. He became the first Lord Burghley. There are some 240 rooms in this great square house built round a central courtyard, and at each corner is a turreted tower. Four more turreted towers comprise the main gate-house. There

are treasures galore in this magnificent house ranging from Old Masters and wood carvings by Grinling Gibbons to silver fire-places and painted ceilings. In all there are more than 700 works of art. Guided tours take visitors through the huge kitchen, the 68 feet long Great Hall and 18 state rooms containing all those treasures.

The Hedda Stone (c.780) showing Our Lord, 3rd from right, with the blessed Virgin Mary on His right and four Apostles

In the Orangery is a licensed restaurant and there is a splendid gift shop. The deer park is close to the house. You can get more information from the House Manager at 0780 52451.

The historical and picturesque town of Stamford is one of the finest medieval towns in Europe, with six of its 17 churches still remaining. It has many 17th century and 18th century buildings designed by such architects as the

Adams brothers and Inigo Jones who lived nearby. It was the first 'Conservation Area' in England and its history goes back more than a thousand years. Detailed information can be got from the STAMFORD ARTS CENTRE in St Marys Street. (Tel 0780 55611).

All Saints Place, Barn Hill, The Bastion, Brazenose Gateway where a 14th century university was set up by student rebels from Oxford, Broad Street, Burghley Hospital and Almshouses, the remains of the castle, the superb George Hotel which is the remains of the castle, the superb GEORGE HOTEL which is an original coaching inn, the High Street, St George's Square, St Mary's Hill and St Peter's Hill should all be visited. You will find architectural gem after gem.

Rutland Water, the largest man-made lake in Western Europe, is off the A1 north of Stamford and is a marvellous leisure centre where you can walk, cycle, picnic, canoe, fish for trout, cruise, study wild-life and enjoy the amenities of the new ANGLIAN WATER BIRDWATCHING CENTRE. A BUTTERFLY AND AQUATIC CENTRE has opened at **Rutland Water**. For details telephone the Tourist Information Centre at Empingham: 0780 8632

13th century Alwalton marble font which was recovered from the Canon's garden in the 1820's

PEAKIRK WATERFOWL GARDENS north of Peterborough are home to 700 waterfowl and the 108 breeds range from ducks to flamingos. A total of 23 ponds, five of them large, offers them plenty of space. Formal gardens add to the centre's beauty.

There is a visitor centre with a viewing area, a shop, refreshments and special art exhibitions. The gardens are open all year except on Christmas Eve and Christmas Day. There is an admission charge and details of the opening times can be obtained from 07333 252271.

HAMERTON WILDLIFE CENTRE is south of the city covering 16 acres of Huntingdonshire Wolds. There are more than 120 species of animals ranging from monkeys of all kinds to wallabies, otters and sloths, and birds that include storks and owls. The centre is devoted to the conservation of rare and endangered animals and more animals are always being added. There is a gift and coffee shops and the centre is open every day except Christmas Day. In Summer it is open from 10.30 am to 4 pm and closes at 4 pm in winter time. Telephone 08323 362 for admission charges.

At **Long Sutton**, near Spalding, is the largest butterfly park in the country, allied with a falconry centre. Five hundred butterflies fly freely among tropical plants, trees, flowers and shrubs growing by streams, pond and waterfalls. Two displays of falconry were given daily with eagles, owls and falcons being flown. There are all kinds of other attractions that range from a mouse house to farm animals and a pets' corner. There is a tea room and tea gardens, a gift shop, a picnic area and plenty of parking. It is open daily from March 13 to October 31. For more details, including admission charges, telephone 0406 363833. You will find it a unique day out.

There are many attractive villages all around Peterborough such as **Castor**, a former Roman settlement. Its church, which has a magnificent tower, is worth exploring. Typical of Fenland villages is **Eye**. **Orton Longueville** has a 700 yard long avenue of trees at ORTON HALL HOTEL. Set in 20 acres of mature parkland in this secluded conservation village, it was previously an estate owned by the Marquess of Huntly, Chief of the Clan Gordon, Scotland's premier clan. It has been tastefully restored to much of its former glory as one of the county's foremost country houses circa 17th century. The renovation has enabled the Edwardian values in style, ambience and service, with a hint of Scottish tradition, to complement the needs of the 20th century hotel visitor. Orton Hall also has a conference centre which offers a variety of spacious, light, airy and above all grand boardrooms with adjacent syndicate rooms in undisturbed tranquillity; ideal for executive meetings, private luncheons and dinners. Across the paved and golden gravel courtyard lies the OLD RAMBLEWOOD INN, originally the stables. A good place to drink or eat hearty food.

The thatched village of **Alwalton** is another pleasant place and here is THE SWALLOW HOTEL. Purpose built in 1988 it is not only ideally situated for anyone wanting to visit or do business in Peterborough, just ten minutes drive away, it is also close to the business park and the East of England Showground. It has 163 luxury bedrooms including three beautiful suites with sitting room, interconnecting family rooms – ideal for the Thomas Tank weekend breaks!

Comprehensive conference and meeting facilities include the Sir Henry Royce Suite - named after this man of Rolls Royce fame who was born at Alwalton.

THE BELL at **Stilton** has stories to tell of a famous cheese, a highwayman and a famous horseman. It should also shout from the rooftops that it is one of the finest inns in the county. It was Samuel Johnson who said ' there is nothing which has yet been contrived by man, by which so much happiness is produced as by a good tavern or inn.' Mine host of The Bell Inn, Liam McGivern would dearly love his establishment to live up to this sentiment. It does! The inn dates back to 1500 and has had some wonderful customers during the ensuing years. Innkeepers, statesmen, outlaws and literary figures have contributed to the inn's fame. One popular tale has it that the highwayman Dick Turpin visited the pub. He is supposed to have hidden within its doors for nine

A sculpture of a mitred abbot on the Knight's Chamber

weeks while the law searched for him. Surprised by a raid, he threw open a window and jumped on to the back of Black Bess before galloping off up the Great North Road.

The great Duke of Marlborough was a notable guest and earlier still, Cromwell's troops were here. In 1725 Lord Harley tasted the cheese here and pronounced it uneatable. Cooper Thornhill was landlord from 1730 until his death in 1759, aged 54. He is invariably referred to as the man who popularised Stilton cheese, which was served, mites and all at The Bell.

Having discovered good hotels and a fine hostelry, I looked for somewhere to visit and discovered at **Sacrewell**, **Thornhaugh**, THE SACREWELL FARM & COUNTRY CENTRE . This is a place for those who seek freedom, space, peace and tranquillity where there is interest and beauty. It is a memorable experience where the past and the present are inextricably linked. Sacrewell tries to explain to visitors the inescapable and binding partnership between farm and human stomach - no future for either without the other.

I have enjoyed myslef enormously returning to Peterborough, a place for which I have a great affection. Not only was I impressed by all that is going on in this progressive city but each day I stayed there and had the opportunity to wander around the countryside, I realised what a splendid place it was in which to live and be able to take advantage of city life and rural beauty.

SWALLOW HOTEL

Hotel, Restaurant, Leisure & Conference Cetnre

Lynchwood, Alwalton,
Peterborough, PE2 6GB.

Tel: (0733) 371111
Fax: (0733) 236725

USEFUL INFORMATION

OPEN: All year, 24 hours
CHILDREN: Welcome
CREDIT CARDS: All Major cards
LICENSED: Full Licence
ACCOMMODATION: 163 bedrooms,
   3 suites

RESTAURANT: Two Award winning
   (AA Rosette) innovative. Prix Fixe
   menus
BAR FOOD: Wide range served in Lounge
VEGETARIAN: Prix Fixe menu
DISABLED ACCESS: Level. Special
   bedrooms, disabled conferences
GARDEN: 11 acres landscaped grounds.
   Pitch 'n' Put, wildlife lake

This hotel, purpose built in 1988 is ideal for visitors to the Business Park and the East of England Showground. It is set in its own landscaped grounds, overlooking an ornamental lake near the thatched village of Alwalton and just ten minutes drive from Peterborough.

The Swallow Hotel has 163 luxury bedrooms including three luxurious suites with sitting room, inter-connecting family rooms - ideal for the Thomas Tank Weekend Breaks! There are also rooms specially designed for disabled guests. Every room has a private bathroom and every modern facility including a mini bar, iron and ironing board and computer telephone links. Fully air-conditioned, the hotel's restaurants and bars give guests a comprehensive choice, and are designed around a modern Romanesque theme. The Laurels Brasserie Restaurant, is open from breakfast time until 10.30pm and features a carving table, cold buffet and charcoal grill. The adjacent Lounge is open all day serving snacks and hot drinks throughout the day. The impressive Cocktail Bar features a pianist most evenings, and is adjacent to The Emperor Restaurant. The menu centres on modern French cuisine, served in a luxurious environment.

Comprehensive conference and meeting facilities include the Sir Henry Royce Suite - named after Henry Royce of Rolls Royce fame who was born at Alwalton. 300 people can be accommodated and it is equally suitable for exhibitions or dinner dances. In addition, the hotel has seminar rooms, boardrooms and ten syndicate rooms. Entry to the Swallow Leisure Club with its indoor swimming pool is free to resident guests with sauna, steam room, gym and beauticians and hair salon.

FLAG FEN BRONZE AGE EXCAVATIONS

Visitor Attraction

Fourth Drove, Fengate, Peterborough,
Cambridgeshire, PE1 5UR.

Tel: (0733) 313414
Fax: (0733) 349957

USEFUL INFORMATION

OPEN: Every day except Christmas Day &
   Boxing Day from 11am- last entry 4pm
ADMISSION: Telephone for current prices
CHILDREN: Yes. Junior Guide booklet
   available. Baby changing facilities
CREDIT CARDS: Access/Visa

RESTAURANT: Light refreshments
DISABLED ACCESS: Site fully accessible
   for wheelchairs. Disabled toilets
GARDEN: Outdoor Picnic area, covered
   picnic area in reconstructed Iron Age
   Roundhouse

Three thousand years ago prehistoric people drove massive posts into the waters of Flag Fen to construct a huge tribal barrier. Around the posts they made offerings and sacrifices to their Gods. Then at about 900 BC the waters rose so fast that everything - seeds, leaves, twigs, even pollen grains became pickled in peaty mud. There is no site like it anywhere in Europe.

The 3,000 year old site was found in 1982 by Dr Francis Pryor whilst examining a Roman road which runs across it. Every year since then, excavations have taken place during the summer months and thousands of pieces of preserved Bronze Age wood have been uncovered, together with pottery, animal bones, and bronze weapons and jewellery. In 1987 the site opened to the public and in 1988 won the Hepworth Heritage Communication Award. The site has been the subject of three, half hour TV programmes and has been in many others ranging from 'Blue Peter' to 'Songs of Praise'.

The Visitor Centre, situated in a man-made lake, provides a picturesque setting in which to enjoy a cup of coffee and browse through the gift shop. It also contains a museum where many of the unique artefacts found on the site are displayed.

Guided tours give visitors up to the minute information about the latest discoveries when excavations are in progress. However most of the site can be enjoyed at a leisurely pace aided with information panels which explain various aspects of the site. Reconstructions of buildings, together with plants and animals of Bronze Age type all help to bring the period to life.

ORTON HALL HOTEL

Hotel & Conference Centre

The Village, Orton Longueville,
Peterborough, Cambridgeshire, PE2 7DN.

Tel: (0733) 391111
Fax: (0733) 231912

Set in 22 acres of mature parkland in the secluded conservation village of Orton Longueville, Orton Hall was previously an estate owned by the Marquesses of Huntly, Chief of the Clan Gordon, Scotland's Premier Clan. The Hall has been tastefully restored to much of its former glory as one of the county's foremost country houses, circa 17th century. The renovation has enabled the best Edwardian values of style, ambience and service to blend with a hint of Scottish tradition to complement the needs of the 20th Century hotel visitor.

The 50 bedrooms answer everyone's needs with all having en-suite bathrooms, some with four-poster beds and several non-smoking rooms. The oak-panelled Huntly restaurant has truly classical and international dishes complemented by a fine selection of wines. The Drawing Room is elegant and restful where one can enjoy an aperitif, coffee or liqueurs. The friendly Library Bar reflects the Hall's Scottish heritage with an abundance of Highland, Island and Lowland malts. However, it is the Conservatory that attracts many people with its 16th Century terracotta floors and latticed windows with the etched glass inscribed with family mottos. It is here that you can enjoy afternoon tea watching squirrels at play on the lawn.

Orton Hall's Conference Centre offers a variety of spacious, light, airy and, above all, grand Boardrooms with adjacent syndicate rooms in undisturbed tranquillity, ideal for executive meetings, private luncheons and dinners. Across the paved and golden gravel courtyard lies the Old Ramblewood Inn, originally the stables - a good place to drink or eat hearty food - families welcome.

USEFUL INFORMATION

OPEN: All year
CHILDREN: Welcome
CREDIT CARDS: Visa/Access/Diners/
  Amex
LICENSED: Full On
ACCOMMODATION: 50 en-suite rooms

RESTAURANT: A blend of Modern and
  Traditional British Country Fayre with
  an International flavour
BAR FOOD: Wholesome & hearty
  English Country fare
VEGETARIAN: Yes. 4-6 dishes
DISABLED ACCESS: Yes. Ground floor
  bedrooms
GARDEN: 22 acres woodland. 2 patio areas

CHARTERS CAFE BAR

Cafe Bar & Restaurant

Town Bridge, Peterborough,
Cambridgeshire, PE1 1DG.

Tel: (0733) 315700
Fax: (0733) 315700

Two minutes from Peterborough Cathedral you come upon an experience! Charters Cafe Bar at Town Bridge is a large, floating, continental barge moored against this historic old bridge on the Nene River. It is an enchanting place to be. The barge was converted by the owner, Paul Hook, in 1990 and it has taken no time to become one of the places to be in Peterborough. You approach it either on the pedestrianised south side of the Cathedral or, if you wish, from the floating pontoon where you may moor your boat before enjoying the pleasures of Charters. It was originally a commercial barge which sailed the rivers and canals of Holland, Germany and Belgium, it carried 616 tonnes of cargo which included sand, grain and other such bulk items.

Below decks the atmosphere is tremendous. Its busy bar can contend with 350 people comfortably. There are always a number of Real Ales as well as wines and spirits. On the upper deck is the restaurant where there is table service and room for 100 covers. Everywhere the atmosphere is informal and relaxed. Charters has earned its reputation and been rewarded for the effort by becoming CAMRA Pub of the Season. The menu is an eclectic mixture of American and Continetal cuisine with a wide choice. It is of a high standard and certainly value for money. There is nothing like it anywhere else within Peterborough and its surrounds.

How did it get where it is? There are many stories but we are told to look for the obvious - by rolling tree trunks, pulled by a herd of African elephants!!!!

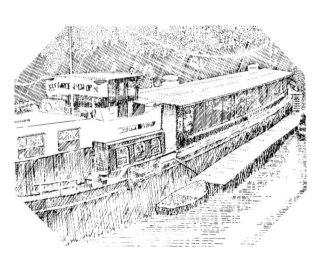

USEFUL INFORMATION

OPEN: 7 days. Lunchtimes & evenings
CHILDREN: Well behaved welcome
CREDIT CARDS: Amex/Visa/Diners/
  Mastercard
LICENSED: Full On & Off
ACCOMMODATION: Not applicable

RESTAURANT: American/Continental
  cuisine
BAR FOOD: Hot and cold in winter.
  Baguettes & salads in summer
VEGETARIAN: Always 3 dishes
DISABLED ACCESS: Restaurant only
GARDEN: Large & shady. BBQ nightly in
  summer, weather permitting

PETERBOROUGH MUSEUM & ART GALLERY

Visitor Attraction

Priestgate, Peterborough,
Cambridgeshire, PE1 1LF.

Tel: (0733) 343329

USEFUL INFORMATION

OPEN: Tues-Sat: 10am-5pm all year except Christmas week
CHILDREN: Welcome. Hands on exhibition in Geology Gallery of particular interest
CREDIT CARDS: None taken

RESTAURANT: No catering facilities
DISABLED ACCESS: Lift available
GARDEN: No

The building in which Peterborough Museum and Art Gallery is housed dates from 1816 and was the private residence of Squire Cooke (see his clock on display). It served as Peterborough Infirmary until 1929, and became the museum in 1931. The Art Gallery was added in 1939. There are three floors of displays, with a costume gallery between the first and second floors.

On the ground floor the friendly receptionists greet you and on the right are two rooms where there are always interesting exhibitions. In the entrance corridor are small temporary displays and at the far end a display about John Clare, the 'peasant poet', Peterborough's most famous son. The Art Gallery has a constantly changing programme of exhibitions, mainly contemporary art, but also of crafts for example cake icing, or other aspects of our culture like science fiction. The first floor is the home of Mark Noble, one of Peterborough's watchmakers in a mock up of his eighteenth century workshop. On the same floor you have Geology and Wildlife on your left and Archaeology on your right. Straight ahead is the Period Shop display where you can see many of the items your grandparents might have used!

The second floor has a display of bone and straw marquetry items made by the inmates in the Napoleonic prisoner of war camp at Norman Cross. It is one of the largest collections in existence and includes the actual fire engine used in the camp. Finally there is a display of Peterborough's social history, telling the story of local industries, schools, entertainment and so forth. This is an excellent outing for anyone.

THE WAYWARD FROG AND RIBITS

Wine Bar and Bistro

29 Bridge Street, Peterborough,
Cambridgeshire, PE1 1HJ.

Tel: (0733) 61999/61996

USEFUL INFORMATION

OPEN: Frog: 11-11pm. Mon-Sat. Sun: please phone. Ribits: 12-2.30pm & 6.30pm till late
CHILDREN: Welcome, children's menu
CREDIT CARDS: All major cards
LICENSED: Full On Licence
ACCOMMODATION: Not applicable
RESTAURANT: Superb choice, individually cooked food, no smoking area, air conditioned
BAR FOOD: Wide choice
VEGETARIAN: Large variety, and different
DISABLED ACCESS: Easy acces. Wide doors, level to washrooms
GARDEN: Not applicable

Just one minute from Peterborough's imposing Cathedral is the intriguingly named Wayward Frog and Ribits. Its name comes from the nickname, 'Wayward' bestowed upon the owner Peter Hayward, and his partner and brother-in-law, a Frenchman; the combination quite easily became 'The Wayward Frog'. For the last twenty five years, this family run business has been giving pleasure to the people of Peterborough and the many visitors who have found its welcoming atmosphere just what is required.

You will find it quite easily, just ten minutes off the A1 and then into the city centre where you will spot the wine bar across the road from the museum which focuses on the RAF in World War II. The old world atmosphere of the wine bar is especially welcoming to business people and senior citizens, probably because it is a nice mixture of the formal and informal. The service is exceptional and the food unusually good for a wine bar. Ribits has great appeal with its cellar lit by candlelight, and it is here you can savour its Mexican food and really juicy steaks, for which it is renowned. The Wayward Frog is somewhere where you can either have a beer, morning coffee, afternoon tea or a snack or a beautifully cooked, and traditional English meal. It is a particularly good venue for lunch when you can indulge in snails, the totally contrasting liver and bacon, a simple omelette or a massive club sandwich. Whichever part of this fascinating establishment you choose to patronise, it is to be recommended.

Great North Road, Stilton,
Peterborough, PE7 3RA.

Tel: (0733) 241066
Fax: (0733) 245173

THE BELL INN
Hotel & Restaurant

The Bell at Stilton has stories to tell of a famous cheese, a highwayman and a famous horseman. It also shouts from the roof tops that it is one of the finest inns in the county. It was Samuel Johnson who said 'there is nothing which has yet been contrived by man, by which so much happiness is produced as by a good tavern or inn.' Mine host of the Bell Inn would dearly like his establishment to justify the sentiment. It does.

The inn dates back to 1500 and possibly before because there is a record of a local innkeeper in 1437. The Bell's main fascination, however centres on the characters associated with it. Innkeepers, statesmen, outlaws and literary figures have contributed to the inn's fame. One popular tale, handed down over the centuries, has the highwayman Dick Turpin visiting the hostelry. He is supposed to have hidden there for nine weeks while hunted by the law. Surprised by a raid, he threw open the window and jumped on to Black Bess to gallop off up the Great North Road.

The great Duke of Marlborough was a notable guest here. Earlier still, Cromwell's troops were here. In 1725 Lord Harley tasted and disliked the cheese sold at The Bell. On October 3rd 1813 Lord Byron slept there. Cooper Thornhill was landlord from 1730 until his death in 1759, aged 54. He is invariably referred to as the man who popularised Stilton cheese which was served, mites and all, at the Bell. Today The Bell still welcomes colourful characters, offers you the warmest of welcomes (be it for a conference, wedding reception or just a drink in the bar) and hopes you enjoy your visit whilst absorbing some of the history of this historic inn.

USEFUL INFORMATION

OPEN: All year
CHILDREN: Welcome
CREDIT CARDS: All Major cards
LICENSED: Full On Licence
ACCOMMODATION: 19 en-suite rooms. Pets not permitted

RESTAURANT: English with French influence. Will cook to order
BAR FOOD: Bar meal. Local produce
VEGETARIAN: 3 set dishes on Restaurant and Bar menu
DISABLED ACCESS: No, difficult
GARDEN: Big garden & courtyard adjacent to bar

Sacrewell, Thornhaugh,
Peterborough, Cambridgeshire, PE8 6HJ.

Tel: (0780) 782222

SACREWELL FARM & COUNTRY CENTRE
Visitor Attraction

Who visits Sacrewell Farm and Country Centre? Those who seek freedom, space, peace and tranquillity, with interest and beauty. It is a memorable experience where the past and the present are inextricably linked. Sacrewell is the home of the William Scott Abbott Trust, set up in January 1964, by Mary Abbott, in memory of her husband William. He farmed Sacrewell from October 1917 until his death in November 1959. It is essentially a well managed farm and the trust is the charity responsible for all that goes on here.

Though the farming is up to date and progressive, there is a responsible attitude to the care of the environment and the Trustees clearly recognise that an important aspect of their educational role, is the creation of better understanding of farming by the general public. Sacrewell tries to explain to visitors the inescapable and binding partnership between farm and the human stomach - no future for either without the other!

Sacrewell Farm is, archaeologically and historically, of more than usual interest, because of the number of people who, for thousands of years, have made it their home. Water in springs, streams and river, was probably a main attraction to early man. There is evidence of habitation before the Roman occupation but the latter brought possibly four homesteads to Sacrewell though these are only discernible in outline. However plenty of artefacts are found regularly. Much has happened over the centuries and more recently history has literally 'flowed' through Sacrewell in the shape of a giant pipeline transporting water from the Nene to Rutland Water. It is somewhere you should visit for the joy of it and for its great interest.

USEFUL INFORMATION

OPEN: All year including Christmas Day
CHILDREN: Lots of hands-on activities. Toys for toddlers, trails, quizes & competitions
CREDIT CARDS: None taken
LICENSED: None

RESTAURANT: Simple snacks. Cream Teas
DISABLED ACCESS: Toilets, ramp, very willing to assist
GARDEN: Picnic site. Maze. Play area

Portsmouth Cathedral

Portsmouth

"All things are literally better, lovelier, and
more beloved for the imperfections
Which has been divinely appointed"

John Ruskin

The City of Portsmouth

by Joy David

Portsmouth or 'Pompey' as it is affectionately known to both servicemen and natives alike, is situated on a peninsula that projects southwards between the two natural harbours of Portsmouth on the western side and Langstone to the east. Like its civilian counterpart, **Southampton**, Portsmouth enjoys certain natural advantages; there is deep water throughout a large part of the harbour, the Isle of Wight offers shelter from much of the Channel weather and the narrow entrance is easily defended. These assets were first recognised by the Romans, who ignored the site of the present day Portsmouth and sailed right up to the top of the harbour, landing at what is now **Porchester**. Here they built PORTCHESTER CASTLE, the best preserved Roman fortress in northern Europe. The massive walls, with many of the original bastions, enclose an area of some nine acres and were built around 290AD. The Roman's successors also appreciated the strategic importanace of the site; King Alfred used it as one of his strongholds in the defence of Wessex and the Normans built a massive keep, which has survived to this day. An Augustinian Priory was founded within the walls during the 12th century. This moved shortly afterwards, but the priory church, now the parish church of St Mary still stands; an

outstanding example of the Romanesque style. The west front is the most beautiful part of the church. It has a simple richness about it. Inside it is austere but there is a fine Norman font and the Royal Arms of both Elizabeth I and Anne.

The castle has been used by succeeding Royals over the centuries. The Plantagenets used it as a base when they were leaving or returning to the country and when they went hunting in the nearby forest of Bere. Queen Victoria is remembered with a lych gate, built to commemorate her diamond jubilee in 1897. It was sold by the Crown in 1632 and had several uses after that, not the least a prison for French prisoners of war whose names you can still detect, carved or scratched on the walls. I have always found the village street leading to the castle with its mainly 18th century facades, a charming spot.

Portsmouth as a community had a relatively late beginning and a somewhat shaky early history. Originally there was a small trading settlement at the mouth of the harbour at what is now known as the Camber area. Then, in about 1180, a local landowner began to develop the area which is now the city centre. A chapel was built to the memory of the recently murdered Thomas a Becket; that site is now where the present cathedral stands. Richard I granted the first charter in 1194 but even by the 14th century Portsmouth was hardly more than a village, relying mainly on agriculture. The area that was to

become the Royal Dockyard was little more than mud-flats, although there had been some attempt at ship-building and repairing, albeit in a somewhat half-hearted way. The little township suffered grievously from the raiding French, being razed to the ground on at least one occasion. Not until the accession of Henry VII (1457-1509) did things begin to change, with the establishment of a dry dock and a number of defensive measures. Henry VIII (1491-1547) did much to continue this development by expanding the navy and building SOUTHSEA CASTLE on the southern tip of the peninsula. His innovations were tested in 1545, when the French set out to revenge the recent capture of Boulogne by the English. Their plan was to defeat the English navy, consisting of some hundred ships, and take the Isle of Wight to act as a bridgehead to invade the mainland. Their force of 150 ships and 60,000 men waiting nearby in additional transports, met with the English just off the harbour mouth. The Battle of Spithead, with Henry watching from Southsea Castle, ended in defeat for the French. Lost during the action, probably because her lower gun ports were not secured while manoeuvring, was the Mary Rose, which turned over and sank, taking her entire crew of 700 with her.

Portsmouth, and to some extent the Royal Navy itself, then fell into a decline, which was only to be ended after the Civil War; the Royal Navy declaring for Cromwell while the town remained loyal. If this sounds odd, it should be remembered that one of the major factors which ultimately turned Englishmen against the crown was the subject of the navy and finance.

Under Cromwell, and later Charles II, the fortunes of both the navy and Portsmouth were restored. Over the years the dockyard expanded to provide all the facilities required; docks, warehouses, rope-lifts, stores, barracks, powder magazines, sail-lofts and the like were all built. By the 18th century, the town was entirely dependant on the Royal Dockyard. After the Napoleonic wars there was a brief period in the doldrums, but the fruits of the Industrial Revolution, the demands of Empire and European expansionism soon brought that to an end. Steam was introduced and iron-clad ships constructed; the humble sailor was becoming a technician and shore-establishments were built to provide him with an education. With much of the fleet serving in the far-flung waters of the Empire, it was felt that Portsmouth might be vulnerable to attack - particularly from our old enemy, the French. A mighty ring of fortresses were built to surround the entire area, from **Gosport** on the western side of the harbour, running right along the crest of **Portsdown Hill** to the north, and down to **Farlington**, at the head of Langstone Harbour.

Out in the Solent four massive sea-forts were built of granite and clad with armour plating. Portsmouth became the most heavily defended city in Europe. Both World Wars served to emphasise the strategic importance of the city, but the much vaunted land defences were of little use, being utilised for headquarters, stores and barracks. Like Southampton, both Gosport and Portsmouth were heavily bombed, with much of the heart being torn out of the city and yet, phoenix like, they have arisen from the ashes of their past and look to a new, and perhaps not

so defence-dependant, future. The Royal Navy is now smaller and more compact, ships are no longer built in the Dockyard and personnel have been drastically reduced. New industries, no longer related to defence have moved into the area and the harbour is used by cross-channel and merchant shipping as well as the sleek grey warships. The city has made a determined effort to find itself a niche by promoting itself as 'The City of Maritime Heritage', and its assests in this area are unequalled.

Approaching from the north, initial impressions, as with Southampton, are unfavourable. The motorway runs down under Portsdown Hill, where houses and factories huddle cramped together under the steep chalk slopes. At the head of the harbour, vast areas of reclaimed marsh now support yet more factories, offices and developments. But consider, these are all signs of life, of a community determined to break free from the old economic order of being dependant on a single source of employment and for that reason, the people of the area should be applauded. Modern development, particularly when rushed, frequently leaves much to be desired and it is interesting to reflect upon the planner's dream of the late fifties and early sixties - the creation of a great new metropolis to be called 'Solent City'. Unfortunately, their carefully structured ideas never came to fruition, but the basis of the idea now exists, insofar as from west of Southampton to east of Portsmouth, it now appears as one continuous community.

Entering the city on a short spur of the motorway, one of the more attractive developments and an indicator of prosperity, is the marina complex PORT SOLENT, built on reclaimed marsh at the head of Porchester Lake. Houses, shops, offices, restaurants, a hotel and boatyard surround a large yacht harbour. One example of the sort

of place one can enjoy here is COLLECTIF at 26, The Broadwalk which has a wonderful position on the waterside. It would be sought after wherever it was housed because it is specialised and very different. On the front of their attractive catalogue is a quotation from Lewis Carroll, 'Oh Kitty, how nice it would be if we could only get through into Looking-Glass house! I'm sure it has oh, such beautiful things in it.' Collectif does not have the key but it does open its doors to the magical world of miniatures. Almost everything for the house in the shop are one twelfth scale minature components which allow the DIY enthusiast to create their own. To complement the miniatures is a wonderful array of teddy bears and dolls. Over 1,000 bears are always in stock from Steiff and Hermann as well as special edition artist bears from Britain and America. It is somewhere which will help you fulfil your dreams - in miniature!

THE YACHT CLUB AND CALM WATER RESTAURANT at The Porthouse is the most welcoming of places. Members, of course, know it well and enjoy everything about it from the social occasions to the pleasure of meeting friends in the bar and eating delicious food in the Calm Water Restaurant. For those in the area for only a short time, temporary membership is available and it takes no time at all to meet new friends.

An earlier example of land reclamation is to be found further down the harbour; HMS EXCELLENT, once the Royal Navy's gunnery school, was built using spoil from dockyard excavation. The original Excellent was Collingwood's ship at Trafalgar and, as a hulk, was the first gunnery school in the navy, firing its cannons out over the mud-flats. A local family, appropriately named Grub, made a good living recovering the cannon-balls, by 'splatching' across the mud at low tide with boards tied to their feet.

Just inland from here is the house where Charles Dickens was born, his father having been a clerk in the Naval Pay Department. THE CHARLES DICKENS BIRTHPLACE MUSEUM at 393 Old Commercial Road, now stands in a quiet cul-de-sac but in 1812 when their first son Charles was born here, it stood on the busy main road into the town. Although Charles Dickens was only associated with Portsmouth for a short time - the family moved away from Portsmouth two years later - the fame of his works meant that every attempt was made to locate the actual house of his birth and it was acquired by Portsmouth Corporation in 1903 and turned into a museum. Considerable structural repair was needed by 1968 and a decision was taken to turn it into a series of period room settings with one exhibition room. The house is displayed to recreate the type of lower-middle class home into which Charles Dickens was born in 1812. Therefore it is not a Victorian house but a Regency one. All the items on display are authentic, none dating beyond 1812. The exhibition room has a small collection of memorabilia and a rotating selection of illustrations from Charles Dickens' published work as well as portraits of the man and his family. The museum has few items that actually belonged to him but pride of place is given to the couch on which he died in 1870 at Gad's Hill Place in Kent. His snuff box, inkwell and paper knife remain as eloquent symbols of his prodigious output which made him one of the best loved authors in the world.

The museum is open from March 1st to October 31st each year from 10.30-5.30pm. For special events contact 0705 827261.

Undoubtedly the best place to start a tour of the city and its heritage is at the ROYAL DOCKYARD which houses three of the world's major maritime attractions as well as an excellent museum. Indisputably the most famous of the three is HMS VICTORY, Nelson's flagship at Trafalgar. Launched at Chatham in 1765, she took six years to build and 3,000 oak trees went into her construction. Beautifully restored and maintained she still serves as Flagship of the Commander-in-Chief, Naval Home Command, manned by officers and ratings of the Royal Navy, making her the oldest commissioned warship in the world.

When you visit HMS Victory you enter another world, that of the Georgian sailor. A guided tour will take you to see the cabins of Captain Hardy and Vice Admiral Nelson, the gun decks where the seamen lived, worked, fought and died, and the Cockpit, where Nelson himself passed away. I always find a visit here a moving experience.

HMS Victory is open every day except Christmas Day March-October from 10am-4.45pm November-February 10.30am-4.20pm. You will find closeby the Victory Gift Shop where you may buy a tot of Pusser's British Navy Rum - for every bottle sold a contribution is made to the Sailor's Fund. Refrehsments are also available close to the ship. The entry fee also includes admission to the Royal Naval Museum.

Close to HMS Victory are the remains of the MARY ROSE upon which experts are still working so that the ship and her treasures may be preserved for future generations. The Mary Rose was Henry VIII's favourite warship and he watched with horror as she foundered. He had expected her to do battle with the French but she sank suddenly taking her 700 men, and all the equipment of war with her. Lost for over four centuries, the raising of the Mary Rose was the world's largest underwater archaeological operation. Divers and archaeologists worked painstakingly for many years - sometimes joined by HRH the Prince of Wales - before she was recovered in October 1982. Now you can see the breathtaking spectacle of this Tudor warship close to where she was built in the 16th century. Restoration to her underwater state continues and an audio guide brings the ship to life once more. The Mary Rose Exhibition displays over 1000 exciting 'treasures' and gives the visitor a fascinating insight into Tudor life. Cannons and longbows, gold coins and pewter plates, navigation instruments, as well as personal possessions including clothing and games. Even the medical chest belonging to the barber-surgeon has been saved. Allow at least two hours as there is so much to experience.

The museum is open at 10am daily except Christmas Day. Closing times vary. March to October 5.30pm July and August 6.45pm and November toFebruary 5pm. There are special events and occasions happening throughout the year. For details ring 0705 750521.

The third historical ship is HMS WARRIOR who saw no battle action, but was the world's first steam-powered, iron-hulled warship and was launched in 1860. As you walk around Warrior it is hard to believe that for 50 years she was used as a floating oil jetty off Milford Haven, with the upper deck covered in a thick layer of concrete. As long ago as 1967 there was talk about restoring Warrior but it was not until August 1979 that restoration began and Warrior was towed to Hartlepool. With all the care of an archeological dig it was intended to restore Warrior as authentically as she appeared during her first commission from 1861-1864. A most invaluable source discovered was a log book belonging to Midshipman

Henry Murray, who at 14 served on the ship and had drawn detailed plans showing where items were kept.

Skilled craftsmen were employed and slowly but surely Warrior was lovingly restored. From the fitting of a newly carved 'figure-head' and the laying of 20,000 sq.ft of pine planking, down to the bowls and plates used by the gun crew, no detail was overlooked. By 1987 the 140 strong Hartlepool workforce had indeed restored HMS Warrior to her former glory. There is something to interest everyone on this 'living museum', from the bathroom and laundry to the boiler and engine rooms. Visitors are encouraged to touch and try things out, sit at a mess deck table, handle a Colt revolver, even examine a cat-o'nine tails! A great experience.

Open all year with the exception of Christmas Day the hours are the same as the Mary Rose.

No visitor should leave the Dockyard without viewing the excellent ROYAL NAVAL MUSEUM. From the Romans to the Gulf War, the story of Britain's Royal Navy, its men, its women, its battles, its ships, unfolds before you. It is like opening up a chest of naval treasures as you see all that is on view. You can chart a course through naval history. You will find it housed in Georgian storehouses, which would have served Nelson's fleet. There are models and relics of ships from the time of King Alfred through the majestic fleets of Elizabeth I to the wooden walls of the Battle of Trafalgar. Here and there are personal possessions of the men who fought and served in times of peace and war. The decisive victories of the golden age of sail as Britannia ruled the waves are presented to you with the panorama of the Battle of Trafalgar. Vivid dioramas of famous naval scenes, medals, letters home from the men and boys of Nelson's navy

captivate the eye and stir the imagination. Queen Victoria's day was different but still it was a hard life for those who served. It is all here for you to see. 20th century naval history comes to life through the personal stories of the men and women who served. It is a stimulating experience.

The Royal Naval Museum is open every day from 10.30am to at least 4.30pm except Christmas Day and Boxing Day. Family tickets are available for all these museums.

Glimpses of the modern navy can be had during 'Navy Days' in August, every other year - the intervening year it is staged in Devonport, Plymouth - when the Naval base takes on a festive air and visitors throng in their thousands to be shown over modern warships and be entertained by displays.

Other aspects of naval and military life are displayed in FORT NELSON near **Fareham**, the splendid ROYAL MARINES MUSEUM in Eastney barracks where you take a fasinating journey through time following the epic and action-packed story of the Royal Marines. See the 300 year history of these elite and famous men unfold from Jutland to D-Day, from Trafalgar to Port Stanley. In the multimedia cinema you can watch the Commandos as they sail South to retake the Falklands.

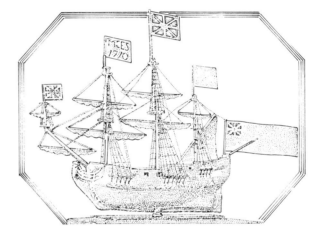

Mounted on a plinth made of oak from HMS Victory, The Golden Barque, above, served as a weather vane from 1710 to 1954, when it was blown down in a gale

It is an impressive story told through their words and previously unseen pictures.

The museum is open 7 days a week throughout the year. 9.30-5pm from Whitsun to August. 10am-4.30pm September to May.

The Royal Marines Museum is one of four naval museums which include the Fleet Air Arm Museum at Yeovilton in Somerset, the Royal Naval Museum here in Portsmouth and THE ROYAL NAVY SUBMARINE MUSEUM, Gosport. Catch a waterbus from Portsmouth harbour to this outstanding museum which will occupy you all day. The service is great. Using just one ticket you can stop off at any one of the museums or famous ships, before rejoining the ferry to complete the Harbour Tour later in the day.

For those with young children, **Southsea**, the southern tip of the peninsula, has much to offer with its promenade, beach and common, which includes a boating lake and attractive gardens. Pleasure cruises around the Solent depart from SOUTH PARADE PIER whch, true to its Edwardian beginnings offers entertainments seven nights a week. THE PYRAMIDS, an indoor leisure complex with all manner of aquatic entertainments, is the new centrepiece to Southsea's waterfront development, while the FUNACRES amusement complex at Clarence Pier offers, amongst other attractions, a roller coaster ride that literally takes your breath away. Alongside the pier the only hover-craft passenger service in the country runs to the Isle of Wight.

THE PORTSMOUTH SEA LIFE CENTRE allows you to experience the thrill of a deep sea dive and discover the magical world of the seas - without getting wet! This watery wonderland is teeming with amazing marine life, sinister sharks, huge stingrays, intriguing sunfish and bizarre wolf-fish to name just a few. A spectacular 14ft high window onto the ocean reveals a sunken wreck and creates the illusion of a genuine walk underwater! You experience the spine-tingling sensation of life beneath the waves as thousands of gallons of water surround you.

If you have been before you may have seen the British Shark display and now you can step through the mighty jaws of a giant shark into the brilliant new shark encounter, filled with fascinating facts and features giving real insight into the life and history of the ocean's deadliest hunters. It is a different adventure every time you visit.

Opening times are 10am-6pm (9pm in summer holidays) 7 days a week, all year except Christmas Day.

Looking for somewhere to stay, WESTFIELD HALL HOTEL at 65, Festing Road, Southsea is a thoroughly nice family hotel with a warm, welcoming atmosphere and an emphasis on quality and value for money. It has been run by the same family for over fourteen years and has 17 prestigious ensuite bedrooms. The hotel is within

easy reach of the city centre and continental ferry port. Car parking is simple and for those who would like to take advantage of a special winter break, there are excellent discounted offers during December, January and February.

ROSIE'S VINEYARD in Elm Grove, Southsea, for many is the only real wine bar on the south coast. It is stunning. It may take you a little effort to find it tucked away but it is more than worth while. It is a lively, unpretentious place, full of atmosphere and if you wonder about the mahogany fruit bins and floral stained glass it is because it had a previous existence as a greengrocers. There are three super bistro bars with a mass of greenery, one of which is a cellar, and at the back there is a fabulous 'Pergola' covered wine garden. Healthy, grape-laden vines entwine themselves round the pergola and while you are sitting at the wooden tables you would be perfectly justified in thinking you were in France, or Amsterdam, even Berlin rather than Elm Grove, Southsea.

The Camber, the original port within the natural harbour, is surrounded by **Old Portsmouth**, an attractive area that had a lewd reputation in years gone by. The streets are quiet now where once the drunken Jacks did their roistering and the drabs and bawds no longer call from the windows to promote their trade. It is something of an oasis amidst a rapidly changing world with good looking, principally Georgian housing, although there are traces of far older construction. The Hard is the epitome of this oldest part of the city. It is close to Nelson's flagship and it was this man's great love for Lady Hamilton that made Bill and Rose Scott embark on the restoration of 21, The Hard which is now known as THE LADY HAMILTON, an inn which has quite a

history. It is one of the oldest buildings on The Hard and was originally the Nag's Head in 1716, and then when it was decided there were far too many hostelries on The Hard in 1920, it was closed - there were, after all, 25 of them! It then became a wine merchants and eventually was sold to Gieves, the famous naval outfitters. As the Lady Hamilton it has become known as the oldest and newest pub in Portsmouth! Here you can drink and eat good wholesome food and stay, if you wish, in one of the bedrooms which are mainly ensuite.

While we are talking about eating there is a very different eating experience to be had at BLU'S at 243 London Road. This is American eating at its best. It is a light-hearted place with good food at sensible prices.

Within an easy drive are two excellent restaurants which certainly warrant your taking the time to reach them. Each time I come to Portsmouth I add more and more delightful eating experiences to my list and these two come high up on it. CHIVES in the High Street at Fareham, once described by Sir John Betjeman as the best example of a High Street in Hampshire. The site has been occupied for more than 2000 years and is strongly connected with Portchester Castle, in that a fording or bridging point was established here on the journey to Winchester. Chives building has evolved over the centuries. The flints exposed on the left hand side of the 3 steps that divide the two restaurant rooms, are the base of a Saxon cottage, (circa 800AD) and made of wattle and daub with a stone base and floor. This, I hope, has given you a taste for the wonderful, historic atmosphere of Chives. however it is only the beginning of the story. The front room is the original medieval cottage. There is a Priest Hole which was uncovered in the 70's and in the first floor sitting room is a very deep, small cupboard in the wall where the wigs were powdered. This was done deep into the cupboard to prevent the iris root and chalk from making the rest of the room dusty. In the same room is a magnificent original Adam fireplace. Too good for the rest of the house, it must have been someone's mad extravagance.

In 1815, a Georgian false front was added when a developer bought this row of Tudor cottages and revamped them in order to sell them as small gentlemen's residences to the dismissed naval officers, who were made redundant by Napoleon's defeat at Waterloo. One can only suggest that you visit this gem. There can be nothing but pleasure in doing so both aesthetically and gastronomically.

My other choice is at **Emsworth** which is about as far east in Hampshire as you can get and lies just outside Portsmouth on the Brighton Road. Once upon a time Emsworth was noted for its oysters but disaster struck at the beginning of the 19th century when oysters were supplied for a banquet in Winchester and were found to carry typhoid, which resulted in several deaths. This was a cruel blow to the town but now it thrives as a busy yachting centre. On the waterfront you can see what Emsworth looked like in Georgian times. There are some very nice houses. In South Street is JULIES, a stone's throw away from the quay. It is housed in a charming building that once was a fisherman's cottage. It has many devoted patrons who come regularly for the food and the friendly, informal atmosphere. One permanent customer is Fred, the resident ghost who can sometimes be smelt, as well as his presence felt; he is quite harmless and merely adds an extra ingredient to the pleasure of being here. In addition to the normal meal times it has become a tradition for people to make a

beeline to Julies on Sunday afternoons during the summer months, to indulge in a fabulous cream tea.

The city centre of Portsmouth, which has suffered harshly during the Second World War, has been largely replaced with modern buildings, but there are a number of survivors. THE CITY MUSEUM was once a barracks, although it resembles a French chateau as designed by a Victorian, while THE GUILDHALL with its classical facade was rebuilt after being gutted in the war. Its 2000 seat auditorium is renowned for the near-perfection of the acoustics.

Finally, there is THE CATHEDRAL, quite unique among its fellows, since not only is it unfinished but it is also made up of three distinct periods; 12th century, 17th century and 20th century. Somehow, the great building seems to represent an apt simile for the city itself; it is organic, its growth has been untidy and inconsistent and yet has to finish, yet it is intensely alive with an eye to the future as well as to the past.

I am indebted to Portsmouth Cathedral Council for lending me a simple book entitled The Guides' Guide to THE CATHEDRAL CHURCH OF SAINT

The Della Robbia

THOMAS OF CANTERBURY. This has been invaluable and has opened my eyes not only to the beauty and interest of the contents but also to the role the cathedral plays.

This is not only the Cathedral, the church where the bishop has his cathedral or seat, and from where his ministry as a focus of unity in the diocese can be seen to be exercised; it is also a Parish church, serving the neighbourhood which includes both the Naval Dockyard and the fairground in Southsea. In addition this is the Civic Church of the City of Portsmouth, where the Lord Mayor and City Council have their seats. The provost is the Chaplain to the City Council. If on the day you go round the cathedral there are no special services, rehearsals, concerts, seminars, school workshops or building work, you have come on an exceptional day; busy days are the rule in this working church.

We readily accept that architecturally the cathedral is a hotch potch but it is a building of great charm and on your journey through it you should take notice of the 13th century eastern transepts and sanctuary. It is the 17th century we have to thank for the beauty of the nave and main transepts. The plain square tower is crowned with an octagonal shaped cupola, with a gilded weather vane. You will find in the new nave, the golden barque which served as a weather vane on the tower from 1710-1954. Sir Charles Nicholson was responsible in this century for the enlargements which still have to be completed, and which are eagerly awaited. The south porch leads us into his nave with its imposing stone arcade in a free Romanesque style. As always I love the light with which the great Perpendicular windows flood the nave. The central tower of the cathedral was part of the old church. There are slender Tuscan piers with round arches in the chancel, a west gallery accommodates the organ and there is a magnificent pulpit of 1693.

What is fitting and perhaps most moving is the constant reminder of the cathedral's association with the navy. Here is a fragment of the White Ensign that flew proudly aboard HMS Victory at Trafalgar and was carried in Nelson's funeral possession. Here too are many other naval flags and regimental colours, memorials and so on to the famous admirals and other officers of the Royal Navy and the Royal Marines. The Cathedral is full of other service souvenirs and none so poignant as the tablet in the navy aisle commemorating all the engagements in which ships called Mary Rose have taken part from 1501 to 1917. A unique funeral service was held here in the summer of 1984 for all those who perished in 1545 and whose remains have been discovered during the lifting of Henry VIII's flagship.

This may be a cathedral of no particular architectural merit but it surely is the most fascinating and rewarding of England's parish church cathedrals. I certainly found it so.

30 South Street, Emsworth,
Hampshire, PO10 7EH.

Tel: (0243) 377914

JULIE'S
Restaurant

South Street is the hub of Old Emsworth and only a stone's throw from the quay. In the street is Julie's, a charming restaurant in a 300 year old building which was once a fisherman's cottage. It has many devoted patrons who come regularly for the food and for the friendly, informal atmosphere. One permanent customer is Fred, the resident ghost who can sometimes be smelt, as well as his presence felt; quite harmless and certainly adding an extra ingredient to the pleasure of coming here.

Kevin Hartley, the Chef/Patron, was Head Chef at Julie's for three years before he purchased the restaurant in March 1993 so his name is well known in the area for the quality of his cuisine. The menu is always changed monthly but whatever the month, fish is always the speciality of the house. Nothing is cooked until it is ordered so you may have to be a little patient but the wait is worth while and can always be helped by a glass or two from the small but well selected wine list. A speciality has been a seasonal Seafood Platter which may well include Emsworth cockles.

Ann, Kevin's mother, runs the front of the house and this cheerful lady makes sure everyone is welcome. She will tell you that her role comes to an end at the kitchen door! It has become quite an institution during the summer months for people to make a beeline for Julie's on Sunday afternoons to have a fabulous cream tea. Horrific for anyone counting calories! Sunday lunches are becoming increasingly popular during the rest of the year. There is a private dining room available for between 2 and 16 people. Ideal for a celebration dinner party or for a small seminar.

USEFUL INFORMATION

OPEN: Tues-Fri: 12-2.30pm. Eves: Tues-Sat: 7-11pm. Sun: 12-2.30pm. Weekday lunches: A la Carte & Table D'Hote, Sunday lunches: Table D'Hote, Eves: A la Carte

CHILDREN: Welcome

CREDIT CARDS: Visa/Access/Master

LICENSED: Restaurant

ACCOMMODATION: Not applicable.

RESTAURANT: Continental bias with a Mediterranean feel. Fish a speciality

BAR FOOD: Not applicable. Cream teas in summer on Sunday afternoons

VEGETARIAN: Always available

DISABLED ACCESS: Level access at rear

GARDEN: Yes a cobbled courtyard with beautiful hanging baskets. Pre-dinner drinks etc

---

15 High Street, Fareham,
Hampshire, PO16 7AF.

Tel: (0329) 234170

CHIVES
Restaurant

Chives has the enviable position of being in the High Street of Fareham, once described by Sir John Betjeman as the best example of a Georgian High Street in Hampshire. The site has been occupied for more than 2000 years and is strongly connected with Portchester Castle, in that a fording or bridging point was established here on the journey to Winchester. Chives building has evolved over the centuries. The flints exposed on the left-hand side of the 3 steps that divide the two restaurant rooms are the base of a Saxon cottage (circa 800AD) and made of wattle and daub with a stone base and floor. This gives you a taste for the wonderful, historic atmosphere of Chives. However it is only the beginning of the story.

The front room is the original medieval cottage. There is a Priest Hole which was uncovered in the 70s, and in the first floor sitting room is a very deep, small cupboard in the wall where the wigs were powdered. This was done deep into the cupboard to prevent the iris root and chalk from making the rest of the room dusty. In the same room is a magnificent original Adam fireplace. Too good for the rest of the house, it must have been someone's mad extravagance!

In 1815, a Georgian false front was added when a developer bought this row of Tudor cottages and revamped them in order to sell them as small gentlemen's residences to the dismissed naval officers who were made redundant by Napoleon's defeat at Waterloo. One can only suggest to you that you visit this gem. There can be nothing but pleasure in doing so both aesthetically and gastronomically.

USEFUL INFORMATION

OPEN: Lunch: Tue-Fri: 12.15-3pm. Dinner: Tues-Sat: 7pm

CHILDREN: Welcome, if well behaved

CREDIT CARDS: All major cards

LICENSED: Restaurant

ACCOMMODATION: Not applicable

RESTAURANT: Large a la carte menu

BAR FOOD: Not applicable

VEGETARIAN: Always available

DISABLED ACCESS: Limited

GARDEN: Not applicable

BLU'S

Diner

243 London Road,
Portsmouth, PO2 9HA.

Tel: (0705) 672268

USEFUL INFORMATION

OPEN: Tues-Thurs: 5-11pm. Fri-Sat: 5-11.30pm. Sun: 5-10.30pm
CHILDREN: Welcome. Children's menu
CREDIT CARDS: Access/Visa
LICENSED: Restaurant
ACCOMMODATION: Not applicable

RESTAURANT: American diner style
BAR FOOD: Not applicable
VEGETARIAN: A selection available
DISABLED ACCESS: Small step. Ground level toilets
GARDEN: No

Just north of Portsmouth's city centre and quite near the ferry terminal is Blu's in London Road. The proprietors, Adrian and Janine, describe Blu's as 'A new experience' and the majority of their first time customers will agree happily with this statement. Happily, because having made the acquaintance of this unusual establishment which transports you to a bygone era of 50's and 60's America, you will more than probably become a habitue.

Against a background of contemporary music, American memorabilia, stars and stripes decor, car number plates, old music scores and bright posters, the furniture battles to have its own say. Old machine tables are covered with red check gingham cloths and there is an aura of cheerfulness which makes this restaurant ideal for families and for business people who want to get away from the stress of their everyday world.

The chef offers traditional American style dishes: chilli, tuna cocktail or corn on the cob make fitting starters for a variety of burgers or steaks. All the main courses are served with a choice of Blu's spuds (fried potato wedges) jacket potatoes or fries. It would not be an American diner if it did not have some of the best ice-cream to be found anywhere as well as 'Thick, Thick Shakes' with a variety of flavours. Everything is cooked to order. The service is fast and friendly and if you have a liking for cocktails, the bar tender will shake you a mean 'Shocking Pink Colada', a 'Black Russian' or an 'Apple Jack'. There are imported American beers and Irish, French, Jamaican and Mexican liquer coffees. Blu's is certainly an experience and a good one!

THE LADY HAMILTON

Inn

21 The Hard,
Portsmouth, PO1 3DU.

Tel: (0705) 870505

USEFUL INFORMATION

OPEN: 11-11pm. Normal Sunday hours
CHILDREN: Welcome
CREDIT CARDS: All major cards
LICENSED: Full On & Off Licence
ACCOMMODATION: 8 rooms, ensuite. No dogs.

RESTAURANT: Not applicable
BAR FOOD: Wide range plus 'Daily Specials'
VEGETARIAN: Always available
DISABLED ACCESS: Level access & accommodation
GARDEN: No

The Hard is one of the oldest streets in Portsmouth and alive with history. The Lady Hamilton occupies one of the oldest buildings and does so with grace and charm. The building has had many uses before it opened its doors to its new vocation just over a year ago. It was originally The Nag's Head in 1716 and then when it was decided there were far too many hostelries on The Hard in 1920, it was closed - there were 25 of them believe it or not! It then became a wine merchants and eventually was sold to Gieves, the famous naval outfitters. As the Lady Hamilton it has become known as the oldest and newst pub in Portsmouth!

Bill and Rose Scott, the landlords, not only have a love for the building but also for Old Portsmouth. The Hard is the epitome of this oldest part of the city and constantly reminds one of how important seafaring life has been here over the centuries. It is close to Nelson's flagship 'Victory' and to the 'Mary Rose'. It was with this thought of the Lady Hamilton's historical past that made Rose and Bill lovingly reconstruct the house, using decor, furnishing and materials that were just right.

The Lady Hamilton offers a superb menu every lunchtime and evening, good, wholesome, home-cooked food at sensible prices, plus 'Daily Specials' and Sunday roasts. They are justly proud to hold Potsmouth Council's Seal of Excellence in good food hygiene standards. The bedrooms are mainly ensuite and very comfortably furnished with colour TV and a beverage tray. The breakfasts are memorable.

THE ROYAL NAVAL MUSEUM
Museum

H.M. Naval Base, Portsmouth,
Hampshire, PO1 3LR.

Tel: (0705) 733060
Fax: (0705) 875806

This excellent museum stands in the heart of Portsmouth's famous Naval Base. Easily reached from the heart of the city and just 15 minutes pleasurable walk from the Anglican Cathedral and ten minutes from the Roman Catholic Cathedral. Portsmouth has been a place of historical interest for many years and people coming here for the first time become very aware of how much it has its roots firmly entwined around the Royal Navy. Many famous people have joined ships from here and it is their lives, and the lives of the sailors for the last thousand years whose story is told in this fascinating group of Georgian storehouses, which would have serviced Nelson's Fleet.

As you wander through you will learn of the life and career of Admiral Lord Nelson; a man hero-worshipped ever since the Battle of Trafalgar. You will discover how tough life was for sailors even until the beginning of World War II. Life in the Royal Navy in the twentieth century is another well documented story; the changing face of the Navy and of its ships and equipment. It is exciting to trace the development from sail to steam and then to the present nuclear submarines. Throughout your visit here you will find yourself learning about the general history of the centuries and seeing how it applied to sailors during those years.

The Museum has over 30 staff whose duties range from hosts to visitors, to curators. They are a welcoming and informative team who aid ones enjoyment considerably. The Museum's buffet serves a wide range of good, wholesome fare from sandwiches to mixed salads and home-cooked hot dishes. Perhaps for the sweet tooth the most tempting are the delicious gateau, cakes and pastries.

USEFUL INFORMATION

OPEN: 10am-5pm daily except Christmas and Boxing Day
CHILDREN: Welcome
CREDIT CARDS: None taken
LICENSED: No

RESTAURANT: Wide range from sandwiches and salads to hot dishes, gateau, cake and pastries
VEGETARIAN: Always a selection
DISABLED ACCESS: Ramped entrance to museum and buffet

COLLECTIF
Miniatures, Dolls & Teddy Bears

26 The Boardwalk, Port Solent Marina,
Portsmouth, PO6 4TP.

Tel: (0705) 214161
Fax: (0705) 214322

On the front of the attractive catalogue of this fascinating business is a quotation from Lewis Carroll, 'Oh, Kitty, how nice it would be if we could only get through into Looking-Glass House! I'm sure its got oh! such beautiful things in it.' No, Collectif does not have the key to get us into Looking-Glass House but it does open its doors to the magical world of miniatures. Almost everything for the house and shop in 1/12th scale plus miniature components which allow the DIY enthusiast to create their own.

To complement the miniatures is the most wonderful array of Teddy Bears and Dolls. Over 1,000 bears always in stock from Steiff and Hermann to special edition artist bears from Britain and America.

It is a bonus having such a wonderful position on the waterside at Port Solent but there can be no doubt that wherever Collectif was situated it would be sought out. In the last two and a half years they have successfully built up this business and have produced a superb catalogue for miniaturists which allows those who can not get to them in person to order what they will. Best of all if you can not get there, you are invited to ring the friendly staff who are more than willing to give their advice and ideas to help you fulfil your dreams in miniature.

USEFUL INFORMATION

OPEN: All year. Every day:10am-6pm
CHILDREN: Very welcome with their parents
CREDIT CARDS: Access/Visa/Master
DISABLED ACCESS: Yes
CAR PARKING: Free
MAIL ORDER: Yes
DIRECTIONS: From the west: Exit M27 Junction 12. From the east: Hilsea exit off A27 and follow signs to Port Solent

THE YACHT CLUB & CALM WATER RESTAURANT

Yacht Club & Restaurant

The Porthouse, Port Solent,
Portsmouth, Hampshire, PO6 4TH.

Tel: (0705) 370164
Fax: (0705) 325892

USEFUL INFORMATION

OPEN: 11-11pm later Friday & Saturday.
Sunday 11-6pm
CHILDREN: Welcome. Play area,
children's menu
CREDIT CARDS: Access/Visa/Diners/
Amex
LICENSED: Full Licence
ACCOMMODATION: Not applicable

RESTAURANT: Excellent choice,
sensible prices
BAR FOOD: Light snacks in Members Bar
VEGETARIAN: Choice at all courses
DISABLED ACCESS: Yes. Toilet & lift.
Assistance available
GARDEN: No. Verandah

The Yacht Club is situated on the top floor of The Port House in Port Solent Marina and offers an idyllic setting with commanding views across the Solent. Visitors to the Yacht Club are made very welcome within its relaxed atmosphere and few would not be tempted to sample the delicious and plentiful bar meals which members have always enjoyed. It is a lively place and provides live music every Friday and Saturday nights in the Member,s bar which is always a popular time.

The Calm Water Restaurant is one of Port Solent's great attractions. If you are lucky enough to get a window table you will be able to sit looking out on beautiful views and overlooking the Marina where 850 boats are berthed. Every day the menus, either A La Carte or Table d'Hote, offer a wide choice of dishes, all freshly cooked and using fresh local produce wherever possible. The service is efficient and friendly.

Within walking distance there is a medieval castle and more closely the Boardwalk offers exciting shops which surround The Yacht Club and with wonderful harbour views and a friendly atmosphere, it is easy to see why The Yacht Club and Calm Water Restaurant is a number one attraction for visitors.

Weddings and Conferences are catered for and organised to a high standard with a Head Chef who takes a pride on the selection of menus he can offer, and guarantees excellent value for money. You will find a visit to The Yacht Club more than worthwhile and temporary membership can be arranged.

PORTSMOUTH SEALIFE CENTRE

Visitor Attraction

Clarence Esplanade, Southsea,
Hampshire, PO1 3PB.

Tel: (0705) 734461
Fax: (0705) 294443

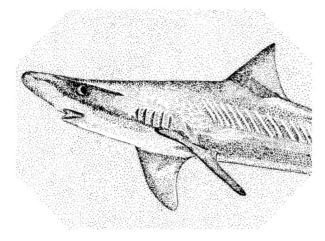

USEFUL INFORMATION

OPEN: Winter: 10am-6pm,
Summer: 10am-9pm
CHILDREN: Welcome. Birthday parties.
Splash pool, play area
CREDIT CARDS: All major cards
LICENSED: Restaurant Licence
ACCOMMODATION: Not applicable

RESTAURANT: Tasty, home-baked,
traditional
BAR FOOD: Not applicable
VEGETARIAN: 10 snacks & main meals
DISABLED ACCESS: All areas. Toilets
GARDEN: Sun terrace & BBQ. Splash
pool and play area

A magical world exists beneath the seas surrounding our own shores ... a world normally only glimpsed by trained divers. At Portsmouth Sea Life Centre, however there is a chance for everyone to experience the marvels of a deep-sea dive without even getting wet. Literally thousands of astonishing sea creatures are featured in spacious displays which recreate their natural habitats. Up to the minute aquarium technology has been employed to provide visitors with unimpaired views, from some amazing angles, of species ranging from simple shrimps and starfish to a variety of British sharks and rays. Even weird and wondrous creatures like the intelligent octopus, the sinister wolf-fish and the voracious trigger fish have their home here, along with the silvery shoals of bass and bream, sleek and dangerous conger eels and many, many more. Myrtle the giant green turtle is a firm favourite for many visitors, an illegal immigrant housed at the Centre on behalf of HM Customs until arrangements are made for her return to the wild off the coast of Florida.

Brand new is a dramatic exhibition - Shark Encounter, a journey through the jaws of a giant shark to see the bizarre contents of its stomach, to watch the unborn baby sharks wriggling in their protective egg cases, and to learn everything you ever wanted to know about the ocean's most efficient and most misunderstood predators. The displays themselves are a constantly moving feast, their occupants changing from time to time to reflect the shifting scene in the wild marine environment just a stone's throw from the Centre's back door! The summer of 1994 will see the opening of the new Sea-Lab enabling visitors to take a closer look and learn fascinating facts about our sea life.

87 Elm Grove, Southsea,
Hampshire, PO5 1JF.

Tel: (0705) 755944

ROSIE'S VINEYARD
Wine Bar & Bistro

For many, this is the only real wine bar on the south coast. It is stunning. It may take you a little effort to find it tucked away in Southsea but it is more than worth while. It is a lively unpretentious place, full of atmosphere and if you wonder about the mahogany fruit bins and floral stained glass it is because it had a previous existence as a greengrocers. The exterior you may feel is almost anonymous, hiding in a row of unimpressive shops and takeaways but inside there are three super bistro bars with a mass of greenery, one of which is a cellar, and at the back there is a fabulous 'Pergola' covered wine garden. Healthy, grape laden vines entwine themselves round the pergola and while you are sitting at the wooden tables you would be perfectly justified in thinking you were in France, or Amsterdam, even Berlin rather than Elm Grove in Southsea.

You are under a total misapprehension if you think Rosie's is the place for a gin and tonic. No spirits or beers ever enter its portals. You are here to savour and enjoy the superb selection of wines. You are welcome for drinks only although you are almost bound to be tempted by the excellent menu which can be anything from a full blown meal from an international menu to a dish of mussels. Just sitting sipping a glass of wine and soaking up the atmosphere is pleasure enough but there are also jazz evenings and other special occasions like the Beaujolais Nouveau run to Beaune or wine tastings which always seem to develop into a good party! Sunday lunchtime is good fun with the addition of jazz.

USEFUL INFORMATION

OPEN: Mon–Sat: 7-11pm. Sun: 12-3pm & 7-10.30pm
CHILDREN: Welcome till 8pm and for Sunday lunch
CREDIT CARDS: Visa/Mastercard
LICENSED: Full on. Wine only
ACCOMMODATION: Not applicable

RESTAURANT: Not applicable
BAR FOOD: Light bites available
VEGETARIAN: Always 2 main courses
DISABLED ACCESS: Small step at entrance. No toilet facilities
GARDEN: Pergola, covered wine garden

---

65 Festing Road, Southsea,
Portsmouth, Hampshire, PO4 0NQ.

Tel: (0705) 826971
Fax: (0705) 870200

WESTFIELD HALL HOTEL
Hotel & Restaurant

Probably Portsmouth's nicest family owned hotel, Westfield Hall has a warm, welcoming atmosphere where emphasis is on quality and value for money. The hotel has been run by the same family for over 14 years. With its additional RAC merit awards for hospitality and comfort, it is considered to be a firm favourite with the many visitors.

The 17 prestigious ensuite bedrooms are designed and furnished with your comfort in mind and include many convenient features, colour television with satellite entertainment, direct dial telephones, tea and coffee bar, and a hair dryer in all rooms.

The licensed restaurant can boast of freshly prepared dishes on the Table d'Hote menu which are changed daily and a wide variety on the A La Carte menu. Complement your meal with a choice from a selective range of wines from various European countries.

You can relax in the comfort of either the elegant front, or garden lounge or a short stroll to the beautiful rose gardens will bring you onto the seafront and promenade. For the continental ferry passengers, breakfast is served from 6.30am. The hotel is within easy reach of the city centre and continental ferry port. Car parking is simple and for those who would like to take advantage of a special winter break, there are wonderful discounted offers during December, January and February. There is also a Christmas celebration programme. Margaret and John Daniels, the owners, will tell you that 'Your Pleasure is our Business.'

USEFUL INFORMATION

OPEN: All year
CHILDREN: Yes
CREDIT CARDS: Visa/Access/Amex
LICENSED: Restaurant Licence
ACCOMMODATION: 17 ensuite. 4 crown commended. 2 star AA & RAC plus Comfort merit award

RESTAURANT: A la Carte & Table d'Hote, changed daily
BAR FOOD: On request
VEGETARIAN: On request
DISABLED ACCESS: Ground floor rooms, but difficult to restaurant
GARDEN: Beautiful private garden. Car parking with space for all guests

Rochester Cathedral

Rochester

"Tis a thing impossible, to frame
Conceptions equil to the soul's desires;
And the most difficult of tasks to *keep*
Hights which the soul is competent to gain."

William Wordsworth

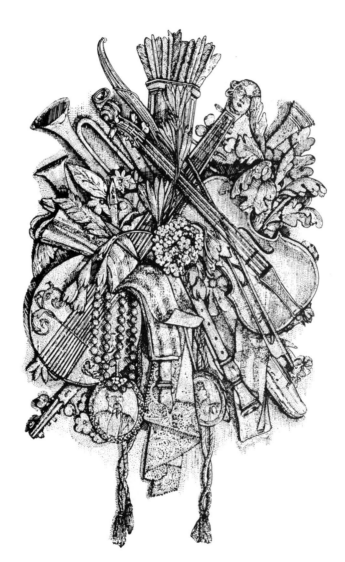

The City of Rochester

by Joy David

The Medway towns have always been places of great interest. Made up of Strood, Gillingham, Chatham and Rochester, they are steeped in history and none more so than the ancient cathedral city of Rochester on the lower reaches of the River Medway. It is a major port and an industrial centre and such a busy place but Rochester's older buildings are clustered around the cathedral and in the High Street, where they were confined by the medieval walls. The city is closely associated with the novelist Charles Dickens, and features more often in his books than any other place, apart from London, although Portsmouth, where he was born, has The Charles Dickens Birthplace Museum. Many great cities have been built around a river. Rochester is no exception; the River Medway winds its way through Rochester, Chatham and Strood which, collectively form the **City of Rochester-upon-Medway.**

Even before the Romans came Rochester had a settlement. Its Celtic name Durubruae means ' the bridges of the stronghold' It was this ability to cross over the Medway, on the route from Dover and Canterbury to London which gave the site its early strategic importance. You can still see traces of the walled city built by the Romans in The Esplanade and in Eagle Alley, where they were incorporated into Saxon and medieval fortifications. Not satisfied with the work of the Romans, the Saxons re-fortified Rochester about AD 600. Shortly after that the CHURCH OF ST ANDREWS was founded as the mother church and became second in importance only to Canterbury which had been established by St Augustine seven years earlier.

Rochester's Norman legacy cannot be missed. The great square keep of the CASTLE towers above the River Medway, a daunting reminder of the history of the city. It was on this site that the Romans originally built the first fort to guard the bridge which connected the Imperial Route of Watling Street, leading from London to Dover.

Many centuries later in 1087, Bishop Gundulf - one of William the Conqueror's finest architects - began construction on the Castle where many of the outer walls followed the same lines as their Roman originals. Now, the castle is known as one of the best preserved and finest examples of Norman architecture in England, measuring 113 feet high, 70 feet square and with walls 11 to 13 feet thick. The keep is the tallest in the country; visitors can wend their way up the circular staircase leading to the battlements and take in superb views of the city and surrounding countryside. The castle remained in the hands of the Archbishop of Canterbury until 1215 when it was seized after a two month siege by King John who used every resource available to gain control of the castle.

He even went to the lengths of mining underneath the South West tower of the keep and using the fat from forty pigs, he set fire to the pit props burning it down and finally gaining entry. Many of the curtain walls were built in the 12th and 13th century. Entry to the Castle Gardens from The Esplanade is via a mock Norman arch which was cut in the outer bastion by the Royal Engineers in 1872. The cannon at the top of the steps is a relic of the Crimean War. It is impressive, stern and imposing and evokes a rich tapestry of historic atmosphere which makes it worth a visit at any time of the year.

The Castle is open Good Friday-30th September, daily from 10am-6pm and from October 1st-31st March. Tuesday-Sunday 10am-4pm.

One of the most dramatic sights to be seen is the CATHEDRAL and Castle closeby each other, from across the Medway. There was a Cathedral here long before the great Norman Castle was built and this much loved building today stands besides the ruins of the Norman fortress. It is a Cathedral that ecclesiastically and architecturally has always been overshadowed by its neighbour at Canterbury. It stands however as 'a thing of beauty and a joy forever' in its own right. There is no longer any trace of the very first cathedral dedicated to St Andrew, though in 1889 some of its foundations were discovered by the west front and its apse is marked out in bronze in the nave. The great Lanfranc, Archbishop of Canterbury, appointed Gundulph bishop, and he set about building a new cathedral at the same time as he was creating his mighty castle. Of this building only the crypt survives. The new cathedral of St Andrew was consecrated in the presence of Henry I. As so often happened to medieval towns fire swept through Rochester shortly after the consecration, indeed as it did again in 1137 and 1179, and badly damaged the church. The nave was all that survived and this was incorporated in the present cathedral.

The West front survived all this, and dating from the first half of the 13th century is the east transept, choir and the presbytery.

In the crypt you will find an altar built for Ithamar, the first English Bishop. All over the place in the crypt you will find that medieval vandals have been at work leaving graffiti. The cuplrits were the soldiers of Simon de Montfort who sacked the Cathedral in 1264. Worth looking out for are the large collection of medieval wall paintings. Whilst many are now in fragments, the Wheel of Fortune in the Quire remains and is stunning.

The 13th century was an eventful time for the cathedral. In 1201 a baker called William of Perth, whose generous care of the poor was noted, was murdered by an ungrateful servant outside Rochester. He was on a pilgrimage to the Holy Land. His standing allowed him to be buried in the cathedral and soon, still grieving at his death, stories from those who came to see his tomb spread and these were of miracles that were occurring at his graveside. The monks, whilst not believing these unfounded tales, were nonetheless anxious to encourage them because more and more people were flocking to the church in order to pray for a miracle of their own. It was bonanza time for Rochester which had for so long been bypassed by the pilgrims on their way to Canterbury.

A shrine was built to the baker and he became known as St William, though he was never officially canonized. With the wealth that came from these visitors the monks were able to enlarge the cathedral during the late 13th and 14th centuries. The nave was completed and the central tower built, capped with a wooden spire. The money was also invested in what has to be the first and greatest of Rochester Cathedral's glories, the incredibly beautiful doorway leading to the chapter-house.

Throughout the centuries the cathedral has been restored, rebuilt, had new additions but it was completed finally in the 16th century. From that time we can still see the nave, the clerestory and great west window which date from the very end of the 15th century and the Lady Chapel from the first decade of the 16th. The dissolution of the monasteries was not kind to Rochester and in common with all our cathedrals it suffered much change. There were few monks there by then and only thirteen to be pensioned off when Henry VIII refounded the cathedral with a new dedication - to Christ and the Blessed Virgin Mary.

Rochester did not suffer as much as Canterbury during the Civil War. The Parliamentary soldiers, some of whom left their greatcoats in the crypt where they can still be seen, left the stonework alone and contented themselves with wrecking the altar rails and fairly minor damage. By the time of the Restoration the Cathedral was in a sad and sorry state and there were attempts from then onwards to repair and improve the fabric. In the 18th century the final touch was when the roof was releaded. George Gilbert Scott, Lewis Leadingham and finally J.L. Pearson were all responsible for restoration in the 19th century and in this year of 1993 the Cathedral has once again undergone a major refurbishment.

This may not be as rich a cathedral in treasures as some of our great Cathedrals but I love it for its sense of peace, of acceptance and tranquillity. I recommend it to anyone who has a love for these great buildings, so much part of our heritage.

The same sense of peace and tranquillity prevails outside the cathedral as it does within. Visitors can stroll through the Cloister Garth Gardens where some of the recently renovated monastic remains can be found. Beside the garden is the ST ANDREWS VISITORS CENTRE which was the original Deanery dating back to 1640.

Today the Cathedral serves the Diocese of Rochester, which resembles the lesser cathedrals of France, where dioceses are smaller than in England but far more numerous. Rochester has 200 parishes in West Kent and the London Boroughs of Bromley and Bexley with a population of well over, 1,000,000 people. Daily services are accompanied by a superb choir and one of the most magnificent organs in the country.

This, the second oldest in England is a regular place of pilgrimage for historians and worshippers alike. It has many visitors from all over the world who delight in its majesty even though it is much altered and reconstructed, with a spire dating only from the early years of this century.

Modern Rochester is a thriving buzzing centre, full of colour and activity. It has a wonderful choice of shops, restaurants and cafes, hotels and pubs, and a wealth of buildings of great architectural and historical interest. Take a stroll along the High Street and you will come across a whole range of architectural glory from CHERTSEY'S GATE. This is one of the old monastery precinct gates which has also been known as Jaspers Gate, Cemetery Gate and College Gate. It featured in Dickens' novel, 'The Mystery of Edwin Drood' as the gatehouse home of Mr John Jasper. In THE ROYAL VICTORIA AND BULL HOTEL you will find yourself drinking in a 400 year old hostelry that Dickens also loved and mentioned in two of his novels, Pickwick Papers and Great Expectations. At that time it would have been known as 'The Bull on the Hoope' however Princess Victoria, then the future Queen of England, stayed there for one night and it assumed its present name.

WATTS CHARITY, once again written about by Dickens, was endowed by Sir Richard Watts, an MP for the city in Elizabethan times, to house, 'six poor travellers' for one night each. Whilst the house is mainly Tudor, the front was added in 1771. It is open from March 1st-31st October from Tuesday to Saturday inclusive from 2pm-5pm.

THE CORN EXCHANGE built in 1698 was originally the Butcher's Market. In 1706 the ornate frontage was added at the expense of Admiral Sir Cloudesley Shovell MP, who lost his life when his ship, laden with treasure, sank off the Isles of Scilly. The original clock, which was smaller and square in shape, was replaced in 1771. It was not until the first part of the 19th century that the building became the Corn Exchange.

Here, too, you will find LA PROVIDENCE, a delightful Victorian square which was restored in 1960 to provide homes for people of Huguenot descent, hence the name.

THE GUILDHALL must be one of the finest 17th century civic buildings in Kent. Here again Admiral Sir Cloudesley Shovell's generosity can be seen at work. It is he who provided the money to decorate, quite magnificently, the plaster ceilings. He was Member of Parliament for the City at the time. His portrait can be found in the main chamber, along with those of other notable MP's for Rochester. Outside, mounted on the cupola on the roof, is a superb gilded weathervane in the form of a fully rigged 18th century warship. This vane has weathered the ever changing climates since 1780. The building houses the main Museum of Rochester since 1979. However in 1993 part of the museum will move to the adjoining CONSERVANCY WING whilst the Guildhall undergoes refurbishment. Using the latest audio visual techniques, the Conservancy Wing brings alive decades of local music halls, theatres and domestic entertainment. Also on display are exhibitions of Victoriana dolls and toys, and old photographs. The Guildhall and Maine Museum re-opened in June 1993 and has striking new display features including a special themed two-tier gallery recreating a Medway Prison Hulk of the Napoleonic period, illustrating the terrible conditions in which the prisoners were held.

The Romans, the Vikings, the Normans all have passed through Rochester, leaving their mark on this historic city which can have few equals. SATIS HOUSE, BAKERS WALK originally was a huge 16th century mansion, a part of which were Longley House, the Friars and the Old Hall. Queen Elizabeth I added her Royal stamp to the house when she visited it in 1573. Ever since it has been known as Satis House. It is not open to the public. Elizaberth I also visited OLD HALL, a house which contains some particularly fine wall paintings. This also is not open to the public.

Then there is THE VINES, once a vineyard frequented by the monks in medieval times now providing a peaceful haven for visitors. BRIDGE CHAPEL on The Esplanade was originally built as a small chapel for the 14th century bridge but is now used as the office of the Bridge Wardens who maintain Rochester Bridge.

I think ST MARGARET'S STREET is well worth visiting. It is a lovely old street which runs southwards from the Cathedral and Castle. BISHOPCOURT, the present Bishop's Palace can be found here; it was initially bequeathed to the Bishops of Rochester in 1674 for 'maintenance of hospitality near the cathedral' THE COOPERS ARMS is a charming old inn which could have been visited by the pilgrims as they passed through Rochester on their way to Canterbury and the Continent. The 15th century medieval tower and belfry of ST MARGARET'S CHURCH are still standing today, whilst the rest of the church was built around them between 1824 and 1840.

The most perfect of Rochester's three surviving 14th century monastic gates is PRIOR'S GATE which leads from St Margaret's Street to Minor Canon Row. One of our great actresses, Dame Sybil Thorndike arrived in Rochester when she was just 18 months old after her father was made a Canon of the Cathedral in 1884. The family lived at No 2 Minor Canon Row, which is a row of seven charming 18th century houses at the rear of the Cathedral, and feature in Dickens Novel 'The Mystery of Edwin Drood'.

All sorts of famous and historical people have visited Rochester. King John led a force of rebel barons who seized the Castle. Henry VIII came here twice during his long reign. The first time was during a visit with Charles V, Emperor of Germany. The second time was to meet his future fourth wife, Anne of Cleves, at the King's Palace for the first time. Sir Francis Drake learnt the laws of seamanship at Chatham, Sir John Hawkins founded a hospital for 'decayed mariners' at Chatham, King Charles II landed at Dover on 25th May 1660 to begin his journey to London where he took up his crown once more. King James II spent his last night under guard at 'Abdication House' now Lloyd's Bank in the High

Street, in December 1689. From here he escaped to the continent and was never to return. Admiral Lord Nelson, started his service in the navy at Chatham when he was 12 years old. Later his most celebrated ship, The Victory, was built at Chatham and launched in 1765. He was known to have stayed in THE MITRE at Chatham.

The Short Brothers set up their aircraft works in 1913 at Rochester Esplanade. They were perhaps best known for their flying boats with such great names as the Empire Flying Boat, Sunderland Flying Boats and Stirling Bombers. Models of the aircraft can be seen in the Guildhall Museum.

Charles Dickens loved Rochester, Chatham and the surroundings. He spent the happiest years of his young life at No 2 Ordnance Terrace, Chatham. The Royal Dockyard was a constant source of fascination to Dickens as a small boy. He was fascinated by the skills of the rope-makers, the blacksmiths, the anchor smiths, and he had a morbid interest in the convict hulks moored out in the Medway. Later he was to record them in Great Expectations. He never forgot the Medway and its towns and it is fitting that he should be equally remembered at THE CHARLES DICKENS CENTRE AND EASTGATE HOUSE. Eastgate House acquired its name from Eastgate Street, the former name of the section of the High Street in which it stands. It was built in 1590 for Sir Peter Buck, once Alderman and Mayor of the City of Rochester and Clerk of the Cheque at Chatham Dockyard. Towards the end of the 18th century the house became a boarding school for young ladies and remained so until well into the 19th century. Dickens would have known the school portrayed in Pickwick Papers as 'Westgate House' in Bury St Edmunds. In 1897 in honour of Queen Victoria's Diamond Jubilee, Eastgate House was established as a museum. In 1979 the City Museum was moved to the Guildhall and THE

CHARLES DICKENS CENTRE was created. Today it is an award winning attraction which uses the very latest audio visual technology to bring to life the vivid characters and scenes of Dickens' novels, depicting much of the grim reality of Victorian England.

The centre contains a dramatic tableau in which state-of-the-art special effects are used to bring to life 'Dickens Dream' based on the famous painting in which many of his characters visit him whilst he dozes in his study. Visitors will also want to visit the theatre which gives regular video presentations of Charles Dickens' life and work.

Standing in the gardens of Eastgate House is the Swiss Chalet from Gads Hill, Dickens' last home. It was presented to Dickens in 1864 by a French actor called Charles Fechter and arrived at Higham railway station packed in 58 packing cases. Dickens used the chalet as a summer house and study and was writing the final chapters of 'The Mystery of Edwin Drood' in the upstairs room just before his death on the 9th June 1870. Unfortunately because the chalet is rather fragile, it is not open to the public but may be viewed from the outside.

Eastgate House and The Charles Dickens Centre are open daily from 10am-5.30pm. Closed Christmas period and New Year.

Found on the ciling of the Nave crossing there are four masks on the bosses, above is the foliate mask

The Maritime past is all important. The city owes its very existence to the River Medway. It is all remembered at THE MEDWAY HERITAGE which tells the story of the River Medway using photographs, paintings, models and artifacts. Visitors can familiarise themselves with every aspect of this busy, working river together with the men and women who worked beside it and sailed upon its waters. Nelson and Drake, Short and Aveling, the Royal Dockyard, the Kent Oil Refinery, the bridges – they all have stories to tell, whether they're about flying boats or steam rollers. Ships play a central role in the exhibition; from HMS Victory which majestically swept along the river's shores, to the barges, steam ships and the very last 'doble'.

If you were under the impression that the song 'Waltzing Matilda' originated in Australia you would be very mistaken. It was in fact a Medway marching song. Sung by the soldiers of the area, it was picked up by the convicts on the hulks and taken to Australia where it became the popular folk song we all know about.

You will find the Centre at St Mary's Church, Dock Road, **Chatham**. It is open Wednesday and Sunday from October to Easter. From Easter to end of September, open every day except Monday and Tuesday. 10am - 4pm weekdays and 2pm-5pm Sundays.

Chatham has many other interesting places including FORT LUTON. This former 'Palmerston Folly' of the 19th century was built like the other Medway Forts, to protect Chatham from a possible French invasion. It has now been restored and contains four and a half acres of gardens, ponds, animals and tunnels full of strange and wonderful models, visiting exhibitions, Victorian street, shops and a tea room. It is open every day except Christmas 10am-4pm weekdays and 10am-6pm weekends and Bank Holidays.

THE HISTORIC DOCKYARD at Chatham has been there for over four hundred years and no less than 400 Royal Navy ships were built here. In 1547 during the reign of Henry VIII, the first storehouse was rented to service the king's ships at anchor in The Medway, many of the ships which took part in the defeat of the Spanish Armada in 1588 sailed from Chatham, having been carefully prepared by the yard's shipwrights.

What you will see today is 80 acres of shipbuilding history spread out before you. There are no less than 47 Scheduled Ancient Monuments, forming the most completely preserved Georgian dockyard in the world. dry docks and covered slips, timber mast houses and seasoning sheds, huge storehouses and the quarter mile long working ropery stand beside the elegant Commissioner's house and garden, officers' terrace and dockyard church. Now a living, working museum this Historic Dockyard tells of the lives of the dockyard craftsmen whose skills - from carpentry and caulking to rigging and forging - made the British fleet the finest in the world. No one can fail to be fascinated by what they see. With seven main attractions plus skills and crafts in action, it is not suprising visitors stay on average 5 hours.

I have no doubt that you will need to drop into the WHEELWRIGHTS RESTAURANT for coffee, tea or lunch. Alternatively there are open and covered picnic areas in which you can relax before continuing your own voyage of discovery. Themed gifts are also available in the three museum galleries or you can order souvenirs from the Dockyard's resident historic artists and craftsmen.

Open: 28th March-30th October, Wednesday-Sunday and Bank Holidays from 10am-6pm 31st October-26th March open Wednesday, Saturday and Sunday from 10am-4.30pm.

Also in Chatham is FORT AMHERST built in 1756 to protect the Royal Naval Dockyard from landward attack. Fort Amherst is a thrilling complex of underground chambers and tunnels. Between 1802-11 it underwent substantial renovation in which French prisoners of war were set to work to extend the tunnels and create vast underground stores and shelters, new magazines, barracks, gun batteries and guardrooms. Finally over 50 smooth bore cannons were mounted, some of which can still be heard on each Sunday throughout the year and every day during the school holidays, as the resident garrison re-enacts scenes from the fort's history.

Visit the towering bastions or the massive gatehouse which has also been restored to its original form and now contains a small museum. The upper floor barrack rooms have been faithfully refurbished to show the exact conditions in which Wellington's 'scum of the earth' had to live. Most Friday evenings lantern light ghost tours wend their eerie way through the fort.

Opening hours are daily except Christmas Day from 10.30am-5.30pm

Also in Chatham is THE ROYAL ENGINEERS MUSEUM which provides a fascinating insight into the debt and the part played by our soldier engineers in our past to the present day. The thinking which led to fortifications such as Rochester Castle and the protective works around the Dockyard are revealed.

The museum's collection has something for everyone; medals, uniforms, weapons, equipment and personal mementos including the map used by Wellington at Waterloo. More unexpected are the treasures collected by the Royal Engineers as they travelled the world with the 19th century Imperial Army, such as the Court Dress presented to General Charles Gordon for his military service to the Chinese Imperial Authorities in the 1860's.

The First and Second World War galleries give visitors a feel for life during the more gruelling parts of the 20th century. The grim reality of life in the First World War trenches, the glaring beams of Second World War searchlights and through a glimpse at a Medway family at home, the tensions of life under threat of invasion in 1940.

Exhibitions, reconstructions, moving models, sound effects - all work to provide an exhilirating experience that will transport some back in time and rekindle memories in others.

Open: All Year. Monday to Thursday plus Spring and Summer Bank Holidays from 10am-5pm.

Throughout the year the city organises a lively programme of events. Some bring the colourful past to life whilst others very much celebrate the present day. Rochester Chimney Sweeps Festival, the Dickens Festival, Medway Sports Festival, Medway Arts Festival, Norman Rochester and the Dickensian Christmas are all superb occasions, beautifully organised and gaining in strength every year. Rochester-upon-Medway is an exciting, vibrant place.

Outside there are many delightful places, including **Strood**, of course. First of all somewhere to stay that is rural and charming. THE OAST MANOR HOTEL at **Hempstead**, **Gillingham** is just off the M2 motorway but stands in beautiful secluded countryside. It is an elegant, country house style hotel. Recently the hotel has been sympathetically refurbished to provide modern facilities without detracting from its unique character and charm.

It is not easy to conjure up the time when Oast Manor was a 19th century oast house used for hop drying and with its attendant cottages built of Kentish Ragstone. The conversion has been done beautifully and the moment you enter the panelled reception area you know that your care and comfort is the first priority of the well trained and friendly staff. The restaurant offers a comprehensive menu but sufficiently limited to make sure that quality is paramount. The dishes are imaginative and beautifully presented. This is a family run hotel in the best tradition.

Mentioned in the Domesday Book, **Burham** is a quiet peaceful, beautiful and very friendly village, just outside Rochester. An ideal place to go for a drink or a meal, THE WINDMILL which started life as a cottage has gradually grown into a full scale village pub. The name is derived from a windmill just a quarter of a mile away. It is a pub to which one could easily become addicted. The landlords, Liz and Derek Powell are two welcoming people who have made a lot of friends in the neighbourhood. Every day you will find cheerful banter at the bar and no one remains a stranger for long. Generally speaking the menu is traditional English but every now and again Jan, the Powell's daughter puts on what her father describes as 'Funny food evenings.' In other words theme menus which may be Italian, Chinese or Mexican. These evenings are great fun and the food is terrific.

Eighteen miles from Rochester and six miles from Maidstone THE SHANT HOTEL & PRINCE OF WALES at **East Sutton** is an excellent hostelry and is known for many miles around. There are 16 bedrooms altogether, all en suite. The dining facilities are extensive and The Shant is very well equipped to deal with conferences, dinners and especially wedding receptions. Pets are allowed in the hotel by arrangement.

There is a wonderful experience to be had at IDEN CROFT HERBS, Frittenden Road, **Staplehurst.** It is lie taking a step back in time. As you wander through beautiful gardens, delicate perfumes fill the air and all is peaceful. It has to be everyone's idea of heaven. It is possibly the largest herb garden in Britain. Well laid out paths take you on a voyage of discovery through a series of lovely gardens, filled with roses and herbs towards a delightful walled garden. Every now and again you will come across seats which allow you to sit and just soak in the calm, aromatic atmosphere. There are thousands of plants for sale and it is with a sense of satisfaction that you leave Iden Croft Herbs, largely because the door to the magical world of herbs has been opened sufficiently to give one the desire to discover more.

THE NATURE RESERVE AND BIRD SANCTUARY north of **High Halstow** village at

The intricacy and splendour of the Gothic Chapter Room door

Northward Hill is an RSPB nature reserve which contains the largest heronry in the UK. Ideally situated, the surrounding marshlands provide a natural habitat for hundreds of species of both well known and rare aquatic birds.

There are several interesting churches in the villages surrounding Rochester. St Helen's Church at **Cliffe** was founded in the late 8th century but the church you see today was built in the 13th century of alternate bands of flint and Kentish ragstone. The decorated pillars and painted walls are particularly worth noting.

At **Cooling**, St James' Church was originally built in the 10th century. Norman additions were made a little later. The graveyard has been immortalised by Dickens who described the '13 lozenge-shaped tombstones'as the graves of Pip's brothers and sisters in Great Expectations. **Hoo** has the 13th century church with a massive tower and elegant shingled spire. In Strood High Street, St Nicholas Church is odd. Whilst the main body of the church was built between 1812-1814, the original medieval tower is still standing..

Upnor is an attractive riverside village worth exploring. It has beome a very popular sailing centre. The 'Arethusa' training ship is based here. UPNOR CASTLE was originally built in 1559 to protect the Naval Dockyard from attack from the river. Although the castle was an important link in the defence line it was not well maintained and proved ineffective when the Dutch sailed up the Medway on the 10th June 1667 to attack the Dockyard. The Dutch met very little resistance, when they left two days later they had destroyed and captured a large number of the Royal Navy ships anchored at Chatham. The Castle became a magazine for ordnance stores in 1668. Since then many more river defences were built to prevent such a disaster ever happening again.

For all the beauty and interest of the surrounding countryside it is the lure of historic Rochester and its fine Cathedral which will make you want to spend as much time as you can here.

Rochester Road, Burham,
Nr. Rochester, Kent, ME1 3RJ.

Tel: (0634) 861919

THE WINDMILL
Public House & Restaurant

Mentioned in the Domesday Book, Burham is a quiet, peaceful, beautiful and very friendly village. The Windmill has added to its charm ever since one of the bars was a cottage; that was back in 1847. The name is derived from a windmill just a quarter of mile away.

Owned by Liz and Derek Powell, two welcoming people who have made a lot of friends in the area and who have an established reputation for the welcoming hospitality that abounds at the Windmill, it is a pub to which one can become easily addicted.

Every day you will find cheerful chatter at the bar and no one remains a stranger for long. It is your choice whether you eat in the attractive restaurant or more informally in the bar. The menu is traditional English, beautifully cooked, well presented and more than generous in its portions. One dish is 'Burham Poacher's Pie' which is a delicious concotion of sausagemeat, herbs and onions on a pastry base with potato and cheese topping. From time to time Jan, the Powell's daughter puts on what her father describes as 'Funny food evenings'! In other words theme menus which may be Italian, Chinese or Mexican. These evenings are great fun and the food is terrific. The wine list, which is small, has some excellent wines at sensible prices. Well behaved children are very welcome.

USEFUL INFORMATION

OPEN: Mon-Sat: 11.30-3pm & 6-11pm. Sun: Normal hours
CHILDREN: Dining room only. Well behaved
CREDIT CARDS: None taken
LICENSED: Full & Supper Licence
ACCOMMODATION: Not applicable

RESTAURANT: Good, traditional English
BAR FOOD: Wide range of snacks. Daily specials
VEGETARIAN: Always available
DISABLED ACCESS: Yes
GARDEN: Seating only. Lawns to play on

Chatham,
Kent, ME4 4TE.

Tel: (0634) 812551
Fax: (0634) 826918

THE HISTORIC DOCKYARD
Visitor Attraction

The skill and thought that has gone into making this historic Dockyard a tourist attraction is undoubted. What they have achieved is an exciting outing for people of all ages which not only intrigues but thrills and informs. There are 80 acres of ship-building history in which you can relive the building of sail-powered warships for the Royal Navy through the award winning Wooden Walls Gallery. With seven main attractions plus skills and crafts in action, it is not surprising visitors stay on average five hours.

Chatham has been a Royal Dockyard for over 400 years providing Britain with over 400 of her great fighting ships, including Trafalgar's finest wooden warships: HMS Victory, Revenge, Temeraire and Leviathan - the 'Wooden Walls of England'. It all started in 1547 when Henry VIII rented a storehouse to service his fleet at anchor in the River Medway. The first warship built for the Royal Navy at Chatham, the Sunne, launched in 1586, was among the fleet sent to meet the Armada. The last, HM Submarine Ocelot, was launched from No 7 Covered Slip in 1962. In 1984 the Dockyard was placed in the care of the Chatham Historic Dockyard Trust. Within its 80 acres stand 47 Scheduled Ancient Monuments, forming the most completely preserved Georgian dockyard in the world. Dry docks and covered slips, timber mast houses and seasoning sheds, huge storehouses and the quarter mile long working ropery stand beside the elegant Commissioner's House, Garden Officers' Terrace and Dockyard Church. Tour by horse-drawn wagon or cruise the River Medway aboard Britain's last working coal-fired paddle-steamer in summer. It is all wonderful.

USEFUL INFORMATION

OPEN: Summer. Easter-Oct 30th, 7 days a week. Feb/Mar/Nov open Wednesday and weekends
CHILDREN: Very welcome. Special prices, play area, baby changing facilities
CREDIT CARDS: Access/Visa
ACCOMMODATION: Not applicable

RESTAURANT: Licensed. Tea Room in summer
VEGETARIAN: Always dishes
DISABLED ACCESS: Very good. Lifts & free helpers
GARDEN: To look at only. Indoor & Outdoor picnic areas

THE SHANT HOTEL & PRINCE OF WALES

Public House, Hotel & Restaurant

East Sutton, Nr Maidstone,
Kent, ME17 3DT.

Tel: (0622) 842235

USEFUL INFORMATION

OPEN: 7 days, 7.30pm until mid night
CHILDREN: Welcome. Family rooms by request
CREDIT CARDS: Access/Visa/Amex
LICENSED: Full On Licence
ACCOMMODATION: 16 en-suite rooms

RESTAURANT: Wide range. Everything is freshly cooked
BAR FOOD: From light snacks to main meals
VEGETARIAN: Looked after individually
DISABLED ACCESS: One step at entrance
GARDEN: Large gardens with seating

The Shant Hotel stands in beautiful rural countryside some six miles from Maidstone and eighteen from Rochester Cathedral. It is a hostelry that is well known not only in East Sutton but for many miles around for its accommodation and for its food. Built in a traditional Kentish style it has a large inglenook fireplace and inside it is heavily timbered. New additions have been made including bedrooms which are only three years old. All the extensions have been done tastefully and carefully in keeping with their surroundings and the bedrooms are all furnished in an attractive Country Style which fits in beautifully.

There are 16 bedrooms altogether, all en-suite and all with colour TV, and that boon to the traveller, tea and coffee making facilities. The dining facilities are extensive and The Shant is very well equipped to deal with conferences, dinners and especially wedding receptions. Pets are allowed in the hotel by arrangement.

Colin and Sue Botley have owned The Shant for nine years and in that time they have made sure that the standard of their food is both extensive and excellent. The menus cover everything from a light snack to a full meal. Everything is fresh and cooked to order. The Shant specialises in Real Ales, always offering at least seven variations whilst the wine list has traditional wines and a very good selection of wines from the New World and even offers a wine grown and produced just half a mile away at East Sutton Wine Garden.

OAST MANOR HOTEL

Hotel

1 Star Lane, Hempstead,
Gillingham, Kent, ME7 3NN.

Tel: (0634) 376615
Fax: (0634) 234360

USEFUL INFORMATION

OPEN: 24 hours, 365 days of the year
CHILDREN: Allowed. No special facilities
CREDIT CARDS: Visa/Mastercard
LICENSED: Full On licence
ACCOMMODATION: 10 bedrooms, ensuite

RESTAURANT: Fresh local produce. Imaginative
BAR FOOD: Traditional pub fare
VEGETARIAN: Always four dishes
DISABLED ACCESS: Level entrance. Ground floor bedrooms. No special facilities
GARDEN: Picturesque and extensive. Patio. BBQ. Pool

The beautiful secluded countryside makes an idyllic setting for The Oast Manor, an elegant country house style hotel. You will find it just off the M2 motorway and close to the host of attractions and pageantry of historic Rochester. Recently the hotel has been sympathetically refurbished to provide modern facilities without detracting from its unique character and charm.

It is not easy to conjure up the time when Oast Manor was a 19th century oast house used for hop drying and with its attendant cottages built of Kentish Ragstone. The conversion has been done beautifully and from the moment you enter the panelled reception area you know that your care and comfort is the first priority of the well trained and friendly staff. The attractive bedrooms are ensuite and every one has colour television, in house video, radio alarms, direct dial telephone and a beverage tray. For a honeymoon or special occasion the 'Peacock Suite' has a wonderful four poster bed and a stay in the 'Dynasty Suite' will always be memorable.

Downstairs the welcoming resident's bar, with its views of the countryside and the Oast Manor's four acres of picturesque gardens, is a pleasureable place to be at any time and especially whilst enjoying a drink before dining. You can enjoy evening meals and lunches seven days a week, including the excellent traditional Sunday lunches. The restaurant offers a comprehensive menu but sufficiently limited to make sure that quality is paramount. The dishes are imaginative and beautifully presented. This is a family run hotel in the best tradition.

City of Rochester upon Medway,
Kent, ME2 4AW.

Tel: (0634) 843666
Fax: (0634) 732756

CITY OF 'GREAT EXPECTATIONS'
Hisroric Attractions

Rochester is dominated by an 11th century castle and cathedral, both built within a few years of each other. Together they serve as dramatic landmarks dominating virtually every view of the city. The cathedral is England's second oldest while the castle is the finest Norman Keep in the country. The narrow streets and alleys that fan out from the castle walls, have been carefully preserved by the city authorities. Retaining the charm that centuries of history have bestowed on them, they form the living stage for a variety of festivals throughout the year including Norman Rochester (August), the Sweeps Festival (May), the Arts Festival (July), Dickens Festival (June), and the increasingly popular Dickensian Christmas weekend in December. Charles Dickens set many of his famous works in Rochester including the Pickwick Papers, Great Expectations and his last, uncompleted, The Mystery of Edwin Drood.

Away from the centre of Rochester there is more to see, much of it reflecting the areas long and proud military traditions. The historic dockyard at Chatham was founded by Henry VIII and played a vital role in defending our shores for over 400 years. Today it is an award winning, working museum reflecting the life, times and skills of maritime England – the 80 acre site is literally 'alive with surprises'. Nearby is Napoleonic Fort Amherst with its tunnels and 18th century re-enactments and the excellent Royal Engineers Museum. Other attractions include Fort Luton, Medway Heritage Centre and the Kingswear Castle Paddle Steamer. The Napoleonic era is also graphically recalled at Rochester's Guildhall Museum, which has undergone considerable internal construction to house a major new exhibit depicting the hardships of being among the French prisoners of war held in the area. They were imprisoned on floating hulks in the River Medway in conditions so appalling that many thousands died. Yet many still managed to create intricate works of art, some of which are on show in the new display, which takes the form of a reconstruction of the interior of one of these dreaded hulks.

Only, 30 miles from London, and 40 miles from the Channel ports, the City's attractions and easy location make it an ideal visit.

Frittenden Road, Staplehurst,
Kent, TN12 0DH.

Tel: (0580) 891432
Fax: (0580) 892416

IDEN CROFT HERBS
Herb Gardens & Centre

Step back in time. Wander through beautiful gardens. Delicate perfumes fill the air and all is peaceful. Everyone's idea of heaven. Where is this perfect place? Iden Croft Herb Gardens and Centre, possibly the largest herb garden in the United Kingdom, run by Rosemary and David Titterington. Paths take you through a series of lovely gardens filled with roses and herbs, towards a delightful Victorian walled garden. Relax on one of the many seats, enjoy the calm, aromatic atmosphere.

There are thousands of plants for sale in well laid out beds. Iden Croft's own information labels help plant collectors to make the best selection, any questions just ask the new information centre. A very special section is home to two national collections of herbs and is planted with Mint, Origanum, Sedum, Thyme and Lavenders. Visitors will be fascinated by the herb shop and with the many interesting herb products on sale.

Rosemary and Gemma (the Jack Russell) enjoy taking children for a woodland walk, visiting the home-made garden gnomes and small play area. Rosemary is always receiving lovely letters from children about the gardens and Gemma has her own fan club; she is always found trotting around the garden.

Disabled people are made very welcome at the centre and Rosemary and David do all they can to make their visit relaxing. Visit the tearooms for light refreshments, cream teas, home-made cakes and real ice cream. Throughout the year, monthly tours and demonstrations are organised. Rosemary and David encourage as many people as possible to learn more about the beauty and use of herbs, and the interest and pleasures to be obtained fom them.

USEFUL INFORMATION

OPEN: All year round. Mon–Sat: 9–5pm
Sundays & Bank Holidays, Mar–Sep 11–5pm
CHILDREN: Very welcome
CREDIT CARDS: Visa/Access
LICENSED: Not applicable
ACCOMMODATION: Not applicable

RESTAURANT: Not applicable
BAR FOOD: Not applicable
VEGETARIAN: Always something on request
DISABLED ACCESS: Full. Garden walks. Toilets, shop
GARDEN: Seating on patio and in gardens. Herb & cottage garden. Garden for the disabled

Salisbury Cathedral

Salisbury

"Thou does preserve the stars from wrong;
And the most ancient heavens, through Thee,
are fresh and strong."

William Wordsworth

The City of Salisbury

by Jane Drake

Approach **Salisbury** from whichever road you choose and you will not fail to see the Cathedral spire. Ride along the ring road, and the Cathedral dominates in a gentle, graceful way, above the old terracotta roofs. Enter the city and you will see the wall of the Close, or the High Street with its gate into the Close, or the river with its walk towards Chuch House, the headquarters of the Diocese of Salisbury. Almost wherever you go in Salisbury you will be somewhere that owes its existance to the Cathedral, so that is the place in which we should start our exploration of this Cathedral City.

SALISBURY CATHDRAL was once described as the most perfect building in Northern Europe. Unlike many other cathedrals which evolved slowly over centuries and therefore show different styles of architecture in one building, the whole of the Cathedral Church of the Blessed Virgin Mary at Salisbury was built in less than one hundred years. This included the spire, which is renowned as one of the tallest of any English Cathedral. John Constable's paintings of the water meadows of the Avon, showing the graceful spire rising above them, are familiar to many and are a well-loved image of England at its most tranquil. Other artists have also been inspired by Salisbury Cathedral, notably Bill Toop, whose

SALISBURY GALLERY in Exeter Street, between the King's Arms and the White Hart, is well worth a visit.

Salisbury Cathedral's great spire was the work of an unknown master mason. If you think about it, it was a truly stupendous achievement. After all, in 1285, or thereabouts, there was none of the modern technology without which we would find it impossible to build any building bigger than a dog-kennel. All the mathematical calculations had to be done 'by hand' (in the old fashioned way using drawn plans and sums). The sixty-thousand odd tons of stone needed for the Cathedral had to be dug from the ground at **Chilmark**, some 12 miles west of Salisbury.

Having performed this Herculean task, the stone had to be squared and transported. The transportation (which took place between March and October to avoid the winter weather) was done at the rate of ten cart loads per day, each cart being pulled by oxen. Imagine all the carters, wheelwrights, smiths and carpenters involved in the transportation of stone, of the thirst and hunger that it would create, and it is immediately clear why Salisbury has so many inns and alehouses.

All this superhuman effort depended, in the final analysis, on the skill of the unknown master mason responsible for the design of the spire. There wasn't anywhere for him to practise spire-building. He had to get it right first time! You can see the interior wooden scaffolding of the spire,

put in place all those years ago and still there today, if you go on a tour of the roof.

In fact, you can see from the tower crossing in the Cathedral (directly below the spire), that the enormous weight caused the four columns that support the tower and spire to bend slightly. To prevent them from collapsing inwards, great strainer arches were built about 135 years later at the entrance to the choir transept.

Our twentieth-century masons still work in the mason's yard outside the cloisters, repairing and refurbishing where necessary. They, of course, have access to modern refinements, and have recently completed essential work to the spire, for which the magnificent sum of £6.5 million was raised. The years of the Spire Appeal are now over, and the scaffolding, so long a familiar sight to Salisbury dwellers, is gone. The masons have done their essential work of repair, following the techniques of the medieval builders who erected it in the first place.

Masonry is not the only ancient skill practised by cathedral craftsmen. In the north choir aisle you can see a leaded window made in the Cathedral workshop, and if you look carefully you will see Ginger, the works cat.

The brilliant, translucent colour of the Prisoners of Conscience Window in the east end of the Cathedral was made in the Chartres workshop of Gabriel and

Jacques Loire (father and son). In 1980 it was installed in Salisbury Cathedral and unveiled by Yehudi Menuhin. It seems impossible that anyone could see its colour and vibrancy - the use of medieval blue glass like that in Chartres Cathedral is striking - and pass by without waiting to know what it means. To paraphrase the Dean of Salisbury, the Very Reverend S.H. Evans, the Prisoners of Conscience are men and women who, at the cost of mental anguish, pysical pain, spiritual humiliation, isolation or premature death, have upheld by non-violent witness the dignity of the human person against falsehood and tyranny. The pull of this window is great. I have never been near it without finding that many other people are near to it too, looking and wondering. The short Pitkin Guide to the Prisoners of Conscience Window is invaluable if you want to know more.

An even newer piece of craftsmanship can be found in the Morning Chapel. Here you will see a memorial to the artist Rex Whistler. A prism of glass engraved by Rex's brother, Laurance, stands within a bronze lantern on a Purbeck corbel, worked in the traditional thirteenth-century manner by an apprentice. The Purbeck stone for the corbel was taken in 1985 from an area that once supplied the Cathedral.

'As many days as in one year there be,
So many windows in one church we see;
As many marble pillars there appear,
As there are hours throughout the fleeting year;
As many gates as moons one year to view;
Strange tale to tell, yet not more strange than true.'

This rhyme is in fact correct, as you can prove to yourself while you walk around the Cathedral. On the way you might like to notice the plate in the north aisle (just around the corner from the north transept) that indicates the water level during a flood in January 1915. The

cathedral, being low lying has been flooded several times and the clergy forced to ride it on horseback.

Outside the nave, the cloisters, it is possible to take brass rubbings. Exact replicas of brasses from English churches have been made by specialists, and for a small fee you can make your own rubbings without fear of eroding the ancient brasses.

In the Chapter House one of the four remaining copies of the Magna Carta is kept on display to the public. The Chapter House itself is remarkable for the beautiful vaulting that rises from a single central pillar. Below the windows run a freize of sixty stone sculptures depicting Old Testament stories. Apparently in the thirteenth century, when they were painted and gilded. Not only the Old Testament sculptures in the Chapter House, but many other parts of the Cathedral too. I remember the first time I entered Salisbury Cathedral quite clearly. There was an overwhelming impression of greyness. It is so lofty, and long, and without any 'clutter' such as you often find in cathedrals that have been added to at different times. It has its colourful corners and details, such as the Moses window above the High Altar, and the wall decoration beneath it, and the vaulting painted with roundels at the choir crossing. They are beautiful, but were whitewashed over in the eighteenth century by James Wyatt, who was

The tomb of Giles de Bridport who was bishop when Salisbury Cathedral was consecrated in 1258

called in to 'restore' the Cathedral. It is easy, with the benefit of handsight, to criticise the work of others. It seems that when the Cathedral was built it was a colourful probably noisy, and certainly very well used place. But religious beliefs changed and medieval stained glass, for one thing, fell foul of ignorant iconoclasts at the Reformation and during the Civil War. So by the time James Wyatt came along the Cathedral must have looked in a very sorry sight and he could only do what seemed right to an ordered eighteenth-century mind.

If you look for the colourful corners you will be well rewarded. The Great West Window contains fifteenth and sixteenth century figure panels brought from France, and six thirteenth century shields. Moving down the South Nave aisle you will come across the tomb of William Longespee, Earl of Salisbury. The illustration beside the tomb shows how it was coloured originally.

Then there's the central crossing vault with the arms of the bishops and royalty of the period, all recently renovated in glorious colour. The choir and the high altar have already been mentioned and there's plenty of colour in the Morning Chapel, some of it quite modern, and evidence on the screen carvings of some that has been lost.

The Audley Chantry (on the north side of the presbytery) is the only chantry chapel remaining in order and in use, and what a blaze of colour it is, with its painted ceiling and striking examples of modern embroidery.In fact, there is a lot of excellent stitchwork in this Cathedral. Much of it is quite recent and created, no doubt, for the same reasons as the spectacular Prisoners of Conscience Window - to beautify the Cathedral and testify to the continuing wish to work to the glory of God.

As you pass the Trinity Chapel in the East End of the Cathedral, there is the brilliant colour of the Prisoners of Conscience Window on the left, and on the right all the colour of the choir leading towards the Great West Window. Walking on down the south side of the choir you can see first of all the tomb of the Earl of Hertford on the left, and then further down the colourful seventeenth-century tomb of Sir Richard Mompesson, whilst above the ceiling shows faint signs of painted roundels which were whitewashed over.

How can I have been so mistaken all those years ago? Salisbury Cathedral is awash with colour if you look properly.

One of the most interesting things in the Cathedral is near the west front in the north aisle. It is the works of the oldest clock in England and was made in about 1386. It doesn't have a face but the huge workings are quite fascinating.

This seems a good enough place to end a brief tour of Salisbury Cathedral. You exit through the south door on the opposite side of the Cathedral, but before you go right outside you would do well to walk round the cloisters, the oldest in any English cathedral, and visit the shop and possibly the refectory.

The Cathedral stands serenely in the largest Close in England. If you come out of it through the door next to the west front you can look straight across to West Walk and the King's House, which houses THE SALISBURY AND SOUTH WILTSHIRE MUSEUM. This beautiful building named in honour of King James I who stayed there on one of this visits to Salisbury, is well worth a visit. Inside are displayed many and various exhibits, the oldest of which is probably the 4000 year old skeleton excavated about 12 miles from Salisbury. Moving still further from our own day, the museum displays will tell you about that most remarkable and well-visited ancient site on Salisbury Plain, STONEHENGE. It is too far out of Salisbury to be included in a chapter on the city but if you can possibly find the time to visit, it will be well worth it.

Another ancient feature of the Salisbury area, but this time a place that featured very strongly in the modern city of Salisbury's pre-history, is given space in the museum. The exhibition which records and explains the presence of Old Sarum, the hill with iron-age earthworks just outside Salisbury, puts the existence of New Sarum (our modern-day Salisbury) into perspective. Apparently the city on Old Sarum hill, inhabited in turn by Romans, Saxons and Normans, had in the end a castle and a cathedral as part of the settlement. Go up there at any time and stand where the old cathedral once stood, and you will soon realize why one of the canons said, 'Let us in God's name descend into the plain.' Not only is the hill wind swept, but water supplies are not handy and water had to be hauled up from below. So, on 28 April 1220, Bishop Richard Poore laid the foundation of his new church in the valley, and in doing so assured the development of the modern city of Salisbury. Soon the Roman and Saxon stones of the old cathedral were used for building a wall around the Close in New Sarum.

The Close is a lovely place to spend some time. Besides the Museum, in which THE HOBNOB COFFEE SHOP (named after the hobbyhorse of the Salisbury giant) is an ideal place in which to digest appetising homemade eatables and the interesting things you have seen in the Pitt Rivers Collection and the rest of the Museum, you can wander up West Walk to the North Canonry. If it is summer you may find open the delightful garden which leads down to the River Avon.

On again to the building known as The Wardrobe (once the Bishop's storeroom) which now houses THE MUSEUM OF THE DUKE OF EDINBURGH'S ROYAL REGIMENT. This is another place with an excellent and low-priced restaurant.

At the end of West Walk Choristers' Green opens out, with MOMPESSON HOUSE (in the care of the National Trust) on the far side. This is one of the finest eighteenth-century houses in the Cathedral Close, 'the almost perfect specimen of a small country town house'. The china collection and eighteenth century drinking glasses, fine period furniture and elegant oak staircase are some of its attractions, but for me the best is the walled garden at the back. Sitting there on a sunny afternoon it is very difficult to realize how near you are to the centre of a busy city.

As you leave Mompesson House to finish your circuit of Choristers' Green before going down North Walk, you will probably notice Bishop Seth Ward's College of Matrons, a long, low red brick building with a colourful cupola in the middle. It was founded in 1682 to house a dozen clergy widows, as it still does today. The reason for its foundation is rather touching - Bishop Ward's proposal of marriage was rejected by a lady whose subsequent marriage to a clergyman resulted in her becoming an impoverished widow. I wonder whether the College was built in time to admit her?

Still in the Close, walk down North Walk with the Cathedral on your right. All houses you see were built to house the Cathedral clergy so would not exist were it not for the Cathedral. Right at the end of North Walk, just to the left of St Ann's Gate (in the chapel of which Handel is said to have given his first concert), is MALMESBURY HOUSE. The interior of this house, which is open to the public at certain times, has been restored to eighteenth-century splendour, and the Orangery is yet another place to sit and eat. An eye-catching sundial in blue and gold, dated 1749, proclaims that 'Life's but a Walking Shadow' high up on the south wall.

Leaving the Close through St Ann's Gate you may think that's the end of the Cathedral and things associated with it, but not at all. When Bishop Poore founded the town in 1220 he laid out a grid-plan of streets which you can still see on today's map, and the building blocks so created were known as 'chequers'. The Cross Keys Chequer (only one reminder of the old chequer system) on the eastern side of the market square, now houses the supermarket Safeway, furniture, music, book and fabric shops and the delightful Cross Keys Restaurant, whose sign proclaims that it was built in about the fourteenth century.

Salisbury's first charter made it a free city under the bishop and it was successive bishops who bridged the rivers and enabled the citizens to come and go freely, and trade. Trade still flourishes here twice a week in the market (held on Tuesday and Saturdays), which is such an essential part of Salisbury life. If you want good fresh fish, fruit and vegetables you cannot do better than to get up early and be in the market by eight o'clock. There are many other things for sale too, of course, and barring large items of furniture you can buy almost everything needed for normal domestic life. The Poultry Cross on

the south-west corner of the Market Square is the only one of the four medieval crosses still remaining. Imagine the hubbub when all of them were in operation, and cattle, sheep, pigs and horses were bought and sold in the Market Square!

Having disgressed a bit from the path I intended to take, we shall now return to St Ann's Gate in Exeter Street, and I commend to you to THE KING'S ARMS, almost directly across the road. This is just one of many excellent pubs in Salisbury offering good food and atmospheric surroundngs. Rumour has it that the escape of Charles II from Worcester was plotted here, but I should not like to swear to it.

Turn left down New Street (having paused to admire the imposing late eighteenth-century WHITE HART on your right) and you will come across yet another couple of ancient pubs - THE WIG AND QUILL and THE NEW INN. The latter looks anything but new but exposes the modern idea of being a non-smoking pub.

At the cross road between New Street, Crane Street and the High Street you can see several shops that I always find difficult to resist going into. On the left is MITRE HOUSE (you can still see the badge on the north wall), which has a clause in its lease which requires it to provide a robing room for each new bishop on his enthronement day. I don't know which room is provided, but there is a

Detail of the wonderful altarcloth on the High Altar, worked by the Wessex Guild of Embroiders

wonderful tea and coffee shop on the ground floor (for the purchase of tea, coffee and their accessories) and an extremely elegant tea room upstairs.

The National Trust Shop almost next door is conveniently situated just around the corner from Mompesson House, mentioned earlier. You will see the North Gate of the Close from here, which still shuts at night. Across the road is BEACH'S BOOKSHOP, always worth browsing through if you like old books, illustrations and maps.

If you go straight on down the High Street, away from the Close, you pass the Old George Mall on the right which has used the ground floor of the Old George Inn as the entry to a modern shopping mall. Then turn right past W.H. Smith's and walk along New Canal. I think this road derived its name from the floods that were fairly common in Salisbury up to the nieteenth century - it probably used quite often to look like a waterway! Along here on the right is the very splendid Odeon cinema. It was built by a wealthy fifteenth-century merchant named John Halle as a dwelling. Inside in the cinema foyer you can see in the wood panelling, window and fireplace, that it was rather grand. In the nineteeth century it was 'done-up' and a mock Tudor facade put on the building! Nevertheless, it is one of Salisbury's endearing features and every time anyone suggests any alteration to it there is a great public outcry.

At the end of New Canal we cross into Milford Street and see the celebrated RED LION HOTEL on the right. With its high arch it is a fine example of an eighteenth-century coaching inn, which for me conjures up an immediate picture of horses, carriages, highwaymen and fine ladies (you have to ignore all the cars parked outside). But in actual fact the Cathedral's influence is felt here because the southern medieval wing (in which you can dine very pleasantly) was built between 1280 and 1320 as a hostel for craftsmen constructing the Cathedral.

Retrace your steps to Queen Street (opposite Benetton) and turn right, taking you to WATSON'S, the fine china and glass shop. This is the beautiful half-timbered house of John A'Porte, built in 1425 and rich both without and within. It is next door to William Russel's, possibly the oldest dwelling in the city (the sign says it was built in 1306) and now also home to Watson's.

The house of John A'Porte looks along Fish Row and Butcher Row (a pedestrianised street full of shops including an old-fashioned baker, butcher and greengrocer). The Tourist Information Centre is here too, behind the Guildhall which opens on to the Market Square and often houses exhibitions of paintings or sales work.

Mentioning the Guildhall reminds me of yet another pub (which is more properly called an inn) - the fifteenth-century PHEASANT. This is in Salt Lane and incorporates Crewe Hall wich was bequeathed to the Shoemaker' Guild in 1638. Good food and ale can be had here, as they have been since 1435.

At the Poultry Cross end of Butcher Row you will see across the road the HAUNCH OF VENISON, labelled 'An Old English Chop House. It can in fact trace its history back to about 1320, though much of the present building dates from the fifteenth-century. From the moment you squeeze yourself in through the narrow double door you know you are in for a treat. The bar is low and old-fashioned and the settles near the fireplace leave you in no doubt that standing is as important as sitting. Up the narrow stairs on the left is another room with settles and, to the initial horror of most people, a mummified serious in this particular chop house! Further upstairs there is a dining room in which dining is well worth while.

Out in the light of day, if you turn left and left again you will walk round the church yard of St Thomas's Church and finally enter the gateway on one of the great glories of Salisbury. The medieval city of merchants - mainly clothiers - rebuilt this church in the later Middle Ages (it was originally a small wooden chapel put up by Cathedral workmen for them to worship in, and dedicated to Thomas a Becket). The interior of the church represents quite clearly the full splendour of the fifteenth century, paid for by wealthy trade guides and merchants. Its most stunning feature is the world famous great Doom Painting over the Chancel Arch, which is thought to be the largest surviving wall painting of the Last Judgement.

Take the pedestrian way past SNELL'S patisserie (if you can bear to pass it) and enter the Maltings, another and very pleasant pedestrianised shopping area. To the right are the swans and to the left is Bishop's Mill (the Bishop again), the site of which has housed a grist mill for flour, tobacco and snuff, a fulling mill for cloth, malthouses (for beer and whisky) and the shortest standard-guage railway in England. It is now an eating house.

If you walk through the Maltings Shopping Centre (which never really feels like a shopping centre because of the proximity of the ducks and swans, the seats on the grass and the fenced in children's playground) you will eventually come to yet another of Salisbury great glories - THE PLAYHOUSE. I don't know what will be playing when you are in Salisbury but in all the years I have been going there I have never seen a bad performance. A measure of the Playhouse's success must be that it is often difficult to get tickets.

The City Hall, opposite the Playhouse, holds popular concerts, wrestling matches, and other entertainments too various to mention. One of Salisbury's great events should be mentioned here, and that is the Salisbury Festival, which takes place during two weeks in September. The City Hall, the Playhouse, the Guildhall and the Cathedral and all used as venues, as are the streets of the city, the Market Square and St Edmunds Arts Centre, which is a little further on than the Pheasant Inn mentioned earlier, and is a venue for many exhibitions and entertainments all the year round. This is a redundant church and very good use has been made of it. Leaflets are always available giving information about current and future events.

Another cheerful 16th century hostelry you might care to visit is THE ANCHOR INN in Gigant Street. This traditional pub serves food at lunchtimes which is both wholesome and inexpensive. Looking for somewhere to stay you will not do better than STRATFORD LODGE at 4, Park Lane. This small hotel was once the home of Jill Brayly who runs it now more in keeping with a country house hotel than anything else. The house is tucked down a quiet lane overlooking a large park, a few minutes from the centre of Salisbury.

For a change of tempo, especially if the weather is fine, I think a walk to Harnham along the Town Path is a very good way to end a tour of Salisbury. If you are in the vicinity of the Playhouse and City Hall go south towards

Fisherman Street. Turn right on to Fisherton Street and then left on a pedestrian street called Water Lane. Walk along beside the ducks until Mill Road curves round in front of you. Go straight across the road and you will find yourself in Queen Elizabeth Gardens. Walking through here you will see the cathedral spire to the left and the backs of some of the lovely buildings in the Close. The path takes in the bridge over the river, on which there are always plenty of ducks, swans, moorhens and coots with an eye for discarded crusts, etc.

The path follows a direct line to its destination in Harnham, although there are several byways that you could explore, taking you over part of the old water meadows that were once so important to live in Salisbury. Fishermen and shaggy dogs chasing sticks are usually in evidence here, along with all the aforementioned bird life that is not queued up at the ornithological equivalent of a soup kitchen.

At the end of the Town Path you will see what I consider to be one of the best sights in Salisbury. THE OLD MILL at **Harnham** has a long low wing faced half-way up in the typical Wiltshire chequerboard pattern, with mellow red bricks above and a slightly sagging terracotta pantile roof. The river flows underneath it and ducks aplenty swim and dive endlessly.

The origins of the Old Mill really are very old, because whatever part of its building was standing at the time was used to store the church monuments in when the cathedral at Old Sarum was moved. The taller part of the hotel is obviously newer (but old, nevertheless!) and may once have been a paper mill. Whatever, it is now an excellent restaurant, in beautiful surroundings. One should not miss visiting THE ROSE AND CROWN HOTEL in Harnham Road. If you have ever heard the anthem 'How lovely are thy dwellings' the words might

well have been written to describe it. It has a timeless beauty set in its own pretty rose gardens on the banks of the river. It has been a hostelry since the 13th century and today it dispenses hospitality with grace and style. There are 28 ensuite bedrooms beautifully furnished and equipped, eight of them in the 13th century building.

Not far from Harnham at **Odstock** is another pleasing hostelry, the 16th century thatched YEW TREE INN. Whilst David and Sheila Reed, the proprietors never allow anyone to forget that this is a true country inn, nonetheless no one can deny that it is renowned for the reputation of its cuisine and wines. For those wanting to spend a little time at The Yew Tree and in the surrounding area there are two comfortable bedrooms available together with a sumptuous English breakfast.

Wilton, a very close neighbour of Salisbury, has its own connection with the Cathedral. The Abbess of Wilton Abbey, seven-and-a-half centuries refused Bishop Poore ground to build his cathedral on, and thus forced him to build it on his own land in Salisbury. So it was she who indirectly caused Salisbury to become the city it is. Because of this, and the close proximity of Wilton and Salisbury, I should not feel comfortable if I did not mention that it would be a great shame to miss Wilton's two major attractions. One is the WILTON ROYAL CARPET FACTORY, probably the oldest carpet factory

The beautiful fan vaulting of the Chapter House (c.1280) rises from the single central pillar

in the world, in which you can take a tour to see how these velvety glorious carpets are made, and the other is WILTON HOUSE. This stately sumptuous building has belonged to the Earls of Pembroke for 400 years, but the fine south front was created in the seventeenth century like the splendid state rooms which are on view. The collection of old masters (Rubens, Rembrandt, Reynolds and Bruegel) is famous, and Chippendale furniture and classical sculptures are also on show. It is easy to spend several hours at Wilton House.

Just beyond Wilton is the small village of **Barford St Martin** where THE BARFORD INN dispenses hospitality as it must have done since its inception as a coaching house in the 15th century. Set in its own grounds it once had its own brewery on the premises and was the main source of employment for the village. This would probably have been at the time that Charles Dickens used the comfort of the Snug Bar to write one of his novels.

North of Salisbury at **Middle Wallop** is one of my favourite places FIFEHEAD MANOR. If you could take a peep at the visitor's book in this lovely manor house you would be left in no doubt that the establishment had many devotees. It is a wonderful place with foundations that are said to date from the 11th century when it was a part of the estates of the Saxon Earl

Godwin. During its history it has been a nunnery and the home of various families. While the historic atmosphere lingers on. Fifehead Manor offers all the amenities of attractive bedrooms with their own bathrooms, a well stocked bar and pleasant reception area. The comfort of visitors is always their main concern. In addition to English, French, German and Dutch is also spoken. It is truly wonderful to drive into the surrounding countryside for a relaxed and peaceful stay away from the cities of Salisbury and Winchester.

Close to Salisbury is the pretty village of **Pitton** with its many thatched cottages. In Whitehill is THE SILVER PLOUGH, a delightful free house, famous for its choice of beers, wide range of English fruit wines, excellent fare and a varied selection of cheeses. It has a superb atmosphere acquired over many years. It was once a farmhouse inhabited by a contented family; this feeling is still there today, nurtured by the present owners and their friendly efficient staff.

One of the three Winterbournes is **Winterbourne Dauntsey**, just 4 miles outside Salisbury on the A338. The only pub there is the very welcoming TYTHING MAN. It is a traditional village pub whose new landlords have rapidly made themselves at home with the locals and are gradually gaining friends and customers from quite a distance away.

Wherever you go the lure of Salisbury and its cathedral will bring you back to bask in its glory.

THE ROSE AND CROWN HOTEL
Hotel & Restaurant

Harnham Road, Harnham,
Salisbury, Wiltshire, SP2 8JQ.

Tel: (0722) 327908
Fax: (0722) 339816

If you have ever heard the anthem 'How lovely are thy dwellings' the words might well have been composed to describe The Rose and Crown. It has a timeless beauty set in its own pretty rose gardens on the banks of the River Avon at Salisbury and overlooking the famous Cathedral. It has been a hostelry since the 13th century and today it dispenses hospitality with grace and style within it walls.

There are 28 ensuite bedrooms beautifully furnished and equipped, eight of them in the 13th century building – these have the original half timbering. The others are spacious and more modern and include family rooms.

Dining at the Rose and Crown is a super experience. You can relax with a quiet drink in the intimate surroundings of the low beamed 'Oak Bar' or the livelier 'Avon Bar' where tasty snacks are served at lunchtime. The charming restaurant has the most spectacular views across the river from your table in the conservatory or you may choose a table in a cosy corner under timbered eaves by an open log fire. There is an excellent choice of dishes on the menu which is guaranteed to suit all tastes. Many include exciting and unusual combinations selected from fresh produce – from wild mushrooms to Avon trout. The wine list is outstanding with no less than 75 bins. Three especially equipped suites are available for conferences and The Rose and Crown is ideal for weddings and dinner dances up to 150 people..

USEFUL INFORMATION

OPEN: 24 hours, 365 days of the year
CHILDREN: Welcome and catered for
CREDIT CARDS: Amex/Diners/Visa/ Access
LICENSED: Fully Licensed
ACCOMMODATION: 28 ensuite rooms. Conference facilities

RESTAURANT: English cuisine with local specialities
BAR FOOD: Full bar menu. Morning coffee. Afternoon tea
VEGETARIAN: Always a selection available
DISABLED ACCESS: Yes. Full facilities
GARDEN: Beautiful riverside gardens

FIFEHEAD MANOR
Country House Hotel & Restaurant

Middle Wallop, Stockbridge,
Hampshire, SO20 8EG.

Tel: (0264) 781565
Fax: (0264) 781400

If you could take a peep at the visitor's book in this lovely manor house you would be left in no doubt that the establishment had many devotees. It is a wonderful place with foundations that are said to date from the 11th century when it was part of the estates of the Saxon Earl Godwin. During its history it has been a nunnery and the home of various families. The American president, George Washington, was a direct descendant of a 15th century Lord of The Manor Wallop Fifehead.

The manor which is such a relatively short distance from Heathrow airport, makes a sensible place for American and other foreign visitors to relax for a night or two before they venture further on their visit to Britain. There are many more reasons for anyone to come here. While the historic atmosphere lingers on, Fifehead Manor offers all the amenities of attractive bedrooms all with their own bathrooms, a well stocked bar and pleasant reception area. A small meeting room can also be made into an attractive private dining room. The kitchens of Fifehead Manor are well known for their delicious and creative dishes. All produce is bought in daily and the absolute freshness of the ingredients is a guarantee for wonderful meals.

Fifehead Manor's staff are well informed, helpful and courteous and guests can at all times expect a warm and friendly welcome. The comfort of visitors is always their main concern. In addition to English, French, German and Dutch is also spoken. It is truly wonderful to drive into the surrounding countryside for a relaxed and peaceful stay away from the cities of Salisbury and Winchester.

USEFUL INFORMATION

OPEN: All year
CHILDREN: Welcome
CREDIT CARDS: Visa/Master/Amex/ Diners
LICENSED: Full On Licence
ACCOMMODATION: 15 rooms with private bathrooms

RESTAURANT: International cuisine
BAR FOOD: Light snacks to full meals
VEGETARIAN: Always one dish. Selection by prior arrangement
DISABLED ACCESS: Yes and accommodation
GARDEN: 3 acres of garden. Croquet

THE YEW TREE INN

Country Inn

Odstock Village, Salisbury,
Wiltshire, SP5 4JE.

Tel: (0722) 329786

USEFUL INFORMATION

OPEN: 12-3pm & 6-11.00 pm
 Sun: 12-3pm & 7-10.30pm
CHILDREN: Welcome
CREDIT CARDS: All major credit cards
LICENSED: Full on & Supper Licence
ACCOMMODATION: 1 double,
 1 family
RESTAURANT: International cuisine,
 Seafood a speciality
BAR FOOD: Full menu with
 delicious home-made specials
VEGETARIAN: Several home-made
 dishes daily
DISABLED ACCESS: Small step,
 willing to assist
GARDEN: Pretty country garden,
 outside seating

This quiet, peaceful village just one and a half miles from Salisbury Cathedral is full of surprises. Its most delightful surprise is the Internationally known Yew Tree Inn. This 16th century thatched hostelry nestles in the Chalke Valley. It is easily found by car, bus or taxi and is somewhere that is visited by tourists from all around the world. The low beamed ceiling, roaring log fire in winter, and the beautiful gardens, which are a delight in summer, all make up the wonderful atmosphere.

Whilst David and Sheila Reed the proprietors never allow anyone to forget that this is a true Country Inn nonetheless, no one can deny that it is renowned for the reputation of its cuisine and wines. The Reed's are perfectionists and the whole establishment is run with a meticulous attention to detail. This is what makes it so special and outstanding. They specialise in Seafood as well as Game in season. Many of the dishes are prepared and cooked at the request of their regular clients - a service that is available to newcomers as well, naturally. Lobster, Sailfish loin, Squab Pigeon are great favourites. The fish is chosen straight off the boats in Emsworth harbour by David's grandfather. The Reed's also try to offer many different fish from other countries. For the truly great trencherman, the huge Yew Tree Inn Mixed Grill is a guaranteed success. There is also an extensive Bar Meal menu and an a la carte Sunday lunch. For those wanting to enjoy a little more of The Yew Tree Inn and the surrounding area, two comfortable bedrooms are available together with a sumptuous English Breakfast.

THE SILVER PLOUGH

Freehouse & Restaurant

Whitehill, Pitton,
Nr Salisbury, Wiltshire, SP5 1DZ.

Tel: (0722) 72266

USEFUL INFORMATION

OPEN: 11-3pm & 6-11pm: Mon-Sat.
 Sun: 12-3pm & 7-10.30pm
CHILDREN: Welcome if well behaved
CREDIT CARDS: Access/Visa/Amex
LICENSED: Full On Licence
ACCOMMODATION: Not applicable

RESTAURANT: Interesting and unusual
 menu
BAR FOOD: Bar menu & daily
 blackboard specials
VEGETARIAN: Separate menu
DISABLED ACCESS: No, but willing to
 assist
GARDEN: Large, attractive garden

Pitton nestles under a hill and is full of thatched cottages living in harmony with more modern developments. In the midst of the village is The Silver Plough, a delightful free house, famous for its choice of beers, wide range of old English fruit wines, excellent fayre and a varied selection of cheeses. It has a superb atmosphere acquired over many years. It was once a farmhouse inhabited by a contented family; this feeling is still there today, nurtured by the present owners and their friendly, efficient staff. It is enhanced by attractive furnishings, including a remarkable bar frontage which is an over mantle dating from 1582, that once graced a manor house in Salisbury. From the beamed ceiling hangs an incredible collection of glass rolling pins.

Situated so near to Salisbury it is somewhere that is popular with people from the city but it also delights the many visitors who flock to Salisbury to see the magnificent cathedral. The Silver Plough stands out as one of the best eating houses in this area. If one had to describe the menu succinctly, the word 'unusual' springs immediately to mind. Great thought and a talented chef have combined to produce dishes which are both exciting and easily acceptable. It is a set price menu in the restaurant either for two courses or three. If time or inclination does not make you decide to eat in the restaurant, the bar has a wide range of food including delicious daily blackboard specials. There is a separate menu for vegetarians.

THE ANCHOR INN

Public House

38 Gigant Street, Salisbury,
Wiltshire, SP1 2BQ.

Tel: (0722) 330680

Where do you go to eat or to enjoy a drink after you have feasted on the beauty if Salisbury Cathedral? There are many places but one within easy reach which is friendly, unpretentious and good value is The Anchor Inn, tucked away in a back street close to the city centre and the Cathedral. The anchor is an original 16th century timber-framed building which has been much altered over the years but still retains great character. The house is surrounded completely by the small family owned Gibbs Mew Brewery, the products of which are part of the pleasure of visiting the pub. The range of beers is excellent and always includes at least three Real Ales.

Inside there are two comfortable bars in which some of the original beams are exposed and in the public bar the stone flagged floors have the sheen of centuries of use. It is not a big pub but seats forty people with ease. Maurice and Nicky Symons are mine hosts and run the pub with the help of a good and cheerful cook who produces some thirty items for the menu.

At the time of going to press not one of the dishes costs over three pounds. The food is fresh and the portions are generous. Traditional pies and other favourites are on offer including a particularly good 'Pork and Apple in Cider'. There is no food in the evenings.

USEFUL INFORMATION

OPEN: 11-3pm & 5-11pm
CHILDREN: Welcome to eat
CREDIT CARDS: None taken
LICENSED: Full Licence
ACCOMMODATION: Not applicable

RESTAURANT: Not applicable
BAR FOOD: Good pub food, value
 for money
VEGETARIAN: On request
DISABLED ACCESS: No
GARDEN: No

THE BARFORD INN

Public House & Restaurant

Barford St Martin, Salisbury,
Wiltshire, SP3 4AB.

Tel: (0722) 742242

The Barford Inn is a 15th century coaching inn set in it's own grounds, approximately 5 miles from Salisbury city centre on the main A 30 just outside Wilton. There was a time when the inn, once called the Dragon Inn, had its own brewery on the premises and was the main source of employment for the village. It would probably have been at this time that Charles Dickens wrote one of his novels in the snug bar.

Those days have long gone but The Barford has lost none of its old atmosphere even though it recently has been completely renovated. This work has been carried out with a complete understanding of the building and has enhanced it with a superb, light, airy restaurant, complete with oak beams imported from a French vineyard. There are times when you can swear that you are inhaling the aroma of grapes; just an added bonus to the existing charm of the pub.

Ido and Alison Davids have been in the catering business for a number of years but the Barford is their first pub. To this venture they have brought not only their skills but an enthusiasm for the trade and a genuine liking for people. They welcome families young and old. The menu is extensive with both traditional favourites like fish and chips and Ploughmans' lunches as well as the more exotic international dishes. Everything is home-cooked, abundant, fresh and delicious. Their prices are sensible. Four ensuite bedrooms decorated and furnished to a luxurious standard are there for those who would enjoy lingering awhile. Certainly it is ideal for anyone wanting to spend time in Salisbury and exploring the Cathedral.

USEFUL INFORMATION

OPEN: Regular pub hours.
 All day Saturday
CHILDREN: Welcome
CREDIT CARDS: All Major cards
LICENSED: Full On Licence
ACCOMMODATION: 4 ensuite rooms

RESTAURANT: Home-made, abundant,
 fresh, delicious
BAR FOOD: Snacks ranging from 95p.
 Will cook to order
VEGETARIAN: Made to order
DISABLED ACCESS: 2 steps down to
 toilet
GARDEN: Large, tables and chairs. Play
 area. Barbecues

275

THE RED LION HOTEL
Hotel & Restaurant

Milford Street, Salisbury,
Wiltshire, SP1 2AN.

Tel: (0722) 323334
Fax: (0722) 325756

USEFUL INFORMATION

OPEN: All year round
CHILDREN: Welcome
CREDIT CARDS: All major cards
LICENSED: Full On Licence
ACCOMMODATION: 56 ensuite rooms

RESTAURANT: Traditional English &
   Continental
BAR FOOD: Available
VEGETARIAN: Catered for with pleasure
DISABLED ACCESS: Yes
GARDEN: Coaching courtyard

The whole of The Red Lion is beautiful and the creeper clad courtyards entrancing. It is seldom that one finds such perfection. This 13th century hostelry was built reputedly to house the draughtsmen working on the cathedral. The original building now constitutes the main body of the hotel which includes the lounge, reception and part of the restaurant. Further wings have been added over the centuries to form the courtyards, which are such a renowned feature of the hotel. It was originally called the White Bear, until 1706 when the name was changed to the Red Lion and Cross Keys, and then again in 1778 to simply The Red Lion which remains to this day.

The Red Lion is probably the longest running, purpose built hotel in the country and yet it has been used as a post office, a customs clearing house and perhaps most famously as a coaching inn. In the reception area can be seen a handbill dated 1777 advertising the 'Flying Machine' a coach which travelled daily to London in thirteen hours.

Since 1913 The Red Lion has been in the capable hands of the Maidment family. There is a unique collection of antiques with a large number of clocks. Do look out for the Parliament clocks and, in particular, the skeleton organ clock in the reception hall. The restaurant with its inviting meals has a delightful ambience. The bars are welcoming and the bedrooms have every modern convenience. There is a lift and a purpose built bedroom wing which includes bedrooms suitable for disabled persons.

STRATFORD LODGE
Hotel

4 Park Lane, Salisbury,
Wiltshire, SP1 3NP.

Tel: (0722) 325177
Fax: (0722) 412699

USEFUL INFORMATION

OPEN: All year round except for Christmas
   week
CHILDREN: Welcome over 8 years
CREDIT CARDS: Mastercard/Visa
LICENSED: Residential and Restaurant
ACCOMMODATION: Beautifully
   furnished, spacious rooms

RESTAURANT: Open to non-residents.
   Traditional & modern English
BAR FOOD: Not applicable
VEGETARIAN: At least one dish.
   Special diets catered for with notice
DISABLED ACCESS: Small step at
   entrance
GARDEN: Pretty, secluded garden

Until Jill Bayly turned Stratford Lodge into the friendly, small hotel that it is today, it was her home. This atmosphere still prevails and it is more in keeping with a small country house hotel than anything else. The house is tucked down a quiet lane overlooking a large park, a few minutes from the centre of Salisbury. A secluded, pretty, lawned garden has tables and chairs which are an enticement in the summer months.

The whole establishment is run with a professionalism that results in everything seeming to run on oiled wheels and with a delightful informality. Every meal is served on beautiful china and the glass sparkles. In a little room off the lounge you will find a grand piano and if you are lucky you will find Jill's friend John playing. What does surprise most people is that what looks like a quite ordinary house from outside is so beautiful inside. The bedrooms are furnished with antiques, the beds covered with beautiful lace bedspreads. The dining room is gracious, the breakfast room is a conservatory with sloping glass ceilings and patio doors. The staff are as friendly as Jill herself, the kitchen is always open for you to see what is cooking and to inhale the wonderful aromas that give you an idea of the meal that is in store for you.

The dining room is open to non-residents and caters for small business lunches, whilst in the evening the menu is exciting and worth studying over the glass of complimentary sherry. There are very few small establishments who can be as justifiably proud of the quality of the food as Stratford Lodge.

THE TYTHING MAN
Public House & Restaurant

Main Road, Winterbourne Dauntsey,
Nr Salisbury, Wiltshire, SP4 6EW.

Tel: (0980) 611306

This pretty village is one of the three Winterbournes. This one is just 4 miles from Salisbury and in its midst is the village pub, The Tything Man. It is not all that old and was built at the beginning of this century but it is a true, traditional English country hostelry, furnished in a comfortable, informal manner with the walls covered in a huge number of plaques which have all come from the Army Camp close by. The local people enjoy welcoming visitors into their circle and you will be encouraged to join in the lively singalong which occurs every Tuesday evening. The music covers all tastes.

In the restaurant which gleams with horse brasses, pots and pans and other utensils, the food is traditional English of the highest standard. There is nothing pretentious about it and everything is freshly cooked. There are small portions for children. The bar menu covers a whole range of dishes with crisply cooked cod and chips, one of the favourites. Whether you want a full meal or just a sandwich you will find the portions generous. The sandwiches which have a variety of fillings, are always well filled. Every day there is a 'Special' which is delicious and inexpensive.

Golf enthusiasts will be delighted to find there is a course nearby and for those who find the ancient stones at Stonehenge appealing, the site is only 4 miles away across country. David and Diane Coker are the landlords, who in the short time they have been here, have built up a regular clientele who know they can expect friendly chatter, good beer, good food and good service.

USEFUL INFORMATION

OPEN: Mon-Thurs: 11-2.30pm & 6-11pm.,
    Sat: 11-11pm, normal Sunday hours
CHILDREN: Yes is eating or well be-
haved,
    small portions available
CREDIT CARDS: None
LICENSED: Full On Licence
ACCOMMODATION: None. Will cater
    for parties and functions

RESTAURANT: Traditional English
BAR FOOD: Wide menu. Daily specials
VEGETARIAN: Always one dish to order
DISABLED ACCESS: Not good. 2 steps
    or via side door
GARDEN: Very large. Eating & drinking.
Car pak

WATSONS OF SALISBURY
Purveyors of China and Glass

8 & 9 Queen Street,
Salisbury, Wiltshire, SP1 1EY.

Tel: (0722) 320311
Fax: (0722) 412903

Who could fail to enjoy visiting or working in this extraordinary business, housed in two historic and striking buildings. It is totally in keeping that beautiful china and glass is sold at Watsons of Salisbury. Watsons is one of the largest, family owned specialists in their field in southern England. It was in 1834, in the reign of William IV, that the firm started to sell its wares in the Salisbury area.

Eight and Nine Queen Street are both historic but with a totally different facade. William Russel's House dates from 1306. Much of the original timber framework has survived, including a large 'hammerbeam' which dominates the first floor showrooms. A small section of wattle and daub infilling has also survived for almost 700 years, and the building boasts a number of original window frames. The frontage of the building, initially rather ordinary, is a fine example of an unusual building material; mathematical tiles. Produced in the 18th century to avoid paying brick tax, they give the appearance of a brick wall; in fact the tiles are nailed to a timber frontage, then mortar-pointed to give the correct finish!

The black and white half timbered, 'Ye House of John A'Port' built around 1425 is the subject of thousands of photographs every year. Extensively restored in 1930 it is a wonderful setting for Watsons. On the first floor, one of the small rooms boasts the superb panelling work of Humphrey Beckham, a 17th century local joiner, whose head-stone in St Thomas' Church is a larger version of the carved panel above the fireplace.

USEFUL INFORMATION

OPEN: 9-5.30pm: Monday to Saturday
CHILDREN: Welcome
CREDIT CARDS: Access/Visa/Amex/
    Diners/Switch
DISABLED ACCESS: Level entrance to
    ground floor
TOILETS: No

St Albans Cathedral

St Albans

"Spirit of Beauty, thou does consecrate
With thine own hues all thou dost shine upon
Of human thought or form."

Percy Shelley

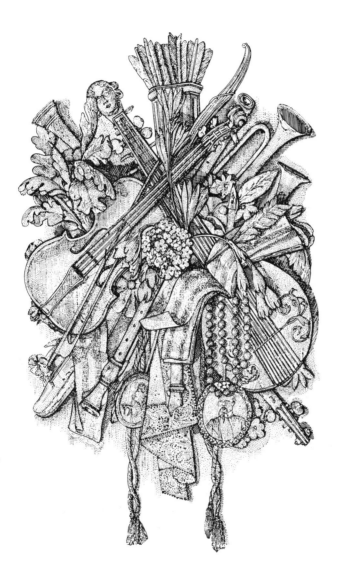

The City of St Albans

by Joy David

Returning to **St Albans** after an absence of twenty five years was to find almost everything had changed except for the old town where all was as it had been for centuries. THE CATHEDRAL AND ABBEY CHURCH OF ST ALBANS which suffered from the 'money is no object' benefaction of a very rich and overpowering man in the 19th century, remains quintessentially a great Norman church.

Almost surrounded by busy motorways, St Albans is easy to reach and having done so you drive into quieter realms and begin to realise that here you are gong to discover in this one place, which offers the unusual combination of the dignity of a Cathedral City and the intimacy of a rural market town, the full span of British history. For a moment or two the sense of history is almost overwhelming.

My first need was to find a good hotel, where I would be well looked after and as a woman, treated properly - not as a second class citizen which is so often the case with a woman travelling on her own. I had been recommended to three and any one of them would have answered my needs. They were all different as you will see from my description but in each case I have no hesitation in putting them forward for your approval.

Taking them in alphabetical order APPLES HOTEL comes first. This family run hotel is at 133 London Road, close to the city centre and to the railway station. It is set back from the A1081 within a stones throw of all local motorways. It is as you enter the gates that you realise you are in a rural setting. The well kept garden of half an acre surrounds the house. Built in the early 1930's Apples Hotel offers very comfortable accommodation and added disabled facilities in 1991. There are nine rooms and it is ETB 4 Crown commended.

The next, THE NOKE THISTLE HOTEL, is on the A405 and is a delightful country style hotel, set in its own grounds. It is a peaceful, tranquil place of great comfort and one of the finest award winning restaurants in the area. Its history is interesting because from time immemorial there has been a manor here. It is recorded even before the Norman Conquest. However it was not until the 16th century that the word Noke came into being - a corruption of the word Oak. Noke was the name of the farm that was part of the Burston Manor estate. In 1880 Burston Manor and Noke farm were sold for £799 pounds five shillings and sixpence! In Victorian times the hotel had only six rooms, it now has 111. It is a hotel that treats everyone as individuals with an old fashioned courtesy and efficiency that is very welcome.

I think that ST MICHAEL'S MANOR HOTEL in Fishpool Street is one of England's loveliest hotels. This would be so wherever it was situated in the country, but added to the ecclesiastical history of St Albans, it makes an outstanding place in which to stay. This 16th century manor house which takes its name from the nearby church of St Michael, celebrated 400 years of history in 1986. It lies in five acres of beautifully tended grounds between the river and Fishpool Street. The original manor house was first built by the Gape family about 1586 on medieval foundations which still form part of the cellars beneath the house. Over the centuries the manor has undergone structural change, but with happily blending styles, and has never been more beautiful with its latest addition, a delightful Victorian-style conservatory.

Fishpool Street itself takes its name from a fishpond that lay near by in medieval times. It is here the monks from the abbey once fished. The Georgian fronts of the houses lining the raised pavements cover much older structures, among them pilgrims' hostels. The delightful ST MICHAELS CHURCH, in **St Michaels village**, has the remains of Saxon windows, a Norman nave and an effigy of Sir Francis Bacon. It is open daily Easter to October 2-5pm.

In St Michael's Street on a site identified in the Domesday Book, is KINGSBURY WATER MILL. The present mill was constructed in the 16th century. Its beautifully restored water-wheel churns the clear water of the River Ver. I was able to take a look at a milling machine, some very old farming implements and an attractive art gallery and exhibition area. I also took advantage of one of the nicest restaurants in St Albans which forms part of the mill.

Opening times are Tuesday to Saturday from 11am-6pm and Sunday from 12 noon until 6pm.

Having decided where to stay I then set about rediscovering old haunts and planning visits to new ones. I was spoilt for choice. It was my intention to visit the Cathedral several times and for that reason I do not intend to write about it until the end of this chapter, leaving the best until last. That is not to say that all the places I was to see were anything less than exciting and rewarding.

The Roman town of Verulamium is west of the city centre, on the banks of the River Ver. The town was a 'municipium' where the citizens had the same rights as those of Rome. Extraordinary things one discovers here. For example the Roman theatre is the only known example in Britain that has a stage instead of an amphitheatre. It probably seated 6,000 spectators. A hypocaust or heating system for a suite of baths, survives and is housed in VERULAMIUM PARK. Sections of the town's 3rd century walls and the remnants of a street of shops also survive.

It is at THE VERULAMIUM MUSEUM that you will find much information about the city and its past. It is set in a 100 acre park on the site of one of Roman Britain's major cities. Here you will learn the story of everyday life in Verulamium. It is also here, within the park, that you will find the remains of the Roman wall and the hypocaust and Roman theatre that I have just told you about. The park gives pleasure to residents and visitors not only because of its history but also for the beautiful setting. Picnics can be enjoyed alongside the lake, or enjoy the small fun fair on Summer days.

Facilities include ample parking and a pleasant cafe/restaurant.

The Verulamium has thrilled many people and has deservedly won three awards in the last year, including a British Travel Authority, 'Come to Britain' Award. The museum tells the story of St Albans' Roman past highlighted by excellent displays which include reconstructed Roman rooms, interactive 'Discovery Areas', an excavation video and one of the finest collections of Roman artefacts and mosaics in the country. Roman skills in every field are seen in other places in Britain but perhaps not as often so well portrayed as at Verulamium. Entrance is free to residents of St Albans District and to friends of St Albans Museum - a wonderful bonus, because a single visit here will never suffice.

Honorary guides undertake guided walks around the park and tours and talks within the museum. For children quiz sheets are available which help them retain the knowledge of the past that they readily absorb while they are there but perhaps would forget equally quickly without some aide-memoire.

Opening times are Monday to Saturday 10am-5.30pm and Sundays from 2pm-5.30pm. The Roman theatre on Bluehouse Hill opens daily from 10am-5pm and 4pm in winter.

A lions head ornament on the south side of the nave

At THE MUSEUM OF ST. ALBANS you can relive the story of the historic city from the departure of the Romans to the present day, through exciting and innovative galleries, each laid out with skill and care. The new 'Tools for the Job' gallery exhibits the renowned 'Salaman Collection' of trade tools. If you have any imagination you will wonder how, with such primitive tools, the artisans and craftsmen produced such extraordinarily effective buildings and artefacts. The wildlife garden is a delightful bonus.

Also on Bluehouse Hill, is GORHAMBURY HOUSE which was built in the 16th century and is now only a ruin in the park. This was the home of Francis Bacon, philosopher and writer. I found the bookstall there very informative and if you have an addiction for books you will enjoy it.

GREBE HOUSE WILDLIFE CENTRE, the home of the Hertfordshire and Middlesex Wildlife Trust is housed in a 16th century timber-framed building and provides interpretive displays illustrating wildlife in the area. Special events are always being arranged and there is a small gift shop. If you are interested in finding out about the special events, I suggest you ring 0727 58901 to obtain the information. Grebe House is open from Monday to Friday 10am-4.30pm and on Saturdays and Sundays 12.00 - 4.30pm.

There is an incredible difference in taking a leisurely stroll around a quiet city on a summer's evening, which is a delightful way of seeing the fine buildings, and the hustle and bustle that you will find during the day. For example the twice weekly street market every Wednesday and Saturday runs the whole length of St Peters Street. It is alive with the cries of market traders and the buzz of customers and onlookers who enjoy its colour as well as its bargains. It would have been equally as busy when it first started in 948AD.

Keen shoppers will love the quality of the shops and the off-street precincts which hold charm in their own right and whose inhabitants have some fantastic merchandise. The Tourist Information Centre is housed in this area and you will find the staff friendly and helpful as well as being informative.

the martydom of St Albans, with angles swinging censers at the west endof his shrine

Eating never poses a problem because the many restaurants offer cuisine from many nations. The gourmet will be satisfied and for those who may prefer the less formal pubs and coaching inns, St Albans is full of them and is the home of CAMRA (the Campaign for Real Ale).

Having enjoyed a good meal it would probably be good for dispensing with unwanted weight if you were to climb to the top of THE CLOCK TOWER in the Market Place. The fine views of the city and the surrounding countryside make it worth the effort. The CURFEW TOWER dates back to 1410. The working clock and curfew bell 'Gabriel' are clearly visible.

Opening times Saturdays, Sundays and Bank Holidays, Easter to Mid-September, 10.30am-5pm.

THE MALTINGS ART CENTRE and THE ABBEY THEATRE offer plays throughout the year and films can be seen at the ODEON CINEMA, London Road or the ALBAN ARENA, the premier entertainment venue which provides a varied programme of ballet, plays, concerts, children's shows etc. Summer time is festival time with a choice of either the St Albans Festival or the bi-annual International Organ Festival; for either, details can be obtained from St Albans Tourism 0727 864511.

THE ST ALBANS ORGAN MUSEUM at 320 Camp Road houses a permanent working exhibition of mechanical musical instruments, which formed part of the private collection of Mr Charles Hart. In 1978 at his request, the charitable trust, now known as the 'St Albans Musical Museum Society' was formed to maintain, administer and make the unique collection available to the public. The magnificent sounds of the mechanical organs by Mortier, Decap and Burgens can be heard every week, together with reproducing pianos by Steinway and Weber. Musical boxes dating from the 1880's are demonstrated together with hand-turned table organettes. A rare Mills Violano-Virtuoso produces its own unique sound of a four string violin and forty four note piano.

Two theatre organs are housed at the museum - a 'Wurlitzer' formerly of the Granada Cinema in Edmonton, North London, three manual organs with ten ranks of pipes plus extensive percussion section. The second theatre organ is a rare survivor of a handful built by R. Spurden Rutt, with six ranks of pipes plus percussion, played from the three manual consoles with their striking illuminated glass surround. Concerts by top organists are a regular feature of the museum's activities.

You will be drawn to the shop at the end of your visit if only to look at the wide range of records and cassettes and possibly more interestingly after looking at the instruments, a range of books devoted to both mechanical and non-mechanical instruments.

The museum is open to the public every Sunday from 2pm-4.30pm during which time there is a live musical performance of the various instruments, given with a descriptive commentary. Concert information is available on 0727 869693.

A totally different venue is THE MOSQUITO AIRCRAFT MUSEUM in Salisbury Hall, **London Colney.** The historic site of moated Salisbury Hall mentioned in the Domesday Book, was chosen by the de Havilland Aircraft Company in 1939 to develop in secret the wooden, high speed, unarmed bomber the Mosquito; with 41 variants of the type the most versatile aircraft of the war. This began the museum's long association with Salisbury Hall making it the oldest Aircraft Museum in the country.

Today the museum has on display 20 types of de Havilland aircraft ranging from a 1917 B.E.2e to modern military and civil jets. Although the museum is staffed solely by volunteers, they have a continuing active restoration programme, and visitors are encouraged to inspect work in progress at close hand. Also on display is a comprehensive collection of de Havilland and other engine types, together with a notable collection of memorabilia.

Visitors to the museum however soon discover that it can offer more than a collection of static aircraft. Close inspection of the exhibits provides a unique hands-on experience. Members are always on hand to assist the visitor and demonstrate the working displays. With a varied programme of regular events that include flying displays, vintage car and motorcycle rallies and model exhibitions, there is always something that appeals to all ages.

The museum is open from the 1st March to the end of October on Thursdays 2-5.30pm, Saturdays and Sundays from 10.30am-5.30pm.

From the air to the ground, THE ROYAL NATIONAL ROSE SOCIETY at Chiswell Green, St Albans on the outskirts of the town invites you to enjoy the world famous 'Gardens of the Rose' at the Society's showground where there is a collection of some 30,000 roses of all types. The 12 acres of gardens are a marvellous spectacle for the casual visitor and fascinating to the rose enthusiast. The gardens are being continuously developed - in particular by associating roses with a great many other plants - to create greater interest for visitors and to stimulate ideas leading to more adventurous gardening.

In addition to the permanent displays of all types of roses with their many companion plants and the RNRS International Rose Trials, other demonstrations and trials are held from time to time. These are designed to show visitors the latest in experimental techniques in horticulture which have an application to the growing of roses. The aim of the trials is to assess new roses for their value as garden plants. They are judged every week during the flowering season and the winners receive Society awards.

The British Rose Festival is a spectacular national event held every year in July. It includes a magnificent display of roses organised by the Society and the British Rose Growers Association on an excitingly new and different theme each year. The competition is for the leading national amateur rose exhibitors and floral artists. All the best of British roses can be seen at this unique show.

The gardens are open Mid-June to late October (inclusive) Monday to Saturday 9am until 5pm. Sunday and August Bank Holiday 10am until 6pm.

If you had taken St Stephens Hill Road towards Chiswell Green you would have passed ST STEPHENS CHURCH which is located on the site of a Roman cemetery, the Church was built by Abbot Ulsinus about a century before the Norman Conquest. You can take a look at it at weekends and Bank Holidays in summer from 2pm-6pm.

The reredos, as basrelief sculpture of marble and paua shell by Sir Alfred Gilbert

And so to the Cathedral where thousands of years of worship have continued here on the site of St Alban's martyrdom. Many centuries ago Alban was the first Christian martyr in this country and his shrine has always attracted pilgrims in search of spiritual and physical healing. It is a beautiful place which emanates strength. You feel as if the Almighty is reaching out for you and endeavouring to pour in to your soul the fortitude shown by St Alban, and at the same time give you hope for the present and peace eternal. I certainly left refreshed in body and spirit. The history is well documented and you will do no better than to purchase the beautifully presented, colourful Pitkin Guide to St Albans Cathedral which will cost you less than £2 and be a constant reminder of your visit.

A huge Norman church was built with the stock of material that the Saxons had accumulated. The Normans thought little of the Saxons' architectural ability and were determined to build bigger and better than anything local people had ever seen. Oddly enough it was the Saxon craftsmen who were the only ones able to create what the new masters required. In the 13th century Abbot John de Cella undertook enormous building works at the west end of the church using newly discovered stone from Totternhoe in Bedfordshire. It was good material to work on and proved ideal for carving. The work did not go smoothly however because of a lack of money and the constant squabbling between the King and the Pope which finally developed in 1213 to a meeting here of disgruntled noblemen, which in turn led to King John's submission and his signing of Magna Carta in 1215.

In 1323, whilst a service was in progress, a catastrophe occurred. Two of the Norman pillars on the south of the nave collapsed outwards. Shortly afterwards the roof of this part of the nave fell in. It was not until 1345 that the rebuilding was completed. In medieval times the choir and presbytery were used exlusively by the monks and for this reason it was customary to screen off the choir from the nave which was frequently used for a variety of secular purposes. The present screen was built about 1360, under Abbot de la Mare, to replace an earlier one damaged in 1323. The two contemporary doors are still used for processional purposes. The screen is a rare survival from monastic times. I found myself just standing before the altar rails and looking at the sheer beauty of this screen with its delicate carving and wonderful, soft colouring. The same delicacy of touch is to be seen everywhere whether it is stone or wood. On the 14th century abbot's door, gnarled with age, the fine tracery is wonderfully wrought. Surrounding it the stonework reminds me of the markings I make with a pastry cutter!

THE RAMRYGE CHANTRY, one of the three chantries in the cathedral is outstandingly beautiful. It commemorates the abbacy of the 16th century Abbot

A rare survival - a 14th century pilgrim badge from the Verulamium museum

Ramyrge. The delicate fan vaulting on the ceiling was the last piece of mason's work in the church before the dissolution of the monastery and dates from about 1520. There is an inscription in the chantry which when translated means 'May the grace of the holy Spirit be with us'. How could it not be in somewhere so divinely beautiful.

It is quite hard to understand how anyone could be so vicious in the destruction of beautiful buildings but this is what occurred when Henry VIII became determined to close all monasteries and he sent Sir Richard Lee, a military engineer in to destroy the monastic buildings of St Albans. The materials were sold profitably for private construction work and for the building of roads. By 1553 the townspeople had had enough and they raised £400 to buy the church. The resources of the small market town were unable to contend with the upkeep and a long slow process of decay set in which must have been heartbreaking. Throughout the next 300 years the decline was unstoppable although the people did try hard especially at essential repairs. It was in 1800 that restoration commenced in earnest by which time the only parts still usable for worship were the choir and presbytery. Having said that much that is Norman still remains, for example the north transept which is Norman except for the part above the balcony.

The south wall of the south transept was completely reconstructed by Lord Grimthorpe in the 1880s. His skill and his money have been invested in the cathedral in many places. The Norman arcading beneath the lancet windows was resited by him from the Norman passageway to the Chapter House. The Michael Stair built in 1986 is a memorial to Bishop Michael Gresford-Jones who was Bishop of St Albans from 1950-1970. It is almost theatrically impressive to watch the choir and clergy descend from the vestries in the Chapter House.

If I had to answer what I find most beautiful about this lovely cathedral, I would find it hard to say but I suppose apart from the sheer magnificence of the whole cathedral, it would be the high altar screen which always leaves me stunned by the intricacy of the carving, the beauty of the figures and the majesty of the whole. My love of this Cathedral will be a life time affair and I have to confess to a love of St Albans as a whole.

133 London Road, St Albans,
Hertfordshire, AL1 1TA.

Tel: (0727) 844111
Fax: (0727) 861100

APPLES HOTEL
Hotel

This small, comfortable family run hotel is set in half an acre of gardens, close to the city centre and main line railway station, just back from the A 1081. It is within a stones throw of all the local motorways and yet it is surprisingly quiet and rural. St Albans Cathedral is five minutes by car or a pleasant stroll would take roughly 20 minutes using the 'Old London Road'.

The hotel was built in the 1930's and completely refurbished in 1988. It has nine en-suite bedrooms offering every modern facility. There is a quiet lounge in which to relax after a day's business or exploration. The friendly residents bar overlooks the outdoor swimming pool. Used quite extensively by business people who find it small conference/seminar facilities very useful, it is also a home from home for many visitors. David and Janet Day are the owners who together with Joel Day, grandmother, Elizabeth and Auntie Gladys look after everyone with efficient friendliness and can boast a collective local knowledge of 300 years. They are more than happy to talk to guests about where to go and what to see.

Good, traditional English fare with the occasional Chef's special to please the more adventurous is what you can expect. Beautifully cooked and always using fresh ingredients, a typical evening menu would offer choices of smoked salmon, melon, camembert wrapped in croissant pastry followed by chicken, steak or pork all served with or without the Chef's excellent sauces, which have found favour with regular guests. Vegetarians are very welcome and there is a wide choice of dishes for them.

USEFUL INFORMATION

OPEN: 24 hours with night access
CHILDREN: Welcome
CREDIT CARDS: Access/Visa/Master/
 Amex/Diners
LICENSED: Restaurant & Residential
ACCOMMODATION: 9 en-suite rooms

RESTAURANT: Traditional English.
 Fresh food only
BAR FOOD: Snacks
VEGETARIAN: Always 5 dishes
DISABLED ACCESS: Yes
GARDEN: Half acre. Ample parking

Hatfield Road, St Albans,
Hertfordshire, AL3 3RR.

Tel: (0727) 819340

MUSEUM OF ST ALBANS
Museum

The Museum of St Albans is to be found on the A1057 Hatfield Road, just a stone's throw from the town centre and a five minute walk from St Albans city station. There is a car park at the museum.

Here you can relive the story of the historic city from the departure of the Romans to the present day, through exciting and innovative galleries, each laid out with skill and care. The new 'Tools for the Job' gallery exhibits the renowned 'Salaman Collection' of trade tools. If you have any imagination you will wonder how, with such primitive tools, the artisans and craftsman produced such extraordinarily effective buildings and artefacts.

The wildlife garden is a delight. Gardening is one of the most popular leisure activities, but gardens are also a refuge and home for many of our wild plants and animals that are finding it difficult to survive in our dwindling countryside. At the museum of St Albans they are cultivating a garden to provide a rich habitat which will support a wide range of animals and plants. The aim is to create a well balanced garden attractive to both people and wildlife and with easy access. The garden has been divided into thematic plots: butterfly garden, herb garden, pond, wall, woodland edge, coppice woodland, hedgerows, mini habitats, compost heap.

St Albans Museum provide a comprehensive service to teachers and schools with museum education officers at both its museums, a school loans service, membership scheme and termly publication 'School News'.

USEFUL INFORMATION

OPEN: Mon-Sat: 10am-5pm. Sundays 2pm-
 5pm. Admission free
CHILDREN: Welcome. Quiz sheets
CREDIT CARDS: Visa/Access
GIFT SHOP: Wide range of gifts and books.
DISABLED ACCESS: No
GARDEN: Large wildlife garden with
 seating, picnic area, beehives

THE NOKE THISTLE HOTEL
Hotel

Watford Road, St Albans,
Hertfordshire, AL2 3DS.

Tel: (0727) 854252
Fax: (0727) 841906

USEFUL INFORMATION

OPEN: 24 hours
CHILDREN: Very welcome
CREDIT CARDS: Access/Visa/Amex/ Diners
LICENSED: Full On Licence
ACCOMMODATION: 111 bedrooms

RESTAURANT: French A la Carte. English Table d'Hote
BAR FOOD: Charcoal grill
VEGETARIAN: Always six dishes
DISABLED ACCESS: Ground floor entrance. Limited facilities
GARDEN: Patio garden. BBQs

Ideally situated on the A405, close to the main motorways, M1 (J6) the M25 (J21a) and the M10, The Noke Thistle Hotel is a delightful country style hotel, set in its own grounds. It is a peaceful, tranquil place of great comfort and one of the finest award winning restaurants in the area.

From time immemorial there has been a manor here. It is recorded even before the Norman Conquest. However it was not until the 16th century that the word Noke came into being – a corruption of the word Oak. Noke was the name of the farm which was part of the Burston manor estate. In 1880 Burston manor and Noke farm were sold for £799 5 shillings and six pence!

Dispensing hospitality since Victorian times when the hotel only had six rooms, it now has 111 beautifully furnished and equipped bedrooms, one of which is called 799 in recognition of the purchase of the original manor in which it is housed. It is a hotel that treats everyone as individuals with an old fashioned courtesy and efficiency that is very welcome. There is a main public bar with a bistro diner and the restaurant which is delightful to dine in and the accompanying food and wine superb. In the summer the patio and garden area at the front of the 'Baltimore Bean Co Bar' enables guests to eat and drink al fresco. There are also barbecues. Many stately homes are within easy access of the Noke Thistle, and the Roman city of St Albans is a wonderful place in which to explore. This hotel would be ideal for a wedding reception, a conference or seminar, or indeed for any special occasion.

ST MICHAEL'S MANOR HOTEL
Hotel

Fishpool Street, St Albans,
Hertfordshire, AL3 4RY.

Tel: (0727) 864444
Fax: (0727) 848909

USEFUL INFORMATION

OPEN: All year round
CHILDREN: Welcome
CREDIT CARDS: Access/Visa/Amex/ Diners
LICENSED: Full Licence
ACCOMMODATION: 12 double, 7 twin, 3 single, all ensuite

RESTAURANT: A La Carte, Table d'Hote fresh produce
BAR FOOD: Not applicable
VEGETARIAN: Always dishes available
DISABLED ACCESS: Ground floor only
GARDEN: 5 acres, award winning

Just twenty miles from London is one of England's loveliest hotels. This would be so wherever it was situated in the country, but added to the ecclesiastical history of St Albans, called 'Verulamium' by the Romans, it makes an outstanding place in which to stay. This charming 16th century manor house which takes its name from the nearby church of St Michael, celebrated 400 years of history in 1986. It lies in five acres of beautifully tended grounds between the river and Fishpool Street. The whole of this hotel is framed in elegance. The rooms are beautifully furnished, everything that can be done for the comfort and convenience of guests has received attention. In the bedrooms, all having ensuite facilities, colour television, radio, telephone, hairdryer and many more thoughtful touches, one is assured of a good night's rest.

For the last three decades the hotel has been owned and lived in by Mr and Mrs Newling Ward who inspire their very professional team to strive for perfection. The head chef provides delicious a la carte and table d'hote menus, with a special 'Chef's Recommendation Menu' in the evening. On Sunday evenings there is a very popular buffet supper. Everything is cooked traditionally, using fresh herbs from the garden.

The original manor house was first built by the Gape family about 1586 on medieval foundations which still form part of the cellars beneath the house. Over the centuries the manor has undergone structural change, but happily blending styles, and has never been more beautiful with its latest addition, a delightful Victorian-style conservatory.

St Michael's, St Albans,
Hertfordshire, AL3 4SW.

Tel: (0727) 819339
Fax: (0727) 859919

VERULAMIUM MUSEUM

Museum

Set in a 100 acre park on the site of one of Roman Britain's major cities, the museum tells the story of every day life in Verulamium. You will find it ten minutes from Junction 21A on the M25 or Junction 9 on the M1. There is an adjacent car park. Within the park are the remains of the Roman wall and the 'Hypocaust' can also be seen with a Roman theatre nearby.

The Verulamium has thrilled many people and has deservedly won three awards in the last year, including a British Travel Authority, 'Come to Britain' Award. The museum tells the story of St Albans' Roman past. It is the story of every day life in Verulamium highlighted by excellent displays which include reconstructed Roman rooms, interactive 'Discovery Areas', an excavation video and one of the finest collections of Roman artefacts and mosaics in the country. The Roman skills in every field are seen in other places in Britain but perhaps not as often so well portrayed as at Verulamium. Entrance is free to residents of St Albans District and to Friends of St Albans Museum - a wonderful bonus, because a single visit here will never suffice.

Honorary guides undertake guided walks around the park and tours and talks within the museum. For children quiz sheets are available which helps them retain the knowledge of the past that they readily absorb while they are there but perhaps would forget equally quickly without some aide-memoire.

USEFUL INFORMATION

OPEN: Mon-Sat: 10am-5.30pm.
Sunday: 2pm-5.30pm.
CHILDREN: Welcome. Quiz sheets available
CREDIT CARDS: Visa/Access
RESTAURANT: Not applicable
DISABLED ACCESS: Yes

Truro Cathedral

Truro

"Fine art is that in which the hand, the head, and the heart go together"

John Keats

The City of Truro

by John Theobald

TRURO CATHEDRAL was the first to be built in England since the completion by Wren of St Paul's in London. Today, eighty years after its completion, the three-spired Cathedral church of St Marys dominates this elegant city and adds great character to one of the most attractive spots in the Duchy. For the Cathedral does not stand in quiet, cloistered grounds away from urban bustle. The precincts of Truro Cathedral are the busy streets, lanes and passages of the county town and you feel that this great church is very much part and parcel of daily life. As indeed it is, for it incorporates part of the Parish church of St Marys that had stood here since the 16th century.

The town had grown round a Norman castle, now long vanished, and by the 18th century it was both prosperous and fashionable, returning two Members to Parliament. Mine owners' families lived in big houses, and wealth rubbed shoulders with fame. When Parliament in the 19th century responded to the petition of Cornish people that they should have their own diocese - they had been without their own Bishop for many centuries - the Bishopric of Truro was created in 1876. The Bishop of Exeter no longer had to make infrequent visits to this distant part of his see.

A little more than a year later Truro was granted city status. It was already an important commercial centre, a port - although its heyday as a shipping centre for the mining industry was over - a shopping centre and a gracious place to live for its prosperous middle class whose lovely Georgian homes give Truro such a distinctive character.

Bodmin was anxious to have the Cathedral, a Royal Commission recommended it should be at St. Columb, and Parliament decided on Truro. The first bishop was Edward Benson who had become headmaster of Wellington College at the age of 29 and went on 15 years later to become Chancellor of Lincoln Cathedral. The Queen approved his appointment to Truro in January 1877, and his residence became Lis Escop - a Cornish name at Kenwyn. Three of his sons became well-known writers. A.C Benson's work included the poem, Land of Hope and Glory; E.F Benson created Lucia and Mapp; and R.H Benson was a prolific Edwardian novelist. Dr Benson, a friend of Gladstone was consecrated at St Paul's in April, 1877, and he was enthroned at Truro on May 1st in St. Mary's Parish Church. Eight Cornish Mayors were in the procession of clergy and others from the town hall, led by the band of volunteers, to the old church which was packed to capacity.

It was no easy task for the new Bishop to have as his Cathedral a modest parish church. A new Act of Parliament

would have been needed to change the site and the Bishop, with the Earl of Mount Edgecumbe in firm support, persuaded the building committee - of which the Earl was chairman - to have a completely new building constructed in place of the old church, parts of which would be incorporated in it.

Wisely the committee chose the distinguished architect John Loughborough Pearson who rose to the challenge of a restricted site - no more than 300 feet long - and a mandate to incorporate part of the old parish church. On this site rose a brilliant creation of a Gothic Cathedral with impressive vaulting, presenting from the outside a bulk that looked far larger than it really was.

One historian has described it as one of the finest Victorian churches designed by one of the best Victorian ecclesiastical architects. Pearson with all his experience made one error. He chose Bath stone for some of the decorative exterior work and it was no match for the fierce south westerlies. Fortunately the Cornish granite used for the main outer walls stood up to any weather. The foundation stone was laid in May, 1880, by the Prince of Wales, later to become King Edward VII. One of the two sons with him and his wife Queen Alexandra, was to become King George V.

The royal party stayed at the home of Lord Falmouth at nearby Tregothnan at TRESILLIAN BRIDGE, after being welcomed by the Lord Lieutenant, the Earl of Mount Edgcumbe. A grand ball was held there on the eve of the ceremony. Bishop Benson welcomed the Prince at noon the next day and the Prince laid the foundation stone at the east end of the site and a memorial stone that is now part of a column in the nave. The day ended with a firework display. The following Sunday an open air service on the site was attended by 4,000 people.

In 1882 Dr Benson was appointed Archbishop of Canterbury and was succeeded by Dr Wilkinson, a London prelate. In 1887 the Prince returned to Truro for the four hour service of consecration and after spending the night on the Royal Yacht in Falmouth Harbour arrived by train to join a congregation of 2,500 that included 19 bishops. Only the two western towers remained to be completed and they were finished in 1910, with one being named after King Edward VII, now dead, and Queen Alexandra. It was fulfillment of a remarkable achievement and an act of great faith. For when the decision to build was taken Cornwall had seen its mining industry in collapse with a third of its population emigrated. No-one could be certain that the money could be raised to pay the huge bills that would have to be met. Pearson had estimated the basic costs to be nearly one hundred thousand pounds, an enormous sum in those days. Ten thousand pounds was needed to buy land and prepare the site. It was not a wealthy community, but it was a community with great pride and of strong religious belief. The final two towers were in fact paid for by a donation from a local widow in memory of her husband.

When the benefactress handed the towers over at a special service it was to the fourth bishop to hold office during the thirty year period its construction had covered. He was Dr William Stubbs. It stands in an area called High Cross for here the townspeople had stood to hear preachers and St Mary's had been the third church to be built here. The fourth was to be a master-piece and another historian has called it a brilliant realisation of the ideal Gothic Cathedral. There is a generous agreement that the Cathedral gives the illusion of being far bigger than it actually is. The great organ is by Willis.

The Bishop's Chair is of Burmese teak and the beautifully carved pulpit is below the 244 feet high tower. (The Bishops Chair, incidentally, in Latin is called a cathedra from the Greek word for chair, and it is from this that the word Cathedral itself comes, as does the phrase ex cathedra, for weighty pronounce-ments.) The acoustic problems caused by the soaring heights above have finally been solved by modern sound equipment.

Detail from Tinworth's terracotta of the Via Crusis

The brass eagle lectern was presented by a local woman whose father had been one of Nelson's captains. The many memorials in the church reflect the history of the town and county through its leading figures who ranged from captains of the mining industry to soldiers and engineers. One of the most prominent is to the Robartes family who made their fortune from tin.

The first Lord Robartes began the building of LANHYDROCK HOUSE, near Bodmin, in the 17th century where the family finally settled in great splendour. It is now one of the National Trust's finest houses in Cornwall. There are guided tours of the Cathedral and refreshments are available in the Chapter House refectory. A shop adjoining the Cathedral has much literature on its history. The Chapter House is a modern building which is both graceful and impressive, harmonising successfully with its neighbour. Two descendants of the Earl of Mount Edgcumbe were present when it was opened in the 1960's to become an important part of diocesan life. I later went to meetings there, in connection with the celebrations of the centennial of the creation of the diocese, when the Bishop was Dr Leonard Graham. He is a man of great learning who went on to become Bishop of London and to lead the opposition against women entering the priesthood.

I hope you will find reading about this cathedral especially interesting having read Bernard Fullerton's chapter on St Pauls for, of course, it was to this Cathedral and its choir school that the young choristers of St Paul's were evacuated during World War II.

More of Truro's history is displayed in the town's MUSEUM AND ART GALLERY in River Street, which is open from 9 am to 5 pm every week-day except Sundays and Bank Holidays. The work of the Cornish painter John Opie, the Court painter to George III, is well represented, and there are many old masters such as Rubens and Constable. There is a first class collection of Cornish minerals and many artefacts covering the long history of this Celtic tip of England.

There is more history in its finest street, Lemon Street, and this is a history carved in the Bath stone used to face its Georgian houses. In a county where its native granite was normally used in building, the stone stands out because of its mellow qualities. At Lemon Street top is a tall monument to the man who discovered the source of the Niger, the explorer Richard Lander.

Born in 1803, the son of a Truro inn-keeper, he was 22 when he joined his first expedition to Africa. As a boy of 11 he had sailed on a merchantman to the West Indies and by the time he was 21 he had travelled much of the world. His work recording the achievements of the first expedition, whose leader had died, so impressed the Government they sent him back to explore the Niger. He died on his third expedition after being wounded by African tribesmen.

Walsingham Place is another good example of Georgian building. It is a great pleasure to explore this pretty Georgian street. But, then I have found it a great pleasure to visit Truro, which I have done on countless occasions. If I want to explore its shopping streets and alleys the west front of the Cathderal is as good a starting point as any. In front of it is High Cross where there was for long a cattle market until it moved to Castle Hill. It took its name from the high cross that stood there. There was once bear-baiting here.

Not far off are the CROWN COURT BUILDINGS which have not long been open and whose outstanding architecture won it a top design award. I prefer to make my way through narrow passages to the Quay, east of the Cathedral.

Oldest of all the lanes in this gridwork of passage-ways is Cathedral Lane. Like Plymouth's Barbican this area has several opes, passage-ways connecting parallel streets. One passage-way has the picturesque name of Squeezegut Alley.

Boscawen Street is the principal shopping and commercial street. Boscawen is the family name of Lord Falmouth. The Falmouth's were great Truro property owners and were the most influential in the town and it was to honour them that the principle street was named in the 1790's when it was built. A new MARKET HALL was opened in 1847 so that the traders whose stalls clogged Boscawen Street would have cover. It was a particularly popular name then. Perhaps the most famous of the family had been Edward Boscawen, who had died in 1761. He was the third son of an earlier Viscount Falmouth.

He was a naval commander known as Old Dreadnought who had a number of celebrated victories over the French, which earnt him the thanks of Parliament and the affection af all Cornishmen, many of whom served with him. You will find in the church of St Michael Penkevil outside the gates of Tregothnan a notable monument to the admiral, as well as others to members of his family. The Boscawens had married into the Godolphin family - one Godolphin had been Lord High Treasurer in the 17th century and the Churchills, one of whom was to become Duke of Malborough.

The Boscawens therefore had great influence in Westminster and Hugh Boscawen, who had married John Churchill's niece, became an MP. He helped put down a Jacobite rebellion, during which he arrested another prominent Cornishman, Sir Richard Vyvyan. Trelowarren on the Helford river was the Vyvyan home and they were notable Royalists.

Sir Richard was locked up in the Tower of London to prevent him supporting the Pretender. For this Hugh was created the first Viscount Falmouth. Four of his sons became a Member for Truro. Much of their land in Truro was sold in Victorian times. TREGOTHNAN is reached from Tresillian at the head of a creek a few miles east of the city. It is a mansion standing in beautiful gardens surrounded by a deer park with magnificent views of the River Fal. It was built by the architect responsible for most of King's College at Cambridge. Here in Boscawen Street in Truro stood the 14th century COINAGE HALL where the tin ingots were weighed, assayed and stamped before being loaded for shipping from the Quay. It was the most important building in the town and on it depended the prosperity of the area. A prison stood next to the Coinage Hall and outside it floggings took place regularly near the public stocks which were used well into Queen Victoria's reign. The offender was tied to a cart tail and then paraded round the town as the flogging continued. Others were sentenced to transportation from **Falmouth.**

Floggings in Boscawen Street continued until early Victorian times. Here also stood the great 16th century town house of the Robartes who had financed the tin industry. They had been the greatest land owners in Truro but their influence waned when Lanhydrock was built and the Falmouth's became the leading family. To this day the Falmouths remain one of the most influential families in the Duchy and the present Viscount is Lord Lieutenant of the county, a man of great public spiritedness.

In Boscawen Street stood the house of another important family of land-owners, the Foote's. This great house, built in 1671 became the famous Red Lion Hotel until its tragic demolition in recent times. For nearly two hundred years the inn was the town's leading hostelry.

Samuel Foote, born in 1720 became a famous actor and playwright and a companion of Dr Johnson who found his wit and satirical humour compelling. Inns played an important part in the social life of what was a hard drinking city. The Fighting Cocks where Richard Lander was born, celebrated the highly popular sport of cock-fighting. A public house called The Ship sponsored Cornish wrestling at which Lander's father was a leading contender. As many as 8,000 would gather on nearby land to watch a championship match. That is a sport popular to this day.

The Lemon family, who were to give their name to Lemon Street, also owned land in Boscawen Street. William Lemon was born in 1696, built a great house in Truro and became Sheriff of Cornwall. His wealth came from mining, too, for he had been granted a mineral monopoly, excluding tin but including copper, for the whole of the country. He controlled production from the ore's extraction to its smelting in the smelting houses. Men such as Lemon had a finger in many other commercial pies, too. Shipping and milling were among them. His grandson, Sir William Lemon, went on to found the Copper Miners Bank in Princess Street.

In Princess Street still stands the fine PRINCES HOUSE built by the first William Lemon. The historic TRURO GRAMMAR SCHOOL is still by the Cathedral and it gave a good education to many Cornish boys from a wide area who later made their mark in the county. The school long ago moved to more spacious premises. Close by the Princes House is THE MANSION HOUSE, built for an associate of Lemon's, Thomas Danniell. Here the rivers Allen and Kenwyn become the Truro which in turn becomes the Fal. They were the source of the power for the many mills that once ground corn and combed wool in this area. They have caused some nasty flooding and destruction in the city at times. There is still some commercial shipping but the river is now used principally by pleasure boats in the summer and is no longer the vital trade route it was for centuries. The trip to Falmouth takes about an hour and well worthwhile it is too.

Stand and stare; there is a beautiful and piercing simplicity about the 14th century Breton Pieta which conveys the mother's dignity and a grief more poignant than any words

There was a Customs House in Truro on the Back Quay until late Victorian times. One commodity on which tax was not levied was the famous oysters from down river which were landed daily on the Town Quay. Vegetables too, came up river.

Commercial cargoes arrived weekly until the arrival of the railways and the growth of Falmouth, one of Cornwall's most attractive towns.

Truro has the unique and outstanding ALVERTON MANOR HOTEL, in Tregolls Road. Not so many years ago it was a convent belonging to the Sisters of the Epiphany and still has the splendid chapel, a popular and sought after venue for wedding receptions and conferences. The hotel is stunning. It is spacious, gracious, beautifully furnished and has a sense of peace which maybe comes from its past but it is more realistic to say that it is achieved by the splendid team work which, headed by partner Michelle Marks, goes into the efficient and smooth running of the establishment. You would expect nothing less than excellent food from such an establishment and you will not be disappointed. It is as exciting as it is innovative and wide ranging.

All food loving travellers should take themselves to MERRIVALE CHARCUTERIE in Coombes Lane.

This is one of the great food success stories in Truro in recent years with an unrivalled reputation in the West Country for the quality and range of their produce. All the meats sold here are locally produced or free range from the West Country. Game of all description in season, from Cornish venison to locally shot woodcock and pheasant. Their famous range of sausages, which make perfect presents, include the spicy Spanish style Chorizo, Toulouse and others.

Truro has a beautiful CITY HALL building right in the city centre and today it houses many unusual and elegant shops, one of which is THE TERRACE, a charming, welcoming good quality coffee shop.

Side-roads off the main road from Truro to Falmouth lead to yachting havens such as **Devoran** and **Restronguet Creek**. Halfway between Truro and **Perranarworthal** at **Playing Place** take the road to the left and it will bring you to the National Trust Gardens of TRELISSICK and also to King Harry's Ferry.

Trelissick is a Georgian House with another magnificent view of the river across the beautiful gardens. Here, too, is Lis Escop, the home of the Bishop of Truro.

Philleigh is a charming and attractive village which one discovers on the way from **Ruan High Lanes** to the King Harry Ferry. From the Truro side of the Fal the ferry will take you and your car across the river and then there is a delightful drive to THE ROSELAND INN, just one and a half miles on the other side. Graham and Jackie Hill have made this 16th century inn a very special place. It is a pub dedicated to the art of conversation and you can talk in

peace whilst enjoying the cheerful chatter of the regulars at the bar. In the winter, log fires burn at either end of the inn and sometimes an antique bagatelle table is produced - a game that most people under 50 will not remember!

Ruan High Lanes has POLSUE MANOR HOTEL which stands totally enclosed in its own grounds. It has a wonderful feeling of seclusion and space. The four and a half acres of gardens, woodlands and orchard just reinforce this. It is the beauty of the grounds that first strikes you as you come down the drive. There is a woodland trail for you to walk through which ends in an orchard and it is here that the colours in Autumn are particularly appealing. Polsue Manor is ideal for a break or a holiday and excellent value.

In Perranarworthal on the right as you enter from Truro is the big house that was the home of the Nobel prize-winning author, William Golding, who died recently. In war-time it was used by General Eisenhower and then became the home of Princess Bibesco, a famous friend of writers such as Proust.

THE NORWAY INN here gets its name from the timber cargoes that were brought here from Scandinavia to creek that is now silted up. The Norwegian Pine was used to make pit props for the Cornish mines.

The next road to the left will bring you to the beautiful waterside village of **Mylor**. William Lemon, who built Lemon Street, had a great family house here which burnt down between the world wars. MYLOR CHURCH and its memorials inside is of great interest.

Nearby ENYS is the estate of another 18th century wealthy Truro merchant, Samuel Enys. Beyond Penryn, just outside **Falmouth**, is **Flushing** where Dutch ship-builders were once established and mailboat skippers lived. Falmouth owes its maritime importance to its great natural harbour and its selection as a station for the Mail Packet Service. Here arrived the fast Falmouth Packets - the local newspaper took its name from them - giving the latest intelligence from abroad.

When Victoria ascended to the throne there were 39 ships taking and bringing mail to and from the America's and the Mediterranean. The service went to Southampton when steam replaced sail and Falmouth never quite regained its importance. But, Falmouth Docks, which were taken over by Peter de Savary, play a vital role in the town's maritime and economic life.

Falmouth is a lovely spot, full of treasures such as the CUSTOMS HOUSE on the Town Quay. Its enormous chimney, the Kings Pipe, was needed to burn vast quantities of contraband tobacco. It has always attracted writers and artists. 'The Wind in the Willows' was written here and its author Kenneth Grahame, stayed at THE GREENBANK HOTEL.

Howard Spring, the best selling novelist, had a beautiful home, The White House, here and he loved this town in which he died. His wife made its gardens memorable. Henry Tuke is perhaps its best known painter.

Falmouth today is a great tourist and yachting centre with many excellent hotels, inns and eating houses. It has, too, its own fishing boats. The Parish Church in the main street has many memorials to the captains of the packet ships who often had to fight their way home against hostile French or American privateers.

There is a memorial to a Cornishman called Sleeman who helped suppress the members of the secret religious order of Thuggee who throttled many thousands of Indian travellers and bequeathed us the word 'Thug'. His work is commemorated in a novel by John Masters.

PENDENNIS CASTLE was built on a headland by Henry the Eighth and added to by Queen Elizabeth the First. It watches over a great stretch of the English Channel and across the estuary known as the Carrick Roads to its fellow fortress, St Mawes Castle on the Roseland peninsula. You can reach **St Mawes** by ferry and explore the harbour by pleasure boat.

The two castles were part of a network of defences designed to keep the French at bay along the whole of the Channel coast from the most distant part of Kent to the very tip of Cornwall.

Two hotels at different levels, I am happy to recommend. The first is the friendly and not wildly expensive BROADMEAD HOTEL in Kimberley Park Road. This is a light, spacious building with attractive decor and well furnished bedrooms. Staying here is very much like a home from home.

The first sight of THE PENMERE MANOR HOTEL in Mongleath Road, conjures up the words, impressive, elegant, superbly positioned and a host of other flattering euphomisms, all of them correctly applied. Over the

twenty five years that the Pope family have owned Penmere, they have extended it with skill and care to provide more bedrooms, a bigger restaurant and the 'Fountain Leisure Club' plus excellent conference facilities. Bolithos Restaurant, open to non-residents is renowned throughout Cornwall. It has everything and more that is expected of a high quality, 3 star hotel.

This area has such a mild climate that back in the 50's and 60's a St Mawes hotelier used to advertise that if any snow fell in the area or fog blanketed it, the guests would not be charged. I don't think Harley Moseley, former American diplomat who fell in love with the place, and bought several hotels, ever paid out.

St Mawes has always attracted many well known people and has been a retreat for peers and those who people the society columns of our newspapers. When I want to stay close to Truro but not in it and equally want to enjoy the Roseland Peninsula with its endless wonderful surprises hidden away, I make for GERRANS BAY HOTEL, originally a large Victorian house which has been carefully extended and modernised to create a welcoming place in which to stay with every possible modern facility. You

The Bapistry; "Gem of the Cathedral", by John Loughborough Pearson

will find it situated on the edge of **Gerrans Village** near Posrtscatho with a view from the front over Gerrans Bay. Here you have the countryside, great beauty, sandy beaches, superb cliff walks and inland creeks which make it a perfect setting for a holiday or a break.

One of the joys about Truro is its central position in Cornwall and the ease with which one can reach either coastline. **Newquay** is a popular holiday resort and for me it is at its best in the quieter times when most of the visitors have gone home. Then you really have a chance to enjoy the beaches for walks and find the scenery thrilling. Watching the waves throw up the surf as they come pounding in from the Atlantic on a winter's day is exhilarating. A favourite hotel of mine in which to stay is PORTH VEOR MANOR overlooking **Porth Beach**. It has a commanding yet sheltered position and is a 19th century house of unique charm and character. This is a wonderful place to stay in the summer, but it is equally attractive out of season and welcomes guests all the year round.

My last recommendation is some distance away in the old fishing village and artist's paradise, **St Ives**. No one should come to Cornwall without seeking out this enchanting place with its narrow streets, superb beaches and unusual light that has brought artists here for generations. I love the place and to round off any visit there, one must have a meal in THE MERMAID SEAFOOD RESTAURANT. This is an eating experience that will live in your mind long after you have left it. It is not just the food which is superb, it is the whole ambience of the place which has been created by the owners, Trevor Smith and his wife, Helen who is the talented chef.

I shall be surprised if you do not fall under the spell of Truro and the many enchanting towns, villages and waterways to which it is the gateway.

Kimberley Park Road,
Falmouth, TR11 2DD.

Tel: (0326) 315704

BROADMEAD HOTEL
Hotel

For anyone wanting to find a comfortable, friendly hotel that is not wildly expensive yet offers every facility, and is conveniently situated, then the Broadmead Hotel must answer that criteria. It stands overlooking the beautiful Kimberley Park, with its myriad of ever-changing colours throughout the seasons and from the hotel it takes no time at all to walk into the town centre or to the beaches.

The Broadmead is a light, spacious building with attractive decor and well furnished bedrooms. Staying here is very much like a home from home. The informality of the owner and staff hides the true professionalism with which the hotel is run. The restaurant and bar is open to non-residents who are as welcome as those staying in the hotel. Every meal is enjoyable with a regular change in the menu. No one will ever leave the table feeling hungry.

Every day people staying here, at any time of the year, can spend their time in Falmouth or quite easily reach Truro with its fine cathedral. St Mawes and Flushing are just across the river; all you have to do is step aboard one of the ferries that leave from the Prince of Wales Pier. Places as far apart as Land's End, The Lizard and Tintagel where King Arthur had his castle, are all within striking distance. Falmouth, of course, is famous for its wonderful harbour - the third largest natural harbour in the world; and the wide beaches and creeks of the Fal and Helford Rivers, ideal for sailing or for boat trips.

USEFUL INFORMATION

OPEN: All Year
CHILDREN: Catered for
CREDIT CARDS: Visa/Access/Amex
LICENSED: Restaurant & Residential
ACCOMMODATION: Comfortable
   ensuite rooms

RESTAURANT: 7-8pm. Open to non-residents
BAR FOOD: Lunctime service for residents
VEGETARIAN: By arrangement
DISABLED ACCESS: New English Tourist Board Category 3
GARDEN: None

Mongleath Road, Falmouth,
Cornwall, TR11 4PN.

Tel: (0326) 211411
Fax: (0326) 317588

PENMERE MANOR HOTEL
Hotel & Restaurant

The first sight of Penmere Manor Hotel conjures up the words, impressive, elegant, superbly positioned and a host of other flattering euphomisms, all of them correct, and enhanced by entering its portals. The main Georgian house was built in 1825 and has always been a happy house, generous in its hospitality, even though over the years it has had many owners. The Bolitho family bought it in 1900 remaining owners until 1948. It became a hotel in 1958 and today, in the capable hands of Andrew and Elizabeth Pope, it is one of the most delightful places to be in the West Country. The Popes have always made it their home as well as their business and have created the delightful, welcoming feeling you get when you stay here.

Over the twenty five years that the Pope family have owned Penmere, they have extended it with skill and care to produce more bedrooms, a bigger restaurant, the 'Fountain Leisure Club' and excellent conference facilities. Bolitho's Restaurant, open to non-residents, is renowned throughout Cornwall. It has everything and more that is expected in a high quality, 3 star hotel.

Penmere is designed for leisure, pleasure and for business. With its five acres of garden and woodland, it is perfect for a wedding luncheon for up to 120. The views from the terrace compliment the luxury of the Georgian house; and the excellent service and cuisine combine to make the day happy and memorable. Every day, every night and every meal is memorable at Penmere

USEFUL INFORMATION

OPEN: All year except 4 days at Christmas
CHILDREN: Welcome. Baby listening etc.
CREDIT CARDS: Visa/Mastercard
   Amex/Diners
LICENSED: Full On Licence
ACCOMMODATION: Twins, doubles, family, all ensuite

RESTAURANT: Superb international cuisine
BAR FOOD: Wide selection, available daily: 12-2pm
VEGETARIAN: Selection available
DISABLED ACCESS: Limited
GARDEN: 5 acres, sub-tropical gardens & woodland

THE ROSELAND INN
Inn

Philleigh, Nr. Truro,
Cornwall, TR2 5NB.

Tel: (0872) 580254

USEFUL INFORMATION

OPEN: 11.30-3pm & 6-11pm. Sun: 12-3pm & 7-10.30pm
CHILDREN: Welcome
CREDIT CARDS: None taken
LICENSED: Full On licence
ACCOMMODATION: None - rooms available next door in farmhouse

RESTAURANT: Not applicable
BAR FOOD: Wide range of super food.
VEGETARIAN: Selection always available
DISABLED ACCESS: Special door at front. Good access to lounge area
GARDEN: Spacious front patio area

Philleigh is a charming and attractive village which one discovers on the way from Ruan High Lanes to the King Harry Ferry. From the Truro side of the Fal the ferry will take you and your car across river and then there is a delightful drive to the Roseland just one and a half miles on the other side.

Graham and Jackie Hill have made the 16th century Roseland Inn a very special place. It was formerly three cottages and the low beams remind one of its age. The cleverly constructed sunken bar is the focal point for locals and a happy discovery for strangers. Everywhere is comfortably furnished in keeping with the age of the inn. Children are very welcome providing they have their parents under control at all times! It is a pub dedicated to the art of conversation and you can talk in peace and enjoy the cheerful chatter of the regulars at the bar. In the winter, log fires burn at either end of the inn and sometimes an antique bagatelle table is produced - a game that most people under 50 will not remember!

The extensive bar menu available during opening times is delicious. You will never find chips on the menu! In the evenings there is also an A La Carte Menu. Recently a glorious seafood menu is available at 24 hours notice based on the Brittany 'Fruits de Mer'. The food is perfectly cooked, imaginatively thought out and well presented and you will never feel that the price was not right. If you take a fancy to the Roseland Inn and want to stay closeby, Graham and Jacquie will introduce you to the local farm next door who have comfortable rooms.

PORTH VEOR MANOR
Hotel & Restaurant

Porth Way, Nr Newquay,
Cornwall, TR7 3LW.

Tel: (0637) 873274
Fax: (0637) 851690

USEFUL INFORMATION

OPEN: All year round
CHILDREN: Welcome
CREDIT CARDS: Visa/Access
LICENSED: Full restaurant licence
ACCOMMODATION: 17 ensuite rooms. Pets by arrangement

RESTAURANT: Traditional English.
BAR FOOD: Snacks available
VEGETARIAN: Always available
DISABLED ACCESS: Yes. Ground floor rooms
GARDEN: Beautiful & overlooking Porth Bay

This is an early 19th century country house of unique charm and character, situated in almost three acres of private grounds overlooking Porth Beach. From its commanding yet sheltered position, magnificent views can be enjoyed over terraced lawns and gardens to beach and valley, and the panoramic vista of the spectacular Cornish coast beyond. The tree-fringed grounds are a haven of peace and tranquillity. A short private path leads to Porth Beach where there is clean sand, rock pools and safe bathing. Newquay is within walking distance, a town that has all the amenities of a large holiday resort and provides golf and most recreational facilities. There are all sorts of reasons for choosing to stay here, including a base for exploring the wealth of scenery which makes up Cornwall. Truro with its magnificent Cathedral is only 15 miles distant.

Porth Veor Manor is wonderful to stay in during the summer months, but it is equally attractive out of season. The bedrooms are all ensuite and fully centrally heated. The welcome is warm at whatever time of year you come. People who come for a break between October and May will tell you that this quieter period is even better for a holiday. There are less people about and although sunning oneself on the beach is not possible, the rewards are there for those who enjoy walking, birdwatching, archeology, fishing or golf and exploring the many quaint villages throughout the county. It is exciting on a stormy day to see the waves pounding against the rocks knowing you can retreat to the comfort of this exceptionally pleasant family run hotel.

GERRANS BAY HOTEL
Hotel & Restaurant

12 Tregassick Road, Portscatho,
Nr Truro, Cornwall, TR2 5ED.

Tel: (0872) 580338

Originally a large Victorian house the Gerrans Bay Hotel has been carefully extended and modernised to create a welcoming place to stay with all modern facilities. All of the hotel's 14 bedrooms, four of which are on the ground floor, are comfortably furnished and provided with tea and coffee making facilities. The double rooms have en-suite bathrooms complete with bath, shower and toilet and the single rooms have private bathrooms, again with bath, shower and toilet.

There is a well appointed lounge to relax in and meet fellow guests; a separate television lounge and a small bar which is stocked with a wide range of both alcoholic and non-alcoholic drinks. There is ample car parking within the hotel grounds and the gardens and lawns at both front and rear of the hotel offer guests a chance to relax and enjoy the peace and tranquillity of their surroundings.

The hotel prides itself in offering a very high standard of home cooked food, using local produce wherever possible. Their bread rolls, soups, pates, sweets etc are freshly made on the premises. The AA have awarded a well deserved red rosette for the standard of food.

Situated on the edge of Gerrans village on the beautiful Roseland Peninsula, the front of the hotel overlooks part of the village to Gerrans Bay itself, whilst the back looks over miles upon miles of open countryside. Here you have great beauty, sandy beaches, superb cliff walks and inland creeks which make it the perfect holiday setting. Within easy reach of the hotel are many National Trust gardens and properties and for those who enjoy more active pastimes, golf, squash, tennis, sailing, wind-surfing, riding and bowls are all available within a few miles of the hotel.

USEFUL INFORMATION

OPEN: April-October plus Christmas
CHILDREN: Welcome.
Dogs - by prior arrangement
CREDIT CARDS: Access/Visa/Amex
LICENSED: Restaurant & Residential
ACCOMMODATION: 14 rooms
all with private bathrooms

RESTAURANT: Traditional English.
AA red rosette
BAR FOOD: Morning coffee, light lunches
& snacks, Cornish Cream Teas
VEGETARIAN: Special diets by prior
arrangement
DISABLED ACCESS: Yes, but limited.
4 ground floor bedrooms
GARDEN: Tranquil gardens & lawns

THE MERMAID SEAFOOD RESTAURANT
Restaurant

21 Fish Street, St Ives,
Cornwall, TR26 1LT.

Tel: (0736) 796816

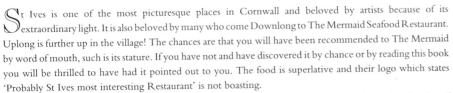

St Ives is one of the most picturesque places in Cornwall and beloved by artists because of its extraordinary light. It is also beloved by many who come Downlong to The Mermaid Seafood Restaurant. Uplong is further up in the village! The chances are that you will have been recommended to The Mermaid by word of mouth, such is its stature. If you have not and have discovered it by chance or by reading this book you will be thrilled to have had it pointed out to you. The food is superlative and their logo which states 'Probably St Ives most interesting Restaurant' is not boasting.

The Mermaid was originally a sail loft and then became 'Tuckers Pop Factory'. A superb collection of old photographs adorn the walls. Solid church pews are in use for the seating, creating booths which have 'modesty curtains' so that your table becomes a place of intimacy. You can see old pop bottles on shelves, from the ceiling hang an assortment of Chianti bottles, and old fishing nets hang everywhere. It all makes for a tremendous atmosphere and made even more astonishing because from the outside it looks a bit like a pub. You will be without soul if you do not enjoy The Mermaid from the moment you step through the doors. At Christmas it becomes a fairy grotto with masses of lights hanging from the ceiling. Trevor Smith, the proprietor creates this every year and has a fabulous display in the window which locals bring their children to see. Trevor and his wife Helen, who is the Chef, have built this wonderful atmosphere in their restaurant over a period of years but they have never forgotten their basic job - to produce first class food.

USEFUL INFORMATION

OPEN: Mon-Sat: 6.30pm until late.
Closed Sundays
CHILDREN: Polite children welcome
CREDIT CARDS: Amex/Visa/Euro/
Mastercard
LICENSED: Restaurant
ACCOMMODATION: Not applicable

RESTAURANT: Speciality seafood &
international cuisine
BAR FOOD: Not applicable
VEGETARIAN: Imaginative, A La Carte
DISABLED ACCESS: Small step.
Willing to assist
GARDEN: Small patio terrace

ALVERTON MANOR

Hotel

Tregolls Road, Truro,
Cornwall, TR1 1XQ.

Tel: (0872) 76633
Fax: (0872) 222989

USEFUL INFORMATION

OPEN: 24 hours, all year
CHILDREN: Welcome
CREDIT CARDS: Amex/Visa/Diners
LICENSED: Restaurant & Residential
ACCOMMODATION: 25 en-suite **rooms**
4 Conference rooms seating 200

RESTAURANT: Superb, innovative &
wide ranging
BAR FOOD: Light bites available
VEGETARIAN: 4-5 dishes daily
DISABLED ACCESS: Yes
GARDEN: 6 acres & a terrace

This unique and outstanding hotel was converted from a convent belonging to the Sisters of the Epiphany and still has the splendid chapel which lends a special aura to Alverton Manor. It is a popular and sought after venue for wedding receptions and more and more businesses are find the Chapel a super place in which to hold a seminar or conference.

The hotel is stunning. It is spacious, gracious, beautifully furnished and has a sense of peace which maybe comes from its past but it is more realistic to say that it is achieved by the splendid team work which, headed by partner Michelle Marks, goes into the efficient and smooth running of the establishment. There are 25 en-suite bedrooms and 4 Conference rooms which can seat 200. Alverton Manor has not gone unnoticed by the AA and RAC who have both awarded it 3 stars. The English Tourist Board gave the hotel 5 Crowns and it is Highly commended by Les Routiers. All this has been achieved in the twelve months in which Michael Sagin and Michelle Marks have been at the helm.

You would expect nothing less than excellent food from such an establishment and you will not be disappointed. It is as exciting as it is innovative and wide ranging. Imagine a 'Gateaux' of fresh crab with marinated cucumber, lemon grass and peppers followed by roast breast of French duckling brushed with a 'rustique' mustard served with a pink grapefruit and orange cream. The desserts are equally delectable and the wines to be relished. Alverton Manor is both an enormous success as a hotel and equally for the standard and quality of its food and wine.

MERRIVALE CHARCUTERIE

Charcuterie

1 Coombes Lane, Truro,
Cornwall, TR1 2BJ.

Tel: (0872) 222227

USEFUL INFORMATION

OPEN: Mon-Fri: 9-5pm, Sat: 9-4.30pm
CHILDREN: Welcome
CREDIT CARDS: None taken
DISABLED ACCESS: Fairly good

Calling all food lovers to Truro, find No 1 Coombes Lane on your map and you will be thrilled to find yourselves standing outside Merrivale Charcuterie. In 1991 they won Guardian Newspaper's National Champion Sausage Makers of the Year, against a field of 500 competitors. Sally organised the opening of this retail outlet in 1992 which was immediately a great success. The quality and range of their produce has an unrivalled reputation throughout the west country.

All meats on sale are locally produced or free range. Also, depending on season, you will find game of all description, from Cornish venison to locally shot woodcock and pheasant. Huw prides himself on cured free range bacon. He also cures and smokes hams which can be purchased on or off the bone.

Their famous range of superb sausages include the spicy Spanish style Chorizo, Toulouse and many others. They also dry-cure their own Serrano style ham. To compliment this wonderful feast and extensive range of quality cheese has been added to the shop.

Many perfect presents can be purchased for that someone special at home, or why not treat yourselves in this gourmets paradise. This special little shop is a wonderful find, you will be delighted with everything within, you will not be able to resist all the tempting treats. Call at the end of your holiday so that you can take your special purchases home with you. This 'mini Fortnums' should be on the itinerary of all food loving travellers.

Ruan Highlanes, Truro,
Cornwall, TR2 5LU.

Tel: (0872) 501270

POLSUE MANOR HOTEL
Country House Hotel

Totally enclosed in its own grounds, Polsue Manor Hotel has a wonderful feeling of seclusion and space. The four and a half acres of gardens, woodlands and orchard just reinforce this. The original manor house was burnt to the ground and replaced by the present, lovely house in 1835. In front of the house still stand some listed carved stones from the original manor house. They are listed because of their symbols which are Christian shapes, but have designs on them of pagan origin. The whole site is very ancient and mentioned in the Domesday Book.

Val and Michael Jones own Polsue Manor. Two people who are friendly and welcoming, excellent hoteliers and passionate about their hobbies. Michael collects clocks and you will see them everywhere about the house. Ducks wander everywhere about the grounds and these are Vals great interest.

The eleven bedrooms are all ensuite and spacious. Indeed the whole house has a sense of space and grace and is light and airy. The food, traditional English, is cooked on an Aga and if you come here for a cream tea, the scones will be freshly cooked for each person - something for which Polsue Manor is famous.

The beauty of the grounds greets you as you come down the drive. There is a woodland trail for you to walk through which ends in an orchard. The colours in Autumn make it particularly appealing. You can play croquet on the lawn and inside there is table tennis and a snooker table. Polsue Manor is ideal for a break or a holiday and excellent value.

USEFUL INFORMATION

OPEN: February to December
CHILDREN: Welcome
CREDIT CARDS: Visa/Access
LICENSED: Residential & Restaurant
ACCOMMODATION: 11 ensuite rooms

RESTAURANT: Good, English, home-cooking
BAR FOOD: Bar lunches available. Cream teas
VEGETARIAN: On request. Prior notice would be appreciated
DISABLED ACCESS: No but willing to assist
GARDEN: 4.5 acres of garden, woodland. orchard

City Hall, Boscawen Street,
Truro, Cornwall, TR1.

Tel: (0872) 71166

THE TERRACE
Coffee Shop

Truro has a beautiful old City Hall building right in the city centre and today it houses many unusual and elegant shops, one of which is The Terrace, a charming, welcoming good quality, coffee shop. This more than useful coffee shop serves Truro very well whether for local people or for the many visitors who have discovered how good it is.

The Terrace has been a labour of love from the very first day that Linda Pearn acquired the property, The decoration was done mainly by Linda herself with the help of her family. It is fresh and attractive and the right setting for those who enjoy home-made cakes and gateaux which are created by Linda again with the help of mum, Marie and sister, Christine. It is very much a family affair.

Open from 10 o'clock until 4.30pm The Terrace caters for customers across the whole spectrum. You can have just a cup of coffee, if that is sufficient, and enjoy it in comfort waited on by a friendly staff. Between 12-2pm there is a minimum price of £2 per person but for that price you can eat and drink very well. Jacket Potatoes with a wide variety of fillings are very popular and the imaginative ingredients for sandwiches makes a decision difficult. Soup of the day - home-made of course - is served with a crusty brown or white roll and butter. The cakes are exceptional and this really is a very pleasant place in which to eat.

USEFUL INFORMATION

OPEN: Mon-Sat: 10-4.30pm
CHILDREN: Welcome. Room for push-chairs, small portions
CREDIT CARDS: None taken
LICENSED: None
ACCOMMODATION: Not applicable

RESTAURANT: Coffee Shop serving hot and cold food & home-made cakes, gateaux, etc
BAR FOOD: A good choice of light bites
VEGETARIAN: Several choices daily
DISABLED ACCESS: One step. Room for wheelchair but not in cloakroom
GARDEN: None

Wells Cathedral

Wells

" - her beauty made
The bright world dim, and everything beside
Seemed like the fleeting image of a shade."

Percy Shelley

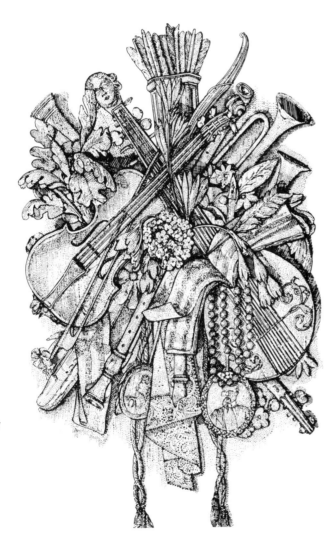

The City of Wells

by Joy David

Every superlative, every adjective must have been used by every writer in an effort to do justice to the thing of beauty that is WELLS CATHEDRAL. It has been called the Queen of Cathedrals, the west front a Gothic masterpiece and without doubt is recognised as the most exquisite among Britain's cathedrals. Richard Lewis, Dean of Wells writes 'Few remain unmoved by the majesty of this sermon in stone.' I cannot imagine anyone being anything but enriched by the experience of just looking at the exterior let alone continuing on a voyage of discovery inside where 'every aspect pleases'.

From a distance you see its three towers standing out against the green foothills of the Mendips. As you come closer approaching through one of the medieval gateways of the city, you are faced with the superb West front, twice as wide as it is high, still carrying 293 pieces of medieval sculpture extending across the whole facade. Such an array of sulptured figures is unique in Europe. Two hundred examples of the genius of the accomplished artists who worked on it so many centuries ago. Recently there has been some controversy about these statues because a massive restoration has been needed to save the west front. On inspection it was found that some of the

statues had gone beyond repair or even recognition. Those that have been replaced have been done so with loving care and meticulous attention to detail by the artists involved. Should the originals have been allowed to stay until they literally crumbled away or was it not better to replace them and allow this wondrous beauty to continue as a whole, healthy building, bringing pleasure to the generations to follow? I have no doubt that it was right to commission replacements particularly when they have been done so beautifully. You will have to look quite hard to pick out the new ones.

The whole story of this controversial restoration project is available for you to see by means of a series of photographs in the Cathedral.

It is difficult to know how those who first saw this wondrous sight would have reacted. I think they would have been stunned and rendered speechless. You can get a better idea possibly if you look at some of the carved capitals in the south transept. I have never seen anything like them in any other cathedral; they are a vibrant tableau of medieval life. They are created as a series. for example the fruit stealers tell the tale of the catching of an orchard thief. On another pillar there is a man who is wishing he could get rid of an aching tooth and he is not the only one. You may wonder why toothache should be the subject of no less than eleven other carvings of our medieval ancestors. It is because the medieval and revered bishop,

the second Bishop Bitton, was venerated as a saint and held accountable for a number of miraculous cures for toothache.

If I take someone with me to the Cathedral who has not been before I always set them a task to find the man with the toothache, and the woman with the thorn in her foot, the farmer, the pedlar with his bag and a string of beads, and finally a very queer monster with his hands on his knees. It is the very best version of the game of Treasure Hunt.

Wells' most famous and unique feature is the celebrated scissor arches with their great curves which transfer weight from the west, where the foundations sank under the tower's weight, to the east where they remained firm. This dramatic solution of a structural problem in 1338 remains effective to this day. William Joy was the ingenious master mason who conceived the answer to what might have been a disastrous end to the Cathedral. The arches look like the giant jaw bones of whales and they dominate any view down the nave, but they are seen to best advantage from the south-east corner of the transept.

By contrast with the comparative plainness of the nave, the quire where daily services are sung, presents a mass of colour. This comes from the glorious east window of 1339, high up in the east wall, known as the Golden Window from its glowing colours. It show's Christ's kinship with King David, son of Jesse. It is among the oldest and finest of Jesse windows in this country. On either side are two windows depicting saints; all four are dated around 1345.

A series of kaleidoscopic windows made up of medieval fragments assembled from glass smashed in the sixteenth and seventeenth centuries in the Quire Aisles lit the processional ways, developed as worship became increasingly theatrical in the 13th century. They lead round the Quire to the retroquire, chapels and Lady Chapel at the eastern end. Here too in the Quire are the embroidered stall-backs worked in 1937-1948 which attract needleworkers from far and near who come especially to examine them; embroidered cushions on the seats; medieval stalls with misericords underneath. These misericords are carved superbly and worth studying. Beyond the Quire are Lady Chapel, with its lovely but fragmented glass, and other chapels, used in turn for the daily eucharist throughout the week. Intriguing vaults are everywhere, including three ribs too many with a stone lion to bite them off.

From the north quire aisle lead the remarkable and much photographed steps up to the Chapter House and beyond. The Chapter House, a gem of the decorated style reduced to its simplest terms, is the official meeting place of the Canons. Beyond it the stairs lead on to the Chain Gate of 1459-1460; a gate so called because it was occasionally closed with chains.

The east walk of the Cloisters supports the Library of 1425. It is 168 feet long and possibly the largest medieval library building in England. Its contents suffered severely in the 16th and 17th centuries but the building was restored and refurnished in 1686. It contains a number of chained books as well as archives and documents from the 10th century onwards. An exhibition room is open to the public at a small charge on four days a week from Easter to the end of September.

In earlier days, the west Cloister supported the Choir School, Audit Rooms and the Grammar School. Young voices may yet be heard there because the Choristers' practice room is still above the west Cloister; but the Choir School and the Grammar School are now united in the Cathedral School of 700 pupils, occupying many buildings to the north of the Cathedral.

Vicars Choral have been an integral part of Cathedral life since the 12th century. In my ignorance, for many years I imagined the term meant 'singing priests' but not a bit of it, the word vicar means deputy. Canons not bound to the cathedral as monks, appointed deputies - or vicars - to do all the tasks that they did not particularly relish doing. Frequently the canon would not be able to sing and so he would choose his vicars for their skill in singing, hence Vicars Choral.

In between the stalls of the Chapter House, one finds a delicious range of carved heads, here a puckish man in a medieval bonnet resides betwixt a king and a patriarch

In 1348 Bishop Ralph of Shrewsbury formed them into a community and drew up for them a code of behaviour. He built Vicar's Close to house them, and Vicar's Hall where they ate and transacted business. In those days they were not free to marry.

Forty two small houses were built in two rows with the chapel at the far end. The 16th century reduced the number of Vicars Choral and also gave them the opportunity to marry if they wished. The small houses were converted into large dwellings to accommodate wives and families. The addition of gardens in the front gave the appearance of a medieval street.

No matter what changes, the work of the Vicars Choral continues today, although their allotted tasks are now strictly choral. They are members of the College of Vicars Choral and still live in Vicars' Close although now they are joined in some of the houses by other members of the cathedral foundation. They continue to sing daily in the cathedral accompanied by the boy choristers. They, with their families, form an important part of the Cathedral community.

Four houses in Vicars' Close are used by the Cathedral School, an almagamation of the Cathedral's medieval Choir School and Grammar School. Boys and girls of all ages attend, and it is famous for its music school.

The Organist - the Cathedral has had an organ since the early 1300's - is also Master of the Choristers, and under the Precentor's direction, responsible for the Cathedral's musical life. He too lives in Vicars' Close.

In spite of the enormous number of visitors who stream

through this most wondrous building every year, it still remains above all a place of prayer. If ever you feel at odds with the belief of the church or in the mood to become an atheist, surely Wells Cathedral must destroy your doubts.

The Cathedral is open every day of the year and admission is free; but because it has few endowments and no state aid it is heavily dependent upon voluntary gifts. Visitors are invited to make a donation towards the maintenance of this great building and its day to day work. Cathedral guides are available by prior arrangement and there are regular guided tours from Easter to the end of October. The Cathedral has a well stocked shop in which you can buy goods ranging from records of the Cathedral choir and organists to Caithness glass, Wedgwood pottery, pewter jewellery and small pieces of silver, as well as guide books, postcards and Christian literature of all kinds.

Beyond the Cathedral shop is THE CLOISTER RESTAURANT in the west Cloister and whether you have spent time in these beautiful surroundings or come directly to the Cathedral having explored Wells, there is one place you should make for and the Cloister Restaurant is that place. Opened in 1984 it was an immediate success and offers a first class menu supported by excellent service. Profits from the restaurant go exclusively to the upkeep of the Cathedral.

The moated palace and its associated buildings of this gem of a cathedral are what gives Wells a very special place in the hearts of all who come here. The fortified palace with its great ruined hall, its chapel and its early Gothic main living block show how feudal it all used to be. No less famous than the palace are the swans who glide along the moat in their stately way, stopping only to raise their beaks to sound the gateway's bell when they

are hungry; a trick they have learned from their ancestors. Some old glass from Nailsea Court suggests that the birds perfected this art almost five hundred years ago. The lawns are wonderfully manicured, the old walls mellow with age. The palace is still the home of the Bishop of Bath and Wells and its garden contains the wells from which the city gets its name.

It is not only the Cathedral and the palace and its environs which are superb in Wells. There are many old houses, picturesquely medieval and Tudor, some with Georgian fronts that stand close to the Cathedral quarter and close to the Liberties north of it.

Small is beautiful when one is talking about Wells. With a population of around 9,400 it qualifies as the smallest of England' cities. It lies sheltered beneath the southern slopes of the Mendip Hills and combines a wealth of historic architecture with its role as a thriving market centre.

The site of Wells was occupied by the Romans but did not become significant until the West Saxon King Ine founded a church by the wells. Although the early history of Wells was always closely associated with that of the Cathedral and its bishops, the city itself has had a long history of its own. It was granted a borough charter by King John as long ago as 1201 and the city has been represented in parliament since the 1930s. City life and the trade guilds used to be focused around the Parish Church of St Cuthbert, with the workers of the once-important wool trade living in Tucker Street. During the Middle Ages the Cathedral was enclosed within the Liberty, an area free from civic jurisdiction until the 1800s.

THE CROWN AT WELLS is in the medieval market place adjacent to the Cathedral and the Bishop's palace.

It is a splendid inn dating back to 1450 approximately when it would have been a medieval coaching inn. You can feel the sense of history the moment you enter its doors. Many famous people have stayed here over the centuries. William Penn, the founder of Pennsylvania, once preached to a crowded market place from one of the hotel bedrooms. Every room, every bar is full of character.

Sadler Street is the home of the elegant WHITE HART HOTEL, with views of Cathedral Green. The hotel was originally known as 'Harts Head' and was first described as an inn in 1497. It is thought to have been the Bishop's guest house. The present owner, Peter Ayton who has recently refurbished the hotel has discovered many interesting features which have been sympathetically restored. There are 13 ensuite rooms, a splendid function suite overlooking the Gothic spires which holds up to 60 people. A dining room with old world charm where one dines beneath beams that are the oldest original example of their kind left in this beautiful little city.

THE FOUNTAIN INN & BOXERS RESTAURANT in St Thomas Street was built during the 16th century to house builders working on the Cathedral. It has charm, character and two friendly proprietors, Adrian and Sarah Lawrence who over the twelve years of their incumbency have built up an enviable reputation for food and wine. If you happen to love cheese you will be in your element; they have an award for their selection of West Country cheese. And there is more. To accompany your cheese, what better than a fine bottle of wine, from their great wine selection, for which they have received recognition winning the Mercier award.

A change of venue and food. THE GOOD EARTH in Priory Road is housed in a red bricked Georgian house, one of the most beautiful buildings in the city. This fascinating restaurant was once a hotel, a past that has allowed its present owner, Christopher Edwards, to use four informal inside rooms as eating areas. In addition he has created another charming spot in the sheltered paved courtyard in which barelled tables and chairs are provided so that in good weather, people may enjoy the sunshine as well as the delicious food. The dishes are totally vegetarian although it does cater in a limited way for vegans. Interestingly enough you will find many non-vegetarians eating here because the food is so good.

Despite its wealth of history, Wells is also very much up to date in terms of facilities, which includes a modern leisure centre and swimming pool, a cinema and an amateur theatre. Regular markets are held in the picturesque Market Square on Wednesdays and Saturdays.

I would recommend a short drive from Wells out to the village of **Panborough**, five miles away, where in its midst is the 17th century PANBOROUGH INN. In this charming atmospheric hostelry, you will always find an interesting mixture of people who have found their way from quite a distance, although there are the faithful regulars who live in this lovely part of Somerset. The peaceful pub is just the place for refreshment after exploring the magnificence and awe inspiring beauty of Wells Cathedral.

Wells is one of Mendips' five towns, the others Frome, Glastonbury, Shepton Mallet and Street all have their own distinctive character and should come into anyone's itinerary when visiting the North East part of Somerset.

Frome is enchanting, it runs up and down and in and out with its narrow streets full of quaint old houses and with a river from which it takes its name. From here you are almost into Wiltshire and everywhere around you there

are some of Somerset's loveliest villages. If there is anything that disappoints me about Frome, it is the PARISH CHURCH which has been there for centuries. It still has a knotwork carving of the Saxon mason and a lion with his tail between his legs. The next oldest thing is the 14th century LADY CHAPEL. It has an 18th century bell with a wonderful inscription.

> *'God made Cockey and Cockey made me,*
> *In the year of our Lord 1743'*

Yes, it does have a lot of beautiful things but it does not have the charm of so many Somerset churches. Somehow it is overdone, there is too much decoration, every quatrefoil has a rose in it, every bit of wood is painted. Inside and out it is ornate. You have to climb up steps from the street to reach it and even these are lined with sculptured groups. There are figures carved on the guttering and somebody told me that if you count you will find no less than 300 stone figures of all sorts, and that is before you look at a monument.

Frome became prosperous as one of the ancient woollen towns of the West Country and in subsequent centuries the town has grown until it is the biggest in the Mendips yet it still only has about 24,000 residents. Wander round the town and you will discover it is a friendly place with some interesting shops. I became reacquainted with CROFTS at 21 Fromefield

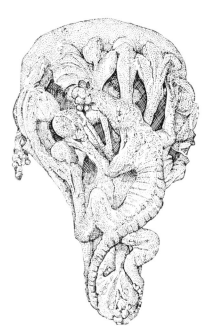

14th century Corbel in the North Transept: a delightfully exquisite design, skillfully carved, of a lizard eating berries

on the main Bath-Frome Road. It is a venue not to be missed and is situated in one of the many Listed buildings, in this case dating back to 1690. Two small, and very individual rooms make up the dining area. Each has a welcoming fireplace, which in winter throws out a wall of warmth. While you are looking at the fixed price menu and sipping your aperitif, you will be offered tiny little nibbles, a mouthful of crumbly pastry flavoured with anchovy, just enough to alert the tastebuds for the treat to come. Wonderful.

Take a look at THE ANGEL INN in King Street. This ancient pub is still obliged to take horses and travellers by a law that has been on the statute books since the 17th century. It seems quite right and proper to have this fine hostelry which has been a public house since the 13th century, in the centre of a conservation area, with medieval streets, which still have water running down the middle.

Shepton Mallett is a wonderful mixture of old and new; a combination of ancient market town and modern industrial community nestling in a fold towards the western edge of the Mendip escarpment. Historically Shepton Mallet has always been strategically well placed; the Roman Fosse Way passes close by; the town's position on the river Sheppey led to its growth during the Middle Ages as a centre for the wool trade, and enabled the brewing industry to be established.

307

Today this location makes Shepton Mallet ideal for anyone wanting to explore the region's many and varied attractions. It was probably at its most affluent as a market and wool-trading centre in the 15th century. Cloth weaving rose to importance in the 17th century. Several wealthy cloth merchants built themselves some fine houses in the town many of which are still there.

The town is not proud of one episode in its history. It happened in 1685 when the Market Cross was the scene for several executions of the unfortunate men of the Duke of Monmouth's 'Pitchfork Army' who were sentenced to death by that dreadful man, Judge Jeffreys.

THE PARISH CHURCH OF ST PETER AND ST PAUL has a fine 14th century tower and the nave roof provides one of the best examples of wagon-roof in England, with 350 panels and 300 bosses, each of a different design. The 50ft high market cross dates from 1500, and nearby is a remnant of the shambles, a 15th century covered market stall. You should also visit COLLETT PARK, which has an attractive lake and an aviary.

Two of the most respected agricultural shows are held at Shepton Mallet. The most famous is the ROYAL BATH AND WEST, held a few miles outside the town on its permanent site. It occurs every May and stretches over four days. Later in the year, on a Saturday in August, the Mid-Somerset Show is held in the town itself. Not so grand as the Bath and West but a great deal of fun. There is also a busy weekly market, every Friday, in the centre of the town around the market cross.

For anyone looking for a good hostelry, the comparatively modern, THE THATCHED COTTAGE has enormous charm. You will find it in Charlton Road. It has a delightful, intimate atmosphere and eight beautifully furnished and decorated bedrooms with enormous bathrooms. Great place to stay or to eat.

The most southerly of the Mendip towns is **Street** which stands just over a mile beyond Glastonbury, across the River Brue. It is right to call it the 'newest' town both in history and appearance. It first gained fame as a tanning centre and for the manufacturing of sheepskin rugs but Street has now gained a worldwide recognition as the home base of the footwear making organisation of C and J Clark Ltd, whose headquarters border on the High Street, and has long been one of the town's principal employers. There is a very interesting shoe museum portraying the history of footwear which is also located on the premises. You can see shoes from Roman times to the present day, also a remarkable collection of snuff boxes, advertising posters, fashion plates, buckles and shoe making machinery of the 19th century. It is certainly different.

The Morlands who dealt in sheep skins, and still do, were the other family who played a large part in the growth of Street. In 1870 Morlands established a working tannery producing first quality skins and by 1906 with the revolutionary growth of the motor car, Morlands were manufactuing coats, rugs, and footwarmers for the discerning motorist. As technology advanced so did the need for more practical ways of keeping warm. In 1919 Morlands started to make boots and slippers. Thirty years on, the company were supplying boots and jackets to the Air Force and, indeed, to the famous Sir Edmund Hilary, who made the first, perilous ascent of Mount Everest. You can look for yourselves in Morland's factory shop to see what they do today. There is ample parking and it is open from Monday - Saturday from 9.30am-5pm. Many shops in the High Street specialise in shoe sales and bargain hunting is popular with residents and visitors. The shopping centre altogether is a pleasant place.

Of the town's older buildings probably THE PARISH CHURCH OF HOLY TRINITY is the finest. Although it was rebuilt in the 19th century, it still has a 14th century tower and chancel. THE FRIENDS' MEETING HOUSE, a dignified building of 1850 is a reminder of the vital role the Quakers played in the industrial wealth of this part of Somerset. The origins of the Clark factory lay in the farming community but it was their strict Quaker upbringing which led them not only to build the factory, but to concern themselves with education, housing, and the welfare of their workers. And even allow a little recreation and fun within the strict confines of Quaker traditions!

Looking at sedate Street it is a little hard to envisage a time when creatures before civilisation itself, roamed the fields before they became extinct a million years ago. There are ten of these historic monsters, a plesiousaurus and nine ichthyosauris which were found in the quarries of blue lias from which the village was made. They are preserved in the museum. Will Street enjoy Jurassic Park or will it give them nightmares? I wonder.

The ruined abbey is the central attraction of the market town of **Glastonbury**. It is also thought of as the cradle of English Christianity, but for me it is a place of legend, history, mystery and an overworked imagination. It may well have been the earliest christian shrine but it is certainly the site of the richest monastery, and to this day still a place of pilgrimage. The Glastonbury legends are told again and again, and over the centuries have no doubt been embellished, but I never fail to feel excited by the thought of a visit here.

Towering over the town is GLASTONBURY TOR, some 521 feet above sea level, and a landmark visible for miles around. ST MICHAEL'S TOWER on the summit is the remains of a 15th century church, the effort of climbing which is rewarded by wonderful views. First the home of primitive man, then a place of Christian pilgrimage, the Tor is still visited by thousands every year. I would advise you to walk up the Tor if it is possible because of the restricted availability of car parking nearby.

One of the legends told is of Christ coming here as a child with his merchant uncle, Joseph of Arimathea. Another is of Joseph coming here with the Holy Grail and yet another of the Apostle Philip sending missionaries from Gaul to establish a church, and of those missionaries finding a church already here, dedicated by Christ Himself. The undoubted Irish influence here is traced back to St Patrick who came first as an Abbot and to whom the lower church in Glastonbury is dedicated. Then there is the story of St Bridget from Kildare, Ireland, who left her bell and wallet behind at Beckery just one mile south west.

It is true that the Tor was occupied in the Dark Ages by someone of taste and wealth who imported wine and oil from the Mediterranean and who also had a liking for meat. How all these things are worked out is always amazing to me. The tradition is that it was the stronghold of Melwas, King of Somerset, who abducted Queen Guinevere and kept King Arthur at bay. That is certainly borne out by traces on the Tor.

All sorts of churches have been built here over the centuries. By 1184, there was more than just a church of wattles. Tradition has it that St David had come with seven bishops but found that the church had already been consecrated by Christ himself; so he built another church and consecrated that. The Welsh seem to have put in an appearance as well with St Gilda being prominent. King Ine who died in 726 built a new church which he dedicated to the Apostles Peter and Paul. This church at the east end of the Lady Chapel was replaced by another built by Abbot Herlwin before 1125.

It was St Dunstan who laid the foundation of Glastonbury's spiritual and economic power. Conventual buildings, a cloister and a chapel are representative of his desire to create a religious community. Three English Kings, Edmund, Edgar, and Edmund Ironside were buried here although Edgar was later moved to the east end of the Abbey church to a magnificent fan-vaulted chapel built by the last two Abbots, Richard Bere and Richard Whiting.

By the time of Domesday, Glastonbury owned an eighth of the county of Somerset covering much of the Somerset Levels, large parts of which were almost immediately drained to bring gain to the Abbot. Norman Abbots continued to add to the building but it was the powerful, rich, Henry of Blois, Bishop of Winchester who built himself lodgings on such a scale that they would have made Buckingham Palace look small. The huge foundations of this building were uncovered not so many years ago. He also built a bell-tower, chapter house and cloister, a great gatehouse and other buildings for the monks. It was also Henry who invited William of Malmesbury to write the history of the house which has helped us to develop the legends of Glastonbury over the centuries. However this magnificent group of buildings was destroyed by fire in 1184 apart

'Shine forth thy light so we may see thy good works': the radiantly beautiful South Quire Aisle, looking east

from the bell-tower, a chamber and a chapel. Those were not the days of insurance but the wealth was such that building started again immediately, beginning with the Lady Chapel on the site of the old church, and now the most complete part of the Abbey church. Hard times came to the monks in 1189 when Royal support dried up and the monks were thrown back on their own resources but the good Lord was smiling down upon them, and legend says that whilst they were digging a grave for a monk, they found between the shafts of two ancient crosses, 16ft down in a wooden sarcophagus, the bones of a large man and a woman who must have been very beautiful; she certainly had long golden tresses – the story said these locks were totally preserved until one monk with straying hands touched them and they fell to dust. The monks were in no doubt that here were the remains of King Arthur and Queen Guinevere. Strangely however, William of Malmesbury had never mentioned Arthur in his 'History of Glastonbury' but the monks were adamant, and for them their acute need for money was immediately alleviated by this lovely, romantic idea. They never looked back.

By 1278 Edward I and his Queen came to the ceremony in which Arthur was finally placed in a great tomb in the choir, and the main part of the Abbey was complete. It must have been wonderful but today only a part of this magnificence survives in the ABBEY MUSEUM. At the Dissolution in 1539 the monastery was still thriving, with over 50 monks. After the mock trial and shocking execution of Abbot Whiting and two monks on the Tor, the buildings were soon used as a quarry. The original Glastonbury Thorn, which immediately burst into bloom when Joseph of Arimathea thrust his staff into the ground, remained until a puritan fanatic decided it was wrong and cut it down in the 17th century but a piece rescued was planted, and today is to be seen in the Abbot's kitchen. I think the Abbots of the past would have been horrified if they had known that the Abbot's Kitchen was used in the 16th century by weavers and in the 17th century as a Quaker meeting house.

Between the Abbey precinct and the Tor is the Abbey Barn, originally one of the Abbey's Tithe Barns, but now houses THE SOMERSET RURAL LIFE MUSEUM. It is full of relics from Somerset's past, and depicts the history and development of a whole range of trades and industries; agriculture, cider-making, peat digging, thatching and other rural crafts, imaginatively laid out and described.

I have always managed to work up a thirst and an appetite after exploring and in Glastonbury I know, without asking, exactly where to find two of the best hostelries.

The Victorian MARKET HOUSE INN is situated directly opposite the ruins of Glastonbury Abbey. This is an establishment much loved by sports touring sides throughout the year. Golf, fishing, shooting and some hunting trips are arranged for guests. It is the garden, which is a suntrap, that I like especially. Here the spreading arms of a 130 year old wysteria are being trained to provide some shade. It is such a restful spot.

In a quiet street just off market Cross is THE MITRE INN. Originally a coaching house, this 300 year old building is said to have the ghost of a highwayman. Take a close look at the tables - they are the antique bases of Singer and Jones sewing machines.

This has been a wonderful wander through some of my favourite countryside and places but the magnet is Wells Cathedral which always draws me back to its inestimable beauty.

21 Fromefield,
Frome, Somerset, BA11 2HE.

Tel: (0373) 472149

CROFTS
Restaurant

Crofts is on the main Bath-Frome road and is a restaurant not to be missed. It is situated in an attractive building that dates back to 1690 and is one of the many Listed buildings in this fine, medieval, market town. Two small and very individual rooms make up the dining area. Each has a welcoming fireplace, which in winter throws out a wall of warmth. The small bar is designed to allow customers to enjoy pre-dinner drinks and an opportunity to relax whilst they study the interesting menu. Everything about Crofts gives you a sense of well-being from the decor, which is in keeping with the feel of the building, to the meticulous attention to detail that has brought it deserved renown very quickly. While you are taking a look at the fixed price menu and sipping your aperitif, you will be offered tiny little nibbles, a mouthful of crumbly pastry flavoured with anchovy or cheese; just enough to alert the tastebuds to what is to come. Everything is home-made including the bread, ice-creams, sorbets and sweetmeats. The emphasis is on English dishes, with the occasional and always interesting, Continental influence. For example you may be offered monkfish with leeks, saffron and coriander or crudities with tapenade.

Margaret Graham is the chef-proprietor and this is a lady with a wealth of experience which she delights in sharing with her customers. Wisely she has made here two dining rooms strictly non-smoking. Well worth seeking out, this delightful, intimate restaurant is open from Tuesday to Saturday in the evenings only.

USEFUL INFORMATION

OPEN: Tues-Sat: 7pm - last orders 9.45pm
CHILDREN: Allowed
CREDIT CARDS: Visa/Access/Master/
Euro
LICENSED: Restaurant
ACCOMMODATION: Not applicable

RESTAURANT: Everything home-made
BAR FOOD: Not applicable
VEGETARIAN: 2 changed weekly
DISABLED ACCESS: No special access
GARDEN: No

Magdalene Street,
Glastonbury, Somerset, BA6 9EW.

Tel: (0458) 832220

MARKET HOUSE INN
Public House & Hotel

This Victorian Market House Inn situated directly opposite the ancient ruins of Glastonbury Abbey and with clear views of the Tor, remains a landmark in the town of Glastonbury. This is where a cross section of customers meet for fine restaurant meals, traditional ales, good company and entertainment. The warm and friendly staff and management maintain high standards of quality and service and with 7 single, double and family rooms will accommodate and entertain guests until the early hours.

Established sports touring sides are welcomed throughout the year. Golf, fishing, shooting and some hunting trips are arranged among many other activities, such as in-house skittles - in the longest alley in the district, visits to the local Cider Farm, picnics to the Tor, for example.

The garden boasts a 130 year old wysteria which is being trained to shade some of the beautiful suntrap of a garden where barbecues, parties and entertainments are staged from time to time. An unique inn, although architecturally typically Victorian, this inn oozes atmosphere and lightheartedness and is complemented by many a selective friendly local who, combined with the standard of service, will make anyone's stay whether for a drink or a week, a memorable one.

The usual facilities of private car park, satellite TV, telephone, full English breakfast, morning coffee and afternoon tea, take-aways and a laundry service to mention but a few are provided in this house and with such competitive pricing and room rates provides extremely good value.

USEFUL INFORMATION

OPEN: Mon-Sat: 11-11pm.
Sun: 12-2.30pm & 7-10.30pm
CHILDREN: Well behaved welcome
CREDIT CARDS: None
LICENSED: Full On
ACCOMMODATION: 7 rooms

RESTAURANT: A la carte & traditional
Devon, Cornwall & Somerset dishes
BAR FOOD: O'Hagans specialist
sausages, traditional baskets and platters
VEGETARIAN: 3-4 dishes
DISABLED ACCESS: No, unfortunately
GARDEN: Large with BBQ area

THE MITRE INN
Inn

27 Benedict Street, Glastonbury,
Somerset, BA6 9NE.

Tel: (0458) 831203

USEFUL INFORMATION

OPEN: 11.30-2.30pm & 5.30-11pm
  Sun: 12-3pm & 7-10.30pm
CHILDREN: Welcome, play area
CREDIT CARDS: None taken
LICENSED: Full Licence
ACCOMMODATION: Not applicable

RESTAURANT: Not applicable
BAR FOOD: Also served on Sunday
  evenings. Daily specials, good home
  cooked dishes.
  Recommended by Egon Ronay.
  Open log fire
VEGETARIAN: Always 6 dishes
DISABLED ACCESS: No
GARDEN: Yes

Glastonbury has a wealth of interesting places to visit including the Abbey ruins - reputedly the burial ground of King Arthur and his Queen Guinevere, beside the 11th century St Benedicts church. In a quiet side street just off the Market Cross is the Mitre Inn. Although not obvious from the front, this old pub has a beautiful walled garden, very tranquil and bathed in sun when the weather behaves.

Originally a coaching house, this 300 year old building is said to have the ghost of a highwayman, but Anne Chichowicz, your host, has never seen it. A medium, however, visiting the pub said she could feel its presence and some days later phoned to say other mediums, while holding a meeting had indeed seen the highwayman 'hanging around'.

Whilst you enjoy a good meal and one of their Real Ales, you sit at very unusual tables - the bases are antique sewing machines, Singer & Jones, treddle stands, in full working order.

The Mitre Inn is the only public house in Glastonbury and surrounding area which is recommended by Egon Ronay. Vegetarian meals are always available; see the daily specials board. Everything is home-cooked using fresh locally produced ingredients. To end a delicious meal, it is impossible to refuse one of their home-made sweets. For vegans there is a special ice-cream which has to be tried.

PANBOROUGH INN
Public House & Restaurant

Panborough, Wells,
Somerset, BA5 1PN.

Tel: (0934) 712554

USEFUL INFORMATION

OPEN: 11.30-2.30pm & 6.30-11pm
CHILDREN: Welcome
CREDIT CARDS: Visa/Access
LICENSED: Full On Licence
ACCOMMODATION: Not applicable

RESTAURANT: Full A la Carte. Home-
  cooked.
BAR FOOD: Snacks, specials, full menu
VEGETARIAN: Always 5 dishes
DISABLED ACCESS: Yes
GARDEN: Beer terrace, with tables

Panborough is truly rural with Glastonbury Tor visible from the car park and the great cathedral of Wells only five miles away. The awe-inspiring beauty of Cheddar Gorge is seven miles from Panborough and the wicked witch of Wookey Hole is just four miles down the road. At Wedmore, three miles away, the remains of a Saxon village have recently been discovered. In the midst of Panborough is the 17th century Panborough Inn, a charming, atmospheric hostelry in which you will always find a mixture of interesting people who have found their way from quite a distance usually, although there are the faithful regulars who live in this lovely part of Somerset. The peaceful pub is just the place for refreshment after exploring the magnificence and awe inspiring beauty of wells Cathedral.

The family partnership of John and Carol Halliwell and Kenneth and Catherine Hargreaves, have spent the last ten years constantly improving this well loved pub. They have made it a very happy place; something one notices immediately on entering its old doors.

Real Ales, Ruddles Best Bitter, the local Butcombe Bitter and sometimes other guest bitters attract aficionados and for wine lovers, the wine list is extensive. The menu offers good, wholesome, home-prepared dishes as well as simple snacks. Every day there are 'House Specials' which are tempting and inexpensive. On Sunday the traditional lunch is a popular institution. In the summer the beer terrace is ideal for a quiet drink.

63-67 Charlton Road, Shepton Mallet,
Somerset, BA4 5QF.

Tel: (0749) 342058
Fax: (0749) 343265

THE THATCHED COTTAGE INN

Inn

This comparatively modern inn has enormous charm. From the day the first brick was laid it was almost a foregone conclusion that it would not be long before it was one of the most popular venues in the Shepton Mallett area. A great deal of thought went into the design of the spacious airy rooms and into the intimate atmosphere of the attractive restaurant. Its thatched roof gives it great character added to by the fascinating structure of the porch that leads inside from the garden. Covered by thatch it is supported by a structure of entwined tree limbs which have been varnished.

There are eight beautifully furnished and decorated bedrooms with enormous bathrooms. Each room is not numbered but called after a bird, somehow just right for an inn in this rural area. Dining in the intimate, panelled restaurant with its pretty drapes and table cloths is an experience not to be missed. The full menu has a particularly good fish section but there is also a three course set price menu which is excellent value for money. In the main bar area one can drink and sample the vast number of dishes available including some very tasty 'Daily Specials'. Everything is well presented, the service is efficient and courteous and at the same time reassuringly friendly. The children have fun in the play area in the garden where tables and chairs are set out for their elders to have a drink in the sun. The Thatched Cottage lives up to its well deserved reputation.

USEFUL INFORMATION

OPEN: Mon–Sat:11–11pm,
  Sun: 12–2.30pm & 7–10.30pm
CHILDREN: Welcome in Middle Room
CREDIT CARDS: Access/Visa
LICENSED: Full On
ACCOMMODATION: 8 ensuite

RESTAURANT: Intimate. Full menu.
  Fish a speciality
BAR FOOD: Extensive menu & daily
  specials
VEGETARIAN: Several choices daily
DISABLED ACCESS: Not to
  accommodation
GARDEN: Large with play area

West Cloister, Wells Cathedral,
Wells, Somerset, BA5 2PA.

Tel: (0749) 676543

THE CLOISTER RESTAURANT

Restaurant

The Restaurant is set in the cloisters of Wells Cathedral, an architectural gem in its own right with a beautiful vaulted roof and fascinating historic memorials. Wells Cathedral, one of the finest Cathedrals in England, or indeed in Europe, is somewhere that no one should miss. The Cathedral contains many unusual and attractive architectural features, such as the Chapter House - the only one in an English Cathedral which is 'upstairs'. The west front of the Cathedral, containing nearly 300 carved stone figures is world famous and much of the stone carving inside is equally fine as are the embroidered panels in the quire. Whether you have spent time in these beautiful surroundings or whether you come directly to the Cathedral having explored Wells, there is one place you should make for and that is The Cloister Restaurant. Jenny Barnes has been the Manager here since the restaurant opened in 1984 and with her supportive and enthusiastic team, many of whom have connections with the Cathedral, she provides a first class menu and service.

There is something for everyone amongst the many attractive dishes. Hot dishes of the day might well be Somerset chicken casserole or a spinach and cottage cheese lasagne. There are home-made quiches, freshly prepared salads, cooked meats and ploughman's etc. as well as some good desserts. Cakes, freshly baked scones and cream teas are available all day. Profits from the restaurant go exclusively to the upkeep of the Cathedral. The Restaurant closes for 2 weeks each year over Christmas and the New Year

USEFUL INFORMATION

OPEN: Mon–Sat: 10–5pm (4.30 Nov–Feb)
  Sun: 2–5pm. Closed Good Friday +
  two weeks at Christmas
CHILDREN: High Chairs, mother &
  baby room nearby. Small portions
CREDIT CARDS: None taken
LICENSED: Wine & cider with meals
ACCOMMODATION: Not applicable

RESTAURANT: Excellent home-made
  fare
BAR FOOD: Not applicable
VEGETARIAN: A choice of dishes
DISABLED ACCESS: Ramp, disabled
  toilet close by
GARDEN: Not applicable

THE CROWN AT WELLS
Hotel & Public House

The Market Place, Wells,
Somerset, BA5 2RD.

Tel: (0749) 673457

USEFUL INFORMATION

OPEN: All year. Food: 10am-10pm,
Drink: 10am-11pm
CHILDREN: Welcome
CREDIT CARDS: Access/Visa/Amex
LICENSED: Full On
ACCOMMODATION: 15 rooms, 4 with
four-posters

RESTAURANT: Bistro style menu
BAR FOOD: Interesting light meals
served in Penn Eating House & Terrace
VEGETARIAN: 3-4 dishes
DISABLED ACCESS: Yes
GARDEN: Patio/terrace for eating &
drinking

Wells without doubt is one of England's treasures. No one comes here without experiencing the thrill of being among so much history and beauty. The Crown at Wells in the medieval market place, which is adjacent to the Cathedral and the Bishop's Palace, is a delightful inn dating back to 1450 approximately and was then a medieval coaching inn. You can feel the sense of history the moment you enter its doors.

Many famous people have been here over the centuries and William Penn, the founder of Pennsylvania, once preached to a crowded market place from one of the hotel bedrooms. Every room, every bar is full of character. If you choose to stay here you will find that four of the fifteen ensuite bedrooms, have four-posters; naturally they have every modern facility but it is all in keeping with the age of the building. This is a family run business which at the moment is undergoing considerable refurbishment but none of it is being allowed to detract one iota from the charm of its old world appearance.

There is a private residents and diners bar. The Penn Bar and Eating House is open from ten in the morning until ten at night and serves light meals, morning coffee and afternoon teas. For residents there is an attractive lounge and in the summer the patio area is very popular for those who want to sit and enjoy the surroundings, have a drink or a meal. The hotel is able to offer excellent facilities for conferences and is a favourite venue for wedding receptions.

FOUNTAIN INN & BOXERS RESTAURANT
Public House & Restaurant

1 St Thomas Street, Wells,
Somerset, BA5 2UU.

Tel: (0749) 672317

USEFUL INFORMATION

OPEN: Weekdays: 10.30-2.30pm &
6-11pm. Sun: 12-3pm & 7-10.30pm
CHILDREN: Welcome. Own menu
CREDIT CARDS: Vsa/Access/Amex
LICENSED: Full Licence
ACCOMMODATION: Not applicable

RESTAURANT: Anglo-French using
local produce
BAR FOOD: Wide range as restaurant
VEGETARIAN: Approx 7 dishes daily
DISABLED ACCESS: Yes - toilets on
first floor
GARDEN: No

Adrian and Sarah Lawrence have been the proprietors of this very nice establishment for 12 years, and have built up an enviable reputation for food and wine using only the very best of local produce. If you happen to love cheese you will be in your element; they have an award for their selection of West Country cheese. To accompany your cheese, what better than a fine bottle of wine, from their great wine selection, for which they have received recognition winning the Mercier award.

The Fountain is situated on the junction of the B3139 to Bath and A371 to Shepton Mallet, just 50 yards from Wells Cathedral, surrounded by many beautiful buildings. After lunch what better pursuit than to wander around the moat to the Bishop's Palace.

The Inn was built during the 16th century to house builders working on the Cathedral. Above the bar is Boxers Restaurant, furnished attractively, with pine tables and Laura Ashley decor. The pub also has a function room which seats up to 30 people.

An extensive menu is available in both the bar and restaurant. There is a huge selection of delicious home-cooked food. There are vegetarian dishes and a children's menu, also vegan dishes on request. In addition to the regular menu, the chef's blackboard specials include tempting dishes. Magret Duckling, venison steak in Cumberland sauce, Mussels or a whole sea bass are to name but a few. Sauces accompanying many of the dishes are very interesting and subtle, a little out of the ordinary and look superb.

THE GOOD EARTH
Restaurant

4 Priory Road, Wells,
Somerset, BA5 1SY.

Tel: (0749) 678600

Wells, known as the smallest city, has a wealth of beautiful buildings amongst which is the listed, red bricked Georgian building, in Priory Road, which houses The Good Earth. This fascinating restaurant was once a hotel, a past that has allowed its present owner, Christopher Edwards, to use four informal inside rooms as eating areas. In addition he has created another charming spot in the sheltered paved courtyard in which barelled tables and chairs are provided so that in good weather, people may enjoy the sunshine as well as the delicious food.

The charm of the Good Earth undoubtedly lies in the informality of the eating surroundings - wooden floors and oak tables allied to the home-made Vegetarian meals, all of which is adjacent to a wholefood store specialising in dried fruits, nuts, cereals, pulses, 50 different varieties of tea plus many more specialised food items. The restaurant has acquired a reputation for its food and has not gone unnoticed by Egon Ronay's 'Just a Bite', 'Family Choice' and 'A Taste of Somerset'. It maintains a consistently high standard and is welcoming to people of all ages. There are high chairs for small children, a baby changing facility and a wheelchair access to all the inside eating areas. The constantly changing menu is all home-made and 100% Vegetarian although it does cater in a limited way for Vegans. Interestingly enough, you will find many non-Vegetarians eating here because the food is so good.

USEFUL INFORMATION

OPEN: Rest & Shop: Mon-Sat: 9am-5.30pm. Closed Sundays & Bank Holidays
CHILDREN: Most welcome
CREDIT CARDS: Visa/Access/Master
LICENSED: Rest: Wine & Beer
   Shop: Off Licence
ACCOMMODATION: Not applicable

RESTAURANT: Home-made, 100% vegetarian. Vegan menu
BAR FOOD: Not applicable
VEGETARIAN: Totally
DISABLED ACCESS: Yes
GARDEN: Paved courtyard seats 20

THE WHITE HART HOTEL
Hotel

Sadler Street,
Wells, Somerset, BA5 2RR.

Tel: (0749) 672056
Fax: (0749) 672056

The charming cathedral city of Wells is home to the elegant White Hart Hotel in Sadler Street, with views of the cathedral green. The Hotel, was originally known as 'Harts Head' and was first described as an inn in 1497. It is thought to have been the Bishop's guest house.

The present owner, Peter Ayton is currently refurbishing the hotel and has discovered many interesting features which have been sympathetically restored. There are 13 ensuite rooms, with tea and coffee making facilities, colour TV and satellite channels. There is a function suite overlooking the gothic spires, which holds up to 60 people. It has every facility needed for business meetings and conferences. An ideal base for anyone touring Somerset with Wookey Hole and Caves, the Gothic Cathedral city of Wells, Bath and Longleat, all near by.

The dining room has an old world charm with its beamed ceilings is the oldest original example of its kind left in this beautiful city. The menus are prepared by the Head Chef from local produce and are unusual but frequently traditional including dishes using wild boar, game casserole, quail and venison. The a la carte menu is noted for its fish dishes and delightful deserts, all at very reasonable prices. The bars are cosy and intimate although less formal. The open log fires and exposed beams make you feel very welcome and you can enjoy traditional bar food in these charming surroundings.

USEFUL INFORMATION

OPEN: 7.30-11.30pm. Lunch 12-2pm, Dinner: 6-10pm
CHILDREN: Welcome
CREDIT CARDS: Visa/Access/Amex/ Switch
LICENSED: Full On
ACCOMMODATION: 13 ensuite with TV, satellite, trouser press & hairdryers

RESTAURANT: 45 covers. No smoking section. Lunch & dinner daily
BAR FOOD: A la carte & table d'hote
VEGETARIAN: 4-5 available
DISABLED ACCESS: Ramp at entrance. No special WC facilities
GARDEN: Not at present

Winchester Cathedral

Winchester

"But thy eternal summer shall not fade,
... So long as man can breathe, or eyes can see,
So long lives this, and this gives life to thee."

William Shakespeare

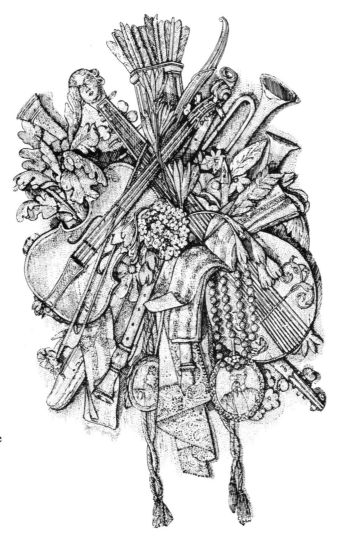

The City of Winchester

by Jane Drake

When John Keats visited **Winchester** in 1819 he wrote that it was 'the pleasantest town I ever was in, and has the most recommendations of any. There is a fine Cathedral, which to me is always a source of amusement.' It seems a rather irreverent way to describe a place as old and venerable as WINCHESTER CATHEDRAL, but Keats was probably thinking of it as a pleasant diversion rather than object from which to derive smiles and laughter. A walk around the Cathedral will soon show that it is a very pleasant and interesting place to visit, full of artistic and architectural manifestations of men's belief in God, who is perceived differently by different ages.

To begin at the beginning of the Cathedral we must start outside, on the grass on the north side of the nave. Etched out in grey stone and red brick are the outlines of the sites of the Old Minster and of the first church built about 650. The red brick of the first church had become by 1000 AD the grey stone of the Old Minister, one of the largest Anglo-Saxon churches in England. Then the Normans conquered England and the then bishop was ordered to replace Old Minster by an even larger church. At the time the new structure measured 535 feet (164m) from end to end, making it the largest cathedral of its

time. If you stand where you can see the Cathedral, including the tower, it almost looks as though the tower should be heightened. Some think that the tower collapsed seven years after the evil King William Rufus (son of the Conqueror) was buried beneath it. In consequence the builders who re-built it may have wished not to tempt fate, and therefore kept it low. Or there may be a completely different architectural reason.

Recently I read a description of the effect that entry into Winchester Cathedral can have on a person. It is such a good description, by Brian Vesey-Fitzgerald, that I have no qualms about repeating it here. 'As you enter the west end the majesty of the whole thing is such that it induces in me at least awe-struck silence. There confronting you are massive pillars, and rising above them a forest of lofty pillars and shafts towering up, and then branching out interlacing in the lovely intricacy of the fan tracery of the roof. It is the spaciousness of Winchester that first impresses, and then you are held spellbound by the height and the vastness of the nave.'

When you have recovered from the first suprise of all this spaciousness, and lightness, you can start to look at some of the details of the Cathedral. The Gilbert Scott choir screen in the nave partly shields the glorious Great Screen behind the High Altar. Whilst in the choir area of any cathedral a close look at the wood carving is almost always very revealing, certainly in Winchester Cathedral the magnificent choir stalls were carved in the early fourteenth century; the carved panels above the stalls depict an

enchanted forest with lions, monkeys and other beasts that we don't usually associate with fourteenth-century Norfolk carpenters. The carpenter in this case was, apparently, a foreigner! The mythical 'green man' peers from the luxuriant foliage, a falconer awaits his prey and a soldier in chain-mail stands to attention, sword in hand. The misericords below (the ledges on which monks could perch during long services) often show the sort of things that fourteenth-century craftsmen found amusing or annoying, because they could carve what they liked in such out of the way places. The stone masons used to do the same, as shown in gargoyles, and the amusing corbels and bosses (best seen with binoculars) in the nave roof.

The tomb with the black top in the choir probably contains King William Rufus, the unpopular son of William the Conqueror, buried in the Cathedral after he was killed by an arrow in the New Forest in 1100. The Great Screen was built in the fifteenth century and contains many statues amidst its delicate carving. The statues are all nineteenth-century but the remains of the original fifteenth-century ones can be seen in the Triforium Gallery (of which more later).

One of the interesting and unusual features in the presbytery is the presence of mortuary chests which sit on top of the presbytery aisle screens. These contain the bones of the pre-conquest monarchs and bishops; they were exhumed in the twelfth century and brought into the Cathedral in lead coffers. The mortuary chests you can see now were made in 1525. It's a bit grizzly really - all the bones must have been handled twice after burial. Is it possible that any might have got mixed up? By a strange twist of fortune Queen Emma's bones now lie intermingled with Bishop Alwyn's; she had to undergo a ghastly ordeal to clear herself of a charge of adultery with him, the story of which I shall tell you further on in our journey round Winchester.

The chantry chapels that flank the High Altar in the north and south aisles are just two of those for which Winchester Cathedral is so famous. I am not going to describe them - they are best come across on a tour around the Cathedral. Each one is so beautiful and evocative of the man for whom it was built that I think it is best to discover them for yourself.

Behind the High Altar is the retrochoir. At the centre of the fourteenth-century retrochoir screen you can see a 'Holy Hole', which allowed pilgrims to the shrine of St Swithun to crawl through a low tunnel beneath the platform on which the saint's remains were displayed. It was necessary to get near to the remains (if you were a medieval pilgrim) because you would expect that curative powers would emanate from them. Not much is known about ninth-century Bishop Swinthun; the single miracle with which he was credited in his lifetime was the restoration of an old woman's dropped basket of eggs to their 'shelly wholeness'! On 15 July 971 his bones were exhumed from their humble tomb and ceremonially translated within the Minster. At that time a violent storm occurred and gave rise to his legendary influence on the weather, and from that time many miracles were said to have happened. Thus began the great attraction of St Swithun's shrine to pilgrims and the sick.

The modern monument of St Swithun stands amid the largest spread of thirteen century floor tiles in England. A lovely sight.

By the opening that leads to the Lady Chapel is a statue of Joan of Arc. It is rather ironic that the chantry chapel of Cardinal Beaufort, who was one of those called to Rome to sit in judgement on her, is nearby.

The statuette on the south side, near Joan of Arc, commemorates that most important man to Winchester, William Walker, the diver. He it was who spent six hours a day under water from 1906 to 1911. Because the east end of the Cathedral had been founded on beech logs that were no longer able to bear the immense weight of the stone, the Cathedral seemed to be in imminent danger of collapse. The walls needed to be underpinned with concrete, below the water level underneath the Cathedral. William Walker worked tirelessly at what must have seemed like an interminable task, and he will always be famous at Winchester as 'the diver who saved the Cathedral'.

There is a charming memorial window to Izaak Walton in Prior Siklstede's Chapel in the south transept. He lived for a long time in Winchester and is buried in the chapel. Jane Austen is also buried in the Cathedral, in the north nave aisle, under a plain black slab that yields no clue to her proficiency as a writer!

Before ending this cursory tour of the Cathedral, I strongly commend the Triforium Gallery with its many Cathedral treasures. It is approached through the South Transept. The Crypt can be entered through the North Transept, provided that it is not flooded. It is so old that it has a peculiar silent awesomeness.

Outside in the open air a visit to the new and well-stocked Cathedral shop is in order. Then double back to walk alongside the Cathedral from the west end. The cloisters used to be here, with a scriptorium in which scribes laboured at the task of copying the Domesday Book for William the Conqueror. It was all destroyed at the Reformation.

A detail from the lavishly decorated memorial to Bishop Samuel Wilberforce (1869 - 73)

Across the grass you will see the REFECTORY, full of coffee and homemade goodies for your delectation.

The buildings in Winchester Cathedral Close are all so old and interesting that it is difficult to know where to start. Walking away from the Cathedral you will see the high-gabled CHEYNEY COURT (very pretty at wisteria time) with the PRIORY GATE next to it. The PILGRIMS' HALL, on the left, was built about 1308. Now it is used by the Pilgrim School, but is open to visitors when they are not using it.

Behind the Close Wall are the ruins of WOLVESEY PLACE, and through the Priory Gate you may turn left through KINGSGATE ARCH into College Street. This will take you to the famous public school, WINCHESTER COLLEGE. Guided tours are arranged daily for visitors during the season (details are available from the Porter).

The best place from which to see the panorama of Winchester is St Giles's Hill, which overlooks the city from the east side. Down towards the left you can see parts of the River Itchen as it meanders through the water meadows which were once such an important part of Winchester life. The meadows used to be flooded at certain times of the year through a complex system of hatches and channels (traces of which are still visible) to provide hay and grazing for sheep and cattle. In the hottest of summers the grass could be prevented from drying out. Further down, to the south, is the hospital of ST CROSS. The poet Keats used to walk along College Walk to the path that leads to St Cross and the water meadows, for the benefit of his health.

The street plan of the centre of Winchester is still as it was laid out in King Alfred's time, 1100 years ago. He is here still, in the form of a bronze statue made in honour of the millenary of his death, standing at the end of the Broadway. From Alfred to the Westgate was the extent of the Saxon and later medieval city. The new Brooks shopping development to the north of the High Street is fairly near to Upper, Middle and Lower Brooks Streets, which were probably laid out by Alfred the Great as part of his defensive measures against the Danes. They had water running through the middle of them (hence the name 'Brooks'), so I suppose they must have been thought to be a fairly effective deterrent against invading Danish hordes. After

Detail from Winchester's Great Screen: above, Bishop Swithin (852 - 62), the famous Saint, is holding the bridge which he built over the River Itchen

all, Alfred was not a man to be faint-hearted about that sort of thing.

Winchester College, the Cathedral, Wolvesey Palace, the layout of the city streets rising to the Great Hall and site of William the Conqueror's great Norman castle, can all be seen from St Giles's Hill. As Keats said, 'From the hill at the eastern extremity you can see a prospect of streets and old buildings mixed up with trees'. I think that is one of the most attractive features of Winchester - the trees, hanging baskets, green parks, flowers and pretty gardens that seem to be everywhere.

Come down St Giles's Hill into Magdalen Hill and turn right into Bridge Street. On the left is Chesil Street, with a lovely old house at the near end. On the beam across the tops of the windows are the words 'Old Chesil Rectory built 1450. The Oldest House in Winchester built 1450.' Not much room for doubt here.

Go down Bridge Street, and on to the bridge itself, under which the River Itchen flows invitingly out towards the Weirs. Ducks abound here, living at the edges of the gardens that descend to the water on the left-hand side, and being fed by the people who walk along the footpath on the right-hand side. A little way along here, on the right, can be seen the only remaining visible section of the city's Roman wall. Winchester is obviously very proud of its

long history, and informative plaques, like the one by the Roman wall, are dotted around the city to inform the visitor of interesting facts.

On the other side of the bridge is the CITY MILL, now owned by the National Trust and used as a Youth Hostel. It has a delightful small island garden and an impressive millrace, and the National Trust shop is one of the best I've seen.

Over the bridge (towards the Broadway) there are shops with the sort of names that make you stop and have a closer look - 'THE PAINTED PAGE' (selling maps, watercolours, picture framing equipment and such like assorted items), and 'COLLECTOR'S CORNER', which specialises in trains, teddies, dolls' houses and rather superior country-style dolls' furniture.

One could be forgiven for supposing that where King Alfred's Statue stands, in the broad area at the eastern end of the Broadway, must once have been a market place. It seems suitable, but in fact there were buildings standing there until 1798.

Just past the statue you can see on the right THE CHURCH OF THE HOSPITAL OF ST JOHN THE BAPTIST. It was built in 1289 as a hall for the poor and needy. ST JOHNS HOSPITAL itself includes the almshouses and medieval chapel slightly to the west on the other side of the road. The Hospital is a richly endowed institution, older than the Hospital of St Cross and quite possibly of Saxon origin, and it owns a substantial amount of property in the city. The hall itself now houses THE CRUSADES EXPERIENCE, a vivid exhibition of the historical conflict between Christian and Muslin. At one time the company in Winchester was so brilliant that such celebrated musicians as Liszt and Paganini were attracted to St John's Rooms. The fine interior decor can be seen once again thanks to the extensive restoration that has been carried out in recent times.

Across the road are the pretty ABBEY GARDENS, where the lands of Nunnaminter, or St Mary's Abbey, founded by King Alfred and Queen Ealhswith, were until the Dissolution of the Monasteries. In Abbey Passage, next to ABBEY HOUSE, the official residence of the Mayor of Winchester, you can still see excavated remains of King Alfred's abbey. Abbey House was given to the city in 1554 as a 'reward' for the huge expense it incurred when Mary Tudor married Philip of Spain in Winchester Cathedral.

THE GUILDHALL, on the far side of Abbey Passage, is a rather extravagant, striking Victorian building in the Gothic style. In summer the hanging baskets provide a riot of colour and seem to give a fitting welcome to visitors who want to go to the Tourist Information Centre in the Guildhall. Guided tours of Winchester, which are well worth going on, start from here. Upstairs, next to the Abbey Bar, an antiques fair is held about once a month, as well as other events and exhibitions in the Guildhall Gallery.

Set into the stone at the base of the right-hand flight of steps leading up to the Abbey Bar is another of those Winchester information boxes, although this one is quite different from the rest. It sets out the geographical facts about the city, with the equipment alongside to prove it:

Height above the sea - 127' 2"
Latitude - 51 degrees 04' North
Longitude - 1 degree 19' West
Real Noon - 5 min 16 sec later than at Greenwich
The Compass points 9 degrees 4' West in 1954

The carvings below the roof line on the Guildhall are of characters historically connected with Winchester. One such is King Canute, whose capital was Winchester and who spoke to the sea at Southampton where, apparently, there are four tides a day, so he evidently knew what he was doing.

Up into the High Street you will see MARKS AND SPENCER on the right, with a plaque on the wall. This tells you that this site was rented by King John (more than 700 years ago) to his tailor who, in return, was to supply yearly a fine coat.

Further up the High Street is THE PENTICE, a covered way with shops on the left. The original Tudor buildings were constructed like this to provide shelter and to avoid ground rent. Many of the shops have cellars with medieval stonework, and a peep into the NATIONWIDE BUILDING SOCIETY will reveal old beams and stonework. The chemist, Boots, is Victorian Tudor, as opposed to the real thing, but is still attractive.

Next to the Nationwide Building Society is THE BUTTER CROSS. Although it dates from the fifteenth century there was probably a cross there before that, from which all public proclamations would have been made. (THE TOWER OF ST LAWRENCE-IN-THE-SQUARE can be seen standing behind the Butter Cross. It is traditionally called the Mother Church of

One of six heavenly guardians at Winchester

Winchester and each new bishop of Winchester visits it for private prayer before his enthronement.) Speaking of proclamations naturally leads to thoughts of the Town Crier, Alan Kinge, who can be seen in his uniform carrying out his duties at special events. The Ancient and Honourable Guild of Town Criers owes its origin to the Statute of Winchester 1285, by which all towns and cities were required to provide a Crier as protection against crime and fire. I expect Mr Kinge's duties are slightly different from that.

Further up the High Street is GOD'S BAGOT HOUSE. If you visit Winchester during fine weather you will probably see several coffee houses with tables out on the pavement, looking very continental. This apparently has something to do with town-twinning, but rather ironically the tables were put outside in July just as the rain which everyone hopes will not fall on St Swithun's Day, July 15, fell.... God's Bagot (or God Begot) House has an ancient and rather strange name which in fact has nothing to do with the Almighty. God here equals good, and the manor of God Begot was given to Queen Emma by her husband, King Ethelred the Unready. The manor was self-ruling, and when her husband died King Canute married Emma. She was very happy until he died, when rumours started to circulate about her and her confessor, the bishop. Her son, the King by that time, ordered her to prove her innocence by undergoing the ordeal of walking barefoot over nine burning ploughshares. This she did, blindfold and praying to St Swithun, and emerged without a mark on her feet. So she gave the manor of God Begot to the Priory of St Swithun, in gratitude.

Royal Oak Passage, next to God Begot House, contains THE ROYAL OAK - the oldest bar in England. The passage leads to a paved area where the outlines of part of St Peter in the Flesh-Shambles, dating from 1000 AD, have been laid in brickwork.

Before you reach the top of the pedestrianised part of the High Street you will pass on the left the bow-fronted offices of the Hampshire Chronicle, established in 1772. Until relatively recently this was one of the few newspapers published independently and using hot-metal type. But progress has overtaken it and its publication is now computerised elsewhere. By the time you reach Winchester it is quite possible that the original Hampshire Chronicle premises will be open to the public and the old machines on show.

Continuing up the High Street you will pass on the left Elizabeth Frink's sculpture of a man on a horse. Not all that far away, on the right, is David Kemp's statue of the Hampshire Hog, made to mark the one hundredth anniversary of the Hampshire County Council and therefore standing outside 'The Castle', as the Victorian red brick offices are known. Note also the gold weather-vane on top of the building which depicts a Hampshire Hog, and the cartoon murals on the blue and white building opposite (just below the Westgate).

Near to the Hampshire Hog statue you will see a grey obelisk. This is the Plague Monument, erected in 1666, on the spot where the inhabitants of Winchester, gripped by the Plague, would leave money in bowls of vinegar to pay for provisions brought in from the country.

The thirteenth-century Westgate, once an important gateway to Winchester, now houses a museum. There are fine views from the roof and the shields on the gate represent the Royal Arms (on the left) and the arms of the city of Winchester (on the right).

Just past the Westgate you can turn left and see the remains of William the Conqueror's great Norman castle, carefully preserved behind a wall. When it stood it was separated by a ditch from the city. In the Civil War, when Winchester was a Royalist stronghold, Cromwell laid seige to it, and finally managed to defeat it. Demolishing the castle turned out to be rather a difficult job it was so strongly built, so quite a lot of the keep wall remains.

Luckily for us the whole of the GREAT HALL, rebuilt in the early thirteenth-century by Henry III, remains. Its most famous asset is King Arthurs Round Table, which has been carbon-dated to about 1280. This means of course that whilst King Arthur himself couldn't have had it made, it may well have been commissioned by Edward I, who was fascinated by chivalric stories. The Tudor Rose in the middle, the Tudor colours in which it is painted, and Henry VIII's head painted in King Arthur's place, show how anxious Henry VIII was to impress the Holy Roman Emperor, Charles V, when he visited. Henry was descended in a direct line from King Arthur and back to Constantine the Great, the first Christian Roman Emperor.

The Round Table has the look of an enormous dart board, and that is how Cromwell's soldiers saw it during the Civil War. It used to hang on the wall at the opposite end of the Great Hall, and when it was moved to its present position the intricate tree showing the Knights of the Shire and the kings reigning at particular times in history was painted. The wrought steel gates that link the Hall with the new Law Courts were installed in 1983 to

mark the wedding of HRH the Prince of Wales to Lady Diana Spencer two years earlier.

A reminder of harsher days than ours is the bench by the entrance to the Great Hall, on which the 'hanging judge', Judge Jeffreys used to sit to pronounce sentence on hapless citizens, when the Hall was used as an Assize Court. Alice Lisle was unjustly condemned to death there in 1685 by the notorious Judge Jeffreys for harbouring two refugees from the Battle of Sedgemoor. She was beheaded in The Square, outside the Eclipse Inn. This miscarriage of justice is depicted in a painting that hangs in the Houses of Parliament.

On the opposite side of the Great Hall is the entrance to 'QUEEN ELEANOR'S GARDEN', a reconstruction of a thirteenth-century garden, based on the records of the palace garden of Queen Eleanor. The garden is a sun trap and is a delightful place to spend a short time.

Leaving the Great Hall this is quite a good point at which to visit the military museums. THE ROYAL GREEN JACKETS, THE LIGHT INFANTRY, THE GURKAS AND THE ROYAL HUSSARS MUSEUMS are all situated in the Peninsula Barracks, reached via an entrance in Romsey Road. THE HAMPSHIRE REGIMENTAL MUSEUM is a little apart from these, off Southgate Street. The Royal Hampshire Regiment and the Royal Green Jackets have long been associated with Winchester, and in recent years the Royal Hussars moved their HQ to Winchester. A central feature of the Royal Green Jackets Museum is a diorama of the Battle of Waterloo, with 22,000 model figures in it. There are many military memorials in and around the Cathedral, emphasising the strong links Winchester continues to have with military life.

Another museum of note in Winchester is THE CITY MUSEUM in The Square. It contains some reconstructed, old, shop interiors (Hunt's, the Chemists, is particularly attractive), and many of the Roman remains and artefacts excavated in the city. There are a few items of Austen memorabilia, since the house in College Street where Jane Austen spent her last few weeks, and died, is not open to the public.

WINCHESTER HERITAGE CENTRE, in Upper Brook Street, has a small permanent exhibition of the history of the city and its buildings, supplemented by regular showings of a specially commissioned film on the city.

In this short chapter it has not been possible to do more than scratch the surface of the City of Winchester and its ancient Cathedral. If you are interested in music you will surely find much to please you in the regular concerts put on in the Cathedral, and an opportunity to hear the world-famous Cathedral Choir, if they are 'at home', must be a bonus. In the summer there is often Morris dancing (Winchester is an important place for this) and St. Giles's Fair, the Folk Festival (April-May) and the Hat Fair (July). All in all, something to interest everyone.

Two hotels that I can happily recommend to you are LAINSTON HOUSE in Sparsholt, Winchester. Here, land belonging to this superb hotel is mentioned in the Domesday Book and a Manor house has stood on the site for hundreds of years. Lainston meaning 'house of stone' dates back to the 17th century and has an infamous previous guest in Elizabeth Chudleigh who was tried for bigamy and whose portrait hangs in the hall. It is due to Elizabeth Chudleigh that marriage banns are read out today. The ruin of the Norman Chapel where the unlawful marriage took place stands in the grounds, close to the house. The hotel is just two and a half miles from the centre of Winchester yet set in 63 acres of beautiful Hampshire Downland. Richard Fannon is the general manager of this outstanding hotel renowned for its comfort and its food. It is he whose assured touch leads

his team in making this such an enjoyable place to stay. He used to run the Hotel La Toc in the Caribbean and can be persuaded to recount amusing tales over a Gin and Tonic!

A majestic chestnut shades the restful garden of THE ROYAL HOTEL and wherever you are in this fine establishment you will find relaxation and a sense of well being. Once a convent, the Royal still exudes an aura of serenity and peacefulness with the bustling High Street only 100 yards away. The hotel was built in 1720 during Stuart times and has a history which provides an atmosphere in keeping with this 'City of Kings'. It was not until the 19th century that it became the Royal Hotel. It is quite superb and has 81 bedrooms and probably the finest conference facilities in the area with trained staff dedicated to the success of every event.

In the quietest and oldest quarter of Winchester, sandwiched between the famous College and the Cathedral is THE WYKEHAM ARMS. This fascinating hostelry is known as the 'Licenced Annexe' to the Cathedral with whom it has a very close relationship - something you will discover when you seek it out. To emphasise the bond, The Wykeham Arms has almost completed its self-imposed task of raising £60,000 towards the Cathedral's Music Foundation. For anyone who has experienced the sheer beauty and excellence of the music that soars to the rafters, it will be impossible for you not to give to this cause. Somewhere in which one may find a new eating

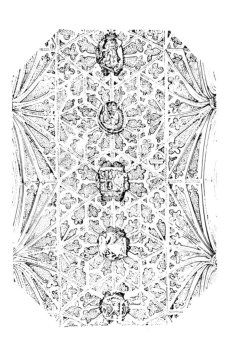

The magnificent roof of hte Chantry of Bishop Fox, d. 1528

experience is SUHEL'S BALTI HOUSE in St Georges Street. 'Never judge a book by its covers' is an old adage. The same should be true of the frontage of Suhel's Balti House; it is not attractive but inside you enter a world of the East. The decor is soft and welcoming, light spacious and modern Indian. There are some striking and beautiful framed Indian landscape prints on the walls. It is always the service that strikes one about the Indians. They have a grace and charm that is often missing amongst Europeans. Here they have perfected the art of unobtrusive service yet are always on hand to help you decide what to have from the large menu. Sometimes to get the right balance is not easy for anyone other than Indians or Pakistanis, from whence Balti originated, and to be advised will certainly enhance a meal.

If, after absorbing the wonders of Winchester and its Cathedral, having been spoilt in hotels and possibly over indulging THE RIVER PARK LEISURE CENTRE will provide you with 'Fun and Fitness for the Whole Family'. It is well equipped and has every facility.

It will be difficult to persuade yourself to leave Winchester but it would be a great pity if you did not explore some of the lovely countryside and sample some of its pleasures and attractions as well. Just to give you a taster there are one or two I would like to bring to your attention.

Beauworth is a village 8 miles east of Winchester and off the Petersfield A272. Here you should seek out MILBURYS, a delightful late 17th early 18th century inn. It is full of charm and has an amazing 300ft well inside the wheel room with a 24ft treadmill over 250 years old. The well mentioned in the Domesday Book is where King Stephen hid his treasure during the Battle of Cheriton. Run as a friendly country inn, it nonetheless is renowned for its first class restaurant in which the international menu offers a delicious assortment of dishes.

Alresford must be one of the most delightful of Hampshire's small towns. It was laid out by Bishop de Lucy of Winchester in 1200 and with a centre shaped like a T, with the aptly named Broad Street, wide enough to accommodate the market. Fire sadly destroyed its medieval houses in 1689 and 1736 but the 17th and 18th centuries did its best to bring back its beauty and with few exceptions the buildings are more than acceptable. It is a town known for its attractive shops, especially antiques, but it should also be known for the excellence of HUNTERS RESTAURANT in Broad Street. The restaurant is also a small wine bar and if you were a stranger walking through its doors for the first time, your immediate feeling would be of the friendliness and the sense of vibrant life that emanates throughout the building.

Now for two places to visit. WHITCHURCH SILK MILL in Winchester Street, **Whitchurch**, was built in 1800 but there has been a mill on the site since Doomsday. A tour will induct you in the art of spinning silk. It is fascinating, educational and a great day out.

Finally one of my favourite places HIGHCLERE CASTLE near **Newbury** which is superb. From outside, Highclere is huge, ornate and typically Victorian. There has been a house at Highclere since the year 900. The original house was the Palace of the Bishops of Winchester when that city was the capital of England. Highclere is the home of the Earls of Carnarvon, who throughout the years have all contributed to the superb collections. The 5th Earl, a respected Egyptologist, discovered the tomb of Tutankhamun. The present Earl is the Queen's Racing Manager. The castle is wonderful, beautifully appointed and has 3,000 acres of parkland created by Capability Brown. The castle is surrounded by spectacular gardens: The White Garden, Monks Garden and Secret Garden and there are a number of follies in the park and gardens. Highclere is somewhere not to be missed.

The beauty and magic of Winchester and its Cathedral will never leave you and will always nag at you until you give in and return, when it will open its welcoming arms and find more magical things and places for you to see whilst making sure that you are reminded of what you saw before.

32 Broad Street, Alresford,
Hampshire, SO24 9AQ.

Tel: (0962) 732468

HUNTERS RESTAURANT

Restaurant

Alresford must be one of the most delightful of Hampshire's small towns. It was laid out by Bishop de Lucy of Winchester in 1200 and with a centre shaped like a T, with the aptly named Broad Street, wide enough to accommodate the market. Fire sadly destroyed its medieval houses in 1689 and 1736 but the 17th and 18th centuries did its best to bring back its beauty and with few exceptions the buildings are more than acceptable. It is a town known for its attractive shops, especially antiques, but it should also be known for the excellence of Hunters Restaurant in Broad Street.

The restaurant is also a small wine bar and if you were a stranger walking through its doors for the first time, your immediate feeling would be of the friendliness and the sense of vibrant life that emanates throughout the building. You are welcome to join in the spirit of the bar before you order your meal or, indeed, to wait for your choice to be cooked to order. You might even be tempted to wander into the superb walled garden of half an acre.

David and Martin Birmingham have been running Hunters for some years and whilst there appears to be no special alliance with the world of hunting there are nonetheless many hunting prints adorning their walls, accompanied by horse brasses. The food on offer reflects their desire for excellence. Every dish is freshly cooked and only the very best of ingredients is used. Lunching or dining here is a sheer pleasure but it is also possible to stay in one of their charming ensuite bedrooms - sometimes a wise precaution if one is to enjoy to the full the number of fine wines on offer!

USEFUL INFORMATION

OPEN: All year. Every day except December 24th-30th
CHILDREN: Welcome
CREDIT CARDS: All major cards
LICENSED: Full On Licence
ACCOMMODATION: Charming ensuite bedrooms

RESTAURANT: Modern English with French influence
BAR FOOD: Light snacks available
VEGETARIAN: Daily selection available
DISABLED ACCESS: Level entrance
GARDEN: Lovely formal gardens and courtyard

Beauworth, Nr Cheriton,
Hampshire, SO24 0PB.

Tel: (0962) 771248

THE MILBURY'S

Inn & Restaurant

Beauworth is a village 8 miles east of Winchester and off the Petersfield A272. To seek out The Milbury's drive through the village and you will come to this delightful, late 17th early 18th century inn. Known in those days as The Hare and Hounds and from the 1850's until quite recently the Fox and Hounds, The Milbury's or 'Mill barrow' is enchanting. Full of old world charm, it has an amazing 300ft well inside the wheel room with a 24ft treadmill over 250years old. The well mentioned in the Domesday Book is where King Stephen hid his treasure during the battle of Cheriton. To prove how deep the well is you can drop an ice cube down the grating and you will discover it takes 8 seconds for it to hit the water.

Run as a friendly country inn, it nonetheless is renowned for its first class restaurant in which the international menu offers a delicious assortment of dishes to tempt even the most difficult palate. The wine list complements the menu perfectly. With the ability to cater for 200 people for weddings in a big marquee or 70 in the restaurant, it is a popular choice. Equally there are a growing number of people who use The Milbury's for business lunches, private functions and meetings. There is no doubt that Jan and Len Larden, the proprietors have brought The Milbury's to a very high standard in the 6 years that they have been here.

In the bar a wide and varied menu is on offer. Sunday brunch, served between 9.30-11.15am, complete with the Sunday papers has become almost a ritual for some regulars. With accommodation also available it would be sad not to make sure of finding this attractive spot.

USEFUL INFORMATION

OPEN: 11-3pm & 6-midnight, 7 days a week
CHILDREN: Welcome. Highchairs, children's room
CREDIT CARDS: Amex/Visa/Access
LICENSED: Full On Licence
ACCOMMODATION: Rooms available

RESTAURANT: International cuisine
BAR FOOD: Extensive bar menu
VEGETARIAN: On request
DISABLED ACCESS: Level entrance
GARDEN: Lovely garden with views

HIGHCLERE CASTLE

Castle & Gardens

Newbury,
Berkshire, RG15 9RN.

Tel: (0635) 253210
Fax: (0635) 254845

USEFUL INFORMATION

OPEN: July-Sept 2pm-6pm, Wed-Sun including Bank Holidays
CHILDREN: Yes. Tutankhamun exhibition - part of the National Curriculum
CREDIT CARDS: None taken

RESTAURANT: Very good country food
VEGETARIAN: A selection
DISABLED ACCESS: Yes to castle & gardens
GARDEN: 3,000 acres. Picnic area in park, outside gardens & castle

From outside, Highclere is huge, ornate and typically Victorian. The architecture is 'Jacobethan' finished off with an Italiante flourish in the tall central tower. Its architect, Sir Charles Barry, called it Anglo-Italian and liked it much better than the houses of parliament he was building at the same time. It was the last years of the 1830's, when Barry was asked by the 3rd Earl of Carnarvon to alter his plain Georgian home into a grand mansion which would impress the world. The design of the grand new house is based on three characteristic Victorian qualities: love of extravagance, love of the past and a love of ancestry. The Earl wanted everyone to recognise that his was an old family, so Barry carved the family motto in Norman French round the facade: UNG IE SERVIRAY (one only will I serve).

There has been a house at Highclere since the year 900. The original house was the palace of the Bishops of Winchester when that city was the capital of England. Every Earl of Carnarvon, has brought something special to the building. The 5th Earl a respected Egyptologist, discovered the tomb of Tutankhamun. At one time the Music Room was full of his finds which he displayed in much the way he might have shown them off to his friends when he returned to Highclere from Egypt. The enormous public interest in this important collection has led to a Themed Exhibition being relocated in the cellars which is seen by visitors at the end of their castle tour. The present Earl is the Queen's Racing Manager. The Castle is quite superb, beautifully appointed and has 3,000 acres of parkland created by Capability Brown. The Castle is surrounded by spectacular gardens; the White Garden, Monks Garden and Secret Garden and there are a number of follies in the park and gardens.

LAINSTON HOUSE

Hotel

Sparsholt, Winchester,
Hampshire, SO21 2LT.

Tel: (0962) 863588
Fax: (0962) 776672

USEFUL INFORMATION

OPEN: All year round. All hours
CHILDREN: Yes. Cots, highchairs, baby sitting
CREDIT CARDS: All major cards
LICENSED: Full On Licence
ACCOMMODATION: 38 en-suite rooms

RESTAURANT: Freshly prepared local produce. Gourmet standard
BAR FOOD: Not applicable
VEGETARIAN: Always four dishes
DISABLED ACCESS: Yes, level entrance. Disabled toilet
GARDEN: Beautiful gardens of 63 acres

Land belonging to this superb hotel is mentioned in the Domesday Book and a Manor House has stood on the site for hundreds of years. Lainston meaning 'house of stone' dates back to the 17th century and has an infamous previous guest in Elizabeth Chudleigh who was tried for bigamy and whose portrait hangs in the hall. It is due to Elizabeth Chudleigh that marriage banns are read out today. The ruin of the Norman Chapel where the unlawful marriage took place stands in the grounds of Lainston, close to the house. The hotel is just two and a half miles from the centre of Winchester yet set in 63 acres of beautiful Hampshire Downland.

Before you even enter the portals of Lainston House you are aware that it is somewhere very special. There are 38 en-suite bedrooms beautifully appointed. The elegant drawing room is a pleasure to sit in and both the Avenue Restaurant and the Garden Restaurant offer food and service that one would expect from a hotel of this standard. For special occasions either personal or business there are private dining rooms to accommodate up to 90 persons. The Cedar panelled bar is a popular meeting place for those who just want a quiet drink or perhaps are joining others for a pre-dinner drink. Conference rooms to accommodate 80 persons theatre style is yet another of the facilities on offer. Lainston House richly deserves its Four Star AA and RAC and 2AA red rosettes for food. Richard Fannon is the General Manager whose assured touch leads his team in making this such an enjoyable place to stay. He used to run the Hotel La Toc in the Caribbean and can be persuaded to recount amusing tales over a Gin and Tonic!

28 Winchester Street, Whitchurch,
Nr Winchester, Hampshire, RG28 7AL.

Tel: (0256) 893882

WHITCHURCH SILK MILL
Working Silk Mill, Shop & Tearoom

Whitchurch Silk Mill on the River Test was built in 1800 but there has been a mill on the site since Doomsday. The whole tour starts in the carpenter's workshop above the waterwheel, where water from the mill stream gives a straight flow to the wheel and additional water can be diverted from the main river along the front of the mill to the wheel, which now powers the winding gear on the top floor.

The silk in use comes from China, the home of silk for 4,000 years. Silk worms fed on mulberry leaves spin cocoons of up to a mile in length of fine silk. The silk is reeled from the cocoons in China and arrives at Whitchurch in hanks. The hanks once dyed are first wound onto wooden bobbins on the water-powered winding machine. The next stage is warping. The silk is led from the bobbins on the creel, which looks like an upturned boat, onto the warping wheel which is then turned until the correct length of warp is reached.

The middle floor houses a small museum area; take yourself back 150 years to see what happened then. On the ground floor the original looms are used to weave a variety of different silks. There is also a small costume display. The Silk Mill's range of fabrics now includes taffetas, organzas and silk ribbons for theatrical costumes, taffetas for curtains for interior designers and National Trust properties, ottomans for upholstery and some spun silks and moire for the mill shop.

A tour will fascinate you, the tearoom on the middle floor serves excellent tea and coffee and light lunches, and on leaving the mill there is an opportunity to walk round the small silk weaver's garden.

USEFUL INFORMATION

OPEN: Tues–Sun: all year round + Bank
    Holidays: 10.30-5pm
CHILDREN: Very welcome, and school
    parties
CREDIT CARDS: Visa/Mastercard/
    Access
LICENSED: None
ACCOMMODATION: Not applicable

RESTAURANT: Tea, coffee & light
    lunches
BAR FOOD: Not applicable
VEGETARIAN: 3 dishes daily
DISABLED ACCESS: Ground floor
    and toilets
GARDEN: For tea room customers
    & visitors

Winchester Cathedral,
Winchester, Hampshire, SO23 9LS.

Tel: (0962) 853224
Fax: (0962) 841684

THE REFECTORY
Restaurant

You will find The Refectory within 100 yards of the Cathedral behind a medieval wall. It is a modern building completed in 1993 and is lucky enough to be in an area of great beauty and tranquility. Opened in November 1993 by Her Majesty The Queen, this welcoming place is an ideal spot in which to end your visit to the Cathedral or for that matter at any time. It was built within one of the gardens of the famous Close where Isaak Walton once lived. The Refectory adjoins the 16th century Coach house which has been attractively renovated to house the Cathedral Shop.

Whenever possible everything is made in The Refectory. You can catch a delicious whiff of freshly baked bread and the tantalising smell of freshly ground coffee as you enter its friendly doors. Throughout the day food is available with a range that takes you from morning coffee to lunches and afternoon teas. The latter is a tempting feast with feather light scones, jam and cream and cakes that can be anything from the tried and tested fruit cake to a carrot cake. Home-made soup served with fresh, crispy bread is always on the lunchtime menu and it is almost a meal in itself. Vegetarians are not forgotten, there is always a hot dish and a variety of salads.

Local people have discovered that The Refectory is ideal for parties, wedding receptions and business functions. In summer the Terrace, which seats up to 40 people, is a popular meeting place.

USEFUL INFORMATION

OPEN: 9.30-5.30pm
CHILDREN: Welcome. Highchairs
CREDIT CARDS: Visa/Access
LICENSED: Restaurant
ACCOMMODATION: Banqueting &
    function facilities

RESTAURANT: Home-made produce
    using fresh ingredients
BAR FOOD: Not applicable
VEGETARIAN: One hot dish & salads
DISABLED ACCESS: Yes. WC and paths
GARDEN: Terrace seats up to 40

RIVER PARK LEISURE CENTRE

Leisure Centre

Gordon Road, Winchester,
Hampshire, SO23 7EH.

Tel: (0962) 869525
Fax: (0962) 851933

USEFUL INFORMATION

OPEN: Daily from 7.30am-11pm
CHILDREN: Welcome. Creche &
forthcoming Day Nursery
CREDIT CARDS: Access/Visa
LICENSED: Full On Licence
ACCOMMODATION: Camp site behind
Park Centre

RESTAURANT: Licenced Cafeteria
BAR FOOD: Good choice of lght bites
VEGETARIAN: Selection of dishes
DISABLED ACCESS: Yes. Lift, 2 in-house
wheelchairs
GARDEN: Surrounded by park and the
River Itchen

The motto of Riverpark Leisure Centre in Winchester is 'Fun and Fitness for the Whole Family'. Certainly every facility is there for a wonderful family outing. The Centre boasts a wide range of leisure activities seven days a week from 7.30am-11pm including:

* 25m Swimming Pool   * 12m Learner Pool   * 4 Squash Courts
* 65m Flume Ride   * Pinks Dance Centre   * Images Health Studio
* 8 Badminton Courts   * 8 Floodlit Tennis Courts

The swimming pool facilities are widely recognised as one of the finest in the South of England. Regular play-pool sessions and the amazing twister flume ride as well as the general and lane swimming sessions, offer a comprehensive service for people of all ages and especially for parents who have children of different ages, all of whom can have great fun here in total safety.

The recently expanded Images Health Studio is well equipped and it is good to see the enthusiasm for Pinks Dance Centre which, with the Fitness Factory, provides the ultimate fitness opportunities for everyone.

For more information you are encouraged to contact The Centre Hotline (0962) 869525. It is operated by D.C. Leisure on behalf of Winchester City Council and is a credit to them. The staff are courteous, efficient and caring. There is a cafeteria and a licensed bar.

THE ROYAL HOTEL

Hotel & Restaurant

St Peters Street, Winchester,
Hampshire, SO22 8BS.

Tel: (0962) 840840
Fax: (0962) 841582

USEFUL INFORMATION

OPEN: All year round
CHILDREN: Welcome
CREDIT CARDS: All major cards
LICENSED: Full On Licence
ACCOMMODATION: 75 ensuite rooms

RESTAURANT: Modern English
and European
BAR FOOD: Bar meals & light lunches,
in conservatory & bar lounge
VEGETARIAN: A La Carte menu
DISABLED ACCESS: Level entrance,
accommodation facilities
GARDEN: Walled garden, summer BBQs

A majestic chestnut shades the restful garden of The Royal Hotel and wherever you are in this fine establishment you will find relaxation and a sense of well being. Once a convent, the Royal still exudes an aura of serenity and peacefulness with the bustling High Street only 100 yards away. The hotel was built in 1720 during Stuart times and has a history which provides an atmosphere in keeping with the 'City of Kings'. It was not until the 19th century that it became the Royal Hotel. Over the past few years it has been sympathetically refurbished to a high standard whilst retaining the original character of the building.

Whether you chose a suite, the half tester, or a newer room overlooking the private walled gardens, you will find style and comfort. All 75 bedrooms have ensuite bathroom, remote colour TV, radio, direct dial telephone and hospitality trays. 24 hour service, shoe cleaning and valeting are some of the little touches that help set the Royal apart from other hotels. The 'Conservatory Restaurant' makes every meal special whether it is a business lunch, a candlelit dinner or just Sunday lunch for the family. At lunchtime lighter meals are served in the bar lounge and on warmer days between May and September, the terrace barbeque is not to be missed.

It may not be apparent to the casual visitor that the Royal Hotel has the finest conference facilities in the area with trained staff dedicated to the success of every event. The hotel is able to accommodate most people's requirements.

8 St Georges Street, Winchester,
Hampshire, SO23 8BG.

Tel: (0962) 862838

SUHEL'S BALTI HOUSE

Indian Restaurant

Never judge a book by its cover is an old adage. The same should be true of the frontage of Suhel's Balti House; it is not attractive but inside you enter a world of the East. The decor is soft and welcoming, light, spacious and modern Indian. There are some particularly striking and beautiful framed Indian landscape prints on the walls. It is always the service that strikes one about the Indians. They have a grace and charm that is often missing amongst Europeans. Here at Suhel's Balti House they have perfected the art of unobtrusive service yet are always on hand to help you to decide what to have from the large menu. Sometimes to get the right balance is not easy for anyone other than Indians or Pakistanis, from whence Balti originated, and to be advised will certainly enhance a meal.

Whilst there are all sorts of dishes on this menu perhaps it would be sensible to try the Balti dishes in which the restaurant specialises and for which it has a well deserved reputation. This is a very popular method of cooking in a traditional Indian stlye. It is always cooked in a cast iron pot which enhances the exotic flavours. For seafood lovers 'King Prawn Bhuna Balti' must come high on the list or for meat, one might choose 'Meat Jalfrazi Balti' - a very hot dish. The 'Chefs House Special' can always be relied on to please.

There is a free home delivery service for orders over £10 if you would rather have a touch of the East in your own homes. It is a good service and the food is always freshly prepared.

USEFUL INFORMATION

OPEN: Mon-Sun: 12-2.30pm & 6-midnight. Closed Christmas Day
CHILDREN: Welcome
CREDIT CARDS: All major cards. Not switch
LICENSED: Full On Licence
ACCOMMODATION: Not applicable

RESTAURANT: Spicy, traditional, specialising in Balti dishes
BAR FOOD: Not applicable
VEGETARIAN: Wide range
DISABLED ACCESS: Easy access. Difficult loos, help available
GARDEN: No

---

75 Kingsgate Street, Winchester,
Hampshire, SO23 9PE.

Tel: (0962) 853834
Fax: (0962) 854411

THE WYKEHAM ARMS

Inn

In the quietest and oldest quarter of the City of Winchester, sandwiched between the famous College and the Cathedral is The Wykeham Arms. This wonderful hostelry is known as the 'Licenced Annexe' to the Cathedral with whom it has a very close relationship - something you will discover when you seek it out for the very first time; probably after a visit to the awe inspiring Cathedral. To emphasise the bond, The Wykeham Arms has nearly completed its self-imposed task of raising £60,000 towards the Cathedral's 'Music Foundation'. For anyone who has experienced the sheer beauty and excellence of the music that soars to the rafters, it will be impossible for you not to give generously to this cause.

For most visitors, coming to Winchester automatically means to the Cathedral. You will hear the sound of many tongues within its walls and frequently in the Wykeham Arms where one may stay in one of the 7 ensuite rooms, which, incidentally, can all be let as singles if required; something that is quite unusual. You will find words of praise written by guests from all over the world, for the hospitality that The Wykeham and its owners, Graeme and Anne Jameson offer.

If you can keep up with the count, you will see that the pub is extensively decorated with 700 pictures, 1500 tankards, military bric-a brac, hats and other items of interest. It is an establishment that has been praised in too many guides to mention, suffice it to say that the imaginatively cooked and served food is delicious, the beer and wines superb, and the whole inn welcoming.

USEFUL INFORMATION

OPEN: All year round
CHILDREN: No children under 14 years
CREDIT CARDS: Amex/Mastercard/ Visa
LICENSED: Full On Licence
ACCOMMODATION: 7 ensuite rooms

RESTAURANT: Fresh, local produce, imaginatively cooked and served
BAR FOOD: Best quality, bread, vegetables, meat & fish, served simply
VEGETARIAN: At least one dish always
DISABLED ACCESS: No
GARDEN: Grassed area. Covered patio

Worcester Cathedral

Worcester

" How lovely is thy dwelling-place."

Psalms

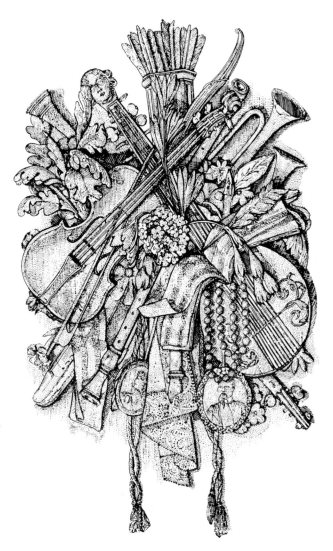

The City of Worcester

by Joy David

The venerable Cathedral city of **Worcester** is capital to the county of the same name and reflects many of the contrasts to be found within the region as a whole with historical associations, architectural contrast and industrial, as opposed to agricultural wealth which is largely the keynote of prosperity in the county. Yet even its industry has a bucolic air to it, for the black smoke and noisome forges of the Industrial Revolution have little place in the manufacture of gloves, Royal Worcester porcelain or that secret blend of 'brown vinegar, walnut ketchup, anchovy essence, soy sauce, cayenne, and shallots' known world-wide as Worcestershire sauce.

This is a city full of interest and always shows a welcoming face, but it has to be said that the twentieth century has not treated it kindly. William Cobbett (1763 - 1835) described Worcester as 'One of the cleanest and handsomest towns I ever saw: indeed I do not recollect to have seen any one equal to it.' Sadly, his description no longer tallies; ring roads, multi-story car parks, power stations and other civic developments have changed forever what was once 'the noblest Georgian townscape in the Midlands'. Nevertheless, there remains much that is good and visitors will find their time amply repaid.

The small, Roman market town known by the tongue-twisting name of Weogornaceaster, was developed, fortified and provided with it's first major ecclesiastical building by a Saxon version of our own Lady Thatcher, one Aethelflaed, Lady of the Mercians. The minster she founded was on the site of the present CATHEDRAL OF CHRIST AND THE BLESSED VIRGIN MARY.

There is no image more quintessentially English than this Cathedral which you see reflected in the broad and tranquil waters of the Severn and overlooking the most beautiful county cricket ground in England. The beauty from afar lessens slightly on closer inspection. It has not always been treated kindly. In the nineteenth century it underwent restoration that has been described as 'the most complete and far reaching of any cathedral'. A.E. Perkins and George Gilbert Scott were the 'improvers' but even they could not alter Worcester's majestic proportions, nor impair the beauty of the tower. It is still strikingly lovely and no cathedral has a more fascinating history.

Worcester Cathedral dates back as far as 680 when Bosel, a priest from St Hilda's Abbey at Whitby, in Yorkshire was consecrated as the first Bishop of Worcester. This community of missionaries survived without flourishing particularly. Around the middle of the 10th century Bishop Dunstan, who went on to greater things at Canterbury and his successor Oswald, refounded the Cathedral, on the same site, as the heart of a new

Benedictine monastery dedicated to the Blessed Virgin Mary. And so it was that for six hundred years Worcester served as both abbey church and cathedral.

There is no longer any trace of Oswald's Cathedral but we know he was much loved and venerated and soon after his death he was canonised. Like all revered bishops, his tomb became a shrine and rapidly the focal point for pilgrims.

In 1041 Worcester was pillaged by the Danish pirates. The raiding party stole the bell and legend has it that the enraged citizens caught the leader, flayed him and nailed his skin on the oak door of the minster. 1062 brought another saintly bishop to Worcester. This time Wulstan, the prior of the abbey and one who was to become the only one of the Saxon bishops to remain long in office after the Norman Conquest. He too was canonised shortly after his death and so Worcester acquired a second shrine. Wulstan had vision and was a great builder, and even today part of his Cathedral remains, most notably the crypt, the largest Norman crypt in England. In it he had built a new shrine to St Oswald, far more glorious than the original, with an ambulatory around the east end to enable pilgrims to file past. It seems that all these early bishops had good marketing instincts. There is no doubt that pilgrimages to any shrine anywhere engendered wealth for the trustees and we should be thankful because it is that wealth, in many cases, which has allowed so much wonderful building in our cathedrals. From the swollen coffers from pilgrimages to Worcester after Wulstan's canonisation, the choir was remodelled and the construction of the richly decorated Lady Chapel was carried out. Much of its original charm and beauty survives although the stained glass and ceiling work belongs to the nineteenth century.

Bishop Wulstan's Cathedral was to suffer heavily from a fire in 1113 and then again in the Civil War during the reign of King Stephen when the city of Worcester was sacked. These medieval vandals and hooligans ' bore the relics of Oswald, our most gentle patron, out of the church'. More disaster in 1175 when the tower collapsed and five years later there was another fire.

In 1203 Wulstan was canonised and then my least favourite king – I am sure I am not alone in my feelings – King John brought good fortune to the city. The king was a frequent visitor to Worcester and when he realised he was dying from dysentry caused by his own over indulgence, he asked to be buried in the Cathedral. This in spite of the fact that the city took sides against him at the time of Magna Carta. So it was that his body was brought here from Newark in 1216 and buried before the high altar in a plain stone coffin between the tombs of two much loved saints, Oswald and Wulstan. The Purbeck marble effigy added sixteen years later shows a lion biting the king's sword tip symbolising the baron's curbing of royal power with Magna Carta, the year before his death. In 1529 a richly decorated tomb was erected around the coffin.

King John was joined in 1502 by Prince Arthur, eldest son of Henry VII. He died at Ludlow castle aged 15 and was entombed in the Cathedral after a lavish funeral. Two years later a magnificent pinnacled chantry was built to house the tomb. It stands to the south of the high altar, just a short distance from the tomb of King John.

Prince Arthur's death probably changed the whole course of the history of England although this is something that historians can only speculate upon. It opened the door for the ebullient Henry VIII to ride roughshod over so many things and people. Suffice it to say that Prince Arthur -named after the legendary king - contracted one of the most important dynastic marriages in history with Catherine of Aragon. Quite evidently, Henry VIII and his ministers recognised this. It was with unseemly haste that the new Prince of Wales, Henry's betrothal to this unfortunate young widow was announced.

For Worcester the good fortune of having the care of Prince Arthur's body and tomb, certainly saved the Cathedral from the wanton destruction of Henry VIII's villains when they came to destroy the shrines of Oswald and Wulstan at the time of the Dissolution.

Early in the fourteenth century it was decided to rebuild the nave and bring it more in line with the style of the Cathedral's east end - itself already remodelled to match the beauty of the Lady Chapel. Work continued along the north side of the nave and then stopped at a time that coincided roughly with the Black Death. The good fortune was that this preserved the twelfth century transitional Norman arches with their ornamental triforium - the upper part of the wall. Look and you will see they clearly differ entirely from all the others. By the

A roof boss in the quire vaulting

end of the fourteenth century the vaults and the west front had been added and about the same time the chapter-house which had been built at the beginning of the twelfth century, was revaulted and embellished with a new door and windows. All major building work came to an end with the erection of the cloisters in the first half of the fifteenth century, apart from the tomb of Prince Arthur.

Whereas many believe that the Black Death brought to a halt the building in the Cathedral there is another school which would have you consider that it might have had something to do with the fact that, most surprisingly, Edward II was being venerated at that time as a saint at Gloucester, which would have sent pilgrims scurrying away from Worcester to the new tourist attraction! If this was so then funds would have dried up and the building would have had to have waited for a better season!

Work may have ceased but the Cathedral was not left unscathed. Henry VIII refounded it as a Cathedral making the last prior, Henry Holbeach, the dean. But the pulpitum was destroyed, the monk's stalls ripped out, statues smashed to smithereens and glass shattered. The seventeenth century saw Worcester vouchsafing the Royal cause. Worcester suffered more than anywhere in the Civil Wars. The Parliamentary army took possession of the city in 1642 and ransacked the Cathedral committing every sort of sacrilege and vulgar abuse. They pulled down the altar with its vestments and furniture, ensuring that nothing remained intact.

After the battle of Worcester in which Charles II made valiant but abortive efforts to regain his throne and subsequently had to flee to France until his restoration in 1660, the Parliamentarians used the Cathedral as a prison and locked up six thousand men. There is a document that says the parliamentary army gave way to 'the most atrocious acts of outrage that the meanness of rapacity could stimulate in the dark mind of the sanguinary puritan'; and although an ostensible authority for a general pillage was not absolutely given by Cromwell, it is as certain that not the least restraint was put upon the brutal violence of his ruffian troups, who fell to ravaging and plundering without mercy, few or none of the devoted citizens escaping their cruelty'.

The stench of blood and death remained in the Cathedral long after the Civil War was a thing of the past. It was almost as if the intensive whitewashing early in the 18th century was the final attempt to get rid of those evil times. Another century was to pass before anyone really got to grips with the restoration of Worcester Cathedral and so we come to the work of firstly A.E Perkins and then of George Gilbert Scott. The latter was such a busy man, something of a workaholic. He is reputed once to have sent a telegraph to his London office from Manchester with the perplexed request 'Why am I here?' He would surely have known why he was in Worcester.

The decay of the local sandstone meant that the Cathedral had to be refaced; the result the total loss of the patina of age. Inside almost everything needed attention. New paving and new windows came first and then a new west door, nave, pulpit and choir screen, bishops' throne and reredos were installed. It cost a fortune, over £100,000, which equated to today's price would be millions. The current resoration appeal is for £10 million pounds and will be raised from donations worldwide. The Cathedral in its new found clothes was re-opened on the 8th April 1874. It is still a joyous and beautiful place of worship and visitation. The crypt remains much as it was in Wulstan's day and nothing can detract from the glory of the nave with its two western bays dating from the end of the twelfth century and the remainder putting the finishing touches on one of the finest Gothic naves to be seen anywhere in the world.

The 19th century certainly brought new life to the Cathedral. Not everyone will approve of the very Victorian feel as a result of this restoraton but it has left us with one of the best collections of Victorian sculpture in the country and some of the most beautiful stained glass. The west window leaves me breathless every time I look at it and I thank these Victorian architects for their foresight in removing the organ and its screen from the entrance to the choir which now gives us an uninterrupted view from one end of the Cathedral to the other. What is also very clear is that had the Victorian restoration not taken place the Cathedral would be nothing but a ruin today.

Two touching reminders of men who loved Worcester almost more than life in this century. Beneath the glory of the west window is a simple stone marking the burial place of the ashes of Prime Minister Stanley Baldwin, a man who will probably be remembered most because of the difficulties he encountered in his premiership in the 1930s during the events that led up to the abdication of Edward VIII and the king's subsequent marriage to the much divorced Wallis Simpson – a story of true love or a tragedy? Who can tell but I firmly believe that this abdication saved the monarchy. I doubt if Edwrad VIII would have held the country together in the manner that his brother, the reluctant, King George VI and his Queen, our beloved Queen Mother, did so during the dreadful years of World War II until his untimely death in 1952.

The second in the north wall is the Elgar window. Illustrating the Dream of Gerontius, it commemorates the most English of English composers who, though a Roman Catholic, loved this Cathedral above all others. For those who perhaps do not know his work, Nimrod from the Enigma Variations and certainly 'Land of Hope and Glory' from his suite, Pomp and Circumstance, and sung with such verve and gusto at that most English of traditions. The Last Night of Proms, annually in the Albert Hall every September, must surely strike a chord!

Elgar would have given his hearty approval to the standard of music in the Cathedral today. The choir broadcasts regularly and has been featured on television. They undertake overseas tours but above all the repertoire at choral services has become much wider, and now includes the whole range of English and a good deal of continental music as well. Commercial sponsoship has become a regular feature of the funding and you may well see choristers wearing badges bearing the names of the benefactors who make their continued music possible.

Thousands of visitors come to this mighty cathedral every year, some of them looking for spiritual comfort but it has to be said most of them to view, in awe, the majesty and the beauty. It is their contribution to the restoration fund that is so vital and for many their personal donations have made them feel as if the Cathedral belongs to them. I would like to take this opportunity of trying to explain to you what needs doing to see that Worcester Cathedral remains a place of worship, a visible and tangible expression of faith. It is not only a reflection of our history, but also a bequest to the future.

Unfortunately the Victorians ran out of money before their restoration was complete. It is also now clear that some of the techniques used by them have been proved to be faulty. The current restoration is almost as massive as that undertaken by the Victorians and the difference in cost £9.99 million!

Take a look at some of the problems the Cathedral has had to face since work on restoration started in 1990. The 4,100 ton central tower was in danger of collapse. It is supported on four piers, which consist of a rubble core, surrounded by a thin stone facing. Over the years, the core has settled leaving large cavities, thus causing uneven loading. This work has taken two years to complete. Seven flying buttresses were replaced. These transmit the thrusts from the vaults to the ground. They were badly decayed and if nothing had been done or is being done, they would fail and the upper nave walls collapse. New slates were required for the Nave roof. and most of all the lead roofs had to be replaced and all gutters and roofs needed to be re-stripped and recovered in accordance with modern standards. Masonry repair is vital on the south west transept and the north porch - falling stone has damaged roofs and caused a potential hazard to people below. £3.5 million has had to be found for stonework alone.

The restoration does not qualify for any government grant. English Heritage are only empowered to assist historic parish churches, not Cathedrals. By law, the Church Commissioners cannot help either. So it is down to us, who visit cathedrals like Worcester for the sheer pleasure of seeing so much beauty and hopefully, finding spiritual sustenance within its walls. Please help if you can. If you are not visiting but would like to donate please send whatever you can afford to the Appeal Office, 10a College Green, Worcester, WR1 2LH.

The Cathedral stands on a rise overlooking the River Severn and the WORCESTERSHIRE COUNTY CRICKET GROUND where traditionally, touring test teams play their first county matches. Ornamental gardens cluster around the WATERGATE at the bottom of the rise where a ferry once ran when the city was walled and a tablet on the gate records the impressive heights gained by the river during floods.

It is a splendidly English backdrop, ideally suited to our summer game but in 1651 the area now dedicated to peaceful recreation would have seen the Royalist forces stumbling in retreat before Cromwell's invincible Model Army. The clash of steel and thunder of guns rang out where leather meets willow today. Relics, displays and mementoes of the battle of Worcester and other

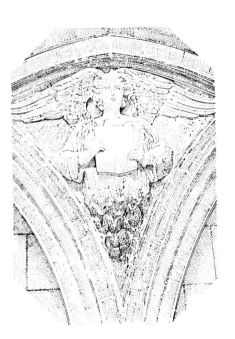

An angel carved in the spandrel in the triforium above the quire

aspects of the Civil War are to be found in the COMMANDERY, at a fine 15th century timber-framed building built on the site of an earlier hospital founded by St Wulfstan, and in the baroque 18th century GUILDHALL with its sumptious assembly rooms.

I have mentioned the friendliness of the inhabitants of Worcester but it obviously does not pay to cross them, since not only do they skin light-fingered Scandinavians but they also have an unpleasant habit of nailing effigies of their enemy's heads to public buildings by their ears. A careful study of the splendid facade of the Guildhall will reveal the likeness of Oliver Cromwell, affixed in the manner described, and on the keystone of the central porch! Further evidence of such bloodthirstiness is to be found in the CITY MUSEUM AND ART GALLERY, which apart from much of general local interest contains THE REGIMENTAL MUSEUM OF THE WORCESTERSHIRE REGIMENT, who rejoiced in the stomach-turning nickname of 'The Vein-Openers'! Their heroism and professionalism in battle earned them the approbation of Wellington, who called them 'the best regiment in this army', while the city's loyalty to the crown was recognised by Charles II, who gave it the motto 'May the faithful city flourish'.

Patriotism of a more peaceful variety is to be found in the music of Sir Edward Elgar who succeeded his father as organist at ST GEORGE'S ROMAN CATHOLIC CHURCH and who was born at nearby **Broadheath**, where his birthplace has been preserved as a museum. Music is an important part of Worcester life and every third year it plays host to the world's oldest musical celebration, the THREE CHOIRS FESTIVAL, which was started in 1717. The other cathedral cities involved are Hereford and Gloucester.

SPETCHLEY PARK on the city's eastern edge is an early 19th century mansion with a deer park and splendid formal gardens that are open to the public. An ancestor of the present owners, one Robert Berkeley, founded the alms houses known as the BERKELEY HOSPITAL in Foregate Street, Worcester. Still in use today, they were built in 1692 and their design is Dutch in style. Architectural styles more familiar to the English eye can be seen in COLLEGE YARD, BRITANNIA and ST GEORGES SQUARES (Regency) and in the splendid half-timbered GREYFRIARS (Tudor with later additions) which has been fully restored under the aegis of the National Trust and which has also a most delightful walled garden. The five hundred year old TUDOR HOUSE FOLK MUSEUM is closeby and has fascinating displays of social history while in Severn Street, the DYSON PERRINS MUSEUM contains examples of Royal Worcester porcelain dating back to 1751 and includes the dinner service made for the Prince and Princess of Wales. The Royal Worcester Company is the oldest factory to manufacture porcelain and was established in 1751.

Two very varied forms of entertainment are offered by the SWAN THEATRE and WORCESTER RACECOURSE, which was founded in 1718. A newspaper report of that time recounts that 'The company that appeared on the Course was very numerous and genteel. Peevishness and Debate were nowhere to be found; but Cheerfulness, Harmony and Universal Satisfaction were everywhere visible.'

Harmony and satisfaction will be yours as well if you visit four places I have chosen. FOWNES RESORT HOTEL in City Walls Road is a hotel of great charm and comfort, with an ability to provide its guests with the opportunity to simply relax, be pampered, wined and dined on excellent food or to be more energetic taking part in various activities that can be arranged. A golfing weekend linked to a visit to the Cathedral would be perfect. Tee times are guaranteed, both weekdays and weekends, booked by reception upon request. Fownes can also provide a ballooning experience you will never forget! You will watch and join in, the spectacle of inflating the balloon. Taking off is an incredible sensation and then you will be given ample opportunity to survey the city of Worcester, the majesty of the Cathedral, and the surrounding countryside. A 'Champagne toast' in flight completes the experience.

An eating experience is within the doors of IL PESCATORE, a stones throw from the Cathedral, where the ebullient Guiliano Ponzi is at the helm of the top Italian restaurant in the area. This likeable, if volatile man, took over, with Latin enthusiasm, a none too promising bistro, and set about refurbishing it, creating a true Italian environment and then opened his doors to discerning people who recognised the very special ambience.

THE WORCESTERSHIRE COUNTRYSIDE CENTRE is well known in its own right but how many people have discovered that REFRESHERS which is part of it, is also somewhere that travellers up and down the M5 should note as somewhere to pull off for a break and to enjoy good food in a super setting. You will find it one mile from junction 7, 2 miles from junction 6 and 5 minutes from the town centre of Worcester.

Nothing to do with hotels or food is THE COBWEB in Friar Street, the oldest part of Worcester, a couple of minutes walk from the Cathedral. This is a world of Dolls' Houses, as delightful a hobby for children of three years to those in their eighties! To step in here is to enter a world of nostalgia and fantasy, a place where dreams come true; what that dream becomes is entirely up to you! The house you have always wanted will cost from £33 to £1,500. The choice of decor and furniture will entrance, from rural style antiques, lacquer work with gold and country style oak, to elegant Georgian, Victorian and Edwardian. There are only a very few times in one's travels that one meets something as enchanting and so different. The Cobweb is such a place.

If you would prefer to stay a little way out of Worcester then THE ELMS on the A443 between Worcester and Tenbury Wells, 2 miles after Great Witley is for you. The Elms stands, majestic, amidst acres of formal gardens in the beautiful Teme valley. Built by the architect Gilbert White, a pupil of Sir Christopher Wren in 1710, it is now a country house hotel of international reputation. It is still an elegant home from home and whatever your purpose a visit here is an experience you will savour for a very long time. Fine antiques grace the public rooms and for the gourmet, the regency Brooke Room Restaurant is a gastronomic delight. Seclusion and calm away from everyday life is offered for private functions in the splendidly appointed Abberley Suite in the main house or alternatively the Crosthwaite Suite in the adjoining Coach House.

Another short and worthwhile visit out of Worcester is to **Ombersley** just off the A449 from Worcester to

Stourport on Severn, and ten minutes from Junction 6 of the M5. Here you will find THE OMBERSLEY GALLERY in one of the oldest buildings of this beautiful village. The rooms display prestigious paintings and crafts by leading British contemporary artists and craft designers. It is full of interest and has a super 'Gallery Restaurant and Tea Room' which has an Egon Ronay recommendation.

In this visit to Worcester the Cathedral took precedence but to end my journey I could not resist making my way north into the very heart of the Malverns. The name is not only applied to the hills but to the straggle of six distinct settlements often referred to collectively as **Malvern**. These are **Little Malvern, Malvern Wells, Malvern Link, Great Malvern, North Malvern** and **West Malvern**. This is an area of extraordinary beauty, interest and entertainment and if you want to stay I have found three excellent hotels. In no particular order of preference however, I am starting with THE MALVERN HILLS HOTEL at Wynos Point, a privately owned country house hotel lying next to the British Camp which was fortified and occupied by the Ancient Britons. The hotel is just four miles from **Ledbury**, a historic town, and 4 miles from the Victorian town of Malvern. The present building has stood since the 19th century but the location has been used as a hostelry for over 500 years. Many establishments with such magnificent views would have relied on the scenery alone to attract custom. But that is not the case at this entrancing hotel which has built up an enviable reputation for comfort and cuisine.

Great Malvern has THE WALMER LODGE HOTEL in Abbey Road. The hotel is of Victorian architecture and when you enter the doors you are immediately aware of the warmth and atmosphere which pervades the whole building.

Built in 1852 it is privately owned by Joseph and Fun Muitt. In the evenings Joseph looks after the guests while Fun runs the kitchen and in the mornings the roles are reversed.

To sip your Earl Grey tea and taste your home made quiche seated at your own table on a railway platform sounds truly fictional, but not so! Three quarters of a mile from Great Malvern town centre is Great Malvern Railway Station which was opened on the 25th May 1860. It has recently been extensively restored to its original splendour and was awarded the 1989 'Heritage Award'. It is here that Terry Page and Margaret Baddeley opened LADY FOLEY'S TEA ROOMS which serves delicious home-made cooking to cater for all tastes, whether it be taken inside the attractive tea room or outside on Platform I. This award winning place also has the 'Brief Encounter' Restaurant which adjoins it. Most of us will remember the 1945 Noel Coward film starring Trevor Howard and Celia Johnson which told the love story of two people who always met on a railway station in the refreshment room. It is an appealing and romantic place to be, but I do hope it will have a happier ending.

Good tea rooms are at a premium so I would like you to take time to find THE KETTLE SINGS at Jubilee Drive, **Upper Colwell**, Malvern. The view from the conservatory style seating area is amazing and if you drive from Great Malvern towards Colwell through the Wyche

The Norman doorway in the refectory building, leading from College Green through to the Cloisters

cutting, it is spectacular where Worcestershire meets Herefordshire and you can see stunning scenes right across to the Black Mountains.

Madresfield meaning the 'Field of the Mowers' is home to the MADRESFIELD AGRICULTURAL SHOW, a delightful local show featuring all manner of events. It is held in the grounds of MADRESFIELD COURT, a handsome Victorian mansion, built on medieval and Elizabethan foundations and which is considered to be the inspiration for Evelyn Waugh's revisited 'Brideshead'. It is also home to HUMPHREYS, a garden centre and coffee shop. The sort of place in which you will be happy to spend quite a lot of time and equally enjoy both the garden centre and the coffee house.

Holywell Road at Malvern Wells is the site of THE ESSINGTON HOTEL, a listed building dating from 1817. Samuel Essington built it for those who were taking the water cure at Holy and Eye Wells 400 yards away. Today the hotel, which is in a conservation area, has been in the hands of Brian and Angela Holt for the last 22 years and they run it with a warm welcome and personal service.

In Malvern Link, THE NAGS HEAD a super pub where everyone is welcome, has accommodation offering a self contained flat which sleeps four. However it is for the food and the drink and the company that I would recommend The Nags Head.

Little Malvern is the smallest and the southernmost of the Malverns and nestles cosly in the lee of the steep slopes. The shifting play of light and shadow on the ancient hills, sometimes dramatic, or often subtle and complex is nowhere better artistically represented than in the wonderful music of Sir Edward Elgar. It seems only right that this man of Worcestershire should be buried, together with his wife and daughter, in the quiet peace of the Malverns at ST WULFSTANS ROMAN CATHOLIC CHURCH.

Great Malvern surrounds Malvern priory church, the sole but impressive remnant of a large priory which dates back to 1088. It is essentially late 18th and 19th century in character and is a product of the period's preoccupation with spa waters. There are distinct parallels with life today; our preoccupation with health, diet, fitness and beauty has led to the establishment of fashionable 'health farms' while the Georgians and Victorians had their spas and hydros.

The first entrepreneur to exploit the area's waters was the founder of the Royal Worcester Porcelain Works, one Doctor John Wall. Dr Wall obviously had a marketing ability that would have made him a target for all major executive recruitment agencies were he still alive today.

> 'Malvern Water, said Dr Wall,
> Is famed for containing nothing at all.'

This was the essence of his campaign and it worked. His premise was quite simply that, since the water was so pure, the cure was effected faster, 'as it could pass more rapidly through the vessels of the body.'

The town quickly became fashionable and hotels, pump rooms and lodging houses were built. The Victorians added a further refinement by introducing a form of 'water cure' that was horrific by anyone's standards. This consisted of being wrapped tightly in cold wet sheets for hours on end, having hundreds of gallons of icy water dropped on you from a great height, cold baths, long walks, a strict diet and naturally nothing but water to drink. Recreation was strictly controlled with even reading being banned as being too demanding. It was a wonder that anyone survived; nevertheless the resort attracted the likes of the Royal Family, Gladstone, Florence Nightingale, Macaulay, Carlyle, Wordsworth and Charles Darwin to name but a few.

It was not long before the more artistic visitors started organising entertainments and concerts, and from these beginnings evolved the MALVERN FESTIVAL. This was closely linked in its early days with the playwright George Bernard Shaw, and is now an internationally known event involving music and drama.

The waters have not been forgotten and are bottled and exported all over the world by Cadbury Schweppes, while the awful Victorian treatments have been replaced by the delights of a 'water activity centre.' THE SPLASH, an indoor complex complete with water-slide, wave making machine and 'beach'.

Malvern is not merely a resort and retirement area, it has a wide range of enterprises but perhaps it will always be remembered for the length and beauty of its hills. You may walk their eight mile length and savour the amazing views to see England at its very best.

For me one of the very best sights in England is the approach to Worcester Cathedral - nowhere is there anything more English.

Great Malvern Railway Station, Imperial Road,
Great Malvern, Worcester, WR14 3AT.

Tel: (0684) 893033

LADY FOLEY'S TEA ROOM
Tea Room

To sip your Earl Grey tea and taste your home-made quiche seated at your own table on a railway platform sounds truly fictional, but not so! Three quarters of a mile from Great Malvern town centre lies Great Malvern Railway Station which was opened on the 25th May 1860. It has recently been extensively restored to its original splendour and was awarded the 1989 'Heritage' award. It is here that Terry Page and Margaret Baddeley opened 'Lady Foley's Tea Room' which serves delicious home-made cooking to cater for all tastes, whether it be taken inside the attractive tearoom or outside on Platform I.

Adjoining the tea room is the 'Brief Encounter' restaurant also run by Terry and Margaret; the name was inspired by the 1945 Noel Coward film, starring Trevor Howard and Celia Johnson which told the love story of two people who always met on a railway station in the refreshment room.

The menu is certainly different, and includes mouthwatering delicacies such as 'Feta and Oregano Tart' as a starter, 'Spicy Pancakes' for a main course with roasted vegetable salad, and as the final delicacy a 'Chocolate Torte'. The wine list matches the excellence of the food. Both establishments are delightful and really should be experienced. You will seldom come across this sort of setting and equally you will find it difficult to discover better service. Do not forget that Brief Encounter is open on Thursday, Friday and Saturday evening from 7-10pm. A very appealing and romantic place to dine. Though one hopes that any romance will have a happier ending than the original 'Brief Encounter'.

USEFUL INFORMATION

OPEN: Mon-Sat: 9am-6pm. Sun: 3pm-6pm.
All year round
CHILDREN: Welcome
CREDIT CARDS: Access/Visa
LICENSED: Full On Licence
ACCOMMODATION: Not applicable

RESTAURANT: 'Brief Encounter' adjoins 'Lady Foley'
BAR FOOD: Not applicable
VEGETARIAN: 4 in restaurant. Daily specials in tea room
DISABLED ACCESS: Yes, and W.C
GARDEN: Railway platform with seating

---

49 Abbey Road, Great Malvern,
Worcestershire, WR14 3HH.

Tel: (0684) 574139
Fax: (0684) 574139

THE WALMER LODGE HOTEL
Hotel & Restaurant

The area surrounding the Malvern Hills is one of the most beautiful parts of England, from the grandeur of the hills themselves to the quiet, sleepy villages that dot the landscape, all with a rich history woven into the colourful tapestry that you will see before you. In the centre of this setting is Great Malvern and situated in a very quiet location and in close proximity to the town centre is The Walmer Lodge Hotel. Built in 1852, it is a private family run hotel owned by Joseph and Fun Muitt.

The hotel is of Victorian architecture which is situated in a conservation area. When you enter the hotel, you can feel the warmth and atmosphere it exudes. The Walmer Lodge is comfortably and individually furnished throughout with all the nine bedrooms ensuite. Each has colour TV and that great boon, tea and coffee making facilities. The rear facing bedrooms have unbelievable views for miles and miles.

The cosy restaurant has a special warmth and the A La Carte four course menu is included in their 'Dinner, Bed and Breakfast Offers'. To the rear of the hotel is a large, perfectly secluded garden with a patio. It is very obvious to anyone who stays here that Joseph and Fun aim to provide a happy, relaxed atmosphere through their friendly and personal attention. In the evenings Joseph looks after the guests while Fun runs the kitchen and in the mornings the roles are reversed! Whichever time of day the food is excellent.

USEFUL INFORMATION

OPEN: All year round
CHILDREN: Well behaved children and pets
CREDIT CARDS: Access/Visa
LICENSED: Restaurant & Residential
ACCOMMODATION: 9 ensuite bedrooms

RESTAURANT: Wide ranging menu with Oriental flavour
BAR FOOD: Not applicable
VEGETARIAN: To order
DISABLED ACCESS: Not convenient
GARDEN: Large, secluded with patio

HUMPHREY'S

Garden Centre & Coffee Shop

Madresfield Garden Centre, The Gardens,
Madresfield, Malvern, WR13 5AU.

Tel: (0684) 574066
Fax: (0684) 566339

USEFUL INFORMATION

OPEN: 7 days a week. Garden centre:
9-5.30pm, 6pm mid-summer.
Coffee shop: 10.30-4.30pm
CHILDREN: Well behaved, welcome
CREDIT CARDS: Access/Visa
LICENSED: Not applicable
ACCOMMODATION: Not applicable

RESTAURANT: Coffee shop with a
delicious menu
BAR FOOD: Not applicable
VEGETARIAN: Always 2-3 dishes
DISABLED ACCESS: Yes, completely
flat area
GARDEN: Delightful garden centre and
nursery

The tiny hamlet of Madresfield, one and a half miles from Malvern, centres on Madresfield Court, a moated Tudor house owned by the Lygon family, Earls of Beauchamp, since about 1160. Humphrey's, named after a cartoon hippopotamus designed by a friend, is the coffee shop within Madresfield Garden Centre.

Hilary Collins, the owner of Humphrey's runs this delightful coffee shop in the former apple store and toolshed. It is most attractive and ideal for a meeting place. Morning coffee, lunches and afternoon teas are served from a menu based on what 'we ourselves would like to eat' says Hilary. The results are highly successful with crisp salads, cakes and bread from a bakery closeby, snacks, sandwiches, generous Ploughmans', tasty smoked salmon quiches and a choice of five hot pies, served with a side salad, baked potato or bread roll. Desserts include a range of delicious hot fruit pies, cheesecakes and gateaux and the piece de resistance the 'Hippo-Lytes' Cream Tea Special.

The Lygons built a Victorian walled garden in the mid-19th century under the directions of their head gardeners, Mr Cox, of the dessert apple fame, and Mr Crump who worked at Blenheim Palace, and bred the Blenheim Orange Melon. The garden became neglected and overgrown by 1987 when Ron and Margery Bithell, with their daughter Hilary, and her husband Stephen Collins, horticultural graduates, took it over and began its restoration. From this the Bithells and Collins have built a nursery and garden centre conserving much of the original Victorian atmosphere.

THE KETTLE SINGS

Luncheon & Tearooms

Jubilee Drive, Upper Colwall,
Malvern, Worcester, WR13 6DN.

Tel: (0684) 40244

USEFUL INFORMATION

OPEN: All year. 10am-5pm
Non Smoking Establishment
CHILDREN: Welcome
CREDIT CARDS: None taken
LICENSED: Licensed for lunch
ACCOMMODATION: Not applicable

RESTAURANT: Home-made food.
Blackboard specials
BAR FOOD: Not applicable
VEGETARIAN: 2 dishes available
DISABLED ACCESS: Small steps.
Willing to assist
GARDEN: Small outside seating area

It may take a little effort to find The Kettle Sings, but it is well worth it. The view from the conservatory style seating area is amazing and if you drive from Great Malvern towards Colwall through the Wyche cutting, it is spectacular where Worcestershire becomes Herefordshire, and you can see stunning scenes right across to the Black Mountains in Wales. For The Kettle Sings, turn left after the Wyche cutting, then left again which brings you to the start of Jubilee Drive which runs to the foot of the Iron Age Hillfort at Herefordshire Beacon, known as British Camp. About a mile down the drive is The Kettle Sings. It was built in 1928 and totally refurbished in 1992. Barbara Teale, the proprietor has taken great trouble to retain the authentic tea room atmosphere, and it is charming.

Lunch is served between noon and 3pm. Barbara has some of the best home-made soups to be found anywhere. There are always several tasty 'Blackboard Specials' such as quiches or seafood lasagne or simply salads, sandwiches and Ploughman's if that is your preference. Toasted teacakes, home-made scones, a selection of gateaux and home-made cakes are all firm favourites with customers. The coffee and walnut cake is renowned.

Whatever time of the day you come here you will be welcome. Barbara Teale has a team of friendly staff who look after everyone extremely well, all the year round.

Wynds Point, British Camp,
Malvern, Worcestershire, WR13 6DW.

Tel: (0684) 40237/40690
Fax: (0684) 40327

MALVERN HILLS HOTEL
Hotel & Restaurant

This privately owned Country House Hotel is set in the tranquillity of the Malvern Hills and lies on the A449 next to the British Camp which was fortified and occupied by the Ancient Britons and an area designated for outstanding natural beauty. The Malvern Hills Hotel is just 4 miles from Ledbury, a historic town and 4 miles also from the Victorian town of Malvern. The present building has stood since the 19th century but the location has been used as a hostelry for over 500 years. Many establishments with such magnificent views would have relied on scenery alone to attract custom, but that is not the case at this entrancing hotel which has built up an enviable reputation for comfort and cuisine.

Walk through the front door and you find yourself surrounded by wood panelling and furniture that is designed for comfort as well as visual appeal with a real, roaring log fire in winter. All 16 en-suite bedrooms are attractively decorated and equipped with every modern convenience one could wish for. A four-poster suite provides an extra luxury for a honeymoon or special occasion. An excellent lunchtime buffet is laid out in the Jenny Lind Lounge, and all tastes are catered for in the tempting spread. In the evening dinner is a memorable and leisurely affair in the Nightingale Restaurant, where fine local produce is used whenever possible. The well chosen wine list is a perfect addition to a meal. Two day breaks at special rates are very popular as are three day Christmas breaks.

In summer the Garden is a popular place and what could be nicer than enjoying a Cream Tea surrounded by immaculate lawns and colourful flower beds.

USEFUL INFORMATION

OPEN: All year round
CHILDREN: Children accepted
CREDIT CARDS: Visa /Access
LICENSED: Full On Licence
ACCOMMODATION: 16 en-suite rooms
+ One with private bathroom

RESTAURANT: Table d'Hote, Good
wholesome food. Local produce used
BAR FOOD: Limited menu
VEGETARIAN: Catered for
DISABLED ACCESS: Unsuitable
GARDEN: Large. Lawns with seating & BBQ

Bank Street, Malvern Link,
Worcester, WR14 2JG.

Tel: (0684) 574373

THE NAGS HEAD
Public House

The Nag's Head is situated in the shadow of the Malvern Hills, in a picturesque area of Malvern Link, which is exceptionally quiet. Mark and Julie Jones maintain that a pub is only as good as the proprietors and staff who run it; this is immediately evident here. The warmth of the welcome, the smooth running of the establishment and the general well being of the place finds favour with the steadfast regular clientele and the many visitors who enjoy The Nag's Head.

Approaching the front door you pass through the terraced patio area from which the views of Worcester are excellent. To the left is the main bar and to the right 'The Nag's Tail Bar' where the locals unfold many an unusual tale. This is a free house and proud of it, serving many first class traditional and guest beers. Lunchtime bar meals are always available with daily specials and mouthwatering sweets and desserts highlighted on the blackboards. Sundays at the Nag's Head is known for the traditional Sunday lunches. Friday and Sunday evenings are devoted to typical folk music which are well patronised. For anyone wanting to stay a night or two to enjoy the pub or revel in the beauty of the Malvern Hills there is a self contained holiday flat with accommodation for four. In addition to the sleeping accommodation, it has a lounge, kitchen and bathroom. An ideal place for children and pets are welcome. You are invited to take breakfast in the pub if you feel like a complete break from cooking. Situated at the rear of the premises is a neatly laid out beer garden complete with a trampoline for the children.

USEFUL INFORMATION

OPEN: Wed-Sat: 11am-11pm. Mon-Tues:
11-3pm & 6-11pm. Sun: 12-3pm
& 7-10.30pm
CHILDREN: Welcome
CREDIT CARDS: None taken
LICENSED: Free House
ACCOMMODATION: Self contained flat,
sleeps 4

RESTAURANT: Not applicable
BAR FOOD: Wide range, good quality
VEGETARIAN: Always 2 dishes
DISABLED ACCESS: Yes. Ramp.
Always willing to assist
GARDEN: Beer garden. Trampoline, large
patio with seating

ESSINGTON HOTEL
Hotel

Holywell Road, Malvern Wells,
Worcestershire, WR14 4LQ.

Tel: (0684) 561177

USEFUL INFORMATION

OPEN: All year round
CHILDREN: Well behaved
CREDIT CARDS: Access/Visa
LICENSED: Full On Licence
ACCOMMODATION: 8 double/twin.
1 single

RESTAURANT: 5 course meals. Fresh
vegetables, cooked to order
BAR FOOD: Not applicable
VEGETARIAN: Always 2/3. 5 courses
if reqired
DISABLED ACCESS: Small entrance
step. Willing to assist
GARDEN: Two and a half acres.
Beautifully laid out

The Essington Hotel, a Listed Building, was built in about 1817 by Samuel Essington as a hotel to accommodate visitors taking the water cures at the local Holy and Eye Wells, 400 yards away. Today the hotel which is in a conservation area, has been in the hands of Brian and Angela Holt for the last 22 years and they run it with a warm welcome and personal service. The hotel is noted for its excellent food which is prepared and served by the porprietors.

Situated in two and a half acres of terraced garden on the side of the beautiful Malvern Hills, the Essington offers magnificent views over the Severn Valley to the Cotswolds, and is an ideal touring centre for the Wye Valley, the Cotswolds and Shakespeare Country. It is within easy reach of Worcester, Hereford and Gloucester with their beautiful Cathedrals, and also just down the road is the internationally famous 'Three Counties Showground'.

All the pretty bedrooms have private bathrooms, hair dryer, colour TV, radio, tea and coffee making facilities. The cosy lounge which has a spacious balcony from which one can feast on the panoramic views, has a brightly burning log fire for the colder days, and leads to the intimate restaurant area. Quite rightly this fine hotel has both Two Star AA and RAC ratings as well as being ETB 3 Crowns Recommended. The Essington is open all the year round and welcomes children. It is ideal too for vegetarians for whom a five course meal can be produced if required.

OMBERSLEY GALLERY
Art/Craft Gallery, Restaurant & Tea Room

ChurchTerrace, Ombersley,
Worcestershire, WR9 0EP.

Tel: (0905) 620655

USEFUL INFORMATION

OPEN: Tues-Sat: 10-5pm. Closed
Christmas eve for 2 weeks approx.
CHILDREN: Welcome if well behaved
CREDIT CARDS: Access/Visa/Switch
LICENSED: None, but bring your own
wine. 50p per bottle corkage fee
ACCOMMODATION: Not applicable

RESTAURANT: Seasonal menu.
Traditional English & continental
BAR FOOD: Not applicable
VEGETARIAN: 3-4 daily
DISABLED ACCESS: Yes but no toilet
facilities
GARDEN: No

This well established gallery, situated in the beautiful village of Ombersley, is housed in one of the oldest buildings, which has been carefully renovated to display prestigious paintings and craft by leading British contemporary artists and craft designers. Three rooms exhibit paintings, etchings, woodwork, furniture, ceramics, jewellery, studio glass and scuplture. The aim of the gallery is to appeal to collectors and visitors alike, offering expert advice, if required, on commissions for business presentations, the home or a special gift. Throughout the year, one-man and group exhibitions are arranged to introduce the latest work of both nationally and locally renowned artists and craftsmen. Should you wish to know about forthcoming exhibitions the gallery will be pleased to forward further details.

Within the gallery complex, customers can be tempted by the Gallery Restaurant and Tea Room. Originally the Priest's house dated 1269 and made of local sandstone, this room presents a really old-English atmosphere with a log burning fire in winter. A variety of quality home-made food is available using fresh and seasonal ingredients ranging from many savoury dishes to delicious cakes and the traditional cream teas. It is somewhere that has been highly recommended both by local people and visitors, and has had an Egon Ronay Recommendation.

You will find Ombersley just off the A449 from Worcester to Stourport on Severn and ten minutes from junction 6 of the M5.

Sidbury, Worcester,
Worcestershire, WR1 2HU.

Tel: (0905) 355071

THE COMMANDERY CIVIL WAR CENTRE
Museum

The first glance that a visitor gets of The Commandery when passing down the busy street of Sidbury is deceptive. The small restored timber framed building gives little inclination of the variety and extent of what lies beyond or of its long and fascinating history. The Commandery is a medieval structure, which stands on the site of earlier buildings, usually known as the Hospital of St Wulstan until the Reformation in the 16th century. The Commandery was then sold to the Wylde family who used it as their country house and altered it in the 17th and 18th centuries. After the Wyldes sold it in the 18th century, it continued to be a large house but parts were adapted for industrial use. At the end of the 19th century it was a college for blind boys and then a printing works for much of the 20th century, until it was purchased by Worcester City Council. It has been greatly restored in recent years and now houses the Civil War Centre.

The Commandery today is a living link with the past that educates and entertains the people of Worcester and visitors alike. The buildings, aided by audio visual presentations, have captured the atmosphere and spirit of the period when Worcester stood alone as the last bastion of the monarchy. The Great Hall was, and still is the focus of life in the Commandery. A fine timber structure, the roof is the dominating feature with moulded beams and carved bosses. Worcester played a vital part in the English Civil War and now the Commandery is Britain's only museum entirely dedicated to telling the story of England's bloody Civil War.

USEFUL INFORMATION

OPEN: Mon-Sat: 10-5pm, Sun: 1.30-5.30pm
Closed Christmas day & Boxing day
CHILDREN: Welcome. Handson Displays
CREDIT CARDS: Access/Visa
LICENSED: None
ACCOMMODATION: Not applicable

RESTAURANT: Tea Rooms
BAR FOOD: Not applicable
VEGETARIAN: None
DISABLED ACCESS: Difficult and not for wheelchairs
GARDEN: Canal site area by tea room. Garden to rear for picnics

---

52 Friar Street,
Worcester, WR1 2NA.

Tel: (0905) 616300

THE COBWEB
Specialist Dolls House

The Cobweb is in the oldest part of Worcester city, a couple of minutes walk from the Cathedral, the city centre, car parks and excellent eating houses. The dolls house world is a delightful hobby for children up to 80 years old! To step into The Cobweb is to step into a world of nostalgia and fantasy, a place where dreams come true; what that dream becomes is entirely up to your own imagination and creativity. The house you have always wanted will cost from £32.62 to £1,500. The choice of decor and furnishings will entrance, from rural style antiques, lacquer work with gold, country style oak, to elegant Georgian, Victorian and Edwardian. All manner of accessories including furniture, wallpapers, dolls, fireplaces, china, glass, foods and shop displays, all to a delightful one twelfth scale are available.

Here you can create the way of life to which you wish to become accustomed! Surround yourself with servants, perpetually angelic children, benevolent grandparents - one can imagine forever and ever. Dreamers and browsers are always welcome. The Cobweb is run singlehanded by Mion Hetherington who has an absolute wealth of knowledge regarding these creations, but beware her wicked sense of humour!

There are only so many times in one's travels that one meets something totally enchanting and very different. Mion Hetherington's Cobweb world is such a place.

USEFUL INFORMATION

OPEN: 10am-5pm Mon-Wed
Thurs-Sat: 10am-5.30pm
CREDIT CARDS: All major cards
DISABLED ACCESS: Two steps. Willing to assist

FOWNES RESORT HOTEL

Hotel & Restaurant

City Walls Road,
Worcester, WR1 2AP.

Tel: (0905) 613151
Fax: (0905) 23742

USEFUL INFORMATION

OPEN: All year round
CHILDREN: Welcome
CREDIT CARDS: All major cards
LICENSED: Full On Licence
ACCOMMODATION: All ensuite rooms,
with every facility

RESTAURANT: English & International.
Open to non-residents
BAR FOOD: Full bar snacks and light
meals
VEGETARIAN: Selection available.
Special diets catered for
DISABLED ACCESS: Yes. Including
accommodation
GARDEN: Courtyard garden

This is a hotel of great charm and comfort, with an ability to provide its guests with the opportunity to simply relax, be pampered, wined and dined on excellent food or to be more energetic taking part in the various activities that can be arranged. A golfing weekend for example is perfect. However, whether you can afford time for a weekends golfing or just want a relaxing game during your stay on business or leisure, the hotel has arranged concessionary green fees at the superbly situated Vale Golf and Country Club, in the heart of the Vale of Evesham, just twenty minutes drive from the hotel. Tee times are guaranteed, both weekdays and weekends, booked by reception for guests upon request, and proof of handicap is not necessary.

If you are looking for a superb idea for a present, Fownes can provide a ballooning experience you'll never forget! You will watch, and join in, the spectacle of inflating the balloon. Taking off is an incredible sensation and then you will be given ample opportunity to survey the city of Worcester, the majesty of the Cathedral, and the surrounding countryside. A 'champagne' toast in flight completes the experience. All of this adds to the great pleasure of staying here and the thrilling experience of visiting the famous Cathedral. The whole ethos of this establishment is to ensure guests enjoy themselves if they are here on holiday and if it is business, then to ease the stress of the cut and thrust of the reason for their stay. The bedrooms are beautifully appointed, the cuisine is English and International and the staff give the service that comes from sheer professionalism and a pride in their hotel.

IL PESCATORE

Italian Restaurant

34 Sidbury,
Worcester, WR1 2HZ.

Tel: (0905) 21444
Fax: (0905) 21444

USEFUL INFORMATION

OPEN: Lunch. Tues-Sat: 12-2pm. Eve.
Mon-Sat: 6.45pm- last orders 10pm
CHILDREN: Well behaved welcome
CREDIT CARDS: Visa/Access
LICENSED: Restaurant
ACCOMMODATION: Not applicable

RESTAURANT: Renowned for fresh fish
& home-made pasta
BAR FOOD: Not applicable
VEGETARIAN: Yes 5-6 dishes
DISABLED ACCESS: Level entrance.
Assistance given
GARDEN: No

Situated a stones throw from Worcester Cathedral and five minutes walk from the city centre is Il Pescatore at 34, Sidbury, Worcester, the top Italian restaurant in the area. At the helm is the ebullient Giuliano Ponzi who with Latin enthusiasm took over a none too promising bistro and set about refurbishing it, creating a true Italian environment and opened its doors to those discerning people who recognise the very special ambience of a good Italian restaurant. It deserves its very high reputation and is somewhere that anyone visiting or living in Worcester should make a bee line for.

The restaurant is renowned for the 'Chef's Own Pasta' and fresh fish dishes. The menu also has the evergreen favourites, Cannelloni, Saltimbocca Alla Romana, Minestrone and Bistecca al Barolo. Fresh mussels are served in abundance and fish dishes may well include marinated salmon, lobster thermidor or a mixture of fish species poached in wine with garlic and parsley. All the ingredients are fresh, coupled with crisp and colourful vegetables.

The amiable atmosphere is very evident throughout this half-timbered building and especially in the cosy but elegant dining room which displays original paintings, all of which are from the brush of Giuliano himself. Il Pescatore is excellent and the service second to none. By the way, do leave room for one of Il Pescatore's delicious desserts.

Worcester Countryside Centre,
Spetchley Road, Worcester, WR5 2LG.

Tel: (0905) 766492

REFRESHERS
Cafe & Gift Shop

For good food in a super setting, travellers on the M5 should look no further than Refreshers at the Worcester Countryside Centre. The prices are totally realistic and offer great value. All day long one can get freshly made teas and coffee, complimented by a tempting range of home-made cakes and slices, including the sticky pleasure of ginger parkin. At lunchtime, from 12 noon until 2pm, the menu ranges from a bacon sandwich, pasty, and well-filled french sticks to one of several delicious home-made dishes. All this means Refreshers is well worth seeking out. You will find Refreshers one mile from Motorway Junction 7, two miles from Junction 6 and 5 minutes from Worcester city centre - just follow the signs for 'Countryside Centre'. For travellers with time to spare there are plenty of opportunities to explore the wood and meadows surrounding the Countryside Centre. Visitors can also take part in one of the many events on the Worcester Countryside Centre's annual calendar. It is a well planned diary with plenty of chances to discover more about the local plants and wildlife in the company of a friendly guide. Every Sunday morning there are busy Car Boot Sales, and there is always plenty to do. Refreshers is very much at the centre of all this activity.
The Centre's adventure play ground area and events field are another bonus for parents. After a walk in the woods, or just a rest from the motorway, children can play safely, burning off all that pent-up energy, while parents enjoy a cup of tea or browse through Refreshers well-stocked gift section. Gift items range from kites to T-Shirts, and jams to greeting cards, as well as many small gifts for children. Refreshers has been carefully planned and the result is admirable. A good find.

USEFUL INFORMATION

OPEN: 7 days: 10-5pm. Later during the season on occasions
CHILDREN: Welcome. Baby changing facility. Play area. Orienteering Course
CREDIT CARDS: None taken
LICENSED: For functions only
ACCOMMODATION: Not applicable

RESTAURANT: Cafe style, home-cooked, inexpensive
BAR FOOD: Not applicable. Snacks & light lunches
VEGETARIAN: 3 dishes always
DISABLED ACCESS: Full access & facilities. Easy trail through woodlands
GARDEN: Seating, play field, woodlands

Index to Places and Venues

Glossary

ABACUS
A flat slabor block of stone or wood forming the top of a capital and supporting an entablature or other load.

ABUTMENT
The part of a stone or brick wall which sustains an arch.

APSE
A semi-circular or polygonal projection

ARCADE
A row of arches, eg between the nave and aisles, or between the choir and aisles, of a cathedral, supporting the main wall which is pierced by windows in a clerestory.

ARCADING
Rows of small arches used mainly for effect, either on the lower part of an internal aisle wall, or as a decorative feature on external walls, below the eaves or parapet.

ARCUATED
A term describing a building in which arches are used to support the structure, a opposed to a 'trabeated' building, where columns and beams ar used. All our Gothic cathedrals are arcuated.

BARREL-VAULT
A continuous semi-circular arch or tunnel, used in English Norman architecture

BELFRY
A bell tower or Campanile.

BOSS
In medieval architecture, a keystone usually carved ornamentally and sometimes painted and gilded, at the intersection of ribs in a vaulted roof.

BUTTRESS
A vertical mass of masonry or brickwork projecting from a wall to resist the outward thrust of a roof-truss or vault or merely to stiffen the wall.

CAMPANILE
A term usually applied only to a bell tower which is detached from a church. These are very rare in England, one example survives at Chichester Cathedral.

CAPITAL
The moulded or carved block on the top of a column. It is often richly ornamented but it actually served a utilitarian purpose - to distribute the weight from above on to the shaft of the column.

CHANCEL
The part of a cathedral or church east of the crossing.

CHAPTER HOUSE
An assembly place for the governing members of an ecclesiastic foundation.

CHEVET
A semi-circular apse with radiating chapels.

CORBEL
A stone block, built into and projecting from a wall to carry the end of a roof-truss or a beam, often carved with grotesque human or animal figures.

CORNICE
A continuous horizontal member, usually moulded, crowning an external wall, or around the top of a room internally.

CRYPT
An underground chamber or cellar, usually vaulted

DOME
A convex roof, usually hemispherical, over a square, circular or octagonal space.

FAN VAULTING
The lates and most elaborate phase of English Gothic vaulting, very complicated and structurally somewhat illogical.

GABLE
The triangular piece of wall at the end of a ridged roof.

GALILEE
A porch or chapel at the west end of a cathedral eg at Ely

KEYSTONE
The wedge-shaped central stone of an arch, on which the efficiency of the arch depends.

LANTERN
A turret or other small structure erected on the top of a tower, a roof or a dome, to give light to the interior of a building eg. at St Pauls or Ely Cathedral.

MISERICORD
In the choir stalls of a medieval church, a bracket (often grotesquely or humorously carved) beneath a hinged seat which, when tipped up, gave some support to a person standing during a lengthy service.

MULLION
A stone or wood vertical bar dividing a window-opening into 'lights'.

NAVE
The main body of a church, with or without flanking aisles; but excluding the chancel and transepts (if any)

OGEE ARCH
A pointed arch of double curvature - convex above concave.

PARAPET
A low wall built around a roof or platform to prevent people falling over the edge.

PILASTER
A flat and often ornamental column, partly built into the wall of a structure, and projecting from it very slightly.

PLATE TRACERY
Primitive form of Gothic tracery, in whch geometrical openings, such as circles, were pierced through a solid slab or plate of stone.

PRESBYTERY
The area near the high altar.

PULPITUM
A screen dividing the choir from the nave.

REREDOS
An ornamental screen above and behind the altar.

ROTUNDA
A term occasionally applied to a dome or to a circular domed building

SANCTUARY
Either the holiest part of a church, ie in the chancel, or any portion of a church in which a medieval fugitive from justice could claim sanctuary and escape arrest, under ancient church law.

SEDILIA
A range of stone seats generally three in number, on the south side of a chancel, for the use of the clergy.

SPANDREL
The approximately triangular space between the outer curve of an arch and an enclosing frame of mouldings etc. Often richly carved with foliage.

TRANSOM
In any large window with mullions, a horizontal bar across the whole window, of the same section as the mullions, to stiffen them tranversely.

TREFOIL
Literally 'three leaved'. Either a carved three leaved ornament, or a three lobed/leaved panel or opening in tracery

UNDERCROFT
A vaulted cellar or range of rooms used for storage

Photograph Acknowledgements

Our particular thanks for the supply of the photographs of the Cathedrals

Birmingham	**Woodmansterne**	Exeter	**Woodmansterne**	Peterborough	**Woodmansterne**
Bristol	**Woodmansterne**	Gloucester	**Woodmansterne**	Portsmouth	**Woodmansterne**
Bury St Edmunds	**Courtesy of the Cathedral**	Guildford	**Woodmansterne**	Rochester	**Woodmansterne**
Canterbury	**Cathedral Gifts Ltd**	Hereford	**Courtesy of the Cathedral**	Salisbury	**Daily Telegraph**
Chelmsford	**Courtesy of the Cathedral**	Leicester	**Woodmansterne**	St Albans	**Woodmansterne**
Chichester	**Courtesy of the Cathedral**	London, St Pauls	**Woodmansterne**	Truro	**Woodmansterne**
Coventry	**Woodmansterne**	London, Southwark	**Daily Telegraph**	Wells	**The Late Mr Hall**
Ely	**Woodmansterne**	Norwich	**Courtesy of the Cathedral**	Winchester	**Courtesy of the Cathedral**
		Oxford	**Woodmansterne**	Worcester	**Courtesy of the Dean & Chapter**

Reader's Comments

Please use this page, or a photocopy of it, to tell us about HOTELS, RESTAURANTS, PUBLIC HOUSES and PLACES OF INTEREST that have appealed to you especially.

We will pass on your approval where it is merited and equally report back to the venue any **complaints**. We hope the latter will be few and far between.

Please post to Joy David, Griffin Publishing Ltd, 24–26 George Place, Stonehouse, Plymouth, PL1 3NY and expect to recieve a book as a token of our appreciation.

Name of Establishment:
Address:

Your comments:

Your Name: ....

Address: ....
                   ....
                   ....

Reader's Comments

Please use this page, or a photocopy of it, to tell us about HOTELS, RESTAURANTS, PUBLIC HOUSES and PLACES OF INTEREST that have appealed to you especially.

We will pass on your approval where it is merited and equally report back to the venue any **complaints**. We hope the latter will be few and far between.

Please post to Joy David, Griffin Publishing Ltd, 24-26 George Place, Stonehouse, Plymouth, PL1 3NY and expect to recieve a book as a token of our appreciation.

Name of Establishment:
Address:

Your comments:

Your Name: ....

Address: ....
....
....

Other Titles Available

An Invitation to The Cathedral Cities of Northern England and Wales	£9.95 + £2.50 p&p
An Invitation to The Vegetarian Guide to Eating Out	£9.95 + £1.85 p&p
An Invitation to Short Breaks in Great Britain	£9.95 + £1.85 p&p

Also written by Joy David

AN INVITATION TO LUNCH, DINE, STAY AND VISIT:
(Potted history of areas, exciting attractions and places to visit)

Devon and Cornwall II	£6.95 + 1.85 p&p
Somerset & Avon II	£7.95 + 1.85 p&p
East Anglia	£5.95 + 1.85 p&p
The Mid-Shires	£5.95 + 1.85 p&p
Heart of England	£5.95 + 1.85 p&p
Wales	£6.95 + 1.85 p&p
Southern England	£6.95 + 1.85 p&p
North East Counties	£7.95 + 1.85 p&p
Edinburgh, The Lothians, Scottish Borders and Northumbria	£7.95 + 1.85 p&p

An Invitation to Devon   £5.95 + 1.85 p&p
(a very readable, gentle meander through Devon)

An Invitation to Plymouth   £7.95 + 2.50 p&p
(A contemporary, easily read book covering all aspects of the City)

Please make cheques payable to **Griffin Publishing Ltd**.

Griffin Publishing Ltd, 24-26 George Place, Stonehouse, Plymouth, PL1 3NY.
Telephone (0752) 256177/188, Facsimilie: (0752) 254314